CHINA'S RELATIONS WITH AFRICA

CHINA'S RELATIONS WITH AFRICA

A New Era of Strategic Engagement

**DAVID H. SHINN
AND
JOSHUA EISENMAN**

Columbia University Press / *New York*

Columbia University Press
Publishers Since 1893
New York   Chichester, West Sussex
cup.columbia.edu
Copyright © 2023 Columbia University Press
All rights reserved

Library of Congress Cataloging-in-Publication Data
Names: Shinn, David Hamilton, author. | Eisenman, Joshua, 1977- author.
Title: China's relations with Africa : a new era of strategic engagement / David H. Shinn and Joshua Eisenman.
Description: New York : Columbia University Press, 2023. | Includes bibliographical references and index.
Identifiers: LCCN 2022050811 (print) | LCCN 2022050812 (ebook) | ISBN 9780231210003 (hardback) | ISBN 9780231210010 (trade paperback) | ISBN 9780231558228 (ebook)
Subjects: LCSH: China—Foreign relations—Africa. | Africa—Foreign relations—China. | Africa—Strategic aspects. | China—Strategic aspects. | Security, International. | Geopolitics.
Classification: LCC DT38.9.C5 S556 2023 (print) | LCC DT38.9.C5 (ebook) | DDC 327.5106—dc23/eng/20221021
LC record available at https://lccn.loc.gov/2022050811
LC ebook record available at https://lccn.loc.gov/2022050812

Cover design: Noah Arlow
Cover images: Getty Images (top), Zuma Press (bottom)

To Herman Pirchner, Jr.
for his steadfast support

CONTENTS

List of Figures and Tables ix

Acknowledgments xi

List of Abbreviations xiii

Map of Africa xix

1 Locating Africa in China's Geostrategy 1

2 Bilateral and Global Relations 21

3 Regional and Subregional Relations 51

4 Party-to-Party Relations 85

5 Africa-Focused Propaganda 119

6 Security Strategy and Interests 155

7 Protecting Interests and Managing Conflict 179

CONTENTS

8 Security Diplomacy 213

9 Maritime Security 255

10 Technology and Information Security 295

11 Projecting Trends in China-Africa Strategic Relations 327

Appendix: China's Establishment of Diplomatic Relations with African Countries 345

Notes 351

Index 457

FIGURES AND TABLES

FIGURES

Figure 1.1　China's interlocking relations with Africa　9
Figure 4.1　ID-CPC bilateral exchanges with African political parties, 2002–2022　95
Figure 4.2　Location of ID-CPC bilateral exchanges, 2002–2022　95
Figure 4.3　African countries with most bilateral exchanges with ID-CPC, 2002–2022　96
Figure 4.4　ID-CPC multilateral exchanges with African political parties, 2002–2022　99
Figure 4.5　Location of ID-CPC multilateral exchanges, 2002–2022　100
Figure 4.6　ID-CPC exchanges with South Africa, 2002–2022　105
Figure 4.7　ID-CPC exchanges with Ethiopia, 2002–2022　110
Figure 4.8　ID-CPC exchanges with Ghana, 2002–2022　114
Figure 5.1　African students in China, 2003–2018　136

FIGURES AND TABLES

Figure 8.1   China's conventional arms transfers to Africa by year, 2010–2021   224

Figure 8.2   China's conventional arms transfers to Africa by country, 2010–2021   225

TABLES

Table 5.1   China-Africa think-tank forums, 2011–2022   140

Table 7.1   China's completed UN peacekeeping participation in Africa as of 2022   206

Table 7.2   China's ongoing participation in UN peacekeeping in Africa as of 2022   206

Table 9.1   Chinese companies' investment in African ports as of 2022   280

Table 9.2   China's naval ship visits to African countries, 2000–2022   282

Table 10.1   China's launch of African satellites as of 2022   302

ACKNOWLEDGMENTS

Although there are many to whom we are grateful, first and foremost, we would like to thank our wives, Judy and Iris, for their understanding and encouragement. We also owe a special debt of gratitude to Herman Pirchner, Jr., whose seventeen years of steadfast support began in 2006 when he helped us secure research funding for our first book. Other than us, Ilan Berman spent the most hours on this book. We are thankful for his detailed editing and comments on the manuscript, which were truly essential. Dominique Reichenbach, Haley Grizzell, Thomas Falci, and Nathan Depew provided critical research assistance and spent long hours updating the China-Africa party-to-party exchanges database and double-checking and harmonizing our citation work. They identified countless edits that greatly improved the book's presentation and content. Mi Siyi provided indispensable assistance to help coordinate our fieldwork in China. Hazik Azam, Rose Benas, Graham Benedict, Kyra Gustavsen, Alice He, Archit Oswal, Joshua Pine, Dan Raleigh, and Krystal Sun all provided important help with research. We are grateful to Caeyln Cobb, Monique Laban, Marisa Lastres, Anita O'Brien, and Eric

ACKNOWLEDGMENTS

Schwartz at Columbia University Press, who were fantastic to work with from beginning to end.

We appreciate the support of Scott Appleby, Ted Beatty, Marc Blecher, Josh Busby, Bobby Chesney, Andrea Ghiselli, Richard Harrison, Eric Heginbotham, Michel Hockx, Caroline Hughes, William Inboden, Rana Siu Inboden, Joshua Kurlantzick, Derek Mitchell, Cliff Mboya, Jonathan Noble, Eric Olander, Kwesi Prah, Nadege Rolland, David Shullman, Michael Sobolick, Isaac Stone-Fish, Jeremi Suri, Annie Swingen, Henry Tugendhat, Wang Duanyong, Catherine Weaver, Brantly Womack, Yun Sun, and Zheng Yu. We would also like to recognize the untimely passing of Devin T. Stewart, a dear friend who provided essential insights and critical support that helped guide our work.

Several institutions provided indispensable financial and organizational support for this book. We are particularly grateful to the American Foreign Policy Council and our home universities, George Washington University's Elliott School of International Affairs and the University of Notre Dame's Keough School of Global Affairs, for their institutional and research support. We are thankful to the University of Texas at Austin's LBJ School of Public Affairs, the Strauss Center for International Security and Law, the Clements Center for National Security, and the Carnegie Council for International Affairs, which funded our fieldwork in China and Africa, and to Fudan University School of International and Public Affairs, which hosted us in China. China House deserves special thanks for their hands-on work helping us administer scores of surveys that provided important insights into the security threats facing the Chinese community in Africa. Finally, we would like to recognize all those who spoke to us candidly and helped two Americans better understand China-Africa relations.

ABBREVIATIONS

ADB	African Development Bank
AI	artificial intelligence
AMU	Arab Maghreb Union
ANC	African National Congress (South Africa)
AQIM	Al-Qaeda in the Islamic Maghreb
ASEAN	Association of Southeast Asian Nations
ATDC	Agricultural Technology Demonstration Center
ATT	UN Arms Trade Treaty
AU	African Union (Addis Ababa)
AVIC	Aviation Industry Corporation of China
BDS	BeiDou Global Satellite Navigation System (China)
BRI	Belt and Road Initiative (China)
BRICS	Brazil, Russia, India, China, and South Africa
CAR	Conflict Armament Research
CARI	China-Africa Research Initiative (Johns Hopkins)
CASC	China Aerospace Science and Technology Corporation
CASCF	China-Arab States Cooperation Forum

ABBREVIATIONS

CASTC	China Aerospace Science and Technology Corporation
CATTF	China-Africa Think-Tank Forum
CCCC	China Communications Construction Company
CCM	Chama Cha Mapinduzi (Tanzania)
CCTV	closed circuit television camera
CDB	China Development Bank
CDC	Africa Centres for Disease Control and Prevention
CDS	College of Defense Studies (China)
CEN-SAD	Community of Sahel-Saharan States
CGN	China General Nuclear Power Corporation
CGTN	China Global Television Network
CHEC	China Harbor Engineering Company
China-Africa Community	China-Africa Community of Shared Future
CI	Confucius Institute
CICIR	China Institutes of Contemporary International Relations
CIDC	China International Development Cooperation
CISAR	China International Search and Rescue
CITIC	China International Trust and Investment Corporation
CMC	Central Military Commission (China)
CMPorts	China Merchants Port Holdings
Community	Community of Shared Future for Mankind
CNNC	China National Nuclear Corporation
CNOOC	China National Offshore Oil Corporation
CNPC	China National Petroleum Corporation
COMESA	Common Market for Eastern and Southern Africa
COSATU	Congress of South African Trade Unions
COSCO	China COSCO Shipping Corporation
COSG	China Overseas Security Group
COSS	China Overseas Security Services
CPC	Communist Party of China

ABBREVIATIONS

CRI	China Radio International
CSCLF	China Soong Ching Ling Foundation
CSGC	China South Industries Group Corporation
CSIC	China Shipbuilding Industry Corporation
CSSC	China State Shipbuilding Corporation
CSTG	China Security Technology Group
CZEC	China Zhongyuan Engineering Corporation
DFID	Department for International Development (UK)
DIA	Defense Intelligence Agency (United States)
DRC	Democratic Republic of Congo
EAC	East African Community
ECCAS	Economic Community of Central African States
ECOWAS	Economic Community of West African States
EPRDF	Ethiopian People's Revolutionary Democratic Front
EU	European Union
FOCAC	Forum on China-Africa Cooperation
Forum Macao	Forum for Economic and Trade Cooperation Between China and Portuguese-Speaking Countries
FRELIMO	Frente para a Libertação de Moçambique (Mozambique Liberation Front Party)
FSG	Frontier Services Group (China)
G-77	Group of 77
GAF	Ghana Armed Forces
GPS	Global Positioning System
HADR	humanitarian assistance and disaster relief
ID-CPC	International Department of the Central Committee of the CPC
ICT	information communications and technology
IGAD	Intergovernmental Authority on Development
IMF	International Monetary Fund
IOL	Independent Online (South Africa)
IORA	Indian Ocean Rim Association
ISA	International Seabed Authority

ABBREVIATIONS

IT	information technology
JEM	Justice and Equality Movement (Sudan)
LNA	Libyan National Army
LNG	liquified natural gas
MEND	Movement for the Emancipation of the Niger Delta (Nigeria)
MFA	Ministry of Foreign Affairs (China)
MIC	Military Industrial Corporation (Sudan)
MINURSO	UN Mission in Western Sahara
MINUSCA	UN Mission in Central African Republic
MINUSMA	UN Multidimensional Integrated Stabilization Mission in Mali
MONUC	UN Mission in Democratic Republic of Congo
MONUSCO	United Nations Organization Stabilization Mission in the Democratic Republic of Congo
MOOTW	military operations other than war
MOU	memorandum of understanding
MPLA	Movimento Popular de Libertacão de Angola (People's Movement for the Liberation of Angola)
NAM	Non-Aligned Movement
NDC	National Democratic Congress (Ghana)
NDU	National Defense University (China)
NECSA	Nuclear Energy Corporation SOC Limited (South Africa)
NEPAD	New Partnership for Africa's Development
NORINCO	North Industries Group Corporation (China)
NPP	New Patriotic Party (Ghana)
NTC	National Transitional Council (Libya)
OAU	Organization of African Unity (Addis Ababa)
OIC	Organization of Islamic Cooperation
ONLF	Ogaden National Liberation Front (Ethiopia)
ONUB	UN Mission in Burundi
ONUMOZ	UN Mission in Mozambique

ABBREVIATIONS

P3	Permanent member of UN Security Council and NATO member (i.e., United States, UK, and France)
PAP	People's Armed Police (China)
PLA	People's Liberation Army (China)
PLAN	People's Liberation Army Navy (China)
PLANMC	People's Liberation Army Navy Marine Corps (China)
POA	UN Program of Action
POC	protection of civilians
PRC	People's Republic of China
PSC	private security company
PTI	Poly Technologies Incorporated (China)
RMB	renminbi (China)
SACP	South African Communist Party
SADC	Southern African Development Community
SALW	small arms and light weapons
SANDF	South African National Defense Force
SANSA	South African National Space Agency
SIPRI	Stockholm International Peace Research Institute
SLOC	sea lines of communication
SNPTC	State Nuclear Power Technology Corporation (China)
SOE	state-owned enterprise
SPLA	Sudan People's Liberation Army (South Sudan)
SWAPO	South-West Africa People's Organization (Namibia)
TEDA	Tianjin Economic-Technological Development Area (China)
TPDF	Tanzanian People's Defense Force
TPLF	Tigray People's Liberation Front (Ethiopia)
UAE	United Arab Emirates
UAV	unmanned aerial vehicles
UHV	ultra-high voltage

ABBREVIATIONS

UNAMID	UN Mission in Darfur, Sudan
UNAMSIL	UN Mission in Sierra Leone
UNCLOS	UN Convention on the Law of the Sea
UNIOSIL	UN Mission in Sierra Leone
UNISFA	UN Mission in Abyei Sudan border
UNMEE	UN Mission in Ethiopia/Eritrea
UNMIL	UN Mission in Liberia
UNMIS	UN Mission in Sudan
UNMISS	UN Mission in South Sudan
UNOCI	UN Mission in Côte d'Ivoire
UNOMSIL	UN Mission in Sierra Leone
UNROCA	UN Register of Conventional Arms
UNSC	UN Security Council
UNTAG	UN Mission in Namibia
UPC	Union des Populations du Cameroon
UPDF	Uganda People's Defense Forces
ZANU-PF	Zimbabwe African National Union–Patriotic Front
ZNU	Zhejiang Normal University (China)

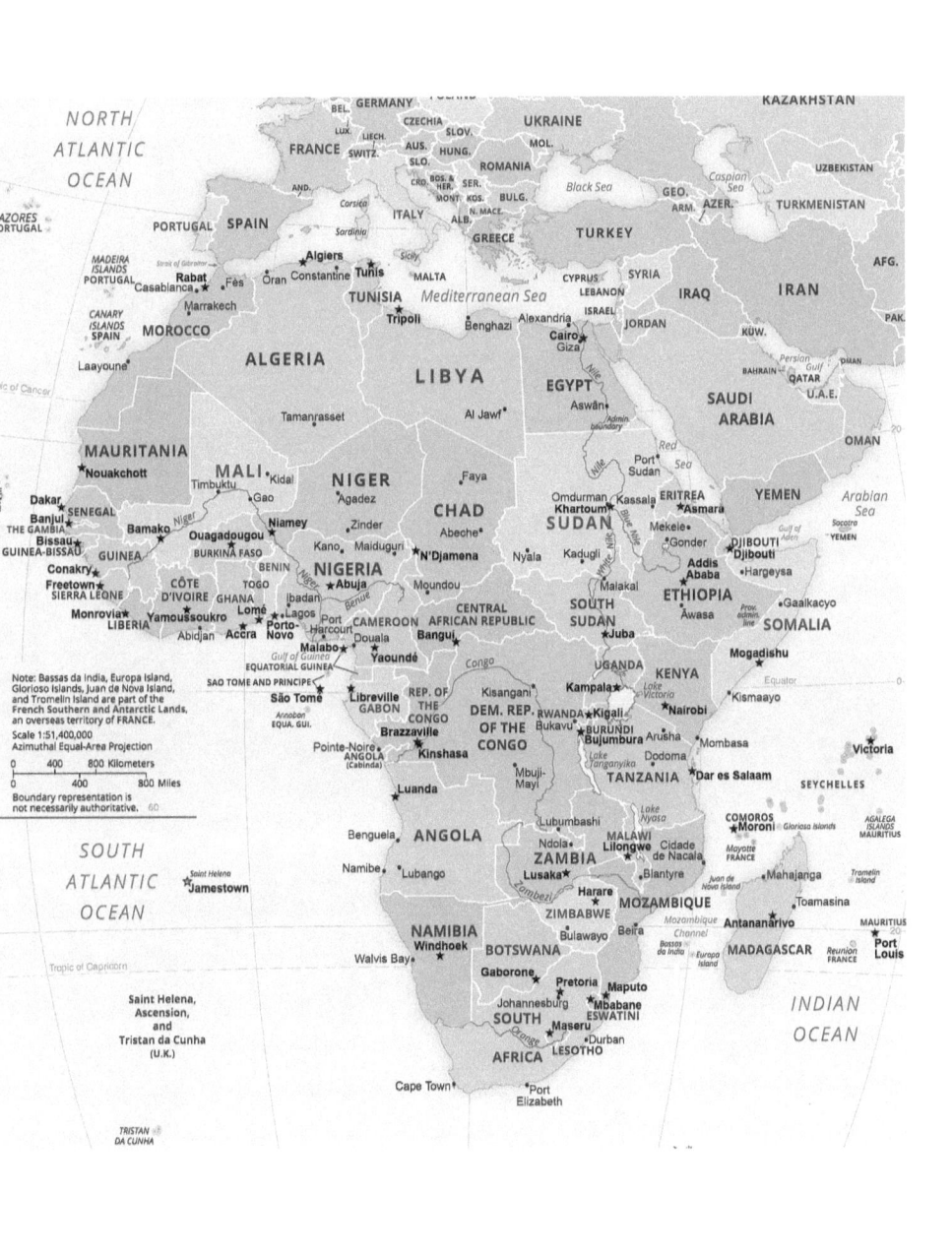

1

LOCATING AFRICA IN CHINA'S GEOSTRATEGY

Although for decades most analysts in Beijing considered Africa a geopolitical backwater, today relations with the continent have emerged as a cornerstone of China's major power engagement with the developing world (i.e., the Global South). Between 2012, when Xi Jinping took power, and the spread of COVID-19 in 2020, nearly every aspect of China's strategic relations with Africa witnessed an unprecedented expansion. Each year Beijing devoted more resources to its party-to-party exchanges, military engagement, and educational and cultural programs with African countries. On a weekly if not daily basis, Africa's political and military leaders landed in China for exchanges and training programs, and People's Liberation Army Navy (PLAN) vessels became regular visitors at African ports.

The pervasiveness of China's influence in Africa can be attributed to its overlapping latticework of relationships with thousands of African elites traversing four distinct levels: bilateral, global, regional, and subregional. At each level, Chinese interlocutors use material support, inclusive rhetoric, and all-expense-paid trips to initiate and perpetuate friendly relations with African partners. This book systematically examines the full scope of these contemporary China-Africa political and security engagements as well as the impact that COVID-19 has had on them.

This introductory chapter is divided into two complementary parts. The first explains Africa's ascendant position in China's geostrategy and identifies two defining features of Sino-African strategic relations: they are multitiered and Sinocentric. We begin by looking at how Chinese leaders' conflation of threats to the party with threats to the country, growing emphasis on relations in the Global South, and focus on countering U.S. "hegemony" have combined to elevate Africa's geostrategic importance.

Next, we introduce the Community of Shared Future for Mankind (人类命运共同体, henceforth the Community), Xi Jinping's principal foreign policy concept. The Community is best understood as a Sinocentric network of relationships based on the exchange of favors between Chinese and like-minded foreign partners. For Africa, Beijing has created a subnetwork within the Community it calls the China-Africa Community of Shared Future (中非命运共同体, henceforth the China-Africa Community). Yet, to benefit from the China-Africa Community, Africans must submit to Beijing's expectations about their proper conduct and obligations based on their subordinate status relative to China.

The second part of the chapter presents the book's research design. It places the book within the academic literature and introduces its research methods and chapter structure. After introducing the book's contribution, our data sources and fieldwork, we conclude by summarizing each forthcoming chapter. Taken together, the topics covered in this book represent a complete assessment of the contemporary China-Africa strategic relationship. We find that by cultivating interpersonal relations with African elites, China gains their support for its core interests and validates its perception of itself as a leader and exemplar for all developing countries.

AFRICA IN CHINA'S STRATEGIC THOUGHT

When China's leaders consider their strategic relations with foreign countries, they do so in the context of the Communist Party of China's (CPC) broader strategic, or "core interests" (核心利益)—that is, "state sovereignty, national security, territorial integrity, and national reunification, China's political system established by the Constitution and overall social stability, and the basic safeguards for ensuring sustainable economic and social development."[1] While there are other interpretations of China's core interests, all assume three basic overlapping geostrategic objectives: to ensure the CPC will continue to rule China, to maintain and defend China's sovereignty and territorial integrity, and to promote a stable international environment conducive to the continued growth of China's comprehensive national strength.

Since China's "going out" (走出去) strategy was initiated in the late 1990s, distinctions between external vs. internal security and traditional vs. nontraditional threats have largely disappeared from Chinese strategic thinking.[2] "Comprehensive security" (综合国家安全), explained People's Liberation Army (PLA) general Xiong Guangkai in 2002, "always gives top priority to national sovereignty and security, further develops the internal political situation of stability and unity, and strives for a long-lasting . . . favorable environment around China."[3] This concept, which was adopted by then general secretary Hu Jintao, has been expanded and rebranded as "holistic security" (总体国家安全) by his successor, Xi Jinping.

"Holistic security," which Xi Jinping introduced at the CPC Central National Security Commission in 2014, takes "the security of the people as compass, political security at its roots, economic security as its pillar, military security, cultural security, and social security as its protections, and that relies on the promotion of international security."[4] This means China's view of "security" now combines traditional national security concerns such as military, homeland, and nuclear security with "political security," "economic security," "cultural security," "social stability," "technological security," "information security," "ecological security," "resource security," and "overseas interests security."[5] In 2016 the Cadre Manual of the Holistic Security Strategy published by the People's Publishing House officially removed distinctions between external and internal, as well as traditional and nontraditional, security threats.[6]

"Although threats to national security in the traditional sense have been declining since the end of the Cold War, threats to the Chinese regime have been on the rise," explain Feng Zhongping and Huang Jing of the Chinese Academy of Social Sciences. In practice, this means that "in nearly every strategic partnership document, concepts such as non-interference in domestic affairs, different understandings of democracy and human rights, or different development paths have been asserted."[7] Such references are common in China's official statements on Africa.[8]

Chinese scholars differentiate the relative status of bilateral relationships based on the characteristics of partner states: specifically, relations with major powers (大国), states on China's geographic periphery (周边国家), developing countries (发展中国家), and multilateral (多边) international forums.[9] The boundaries between these categories are somewhat amorphous, and many states straddle two or more of them. Major powers are large, economically developed states, a category that includes the United States, Japan, Russia, Germany, Britain, and the European Union (EU) as a whole. The "strategic periphery," which is defined by physical proximity to China, has traditionally included Russia as well as countries in East Asia, Central Asia, South Asia, and Southeast Asia. In 2004 General Secretary Hu Jintao stated: "Major powers are the key, surrounding (peripheral) areas are the first priority, developing countries are the foundation, and multilateral forums are the important stage."[10] Under Xi Jinping, China's conception of what constitutes the "greater periphery" (大周边) has expanded apace with the country's growing power and influence to include parts of East Africa.[11]

In 2016 He Yafei, a former deputy minister of foreign affairs, argued that developing countries should remain "the bedrock and strategic focus of China's major-country diplomacy." He observed that China works to build partnerships with developing countries that also seek a "multi-polar world and democratic international relations" and the "reform of global governance." Moreover, he noted, China's relations with developing countries will continue to expand and deepen as those nations narrow their capability gap with developed countries.[12] China's 2019 Defense White Paper affirms this assessment: "As the realignment of international powers accelerates and the strength of emerging markets and developing countries keeps growing, the configuration of strategic power is becoming more balanced."[13]

LOCATING AFRICA IN CHINA'S GEOSTRATEGY

Although Deng Xiaoping's "low-profile" (韬光养晦) strategy to maintain a peaceful international environment suitable for China's continued rise to great power status has never been officially repudiated, over time it has gradually given way to a more assertive vision.[14] "From 2012 to 2014, Chinese diplomacy transformed from 'keeping a low profile' to 'striving for achievements,'" Yan Xuetong of Qinghua University has observed.[15]

As China's major power engagement has gone global, Beijing has adopted a more nuanced view of developing countries. Beijing now differentiates "major developing states" (发展中大国) or "newly emerging powers" (新兴大国) from "other" developing states.[16] In each region of the Global South, China cultivates relations with these larger and strategically important "hub" states, to which it affords special attention. In Southeast Asia, they include Indonesia, Singapore, and Thailand; in South Asia, India and Pakistan; in Central Asia, Kazakhstan; in Africa, Egypt, Ethiopia, Nigeria, and South Africa; in the Middle East, Iran and Saudi Arabia; and in Latin America, Argentina and Brazil.[17] This list is not definitive, has evolved over time, and will continue to do so. Although traditional international relations theorists would not consider these countries major powers, their size compared to their neighbors gives them a consistent leading voice and a strong normative influence in both regional and subregional institutions. Thus whether these countries' leaders decide to make common cause with China can either facilitate or frustrate its initiatives in their respective geographic areas.

In the 2000s and 2010s China's political and military engagement with developing countries was not intended to subvert the international order, nor to serve as "hard balancing" against the United States and its allies.[18] However, amid rising tensions with Washington, Tokyo, New Delhi, London, Canberra, and Brussels, many in Beijing believe that the obstacles to justice and peace are hegemonism, power politics, and the self-serving behavior of "a few Western states" led by the United States.[19] According to China's 2019 Defense White Paper: "International strategic competition is on the rise [and] the United States has adjusted its national security and defense strategies, and adopted unilateral policies."[20] It is within this geostrategic context that African partners are seen as essential

5

assets in Beijing's strategy to advance its interests and constrain Washington through the creation of a more "democratic" and "multipolar" world order.[21] These goals are to be accomplished via the Community or, in the African context, the China-Africa Community, which advances Chinese interests and opposes American "hegemony," explains Lei Yu of Liaocheng University.[22]

A NEW TYPE OF INTERNATIONAL RELATIONS

The Community is more than a mere propaganda slogan; it is Xi Jinping's most important international relations formulation (提法).[23] To realize the "Chinese Dream" (中国梦) of building a strong, civilized, harmonious, and beautiful China, Beijing is creating an ever-expanding network of relationships with like-minded foreigners—that is, the Community. Like its predecessors, such as "harmonious world" (和谐世界) and "peaceful rise" (和平崛起), the inclusive yet nebulous concept of the Community is intended to advance China's desire to reshape international relations and governance norms in ways that acknowledge the nation's superior status and core interests.[24] Ever since Xi first coined the term at the Bo'ao Forum in 2013, China's leaders have regularly referenced it when addressing foreign counterparts.[25]

The Community challenges the dominant Western liberal world order by offering one that is ostensibly better, fairer, and more inclusive.[26] It intends to "reshape international relations" (重塑国际关系) in a fashion befitting Chinese, rather than Western, notions of the proper status of actors and their corresponding responsibilities to one another. Xi Jinping set forth this objective in his speech at the Nineteenth Party Congress in October 2017, in which he vowed that the Community would make China "a global leader in terms of comprehensive national strength and international influence." "China champions the development of a Community with a Shared Future for Mankind, and has encouraged the evolution of the global governance system. With this we have seen a further rise in China's international influence, ability to inspire, and power to shape."[27]

The Community is a global network of foreign partners who want to work with China in a "win-win" fashion—that is, to build relations that serve both sides' interests. In December 2017 Xi told a gathering of foreign political parties in Beijing that the Community is a "harmonious family" around the world.[28] Echoing Xi, Fu Ying, chair of the National People's Congress Foreign Affairs Committee, extolled the virtues of China's non-expansionist and conflict-averse "traditional strategic culture," which makes the Community's "cooperative security" concept more attractive than the West. Fu described an "extended family coexisting harmoniously that does not duplicate the old game of geopolitics," and which is fluid and open, unlike rigid traditional Western alliance structures."[29] China, Fu said, is promoting the Community as a bold new framework for a new international order based on cooperative security, common development, and political inclusiveness.[30]

Although the Community emerged in response to China's expanding overseas economic interests, it is increasingly "based on political and security arrangements," explain Xu Jin and Guo Chu of the Chinese Academy of Social Sciences. China's 2019 Defense White Paper emphasizes that its strong military is a force for building the Community.[31] Although most partners join the Community for the material and financial benefits, over time, to advance their own interests, they are encouraged to enhance their strategic cooperation with China. According to Xu and Guo, after repeated exchanges with Chinese partners, members of the Community gradually develop a sense of belonging and a positive view of China and come to perceive Beijing's growing influence as both "inevitable and the right thing." Through reciprocity, Chinese partners cultivate foreign partners, until the latter "become accustomed to China playing the role" of a regional and global leader.[32] Although foreigners' affirmations may begin as purely performative—that is, intended to ingratiate themselves with their Chinese counterparts—if done repeatedly and deliberately over time, they become habitual such that what began as instrumental behavior gradually brings about their enthusiastic participation.[33]

BUILDING THE CHINA-AFRICA COMMUNITY

During his visit to Tanzania in 2013, Xi Jinping offered his vision for the China-Africa Community: "China and Africa have always been a community of shared destiny, and our common historical experience, common development tasks, and common strategic interests have closely linked us. We all regard each other's development as our own opportunities, and we are all actively promoting common development and prosperity through strengthening cooperation."[34]

In 2018 Xi again called for Chinese and African partners to "work together to build a China-Africa Community with a shared future for win-win cooperation . . . and safeguard the common interests of China and Africa and the vast majority of developing countries."[35] He did the same in his keynote speech at the Forum on China-Africa Cooperation (FOCAC) in 2021 titled: "Uphold the Tradition of Always Standing Together and Jointly Build a China-Africa Community of Shared Future in the New Era." Chinese officials at all levels regularly reference the Community when meeting with their African counterparts, and Chinese scholars argue that the China-Africa Community has a "fundamental position" within it.[36]

Multitier and Interlocking

The China-Africa Community has two primary structural features. The first, which He Yafei articulated, is that China's foreign relations comprise "multi-centric, multi-layered and multi-pivotal sub-networks of regional and international cooperation that are interconnected and interwoven."[37] China's interlocking, overlapping latticework of relationships with Africa policy makers, which we detail in chapters 2 and 3, traverses all four levels: bilateral, global, subregional, and regional (figure 1.1). Together, they constitute a dense social network that seeks to "promote *guanxi* connections with African current and future leaders," Lina Benabdallah of Wake Forest University explains.[38] Through this network, Chinese interlocutors share the "knowledge" and "public goods" that African and other developing countries require but the West has failed to provide.[39]

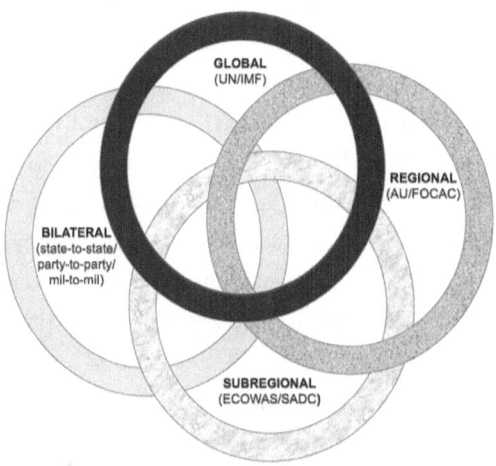

FIGURE 1.1 China's interlocking relations with Africa.

China's bilateral ties with African states remain the foundation of its relations on the continent. They include a diverse and expanding array of state-to-state, party-to-party, military-to-military, and people-to-people engagements that vary depending on the country's size, location, and the extent of Chinese interests there. Within each African subregion, Beijing prioritizes relations with countries where geography, politics, or economic interests make relations particularly propitious. In eastern Africa, these include Djibouti, Ethiopia, Kenya, and Tanzania; in southern Africa, Angola, Namibia, South Africa, and Zimbabwe; in West Africa, Ghana, Senegal, and Nigeria; and in North Africa, Algeria and Egypt. China attaches the most political importance to the largest African states—Egypt, Ethiopia, Nigeria, and South Africa. Other states—such as Namibia, Tanzania, and Zimbabwe—receive special attention due to their ruling parties' long-standing close relations with Beijing. Still others, like Kenya, Angola, Ghana, Senegal, and Algeria, are seen as important subregional influencers as well as trade partners and investment destinations. As the location of China's only overseas military base, Djibouti has unique strategic significance.

At the global level, China is shaping international relations among nations to suit its interests and those of its African partners. Beijing regularly affirms its "UN-centered diplomacy," calls on all states to observe the UN Charter, and contributes peacekeepers to UN forces in Africa. Such participation reassures African and other developing countries that China is committed to the existing international system and highlights Beijing's leadership and solidarity with them. But if a global institution makes a decision that runs contrary to China's interests or those of its African friends, Beijing is prepared to obstruct, attack, and question both its legitimacy and its jurisdiction. In 2005, for instance, Beijing vetoed UN sanctions on Zimbabwe's Robert Mugabe, and it threw a diplomatic lifeline to Sudan's Omar al-Bashir by hosting him in 2011 and again in 2015, despite his conviction by the International Criminal Court.[40] In 2022 China lambasted another UN report—this one describing torture, sexual assault, and forced labor in Xinjiang—as "wholly illegal and invalid" and "manufactured firsthand by the U.S. and some Western forces."[41]

China's regional-level interaction with the Global South can be traced back to 1996, with the establishment of the ASEAN+1 framework with Southeast Asian nations. This effort to build relationships with entire regions of the Global South was formally initiated after the Fifteenth Party Congress in 1997, at which General Secretary Jiang Zemin determined that the constraints associated with multilateral frameworks "were preferable to the risk of isolation and encirclement, and could help foster a reputation for responsible international behavior," explains Andrea Ghiselli of Fudan University.[42] In 1998 Jiang instructed China's ambassadors: "All major countries rely on regional organizations for their own development and try to use multilateral contexts to achieve what they cannot accomplish through bilateral means. We need to place greater emphasis on this."[43] Since then, China has gone on to create similar frameworks with nearly every developing region, including FOCAC with Africa in 2000, the Shanghai Cooperation Organization with Central Asian nations in 2001, the China-Arab States Cooperation Forum in 2004, the 16+1 Cooperation between China and Central and Eastern European Countries framework in 2012, and the China-Caribbean Economic and Trade Cooperation Forum in 2015.

FOCAC is a proprietary, Africa-wide initiative that China underwrites and uses to coordinate and synchronize its relations across the continent (see chapter 3). It is China's primary institutional conduit for engaging and providing resources to Africans: at the FOCAC meetings in 2018 and 2021, China pledged a combined $100 billion in financing for Africa.[44] As noted above, Xi Jinping's speech at the Eighth FOCAC Ministerial Conference in 2021 called for both sides to advance the China-Africa Community by "injecting strong impetus into the China-Africa comprehensive strategic and cooperative partnership."[45] China has also contributed substantially to the African Union, including funding and building its $200 million headquarters in 2012.[46] In 2019 Beijing hosted the China-Africa Peace and Security Forum, which included more than a hundred officials representing fifty African countries and the African Union.[47] By creating and funding these and other continent-wide initiatives, Beijing not only builds relationships but also ensures it remains informed about any relevant developments that might affect its interests.

China's relations with African subregional multilateral groupings (e.g., the Economic Community of West African States, or ECOWAS, and the East African Community, or EAC) are a feature of its multitier engagement that is unique to Africa. Beijing has provided millions of dollars in grants to support its preferred subregional organizations and is building a new multimillion-dollar headquarters for ECOWAS.[48] Beijing uses these organizations to build relationships with well-placed African political partners, while ensuring they do not become venues for collaboration against Chinese interests.

Sinocentric

A second structural feature of the China-Africa Community is Sinocentrism. "The Sinocentric-system is a hierarchy," writes Qin Yaqing of China Foreign Affairs University, one that is fundamentally different from "the relationship of equality among sovereign states [that] defines the Westphalian system."[49] James P. Harrison of Hunter College uses the term "culturalism" to describe Beijing's worldview, which emphasizes Chinese virtues and wisdom and juxtaposes them with foreigners' iniquity and ignorance.[50] According to Zhao Suisheng of the University of Denver, this belief that notions of Chinese cultural and political superiority ought to be "universal" can be traced back to imperial times:

> China's cultural superiority was based on the belief that the Chinese imperial system and Confucian ideology preserved domestic social order and political stability and therefore extended to the surrounding areas. The hegemonic nature of Chinese culture gave rise to a false sense among the Chinese that their hierarchy was universal. There were no other hierarchies and no other sources of power in the world. All countries within the tributary system were culturally subservient to China.[51]

Lucian Pye of the Massachusetts Institute of Technology observes how this thinking influenced China's foreign relations: "The Chinese, with their Confucianism, created an elaborate intellectual structure of an ethical order which all enlightened peoples were expected to acknowledge and respect."[52] Small nations on China's periphery that accepted Chinese cultural and moral superiority could retain their local political autonomy while enjoying the economic benefits of the China-led hierarchical order, known in imperial times as *tianxia* (天下) or "all-under-heaven," writes James C. Hsiung of New York University.[53]

Within an "all-under-heaven common community" (天下共同体), the center protects the periphery, and the periphery subordinates itself to the center (中心保护周边，周边藩屏中心), forming a pattern of interdependence, coexistence, and coprosperity.[54] "The *tianxia* system structure is hierarchical because only such an arrangement could sustain its stability and harmonious order," Qin Yaqing explains.[55] Harmony is based on interdependence and reciprocal improvement, that is, "win-win," observes Zhao Tingyang of the Chinese Academy of Social Sciences.[56] *Tianxia* is a "utopian cosmological order" that brings each level of China's foreign relations under the same "moral rationale."[57]

Today, China's leaders continue to see their nation as the core of an international coalition of developing countries working to bring about what John Eperjesi of Kyung Hee University described as an "era of Sino-centered economic prosperity and alternative Chinese modernity."[58] Zhao Suisheng has also identified the reemergence of a distinct "Chinese world order" bound together by an "ethical hierarchy, maintained by the power of Chinese civilization." Beijing, he writes, has "set a nineteenth century agenda for China in the twenty-first century—to restore the regional hierarchy of imperial China." According to Zhao, China seeks to "reassume its traditional place at the center," to rebuild "the old tributary system . . . in a modern form," and for "contemporary ideas of racial hierarchy [to] be redrawn and China's age-old sense of superiority [to] reassert itself."[59] In this way, China's demands for constant reaffirmations of its superiority and leadership alter "the way that international relations and the global order are organized, or more correctly *should* be organized," argues Shaun Breslin of the University of Warwick.[60]

The Chinese order "consists of formal hierarchy but informal equality" whereby China, as the "central state," elicits "bandwagoning" from other nations, Hsiung explains.[61] The objective is to catalyze "friendly relations and motivational orientations" and generate feelings of cooperation from foreign guests.[62] According to Ilaria Carrozza of Peace Research Institute Oslo and Benabdallah, Chinese officials use political nostalgia and inclusive terms like "brotherhood," "friendship," "equality," and "win-win" to create an "imagined . . . South-South solidarity between 'fellow sufferers.'" They make repeated references to "Global South solidarities and representations of African states as states that share China's quest for development, its historical struggle, and aspiration for a prosperous future."[63] As the self-designated superior partner, Chinese officials strive to project modesty, benevolence, and generosity in order to elicit compliance and obligation from the African side. Just ahead of FOCAC 2021, for instance, China released a White Paper titled "China and Africa in the New Era: A Partnership of Equals."

In addition to rhetoric, Chinese officials employ what Chen Dongxiao of the Shanghai Institutes for International Studies calls "host diplomacy" (主场外交) to create a friendly environment and connote their superior position.[64] They generally meet African officials at or above their rank in elaborate, climate-controlled meeting rooms with plush furnishings, wall-size hand-painted Chinese landscapes, ornate chandeliers, and elaborate flower displays arranged in porcelain vases. Senior officials warmly welcome each guest in order of their relative status with a handshake and a smile. Participants then sit according to rank in rows of oversized chairs facing each other. The two leaders sit at the front of the room with a large flower display and perhaps a translator between them. The highest-ranking Chinese official wields the prerogative to conduct the meeting as they choose.

Sinocentrism is also observable at banquets, during which each delegation member is seated in a particular location around the table based on their relative status. The Chinese host, who faces the door to greet their guests, orchestrates the discussion, begins the toasts, and decides when the meal has ended. "Practices of food-sharing play a distinct role in informalizing interactions—especially, in transforming diplomatic relations into interpersonal ones and drawing foreign representatives into establishing friendship ties," explains Emilian Kavalski of Jagiellonian University.[65] This strategy of dulling the criticism of others through good treatment is captured in the Chinese expression "the mouth that eats the food of others is softened, the hand that takes the possessions of others is shortened" (吃人家的嘴软，拿人家的手短).

Chinese officials regularly accompany their African guests on provincial tours, which, as Benabdallah observes, serve as "business cards for China's rich cultural heritage but also a testimony of China's successful development model."[66] During these tours, Chinese interlocutors encourage their visitors to inquire about the types of material and financial support China might be able to provide. According to Yun Sun of the Stimson Center, Beijing uses such economic enticements to lure African partners "into the Chinese orbit." She identifies "a popular perception in China that Africa's support of China's foreign policies can be easily acquired through economic enticement and reward." China's "catering to African needs lays the foundation for Africa's warm reception and benevolent interpretation of China's agendas. The political support of Chinese policies can usually be acquired through generous offers of Chinese aid, loans, and investment," Sun explains.[67]

LOCATING AFRICA IN CHINA'S GEOSTRATEGY

RESEARCH DESIGN

ACADEMIC LITERATURE

Scholarship on China's strategic relations with Africa has evolved considerably since the 1960s and 1970s, when the United States, the Soviet Union, and China were engaged in an ideological struggle for influence in what Mao Zedong called the Third World. From 1963 to 1966 at least four books were written in English on China's foreign policy toward Africa, all touting what one author called *Red China's African Offensive*.[68] In the 1970s China's political and security relations with developing countries were well-covered in various surveys of Chinese foreign policy,[69] and several books dealt specifically with Beijing's ties with African countries and revolutionary movements.[70]

During the 1980s and 1990s, as China looked toward the West, the academic literature on China's engagement with Africa dwindled.[71] While relations with major powers such as the United States, Russia, and Japan received due attention, with a few exceptions books on China and the Global South receded from view.[72]

Since the turn of the millennium, many researchers and experts have recognized the importance China attaches to its relations in the developing world, especially Africa.[73] During the 2000s China's rapidly growing economic relationships with African countries generated a flood of media reports and policy and academic studies, yet there was little effort to contextualize these developments within China's overall foreign policy and history on the continent. Indeed, that was the goal of our first book, *China and Africa: A Century of Engagement* (2012), which covered the full range of topics—from trade and investment to military diplomacy and Chinese communities in Africa.[74] Although this volume looks at a narrower subject than its predecessor—Sino-African political and security relations—it too seeks to contextualize and interpret that phenomenon within China's larger geostrategy and history with Africa.

Since 2012, in addition to countless policy and press reports, a growing number of mostly edited books have been published on China's relations with developing countries.[75] Numerous books touching on various aspects of China-Africa strategic relations have also appeared.[76] These publications traverse an ever-wider range of academic fields, including political science, economics, sociology, and anthropology, among others. Some of them focus on China's relations with individual African countries.[77] Yet despite both the growing body of academic research and the rapid expansion of Sino-African political and security relations, compared to trade, aid, and investment only a small portion of the contemporary literature examines these topics.[78] Since 2010 one edited volume has focused on the broader China-Africa security relationship, while three books have sought to contextualize China-Africa political relations within Beijing's larger geostrategy.[79] This is the first book to examine these two topics together and to capture their full breadth under one cover.

This relative dearth of research is understandable, since all states, and few more than China, consider political and security-related matters to be sensitive, making them among the most difficult to research. The problem has been exacerbated in recent years by the deterioration of China's relations with Western countries, particularly the United States. Even before the advent of COVID-19, China had begun imposing stricter limitations and surveillance on foreign researchers, making fieldwork there increasingly difficult if not impossible.[80] As a result, academic publications on China-Africa strategic relations have been relegated to topics that can be observed from afar, or those for which data or Chinese language research is already available.

Still, limiting academic studies of contemporary China-Africa strategic relations to only those topics for which data is already available is akin to searching for one's keys under an increasingly crowded lamppost. Such an approach is especially problematic when the darkness is expanding, along with our questions about what lurks there. Indeed, China's strategic relations with Africans were expanding rapidly prior to COVID-19, and although they were constrained by the virus, they are primed to grow precipitously again as China reopens to foreign visitors.

LOCATING AFRICA IN CHINA'S GEOSTRATEGY

SOURCES AND STRUCTURE

This book is based primarily on six types of sources: systematic data, informal in-person interviews, online surveys, official documents and statements, media reports, and scholarly publications. The best example of systematic data is our proprietary database of all reported meetings between the International Department of the Central Committee of the CPC (ID-CPC) and African political parties covering 2002–2022. Between 2017 and 2020 we conducted informal interviews in China, South Africa, Ghana, Egypt, Ethiopia, Djibouti, Namibia, and Morocco with more than two hundred Chinese and African elites and third-country nationals, including party and military leaders, government officials, academics, journalists, and civil society representatives. In 2019 and 2020 we worked with China House, a Nairobi-based NGO, to deploy Chinese researchers and online surveys to determine the security concerns of residents of Chinese communities in twelve countries—Algeria, Angola, Cameroon, Democratic Republic of Congo, Egypt, Ethiopia, Kenya, Nigeria, South Africa, Sudan, Tanzania, and Zimbabwe.

Chapter 2 explores China's bilateral and global diplomacy with Africans. Our analysis includes traditional government-to-government diplomacy, high-level visits, as well as cooperation at the United Nations. We present a detailed examination of China's core interests and issues of concern for African governments before concluding with an examination of African agency vis-à-vis China.

Chapter 3 looks at China's relations with African regional and subregional organizations. Engagement with multilateral African institutions provides opportunities for China to communicate with several countries at once. To coordinate its political and security programs and positions faster and more efficiently, China financed FOCAC—its own Africa-focused organization. China's interaction with preexisting regional and subregional organizations varies, yet each offers another venue for Beijing to advance its interests and build relationships with African elites.

The fourth chapter examines the CPC's relations with African political parties. It includes our database spanning two decades of exchanges between the ID-CPC and African political parties. The data and descriptions of these meetings helped us analyze the ID-CPC bilateral and multilateral exchanges with African political parties. We conclude with country case studies of party-to-party relations in South Africa, Ethiopia, and Ghana and what they tell us about how China engages African parties under different national and political conditions.

The fifth chapter analyzes Beijing's Africa-focused propaganda work. After summarizing how party leaders conceive of foreign-focused propaganda work, we explore how they apply these concepts and tactics in the African media, education, and cultural spheres. These activities reinforce China's relationship building with elites across African societies with an eye toward advancing and defending Chinese interests, countering the United States, and, increasingly, promoting China's own model of political governance as superior to liberal democracy.

Chapter 6 links China's holistic security concept with its development priorities in Africa. Continued access to energy and critical minerals such as cobalt, tantalum, platinum, and manganese is essential to maintaining economic growth, and with it China's rise to great power status. Chinese companies source large quantities of these and other resources from African countries and are investing in Africa's earth supply chains, agricultural lands, commercial fishing, and deep seabed mining in the Indian Ocean.

The seventh chapter explores how military modernization and the development of expeditionary forces have become essential to protecting China's overseas interests. We document how China's expansion in Africa has created new security challenges. In many countries, private security companies are being employed to thwart attacks on Chinese nationals and property. When and where its own efforts and those of African governments have proven insufficient, China has been compelled to evacuate its expatriates. Concern over the safety of Chinese nationals has also pushed Beijing to take a more active, albeit still limited, role in conflict prevention, management, and mediation. China's participation in UN peacekeeping operations supports stability on the continent while also allowing the PLA to obtain much needed practical experience and station its personnel nearby to assist Chinese nationals in case of an emergency.

LOCATING AFRICA IN CHINA'S GEOSTRATEGY

In chapter 8 we detail China's security diplomacy, training, and joint exercises with the military in African countries. China has increased its counterterrorism and intelligence-sharing cooperation in Africa. Until the outbreak of COVID-19, China's security diplomacy included a growing number of military exchange visits, and holding two regional security forums in 2018 and 2019. China hosts training exercises with African military and police, although such collaborations remain limited in scale and frequency. Arms sales are another way the PLA interacts with African security forces, although the value of these purchases has declined in recent years. In some African countries Chinese construction companies are building military and police facilities. Although China remains a minor player in disaster relief, the PLA is expanding its humanitarian assistance work in Africa.

Chapter 9 looks at maritime security. We begin by explaining how China's expanded naval security deployments in the western Indian Ocean reflect its geostrategic rivalries with the United States and India. Next, we review and explain the strategic importance of China's antipiracy activities in the Gulf of Aden and the Gulf of Guinea, joint exercises and training with African navies, and PLA Navy port visits and investments in Africa. The chapter concludes with a discussion of China's first overseas military base in Djibouti and the prospects for additional military facilities in Africa.

Chapter 10 examines China-Africa security cooperation in a range of high-technology sectors with important security implications for both sides. Chinese companies like Huawei and ZTE remain the continent's leaders in the field of information technology equipment and information technology network development. China's firms are also expanding their presence in artificial intelligence, surveillance technology, and cyber security, fields in which Beijing hopes to control global standards. China-Africa nuclear, space, and satellite cooperation remains at an early stage and faces considerable competition from Western countries and Russia.

In the book's final chapter we extrapolate from our findings to identify nine emerging trends that we believe will continue to shape China's political and security relations with Africans in the decade to come.

2

BILATERAL AND GLOBAL RELATIONS

The strength of China's relations with African countries lies in the solid ties it has developed over the years with African governments. China requires an official government-to-government relationship before it will begin building bilateral political and security ties with a country, including party-to-party relations (see chapter 4), people-to-people relations (see chapter 5), and security relations (see chapters 8, 9, and 10). In this way, diplomatic ties are the bellwether of China's bilateral relationships, and in Africa they are strong. This is demonstrated by China's almost universal diplomatic representation in Africa, the number and quality of its high-level exchange visits, and the support it receives from Africa at the United Nations and in other international forums. China's long-standing focus on state sovereignty and reluctance to interfere in the internal affairs of other nations have assisted its ability to develop cordial ties with African leaders. As emphasized in chapter 1, the Xi Jinping era has updated these relationships by underscoring the China-Africa Community of Shared Future and linking Africa to the concept of the Chinese Dream. China has cordial relations with every government in Africa except for one that recognizes Taiwan.

BILATERAL AND GLOBAL RELATIONS

This chapter explores the current state of diplomatic ties, the influence created by financing and building key government buildings, the importance of high-level visits, and China-Africa collaboration at the United Nations. Yet China-Africa relations are not trouble free at the bilateral level. China's professed policy of noninterference in African affairs has undergone change because of its more assertive foreign policy and increasing threats to its nationals and interests in Africa. Beijing continues to insist that African governments not interfere in Chinese "core" issues, which as a practical matter means they must either carefully avoid them or back Beijing's positions. Those issues include Taiwan, human rights, Tibet, mistreatment of Muslim minorities, the South China Sea, and Hong Kong. Tensions between China and African governments have also increased in recent years, as a considerable number of African states experience large, persistent trade deficits with China and face unsustainable debt, much of it held by Chinese financial institutions. This chapter suggests that there is growing concern in Africa regarding the asymmetric nature of bilateral ties and a desire to increase African agency.

DIPLOMATIC TIES

China has diplomatic relations with fifty-three of the fifty-four countries in Africa. (The African Union recognizes fifty-five countries, including the Western Sahara, which Morocco claims and administers but China does not recognize.) Throughout the last half of the twentieth century and extending into the twenty-first, China devoted much of its diplomacy in Africa to convincing countries to recognize Beijing and not Taipei (see appendix).[1] China has won this battle. Only Eswatini, formerly Swaziland, continues to formally recognize the Republic of China (Taiwan), which maintains trade offices in several African countries. Besides Eswatini, China has an embassy in all fifty-three countries, and all those African nations have embassies in Beijing. While all fifty-four African countries recognize

BILATERAL AND GLOBAL RELATIONS

the United States, China has more embassies in Africa, and not every African country recognizing the United States has an embassy in Washington.

China has not always had such cordial bilateral ties with African countries, however. The past is replete with contentious competition from Taiwan for diplomatic recognition, as well as political missteps by Beijing. In the 1960s, for example, Ghanaian president Kwame Nkrumah welcomed Chinese military advisers to train dissidents committed to overturning governments in several independent African countries in the basics of guerrilla warfare. This collaboration ended in 1966, when Ghana's military deposed Nkrumah while he was being hosted in Beijing. The new Ghanaian government eventually suspended relations with Beijing, and all Chinese staff departed the embassy in Accra. Ghana published two white papers detailing China's military assistance and the secret guerrilla training camps before it restored ties with China in 1972.[2] More blatant interference occurred in Cameroon throughout the 1960s, when China supported an armed struggle by the Marxist leader of the Union des Populations du Cameroon (UPC), Félix Moumié, against the conservative elected president, Ahmadou Ahidjo. The Ahidjo government crushed the UPC in 1970 and the following year established diplomatic relations with Beijing.[3]

China and Libya experienced a difficult diplomatic relationship until recently even though the two nations established official ties in 1978. In 2006, when Libyan leader Mu'ammar al-Qadhafi was hosting China's foreign minister in Libya and confirming his country's commitment to the One China Principle, his son, acting as his father's envoy, met Taiwanese president Chen Shui-bian in Taipei and invited him to Libya to facilitate bilateral ties. President Chen subsequently made a transit stop in Tripoli, angering China. Two years later Taiwan opened a commercial office in Libya. At the ministerial Forum on China-Africa Cooperation in Egypt in 2009, Libya's foreign minister, Moussa Koussa, complained about China's "divide and rule" of African countries. The same year Koussa suggested that China is engaged in "something akin to a Chinese invasion of the African continent."[4]

Burkina Faso, the most recent country in Africa to switch recognition from Taipei to Beijing, did so in 2018 because of China's economic incentives and peer pressure from neighboring African countries. Five nations—Burkina Faso, Chad, Mali, Mauritania, and Niger—created the G5 Sahel Joint Force to combat terrorism in the region. China expressed a willingness to help fund the G5 but signaled that Burkina's relationship with Taiwan posed an obstacle to doing so. Ouagadougou's recognition of Beijing solved that problem.[5]

China has made enormous progress in its diplomatic relations with Africa since the 1960s and 1970s. This is due to its more pragmatic and less ideological foreign policy, increased experience in dealing with Africans, and especially the fact that China became a major trading power and has large amounts of capital to lend and invest in Africa. The improvement in the quality of China's diplomatic representatives in Africa over the years has also been striking. Many of its early representatives had little knowledge of the continent and often a poor command of the local lingua franca. Now Chinese Embassy representatives often serve multiple tours in Africa and usually have solid language skills.[6] In 2017, for example, the Chinese ambassador to Somalia was the only Somali speaker among the twenty-two ambassadors to the country.[7]

China can move resources quickly and has learned over the years how to use them effectively to advance diplomatic ties. Djibouti is an example of this flexibility: there, China has established its only military base outside the homeland and become the country's primary economic partner. As a result, Djiboutian president Ismaïl Omar Guelleh has commented that "the reality is that no one but the Chinese offers a long-term partnership in Djibouti."[8] Similarly, Cape Verde's prime minister, José Ulisses de Pina Correia e Silva, stated that his country's favored security partner is the United States, its favored trade partner is Europe, but its favored economic development partner is China.[9]

Ethiopia offers another example of China's ability to effectively leverage its economic resources. The United States was Ethiopia's preferred partner during the 1990s while China's engagement at that time was modest. This changed dramatically in the twenty-first century, however, with China becoming Ethiopia's largest trading partner, most important source of foreign direct investment and loans for infrastructure, and an important party-to-party relationship (see chapter 4). In January 2018 an Ethiopian with close ties to the country's ruling political party said that China's influence in Ethiopia is "hands down" greater than that of the United States because it is "system wide."[10] A change of government in Ethiopia a few months later, however, resulted in a prime minister who looked more favorably on Washington, changing the equation, and opening the door for a return of U.S. influence. But as Washington struggled to identify significant new funding for Addis Ababa, China organized several high-level exchange visits, rescheduled part of Ethiopia's debt, and quickly funded some of the prime minister's pet projects.[11] These maneuvers had their desired effect: while attending the Belt and Road Forum for International Cooperation in Beijing in 2019, Prime Minister Abiy Ahmed hailed China as Ethiopia's most reliable friend and most cherished partner.[12]

China has established categories of partnerships with countries around the world. They range from broad strategic partnerships to those that cover select categories of cooperation. The category called "comprehensive strategic partnerships" includes the African Union and ten African countries (South Africa, Algeria, Egypt, Mozambique, Zimbabwe, Ethiopia, Kenya, Sierra Leone, Tanzania, and Namibia). Despite their ideological and social differences, these countries maintain stable, wide-ranging, and multifaceted strategic cooperation with China. Beijing has lower-level "strategic partnerships" and "comprehensive cooperative partnerships" with the Republic of Congo, Angola, Gabon, Guinea, Senegal, Djibouti, Nigeria, Morocco, and Sudan.[13] A former Moroccan minister explained the difference by comparing China's relations with Algeria and with Morocco. Algeria has a strong military relationship with China and buys much of its military equipment from China, and Chinese companies build most of its infrastructure. Morocco is strategically located and has significant commercial ties with China but otherwise looks to cooperate primarily with Europe and the United States.[14]

GOVERNMENT BUILDINGS DIPLOMACY

China has a long history of constructing government buildings, such as presidential palaces, parliaments, ministerial headquarters, military facilities, and media headquarters, across Africa. Chinese companies build the structures, most of which appear to be motivated by profit, often under contracts funded by a loan from China at commercial or concessionary rates. Some of them, however, are gifts from China where there is reasonable expectation of currying favor with African officials and recipient governments. Interest-free loans, which in some cases China eventually cancels, fund others. This effectively makes the building a gift. When, for example, China provides grant funding or an interest-free loan to build a presidential palace or Foreign Ministry, it raises questions about the objectivity of the recipient country's foreign policy. A study by the U.S.-based Heritage Foundation in 2020 identified nineteen African countries where China has built the presidential palace or office; seventeen, the Foreign Ministry; and thirteen, other ministerial headquarters (see chapter 8).[15]

It is usually not possible to determine how an African government pays for a Chinese-built structure, but there are cases where it is known China has built presidential palaces and foreign ministries either free of charge or with an interest-free loan. In 2019 China turned over a $22 million presidential palace to the government of Burundi as a gift. On that occasion, Burundi's foreign minister said that "it proves the strongest political and diplomatic relations existing [sic] between Burundi and China."[16] In 2014 China replaced Sudan's historic presidential palace with a modern one funded by a grant for an unspecified amount.[17] China also funded presidential palaces in Togo and Guinea-Bissau, providing either grants or interest-free loans.[18] In 2022 it turned over a new parliament building and conference center to Zimbabwe as a gift.[19]

In 2004 China completed a Ministry of Foreign Affairs headquarters for Uganda, funded by a $6.5 million grant.[20] The same year China provided a $12 million grant for construction of the Foreign Ministry building in Mozambique.[21] In 2012 the Shanghai Construction Company completed

Sierra Leone's new Foreign Ministry with a $10 million grant from China.[22] The Chinese-built Ministry of Foreign Affairs and International Cooperation in Equatorial Guinea also received Chinese assistance.[23] In 2021 Kenya's principal secretary at the Ministry of Foreign Affairs and China's ambassador to Kenya, Zhou Pingjian, announced a Chinese grant of $38 million to construct a new ministry headquarters. Zhou made the announcement as he donated two VIP buses to the ministry, adding that 2021 marks the fiftieth anniversary of Beijing replacing Taipei in the United Nations, a vote that Kenya supported.[24] That same year Ethiopian prime minister Abiy Ahmed inaugurated a $50 million African Leadership Excellence Academy (two-thirds funded by a gift from China), built by a Chinese company.[25] And in 2022 China handed over the Tunisian Diplomatic Training Academy, which received Chinese financial aid.[26]

China's most publicized African building projects are the headquarters for the African Union (AU) in Addis Ababa, Ethiopia, and for the Economic Community of West African States (ECOWAS) in Abuja, Nigeria. The AU headquarters opened in 2012 while groundbreaking for the ECOWAS headquarters took place in 2022. China provided grant funding for both projects. The $200 million AU building sparked a major controversy in 2018 when *Le Monde* reported that Chinese technicians at the AU had been downloading and sending to Beijing each evening for several years the organization's confidential communications. Both China and the AU denied the story, which is widely believed to be accurate (see chapter 10).[27]

HIGH-LEVEL VISITS

As part of its focus on building relationships, China has relied on high-level visits as a key component of its diplomacy dating back at least to Premier Zhou Enlai's ten-country tour of Africa in 1963–1964. This historic event signaled the beginning of China's policy of emphasizing regular, personal contacts with senior African leaders.[28] China's approach to diplomacy "possess[es] an awareness and ability to plan the agenda," explains Chen

Dongxiao, president of the Shanghai Institutes for International Studies. During "diplomatic activities (especially multilateral events) [Beijing] skillfully makes use of 'host advantages,' thus amplifying the function of diplomatic activities. . . . These activities must help maintain and even expand the host country's national interests and have some effects that common diplomatic activities are unable to produce."[29] The outbreak of COVID-19, however, significantly reduced the number of visits in both directions.

China uses this approach routinely to cultivate relationships with large numbers of senior African government officials, party cadres, and military leaders.[30] Every year since 1991 China's foreign minister has made his first visit outside China to a country in Africa. In 2020 Foreign Minister Wang Yi went to Egypt, Djibouti, Eritrea, Burundi, and Zimbabwe.[31] In 2021 he visited Nigeria, the Democratic Republic of Congo (DRC), Botswana, Tanzania, and Seychelles, and in 2022 Eritrea, Kenya, and the Comoro Islands.[32] In January 2023 China's new foreign minister, Qin Gang, visited Ethiopia, Gabon, Angola, Benin, and Egypt.

Between 2007 and 2018 China's top leadership made seventy-nine visits to forty-three African countries. South Africa received the most visits, with a total of seven. Tanzania, Zambia, Namibia, Senegal, and, surprisingly, Chad received three or more.[33] Soon after becoming president in 2013, Xi Jinping went to Tanzania, South Africa, and the Republic of Congo. In 2015, preceded by a visit to Zimbabwe, he returned to South Africa to participate in the Johannesburg summit of the Forum on China-Africa Cooperation. In 2018 he again went to South Africa to attend the BRICS summit, and made stops in Senegal, Rwanda, and Mauritius. China invites large numbers of African leaders on bilateral visits or to attend multilateral meetings (see chapter 3). In 2016 alone, Xi Jinping received the heads of state of Egypt, Nigeria, Mozambique, Togo, Republic of Congo, South Africa, Chad, Senegal, Zimbabwe, Gabon, Sierra Leone, and Guinea.[34]

China frequently uses high-level visits for strategic purposes, such as to mitigate or reverse potential diplomatic setbacks. Ethiopia offers excellent examples in this regard. In 2016, at the height of internal conflict in the country when Chinese investments and personnel were threatened, Vice

President Li Yuanchao spent almost a week in Ethiopia to advise on the best way to respond to the crisis.[35] In 2018 Ethiopia elected a new prime minister, Abiy Ahmed, whose public comments suggested that he wanted to reach out to Western countries. The chairperson of China's Standing Committee of the National People's Congress, Li Zhanshu, quickly led a delegation to Ethiopia to shore up bilateral relations.[36]

African leaders welcome this high-level interaction and sometimes compare it favorably to the fewer visits conducted by senior American officials and fewer invitations received from the White House. A senior official in Ghana's Foreign Ministry noted that the president and foreign minister have good relations with their Chinese counterparts, which serves as the basis of Ghana's solid ties with China and underscores the importance that China attaches to personal relationships.[37] Only five African countries—Tanzania, Burundi, Democratic Republic of Congo, Eritrea, and Algeria—did not send their most senior official to the 2018 Forum on China-Africa Cooperation in Beijing, although three of the five sent their prime ministers.[38] By contrast, a senior African Union staff member remarked during the Trump administration that an invitation to the White House was no longer highly valued because it only generates a photo opportunity, while an invitation to Beijing usually results in a commitment of "goodies."[39]

CHINA-AFRICA COLLABORATION AT THE UNITED NATIONS

Since 1971, when twenty-six African UN members supported China's admission to the body to replace Taiwan, Beijing has worked hard to cultivate African votes.[40] Its policy of refraining from criticism of African human rights abuses and eschewing involvement in the internal affairs of African states, together with its increasing financing of African infrastructure, has aided this policy. As a result, the voting pattern of the three African countries serving as rotating members on the UN Security Council and the thirteen African members of the UN Human Rights Council has become more closely aligned with that of China than with the United States, France, and the United Kingdom, the three permanent members of the Security Council (P3), which are also NATO members. A senior member of the U.S. Embassy in Pretoria commented, for example, that South Africa consistently votes with China against the United States.[41]

When African security issues have come before the UN Security Council, the three rotating African members, the P3, and China often vote the same way. But there have been important exceptions, where China took a different position from the P3. Beginning in 2004, for instance, China consistently removed or tried to remove language in UN resolutions favored by the P3 that criticized Sudan for its ethnic cleansing in Darfur. Under heavy pressure from Western countries in the run-up to the Beijing Olympics in 2008, China voted more in line with the P3, but it usually abstained on resolutions dealing with Sudan.[42] Similarly, in 2008 China and Russia vetoed a Security Council resolution that sought to impose sanctions on Zimbabwe. South Africa and Libya joined China in opposing the sanctions, but Burkina Faso, which recognized Taiwan in 2008, supported the P3 position.[43]

In thirteen resolutions dealing with Sudan from 1996 to 2016, China voted contrary to both the African and the P3 position; abstaining on four of them. It also abstained on three others where two of the three African countries voted yes. China completely aligned its record with the Africans on seven South Sudan resolutions from 1996 to 2016, except for one where it abstained while two Africans voted yes. The UN Security Council proposed four resolutions on Burundi from 2014 to 2016; China voted with the three African countries and the P3 on three of them. It then abstained on a fourth where two African countries also abstained. There were five resolutions on Mali from 2012 to 2016; China voted for all of them, as did all the African countries and the P3. The six resolutions on Libya from 2011 to 2016 also resulted in agreement by the Africans, China, and the P3, except for one where China abstained.[44]

The alignment between China and Africa on resolutions before the UN General Assembly has been close as well. From 1971 to 2017 at least ten African countries voted with Beijing 89 percent of the time or more. These nations included Somalia, Djibouti, Zimbabwe, Sudan, Comoros, Guinea, Namibia, Mauritania, Niger, and Morocco. Only one African country—South Sudan—was among those in least agreement with China. The voting pattern for resolutions considered by the U.S. State Department as "important" between 1992 and 2017 was similar. Out of 192 ranked countries, nine in Africa—Zimbabwe, Republic of Congo, Sudan, Namibia, Mali, Nigeria, Uganda, Somalia, and Tanzania—were in the top twenty, having voted in agreement with China on UN resolutions more than 80 percent of the time. No African country was in the bottom twenty.[45]

Voting in the UN Human Rights Council is especially instructive because China and some African states routinely receive criticism on their human rights practices, especially from Western countries. The United States withdrew from the Human Rights Council in June 2018, stating that it made a mockery of human rights, and only rejoined in February 2021 following the election of President Joe Biden. One study looked at votes on seven proposals advocated by China at the council from 2016 to 2018. China sponsored two resolutions on development and human rights, which won the endorsement of a majority of members. It cosponsored five amendments designed to enhance the principle of noninterference or weaken protections for civil society groups, all of which failed to receive a majority. Western countries voted against both resolutions and all five amendments. For the two resolutions that passed, all thirteen African countries voted in favor of one, and twelve voted in favor on the other, while one abstained. The voting on the amendments was mixed but still favored China's position over that of the P3.[46]

China also looks to Africa and its fifty-four members for support of its candidates to lead the UN's specialized agencies. Of fifteen such agencies, a Chinese national headed four in 2021: the Food and Agriculture Organization, the International Civil Aviation Organization, the International Telecommunication Union, and the United Nations Industrial Development Organization.[47] The election in 2019 of Qu Dongyu as director general of the Food and Agriculture Organization was especially illustrative of the power dynamics. The Cameroonian candidate for the position, Medi Moungui, who had the backing of the African Union, withdrew from the race a month after a senior Chinese official visited Cameroon and announced that Beijing would cancel $78 million in debt owed by the country.[48]

As China's influence in both Africa and the United Nations increases, it opens itself up to more criticism. A case in point was the 2020 dispute between Kenya and Djibouti for representation on the UN Security Council in 2021–2022. African seats are usually filled after the African Union proposes a consensus candidate to the UN General Assembly. In this case, the African Union chose Kenya, but Djibouti cried foul. On separate occasions, different Chinese officials alternately implied publicly that China intended to support Kenya and Djibouti. This irritated both countries, prompting China to declare neutrality over a dispute that it said Africans must resolve themselves. Foreign Minister Wang Yi subsequently told his Kenyan counterpart that China "supports Africans to solve African problems in an African way."[49] Kenya ultimately won the seat in a secret ballot.

CHINA'S CORE INTERESTS

China's relations in Africa should be understood in the context of its stated "core national interests" (国家核心利益). While there are various formulations of this concept, all assume three basic overlapping objectives: to ensure the CPC will continue to rule China, to maintain and defend China's sovereignty and territorial integrity, and to promote a stable international environment that is conducive to China's continued economic growth.[50] The second category includes several controversial issues (Taiwan, human rights, Tibet, the mistreatment of Muslim minorities, the South China Sea, and Hong Kong) that are not criticized publicly and probably are rarely, if ever, addressed privately by African government officials. While this is largely because these issues are not salient in Africa, it is nevertheless noteworthy that, with one exception, not a single African government that recognizes Beijing has publicly contested any of them in more than ten years. In fact, many governments have publicly supported China's position on one or more of them. China, for its part, takes every opportunity to elicit their support. For example, when Tanzania's chief of defense forces called on Liang Guanglie, Chinese state councilor and defense minister, Liang hailed Tanzania's support on Taiwan, Tibet, and China's other "core interests."[51]

This asymmetry of concern, which is compounded by a vast asymmetry of power, means that China's ability to secure the support—or at least silence—of African governments should come as no surprise. Through its extensive economic and political engagement, China has successfully neutralized the willingness of these governments to publicly criticize issues that Beijing views as vital to its sovereignty, global status, and territorial integrity. African governments also welcome China's appeals to state sovereignty and noninterference in internal affairs. But while Beijing wields considerable power over what Africa's governments say on these topics, African civil society organizations, opposition political parties, and former government officials have occasionally criticized China.

Many of the African governments that support China's positions have serious human rights problems of their own, and some have autocratic governments. Most of them rely heavily on China for financing, aid, investment, and political backing. Their support or inaction is thus a consequence of their own vulnerability to criticism, relative weakness, and lack of concern about faraway territories over which China emphasizes its dominion. Nevertheless, China has impressed on African governments that its internal affairs are off the table for criticism.

If an African government crosses China on one or more of these sensitive domestic matters, Beijing's response can vary widely. For any country, large or small, recognizing Taipei means an end to official engagement with Beijing and a cessation of all aid or support. Beijing's responses to African transgressions on the other issues are less clear and depend on the severity of the "offense" and the nature of the country's relationship with China. This ambiguity of response serves as a deterrent in and of itself. An important country, say South Africa or Egypt, has more leeway than does a small one like Togo. Consequently, even the visit to South Africa by exiled Tibetan president Lobsang Sangay did not disrupt bilateral relations. Had this happened in Togo, for example, Beijing's response may well have been different. Ultimately, we found that African governments take extraordinary steps to avoid offending China and, in fact, go out of their way to ingratiate themselves with Beijing.

TAIWAN

The One China Principle has long been central in China-Africa relations and exemplifies Beijing's ability to exert influence. In 1971 Beijing received the support of twenty-six African states (34 percent of those voting affirmatively on the issue) in the United Nations General Assembly to serve as the sole legitimate representative of China, ousting Taipei from the seat. Over the next few years, ten of the fifteen countries that supported Taipei subsequently recognized Beijing.[52] Since Xi Jinping came to power in 2012, Gambia, São Tomé and Principe, and Burkina Faso have switched their recognition from Taipei to Beijing as well. Only Eswatini in southern Africa still recognizes the Republic of China (Taiwan), and China has stepped up its pressure on the government there to reverse this position. In 2020 Beijing announced that holders of Eswatini passports could obtain a visa for China only at the Chinese Embassy in Pretoria; previously, they could also obtain them from Chinese consulates in South Africa.[53] Some observers interpreted this decision as an effort to pressure those in Eswatini's business and economic sectors to press the country's leaders to switch recognition to Beijing.[54] Chinese officials routinely express appreciation to African governments for their near universal support for the One China Principle.

Beijing insists that Taipei confine its engagement in Africa to commercial activities. As is the case in other parts of the world, Taipei has six semiofficial, government-sponsored trade offices in Africa, located in Abidjan, Algiers, Cairo, Johannesburg, Lagos, and Nairobi.[55] China itself has significant commercial engagement with Taiwan and does not object to these trade offices, so long as they do not formally engage in diplomatic activity. The Taipei Trade Office in Nigeria has experienced considerable controversy in this regard. Located in Lagos from 1991 to 2001, it then moved to the country's new political capital in Abuja, where it came under pressure from Beijing to return to the commercial capital of Lagos.[56] In 2017

Beijing succeeded in convincing the government of Nigeria to relocate the office back to Lagos, which occurred at the beginning of 2018.[57]

In 2020 the foreign minister of Somaliland, which declared unilateral independence from Somalia in 1991, but which no country recognizes, visited Taiwan. The foreign minister of Taiwan announced that Taipei agreed to establish a "Taiwan Representative Office" in Somaliland—a step short of formal diplomatic relations.[58] The Chinese Embassy in Somalia, which still claims Somaliland, quickly responded that "we resolutely oppose two Chinas, one China, one Taiwan, Taiwan independence, and the separatist forces advocating Taiwan independence and their separatist activities."[59] China subsequently sent a high-level delegation to Somaliland to discuss economic cooperation and trade. More important, Beijing wanted to ensure that Somaliland treat Taiwan as a business partner, and not as a political one.[60] Somaliland is the only one of these special offices in Africa where "Taiwan" appears in the name instead of "Taipei."[61] China's Foreign Ministry spokesperson subsequently stepped up the hostile rhetoric, stating in response to a question about Somaliland that "those going against the trend to challenge the one-China Principle will get burned and swallow the bitter fruit."[62]

Taiwan's relationship with South Africa, which follows the One China Principle, is more developed than with any other country in Africa, except for Eswatini. In addition to its trade office in Johannesburg, Taipei has liaison offices in both Pretoria and Cape Town. Taipei additionally has a sister city relationship with Pretoria. An estimated seven to eight thousand Taiwanese reside in South Africa, and there are about eight hundred Taiwan businesses there.[63] Due to the political and economic importance of South Africa and the unique history of Taiwan's community there, China seems to accept more flexibility in its application of the One China Principle than it does in other African countries.

HUMAN RIGHTS

China's approach to human rights differs in important ways from the Western interpretation of the concept, which is based on universality, indivisibility, and interdependence. China, by contrast, has what it calls "human rights with Chinese characteristics," which prioritizes economic development over individual civil and political rights. Rather than universal human rights, Beijing insists on a relativistic approach based on each country's unique history, culture, values, and political system.[64] Although African elites experienced Western conceptions of human rights during and after the colonial period and many continue to accept these values, the Chinese definition has proven more attractive to many African leaders.

The reasons are understandable. From a Western perspective, both China and many African countries have poor human rights records. African countries facing Western criticism and even sanctions for human rights abuses routinely look to China for support at both the UN Security Council and the UN Human Rights Council. China, for its part, enlists the support (or at least secures the silence) of African members of the UN Human Rights Council and of the three rotating African members on the UN Security Council, on issues such as its suppression of the media, the detention of political opponents and human rights activists, the mistreatment of Christians, and mass surveillance. China has taken the issue a step further, however, and enlisted the support of African countries in criticizing the United States and Western nations for violating human rights and expressing serious concern about systematic racial discrimination. In 2020 China made a joint statement before the Third Committee of the UN General Assembly to this effect on behalf of twenty-six countries, including Angola, Burundi, Cameroon, Equatorial Guinea, Eritrea, Namibia, South Sudan, Sudan, and Zimbabwe.[65] While the issues of Tibet, the mistreatment of Muslim minorities, and Hong Kong all have significant human rights implications, we address them separately because of the importance Beijing attaches to them.

TIBET

Tibet is far from Africa and attracts little interest from the countries of the continent. It is an easy topic for most African governments to ignore. Nevertheless, the issue has arisen in South Africa. In 2009, for instance, South

African opposition parties invited the Dalai Lama for a visit. But, under pressure from China, the South African government denied his visa. In 2011 the Dalai Lama was invited to attend the eightieth birthday of Archbishop Desmond Tutu and give public lectures. The South African government again denied the visa.[66] In 2014 the Dalai Lama hoped to attend the fourteenth world summit of Nobel Peace laureates in Cape Town, but the government denied his visa a third time, for which China's authorities expressed appreciation.[67]

In 2018 South Africa permitted the visit by the exiled president of the Tibetan government, Lobsang Sangay, who travels on a U.S. passport. After his arrival, however, the government canceled all public events as a result of protests by South Africans and members of the local Chinese community. The Chinese Embassy issued a strongly worded statement that Sangay's visit "undermined the political trust between China and South Africa" and would discourage Chinese investment, angering the South African government in the process.[68] Sangay returned to South Africa in 2019, when he met with the country's former president, F. W. de Klerk.[69]

In 2017 Botswana had its own controversial interaction with China when the U.S.-based Mind and Life Institute invited the Dalai Lama to address a human rights conference and to meet President Ian Khama. China pressured Botswana to cancel the visit; the Dalai Lama ultimately bowed out, citing fatigue, but an angry President Khama, whose cabinet was divided on the issue, invited the Dalai Lama to visit Botswana in the future.[70] Khama completed his ten-year term in 2018, however, and there is no indication that his successor has issued an invitation.

MISTREATMENT OF MUSLIM MINORITIES

China has worked hard over the years to establish good relations with Muslim countries and has succeeded in doing so.[71] More than half of Africa's fifty-four countries are predominantly Muslim or have large Muslim minorities. China has made clear that it does not want any country to interfere with its policies toward its Muslim minorities, including the building of a chain of gulags that it calls "re-education centers" for the Uighur population in Xinjiang.⁷² That message has been received; to date, on only one occasion has an African country joined Western critics and a few others (such as Turkey and Japan) in criticizing China's treatment of its Muslim minorities. Nor has the issue resonated with African publics. Even leaders in overwhelmingly Muslim countries, like Egypt and Djibouti, have expressed no public criticism of China's policies.⁷³ One Moroccan analyst explained the rationale behind this silence: "What is the incentive to criticize China's policy towards the Uighurs? There is none."⁷⁴ Moreover, the governments of some of the Muslim countries that have supported China's policies in Xinjiang oppose political Islam, which they associate with terrorism, and have therefore accepted China's argument that the Uighur crackdown is a counterterrorism campaign.⁷⁵

The official reaction from African countries has been a *defense* of China's policy toward its Muslim minorities. The Organization of Islamic Cooperation (OIC) adopted a resolution in March 2019 that commended China for "providing care to its Muslim citizens" and looked forward to additional cooperation between the OIC and China.⁷⁶ Half of all African countries are members of the OIC. The Independent Permanent Human Rights Commission of the OIC, which met in Jeddah, Saudi Arabia, in April 2019, issued a press release that encouraged Uighurs and the government of China "to continue to engage positively" on all issues of mutual interest, including protection of the rights of Uighur Muslims. Yet the same report also called for sustained international pressure on the government of Myanmar to ensure it fulfills its obligations under international law to respect the rights of the Rohingya Muslim minority.⁷⁷ A Djiboutian Foreign Ministry official confirmed that his country supported the condemnation of Myanmar for its treatment of the Rohingya because, among other things, Myanmar, unlike China, has little influence in Africa.⁷⁸

In July 2019 the ambassadors of twenty-two mostly Western countries sent a letter to the president of the United Nations Human Rights Council urging China to stop its arbitrary incarceration of Uighurs and members of the country's other Muslim minority communities.⁷⁹ China quickly organized a response: the ambassadors of thirty-seven countries—seventeen of them African—sent a letter to the council stating that security had returned to Xinjiang and the fundamental human rights of people of all ethnic groups there had been safeguarded. More countries subsequently signed on to the letter.[80] Many countries, including predominantly Muslim ones, agreed to sign to demonstrate solidarity with the noninterference principle and not to jeopardize access to China's aid and financing.[81]

In October 2019 China's Foreign Ministry circulated documents on the issue to African media houses, including a white paper titled "The Fight Against Terrorism and Extremism and Human Rights Protection in Xinjiang."[82] The following month twenty-three predominantly Western countries submitted a joint statement at the United Nations that was extremely critical of China's persecution of the Uighurs. China orchestrated another response, this one signed by fifty-four countries, including twenty-eight from Africa, which praised "China's remarkable achievements in the field of human rights by adhering to the people-centered development philosophy and protecting and promoting human rights through development" while also citing the "challenge of terrorism and extremism" in Xinjiang.[83]

In October 2020 Cuba's permanent representative to the United Nations read a statement before the Third Committee on behalf of forty-five countries, including twenty-one in Africa, defending China's human rights policies in Xinjiang. Curiously, eight countries (Burkina Faso, Chad, Djibouti, Mauritania, Niger, Nigeria, Sierra Leone, and Zambia) that signed the November 2019 letter in the previous paragraph were not part of the October 2020 statement. All of them except Zambia have significant Muslim populations. Madagascar and Morocco joined the October 2020 statement but did not sign the November 2019 letter. By contrast, no African country joined a competing statement critical of China's policy in Xinjiang read by the German permanent representative to the United Nations.[84]

China continued to press its case for Xinjiang with Africans in 2021. Zimbabwe's ruling political party expressed its support for China's "measures to protect and bring prosperity" to the people of Xinjiang.[85] Beijing-based ambassadors from Burkina Faso, the Republic of Congo, and Sudan all spoke out in favor of China's policies at an event called "Xinjiang in the Eyes of African Ambassadors to China." Burkina Faso's ambassador to China said that Western allegations of "forced labor" and "genocide" are groundless, while Sudan's ambassador added that the Xinjiang issue is not about human rights but instead is a political weapon Western countries use against China.[86] Chinese embassies in Africa also launched a full-scale social media campaign to rebut allegations of genocide and widespread human rights violations in Xinjiang.[87] In June 2021 Canada presented a joint statement on behalf of forty-four members of the UN Human Rights Council expressing grave concerns about the situation in Xinjiang. Not a single African country supported the document.[88]

The solitary case in the last ten years of an African country's objection (other than Eswatini, which recognizes Taiwan) to China's human rights policies in Xinjiang occurred in October 2021 when Liberia joined forty-three states in a joint statement sponsored by France in the Third Committee of the UN General Assembly. The Chinese ambassador responded that Beijing is "shocked and disappointed" by Liberia's support for the joint statement, noting that Liberia is dependent on China for most of its trade and infrastructure and citing Beijing's past assistance.[89]

SOUTH CHINA SEA

China's construction of contested islands in the South China Sea has led to tensions with the United States, as well as with those Asian nations that claim the same territory and waters. The controversy, however, has no resonance in Africa. While it is unsurprising that Africans would ignore the issue, this has not stopped China from soliciting and obtaining African support for its position. In May 2016 ten African countries signed the "Doha Declaration" of the seventh ministerial meeting of the China-Arab States Cooperation Forum (see chapter 3), which expressed appreciation for China's efforts to resolve territorial and maritime disputes with neighboring countries through dialogue and negotiation. The declaration added that signatories of the UN Convention on the Law of the Sea should have the right to choose their own approach to resolving the issue, a stance that ran counter to efforts by the Philippines to turn the matter over to a UN arbitration panel.[90]

BILATERAL AND GLOBAL RELATIONS

A substantial number of African countries that did not sign the "Doha Declaration" made separate statements, and several countries did both. Some statements, such as those made by Kenya and Gambia, explicitly supported China's position. Most African countries, including South Africa, Lesotho, and Ethiopia, supported half measures that called for resolving the disputes through consultations and negotiations, while also following the China-approved Declaration on the Conduct of Parties in the South China Sea.[91] By mid-2016 thirty-nine African countries had made at least one public statement supporting China's position on the South China Sea, according to a survey by China's Renmin University.[92]

HONG KONG

In 2019–2020 protests in Hong Kong over the erosion of local rights and freedoms posed a challenge for Beijing. To press its case, China went on a global media blitz that stressed the importance of the "one country, two systems" principle and called out any country that supported the protesters.[93]

In October 2019 Uganda's Ministry of Foreign Affairs issued a statement saying that it "firmly supports the one country, two systems policy of the People's Republic of China on the matter of Hong Kong and other areas." The statement added that "Hong Kong is part of China. Hong Kong's affairs are China's domestic affairs."[94] The following day Tanzania's chief government spokesperson told Xinhua that Hong Kong is an internal matter within China, and that Tanzania supports the one country, two systems approach. He added that the steps taken by the Hong Kong government were the best approach to the situation, and other countries should support China.[95] Tanzania's constitution and legal affairs minister likewise reaffirmed the country's full support for the one country, two systems policy.[96] In January 2020 Namibia's minister of land reform commented at the Chinese Spring Festival dinner in Windhoek that his country is closely following developments in Hong Kong and fully supports the sovereignty and territorial integrity of China, which includes Hong Kong.[97]

Similarly, during a visit to Lusaka in 2019 by a Chinese assistant foreign minister, Zambia's foreign minister reportedly backed China's position on Hong Kong. China's ambassador in Lusaka thanked Zambia for its support on Hong Kong, which demonstrated the "high level of bilateral friendly cooperative relations."[98] A member of China's National People's Congress Standing Committee, on a visit to Liberia, stated that senior Liberian officials supported China's position on Hong Kong.[99] In a meeting with Ghana's minister of foreign and regional integration, China's ambassador to Ghana expressed appreciation for the minister's support of China's one country, two systems policy on Hong Kong.[100] Commenting on a 2021 phone conversation with Xi Jinping, China's Ministry of Foreign Affairs stated that Burundi president Evariste Ndayishimiye firmly supported China's position on its core interests, including Hong Kong, Taiwan, Xinjiang, and the South China Sea.[101] Yet when the coverage of these meetings comes only from China's official media, it raises questions about whether liberty has been taken when reporting the African interlocutors' comments.

In June 2020 Cuba and the United Kingdom presented competing statements before the UN Human Rights Council that respectively supported and opposed China's new national security law for Hong Kong. Fifty-three countries, including twenty-five in Africa, backed the new Hong Kong security law, while not a single African country supported the UK statement criticizing the measure.[102] Several other African countries, although not voting with China, voiced support for the national security law in Hong Kong.[103]

The June 2020 Joint Statement of the Extraordinary China-Africa Summit on Solidarity Against COVID-19 contained one of the most surprising pledges of African support for China's position on Hong Kong. Thirteen African presidents and prime ministers, including leaders from South Africa, Nigeria, Egypt, Kenya, and Ethiopia, as well as the chairperson of the African Union Commission, participated in the virtual summit. The Joint Statement contained the following reference, which is totally unrelated to COVID-19: "The African side supports China's position on Taiwan and Hong Kong and supports China's efforts to safeguard national security in Hong Kong in accordance with law."[104] In October 2020 the Pakistani permanent representative to the United Nations read a statement supporting China's position on Hong Kong before the Third Committee backed by fifty-four countries. Half of the countries in Africa joined the statement. Not a single African country signed a competing statement critical of China's position in Hong Kong proposed by the German permanent representative to the United Nations.[105]

Most African governments support China's core interests because it is an easy way to strengthen ties with China without compromising their own priorities. Opposing China's positions on these issues would jeopardize billions of dollars in Chinese financing, aid, and investment, for no gain.[106] This situation, however, can also provide ammunition for the political opposition in African countries. As one prominent member of Uganda's parliament explained, by unquestionably supporting Beijing, President Yoweri Museveni "has mortgaged Uganda to China."[107]

ECONOMIC CHALLENGES BECOME AFRICAN POLITICAL CONCERNS

There are two economic issues in the China-Africa relationship that now raise serious political concerns among African governments and civil society: large and persistent trade deficits with China in many African countries, and China's contribution to a high debt load in others.[108] The coronavirus pandemic has aggravated both problems. As Africa's largest trading partner and most important bilateral source of loans, China plays an outsized role in African economies. Both issues, especially the debt question, are complicated and have caused a growing number of African governments to reassess their financial relationship with China. They have implications for China's political and even security links with African countries, given that China takes a comprehensive approach to security (see chapters 1 and 6). Djibouti's large indebtedness to China, for example, inhibits its ability to maximize the leverage offered by its geostrategic position and helped Beijing establish its first overseas military base in the country. Meanwhile, large, sustained trade deficits have become sensitive political issues in important countries such as Egypt, Kenya, and South Africa.

AFRICAN AGENCY

The asymmetric relationship between China and all African countries means that the latter must negotiate from a position of weakness. Although African governments face similar power inequities when engaging other major powers, the situation is particularly acute with China because of its ubiquitous relationships and role as the principal bilateral lender. The issue of agency is also important as China interacts with Africans in the African Union, the Forum on China-Africa Cooperation, the Belt and Road Forum for International Cooperation, and other groupings discussed in chapter 3.

Agency on the part of African countries becomes most salient during negotiations with China over the terms of loans, the percent of Chinese labor permitted to work on Chinese-financed projects, the terms for extracting energy and minerals, enforcement of local labor and safety laws, and local environmental standards. African agency, or the lack thereof, also affects important local questions, such as the number of Chinese small traders allowed in African markets, preventing the entry of counterfeit goods, maintaining control over African intellectual property, and the transfer of skills to Africans.

Africans understand that China pursues its own interests as it interacts with their countries.[109] A large, well-financed government with a deep and experienced bureaucracy and established institutions, China comes to the table with significant advantages over any African counterpart. The leadership of a Ghanaian think tank explained, for example, that a large delegation from China proposed a $15 billion loan. China came with all kinds of data and "razzle-dazzled" us, they said. Ghana's delegation in those talks, by contrast, consisted of just three persons. The position taken by the government of Ghana at that time was do whatever you want.¹¹⁰ Other Ghanaians agreed that Ghana is not well prepared when it sits across the table from China because the bureaucracy is broken, and Ghana faces political divisions. As a result, the Ghana-China relationship is "asymmetric and unsustainable."¹¹¹

Some Africans are self-critical about the degree to which they fail to exercise agency. A common complaint is that most African nations do not have a strategy for dealing with China. Ibrahima Diong, a former regional coordinator for Africa at the World Bank, said China knows what it wants from Africa, but most African countries do not have a strategy vis-à-vis China. Africans themselves need to get better organized, she noted.¹¹² Carlos Lopes, the former executive secretary of the UN Economic Commission for Africa, added that it "is critical for African leaders to become more strategic in their relationship, by articulating a unified China policy."¹¹³ For his part, Alfred Dube, the former director of the Institute for Security Studies in Addis Ababa and Botswana's former ambassador to China, explained that Africa must have a strategy for dealing with China and getting the most out of FOCAC. Going to Beijing with a "begging bowl" will not work any longer, according to Dube.¹¹⁴ A Ghanaian scholar, meanwhile, explained that Ghana lacks a strategic vision, and African countries have little interest in developing strategic policies. Rather, Africans focus on short-term, self-interested outcomes.¹¹⁵ James Shikwati, who runs a think tank in Kenya, similarly blamed Kenya's bad deals with China on a predatory elite culture that he called "tenderpreneurship."¹¹⁶

A case study of a $300 million China Export Import Bank loan for building roads in Mozambique is instructive in this regard. The Mozambique side made little use of its limited agency, entering negotiations with the goal of securing funding for the project with minimal concern about the Export Import Bank's standard terms, such as requiring a Chinese contractor, mostly Chinese materials, and all Chinese skilled labor. As a result, it was less of a negotiation than an agreement. The Mozambique side functioned as though the cards were dealt before the negotiations began; its priority was to get the project done quickly and efficiently. Mozambique's leverage was limited by the fact that its domestic construction companies were not important to the country's political elite and there was no incentive to enhance their role in the project. This is not an uncommon situation in African countries.[117]

African institutions such as the governmental bureaucracy, banks, and trade unions that operate with a minimum of corruption can contribute significantly to African agency. Unfortunately, most African countries are weak in these areas. South Africa is an exception, but even its government and trade union failed to protect the textile industry from Asian, especially Chinese, imports.[118] Ghana's strong trade unions, on the other hand, forced China to allow workers to exercise their rights in the Bui Dam project, which was financed and built by a Chinese company.[119] Kenya accepted Confucius Institutes before it had created regulations for international higher education, leaving it open to questionable behavior on both the Chinese and Kenyan side.[120] Some African countries have good environmental laws and regulations that Chinese companies are expected to observe, but their corruption, ineffective bureaucracies, and understaffing make them hard to enforce. Consequently, Chinese companies can choose to follow the regulations or ignore them.[121]

A 2017 study of African agency in the uranium sectors of Niger and Namibia demonstrated that Namibia did better than Niger in its interaction with Chinese companies. The authors suggested the outcomes were different because of government capacity, the differing histories of trade unions, the comparative nature of colonial relationships, population size and distribution, and the diversity and geographical distribution of resources.[122] African governments can affect some of these factors. Others, however, are out of their control. Another study involving the Chinese-built and financed railway in Ethiopia concluded that Ethiopian officials exercised agency at various stages of design and construction. At the same time, limitations of capacity and technical expertise constrained Ethiopia's agency.[123] A study of Chinese-financed wind farms in Ethiopia concluded that its authoritarian state system gave Addis Ababa significant agency.[124]

Some African countries have agency for special reasons, such as natural resources, unused arable land, human capital, and sizeable markets for Chinese exports.[125] Djibouti is strategically located, which aided its negotiating position with China and other major powers for respective military bases.[126] One study on Djibouti's agency vis-à-vis China, France, and the United States concluded that, by balancing its ties among the three, it was able to "exert some agency" with all of them.[127] Similarly, the small Indian Ocean archipelago of Seychelles has exercised agency by taking advantage of Sino-Indian rivalry in this strategic waterway, which has become increasingly important to the PLA Navy.[128] By balancing relations between India and China, the Seychelles has maximized the benefits it has received from both countries.[129] Benin enhanced its agency by strategically organizing its bureaucracy and negotiators during talks with China for financing and building a business center.[130]

Other nations, such as Angola and Nigeria, have the potential to exercise agency because they hold large oil reserves that are of interest to China.[131] Angola, Africa's largest supplier of crude to China, signed infrastructure-for-oil deals while limiting China's influence on their relationship. It managed to negotiate an attractive interest rate on several of its loans with repayment at the London Interbank Offer Rate plus 1.25 percent, as well as increasing the repayment period to fifteen years.[132] In the case of Nigeria, endemic corruption undermines much of the agency that the country's oil might otherwise have provided.[133] Similarly in the DRC, if not for corruption, strategic minerals such as cobalt might have had a positive effect on African agency.

Our discussions with a variety of Africans suggest there is some agreement about countries that have been more strategic and done a better job in exercising agency vis-à-vis China. South Africa, Egypt, Ethiopia, and Rwanda are most frequently cited as examples in this regard. Ethiopia has used its strategic partnership with China to implement an ambitious program of industrialization. The government also leverages its relationship with China as a bargaining chip in its negotiations with European donors.[134] Some Kenyan trade unions have interacted effectively with Chinese companies. Trade unionists use the dispute mechanism effectively even when Kenyan government officials are more concerned with preserving good relations with China.[135] One recent study on African agency concluded that "the relationship between China and Africa is simultaneously highly unequal in economic terms, and yet contains an element of striving to realize sovereign equality as a form of South-South cooperation."[136] African governments also exercise agency by playing China and Western development partners against one another.[137]

African agency came into play in an intriguing way when China mishandled its African residents at the beginning of the COVID-19 outbreak. After treating Africans in China poorly, there was a backlash from several African governments and more generally from civil society organizations and the independent media. To make up for these missteps, China seemed to be more amenable, at least in the immediate aftermath of the problem, to discussions about debt relief with countries such as Zambia and Ghana.[138]

It remains up to African governments, however, to maximize the leverage they have. Africans are beginning to ask whether Africa needs China more than China needs Africa and concluding that the answer is "no." As one Zambian journalist put it, the relationship between Africa and China has been mutually beneficial. The challenge, he wrote, is that Africans have either not leveraged their natural resources, or their leaders are pocketing China's money and allowing China to take advantage.[139] What remains, however, is for Africa to develop a strategy for interacting with China.[140] African countries with critical raw materials will undoubtedly find this task easier, as will countries like Djibouti, Seychelles, and Egypt, which can leverage their strategic locations.

Notably, all African countries can use their ties to the European Union and North America, as well as newer arrivals to continental politics such as India, Brazil, Turkey, Malaysia, and the Gulf States, to get a better deal with China.[141] One regional study in 2020 found that a huge Chinese loan to the DRC gave the government of former president Joseph Kabila leverage in its interaction with other external actors between 2007 and 2009. This agency, however, subsequently disappeared as China became more cautious in its loan policy and stopped providing enormous loans to the DRC.[142] As Kingsley Moghalu, former deputy governor of Nigeria's Central Bank, has concluded: "China feels its future and image as a global power is tied significantly to Africa. This gives Africa bargaining power."[143] Similarly, the Centre for African Studies at Nanyang Technological University in Singapore wrote that "China cannot afford to let Africa fail," and the postcoronavirus world may allow African states to improve "their balance of power" with China.[144]

* * *

China has achieved almost universal diplomatic recognition in Africa and leveraged its influence by constructing, sometimes free of charge, key government buildings such as presidential palaces and foreign ministries. The frequency of high-level visits between Chinese and African leaders, as well as their collaboration in the United Nations, reflects the importance that China places on relations with Africa generally and the value it attaches to personal relationships with African leaders. However, China's ostensibly noninterventionist approach to relations with African countries has been shifting. China regularly rewards or penalizes them depending on their public position on China's core interests, including Taiwan, Tibet, human rights, Muslim minorities in China, the South China Sea, and Hong Kong.

The financial advantages that African countries obtain from China sometimes result in large and unsustainable trade deficits and/or debt that is increasingly difficult to repay. Both issues have led to tension in African countries' respective relationships with China and complicated African attempts to assert agency. The strength of African agency also varies widely from country to country. Much of it depends on whether a country is a major source of critical raw materials or occupies a geostrategic location. Nevertheless, China, because of its political and economic power, almost always comes to the negotiating table with a significant advantage. One study on the subject concluded that although African agency is increasing, "the power gap between China and African countries, nonetheless, is real."[145] If African nations develop a coherent, and ideally more unified, strategy toward China, they should be able to increase their agency and their ability to negotiate more effectively with Beijing.

3
REGIONAL AND SUBREGIONAL RELATIONS

Under the leadership of Xi Jinping, China has increased its interaction with African and Arab states through regional and subregional organizations. China initiated some of these institutions, although African and Arab countries created most of them. China created the Forum on China-Africa Cooperation (FOCAC), the China-Arab States Cooperation Forum (CASCF), the Belt and Road Initiative (BRI) Forum, and the Forum for Economic and Trade Cooperation Between China and Portuguese-Speaking Countries (Forum Macao).

The African Union (AU) recognizes eight subregional communities that include African and Arab states: the Arab Maghreb Union (AMU), the Common Market for Eastern and Southern Africa (COMESA), the Community of Sahel-Saharan States (CEN-SAD), the East African Community (EAC), the Economic Community of Central African States (ECCAS), the Economic Community of West African States (ECOWAS), the Intergovernmental Authority on Development (IGAD), and the Southern African Development Community (SADC).[1] China also engages with organizations that have African and non-African members, among them, the Organization of Islamic Cooperation (OIC), the Group of 77 (G-77) and China, the Non-Aligned Movement (NAM), the Indian Ocean Rim Association (IORA), and Brazil, Russia, India, China, and South Africa (the BRICS). Most of these organizations began with a predominantly economic agenda, but today all of them have political goals, and most have become important in the security arena as well.

Yet in almost every situation, China's engagement with individual African countries is more important than its relationship with these organizations. It is in the bilateral context that China has greater power asymmetry and can more successfully pursue its interests.[2] Nevertheless, the regional and subregional organizations mentioned provide opportunities for China to communicate simultaneously with multiple countries and, in some cases, to coordinate its programs and positions faster and more efficiently.[3] Those organizations established by African and Arab countries are also useful to Beijing because they engage with many countries other than China.

This chapter analyzes China's interaction with all these organizations and evaluates the significance of its engagement with each, which varies enormously. China's interaction with several of them has also evolved over time. For example, Beijing now pays less attention to the NAM than it did in prior years. In most cases, however, China is more engaged than before with these organizations. China's historical support for African liberation movements and its self-identification as a developing country have made it easier to engage with many of these groups.[4]

China's participation in these forums and organizations offers multiple opportunities for Beijing to underscore its messages of "win-win" cooperation and its expressed desire to interact with African countries on an equal basis. More important, however, it allows China to pursue one of the themes of this book: placing itself at the top of a hierarchy of developing nations, although this is not the public message that China wishes to convey.

REGIONAL AND SUBREGIONAL RELATIONS

CHINESE-INITIATED REGIONAL ORGANIZATIONS

China was behind the creation of FOCAC, the CASCF, the BRI Forum, and Forum Macao and serves as the principal source of financing for them. As a result, Beijing exercises more leverage over these organs than over groups established by Arab and African states or those that evolved organically based on common interests. For instance, China controls the agenda of the BRI Forum and Forum Macao and significantly influences the agendas of both FOCAC and the CASCF. More important, it tends to use organizations that it has inspired to initiate and drive policy. Member states meet regularly in China, but in some cases one of the other members hosts the meeting. Nevertheless, Beijing usually controls the time and place of the gathering. When the meetings do take place in China, they provide an opportunity for visiting African officials to also meet bilaterally with Chinese officials and visit various regions of the country. African membership in the groups varies widely. All fifty-three African countries that recognize Beijing are members of FOCAC, while only ten belong to CASCF. As of 2022, forty-nine African countries had signed on to the BRI, although fewer have participated so far in the BRI Forum. Only five Portuguese-speaking African countries are members of the Forum Macao.

FORUM ON CHINA-AFRICA COOPERATION

Created in 2000 at the China's initiative, FOCAC is the premier regional coordinating mechanism for Beijing's engagement with Africa.[5] All African countries except Eswatini, which recognizes Taiwan, are members. FOCAC meets every three years at the ministerial or summit level, alternating between Beijing and an African venue. Because of COVID-19, the eighth and most recent session took place mostly by video in Beijing and Dakar in 2021. A detailed three-year action plan and a Chinese pledge of new loans, grants, and export credits follows each meeting.[6] Xu Jinghu, China's special representative on African affairs, has described FOCAC as "the most effective and practical platform for Sino-African cooperation."[7] The AU links African engagement with China in FOCAC.

Trade, investment, infrastructure, and development assistance have been constant FOCAC themes, but the group's priorities have changed over time. Cultural cooperation appeared as an area for cooperation in 2003. In 2009 FOCAC highlighted climate change, poverty reduction, and think tank exchanges. The 2012 FOCAC underscored the importance of peace and security cooperation, which has continued as a high priority. China's assistance for African industrialization was a central theme in 2015, while the 2018 FOCAC highlighted agricultural development. Other focus areas have included education, public health, energy, natural resources, people-to-people contact, and debt relief.[8]

Since the first FOCAC in 2000, one important theme has been political cooperation—that is, "political exchanges" and high-level exchange visits have been important to elicit African support for the One China Principle and to demonstrate China's support for the AU and UN peacekeeping operations in Africa.[9] The most recent FOCAC Action Plan (2022–2024) declares that "the two sides will maintain close high-level exchanges to deepen traditional friendship, enhance political mutual trust, strengthen strategic coordination and cement the political foundation of China-Africa relations." Parliamentary dialogue is a major focus; the two sides committed to enhancing exchanges between the National People's Congress of China and between the National Committee of the Chinese People's Political Consultative Conference and African parliaments, the Pan-African Parliament, and the African Parliamentary Union. Both sides also pledged to strengthen relations between the CPC and African political parties.[10]

China used the 2012 FOCAC to announce its new security policy toward Africa.[11] It unveiled the "Initiative on China-Africa Partnership for Peace and Security," which provided financial and technical support to the African Union's peace support operations. The 2015 FOCAC expanded on these themes by referring to the settlement of disputes through dialogue and consultation, emphasizing a collective response to nontraditional security threats such as terrorism and food security, and implementing the peace and security initiative launched in 2012.[12] China also promised $60 million in military assistance for the African Standby Force.[13]

The 2018 FOCAC accorded still more importance to peace and security issues. China and Africa agreed to enhance cooperation on public security, peacekeeping, cyber security, antipiracy, and counterterrorism. China promised to launch fifty assistance programs under the BRI and in the areas of law and order, UN peacekeeping missions, fighting piracy, and combatting terrorism. It committed $100 million in military assistance for the African Standby Force and African Capacity for Immediate Response to Crisis, and agreed to set up a fund to increase cooperation on peace, security, peacekeeping, and law and order. Beijing also pledged to continue military aid to the AU and support countries in the Sahel region, as well as those bordering the Gulf of Aden and the Gulf of Guinea, in combatting terrorism. China agreed to provide equipment and short-term law enforcement training courses to African police and boost joint exercises and training to improve African law enforcement's ability to "protect the safety of Chinese nationals, Chinese companies and major projects."[14] COVID-19 focused the 2021 FOCAC on health diplomacy, but there was also continued emphasis on political and security cooperation, especially in cybersecurity and training and support for African police.[15]

Africans tend to speak favorably about FOCAC. One professor at the University of Johannesburg commented that FOCAC offers a better way of communication than any forum currently available in the West.[16] A senior official in Ethiopia's Ministry of Foreign Affairs acknowledged that, while some African countries complain that FOCAC has not aided them, this has not been Ethiopia's experience. Rather, he said, his country has found FOCAC the best venue for China-Africa cooperation.[17] On the other hand, a senior official in Ghana's Ministry of Foreign Affairs was less enthusiastic, suggesting that FOCAC is not really a multilateral organization, but a useful way to reduce bilateral visits.[18] A China-Africa scholar at the University of Witwatersrand noted that FOCAC is a unique diplomatic mechanism that has benefits for both China and Africa. He added, however, that Africa needs to work harder to fully benefit from the FOCAC process.[19]

CHINA-ARAB STATES COOPERATION FORUM

The CASCF has twenty-one member countries, the same number and composition as the League of Arab States minus the Palestinian Authority. Ten of the members are African and members of FOCAC: Algeria, Comoros, Djibouti, Egypt, Libya, Mauritania, Morocco, Somalia, Sudan, and Tunisia.

In 2004 President Hu Jintao established the CASCF during a visit to the Arab League headquarters in Cairo. Foreign ministers from member states now meet every two years in China or an Arab state. The meeting usually discusses strengthening political, economic, and security cooperation between China and the Arab countries. Senior officials from member countries also meet annually to prepare the organization's ministerial meeting and to implement its resolutions. As of early 2023, nine ministerial-level meetings and seventeen senior official meetings had taken place. Additionally, the CASCF hosts ten subgroups, such as the China-Arab Relations and China-Arab Civilization Dialogue, which usually meet every two years.[20] A senior Chinese Foreign Ministry official serves as ambassador for the CASCF.

In 2008 the action plan for the third CASCF ministerial meeting outlined that the two sides would enhance political consultation under the Senior Officials Meeting, where China's Ministry of Foreign Affairs and the Secretariat of the League of Arab States agreed in advance on the topics. The CASCF recognized the positive role played by the China-Arab Friendship Association, which held its first meeting in Khartoum in 2006.[21] The fifth ministerial conference took place in Tunisia in 2012, at the height of the "Arab Spring," and resulted in an action plan that focused on political cooperation, economics, and various forms of social and educational engagement. The conference downplayed security cooperation, although the Egyptian delegates urged China to support internal Arab country security concerns.[22]

At the sixth conference in Beijing in 2014, Xi Jinping proposed to make energy security the principal topic of the gathering, followed by infrastructure construction and trade. He suggested that other key issues should be nuclear power, aerospace and satellites, and new sources of energy.[23] China's former ambassador for the CASCF commented prior to the conference that China and the Arab countries should also establish a dedicated security cooperation seminar.[24] In 2016 the seventh CASCF conference in Doha emphasized China-Arab economic development and joint construction of the BRI.[25] As noted in chapter 2, the conference passed the Doha Declaration, supporting China's position on island building in the South China Sea.

The eighth conference took place in Beijing in 2018. The theme was the BRI. China pledged $20 billion in loans for economic development and $3 billion in loans for the financial sectors.[26] The subsequent action plan covered 2018–2021 and has sections dealing with a wide range of issues, including political cooperation and energy security. There was no section on security cooperation, but the one covering political issues called for safeguarding the sovereignty and stability of Arab countries based on the principles of noninterference and the Community of Shared Future for Mankind. The two sides also agreed to strengthen the forum's political consultation mechanism under the framework of ministerial meetings and "senior political" dialogues.[27]

In 2019 CASCF senior officials met for the sixteenth time and the Strategic Political Dialogue for the fifth time. The Chinese side expressed appreciation for Arab countries' support on Xinjiang and said China was ready to enhance coordination with Arab states in countering terrorism and extremism.[28] In 2020 the ninth CASCF ministerial conference was held online because of the coronavirus pandemic. Cohosted by Jordan and China, it offered little more than China's assistance to member states in combating COVID-19. The Arab countries, for their part, said they remained committed to the One China Principle and supported China's "just position" on Hong Kong and Xinjiang.[29]

China's principal goals in the CASCF are expanding its influence in the Arab world and ensuring its energy security. Coordinating views on key political issues such as countering terrorism, which concerns both China and the Arab states, is also important. China likewise seeks the support of CASCF members to resist Western countries criticism of its mistreatment of its Muslim minorities. By contrast, except for arms sales, engagement in Middle East military and security issues has been a low priority for China, although Beijing has contributed personnel to the UN peacekeeping operation in Lebanon. Compared to FOCAC action plans, those for the CASCF are notable for their absence of discussion on security cooperation. Yet stability and security in the Middle East and North Africa remain important for China, and the country's strategic engagement has expanded accordingly.[30]

BELT AND ROAD FORUM FOR INTERNATIONAL COOPERATION

During a visit to Kazakhstan in 2013, Xi Jinping proposed the idea of a Silk Road Economic Belt connecting China by land to Europe. A month later in Indonesia, he suggested a twenty-first-century Maritime Silk Road connecting China to Europe by sea. These two concepts eventually became known as the BRI. The official objectives of the initiative are to "promote the economic prosperity of the countries along the Belt and Road and regional economic cooperation, strengthen exchanges and mutual learning between different civilizations, and promote world peace and development."[31] In 2017 the Nineteenth Party Congress enshrined the BRI in the CPC's constitution, and it has remained central to China's foreign policy.

There is widespread agreement regarding the significance of the BRI. A researcher at the Shanghai Academy of Social Sciences called it a "guideline of China's foreign policy."[32] Nadège Rolland, of the National Bureau of Asian Research, has concluded that China's ultimate objective for the BRI is to enhance infrastructure connectivity across Eurasia and to "move toward a community of common destiny and embrace a new future." She adds that it has become the "most prominent feature of China's foreign policy" and is now considered by Chinese officials "as the backbone of an emerging order in which China has become the preponderant power."[33] Paul Nantulya of the Africa Center for Strategic Studies has described the BRI as "strategic and comprehensive in scope and an essential component of the Communist Party of China's twin objectives of achieving national rejuvenation and restoring China as a Great Power."[34] China's *Blue Book of Non-Traditional Security* (2014–2015), meanwhile, outlines that two of the goals of the BRI are to mitigate American-led geopolitical machinations and to promote a new world order that enhances Chinese power.[35] Some scholars argue that the BRI may produce greater African dependency on China.[36]

Africa was, however, an afterthought for the BRI. Soon after the BRI's announcement, the official Xinhua news agency released a map that showed the initiative's Maritime Silk Road crossing the Indian Ocean to Kenya and continuing north to Djibouti before passing through the Red Sea and Suez Canal to the Mediterranean Sea.[37] In the beginning, however, there was no formal mention of Africa's role in the BRI. China's December 2015 Africa policy paper, for instance, made no reference to the initiative.[38] The 2015 BRI Action Plan did mention Africa five times, but only in the context of generic statements referring to "Asia, Europe, and Africa." While the action plan identified the CASCF as a mechanism for multilateral cooperation, there was no mention of FOCAC in the document.[39] A government-affiliated think tank in Ethiopia subsequently wrote that "it is something of a disappointment that Africa's role in the initiative has yet to be explicitly outlined." The study added that some Chinese officials prefer to concentrate on FOCAC and leave the BRI opaque, perhaps fearing that China would be suspected of imperial ambitions.[40]

It was only after African leaders began asking how the BRI would benefit their countries that China decided to include Africa. China's "Vision for Maritime Cooperation Under the Belt and Road Initiative" in 2017 noted that ocean cooperation will focus on building the China-Indian Ocean-Africa-Mediterranean Sea Blue Economic Passage and setting up marine disaster warning systems in the Red Sea and Gulf of Aden. Importantly, it emphasized the need to forge port alliances and said that Chinese enterprises would help construct and operate ports along the BRI (see chapter 9). It identified FOCAC as a mechanism for ocean cooperation and outlined that China had signed an agreement to this effect with South Africa. It further added that projects under the BRI Vision for Maritime Cooperation should include the railway linking Djibouti and Addis Ababa, the railway from Mombasa to Nairobi, and the Suez Economic and Trade Cooperative Zone. Notably, however, all these projects were underway or agreed upon before the announcement of the BRI in 2013.[41]

In 2017 China held the first Belt and Road Forum for International Cooperation in Beijing to coordinate BRI activities. Just two African heads of government, those of Ethiopia and Kenya, attended this event. The joint communique issued at the conclusion of the forum seemed to marginalize Africa, stating that the BRI enhances connectivity between Asia and Europe but is "also open to other regions such as Africa and South America."[42] In 2018, at the eighth ministerial meeting of the CASCF, China and the Arab states signed a "Declaration of Action on China-Arab States Belt and Road Cooperation" that spelled out current and future cooperative projects.[43]

In 2019 the heads of government from Djibouti, Egypt, Ethiopia, Kenya, and Mozambique participated in the second Belt and Road Forum for International Cooperation.[44] In his meeting with Egyptian president Abdel-Fattah al-Sisi, Xi Jinping underscored China's willingness to participate in the development of the Suez Canal Corridor and said the two sides should deepen antiterror and security cooperation and enhance people-to-people and cultural exchanges. For his part, Kenyan president Uhuru Kenyatta expressed appreciation to Xi for promoting regional peace in Africa, while Ethiopian prime minister Abiy Ahmed described China as "the most reliable friend and the most cherished partner of Ethiopia." The leaders of Djibouti and Mozambique were also effusive in their praise of China and the BRI.[45]

The second Belt and Road Forum for International Cooperation identified 283 financing and investment projects, agreements, or initiatives. There was a reasonable representation of African countries. For example, China signed a tax treaty with Kenya and cultural cooperation documents with Niger, Namibia, Nigeria, Mauritius, and Guinea. At the same time, China's Ministry of Ecology and Environment jointly launched the BRI International Green Development Coalition with the environmental agencies of twenty-five countries, among them Angola, Ethiopia, Gambia, Kenya, Mauritius, Niger, and Togo. Beijing likewise established the BRI Energy Partnership with twenty-eight countries, including Algeria, Equatorial

Guinea, Niger, Sudan, Gambia, Cape Verde, Republic of Congo, and Chad. China's National Development and Reform Commission, meanwhile, signed investment projects with Egypt, Mozambique, and Uganda.[46] While all these projects and initiatives now appear under the umbrella of the BRI, China negotiated some of them on a bilateral basis, and many others probably would have happened even without the forum. An Ethiopian Foreign Ministry official described the BRI as an "add-on" to China's Africa policy, while another official in the prime minister's office said it seemed to be a program that pulled together ongoing projects.[47] Simply put, the BRI has not yet had a transformative economic impact on Africa.[48]

Nevertheless, by 2023 most of Africa had joined the BRI.[49] Although there is no official list of BRI countries, as of 2022 forty-nine African states had signed BRI memoranda of understanding (MOUs) with China.[50] Although these MOUs vary from country to country, they are general in nature and cover similar issues. The MOU with Liberia aims to enhance political, economic, and security cooperation, and people-to-people exchanges; strengthen regional connectivity; and establish a framework to maintain regional peace and development.[51] Morocco's MOU cites mutual support on issues of sovereignty and territorial integrity and includes a willingness to expand cooperation on politics, military, security, and antiterrorism issues.[52] The COVID-19 pandemic will affect the BRI in ways that are not yet clear but may well result in a slower and even scaled back implementation of the proposed projects.[53] By 2022 there were also indications that Xi Jinping was combining the BRI with his new Global Development Initiative.[54]

China's official media has said little about the security implications of the BRI. As of 2018, a search of Chinese military newspapers, service newspapers, and military academic journals provided few references to the BRI, and *China Military Science*, the People's Liberation Army's most authoritative journal, had yet to refer to the initiative. To the extent that the military has shown interest, it has been primarily related to the BRI's maritime component. The absence of discussion may be due to a lack of PLA senior-level consensus, a concern that security implications will detract from economic and diplomatic priorities, or a reflection that Beijing considers the topic to be sensitive.[55] Wu Zhengyu of Renmin University argued that China intends for the BRI primarily to enable its economy to overcome current limits and bottlenecks by providing access to new markets and securing supplies of energy and raw materials. This requires a corresponding shift in naval strategy to ensure the safety, security, and ultimate success of projects in the Indian Ocean region and beyond. This, Wu says, has caused Beijing to refocus its attention from land routes to sea routes.[56]

At a minimum, the BRI is extending China's interests and presence globally, including to Africa, using its strong economic relations to broaden its political and security engagement.[57] As the BRI's footprint grows, that of the PLA Navy will likely follow, requiring the building of logistical infrastructure at strategic locations such as Djibouti.[58] Some argue that China's BRI creates a larger stake for Beijing in maintaining peace and security in Africa; the idea is logical, insofar as a more active involvement in security issues serves China's own geostrategic interests.[59] There is widespread agreement that the BRI-driven extension of supply lines into the region increases the Indian Ocean's strategic importance.[60] BRI investments and infrastructure projects such as ports and storage facilities in Africa may also have dual-use potential and be utilized to sustain PLA Navy deployments.[61] The growing strategic importance of the Indian Ocean region will encourage more African countries to send high-level delegations to future meetings of the Belt and Road Forum for International Cooperation.

FORUM FOR ECONOMIC AND TRADE CO-OPERATION BETWEEN CHINA AND PORTUGUESE-SPEAKING COUNTRIES (FORUM MACAO)

Launched in 2003 by China's Ministry of Commerce, Forum Macao takes advantage of China's Portuguese-speaking enclave and includes eight other countries: Angola, Cape Verde, Guinea-Bissau, Mozambique, and São Tomé and Principe from Africa, as well as Portugal, Brazil, and Timor-Leste. To date, there have been six ministerial-level conferences of the forum, all of them in Macao, which is also the location of the body's permanent secretariat. The forum's members usually issue an action plan after each conference, which covers topics including trade, investment, production capacity, agriculture, forestry, fisheries and livestock, infrastructure, energy and natural resources, education, finance, development, tourism, transport and communication, culture, media, health, maritime affairs, and cooperation among provinces and municipalities.[62] The most recent ministerial conference took place in 2022 by video link and focused on the COVID-19 pandemic.[63]

To date, political and security issues have not been an important part of Forum Macao's activities, but China is trying to forge a closer link between it and the BRI.[64] Its activities are also complementary to FOCAC. The forum's five African members can facilitate negotiations at the bilateral level and achieve more direct results, given that it belongs to the Ministry of Commerce and targets economic and trade cooperation while FOCAC deals with a wider range of strategic issues. Forum members have permanent representatives in Macao who can engage in a common language. Nevertheless, the Lusophone countries still favor their bilateral relationship with China.[65] In 2006 an "unofficial observer" from São Tomé and Principe, which recognized Taipei at the time, attended the ministerial meeting of the forum in Macao. This gathering may have begun the process of São Tomé and Principe's recognition of Beijing, which occurred in 2016.[66]

AFRICAN AND ARAB REGIONAL ORGANIZATIONS

China continues to emphasize its support for the AU and for most of Africa's subregional organizations, especially their efforts to promote peace, political stability, and development. Both China's first policy statement on Africa in 2006 and its second policy document on the subject in 2015 underscored the importance of cooperation with these organizations.[67] Close collaboration with the AU and African subregional actors is especially attractive to China because they function largely independent of Western influence.[68] China provides personnel only for UN peacekeeping operations, not for missions managed by African organizations, which rely on Western financing, or coalitions of the willing such as the U.S.-led operation in Somalia in 1992–1993.[69] As it pursues its political and security agenda in Africa, China seeks maximum control.

African and Arab regional and subregional organizations give African countries additional leverage when they interact with China. Some African leaders believe that, in a globalized world, interacting bilaterally at the nation-state level is not the most effective. Former Zimbabwe deputy prime minister Arthur G. O. Mutambara argued that subregional groups such as the EAC, COMESA, SADC, AMU, and ECOWAS are better frameworks by which to engage China. Their scale, market size, pooling of resources, and regional consensus strengthen bargaining power. Mutambara emphasized that Africans "need regional strategies and policies to effectively respond to China."[70]

China's interaction with these regional and subregional groups varies considerably. The most important organization for China is the AU, which represents all states in Africa. The League of Arab States is much less important to China as it includes many fewer states and there is less unity among its members than is the case with the AU. Of the subregional groups, China prioritizes the SADC, ECOWAS, and COMESA. China's interest in IGAD is confined mostly to its role in the South Sudan conflict, where China has significant petroleum interests. Its engagement with the EAC is likewise limited but growing. Not surprisingly, China has little or no involvement with three weak and/or dysfunctional subregional groups: the ECCAS, the CEN-SAD, and the AMU.

AFRICAN UNION

In 1963 thirty-two African heads of state met in Addis Ababa and agreed to establish the Organization of African Unity (OAU), which focused on the decolonization process. Its members subsequently decided to emphasize Africa's economic development and in 2002, they created the AU to replace the OAU. The AU voted to recognize fifty-five countries, including the Sahrawi Arab Democratic Republic (Western Sahara), territory that

Morocco controls. China does not recognize the independence of the Western Sahara, and AU member Eswatini has diplomatic relations with Taipei. China, however, has formal diplomatic relations with all other members of the AU. The AU, which had previously held observer status, became a full member of the FOCAC in 2011. The 2015 FOCAC Johannesburg Action Plan identified the significant role played by the AU in safeguarding peace and stability in Africa, a goal China supports. The AU sees itself as the essential platform through which China and other non-African partners contribute to security on the continent.[71]

From an early stage, China appreciated the importance of the AU to its Africa policy. In 2006 it worked with the AU Task Force on Africa's Strategic Partnership with Emerging Powers. During this exercise, it heard African concerns about China's approach to the continent. The AU Task Force stated that partnership between two "unequals is tricky" and warned that Africa should not develop a partnership that mortgages its future. The Task Force recognized that African countries prefer bilateral relations with China over multilateral ties and argued for a long-term vision that outlines an effective partnership complete with clear strategies for implementation.[72] It offered a cautionary tale for both African states and China, concluding that "the strategic partnership should address what Africa can do with China as a partner, rather than what China can do for the continent."[73] In 2013 Zimbabwe's deputy prime minister argued that there must be an Africa-wide strategy and negotiations with China at the level of the AU.[74] Several African scholars concluded that Africa "should come up with a clearly defined BRI response strategy to strengthen its bargaining power."[75] Even today, however, neither the AU nor most individual African countries have developed a long-term strategic vision for dealing with China.[76] Likewise, China seems to be less interested in a real strategic partnership with the AU than in pursuing its own interests in Africa via the organization.

The AU has become China's most important regional interlocutor in Africa and is especially important for cooperation on political and security issues. China established a strategic dialogue mechanism with the AU more than a decade ago. The first meeting took place at the AU headquarters in 2008. At the second dialogue in Beijing in 2009, AU secretary general

Jean Ping stated the AU would "continue to stand by China on major issues concerning China's sovereignty and territorial integrity."[77] In 2012 China solidified its political relationship with the AU by completing construction of the new AU headquarters in Addis Ababa, all $200 million provided by Beijing.[78] The fifth FOCAC action plan (2013–2015) included a section on the expansion of China-AU relations and another that focused on peace and security. As part of that framework, China agreed to provide "financial and technical support to the African Union for its peace-support operations, the development of the African Peace and Security Architecture, personnel exchanges and training in the field of peace and security and Africa's conflict prevention, management and resolution and post-conflict reconstruction and development."[79] Subsequent FOCAC action plans have continued to emphasize China's political and security cooperation with the AU. China further formalized its relations with the AU in 2015 when it established a permanent mission to the organization in Addis Ababa.

China and the AU are trying to improve their political dialogue. In 2018 Chinese foreign minister Wang Yi and AU Commission chairman Moussa Faki Mahamat held the seventh round of the China-AU strategic dialogue. There, China committed to working with the AU to strengthen strategic communication and "deepen political trust." Wang Yi also used the occasion to link the development goals established by the Nineteenth CPC National Congress with those in the AU's 2063 Agenda, which provides a fifty-year plan for Africa's development.[80] Later that year Mahamat met with Xi Jinping, who welcomed the opening of an AU office in Beijing as a tool for strengthening the strategic partnership between Africa and China.[81] In 2020 China increased its ties with the AU by beginning construction on the African Centres for Disease Control and Prevention headquarters in Addis Ababa, an $80 million project entirely funded by Beijing.[82]

China has made important financial contributions to the AU peace and security budget and to various discrete peacekeeping activities. In 2012, for instance, China pledged $100 million over three years to the AU to enhance peace and security in Africa. Then, in 2015, it announced at the United Nations that it would provide $100 million in military assistance for peace-keeping missions over a five-year period. Later the same year, at the

Johannesburg FOCAC, China committed $60 million in military aid over three years to support the AU's Peace and Security Architecture.[83] The 2019–2021 FOCAC Action Plan stated that China would implement $100 million in military assistance to support the African Standby Force and African Capacity for Immediate Response to Crisis. However, this appears to encompass financial commitments previously announced by Beijing. Chinese officials frequently repeat funding announcements that, in fact, they made months or even years earlier. Nor is it clear how this money has been allocated, although the AU did use $25 million of it to purchase military equipment for its logistics base in Cameroon.[84]

China periodically provides smaller grants to AU peacekeeping operations, such as $4.5 million worth of equipment to the AU Mission in Somalia and $1.8 million to the AU Mission in Sudan.[85] From 2011 to 2019 the AU calculated that China supported the Somalia operation with about $1.2 million annually in financing and equipment.[86] China repeatedly expressed its support for the AU's peacekeeping mission in Darfur, and in 2007, when it became a hybrid AU/UN mission, China contributed troops.[87] According to a former commander of the AU Mission in Somalia, China had minimal involvement, providing small arms, ammunition, and buses but otherwise keeping its distance.[88] China does not always support AU peacekeeping efforts, however. In 2015 the AU wanted to deploy 5,000 East African Standby Force peacekeepers to protect civilians during a crisis in Burundi, but the country's president objected to the operation, which required UN Security Council approval. Rwanda and Tanzania subsequently announced they were not prepared to contribute troops. China and Russia then agreed to veto any resolution infringing on Burundi's sovereignty. The AU did not end up implementing the operation.[89]

The New Partnership for Africa's Development (NEPAD) is the implementing arm for the AU's Agenda 2063, Africa's blueprint for transforming the continent. Agenda 2063's focus is on economic development, but it includes prioritization of regional peace and security. The AU Assembly and a dedicated Steering Committee oversee NEPAD. The OAU adopted the plan in 2001, and its authors promoted it as an African Marshall Plan. But, predicated on a massive infusion of foreign aid, NEPAD has not lived up to expectations.⁹⁰ Nevertheless, China regularly acknowledges their importance and pledges support for both NEPAD and Agenda 2063.⁹¹

Despite China's increased support for the AU security mechanism, Beijing remains concerned over whether the AU can live up to its promise of Africa-wide leadership.⁹² China is also frustrated because it has found the AU to be too bureaucratic.⁹³ A senior AU official acknowledged that the organization cannot achieve unity among its members on key issues related to China.⁹⁴ Well-informed Africans understand that China is not the major funder of the AU and that the European Union and the United States provide more financing. However, the impression persists that China is the largest donor because it paid for and built the new headquarters.⁹⁵

China also influences the AU via the press. AU officials prefer Chinese media over Western media outlets because they tend to write more positive stories about the organization.⁹⁶ On the other hand, there is a history of embedding Western experts in the AU peace and security apparatus, while there have been comparatively few Chinese experts deployed in this fashion. However, the frequent exchanges between AU and Chinese officials, almost always funded by Beijing, seem to have offset this Western advantage.⁹⁷

LEAGUE OF ARAB STATES

Established in Cairo in 1945 and commonly called the Arab League, the League of Arab States has ten African members and includes Eritrea as an observer. Most of the Arab League's substantive interaction with China occurs in the CASCF. As in the case of the AU, Arab League members each have their own bilateral relations with China; there is rarely a unified Arab position.⁹⁸ On the other hand, there is a lengthy history of high-level exchanges between Arab League and Chinese officials unrelated to the CASCF. The secretary general of the Arab League first went to China in 1993; later that year the organization established an office in Beijing. In 1996 President Jiang Zemin visited the Arab League headquarters in Cairo, and the following year China's vice premier, Qian Qichen, met its secretary general in Cairo. In 1999 China's foreign minister signed a MOU with the Arab League's secretary general establishing a mechanism for bilateral political consultation.[99] Subsequently, in 2002, Premier Zhu Rongji called on the secretary general during his visit to Egypt.

President Hu Jintao's 2004 meeting in Cairo with twenty-two Arab League delegates resulted in the creation of the CASCF. Arab League secretary general Amr Mahmoud Moussa praised China, commenting that it has won the admiration and support of all developing nations.[100] Chinese and Arab League representatives continued lower-level contact until Xi Jinping's speech on China-Arab relations at the Arab League in 2016, which coincided with the issuance of China's first Arab Policy Paper. The document underscored the importance China attaches to the Arab League, especially the league's efforts to maintain regional peace and stability and to promote development.[101] In a wide-ranging MOU in 2018 concerning the BRI, China's foreign minister and the Arab League secretary general agreed to work to safeguard freedom of navigation, protect maritime routes, and combat piracy.[102] In 2020 Wang Yi urged the Arab League secretary general, Ahmed Aboul Gheit, during a meeting in Cairo to build "a China-Arab community with a shared future" and to "deepen the strategic partnership." He also expressed appreciation for the support the Arab League has given China on Xinjiang. Gheit replied that the Arab League understands China's position on Xinjiang and opposes any interference in its internal affairs.[103] This early, frequent, and high-level interaction by China with the Arab League has helped strengthen its relations with Arab countries in Africa.

SUBREGIONAL ORGANIZATIONS

SOUTHERN AFRICAN DEVELOPMENT COMMUNITY

Created in 1992 by eleven countries, SADC now comprises sixteen member states: Angola, Botswana, Comoros, Democratic Republic of Congo, Eswatini, Lesotho, Madagascar, Malawi, Mauritius, Mozambique,

Namibia, Seychelles, South Africa, Tanzania, Zambia, and Zimbabwe. Its main objectives are development, peace and security, economic growth, and the alleviation of poverty. With the passage of time, however, regional peacekeeping has become an increasingly important part of the SADC's agenda.[104] South African and Botswanan forces intervened militarily in Lesotho in 1998 following tense elections. South Africa claimed the intervention was a SADC humanitarian peacekeeping mission, but the effort had no official SADC sanction. By contrast, in 2012 the SADC deployed troops from Tanzania, Malawi, and South Africa at the request of the Democratic Republic of the Congo to counter a rebel threat.[105]

China has a long relationship with the SADC, mostly in the development area, and even provides an annual $100,000 grant to the SADC Secretariat to support its operational needs.[106] Drawing on funding that China provided to the AU Peace and Security Architecture, the SADC requested money to construct its regional logistics depot in Botswana as part of the AU standby force to support regional peace operations. The purpose of the depot is to provide military stocks on a timely basis to meet the rapid deployment capability of the SADC standby force. China reportedly agreed to authorize the funding, but the project has not yet been implemented.[107] While China's cooperation with the SADC on strategic issues has been limited, they are likely to increase as the organization takes on more responsibility for security and as China's interests expand in southern Africa. SADC also provides a venue to raise political issues of concern to both parties. China's ambassador to Botswana represents it at the SADC.

ECONOMIC COMMUNITY OF WEST AFRICAN STATES

Established in 1975, ECOWAS has fifteen members: Benin, Burkina Faso, Cape Verde, Côte d'Ivoire, Gambia, Ghana, Guinea, Guinea Bissau, Liberia, Mali, Niger, Nigeria, Senegal, Sierra Leone, and Togo. ECOWAS focuses primarily on economic development and subregional integration. It also operates ten specialized agencies, including the Inter-governmental Action

Group against Money Laundering and Terrorist Financing in West Africa. In 1993 ECOWAS concluded that political and social stability in the region are crucial ingredients of building sustainable development and expanded the power of its directorate of political affairs, peace, and security. The directorate's mandate includes strategic issues such as maritime security, terrorism, genocide, human rights, elections, bad governance, and the ECOWAS Standby Force, which includes dedicated military units from member states.[108]

Most of China's involvement with ECOWAS has been in the trade and investment arenas. ECOWAS engages both Beijing and Chinese provinces on economic issues.[109] In 2003 China accredited its ambassador in Nigeria to ECOWAS.[110] The first China-ECOWAS Economic and Trade Forum took place in Beijing and Wuhan in 2008. Attended by 450 Africans, it focused on infrastructure projects and possible joint ventures. The second occurred in Accra in 2012 and again emphasized infrastructure.[111] In 2012 China and ECOWAS signed an agreement for cooperation in infrastructure development, trade, and investment. Four years later a Chinese conglomerate, the CGC Overseas Construction Group, signed five MOUs with the ECOWAS Commission encompassing the construction of railways, highways, telecommunications, aviation, and the ECOWAS headquarters.[112] In 2018 ECOWAS approved a $31.6 million grant from China to build its new headquarters in Abuja, Nigeria; groundbreaking took place in 2022.[113] Although some member states have, over the years, recognized Taipei, the ECOWAS Commission became an early proponent of the One China Principle.[114]

ECOWAS has a history of intervening in West African crises and coordinating the actions of member states on regional security challenges.[115] In 1990 it deployed the ECOWAS Monitoring Group to Liberia following the outbreak of civil war and the collapse of the central government there. ECOWAS subsequently sent forces to Sierra Leone (1997–2000), Guinea Bissau (1998–1999), and Côte d'Ivoire (2003–2004).[116] In 2004 China provided $125,000 for ECOWAS peacekeeping activities and subsequently contributed to the ECOWAS peace fund.[117] Following an insurgency in Mali in 2012, ECOWAS wanted to deploy forces to that country but lacked the capacity to do so. French troops initially filled the void; ECOWAS then tried to mediate the dispute and imposed sanctions.[118] China supported ECOWAS's mediation while avoiding the issue of sanctions, and it did not offer any material support to the proposed ECOWAS force.[119] In 2013 China contributed troops to the UN peacekeeping mission to Mali.

China is increasing, albeit modestly, its support for ECOWAS peace and security activities. Beijing reluctance to provide more military support may be explained by concern with ECOWAS's interventionist approach, for example, intervening militarily in Gambia in 2017.[120] In 2014 the two parties established a strategic consultative mechanism to improve cooperation in capacity building, peace and security, counterterrorism, and transnational crime.[121] In 2016 China donated $5 million worth of nonlethal military equipment and vehicles to the ECOWAS Standby Force.[122] The following year China gave ECOWAS a $200,000 capacity building grant. The president of the ECOWAS Commission thanked China for the gift but urged Beijing to interact more comprehensively with the organization.[123] These overtures reflect an abiding Chinese strategic interest: mitigating piracy and theft in the Gulf of Guinea, which have affected Chinese ships and crews. China is cooperating with ECOWAS to combat the problem and on at least one occasion has participated in a naval exercise with ships from ECOWAS countries.[124]

COMMON MARKET FOR EASTERN AND SOUTHERN AFRICA

COMESA, which in 1994 replaced the Preferential Trade Area for Eastern and Southern Africa, has twenty-one members: Burundi, Comoros, DRC, Djibouti, Egypt, Eritrea, Eswatini, Ethiopia, Kenya, Libya, Madagascar, Malawi, Mauritius, Rwanda, Seychelles, Somalia, Sudan, Tunisia, Uganda, Zambia, and Zimbabwe. Its primary goal is to promote regional integration through trade and the development of natural and human resources. It achieves this objective by working to create a free trade area that guarantees the free movement of goods and services produced within COMESA and the removal of all tariffs and nontariff barriers. Goods and services that enter the customs union from non-COMESA countries face a single tariff in all member states. It encourages the free movement of capital and investment supported by a common investment area.[125]

In 1999 COMESA decided to address the question of peace and security to facilitate its core objective of subregional integration and development. It established a structure consisting of a committee of officials, ministers of foreign affairs, and heads of state and government to address issues of peace and security in coordination with the AU and subregional organizations. The focus of this structure is conflict prevention, conflict management, postconflict reconstruction, anti–money laundering, counterterrorism, and support for democracy and governance through election observation programs.[126] COMESA claims as successes the establishment of a conflict early warning system, best practices for elections, a pool of trained election observers, software programs to combat money laundering, training to improve financial investigation and prosecution, and the development of laws to suppress illegal mineral exploration among member nations.[127]

China is COMESA's largest bilateral trading partner and in 2011 designated its ambassador to Zambia to serve concurrently as its special representative to COMESA, which has its headquarters in Lusaka. China holds 9 percent of the shares in COMESA's Trade and Development Bank.[128] While Beijing offers minimal financial support to COMESA and focuses on the trade relationship with member states, the two sides make a point of complimenting each other. COMESA Secretary-General Sindiso Ngwenya praised Chinese-financed infrastructure projects in member countries and frequent political exchanges, which have deepened the relationship. He added that it is "disingenuous for those who only yesterday and for centuries participated in the enslavement of Africans and exploitation of natural resources to turn around and proclaim that they have clean hands and that China's partnership is based on the model of exploitation that they know."[129]

INTERGOVERNMENTAL AUTHORITY ON DEVELOPMENT

Begun in 1986 as a drought and development agency, IGAD subsequently refocused its efforts on addressing political and socioeconomic challenges in the region. Its mission is to promote subregional cooperation and integration through peace, security, and prosperity. The organization's members are Djibouti, Ethiopia, Kenya, Somalia, Sudan, Uganda, South Sudan, and Eritrea. IGAD's peace and security program includes conflict early warning and response, preventive diplomacy and mediation, transnational security threats, governance, democracy, rule of law, human rights, humanitarian affairs, postconflict reconstruction and development, and gender equality. IGAD played an active role in achieving the Comprehensive Peace Agreement between Sudan and South Sudan in 2005, restoring a functional government in Somalia, and efforts to end internal conflict in South Sudan.[130]

China is not a significant funding source for IGAD, does not have observer status in it, and has limited, albeit increasing, interaction with the organization.[131] Rather, IGAD's principal international funders are the European Union and the Gulf States. The organization is responsible for implementing the costly AU peacekeeping mission in Somalia, which is funded primarily by the European Union, United States, and United Nations.[132] China's contributions to IGAD consist of small, periodic cash grants. In 2011 China signed a MOU with IGAD that included a pledge of $100,000 for operational costs.[133] China's ambassador to Djibouti turned over an additional $100,000 to IGAD in 2013 and again in 2018, accompanied by the requisite photo opportunities. IGAD's secretary general acknowledged "China's growing partnership with IGAD Member States entrusted in win-win and strong bilateral relations."[134] An Ethiopian with a think tank in Addis Ababa explained that IGAD has not reached out to China, which, in turn, has been reluctant to associate too closely with IGAD because of its ties to Western countries.[135]

China took an active interest in IGAD's effort to mediate the civil war in South Sudan, where a Chinese state-owned oil company has extensive investments. China seconded military personnel to the IGAD Monitoring and Verification Mechanism responsible for overseeing cessation of hostilities and participated in the expanded mediation group known as IGAD Plus, which resulted in a peace agreement in 2015.[136] In 2018 China provided $500,000 to the IGAD forum supporting the South Sudan peace process.[137] By playing a lead role in the peace process, IGAD provides political cover for China, which prefers to avoid direct involvement in internal conflicts.[138] China continues to engage with IGAD on this issue to enhance the safety of Chinese nationals and oil interests in South Sudan. Senior IGAD officials from Ethiopia, Sudan, and Uganda have spoken favorably about China's role in South Sudan. Privately, however, some officials involved in the IGAD peace process lamented that China is only interested in protecting its oil interests.[139]

EAST AFRICAN COMMUNITY

The current iteration of the EAC dates from 2000. Its members are Kenya, Tanzania, Uganda, Rwanda, Burundi, South Sudan, and the DRC, and its objective is to deepen economic, political, social, and cultural integration through increased competitiveness, value-added production, trade, and investment. The organization's foremost goal, so far unachieved, is political integration based on common foreign and security policies, good governance, and effective implementation. The EAC has a peace and security component. Members of the EAC Partnership Fund include the European Union, Canada, Japan, and eight European countries but not China.[140] Unlike IGAD, the EAC, which shares three members with IGAD, has played a minimal role in efforts to resolve regional security and political conflicts.

China is the largest trading partner of the bloc's member states, and trade consists overwhelmingly of China's exports to the region.[141] One study concluded that "China's role in facilitating the regional integration through trade is questionable at best and detrimental at worst." While China has extensive bilateral engagement with EAC members, especially in the financing and building of infrastructure, it has not been closely engaged with the regional organization.[142] In 2011 China accredited its ambassador in Tanzania to the EAC, and later that year signed a framework agreement with the organization to increase trade, investment, infrastructure, and human resource development.[143] As in the case of IGAD, Beijing has made small, sporadic donations to the EAC. In 2016 China gave the EAC $200,000 to facilitate dialogue to end the crisis in Burundi.[144] In 2017 it provided $200,000 for the EAC's integration agenda.[145] In 2019 it donated twelve vehicles worth $400,000 for use in EAC capacity-building programs.[146]

ECONOMIC COMMUNITY OF CENTRAL AFRICAN STATES

Established in 1983, ECCAS has eleven members: Angola, Burundi, Cameroon, Central African Republic, Chad, DRC, Republic of Congo, Equatorial Guinea, Gabon, Rwanda, and São Tomé and Principe. While focused on economic integration, it has tried with minimal success to pursue a peace and security agenda in an especially troubled part of Africa. To this end, ECCAS created a Council for Peace and Security in Central Africa and has a nonpermanent Central African Multinational Force. Experts from ECCAS and ECOWAS have met in efforts to combat terrorism and violent extremism in both regions. ECCAS has not lived up to expectations, however, especially in the peace and security arena.[147]

China has good relations with all ECCAS members but has shown little interest in the subregional organization itself. On a bilateral basis, it aided participants of the ECCAS multinational force in the Central African Republic.[148] Beijing continues to pay occasional lip service to ECCAS and to express its willingness to help the organization bring peace and security to the Central African Republic.[149]

COMMUNITY OF SAHEL-SAHARAN STATES

Beginning with only six members in 1998, CEN-SAD has expanded to its current membership of twenty-eight and has a headquarters in Tripoli, Libya. Member countries range from Africa's west to east coast, and all of them belong to other African subregional groups. CEN-SAD's original goal was to create a comprehensive economic union. This has evolved into a greater focus on regional security and sustainable development.[150] It undertook a peace operation in the Central African Republic from 2001 to 2003. Morocco and Egypt subsequently began emphasizing CEN-SAD's counterterrorism role. In 2018 Egypt inaugurated a CEN-SAD antiterrorism center in Cairo.[151] However, CEN-SAD has yet to become an effective organization, a situation exacerbated by the fact that its headquarters is in conflict-ridden Libya.

There is no public indication that China has had any substantive engagement with CEN-SAD. This is not surprising, given the difficulty of doing business in Tripoli and the relative ineffectiveness of CEN-SAD. China has good bilateral relations with all CEN-SAD members and appears to have concluded that an institutional link with the organization is not necessary.

ARAB MAGHREB UNION

In 1989 Algeria, Libya, Mauritania, Morocco, and Tunisia approved a treaty creating the AMU, which emphasizes sustainable development and the possibility of solidarity among Arab states. Subsequently, in 1992, the general secretariat of the organization moved from Libya to Morocco. The AMU held six summit meetings, the last one in 1994. Since then, however, Morocco's annexation of the Western Sahara has paralyzed the AMU because member state Algeria supports the territory's independence. The Arab Spring in the Maghreb in 2011 added to the AMU's challenges as the initial outbreak of conflict in Tunisia threatened to spread to other member countries. Algeria is not active in the organization, and internal problems continue to overwhelm Libya. The AMU has a secretary general and small staff but has yet to achieve any of its goals.[152]

China has bilateral relations with the five member countries but has had no discernable interaction with the AMU itself. This is understandable given the AMU's dysfunctionality, Beijing's desire to remain aloof from the Western Sahara dispute, its effort to avoid alienating Algeria, and the fact that all member states participate in the CASCF.[153]

OTHER ORGANIZATIONS THAT INCLUDE AFRICAN MEMBERS

China is a member, observer, or affiliate of several organizations that have African and non-African members. They include the OIC, the G-77 and China, the NAM, the IORA, and the BRICS. The importance which China attaches to these groups has varied over time. China has become less committed to the G-77 and China and to the NAM, while showing more interest in the OIC and the BRICS. Since the announcement of the BRI, China has also given higher priority to the IORA. In each case there are practical political, economic, and security reasons for this decreasing or increasing interest. These forums provide China's officials additional opportunities to interact with African countries and establish personal relationships.

ORGANIZATION OF ISLAMIC COOPERATION

Founded in 1969 at a summit in Morocco, the OIC has grown from thirty to fifty-seven members, including twenty-seven African countries: Algeria, Benin, Burkina Faso, Cameroon, Chad, Comoros, Côte d'Ivoire, Djibouti, Egypt, Gabon, Gambia, Guinea, Guinea Bissau, Libya, Mali, Mauritania, Morocco, Mozambique, Niger, Nigeria, Senegal, Sierra Leone, Somalia, Sudan, Togo, Tunisia, and Uganda. Priority OIC issues include peace and security, counterterrorism, food security, human rights, and good governance, particularly among member states in the Middle East and South Asia but also in Africa.[154]

China claims to have attached importance to the OIC ever since Premier Zhou Enlai sent a congratulatory message to the organization in 1974 on its second summit. Following an inactive period in China's relationship with the OIC, Beijing began to realize the value of interacting with the organization on counterterrorism, a point China's foreign minister made to the OIC chairperson in 2001. The CPC-controlled Islamic Association of China has been an important official interlocutor with the OIC. By 2009 Beijing began discussing ethnic minority issues with the OIC, and soon thereafter high-level exchange visits took place. In 2012 Premier Wen Jiabao went to the OIC headquarters, where he urged greater cooperation. In 2014, during a meeting with the OIC secretary-general, Foreign Minister Wang Yi called for the strengthening of political exchanges. China has identified the OIC as a partner in the BRI. In 2016 Xi Jinping visited the OIC's headquarters, where he described the organization as a bridge for the development of China's relations with Islamic countries. The OIC secretary general responded that his organization and China hold similar positions on international matters. Xi Jinping's 2019 congratulatory message to the OIC summit reiterated his belief that it as an important bridge for cooperation between China and the Islamic world.[155]

Beijing is most interested in the OIC because of the role it plays in mitigating Western criticism of China's mistreatment of its Muslim minorities (see chapter 2). So far, the OIC's statements on the topic have supported China's position. In 2019 a Chinese Foreign Ministry spokesperson praised the OIC's resolution that commended Beijing on the care it accords Muslims in Xinjiang, adding that China is ready to work with the OIC to build a model for cultural exchanges and South-South cooperation.[156] Beijing requested OIC observer status in 2012, but it was not until 2022 that the OIC invited China's foreign minister to attend the forty-eighth session of the Council of Foreign Ministers in Islamabad.[157]

GROUP OF 77

Established in 1964 by seventy-seven developing nations, the G-77 is the largest intergovernmental organization of developing countries in the United Nations. It provides a forum to articulate and promote their collective economic interests and enhance their joint negotiating ability on economic issues within the UN system and to promote South-South cooperation for economic development. As of early 2023 the organization had 134 members, including all countries in Africa.[158]

While the G-77 continues to meet and issue declarations and recommendations on a range of political and security matters, it has minimal impact.[159] China provides financial support and pays lip service to the group. In 2017 China's deputy permanent representative to the UN said the G-77 and China will maintain "unity and collaboration in promoting common development and safeguarding common interests."[160]

NON-ALIGNED MOVEMENT

The Non-Aligned Movement grew out of the collapse of the colonial system and the independence movements in Africa, Asia, and Latin America. The Asia-Africa Conference in Bandung, Indonesia, in 1955 assembled twenty-nine heads of state and launched the NAM. However, the first NAM summit did not occur until 1961, when twenty-five countries convened in Belgrade, Yugoslavia. Although it does not have a headquarters, constitution, or secretariat, since 1970 the organization has convened a summit every three years in a member state. The NAM now has 120 member countries, seventeen observer countries, and ten observer organizations. All fifty-four African countries are members, except South Sudan.[161]

Although China was never a formal member of the NAM, Premier Zhou Enlai led the Chinese delegation at the Bandung Conference, which incorporated the PRC's "Five Principles of Peaceful Coexistence" into the "Ten Principles of Bandung." Bandung was a watershed for Chinese diplomacy, including its relations with newly independent and soon to be independent African states.[162] China became an observer of the NAM in 1992 and has subsequently attended the organization's summits. In 2005 President Hu Jintao attended the fiftieth anniversary of the Asia-Africa summit at Bandung, stating in Jakarta that the NAM was important in establishing a new, fair, and rational international political and economic order.[163] In 2015 President Xi Jinping represented China at the sixtieth anniversary of the Asia-Africa summit, using the occasion to promote the building of a Community of Shared Future for Mankind and the BRI.[164]

REGIONAL AND SUBREGIONAL RELATIONS

In 2016 Chinese officials attended the seventeenth NAM summit in Venezuela. A Foreign Ministry spokesperson commented that China has always endorsed the purposes and principles of the NAM and attached great importance to the role it plays in international affairs.[165] While the Chinese media covered the eighteenth NAM summit in Azerbaijan in 2019, there is no indication that Chinese officials attended or commented on the outcome.[166] Working with the NAM offers China an excellent opportunity to claim that it is still a developing country. Although China continues to attach considerable importance to commemorating the Bandung Conference, over time the NAM has become a less important venue for China to interact with the developing world, including African nations.

INDIAN OCEAN RIM ASSOCIATION

The IORA was formed in 1997 to foster cooperation among countries with a particular interest in commercial shipping and sea lane security. It has twenty-three members, including nine from Africa: Comoros, Kenya, Madagascar, Mauritius, Mozambique, Seychelles, Somalia, South Africa, and Tanzania. In 2001 China became one of ten dialogue partners for the bloc. Mauritius hosts the IORA secretariat. The IORA is the only ministerial forum that covers the Indian Ocean and includes dialogue partners, which provide technical cooperation, help on environmental issues, and promote trade and investment. India, which is concerned about China's motives in the Indian Ocean, tends to set the IORA agenda. Except for South Africa, the IORA's African members have played a minor role in the group because of their limited capacity. In 2011 the IORA for the first time included security-related issues such as counterpiracy, protection of sea lanes, and disaster relief on its agenda. It has since held numerous seminars dealing with terrorism, piracy, drug smuggling, transnational crime, illegal fishing, cyber security, democracy, and good governance.[167]

China regularly attends IORA council of minister meetings and has been expanding cooperation with the organization. In 2017 China's special representative for African affairs participated in the council of minister's session in South Africa, where she emphasized the importance China attaches to the IORA and urged its members to engage actively in the BRI. China has also used the forum to promote the Community of Shared Future for Mankind, to develop a comprehensive and sustainable maritime security program to counter piracy and other crimes, and to establish a maritime disaster risk information and emergency system. China's white paper on its vision for maritime cooperation under the BRI identifies the IORA as a partner for multilateral oceanic cooperation.[168]

The emerging strategic importance of the Indian Ocean rim and the BRI are driving China's efforts to deepen relations with the IORA (see chapter 9). China's economic and energy security interests in the region include keeping open sea lines of communication and insuring unimpeded expansion of international trade. China says it accepts the IORA's goals of combatting illegal fishing, piracy, marine pollution, and drug, people, and wildlife trafficking. The IORA provides a forum where China can present itself as a responsible global power and reduce the fear of some countries, especially India, about its naval presence in the Indian Ocean. In 2022, at the Council of Ministers meeting in Bangladesh, the Chinese representative said the Global Development Initiative and Global Security Initiative offer solutions for world peace and development.[169]

BRICS

At the beginning of this century, Goldman Sachs coined the term BRICs (Brazil, Russia, India, and China). In 2009 the first summit of the BRICs took place in Russia. The following year the foreign ministers of the four countries, led by China, agreed to invite South Africa as the fifth member, changing the acronym to BRICS with a capital "S." The BRICS focused on the need for emerging powers to have a greater voice in global governance and the reform of international financial institutions. Their agenda has expanded and includes separate meetings for finance ministers, central bank governors, national security advisors, science and technology ministers, and disaster response authorities. The ruling political parties of each member nation also meet regularly. South Africa is pressing the BRICS to expand their security cooperation as well. Initially a forum for discussion, the first major success of the BRICS was the creation of the New Development Bank, which began with $50 billion in capital and a $100 billion Contingent Reserve Arrangement.[170]

China and India, ranked second and fifth globally by total GDP, are the two heavyweights in the BRICS. By contrast, it is questionable whether South Africa, ranked thirty-seventh globally by GDP, should even qualify as a member. To be sure, it had the largest GDP in Africa when admitted, but it has since fallen behind Nigeria. Put another way, the economic output of the city of Beijing is equivalent to that of South Africa. Pretoria views its invitation to join BRICS as a desire by China and the other members to use South Africa as a gateway to southern Africa. There is little evidence so far, however, that South Africa has played this role for China or any other BRICS member.[171]

★ ★ ★

While bilateral interaction with African countries continues to dominate China's strategic engagement on the continent, regional, subregional, and international organizations have become increasingly important as well. Organizations such as FOCAC and the BRI Forum for International Cooperation, which China primarily inspired and funded, offer additional avenues to initiate policy objectives, as well as to solidify China's interests in Africa. Well-established African continental organizations such as the AU, and subregional organizations such as ECOWAS, while providing China less leverage, offer opportunities to counter Western influence in Africa, prioritize China's regional security concerns, expand its relationships, and validate its position on core issues, such as the handling of the Uighurs in Xinjiang.

Due in part to China's growing physical presence in Africa and its extensive investments there, continental security has become an important aspect of its Africa policy. This has resulted in greater efforts by Chinese officials to achieve Beijing's political goals and to address China's security concerns. The funding and construction of the AU and ECOWAS headquarters, in turn, underscore the high value that China places on these organizations. Yet China seems more focused on using them to achieve its own ends, rather than engaging with them to advance the goals of African nations or creating joint initiatives based on equality.

4

PARTY-TO-PARTY RELATIONS

Since Xi Jinping became general secretary of the Communist Party of China (CPC) in 2012, he has prioritized relations with political parties throughout the Global South, especially in Africa.[1] This chapter examines the bilateral and multilateral exchanges and training workshops carried out by the International Department of the Central Committee of the CPC (ID-CPC) with African political parties. We use Chinese and African party officials' public statements, our interviews with them, and two decades of systematic data from the ID-CPC's website to shed light on why and how the department is using these engagements to build relationships with African political parties.

The following section introduces the ID-CPC and shows how, under Xi Jinping, it was empowered and its activities expanded. The department has become the primary CPC organ tasked with perpetuating relationships with African political parties. Its cadres use the repeated reciprocal exchange of favors to create an extensive network of interpersonal relationships with foreign (in this case, African) political elites and reward their compliance and deference. African parties, regardless of their political persuasion, can maintain good relations with Beijing so long as they support the creation of "a peaceful and stable international environment favorable to China's development."[2]

The second section elucidates the ID-CPC's bilateral and multilateral exchanges and "cadre training" (干部培训) workshops for African political parties. Here, we present our original database spanning two decades (January 1, 2002, to December 31, 2022) of ID-CPC engagements with African interlocutors, including a total of 881 distinct ID-CPC interactions (807 bilateral and 74 multilateral) with at least 130 African parties. This analysis is informed by public statements and our own informal interviews conducted with party cadres, policy makers, and experts during fieldwork in China, Djibouti, Egypt, Ethiopia, Ghana, Morocco, Namibia, and South Africa between 2017 and 2020, and it builds on our previous fieldwork a decade before in Angola, China, Egypt, Ethiopia, Kenya, South Africa, Sudan, and Eswatini.

We uncover three trends in China-Africa party-to-party relations. First, both bilateral and multilateral exchanges have expanded considerably under Xi Jinping. Second, before COVID-19, the department was hosting more African delegations than ever before, and many more than it was sending to the continent. Third, after the pandemic began, these programs shifted almost entirely online, but while the number of bilateral exchanges fell precipitously, multilateral engagements continued at constant, albeit low, levels. The CPC-funded Julius Nyerere Leadership School, which was completed in 2022 in Tanzania, is poised to emerge as the premier venue for building China-Africa party-to-party relations on the continent.

In the third section, we examine how the ID-CPC has built relationships with political parties in three diverse African countries where we conducted fieldwork: South Africa, Ethiopia, and Ghana.[3] We present the ID-CPC data for each country, review relevant public statements, and analyze our interviews with party representatives in China and the three African countries. These interviewees include ID-CPC cadres working on Africa and members of CPC partner parties in South Africa (the African

National Congress [ANC] and the South African Communist Party [SACP]), Ethiopia (the Ethiopian People's Revolutionary Democratic Front [EPRDF] and the Tigray People's Liberation Front [TPLF]), and Ghana (the National Democratic Congress [NDC] and New Patriotic Party [NPP]).[4] Each of these three case studies offers important insights into how the CPC builds relationships with political parties in different African countries.

South Africa offers an example of how the CPC's close relationship with the ANC and its smaller partner party, the SACP, facilitates the sharing of social resources that create "win-win" outcomes for both sides. Similarly, in Ethiopia, the CPC worked for decades to fortify both the EPRDF and its leading party, the TPLF. The collapse of the EPRDF in 2019 and the subsequent civil war with Tigray precipitated a temporary reduction in Beijing's ability to understand, react to, and influence developments in that country. Still, in 2020 the CPC held its first training workshop for the ruling Prosperity Party. In Ghana, a liberal democracy, Beijing takes advantage of the free political environment to maintain relations with both the NDC and NPP.

By identifying cross-cutting consistencies in the ID-CPC's strategic engagement that traverse these three diverse African countries, our comparative analysis reveals how the department is creating a network of reliable partner parties. The CPC cultivates interpersonal relationships with politically powerful and dependable Africans whom it calls on to validate the superiority of China's political system, adopt methods of governance similar to the CPC, support Beijing's territorial claims, help advance Chinese interests in their country, and oppose U.S. "hegemony." For their part, African parties receive all-expenses-paid junkets to China, attend cadre training workshops, obtain material support and educational opportunities at Chinese universities, and can leverage relations with the CPC to strengthen their domestic political position. But to benefit from working with Beijing, African interlocutors must show deference to China's "core" interests and affirm the superiority of its political system (see chapters 1 and 2).

PARTY-TO-PARTY RELATIONS

THE ID-CPC'S EXPANDING ROLE IN CHINA'S FOREIGN POLICY

China's political system is best understood as a three-legged stool that includes the party, the government, and the military.[5] In foreign affairs, as in all other areas, both the government and the military remain subordinate to the party's leadership, with Xi Jinping at its core.[6] While the Ministry of Foreign Affairs (MFA) and the People's Liberation Army maintain their own distinct channels through which they conduct China's state-to-state and military-to-military diplomacy, respectively, the ID-CPC is the primary institution tasked with cultivating relations with foreign political parties. The ID-CPC website underscores its unique role as "a research institution of international studies, influential with distinct characters both at home and abroad, providing policy recommendations to the central committee for its foreign policy decision making and running of the party and state."[7]

Under Xi Jinping, party organs have gained influence relative to state institutions in many areas, including foreign affairs.[8] In 2015 Song Tao, a longtime protégé of Xi, replaced Wang Jiarui as ID-CPC minister, suggesting Xi had taken a personal interest in the department's work.[9] In his speech before the Forum on China-Africa Cooperation summit in Johannesburg in 2015, Xi identified "five major pillars" of the China-Africa relationship, the first being "political mutual trust."[10] Subsequently, in 2017, China's "core" leader elevated the ID-CPC's status in his keynote speech at the CPC in Dialogue with World Political Parties High-Level Meeting in Beijing. Addressing the leaders of more than three hundred political parties, including dozens from Africa, Xi laid out a vision for "a new type of party-to-party relations":

> We political parties in various countries should strengthen mutual trust, dialogue, and coordination. On the basis of a new form of international relations, we should explore the building of a new type of party-to-party relations that seeks to expand common ground while reserving differences and enhances mutual respect and mutual learning, and we should

build a multiform, multilevel international network for party-to-party exchanges and cooperation."[11]

He added that the ID-CPC would hold fifteen thousand or more party-to-party "interactions" over the next five years and pledged to "share practices of party-building and enhancing state governance" with foreign political parties.[12] Party propaganda outlets hailed Xi's call for the ID-CPC to bring together political parties from different countries to "work together for an international network of cooperation and exchange in various forms and at multiple levels."[13] The official ID-CPC website affirms that "direct guidance and personal involvement of the Party and State leaders have given a powerful push to the development of the Party's external work."[14]

In accordance with these instructions, the ID-CPC has become the primary party organ tasked with creating "a new pattern in the Party's international relations characterized by all-round, multichannel, wide-scope and in-depth party-to-party exchanges and cooperation" with foreign political leaders.[15] No other outward-facing institution rivals the department's volume of activities, its untold financial resources, the scale of its overseas network, and its leadership's close connections to Xi Jinping.[16]

In almost every country, the ID-CPC maintains relationships with members of the leading political party or parties, through which it is able to initiate and perpetuate the continued exchange of favors. As of 2019 the ID-CPC maintained relations with more than six hundred political parties and organizations from more than 160 countries around the world, and that "circle of friends continues to grow," explained Luan Jianzhang, director general of the ID-CPC Policy Research Office.[17] As of 2021, Beijing claimed to have relations with 110 African political parties across 51 countries.[18]

The department is divided into fourteen offices, eight of which are geographic regional bureaus. The two most directly relevant to Africa are Bureau III and Bureau IV, which cover West Asian and North African Affairs and African Affairs, respectively. Other bureaus that work on Africa include the Research Office, which carries out theoretical, strategic, comprehensive, and policy-oriented studies, and the Protocol Office, which organizes "reception arrangements for visiting foreign delegations."[19]

Unconstrained by diplomatic or military protocol, party-to-party engagements are more flexible, less formalized, and receive less public and media scrutiny than formal diplomatic engagements. These attributes make them ideal for building and maintaining relationships. Creating a welcoming environment for foreign visitors elicits "friendly relations and motivational orientations."[20] To that end, ID-CPC officials use what Chen Dongxiao, president of the Shanghai Institutes for International Studies, has called "host diplomacy" (主场外交) to shape foreign partners' perceptions of China, help them "rectify" their incorrect ideas, and reform their systems based on Chinese conceptions of good governance.[21] Hosting African delegations gives the department a "home field advantage," allowing it to set the agenda, Chen explains: "Just as sports teams enjoy a so-called 'home field advantage,' 'host diplomacy' means that the host country can take advantage of favorable 'timing, geographic and human factors' in order to grasp or strengthen its say in international affairs, plan topics or agendas to its advantage, push for the construction of international rules or orders favorable to its own interests and then realize its own diplomatic targets."[22] Hosting not only gives the department control over the schedules of foreign guests and provides opportunities for collecting information on them but also reduces Chinese officials' wasted man-hours and needless expenditures and minimizes their opportunities for unauthorized activities. Examples of restrictions on ID-CPC officials implemented prior to COVID-19 include a limitation on the number and duration of their overseas visits and restrictions on personal travel outside China.[23]

While visiting China, African party delegations may take advantage of the ID-CPC's vast network to set up meetings with other party organs, government ministries, or official institutions such as policy banks, research institutes, or state-owned firms.[24] At the staff level, each visiting delegation requires extensive previsit planning and coordination with counterparts in the MFA, Ministry of State Security, Ministry of Propaganda, United Front Work Department, and other relevant party and security bureaus. Upon arrival, African party delegations are presented with an itinerary with the CPC's logo on the cover and a rank order of delegates on the back page. In Beijing, they often reside at the Wanshou Hotel, which was renovated before the inaugural Party and the World Dialogue in 2014 and has more than three hundred guest rooms and twenty conference rooms.[25] The hotel, which also hosted the Party and the World Dialogues in 2017 and 2019, was the ID-CPC's go-to venue for hosting African delegations prior to COVID-19. African delegates we spoke with at the Wanshou Hotel lauded the department's professionalism and preparation.[26]

Conversely, when the ID-CPC sends a delegation to an African country, it expects its local host will reciprocate by helping to arrange meetings with government, military, and business leaders in its relational network.[27] "Political parties," says Wang Heming, deputy director of the ID-CPC's African Division, "are not only decision makers for their country's policies, but also executors." The ID-CPC, Wang explains, acts as a conduit that enhances the party's influence and knowledge because political parties make policy decisions across a range of issues: "As political parties govern the country, they accumulate experiences and lessons, which are valuable for sharing with other countries. Communication between political parties, especially between ruling parties, plays a very positive role in promoting national diplomatic relations. We know that political parties make decisions for national policies on all fronts."[28]

The involvement of political parties across "all fronts" means they can provide timely information on local developments and support via their social network to help the CPC identify opportunities or mitigate adverse effects on its interests or its African partners.[29] In this way, by building relationships the ID-CPC enhances what James C. Scott of Yale University termed its *legibility*. According to Scott: "Legibility is a condition of manipulation. The greater the manipulation envisaged, the greater the legibility required to effect it."[30] Beijing's ambitious plans in many African countries require relationships that provide knowledge about local conditions—that is, a high degree of legibility. The stronger the department's relationships are with cadres in a particular African political party, the greater its legibility in that country, and hence the greater its capacity to pursue its interests there. Luan Jianzhang explains: "We have created a network for the CPC to hold exchanges with other parties in the world. So, we hope to promote such exchanges and communication. Political parties serve as the most fundamental political organization in the majority of countries around the world . . . [and] act as policy makers, as well as representatives who guide public opinion."[31]

African parties' ideologies run the gamut from leftist radicalism to Islamist dictatorships to rightist authoritarianism. Amid this mix, the department has emphasized flexibility and cultivated ties with as many strong and influential political parties as possible—regardless of their ideological persuasion.[32] This policy of avoiding ideological differences is articulated on the ID-CPC's website: "The CPC associates with not only the communist parties and other left-wing parties of the world as it originally did but also national democratic parties of the developing countries and political parties and statesmen of various ideologies and natures such as socialist, labor and conservative parties."[33]

Instead of ideological affinity, the ID-CPC seeks to build relationships with as many "high-quality" partners as possible. But just because the ID-CPC will work with parties across the political spectrum does not mean its engagements are apolitical. For instance, Zhong Weiyun, then division chief of the ID-CPC Bureau of African Affairs, explained how free elections have undermined Beijing's relations with African ruling parties: "In the early 1990s, a wave of multi-party democracy swept the African continent and posed certain negative impact on Sino-African inter-party exchange. After years of sustained communications, many of the long-reigning parties with which China had invested much time and energy developing relationships were replaced."[34]

Today, ID-CPC cadres continue to work to improve African perceptions of China, "debunk misconceptions," and discredit liberal democracy, especially the U.S. system. From Beijing's perspective, Western governments, universities, and media promote liberal values that predispose Africans to see China's political system unfavorably.[35] In response, at the opening of the Nineteenth CPC National Congress in 2017, Xi Jinping formally announced his decision to "offer" China's political system to developing countries: "The path, the theory, the system, and the culture of socialism with Chinese characteristics have kept developing, blazing a new trail for other developing countries to achieve modernization. It offers a new option for other countries and nations who want to speed up their development while preserving their independence; and it offers Chinese wisdom and a Chinese approach to solving the problems facing mankind."³⁶

In 2018 Xi explained that China's "system of multiparty cooperation led by the CPC" offers "a new type of party system growing from China's soil" and touted its advantages over liberal democracy: "The Chinese system is new . . . because it pools ideas and suggestions through institutional, procedural, and standardized arrangements and develops a scientific and democratic decision-making mechanism. It steers away from another weakness of the old-fashioned party system, in which decision making and governance, confined by interests of different political parties, classes, regions and groups, tears the society apart."³⁷

Song Tao reiterated this point in 2020 and applied it specifically to Africa, arguing that "the Chinese system . . . can serve as a reference to all developing countries including African countries in their pursuit of independent progress."³⁸ By building durable relationships with African political leaders regardless of their ideological persuasion, China gains their validation for its claim that, among other things, its autocratic political system is superior to U.S.-style liberal democracy.³⁹

PARTY EXCHANGES AND TRAINING WORKSHOPS

BILATERAL

The ID-CPC underwrites exchanges and short-term training programs for both senior-level and mid-to-junior-level party cadres from dozens of African political parties. According to Lina Benabdallah of Wake Forest University, the department uses these workshops, which generally last about two weeks, to disseminate "norms, produce knowledge, and increase networking and social power for China."⁴⁰ The goal, writes Yun Sun of the Stimson Center, "is to educate African political parties on China's experience in economic development and political governance."⁴¹ The department,

Sun explains, "systematically trains [African cadres] on how to emulate China's paths to success. The conscious effort made by China to help African elites absorb, assimilate, and duplicate the Chinese experience does constitute a different type of ideological push. It is geographically expansive, institutionally systematic, and will have a profound psychological and political impact over the choices and preferences of African political parties, and thus over the African political landscape.[42]

The data reveal that between 2002 and 2022, the ID-CPC conducted bilateral exchanges with political parties from all African states except Eswatini, which has diplomatic relations with Taipei, and Somalia, which remains unsafe. Figures 4.1 and 4.2 show two important trends in ID-CPC party-to-party exchanges with African parties that began when Xi took power, but ended with the onset of COVID-19 in 2020. First, as shown in figure 4.1, the number of ID-CPC bilateral exchanges with African political parties increased gradually, from thirty-six in 2011 to a peak of eighty in 2018. After funding fifty-three bilateral exchanges in 2019, due to the pandemic the ID-CPC conducted only seventeen exchanges (sixteen of them virtual) in 2020, thirty-one (twenty-nine virtual) in 2021, and twenty-one (twenty virtual) in 2022.

Second, as shown in figures 4.1 and 4.2, between 2013 and the onset of the pandemic, ID-CPC bilateral exchanges increasingly emphasized hosting African parties rather than sending delegations to the continent. Under Xi's predecessor, Hu Jintao, more ID-CPC delegations visited Africa (191) than African delegations were hosted in China (179). China sent more or the same number of delegations to Africa than it hosted between 2002 and 2005 and between 2008 and 2010, with the greatest disparity coming in 2012, when China sent twenty-eight delegations to Africa and hosted twenty-one African delegations. That trend was reversed in 2013, however, when China received twenty-one African delegations while sending only twelve to the continent. Before COVID-19, Xi's China hosted many more African delegations (257) than it sent to Africa (111), with the greatest disparity coming in 2018, when the ID-CPC hosted forty more delegations in China than it sent to Africa. Between 2015 and 2019, the ID-CPC increased its bilateral host diplomacy at an unprecedented rate, welcoming twenty-six

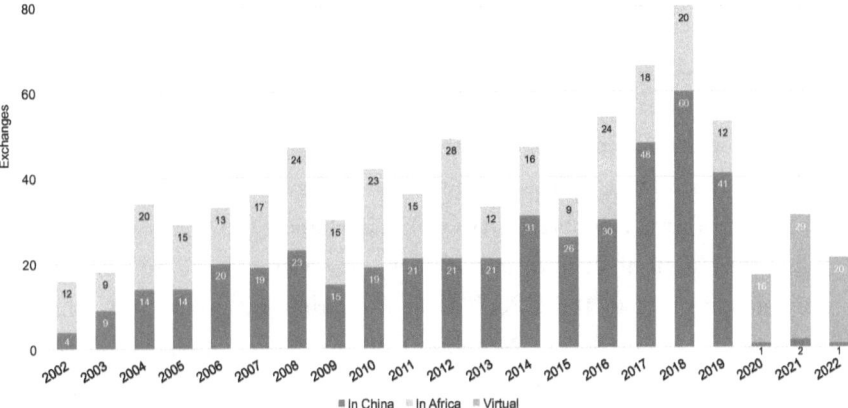

FIGURE 4.1 ID-CPC bilateral exchanges with African political parties, 2002–2022. Source: ID-CPC, https://www.idcpc.org.cn.

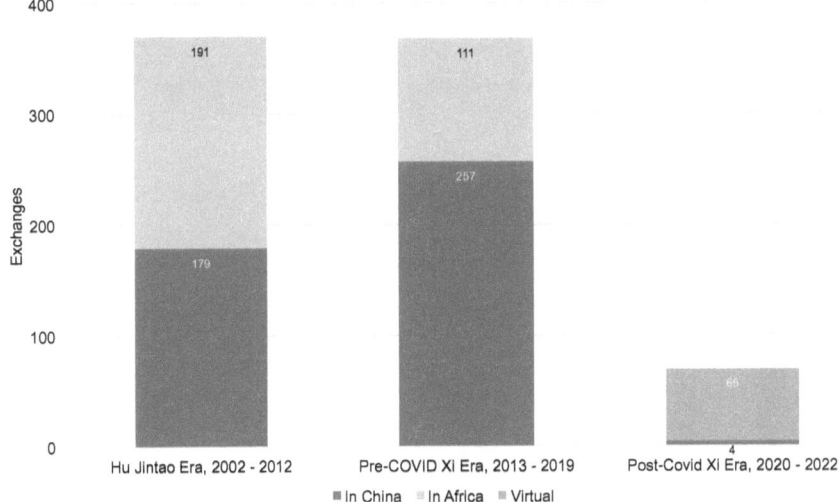

FIGURE 4.2 Location of ID-CPC bilateral exchanges, 2002–2022. Source: ID-CPC, https://www.idcpc.org.cn.

African delegations in 2015, thirty in 2016, forty-eight in 2017, sixty in 2018, and forty-one in 2019. After COVID-19 began spreading in 2020, however, the number of bilateral exchanges fell and they were moved online until 2023.

Of the twenty foreign partner parties with the most exchanges with the ID-CPC as of 2020, seven were African political parties.[43] Figure 4.3 shows that between 2002 and the end of 2022, the ID-CPC's most frequent African exchange partners were from South Africa (sixty-nine), Sudan (fifty-six), Ethiopia (forty-four), Tanzania (thirty-seven), Egypt (thirty-five), Zimbabwe (thirty-three), Namibia (thirty-two), and Morocco (thirty-two). The ruling parties in all of these countries, except for Morocco and Sudan, have long-standing ties to the CPC.[44] ID-CPC cadres are posted to China's embassies in South Africa, Namibia, Ethiopia, Egypt, Tanzania, Niger, Ghana, and "a few others," according to Cao Zhigang, then second secretary of China's embassy in the United States.[45] Figure 4.3 suggests a positive correlation exists between where ID-CPC officials are posted in Africa and the number of exchanges with that country's political parties.

To enhance their appeal, African cadre training workshops are designed to highlight the CPC's accomplishments and the specific messages it wants to convey to visitors. Delegations usually visit Beijing and a province selected

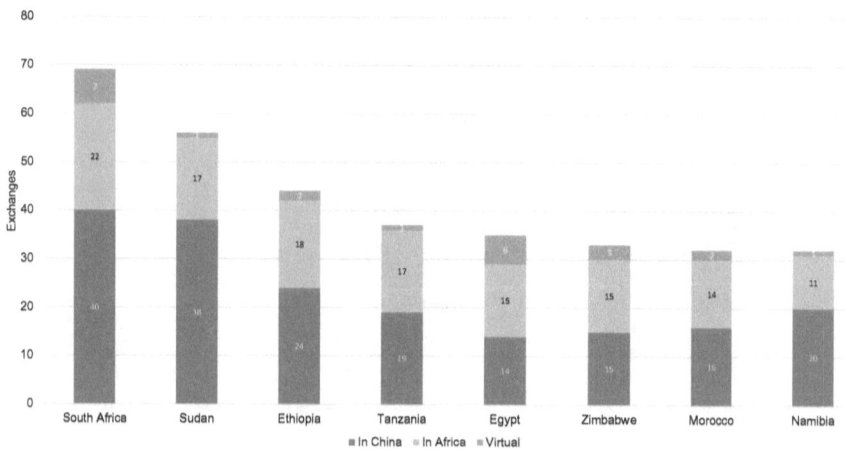

FIGURE 4.3 African countries with most bilateral exchanges with ID-CPC, 2002–2022. Source: ID-CPC, https://www.idcpc.org.cn.

based on their preferences, the department's objectives, and the locale's administrative capacity. In China, African guests may attend lectures at one or more of the CPC's training institutions, visit local sites, attend cultural programs, and meet with officials.[46] Examples of previous lecture topics for Africans include "grassroots party building," "the training and selection of young leading cadres," "party discipline and scientific management," and "the construction and development of the party school system." One class on the "Theory and Practice of the CPC's Strengthening the Construction of the Ruling Ability" covered "the main reasons, main contents and tasks and historical experience of the CPC's strengthening the ruling ability."[47]

Chinese reports on these training programs regularly claim that African "participants said that they benefited from what they learned and gained a lot from the seminars."[48] But this can be misleading because Beijing rewards foreigners who engage in public displays of admiration that validate China's political system. These affirmations, or *biaotai* (表态), provide external legitimacy for the CPC and reflect its own desirable perception of itself as a benevolent exemplar for African parties that are eager to learn from "China's expertise with regards to state governance and party-building."[49] An example of this rhetoric came from Raphael Tuju, secretary general of Kenya's now-defunct Jubilee Party, who in 2020 said: "The CPC is the biggest political party in the whole world. Its grassroots organisation is second to none. Jubilee Party can only aspire, and where possible learn some lessons. It is unlikely that in our lifetime, Jubilee Party can get anywhere close to the organisational levels of the CPC."[50]

There are countless other instances of African partners affirming China's political system and territorial claims.[51] Still, African responses to ID-CPC exchanges are not uniform. One official who participated in several ID-CPC training programs explained how they are designed to demonstrate the CPC's accomplishments and create an affinity and deference among the visitors:

> China will never feel safe as long as there are strong and well-functioning democracies in the world, so they are using every possible means not only to be accepted but to be popular among peoples of many African and

Middle Eastern countries because we are among the biggest tyrant factories in the world, so we are a very good soil to grow their seeds and thoughts. I believe the long-term purpose for these training is eventually making the Chinese model of governance more acceptable. The amazing economic welfare figures they show us in the training rooms and the fancy infrastructure we see there is definitely makes the majority of us say, we don't want democracy we need economic development. In the lectures room they adopt a twisted technique by affirming that they are a developing country like us and the West will never understand us and our needs like the Chinese will.[52]

MULTILATERAL

Prior to COVID-19, the ID-CPC had been arranging a small but growing number of party-to-party exchanges and training workshops involving members of political parties from two or more African countries. According to Chen Dongxiao: "Hosting a multilateral international conference can help the host nation exert influence on the topics and agendas in international affairs. At the same time, the number of participating countries and the seniority of representatives attending will also serve as important indices to gauge the host nation's international influence."[53]

As Wang Heming explained, the ID-CPC's hosting of multilateral delegations provides "a platform for the exchange and communication of theories and philosophies."[54] By positioning itself as a central node in their relational network, the ID-CPC intentionally creates a "group-think" effect among African visitors that reinforces and normalizes Sinocentric conceptions of international relations and rewards its supporters' compliance.[55]

In 2017, for example, the ID-CPC hosted nineteen African political parties for the Third China-Africa Political Party Theory Seminar in Beijing on "Building a Community of Shared Future for China and Africa: The Mission and Role of Political Parties."[56] And in 2019 the ID-CPC brought thirty French-speaking African political party leaders to receive training at the Party School of the Kunshan Municipal CPC Committee on "the theory and practice of the CPC in governing the country." The group's leader,

PARTY-TO-PARTY RELATIONS

Madagascar's former prime minister Ratsirahonana Norbert Lala, said: "We learned worthwhile new concepts and experiences in Kunshan and hope to continue to deepen China-Africa cooperation and help build a closer community of common future between China and Africa in the new era."⁵⁷

Like bilateral exchanges, the number of multilateral party-to-party exchanges with Africans rose between 2012 and 2022, and they were increasingly being held in China until 2020 when COVID-19 forced them online. Figure 4.4 shows that ID-CPC's multilateral exchanges with African parties took place in Africa in 2002 (one), 2012 (one), 2013 (one), 2015 (two), 2018 (three), and 2022 (one). Yet while the number of bilateral exchanges dropped considerably amid COVID-19, the department maintained a consistent, albeit relatively low, number of multilateral exchanges with African parties in 2020 (six), 2021 (ten), and 2022 (ten). As shown in figure 4.5, of the seventy-four multilateral exchanges held with African parties between 2002 and 2022 forty-four of them (60 percent) were conducted in China. Under Hu Jintao, the department held sixteen multilateral exchanges at home and only two in Africa; before the pandemic under Xi, the ID-CPC hosted twenty-four multilateral gatherings in China and only six in Africa;

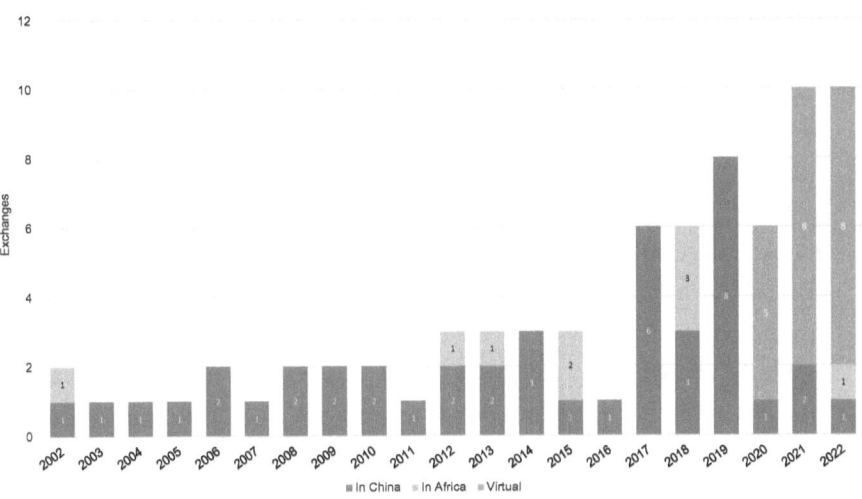

FIGURE 4.4 ID-CPC multilateral exchanges with African political parties, 2002–2022. Source: ID-CPC, https://www.idcpc.org.cn.

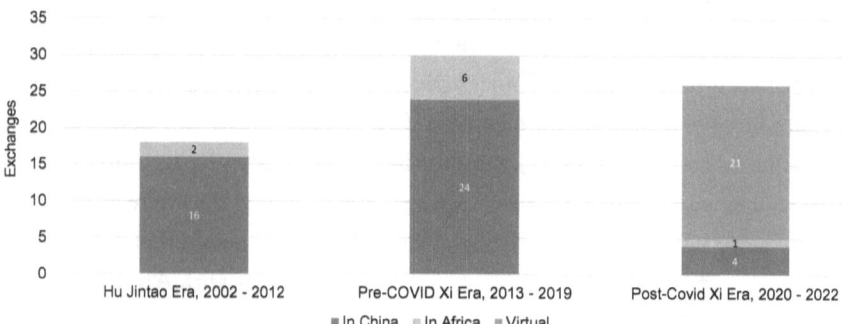

FIGURE 4.5 Location of ID-CPC multilateral exchanges, 2002–2022. Source: ID-CPC, https://www.idcpc.org.cn.

and between 2020 and 2022 the ID-CPC hosted twenty-one online multilateral exchanges, as well as four in-person exchanges in China and one in Africa.

To achieve a generational shift in African perceptions of China, Beijing created the Sino-Africa Young Political Leaders Forum. After training more than two hundred young African leaders between 2011 and 2015, the program was expanded in 2016 to train a thousand more in China by 2018.[58] For instance, the third Young African Leaders Training Course, held in 2019 at the Chongqing Party School, included twenty participants from various African ruling parties who attended presentations on "Training and Selection of Young Leading Party Cadres," "Youth Work," and "70 Years of New China's Achievements." The school's executive vice president urged the African trainees to "gain inspiration and experience, happiness and friendship from the 'China Story.'" "African friends" asked the "teachers" questions about "how to promote these experiences in Africa" and said they would "share what they have seen, heard, and learned." One Botswanan participant said her visit "opened up the horizon" and revealed the "CPC's strict discipline and scientific management."[59]

The ID-CPC has financed the Julius Nyerere Leadership School in Kibaha, Tanzania, which represents both a natural outgrowth and, in some ways, a notable departure from its host diplomacy and cadre training programs in China.[60] The school was built by China's construction firms for approximately $40 million.[61] As a venue in Africa created together with African parties, it places the CPC at the physical center of a multinodal network of likeminded political partners.

The process of developing a party school with African parties began in 2014, when the ID-CPC hosted fourteen cadres from various political parties for the African Political Party School Construction Special Training Course at the Zhejiang Provincial Party School. The school's vice president held a banquet for the African delegation and introduced the "construction and development of the party school system in Zhejiang, and arranged for an in-depth and meticulous exchange with the members of the delegation on the teaching management of the party school and the cadre education college."[62]

Discussions continued in China the following year, when ID-CPC vice minister Xu Luping hosted leaders from six African parties—South Africa's ANC, Tanzania's Chama Cha Mapinduzi (CCM), Zimbabwe African National Union–Patriotic Front (ZANU-PF), Namibia's South-West Africa People's Organization (SWAPO), the Mozambique Liberation Front Party (FRELIMO), and the People's Movement for the Liberation of Angola (MPLA)—to discuss building a joint party school in Africa. Song Tao met with the general secretaries of these six parties in Chongqing just prior to the CPC and World Dialogue in 2016, where they pledged "to further strengthen friendship, unity and cooperation with the CPC, learn from each other's experience in governing the country, and push bilateral party and state relations to a new height."[63]

In 2018 Song Tao and the general secretaries of the aforementioned six African parties traveled to Tanzania to participate in the groundbreaking ceremony for the Julius Nyerere Leadership School. Nearly a hundred party leaders from about forty African political parties and organizations attended the event, at which MPLA general secretary Antonio Paul said, "The CPC has come at the right time where we need transformation in the basic areas of our societies."[64] Song Tao read Xi Jinping's letter of congratulation, which identified the school as essential to the "construction of a closer community with a shared future for China and Africa."[65]

At the Nyerere School's inauguration ceremony in February 2022, Song Tao stressed the CPC's desire to "strengthening exchanges and cooperation" with African political parties in his virtual address to the approximately two thousand in-person attendees.[66] That June, the department sponsored the school's first in-person "ideology exchange program," the twelve-day "Former Liberation Movements of Southern Africa Leading Cadres Workshop," which included 120 representatives from the six parties.[67] A send-off ceremony was held at ZANU-PF headquarters for the twenty Zimbabwean cadres that the ID-CPC funded to attend.[68] "What we want to do is to get their experiences. China is bigger than Zimbabwe in terms of economy and their party as well, so we have a lot to learn from them than they have to learn from us," Emmanuel Mahachi, chairman of the ZANU-PF Harare Youth League, said at the event.[69] Although COVID-19 travel regulations did not permit ID-CPC officials to join the workshop in person, going forward the CPC is betting the school will become an important venue for building relations and sharing governance lessons with African political parties.

CASE STUDIES: SOUTH AFRICA, ETHIOPIA, AND GHANA

To identify consistencies in the CPC's engagement with African political parties, this section traces how the ID-CPC builds and maintains relationships in three of China's most important African partner countries: South Africa, Ethiopia, and Ghana. In addition to their strategic importance, these three countries also exhibit variation across several characteristics: state size, political system, geographic location, colonial legacy, language and culture, etc. Examining how the ID-CPC builds relationships in these diverse countries reveals cross-cutting consistencies and differences in its methods and objectives.

PARTY-TO-PARTY RELATIONS

SOUTH AFRICA: ANC AND SACP

This section covers the CPC's relations with the ANC and the SACP since the end of apartheid in 1994. It provides an illustrative account of how the CPC has offered political support and cadre training to these South African political parties, which, in return, have provided their support on issues, like Taiwan, that are important to China. The CPC-SACP relationship is among the clearest cases of a mutually beneficial, that is, "win-win," party-to-party relationship. It also reveals how Beijing guides its African partners to adopt Chinese, rather than Western, concepts and methods of party governance.

The ANC political coalition, which includes the SACP, has enabled the CPC's expanded relations with both parties. SACP leaders have long-standing relationships with their ANC counterparts and sometimes simultaneously hold senior positions in both parties. The SACP facilitates CPC-ANC relations and helps mitigate political pressure from the South African left that Beijing might otherwise face for its trade, human rights, and debt practices. Unlike the SACP, the Congress of South African Trade Unions (COSATU), another ANC coalition member, has been critical of China's policies toward South Africa. COSATU has spoken out against the negative effects on South Africa workers of illegal Chinese migration, imports of "cheap Chinese goods," and "extortionate" loans from China.[70] But while SACP cadres privately shared concerns about China's "capturing African elites," we were unable to identify an incidence when the party publicly voiced these or any other concerns about China's activities in South Africa.[71]

Instead, the SACP has successfully leveraged its relationship with the CPC to supplement its limited domestic political power and enhance its influence within the ANC coalition. Like the CPC, the SACP has Marxist roots but has increasingly shown itself willing to evolve ideologically toward more "pragmatic" conceptions of socialist governance. The SACP focuses primarily on acquiring governance lessons from the CPC experience.[72] They take advantage of the CPC's vast resources to obtain material support and training to improve their party's organization and structure.[73] Several SACP cadres have received degrees in China, including at the MA and PhD levels, and as of 2018 Beijing was providing three scholarships per year for younger SACP cadres to study in China.[74]

After apartheid, CPC-SACP relations expanded rapidly. SACP leaders took advantage of Beijing's desire for Pretoria to cut ties with Taipei to establish itself as the primary conduit for Sino–South African rapprochement. Prior to the 1994 elections, in which the ANC won 63 percent of the vote, the CPC reached out to the ANC via the SACP.[75] At that time many top ANC leaders either had close ties to the SACP or, like Thabo Mbeki, simultaneously held leadership positions in both parties.[76] This overlap in the two parties' leadership allowed the SACP to act as a go-between in CPC-ANC relations, thus catalyzing the normalization of diplomatic relations. According to a senior SACP leader: "The SACP played a much deeper and critical role on the recognition of the ANC's One China Policy."[77]

According to the senior cadre, long-serving SACP general secretary Blade Nzimande, who at the time was both a member of the ANC's International Relations Committee and acting chairman of the SACP, "led the process for the recognition of the PRC versus Taiwan." "Nzimande authored a report to the country's new leadership calling for the switch [to Beijing] and actually sparred against President Mandela who indicated that Taiwan had donated [R10 million] to the electoral success of the ANC."[78]

In early 1996 Beijing hosted South African foreign minister Alfred Nzo, who had served for decades both as ANC secretary general and as a member of the SACP Central Committee. In November 1996 Mandela announced that, starting in January 1998, Pretoria would switch recognition from Taipei to Beijing, and in late 1997 Nzo hosted Foreign Minister Qian Qichen to sign the joint communique establishing bilateral relations. General Secretary Jiang Zemin singled out the SACP's contribution during a meeting with Nzimande in Beijing and thanked him for pushing the ANC to recognize Beijing.[79]

After the establishment of bilateral relations, China launched a relationship-building campaign that garnered South African support for the creation of FOCAC in 2000.[80] Figure 4.6 reveals that, throughout the 2000s, a robust expansion of party-to-party exchanges occurred between the CPC and the ANC, the SACP, and sometimes both parties together.[81] In 2001, for instance, the ANC general secretary visited China

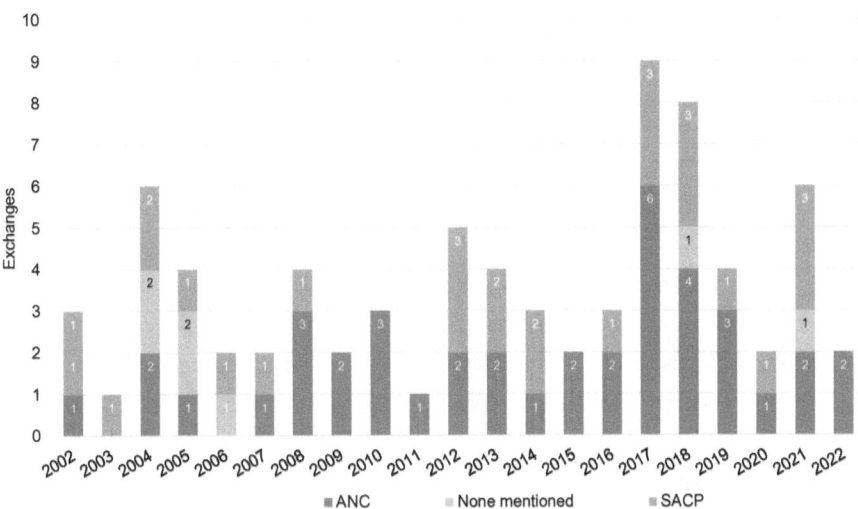

FIGURE 4.6 ID-CPC exchanges with South Africa, 2002–2022. Source: ID-CPC, https://www.idcpc.org.cn.

twice, the SACP leadership visited once, and the ID-CPC sent at least one high-level delegation to Pretoria. In 2007 Wang Dongming, a member of the CPC Central Committee, led a CPC delegation to South Africa to address the SACP's Twelfth National Party Congress. Jacob Zuma traveled to China in 2004 and 2008 as deputy president and president of the ANC, respectively, and again in 2010, as both president of South Africa and leader of the ANC.[82] During his visit in 2008, Zuma praised the party-to-party relationship, adding that he hoped the CPC could host training workshops for senior ANC cadres to learn about cadre development and party organization.[83]

After Zuma's 2008 trip, the ANC and the CPC inked a four-year deal to enhance cadre training through 2012. Ultimately, during that period, four groups (including a total of fifty-six members of the ANC National Executive Committee) would visit China for training on the "theories and practice of the ruling parties in China and in South Africa."[84] In 2009 the CPC Central Party School hosted South Africa's current president, Cyril Ramaphosa, then a member of the national executive committee of the

ANC, for a two-week "study tour" under the theme "From Revolution to Governance; Theories and Practice." According to the ANC delegation's posttrip report, while in China the eighteen-member group met with ID-CPC leaders for discussions on topics including "the theoretical basis for 'socialism with Chinese characteristics,' the party-building experience, experiences in political education, party discipline, and combating corruption."[85]

While visiting Beijing in 2015, the ANC signed a five-year party-to-party cooperation agreement with the CPC and released a policy paper identifying the CPC as the "guiding lodestar of our own struggle" toward government centralization and a "post-Western," "new world order."[86] In 2015, after traveling with an ANC delegation to study CPC organizational structure and local governance in Beijing, the ANC's secretary general said the party "is willing to learn from the CPC's 65 years of governance of China."[87] The ANC's head of research recalled that the ANC guests were treated "like royalty" and explained the purpose of CPC training and its influence on the ANC: "The advanced study tour was intended to soak the leadership in the latest development models of China, expose them to its political system, [and] party-building models. We left China excited and invigorated, with a view to shaping our organisational thinking going forward."[88] In 2020 China's embassy in South Africa distributed a thousand food parcels via the ANC Women's League, whose president thanked "the CPC for their benevolence" and, alluding to decades of support, said: "Comrades in China have done a lot for us. They have walked with us a long journey. We are grateful for the donation and we see it is from their heart. Thank you, China, thank you."[89]

The CPC is also training SACP cadres. Each year between 2013 and 2019, China hosted two bilateral training workshops for about twenty SACP cadres.[90] In 2018, for instance, the SACP politburo spent two weeks receiving "political education training" in Beijing. A senior SACP cadre told us that they "learn from admirable CPC practices such as efficiency, commitment, discipline, and party-loyalty" and emulate the conduct of CPC members, which are "humble, patriotic, and not materialistic." Topics studied included "learning party building skills," "how to organize the party," and "how to organize a party in government," and "anti-corruption." A report obtained from the SACP on their 2018 training program highlights the CPC's role in "cadre development" and "ideological training." It begins: "Enjoined by communist ideals, bilateral relations between the SACP and the CPC have resulted in cadre development efforts between the SACP and CPC. Delegations of the SACP leadership under the guidance of Central Committee Members have passed through ideological training that includes a visit to China."

According to the report, SACP first deputy general secretary Solly Mapaila and Central Committee member Reneva Fourie led twenty-two SACP cadres to visit Beijing and the Party School in Nanning, Guangxi. The SACP delegation included members from all nine South African provinces, nine male and thirteen female delegates, and Provincial Executive Committee members, leaders from districts, and the SACP Head Office staff. "The delegation comprised members who serve in important institutions of our democracy: provincial legislatures, public entities, municipalities, non-governmental organisation as well as trade unions," the report explained. In Beijing, SACP delegates met with ID-CPC vice minister Guo Yezhou before leaving for Guangxi, where they spent five days receiving lectures on topics including "Xi Jinping's Thought on Socialism with Chinese Characteristics for a New Era," "CPC Experiences and Practices of Strengthening the Governing Ability," "The Party and Marxism," and "Organisational Discipline and Ethics."[91]

In 2020, as the coronavirus pandemic spread around the globe, the ID-CPC conducted an online senior cadre training workshop for the SACP. "China is ready to share its practice with South Africa [and] consolidate the special friendship of comrades and brothers," said ID-CPC assistant minister Li Mingxiang.[92] Subsequently, in 2021, the ID-CPC and SACP held a joint centennial celebration webinar at which Li commended both parties for their "century-long struggle," through which they are "proving the validity of Marxism and demonstrating the strong vitality of socialism."[93] During the SACP's Fifteenth National Congress in 2022, Li again delivered virtual remarks praising the SACP and calling for more cooperation between the two parties.[94]

It is noteworthy that the CPC's years of close engagement with the SACP, a self-proclaimed "vanguard" communist party, have not produced more ideological tensions between them. When we asked about the role of ideology in the relationship, SACP cadres acknowledged that the CPC's "state capitalist" political system is quite different from South Africa, but said those differences have not impeded party-to-party relations. They said the CPC perceives the SACP as a "traditional" communist party and is working to help its cadres "modernize" their view of socialism.[95] According to the aforementioned SACP report, it is "important to remain ideologically grounded in order to provide an ideological defence on the constant attacks by capital and imperialist forces [sic]." This language, coupled with similar comments from ANC cadres, suggests that rather than communist ideals, shared opposition to Western "imperialism," especially the United States, is now the ideological glue that binds the CPC with both the ANC and SACP.

Both South African parties' close relations with the CPC have led some to question their Marxist credentials. One editorial, entitled "Why Is the ANC Following the Example of the Chinese Communist Party?," concluded that ANC leaders have pledged their party "will rule until the second coming of Christ. If that means learning the authoritarian measures used by the Chinese Communists against the Tibetans, or the democracy protesters in Hong Kong, then so be it."[96] In his book *The Big Sell Out*, Dan Mokonyane argues that just as the CPC abandoned communism in the 1980s, "what the ANC/SACP stood for, even in 1990, has long been forgotten or quietly dropped."[97] Yet, despite its oft-professed desire to learn CPC methods to enhance party cohesion and discipline, the ANC continues to suffer from corrosive internal fragmentation and widespread corruption.[98]

ETHIOPIA: EPRDF AND TPLF

Although Ethiopia is very different from South Africa in terms of language, location, history, culture, climate, and political system, there are notable similarities between the CPC's objectives and patterns of relationship building with the ANC and SACP and its engagement with the EPRDF, Ethiopia's ruling party between 1991 and 2019, and the TPLF, which led the now-defunct EPRDF political coalition. In Ethiopia, as in South Africa, the CPC accessed the larger ruling party, the EPRDF, via the smaller vanguard party, the TPLF—which until 2018–2019 made all the important decisions in Ethiopia.[99] As it did with the ANC and SACP, the CPC spent considerable resources engaging and training members of the EPRDF and the TPLF. The CPC also viewed the EPRDF, like the ANC, as a priority partner in Africa; and like the SACP, the TPLF provided a subgroup with overlapping membership that the CPC used to access and influence the larger ruling party.

The EPRDF, like the ANC, saw the CPC as a "political mentor," especially on questions of economic development and party governance. While the EPRDF does not appear to have received direct cash payments from the CPC, its members did accept various types of in-kind largesse. We were told that Beijing-financed construction projects helped enrich EPRDF leaders, and many of their children received scholarships to study at Chinese universities.[100]

Like South Africa, China prioritizes Ethiopia in its Africa strategy. According to the former Chinese ambassador to Ethiopia, Ai Ping, the country "plays a very unique and important role in both the sub-region and the continent as a whole."[101] As former CPC general secretary Hu Jintao explained: "Ethiopia could play a pivotal role in enabling China to consolidate its cooperation with other African countries."[102] "China believes Ethiopia is a key pillar of peace and security in the East Africa region," said Liu Jianchao, who took over from Song Tao as ID-CPC minister in June 2022.[103] Seifudein Adem of Doshisha University explains that "behind China's elevated interest in Ethiopia . . . is the diplomatic clout Ethiopia is said to enjoy in Africa, part of which emanates from the history of Ethiopia as symbol of black freedom and stimulator of pan-Africanism. Also relevant is the fact that Addis Ababa is the seat of the headquarters of the African Union and other regional institutions. China's strong foothold in Ethiopia would presumably help the former in projecting its influence onto the rest of Africa."[104]

Because until 2019 China and Ethiopia both had autocratic political systems and were led by revolutionary-cum-ruling parties seeking to maintain power while modernizing large and dynamic developing countries, some reasoned that CPC governance lessons and methods were particularly applicable in Ethiopia. Like the CPC, the EPRDF leadership viewed economic development as a means to affirming the party's political legitimacy.[105] Tang Xiaoyang of Qinghua University, for instance, argued that no African party hewed closer to the CPC model of a strong ruling party than the EPRDF.[106]

Senior EPRDF cadres first visited Beijing in 1994 and, like the ANC, soon began regular party-to-party exchanges with the CPC.[107] In 1995 Meles Zenawi, the leader of both the EPRDF and the TPLF, visited Beijing, and the following year General Secretary Jiang Zemin visited Addis Ababa. Between 2003 and 2010 the ID-CPC and EPRDF held eleven bilateral exchanges, about one or two per year. In 2008, for instance, Meles invited a senior delegation of CPC cadres to attend the Seventh EPRDF Organizational Conference, and they returned in 2010 for the Eighth EPRDF Organizational Conference.[108] Party-to-party exchanges accelerated noticeably in 2011, when the ID-CPC and EPRDF met four times, and between 2013 and 2019 the two parties had a total of twenty-six engagements (figure 4.7). This expanded volume of exchanges was driven by the

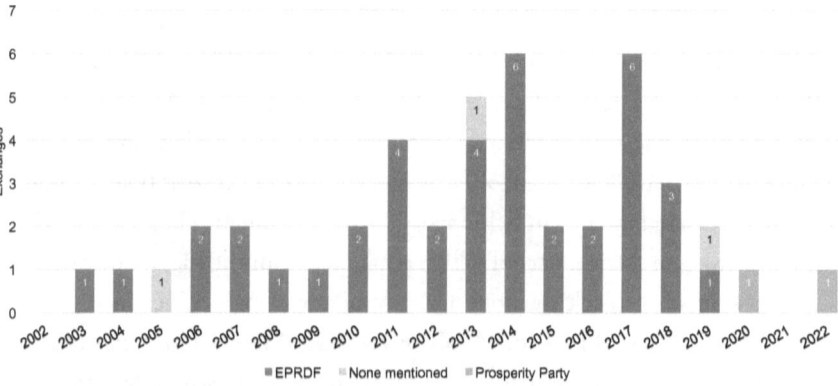

FIGURE 4.7 ID-CPC exchanges with Ethiopia, 2002–2022. Source: ID-CPC, https://www.idcpc.org.cn.

aforementioned emphasis on ID-CPC work in Africa, as well as Beijing concerns about Ethiopia's future without Meles, who died in 2012.

Before 2020 the ID-CPC and the Central Party School in Beijing also hosted annual training workshops for EPRDF cadres on party organizational structure, ideological work, propaganda, cadre education, and central-local relations.[109] The EPRDF delegation to China in 2013 focused on cadre management; the training program in 2015 taught the EPRDF how the CPC monitors, guides, and manages public opinion through propaganda, including organizational, technology, legislation, and media relations; and the 2016 delegation focused on youth management.[110] Speaking at the Shanghai Forum at Fudan University in 2017, Arkebe Oqubay, minister and special advisor to the prime minister of Ethiopia and a senior member of both the EPRDF and TPLF, said party-to-party relations were at the center of China-Ethiopia relations.[111]

In May 2018 the chair of the Standing Committee of the National People's Congress, Li Zhanshu, visited the new Ethiopian prime minister, Abiy Ahmed Ali, whom he urged to "keep control of politics" and to do everything possible "to prevent chaos."[112] In September 2018 Xi Jinping hosted Abiy in Beijing, and they agreed to maintain political exchanges and deepen cooperation.[113] In October 2018 ID-CPC deputy minister Ge Yezhou led a delegation to Ethiopia to represent the CPC at the EPRDF's Eleventh National Congress.[114] In December 2018, even while the EPRDF was riddled with internal strife, the ID-CPC hosted an EPRDF "cadre study group" led by Melese Alemu Hirboro, vice head of the EPRDF, who met with Song Tao "to enhance exchanges of experience in party governance and state administration." Six months later, in April 2019, with the EPRDF crumbling, Song Tao hosted another EPRDF cadre study group, this one "marking the 25th anniversary of the partnership between the CPC and the EPRDF." Song told them: "China supports the EPRDF . . . and is willing to continue providing assistance."[115] This pledge, which came despite the EPRDF's impending collapse, suggests that the CPC, having invested heavily in the relationship, was reluctant to abandon its long-time partner.

The EPRDF's disintegration seems to have disrupted the CPC's knowledge of developments in Ethiopia. One senior Ethiopian who met with an

ID-CPC delegation that attended the EPRDF's final party congress described them as, "clueless and desperate about making sense of what was happening in the country. It sounded to us that they were completely cut off, and mind you the TPLF was still relevant in the leadership." He said that amid growing political tensions, the CPC skipped the TPLF "45 Years of Journey" celebration in order to avoid damaging country-to-country relations: "If they [the CPC] have any relationship with TPLF, they would keep it unnoticeable and in hibernation for a while."[116]

In late 2019 Prime Minister Abiy Ahmed's Prosperity Party completely displaced the EPRDF and TPLF, which reorganized in the Tigray Region, where it won regional elections in 2020, leading to a civil war between Tigray and the government in Addis Ababa. This power transition, coupled with COVID-19, can explain why there were only two party-to-party exchanges between 2020 and 2022 (figure 4.7). In 2020 the ID-CPC held its first online training workshop for the Prosperity Party, which was attended by Li Mingxiang and by Awolu Abdi, head of public and international relations for the Prosperity Party, who said that "the workshop was an important initiative for exchanges and cooperation between the two Parties."[117] Although no meeting appears to have taken place in 2021, in 2022 Liu Jianchao and Prosperity Party vice president Adam Fara held a virtual meeting and agreed to build a "strategic partnership." Fara said his party "has been learning from the CCP and will continue to do so," and Liu committed to "strengthening ties with the Prosperity Party."[118] Still, the CPC has yet to develop the same level of collaboration with the Prosperity Party that it had with the EPRDF/TPLF.

The South Africa and Ethiopia cases suggest that China's biggest problem may not be countering U.S. "imperialism" in Africa, but rather the internal fragmentation of long-standing partner parties like the ANC and the collapse of others like the EPRDF. In the case of Ethiopia, such splintering not only injects uncertainty into state-to-state relations but also calls into question the value of CPC training when its purported "best student" falls apart after years of lessons on strengthening party governance.

PARTY-TO-PARTY RELATIONS

GHANA: NDC AND NPP

Ghana is an example of ID-CPC relationship-building in an African electoral democracy that has seen peaceful transitions of power. Although in autocracies like Ethiopia the CPC's relations with opposition parties are subordinated if they jeopardize ties with the ruling party, in multiparty democracies like Ghana Beijing can safely build relations with both the governing party and the opposition. Through its relationships with opposition parties, the CPC is able "to keep track of domestic politics" and "establish contacts with a wide range of politicians and experts who subsequently staff governments after they come to power," observes David Shambaugh of George Washington University.[119] Relations with opposition parties serve as a hedge, ensuring that a relationship already exists in case the opposition assumes power. As the ID-CPC's Zhong Weiyun explains: "Many state leaders, before they assume office, had already been China's friends. After they assume office, they have made active efforts in advancing friendship with China. Through contact with young political figures, the CPC has laid foundations for future state-to-state relations."[120] In Ghana, the CPC maintains ties with both the NDC and the NPP. Figure 4.8 shows that between 2009 and 2022, the meetings posted on the ID-CPC official website are only with those with the ruling party at that time. Our meetings with NDC officials in 2018 revealed, however, that quiet contacts continued even after the NPP took power in 2016.[121]

For the CPC, "improved relations with the NDC have been reflected in the posture and attitude of the Ghanaian government," while for the NDC, its relationship with the CPC has been "all about party building," according to one senior NDC leader. The CPC-NDC relationship began slowly in the mid- to late 1990s through interlocutors at China's embassy in Accra. In 1997 the NDC's director of international relations, Kofi Attor, led a delegation of party leaders to Beijing and signed an MOU between the two parties. Over the next two decades, as the NDC consolidated political power, its relationship with the CPC grew apace to include "numerous party-to-party exchanges and a lot of types of cooperation."[122]

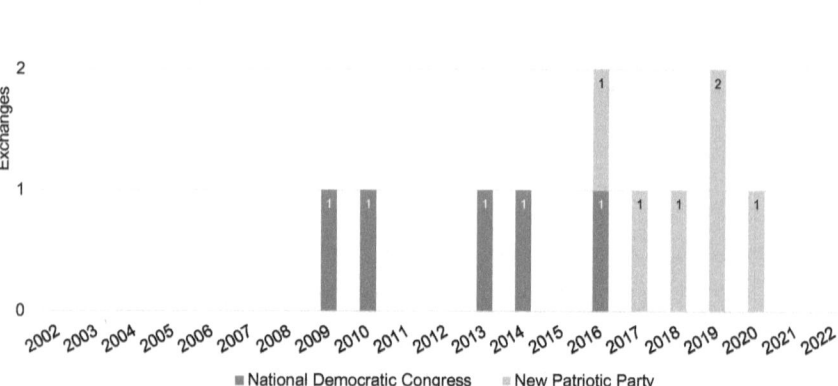

FIGURE 4.8 ID-CPC exchanges with Ghana, 2002–2022.
Source: ID-CPC, https://www.idcpc.org.cn.

As it did in South Africa and Ethiopia, the CPC advances its relations with Ghanaian political parties using party-to-party exchanges, training workshops, and various types of material support. NDC leaders said their party had not accepted cash, but that "the CPC had provided many gifts." This in-kind support has included laptops, projectors, cell phones, various types of communications technology, office furniture, and equipment.[123]

But the CPC's most substantial contribution to the NDC is its party headquarters in Accra.[124] The building's construction by the China State Construction Company raised questions about the funding source, because before the NDC came to power in 2009 it was facing eviction from its previous headquarters for unpaid rent.[125] These concerns were amplified when the NDC's general secretary refused to submit the party's financial accounts to the national electoral commission and denied owning the building.[126] NDC officials told us they had wanted to make a public statement thanking Beijing for building the headquarters, but the Chinese Embassy asked them not to.[127]

Over the years the NDC has sent scores of cadres to the CPC Central Party School. As of 2018, between two hundred and three hundred NDC party members had received training in China on topics such as party organization and management, cadre recruitment, and women and youth outreach.[128] These experiences had a profound impact on the NDC, explained Kwesi Quartey, who served as secretary to former Ghanaian president John Mahama and deputy foreign minister under the NDC-led government until 2017.[129] Quartey believes that "China has been an example to Africa and to the rest of the world."[130]

This appreciation for the CPC's achievements inspired the NPC to create its own institution to teach its cadres organizational, recruitment, and leadership skills. In 2014, upon returning from leading a six-member delegation to Beijing, NDC general secretary Johnson Asiedu-Nketia announced that he had held discussions with the CPC about establishing an NDC party school.[131] The NDC would replicate the CPC approach, Asiedu-Nketia said, "so that through the party school, we will be able to train our cadres and our students... about how to go about the business of running the political party first and how to prepare our youth for leadership positions in the future."[132]

Completed in 2016, the NDC's party school is located within its Chinese-built headquarters and was furnished by Beijing with instructional materials, desks, and chairs. The courses have been adapted from those taught at the CPC's Central Party School so the NDC can train more cadres at home and send fewer to China.[133]

The relationship with the NPP provides a window into the CPC's cultivation of ties with an opposition party-cum-ruling party. Soon after the NPP won national elections in 2016, the CPC moved to enhance party-to-party relations. While visiting the NPP's headquarters in 2018, we were shown numerous "gifts," many with tags still attached, provided via the Chinese Embassy in Accra, including TVs, laser printers, copy machines, laptops, cameras, cell phones, desks, office chairs, and a prominently displayed copy of Xi Jinping's book *Governance of China*.[134] As it did for the ANC in 2020, at the height of the COVID-19 pandemic, the ID-CPC delivered six thousand boxes of face masks directly to the NPP. While presenting them to NPP Chairman Frederick Armah Blay, the chargé d'affaires of the PRC Embassy, Zhu Jing, said the "supplies arranged by the ID-CPC were to support the NPP to prevent the spread of the pandemic among its members and officials." Blay thanked the ID-CPC for its "solidarity with the NPP."[135]

NPP cadres have also attended programs such as the ID-CPC-organized multilateral party meetings in Tanzania in 2018. At that time, the NPP had yet to receive bilateral training from the CPC, but pursuant to an ID-CPC outreach submitted a proposal highlighting its desire to "improve party capacity and deepen its ideological skills," and received in invitation to visit China from the embassy. One NPP party leader said he hoped to learn more about party structure, organization, discipline, and how to create a hardworking contingent of loyal cadres like the CPC. The NPP also expressed interest in replicating the CPC's party school model of midcareer cadre training. "NPP needs to build a strong party to have a strong government," said one NPP official. The NPP, like the aforementioned African parties, is also most interested in "learning party management and discipline," said another official working on China policy.[136]

When asked what, if any, challenges the CPC faces in Ghana, NPP officials identified three important differences that limit the applicability of the CPC's party-building lessons. First, China's "noncompetitive, closed political system" is not comparable to Ghana, which is a parliamentary democracy. Second, the CPC's weak human rights record means that many of its policies are not feasible in Ghana. "The NPP is a center-right party, we believe in democracy, rule of law, and individualism," the NPP official explained. Third, the CPC's efforts to encourage the NPP to become "anti-U.S." were not effective because the NPP is committed to creating a balanced "middle-of-the-road foreign policy."[137]

* * *

Based on primary sources, interviews with Chinese and African officials, and two decades of official data, this chapter sheds light on how the ID-CPC builds relationships with scores of African political parties. Prior to COVID-19, each year the ID-CPC was hosting dozens of bilateral and multilateral dialogues and trainings to expand the depth and breadth of its relations with a growing network of African political leaders. Gradually, delegation by delegation, workshop by workshop, ID-CPC cadres build relationships with African political elites and reward their compliance and deference with material and political support. Although COVID-19 temporarily halted in-person China-Africa bilateral and multilateral party-to-party exchanges and trainings, they were resumed after travel restrictions were eased in January 2023. Meanwhile, the Julius Nyerere Leadership School seems poised to emerge as a principal venue for exchanges and training between the ID-CPC and like-minded African parties.

Prior to COVID-19, the CPC was building relations with as many high-quality African parties as possible in order to establish itself as the central node in an expanding multinational network. Hosting African parties in China enhances the Chinese side's agenda-setting power and provides a controlled venue for policy coordination and the exchange of political favors and material support. The ID-CPC uses these engagements to gradually normalize Sinocentrism and reciprocal obligations in asymmetric relationships (see chapter 1). Beijing wants its African partners to legitimize its authoritarian political system, adopt concepts and methods of governance akin to the CPC, support China's territorial claims, help advance Chinese interests, and oppose the United States and the liberal values it promulgates. As we heard in Addis Ababa, working with the CPC requires "understanding the Chinese way of thinking," which Ethiopian officials said prioritize interpersonal relationship building and promote economic development to maintain political stability.[138]

For their part, African parties receive opportunities to visit and attend cadre training workshops in China, receive financial or in-kind largesse, gain educational opportunities for their children, and can leverage their relationship with the CPC to enhance their political influence at home. Ultimately, however, African political parties in South Africa, Ethiopia, and Ghana all said the CPC offers resources and methods of political governance and cadre oversight that could allow them to retain power.

5

AFRICA-FOCUSED PROPAGANDA

This chapter examines China's ongoing involvement in the African media, education, and cultural sectors, which are intended to improve African perceptions of the country and its political system, while doing the opposite for the United States. The Communist Party of China's (CPC) "Africa-focused propaganda" (对非宣传) targets a much broader audience (e.g., journalists, doctors, students, teachers, scholars, businesspersons, performers, and artists) than do traditional diplomatic, party-to-party, or military-to-military engagements. These African "opinion-setters" generally have less preexisting knowledge of China's strategic interests than those in the government or military, thus making them more impressionable targets for the "multifaceted, adaptive, and complex set of tactics" detailed in this chapter.[1]

Africa is currently home to 1.46 billion of the world's 8 billion people. By 2050 the continent's population will nearly double, to 2.48 billion. By 2100, 4.4 billion of the projected 11.2 billion people on Earth will be African.[2] Africa is also the world's youngest continent, with a median age of just 19.5, and 41 percent of its population under the age of 15.[3] It is amid this demographic expansion that China uses Africa-focused propaganda to "nurture greater cooperation, friendship, and partnership" with each successive generation of African elites.[4] The rapid expansion of virtual platforms such as satellite TV, online streaming services, and phone applications, coupled with the availability of cheap headsets, gives young Africans access to more online material than ever before.[5] To entice them, Chinese propaganda outlets are hiring Africans to localize their content, hosting delegations and training workshops, and offering long-term educational opportunities. According to Xi Jinping, this new propaganda strategy intends to create "a new type of mainstream media" that is "powerful, influential, and credible."[6]

CPC propaganda promotes positive views of the party, its leaders, and policies, counters hostile foreign forces, and asserts China's territorial claims over Taiwan, Hong Kong, Tibet, the South China Sea, etc.[7] But as Beijing's foreign policy has grown more assertive, its propaganda has also increasingly confronted "the Western media's distortion of the Chinese presence on the continent," explained one former CGTN editor in Africa.[8] The lead narrative is that China's political system is superior to Western liberal democracy, especially the U.S. system, because it is responsible for the nation's rapid economic growth and political stability.[9] This specifically anti-American messaging portrays China as a rising power and the United States as an aggressive, hypocritical hegemon facing an inevitable decline.[10]

We begin by introducing how the party conceives of its foreign-focused propaganda work and the bureaucratic apparatus that creates and manages it. Then, in the three sections that follow, we identify and analyze China's Africa-focused media, educational, and cultural propaganda programs and how they seek to improve African elites' views of China and build relationships to advance Beijing's interests and counter the United States. We conclude by evaluating the effectiveness of China's Africa-focused propaganda activities, based on how Africans are responding to them and whether they are achieving Beijing's objectives.

AFRICA-FOCUSED PROPAGANDA

CHINA'S PROPAGANDA APPARATUS

Since its founding in 1921, the CPC has used propaganda to "educate the masses" (教育群众) and "mobilize friends to strike at enemies" (动员党的朋友打击党的敌人). Unlike in liberal democracies, the term *propaganda* does not carry a negative connotation in the CPC lexicon. Rather, it is viewed as one among many instruments of coercive power that party cadres use to achieve their desired ends—or, as David Shambaugh at George Washington University described it, "a legitimate tool for transforming and building the kind of society sought by the Party."[11] In keeping with the "holistic security" concept introduced in chapter 1, CPC leaders take threats to their regime as their highest security priority. This emphasis on regime security dominates every aspect of China's foreign-focused "political, economic, security, cultural, and educational activities," which are considered strategic communications and fall under the party's exclusive purview.[12]

The Propaganda Department of the CPC Central Committee (中共中央宣传部), which controls all public information in China, is a sprawling bureaucracy that penetrates every conceivable social space. It administers "a politically weaponized system of censorship... refined, organized, coordinated and supported by the state's resources," explains Xiao Qiang of the University of California, Berkeley. It is "a powerful apparatus to construct a narrative and aim it at any target with huge scale. No other country has that."[13]

As Xi Jinping emphasized at the National Meeting on Propaganda and Thought Work in 2013, China's foreign-focused propaganda "uses innovative outreach methods to tell a good Chinese story and promote China's views internationally."[14] Beijing is developing "the ability to influence and control international public opinion," or what former China Radio International (CRI) director-general Wang Gengnian, called "international discourse power." According to Wang: "Mastering discourse power can influence and guide the direction of international public opinion, influence international mainstream society and mainstream media, and give China's development a good international environment."[15] Wang describes the information space as a "battleground" (战场), with the enemy being U.S.-led Western "discourse hegemony" (话语霸权).[16]

Since the 1980s the CPC Central Committee Foreign Propaganda Small Group, which includes senior party leaders, has set the agenda for China's foreign-focused propaganda work. These plans are then implemented by the Propaganda Department—the sprawling, multilayered bureaucracy that "extends into virtually every medium concerned with the dissemination of information."[17] Foreign-focused cultural propaganda work is administered by the Ministry of Culture, while foreign-focused education propaganda is handled by the Center for Language Education and Cooperation (known as the Confucius Institute Headquarters, or Hanban, until 2020), housed under the Ministry of Education.[18] Each university has its own office to deal with issues related to foreign students and faculty, and provinces and larger municipalities each have offices that administer their foreign-related activities, such as hosting prominent foreign guests and delegations.[19]

China's media outlets (e.g., newspapers, radio, and TV), traditionally regarded as the primary purveyors of propaganda, remain its most readily observable feature. The Chinese conception of propaganda is much broader, however, including but not limited to

> newspaper offices, radio stations, TV stations, publishing houses, magazine, and other news and media departments; universities, middle schools, primary schools, and other vocational education, specialized education, cadre training, and other educational organs; musical troupes, theatrical troupes, film production studios, film theaters, drama theaters, clubs, and other cultural organs, literature and art troupes, and cultural amusement parks; cultural palaces, libraries, remembrance halls, exhibition halls, museums, and other cultural facilities and commemoration exhibition facilities.[20]

From this list, we identify the three overlapping subcategories of China's propaganda work—media, education, and culture—which we examine in the African context in the sections that follow. After identifying "Africa-focused propaganda" as a regional subgrouping under "foreign-focused propaganda," (对外宣传) we examine its three subcategories: "Africa-focused media propaganda" (对非媒体宣传), "Africa-focused educational propaganda" (对非教育宣传), and "Africa-focused cultural propaganda" (对非文化宣传).[21]

MEDIA

OUTLETS AND APPLICATIONS

Over the past two decades, and especially with the expansion of financing under the Belt and Road Initiative, China's companies, led by Huawei and ZTE, have laid digital communications infrastructure in dozens of African countries.[22] As we discuss in detail in chapter 10, between 2000 and 2014 Chinese firms and agencies committed around $4.8 billion to support more than a hundred telecommunications projects in Africa.[23] Africans, especially young urbanites, are online more than ever before. In 2019 there were approximately 437 million internet users in Africa, and by 2025 that number is expected to top 700 million.[24]

China's "big four" party-controlled media outlets—Xinhua, *China Daily*, China Radio International (CRI), CGTN (China Global Television Network, known as China Central Television International until 2017)—target this growing African audience in various countries, regions, and linguistic groups. They receive vast state resources that allow them to cover more stories using more mediums (print media, television, radio, and online) in numerous local languages and all six UN languages—Arabic, English, French, Spanish, Russian, and Chinese—four of which are official languages in at least one African country.[25] They do not identify themselves as CPC propaganda outlets, and each has numerous multilingual, outward-facing social media accounts on platforms that are blocked in China, such as Twitter, Facebook, YouTube, and Instagram.[26] In early 2023, CGTN's French-language Twitter account had a million followers; CGTN Spanish, 586,000; and CGTN Arabic, 678,000. These accounts have even more followers on Facebook, where CGTN French had twenty million followers, and CGTN Spanish and CGTN Arabic had between sixteen and seventeen million followers each.

Although official figures are not available for China's foreign-focused propaganda expenditures, in 2017 Shambaugh valued them at about $10 billion.[27] In 2020 Sarah Cook of Freedom House estimated that China spends "hundreds of millions of dollars a year" on foreign-focused media propaganda alone. Between 2017 and 2020 she identified "a dramatic expansion in [China's] efforts to shape media content and narratives around the world, affecting every region and multiple languages."[28] To be sure, whatever the pre-COVID baseline figure was, China's 2020–2022 public relations blitz required a substantial injection of resources. In 2022 Freedom House estimated that Beijing was "devoting billions of dollars a year to its foreign propaganda and censorship efforts." There are no estimates available for the Africa-focused portion of China's propaganda expenditures.[29]

To reach more Africans, China's elite universities are expanding training in African languages for Chinese students.[30] In 2017 Beijing Foreign Studies University, for instance, started offering five African languages—Comorian, Tswana, Ndebele, Shona, and Tigrinya—and subsequently added Kinyarwanda in 2019.[31]

In 2006, the year China celebrated "The Year of Africa," Xinhua relocated its Africa editorial office from Paris to Nairobi, and CRI established a radio station there broadcasting in English, Chinese, and Swahili. China's media presence in Africa began expanding markedly after the 2008–2009 global financial crisis. While budget cuts forced many Western news outlets to reduce their Africa coverage, China launched a worldwide $7.25 billion campaign, known as "Big Foreign Propaganda" (大外宣). During the campaign, Xinhua increased the number and size of its foreign bureaus, the *Global Times* started an English-language edition, and CCTV began broadcasting in Arabic.[32] *China Daily Africa* and the glossy magazine *ChinAfrica* were both launched in 2012.

By 2014 Xinhua had thirty bureaus, sixty journalists, and four hundred local employees in Africa; and as of early 2023 it was operating thirty-seven bureaus, more than any other media agency on the continent.[33] By 2019 CGTN Africa had approximately 150, mostly African, employees. That year, in Kenya, China's big four media outlets employed more than a hundred local staff, and the sixteen-story Xinhua Tower was completed in Nairobi to house the agency and about forty Chinese staff and their families.[34]

CRI, which has been active in Africa for decades, broadcasts in at least nine African languages and has regional African bureaus in Harare (Southern Africa), Lagos (West Africa), and Cairo (North Africa).[35] In 2018 the Propaganda Department combined CRI with its domestic sister station, China National Radio, to create the Voice of China, which is tasked with "propagating the party's theories, directions, principles and policies" and "telling good China stories."[36]

Television remains a primary conduit for China's media propaganda. Soon after China Central Television International established its Africa bureau in Nairobi in 2011, visiting CPC minister of propaganda Li Changchun called for it to become the largest international television broadcasting center in Africa. At the opening of the station's new studio facilities in 2012, Ambassador Liu Guangyuan in Kenya instructed reporters to "tell Africa a good Chinese story."[37] The bureau quickly began recruiting African anchors and local staff and by the end of the year had over a hundred employees, including about seventy Africans (primarily Kenyans) and forty Chinese.[38] To improve the attractiveness of its broadcasts and compete with the likes of BBC, CNN, and al Jazeera, CGTN continues to invest in its studios and in enhancing the production value of its graphics and video packages.

Since it began operating in Rwanda in 2008, StarTimes, a semiprivate pay TV company with links to Beijing, has acquired more than thirteen million subscribers in thirty African countries. Although the scale of the company's presence varies, it is the primary provider of satellite TV in more than two dozen African countries, and in about twenty it has facilitated the transition from analog to digital transmission.[39] Subscribers pay as little as $2 per month for digital TV programming that prioritizes China's state media and local channels over Western news networks, which are available at a markup.[40] The content offered by StarTimes includes Chinese Super League football, as well as kung-fu movies and Chinese soap operas, which are translated into African languages such as Hausa and Swahili.

The company continues to produce an increasing amount of original content for African audiences.[41]

Another Chinese firm, Opera, delivers personalized "soft" content directly to Africans mobile devices.[42] The app, which allows users to curate their own news and video feeds, was launched in Nigeria and Kenya in 2018 and has since expanded to Egypt, South Africa, and Ghana. The company has grown from twenty-one million monthly users in 2019 to more than two hundred million in 2021.[43] Another semiprivate Chinese company, Transsnet, created Vskit—a short-video platform like TikTok aimed at younger Africans that went from ten million users in 2019 to more than fifty-one million in 2021.[44] In South Africa, the Alibaba Group's Alipay teamed up with Vodacom to create a "super app" similar to WeChat that offers banking and payment services to low-income residents.[45] The growing number of users suggests Africans find the soft content and consumer services offered by these semiprivate Chinese platforms more appealing than the traditional propaganda content distributed by the big four.

THE EDITORIAL LINE

In his New Year's speech to the Political Bureau of the CPC Central Committee in 2014, Xi Jinping described the image the party's foreign-focused propaganda work should convey:

> China should be portrayed as a civilized country featuring rich history, ethnic unity and cultural diversity, and as an Eastern power with good government, developed economy, cultural prosperity, national unity and beautiful mountains and rivers. China should also be marked as a responsible country that advocates peaceful and common development, safeguards international justice, and makes contributions to humanity, and as a socialist country which is open, amicable, promising and vibrant.[46]

At the inauguration of the China-Africa Institute in 2019, State Councilor Yang Jiechi said China's propaganda work "fosters favorable public opinion for the friendship and cooperation between China and Africa."[47] In addition to positive reports, according to Ambassador Liu Guangyuan, CPC propaganda also works to counter the "ongoing conspiracy" whereby a "small number of countries monopolize the international media discourse."[48] This is because, as Wang Gengnian explained, "over the last ten years, the U.S. and some major Western countries have used radio, satellite television, and other emerging media to create a comprehensive and three-dimensional siege network encircling China." In response, he said, Beijing must "enhance the competitiveness and influence of China's international communication."[49]

In Africa, as elsewhere, CPC cadres dominate the editorial process and ensure that stories glorifying party leaders and those undermining the United States receive top billing.[50] Emeka Umejei of the University of Ghana identified two types of Chinese staff working at CPC media outlets in Africa: officials from the Department "masquerading as journalists" and "professional journalists." Although the former lack journalism training, they make the editorial decisions and oversee both the African and the Chinese journalists.[51]

Working with their colleagues in Beijing, propaganda cadres at African bureaus distinguish between public content, which is released among Xinhua's scores of daily reports, and "internal reference" reports, which cover sensitive topics and are only distributed to relevant government and party organs. In this way, China's propaganda outlets enforce the party line while channeling proprietary information and analysis back to Beijing.[52] An African working at CGTN explained how the Department dominates the editorial process:

> The deputy bureau chief of CGTN in Nairobi, Kenya, can call the shots professionally but he does not participate in the Wednesday meeting, which is strictly for members of the CPC. It is at that meeting that a lot of important decisions are taken, which means that if you're not present you cannot function. He is not a member and he is basically an outsider. No African journalist attends this meeting and most times, work has to stop during the meeting.[53]

Africans journalists working for China's big four cannot cover topics propaganda cadres deem "sensitive." After joining a Chinese state-media outlet, they quickly learn that hard-hitting reports are unwelcome if they cast China or its partners in a negative light. The editorial line looms over journalists, as one African reporter at *China Daily* put it: "Within the periphery of the editorial policy, you have every freedom . . . outside the editorial policy, it is impossible to do any story." An African CGTN journalist concurred: "We know what is acceptable and what is not acceptable. These things will be made clear to you when you join as to what kind of reporting is expected of you and what direction you are expected to take."[54]

Department officials also collaborate with Chinese embassy personnel to discourage or deride any publications that might make Africans reconsider engaging with China. The head of the foreign desk at Nigeria's *This Day* newspaper described this "top-down strategy" to silence critical African voices. Unlike diplomats from the United States and European countries, he said, staff at China's embassy "will locate the editor-in-chief. And once they do that, as a reporter you are threatened and even when you report, it might not be used."[55] When negative comments from African thought leaders are published, they often face direct criticism and censorship. In 2022, for instance, the big four deleted comments from the director-general of the World Health Organization and former Ethiopian foreign minister Tedros Adhanom Ghebreyesus and labeled him "irresponsible" after he questioned the sustainability of Beijing's "zero-COVID" strategy.[56]

Looking forward, China's big four outlets in Africa face a growing contradiction between their ever-expanding editorial line and their desire to compete with Western media. China's shrinking domestic information space is increasingly constraining their international coverage. As Chinese interests in Africa grow, they will receive more resources, yet more African interests and partners mean an ever-increasing number of "sensitive" topics are likely to be deemed off-limits or required to be reported according to the editorial line.

CONTENT LOCALIZATION

One way China's foreign-focused propaganda strategy "uses foreign strength to promote China" (利用外力为我宣传) is to court influential and recognizable African voices to disseminate and authenticate its content.[57] To give its broadcasts an authentic flavor, CGTN headhunts recognizable African

AFRICA-FOCUSED PROPAGANDA

TV personalities and reporters and offers them well-paid jobs. Working with Africans helps party propagandists learn "the ways overseas viewers customarily receive information [to] constantly enhance the appeal and affinity of overseas propaganda," explains Liu Yunshan, former minister of the CPC Central Propaganda Department.[58]

Another way to gain audience and credibility is for Chinese interlocutors to "forge close partnerships of mutual advantage with highly prominent foreign figures" such that "every country now has some prominent figures whom the CCP has designated 'friends of China,'" writes Anne-Marie Brady of the University of Canterbury.[59] These "friends" then appear regularly on air and provide quotes or write articles for the big four pushing the party line. In return, they may receive all-expense-paid trips to China and other perquisites.

China increasingly uses business transactions to create a "multiplatform" that matches party-controlled media conglomerates with African outlets that disguise its reports in ways that "make them appear native to the independent publication," Sarah Cook observes.[60] "Experience has shown that it is better when China's cultural products are 'sold out' rather than 'sent out,'" explains Liu Qibao, who succeeded Liu Yunshan as CPC Central Propaganda Department minister until 2017.[61] To attract African outlets, China's state media use various content sharing agreements, advertising buys, paid propaganda inserts, and mergers and acquisitions.[62]

The practice of using content sharing agreements to provide cheap or free reports to entice African media outlets into voluntarily disseminating CPC propaganda can be traced to at least 2006.[63] In 2007 the heads of the state news agencies of Senegal, Togo, and Benin visited China, where they met with Xinhua's president, signed "news exchange agreements," and pledged to "learn from Xinhua experiences and strengthen cooperation with Chinese state media."[64] As of 2022 news organizations in Zimbabwe, Zambia, Kenya, Egypt, Nigeria, and Ghana are among those that have also signed media-cooperation and content-sharing agreements with Xinhua.[65]

Some smaller African media houses use Xinhua's international content, which they obtain via syndication agreements with larger African outlets or state broadcasters.[66] For cash-strapped African outlets, cheap content from China's state media sources can be an economic lifeline. For Beijing, however, African outlets' tight budgets offer an opportunity to amplify and disguise its propaganda beneath a veneer of grassroots legitimacy.[67] Another tactic, known in English as "astroturfing" and in Chinese as "borrowing foreign media" (借用海外媒体) or "borrowing boats to reach the sea" (借船出海), launders CPC propaganda through either friendly or unwitting local media outlets.[68] It has been observed across the Global South from Thailand and Laos in Asia to Peru and Panama in Latin America.[69]

In 2017 CRI had secured content-sharing agreements with at least seventy overseas radio stations and eighteen global internet providers.[70] In Liberia, for instance, CRI broadcasts over the Liberia Broadcasting System, and in Togo Radio Lome broadcasts its French language reports.[71] In Senegal, Niger, and Mauritania, CRI has built relay stations that carry its broadcasts to a wider audience.[72] China has also provided equipment for ailing African state broadcasters, including the Ghana News Agency, Somalia's national broadcaster, and the Liberia Broadcasting System.[73]

China's firms have used equity investments to enhance its influence over independent African publications.[74] In 2013, for instance, StarTimes acquired a majority stake in the South African satellite company TopTV.[75] And the firm's partnership with TopStar, a Zambian state broadcaster, allowed it to obtain licenses for signal distribution and content provision.[76] The China-Africa Development Fund and the state-owned China International Television Corporation own a 20 percent stake in South Africa's Independent Online (IOL).[77] IOL has become the official media partner of the Chinese Embassy and "acts as an extension of Xinhua" in South Africa.[78] For example, in 2018 IOL columnist Azad Essa was fired after he criticized China's persecution of Muslims in his column.[79]

HOSTING AND TRAINING AFRICAN MEDIA

In the Forum on China-Africa Cooperation (FOCAC) Dakar Action Plan (2022–2024), China committed to

> training and capacity building programs for African media practitioners, help African countries train high-caliber professionals in news,

AFRICA-FOCUSED PROPAGANDA

broadcasting and television, and ... training and capacity building seminars for African countries' media officials and journalists, promote more exchanges between Chinese and African media personnel, support the capacity building of radio and television media in Africa, promote the integrated development of African media, and advance practical media cooperation between China and Africa."[80]

This approach, which Bob Wekesa of the University of Witwatersrand calls "media-based public diplomacy," includes "anything where China lobbies the media industry of an African country for cooperation in the media sector itself—for instance, exchange visits, trips, short-term training and others."[81] The objective of these exchanges and trainings, according to Nie Chenxi, party secretary of the National Radio and Television Administration and deputy director of the Propaganda Department, is to "cooperate more in media operations, program production, technical services and personnel training."[82] Li Qiangmin, then deputy director general of the African Department of China's Ministry of Foreign Affairs (MFA), described these programs as "key components of China-Africa human resource cooperation."[83]

China conducts both bilateral and multilateral media training sessions to generate positive reporting and build partnerships with African media professionals. This initiative began in earnest between 2004 and 2011, when China hosted at least eight major training workshops for African media.[84] By 2011 the CPC had trained over three hundred African media officials from forty-eight countries, each of whom had spent at least two weeks in China taking courses on topics such as "China's Experience and Achievements on Economic Reform and National Development," "The Taiwan Question," and "China's Journalistic View and the Operation of Chinese Press."[85]

In 2012 these annual African journalist training workshops were upgraded to the first Forum on China-Africa Media Cooperation and placed under FOCAC. Beijing hosted the second forum in 2014, and the following year the China-Africa Media Summit was held in Cape Town prior to the FOCAC Summit.[86] The third forum, cosponsored by the MFA and Propaganda Department, was held in Beijing in 2016 and included more than three hundred media professionals and officials from forty-four African countries.[87] At the opening ceremony Cai Fuchao, minister of state administration of radio, film, and television, stressed that media cooperation remains "a powerful driving force behind China-Africa Cooperation."[88] The fourth Forum on China-Africa Media Cooperation, held in Beijing before the FOCAC Summit in 2018, included more than four hundred officials and heads of media organizations from forty African countries, focused on digitization and content development.[89] Another, smaller China-Africa Media Cooperation Forum was held in Nairobi in 2020 with over 120 government officials from China and eleven African countries under the theme "China-Africa Media Cooperation in the Digital Age."[90] Then, in August 2022, China hosted the fifth forum in Beijing, with nearly all the African participants (representing more than forty countries) attending virtually.[91]

The BRI has also provided opportunities for Sino-African media collaboration. In 2018 the All-China Journalists Association convened the BRI Journalists Forum with nearly one hundred representatives from media organizations in forty-seven developing countries. Speaking at the forum, Abdulwaheed Odusile, president of the Federation of African Journalists, said China is training African journalists to "tell their own story."[92] According to its organizers, the gathering "improved relationships" and "enhanced communication and mutual learning among media organizations and correspondents and editors."[93] In 2019 *People's Daily* launched the Belt and Road News Network, which includes media organizations from twenty-five countries, among them Egypt, Ethiopia, Nigeria, South Africa, Sudan, Tanzania, and Zambia.[94]

In addition to these grander engagements, China also underwrites smaller bilateral and multilateral training sessions for African journalists. These working-level seminars provide a private environment to build interpersonal relationships. Having been feted in Beijing, many attendees naturally feel reluctant to produce content that impugns China when they return home. Although China's "zero-COVID" strategy temporarily paused these gatherings, Beijing continued them virtually, albeit less frequently and less effectively. In 2021, for example, the Hunan Province

Professional Institute of Foreign Trade, the Hunan Film and Television Group, and the Ministry of Commerce jointly hosted a two-week online training session for sixty-five French-speaking African journalists from the Democratic Republic of Congo, Senegal, Cameroon, and Gabon.[95] Still, online training seminars cannot replace the comradery of in-person gatherings, which resumed after China lifted its "zero-COVID" travel restrictions in early 2023.

EDUCATION

TEACHING LESSONS AND BUILDING RELATIONSHIPS

Our first book, *China and Africa: A Century of Engagement*, traced the history of China's use of educational and training programs to cultivate relationships with African partners from their inception in the early 1960s through the end of the Hu Jintao era in 2011.[96] Here we pick up that analysis, explaining how the party's contemporary educational and training programs build relationships with African "friends."

According to Chinese tradition, "students defer to teachers, children to parents, subjects to leaders, and all to the emperor," observes Kenneth Lieberthal of the University of Michigan.[97] Students are expected to show deference to their teachers, especially in public, where pointed questions can be seen as challenging their authority.[98] Moreover, as discussed in chapter 1, Sinocentrism has long pervaded Chinese relations with foreigners. The imperial emperor, for instance, required foreigners to engage in ritualistic prostrations (*koutou*) that conveyed their submission to his preeminence. By treating foreigners as ignorant supplicants, Chinese leaders distanced themselves from the outsiders, thus affirming their cultural and moral superiority, explains James Hevia of the University of Chicago.[99]

Beginning in the 1980s with China's Reform and Opening Up (改革开放), Beijing adopted the posture of an eager learner in its educational engagements with foreign countries. Deng Xiaoping and his successors encouraged Chinese students to go abroad to obtain Western knowledge to overcome the nation's geostrategic weakness.[100] Having risen out of backwardness to regain "major power status," China now sees itself as a benevolent teacher who is ready to share their knowledge with African countries.[101] The objective "has refocused on imperial China's continuous glory, interrupted only by Western imperialist powers," explains Zhao Suisheng of the University of Denver.[102] Contextualized within this "return to grandeur" narrative, the party's expansion of educational programs for Africans not only builds relationships but also legitimizes its rule by reinforcing the narrative of Chinese national rejuvenation, that is, the Chinese Dream discussed in chapter 1.

TRAINING AND HIGHER EDUCATION

Before COVID-19, China was rapidly expanding the scope and scale of its educational programs for Africans. These include two overlapping types of programs: short-term professional and vocational training workshops for midcareer professionals and officials, and degree-granting programs (BA, MA, or PhD). Although both types are ostensibly focused on human capital development, they are differentiated in that the former last just two to three weeks and are hosted by an official government or party organ, perhaps with a university's assistance, while the latter are generally multiyear programs housed at a particular department or school within a Chinese university.

Successive FOCAC action plans have featured lofty yet ill-defined Chinese commitments for both short-term training opportunities for African professionals and scholarships for degree-granting programs in numerous fields, including health, sports, agriculture, the arts, diplomacy, journalism, and public administration. In the FOCAC Johannesburg Action Plan (2016–2018) Beijing committed to train two hundred thousand local African vocational and technical personnel, provide forty thousand Africans with training opportunities in China, offer two thousand opportunities for Africans to receive degrees in China, fund thirty thousand government scholarships, and bring two hundred African scholars per year to China. It also reaffirmed support for the 20+20 Cooperation Plan for Chinese and African Institutions of Higher Education, which was established in 2009 to enhance collaboration between Chinese and African universities.[103]

In the FOCAC Beijing Action Plan (2019–2021), China pledged to "continue to implement" the 20+20 Plan and agreed to provide fifty thousand training opportunities in China via seminars and workshops, training for a thousand "high-caliber Africans," and fifty thousand government scholarships for African professionals across a range of disciplines.[104] In the FOCAC Dakar Action Plan (2022–2024), China also vowed to "continue to provide short-term seminars and training opportunities" and "education with academic degrees," and implement the 20+20 Plan. Perhaps due to COVID-19, however, the most recent plan does not include specific commitments beyond a pledge to hold seminars and workshops with ten thousand high-level African professionals.[105] Ultimately, beyond anecdotal accounts and spotty official data, there was no way for us to independently verify whether Beijing has met these training commitments.

China's training workshops build personal relationships with "African political, economic, social elites, and opinion leaders that will shape the future of the continent and its relations with China," explains Yun Sun of the Stimson Center.[106] According to a Ministry of Commerce manual, they "complement China's comprehensive foreign policy needs [by] helping train the human capital of developing countries and drive forward friendly relations."[107] Lina Benabdallah of Wake Forest University, who conducted fieldwork in China in 2014, observed "a proliferation of professionalization training workshops hosted in Beijing for delegations of African political elites, civil servants, and occasionally cohorts dressed in military uniforms." Having been "granted access to attend many of these workshops," she identified their three target audiences: ministerial level officials, senior civil servants, and well-connected Africans she called "unofficial officials." This "human resource development" approach, writes Benabdallah, "is not only a hallmark of China's foreign policy in Africa but also with developing countries more broadly."[108]

The results of China's degree-granting programs for African students have indeed been dramatic. Between 2008 and 2018 the number of African university students pursuing degrees in China rose by a factor of ten, from 8,799 (4 percent of all international students in China) to 81,562 African students, or more than 16 percent of the total (figure 5.1). In 2016 more students from Anglophone Africa were studying in China than in either the United States or the United Kingdom.[109] That year, for instance, Zambia sent 3,248 students to China, compared to 469 to the United States.[110] But while the Ministry of Education stopped publishing this data after 2018, there is strong evidence that COVID-19 reversed these growth trends. Beijing canceled all visas in 2020, forcing thousands of African students to return home.[111] Throughout 2021 and 2022, foreign student visas were not being granted, forcing thousands of often frustrated Africans to abandon their studies or, when possible, complete them online.[112]

One consequence of prioritizing politics when awarding scholarships is that the quality of African students who receive them can vary. This is because,

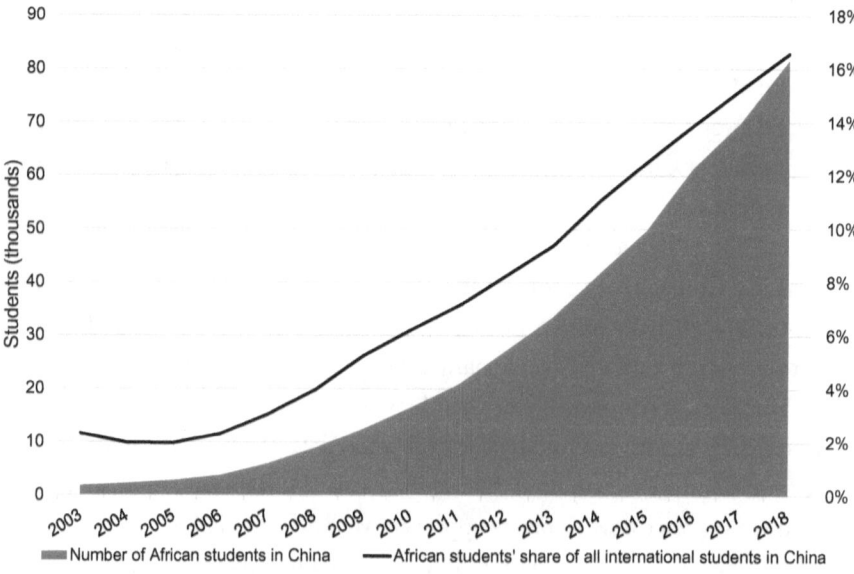

FIGURE 5.1 African students in China, 2003–2018. Source: Ministry of Education, People's Republic of China.

rather than a coherent, merit-based system to award scholarships, China's diplomats use scholarships to lure elites with whom they want to cultivate relationships. Over time, prioritizing well-connected over well-qualified African students has produced wide disparities among scholarship recipients.[113] The "traditional mindset among some Chinese officials is that they still think the most important thing is to leave enough quota, enough scholarships, to give to special persons, the elites. They go to officials' children or special connections," said one Chinese researcher. This creates "a very bad cycle," whereby African elites take the educational opportunities that China offers but then decide to "leave the relationship," thus requiring the Chinese side to continuously pursue new partners.[114]

THINK TANK AND SCHOLAR EXCHANGES

Whereas in the United States, Britain, and other Western countries think tanks are research institutions *outside* the formal structures of government, like everything else in China they too fall under CPC leadership. The China Institute of International Studies, "China's first academic institution specializing in foreign affairs and international studies," for example, is "affiliated with the MFA."[115] The China Institutes of Contemporary International Relations (CICIR) is part of the Ministry of State Security; and the China Center for Contemporary World Studies is located within the International Department of the CPC Central Committee.

According to CICIR's then president Yuan Peng, China's foreign-focused think tanks are "an intelligence platform for China's international strategy in the new era."[116] Yuan, who also goes by Yuan Yikun, was named vice minister of state security in 2023. Nadège Rolland of the National Bureau of Asian Research describes them as "essential tools for propaganda."[117] The CPC uses think tanks for the "formation, dissemination, and persuasion of public opinion," writes Wang Lili of Renmin University.[118] Compared to China's think tanks, their African counterparts tend to be more autonomous, much smaller, and minimally resourced. Unlike in China, for instance, some African think tanks accept funding from foreign universities, private donors, and/or civil society organizations. Each African think tank's unique leadership and regulatory environment determines its receptiveness to overtures from Chinese counterparts. Institutions that are more closely tied to governments may have more influence among policy makers, while those that are more autonomous, but willing to accept foreign patronage, may have less constraints on their collaborations.

Chinese institutions use a combination of host diplomacy and financial largesse to place themselves at the center of a constellation of African scholarly social networks.[119] Good relations with influential African scholars "provide [a] strong complement to official diplomacy," Patrick Ho, then secretary general of the China Energy Fund Committee, told the 2015 Think-Tanks Alliance Silk Road Forum. Ho said "experts from various countries" create "bridges," and he called for think tank partners to hold "regular closed-door seminars that will facilitate the members to exchange views on issues and future plans."[120] One Chinese think tank, the Shanghai Institutes for International Studies, "raises its international influence" by creating "a series of high-end dual-track intellectual platforms" to "conduct international exchanges and joint research" with developing countries.[121] Such collaborations are intended to "win over policy support and participation of people from different countries in the way of actively cooperating with the government's motives," explained Ho, who is currently serving a three year sentence in a U.S. prison for bribing African officials.[122]

To this same end, China has created several multilateral think tank forums to engage partners in the Global South. The Silk Road Think Tanks Network was launched in 2015, and the BRICS Think-Tank Forum was first held in 2017 at Fudan University.[123] For Africa, both the 2016–2018 and 2019–2021 FOCAC action plans include commitments to "invite 200 African scholars to visit China each year."[124] While the 2022–2024 FOCAC Action Plan does not specify the precise number of African visitors, like its predecessors it too affirms the China-Africa Think Tank 10+10 Partnership Plan to "strengthen joint research and exchanges between Chinese and African think-tanks."[125]

China created the China-Africa Think Tank Forum (CATTF) in 2011 and hosted its first gathering at the Institute of African Studies at Zhejiang Normal University (ZNU) (see table 5.1). The forum works to shape

"African elites' perceptions and understanding of China through direct bilateral communication, without the interference of Western values or idiosyncrasies," Yun Sun explains.[126] At the inaugural meeting, Zhai Jun, vice minister of foreign affairs, called it an "important measure to strengthen academic exchanges and cooperation."[127] In 2018 the two-day CATTF was held at the prestigious Diaoyu State Guest House in Beijing and included more than 380 representatives from 44 African countries.[128] In 2019 the forum was again held in Beijing, but in 2020, 2021, and 2022 it was held virtually due to China's "zero-COVID" travel restrictions, albeit each time with hundreds of online participants.[129]

CONFUCIUS INSTITUTES

In 2004 China began opening Confucius Institutes (CI) to attract foreign students through a combination of Chinese language courses, research funding, scholarships to study in China, and cultural exchanges.[130] Each CI is a collaboration between a Chinese university and a local host university facilitated by China's Ministry of Education Center for Language and Cooperation.[131] In Gambia, for instance, the University of Gambia, the country's only public university, signed an MOU with Guizhou University in 2018 to create a CI and "strengthen bilateral ties through the cultural promotion of language, exchange of faculty, staff and student visits, and short-term training."[132] Taken together, CIs constitute a global network of Beijing-funded institutional partnerships through which "the CPC forms relationships with political, economic, and societal elites and groups in other countries," Shaun Breslin of the University of Warwick explains.[133]

Although CIs in African countries represent a small fraction of the approximately 550 CIs that exist in 154 countries around the world, they have gradually risen in number, from 42 in 2015 to 46 in 2017 to 54 in 2018 to 64 in 2022.[134] South Africa is home to six CIs, the most of any African country.[135] The first CI in Africa, a cooperation between the University of Nairobi in Kenya and Tianjin Normal University, opened in 2005. Since then, its student enrollment has grown from about twenty students per

TABLE 5.1 China-Africa think-tank forums, 2011–2022

DATE	THEME	HOST AND LOCATION	RANKING CHINESE PARTICIPANT	AFRICAN AND OTHER PARTICIPANTS
October 2011	China-Africa relations in the second decade of the new millennium	Hangzhou and Jinhua, Zhejiang Normal University, Hangzhou, China	Zhai Jun, vice minister, Ministry of Foreign Affairs (MFA)	Researchers from 27 African countries
October 2012	Current issues and future perspectives in governance, peace, and security	Addis Ababa University, Addis Ababa, Ethiopia	Zheng Jiwei, vice governor, Zhejiang	80+ Chinese and African officials and scholars
October 2013	Upgrading Sino-African relations and constructing Chinese and African soft power	FOCAC Secretariat, Beijing, China	Yang Jiechi, state councilor	16 think tanks from China and Africa
September 2015	New development trends under African Vision 2063	South Africa Mapungubwe Institute for Strategic Reflection, Pretoria, South Africa	Dai Bing, deputy director-general, Dept. of African Affairs, MFA	Representatives from 50 African countries
April 2016	China-Africa production capacity cooperation and industrialization of Africa	ZNU and Yiwu Municipal Government, Yiwu, Zhejiang, China	Liang Liming, vice governor, Zhejiang; Lin Songtian, director general, Dept. of African Affairs, MFA	300+ Chinese and African participants
June 2017	Fighting against poverty: learning from the experience of poverty alleviation in China and Africa	ZNU and African Union Leadership Academy, Addis Ababa, Ethiopia	Wang Yi, foreign minister	H. E. Mousa Faki, chair, African Union Commission; members of Permanent Representative Committee and African Union Partners' Group

Date	Theme	Location	Chinese Host/Speaker	African Participants
July 2018	China-Africa relations over the course of reform and opening-up	FOCAC Secretariat, Beijing, China	Chen Xiaodong, assistant minister, MFA	Researchers from 52 African countries
August 2019	Jointly building a closer community of shared future between China and Africa	FOCAC Secretariat, ZNU, China-Africa Institute, and China Institute of International Studies, Beijing, China	Chen Xiaodong, assistant minister, MFA	400+ participants representing 51 African countries
November 2020	Sino-African solidarity in the fight against COVID-19 and public health security	FOCAC Secretariat, Beijing, China (virtual)	Deng Li, assistant minister, MFA	3,000 mostly virtual participants from African countries
October 2021	Unity, cooperation, innovation and development, and jointly building a China-Africa community with a shared future	FOCAC Secretariat, Hangzhou, China (virtual)	Zhu Congjiu, vice governor, Zhejiang	Abdoulaye Diop, minister of foreign affairs, Mali; Felix Mbayu, minister of external relations, Cameroon; 200+ scholars and political and business leaders from 15 African countries
July 2022	Promoting the spirit of China-Africa friendship and cooperation and jointly implementing the global development initiative	FOCAC Secretariat, China-Africa Research Institute, Peking University, and ZNU, Beijing and Jinhua, China (virtual)	Zhao Qi, secretary general, Chinese Academy of Social Sciences	Moussa Mara, former prime minister, Mali; 200+ scholars and politicians from 19 African countries

semester to more than 500 in 2020, when it was named a "Model Confucius Institute." Speaking at the institute, Minister Counselor Zhao Xiyuan of the Chinese Embassy in Kenya said: "Over the past 15 years, more than 90,000 people have experienced Chinese cultural activities, more than 18,000 people have participated in various Chinese training courses, and more than 500 people have won various scholarships to study in China."[136]

Chinese language classes are CIs' most important programs.[137] Beijing provides "financial support to improve Chinese language teaching in [African] countries as part of bilateral cooperation," Xinhua reports.[138] Although many Africans see learning Chinese "as a window of opportunity," for Chinese, teaching their language to Africans affirms their nation's cultural appeal. Official reporting stresses that Chinese language instruction is offered to meet popular demand, not imposed from Beijing. For example, according to Xinhua: "The growing popularity of the Chinese language among Uganda's youths and the working population has inspired policymakers to include it in the national curriculum for schools."[139]

Both the Ugandan and Chinese governments are contributing to support Chinese language instruction. After a CI was established with the Makerere University in Kampala in 2015, it signed an agreement with the Luyanzi Institute of Technology to create a nine-month teacher-training program for Ugandans to learn to teach Chinese. In 2022 the director of the National Curriculum Development Centre, Grace Baguma, told the graduation ceremony of the institute's fourth cohort, including forty teachers, that the government would hire them. "The training will prepare them to teach the Chinese language in the lower secondary curriculum," said Baguma, adding that her ministry "plans to adopt" a Chinese expert to make teaching Chinese sustainable nationwide.[140] Still, given the difficulty of learning any foreign language, let alone Chinese, small, short-term training programs simply cannot achieve widespread adoption.

This is the case in Cameroon, which incorporated Chinese into the national curriculum in 2012 and as of 2019 taught the language in 140 middle schools.[141] By 2021 there were about thirty thousand Chinese language learners in Cameroon, but the program faces numerous problems, including a "lack of Chinese knowledge, lack of understanding of Chinese culture, lack of Chinese teaching ability, lack of enthusiasm for teaching, lack of professional development resources and support measures." One student complained that her teacher "just writes the contents on the blackboard every time and let us copy them"; another, that the "teacher uses French completely when he's giving [Chinese] lessons."[142] Between 2020 and 2022 these problems were compounded by COVID-19, which pushed instruction online and forced many children out of school.

Meanwhile, an unknown number of secondary schools in South Africa, Tanzania, and Kenya have also added Chinese to their curriculum.[143] "Language is key to enhancing mutual understanding and friendship between the two peoples. It has promoted exchanges and cooperation between China and South Africa," explained Angie Motshekga, South Africa's minister for basic education. Raphael Tuju, secretary general of Kenya's then ruling Jubilee Party, "has been squeezing" Chinese instruction into the national curriculum, an effort he initiated after "frequent official visits to China" cultivated his "strong attachment to the culture, political and economic system."[144] But while Beijing hopes more African countries will add Chinese to their national curriculum, given the widespread use of European languages and the challenges of having nonnative speakers teach Chinese, it is inconceivable that the language will become common anytime soon.

CULTURE

CULTURE AS POLITICS

To build relationships and improve its image with Africans, the CPC underwrites what it calls "people-to-people exchanges" on various cultural topics, including literature, arts, education, movies, libraries, museums, holidays, and festivals. Every year, Chinese embassies and consulates around Africa coordinate the activities of the party's numerous cultural organs, including CIs, Chinese cultural centers, and culture-related front groups. These groups produce two broad types of content: people-to-people cultural exchanges (e.g., official delegations, performing troupes, artists, and performers), which account for the lion's share of expenditures, and print materials and online content (e.g., books, pamphlets, videos, and audio materials).[145]

The CPC's use of culture for political purposes predates the People's Republic of China's establishment in 1949. "The philosophy of the new government was to transform everything, including culture, and to make a brand new society," Liu Haifeng of Peking University explains.[146] "Given their origin, cultural exchanges with other countries were not simply for the sake of culture *per se*; on the contrary, they had been formulated as political tasks from the beginning." Mao Zedong instructed that China's foreign-focused cultural propaganda should publicize the party's achievements and develop and reinforce relationships with foreign youth.[147] Thus the CPC's strategic use of foreign-focused cultural engagements grew out of the foundational belief that, like all things, they too should serve the party's strategic ends.[148]

Beijing's use of cultural propaganda to "make foreign things serve China" (洋为中用), formally began at the Asian-African Bandung Conference in 1955, where Zhou Enlai's call for "cultural cooperation" to advance political solidarity against the West was written into the final communique.[149] By using cultural engagements to help break China's diplomatic isolation, Zhou demonstrated that they could advance geopolitical objectives.[150] To this end, the Chinese People's Association for Cultural Relations with Foreign Countries was created in 1954.[151] Today the association's "missions" remain "leading people-to-people diplomacy, serving as the mainstay in public diplomacy and promoting exchanges between Chinese and foreign local governments," according to its president, former ambassador to South Africa Lin Songtian.[152] This approach differs starkly from Western notions of "cultural diplomacy," which Milton Cummings Jr. of Johns Hopkins University described as "the exchange of information, art, lifestyles, other aspects of culture and of ideas, value systems, traditions, beliefs 'among collectives' to foster mutual understanding."[153]

To "match with China's prestige and position," Beijing should use culture as an "important element" of the country's "national power," General Secretary Jiang Zemin declared in 1997.[154] Xi Jinping's predecessor, Hu

Jintao, identified cultural diplomacy as a foreign relations priority.[155] At the Sixteenth Party Congress in 2002 culture-building and "strategic reform of the cultural system" were elevated to "an urgent strategic position."[156] Party leaders also identified a "serious excess of cultural imports over exports" and claimed this "extremely high deficit" posed "severe challenges to the Chinese government." In response, they felt "the necessity of revealing China's own cultural achievements."[157]

In 2011 the Seventeenth Central Committee of the CPC met to discuss the promotion of Chinese culture, with the final statement setting the national goal to "build our country into a socialist cultural superpower."[158] At the Eighteenth Party Congress in 2012, the new party leadership called for the use of cultural exchanges to expand "win-win" relationships.[159] China now seeks to become a "cultural major power" (文化大国), and Xi Jinping has repeatedly called on the party's propaganda apparatus to enhance China's "soft power" (软实力) by creating a compelling Chinese narrative and strengthening the capacity to convey its messages to foreign audiences.[160]

In 2018 Xi said that Chinese traditional culture is the foundation of the nation, and that "its vision, concepts, values, and moral norms not only constitute the ideological and spiritual core of Chinese but are also valuable for addressing the issues that humanity faces."[161] In keeping with Mao's methods, Xi instructed CPC propagandists "in the art and cultural sectors to produce masterpieces that laud the Party, the motherland, the people, and the heroes" and then "send culture out into the world."[162] In 2021 the Propaganda Department announced that it would broaden the appeal of Chinese "cultural products" to foreign audiences using "overseas new media platforms" such as "films, TV episodes, and video games" to "carry out cultural investment and cooperation abroad, build international marketing networks and branches, and expand the scale of quality cultural assets abroad."[163]

Cultural Exchanges

Rather than precipitating cultural exchanges for their own sake, the party's Africa-focused cultural propaganda uses them to spread the party line and build political relationships. As their name suggests, the CPC's

Africa-focused United Front groups (e.g., the Chinese-African People's Friendship Association) portray themselves as grassroots organizations to deceive their local partners, who are usually actual community organizations. By projecting the false image of popular organizations, these top-down party-sponsored groups nest political objectives into ostensibly innocuous cultural exchange activities.

The websites of CPC front groups are designed to improve Africans' perceptions of China and stimulate them to consider working with Chinese entities. China is depicted as a friendly country (e.g., smiling faces and delicious foods) that has made cultural contributions (e.g., pagodas, the Great Wall, Chinese New Year celebrations) and created a desirable development model (e.g., high-speed trains and skyscrapers). Alongside images of Africans happily embracing partnership with China, these websites include links to visitor programs and educational opportunities.[164] Chinese embassies and friendship organizations in Africa use similar imagery and messaging on their Facebook pages.[165]

The first China Cultural Center opened in Mauritius in 1988, and by 2017 Beijing had also established them in Egypt, Benin, Tanzania, and Nigeria. These centers host a range of events, including folk music and dance performances, traditional art demonstrations, lectures, and Chinese food tastings. They provide language and cultural training programs for Africans and hold Chinese competitions in which the winner receives an all-expense-paid "China Cultural Center Students Award Tour" to visit "scenic spots, historical sites, museums and theaters in Beijing, and try traditional Chinese art and crafts, such as painting, weaving, dyeing and potteries." In 2017, for instance, all the centers coordinated a weeklong program called "Inheritance and Innovation: Chinese Intangible Cultural Heritage." Every year the Ministry of Culture's Bureau for External Cultural Relations selects speakers to participate in its Chinese Culture Talk lecture series held at Chinese embassies, consulates, and cultural centers. Topics include Chinese philosophy, religion, literature, cuisine, and medicine.[166]

In 2001 the Ministry of Culture began its "Happy Chinese New Year" program, which coordinates dozens of exhibitions, expos, and performances each year.[167] In 2020, just before the COVID-19 outbreak, Chinese New

Year events were held in African countries including South Africa, Tanzania, Kenya, Botswana, and Mauritius. In Kenya, the Chinese Embassy, the Confucius Institute at the University of Nairobi, and the Erdemann Chinese Culture Centre in Nairobi jointly organized a five-day exhibition and Chinese cultural activities, including a costume photo booth, kids' Chinese zodiac center, food, an art class, and dragon dances. *China Daily*'s reporting on the event stressed the attendance of two Kenyan ministers, noting that "mutual political trust between the two countries has deepened, and exchanges and cooperation between governments, political parties and legislatures have become closer." The Kenyan side "expressed gratitude to the deepening relationship between China and Kenya that has exposed rich Chinese culture to the locals." In South Africa, the embassy's cultural festivities brought together "hundreds of guests including senior government officials, political activists, academics and school children among others."[168] These official reports on China's cultural propaganda activities in Africa show how, like the media and educational engagements discussed above, China uses culture as a pretext to spread its political narratives and develop ties with well-connected Africans.

The same intentions motivate Beijing's feting of African youth, which began in 2004 when the Communist Youth League of China and All-China Youth Federation hosted 132 "youth organizations, statesmen and entrepreneurs" from forty-four African countries for the first China-Africa Youth Festival in Guangzhou.[169] In 2016 some six hundred youths from thirty-six Asian and African countries attended an event intended to rekindle the Bandung spirit of Afro-Asian solidarity.[170] In 2019 the MFA and the China Soong Ching Ling Foundation (CSCLF), a foreign-focused CPC front group, hosted the Fourth China-Africa Youth Festival in Beijing with more than three hundred representatives. In his keynote, CSCLF chairman Wang Jiarui, the former ID-CPC minister, said the festival would "inject vitality into the development of China-Africa relations."[171]

China hosted the 2020 China-Africa Youth Festival in person, including guests from forty-two African countries, despite the spread of COVID-19. This time the Jiangxi provincial government joined the MFA and CSCLF in cosponsoring the delegation, which toured companies and industrial parks and "attended various activities showcasing Chinese culture." The two-hundred-person welcome banquet included dozens of dignitaries, among them Deng Li, assistant minister of foreign affairs, who called on youth from China and African countries "to forge deeper cooperation." At the event, Wang Jiarui again urged participants to enhance "exchanges and mutual understanding among Chinese and African youth."[172]

The Sixth China-Africa Youth Festival in 2021 was also hosted by CSCLF and held in person in Beijing but was a scaled down affair including only forty-five African students. The event celebrated the "CPC centenary, the wisdom and responsibility of youth, and a new chapter in common development between Africa and China." Deng Li addressed the audience, calling on each participant to become "a builder and promoter of the China-Africa community of shared future."[173]

In some countries, China's African friends have formed "interest and propaganda groups that continuously serve as a buffer between any anti-Chinese rhetoric and pro-Chinese agenda," explain Steve Hess of Transylvania University and Richard Aidoo of Coastal Carolina University. "These groups monitor the relationship between government actors and Chinese business interests, and are quick in their response to any anti-Chinese fervor that seems to be gathering." They exploit their local knowledge and contacts in "popular media" and of "various domestic laws and policies" to help safeguard Chinese investments and interests. In Ghana, for instance, the Ghana-China Friendship Union and the Ghana-China Business Chamber of Commerce "contribute positively to the popular discourse and dialogue on Chinese businesses and engagements."[174]

EVALUATING CHINA'S AFRICA-FOCUSED PROPAGANDA

China has put vast human and financial resources into its Africa-focused propaganda programs. This investment contrasts starkly with that of African countries, none of which has developed a coordinated response to China, let alone its own commensurate programs to influence Beijing. Thus a distinct power asymmetry exists between China's well-capitalized and coordinated propaganda strategy and the atomized Africans whom they engage. While these lopsided relationships create opportunities for some Africans, others view them as condescending, or worse.[175] As a result, China's propaganda programs have produced a range of reactions among Africans—from sycophantism to skepticism—with many Africans finding as much to criticize as to admire.[176]

Despite setbacks due to COVID-19, China's Africa-focused media propaganda has never been better resourced, yet measuring its impact on African audiences remains difficult. What evidence does exist suggests its direct effect on African perceptions has been minimal.[177] In 2021 roughly 2 percent of Kenyans and South Africans said they listened to CRI or read the *China Daily*, and about 7 percent of Kenyans and 6 percent of South Africans watched CGTN. Not surprisingly, those who consume Chinese media tend to hold more positive views of China.[178] This limited reach may help explain the decline in favorable opinions of China in these two countries between 2013 and 2019—down from 78 percent to 58 percent in Kenya and from 48 percent to 46 percent in South Africa, according to the Pew Research Center. At the same time, the percentage of Nigerians holding favorable views of China fell from 76 to 70 percent.[179]

Yet, African views of China and its role on the continent remain largely positive. Between 2019 and 2021, an in-person survey conducted by Ghana-based Afrobarometer found that 63 percent of Africans interviewed viewed China positively as compared with 60 percent who saw the United States in a favorable light.[180] An online survey conducted in June and July 2022 by the Central European Institute of Asian Studies (CEIAS) found that majorities of respondents in Angola (59 percent), Egypt (52 percent), Ghana (57 percent), Kenya (55 percent), and Nigeria (70 percent) had positive perceptions of China. In all the African countries CEIAS surveyed, however, China was viewed less favorably than the United States, which had a definitively positive image in Angola (80 percent), Egypt (57 percent), Ghana (80 percent), Kenya (82 percent), and Nigeria (88 percent). Even in Tunisia, where less than half of respondents viewed the United States favorably (47 percent), even fewer (42 percent) held positive views of China. "China's influence on democracy in other countries, its military power, and its environmental impact are all perceived comparatively negatively," the CEIAS report concludes.[181]

Before COVID-19, the increasing number of sponsored exchanges, syndication agreements, and media training programs suggested that Chinese propagandists believed their outreach to African journalists and editors was working. Indeed, dozens of African media professionals do republish or share China's propaganda content. These cheerleaders legitimize the party's rule over China, advance Beijing's claims to lead the Global South, deflect criticism of China and its African partners, perpetuate anti-American narratives, and question the effectiveness of liberal democracy. As China's African "friends" gain resources and influence, the predictable result is that—even as concerns about China's intentions continue to mount in Western capitals—media in countries such as Kenya, Ghana, and Malawi are reprinting increasing amounts of Xinhua content.[182]

Still, the reach of China's propaganda in Africa should not be overstated. After analyzing China's influence on media coverage in thirty African countries in the first half of 2020, Dani Madrid-Morales of the University of Houston concluded that "Chinese sources appear to be much less influential" than French or British outlets, but more influential than U.S. media. He identifies "a very significant gap between prevailing themes found in news converge about China and COVID-19 in the Chinese media, and the most common themes in African media." China's official outlets, Madrid-Morales finds, have "limited transnational intermedia agenda setting capabilities in Africa."[183]

Before COVID-19 the increasing size and number of Africa-focused media outlets, training programs, and cultural exchanges suggested that Beijing believed its efforts to cultivate African elites were at least somewhat effective. Although each engagement may yield only a few fruitful relationships, over the years they have created ties with scores of influential African opinion-setters who advance China's narratives and provide political support. Zhang Yanqiu, director of the African Communications Research

Center at the Communication University of China, explained that, after attending China's media training programs, "students work like a bridge between the two countries."[184] They join a list of ready interlocutors that Beijing can contact to participate in future cooperative activities. These African "friends" are regularly called on by the big four to provide comments that legitimize the party's rule, advance Beijing's claims to lead the Global South, deflect criticism from China, perpetuate anti-U.S. narratives, and question universal values and liberal democracy.

One example is Kojo Amoo-Gottfried, president of the Ghana-China Friendship Association. In 2014 Amoo-Gottfried hosted a welcome reception for incoming ambassador Sun Baohong. At that event, Sun thanked him and his organization for "promoting China-Ghana friendship and great support to the embassy."[185] In 2017 the embassy invited Amoo-Gottfried to attend the Global Confucius Institute Day Celebration as a distinguished guest.[186] In 2018 he hosted an event marking the fifty-seventh anniversary of the signing of the China-Ghana Treaty of Friendship that was attended by the Chinese ambassador and "high ranking [Ghanian] officials including Members of Parliament."[187] And amid the COVID-19 pandemic in 2020, Amoo-Gottfried appeared in Xinhua alongside the chargé d'affaires at China's embassy in Accra to accept medical supplies. He thanked China and said: "The relationship between China and Ghana has been improving from year-to-year and we intend to lift it higher."[188]

The CPCs short-term trainings are perhaps its most popular propaganda programs among Africans. Having interviewed "many African diplomats about the workshops and their impressions of them," Lina Benabdallah found their perceptions to be "overwhelmingly positive." A Nigerian who participated in two training programs said "African delegations were treated as equals, with respect and care, by their Chinese hosts."[189] According to Erastus Mwencha, deputy chairperson of the African Union Commission: "The knowledge that they [Africans] garner from [studying in China] is invaluable and once they have completed they can return back to Africa and assist in the growth of our continent."[190]

Africans who have pursued degrees in China tend to be less sanguine. "Young Africans are not robots and *tabula rasa* such that the Chinese will just stuff them with whatever they want. The students will take the best of China and leave the bad there in China and go back to Africa," observes Adams Bodomo of the University of Vienna.[191] In 2013 South African journalist Simon Allison interviewed more than twenty African master's degree students in China. Despite Beijing's regular proclamations that its educational exchanges are based on equality, he found that "China and Africa are, quite conspicuously, not at the same level of development, no matter how often African and Chinese leaders express their fraternal solidarity."[192] According to Allison, "cognitive dissonance between the image projected by China in Africa and the reality experienced by [African] students can generate feelings of wariness and caution." A Rwandan MA student in China said that her initial ignorance about China was replaced with fear. A Tanzanian student pursuing an MA explained that in China "there is a kind of framing sometimes, trying to push you into viewing the world in a certain light." "China has gone very far ahead," and many Chinese "feel like maybe they are in heaven," he said, adding: "We'll be influenced by our time here, but that does not mean we'll be totally in favor of them. It's not like a father and child. We are the future leaders of our countries and we'll have to look for the future benefit of our countries."[193]

Several African students we interviewed in China said they had encountered negative social attitudes. Most had trouble making Chinese friends, and some cited specific acts of racism. "One time I discovered a picture of myself online with exaggerated gorilla features and a banana in my nose!" recalled a Nigerian PhD student in Shanghai.[194] In 2019 more than twenty African graduate students at Beijing Normal University expressed their collective concerns about the constrained academic environment and their difficulties in finding a suitable thesis advisor.[195] Some lamented limits on the academic and internet environment constrained both their research topics and access to materials.[196] Others complained that Chinese professors invest little in mentoring African students, who will likely leave the country after completing their degrees.

Anecdotal observations during 2020–2022 suggest a dip in favorable perceptions of China among Africans. As was the case elsewhere in the world, in Africa anti-Chinese views spread apace with COVID-19. These negative

AFRICA-FOCUSED PROPAGANDA

perceptions were further stoked by the subsequent expulsion of Africans living in China, the strict COVID-19 lockdowns and resulting mass protests in dozens of Chinese cities, and the proliferation of online videos showing Chinese bosses abusing their African employees.[197] Although China has long faced criticism from African civil society and workers' rights groups, some previously reticent African policy makers have begun raising contentious issues such as tax evasion and illicit mining with their Chinese counterparts. One disgruntled African student said that "All my support for China has changed totally. We loved China so much. I was always defending China when friends and family back home blamed Chinese people's eating habits for the virus and when they made hate speech."[198]

Finally, it is important to identify several high-profile blunders in the cultural sphere. In 2017, for instance, an exhibit at the Hubei Provincial Museum titled "This Is Africa" and comparing images of Africans to those of wild animals was cancelled after it prompted widespread African anger.[199] In 2018 the Chinese New Year's Gala was criticized for featuring an African man dressed as a monkey and a Chinese actor in black face with an enlarged fake posterior heaping praise and appreciation on China.[200] In 2022 Zambia extradited a Chinese filmmaker, Lu Ke, to Malawi for making and selling racist videos in which Malawian children were made to chant in Chinese, "I'm a black monster. My IQ is low." Lu claimed he made the videos "to spread Chinese culture to the local community."[201] Taken together, such incidents underscore that many average Chinese continue to view and depict African countries and peoples as "primitive," "subpolitical," and "ritualized."[202]

* * *

The CPC has long considered managing international public opinion to be a top priority in its international relations. Beijing's Africa-focused propaganda, including its seminars and trainings for African youth and midcareer professionals, are billed as capacity-building opportunities for Africans, but their content reveals that the CPC exploits their flexibility and informality to share its methods of political governance and vision for a new type of international relations. CPC media, educational, and cultural propaganda affirm Chinese leadership and the superiority of its authoritarian political model compared to Western liberal democracy and cultivate "win-win" relationships with African participants to oppose U.S. "hegemony." The goal is not only to improve African opinion-setters' perceptions of China, but also to entice them into building "win-win" relationships with Chinese interlocutors and ideally adopt and promulgate the CPC party line. Although for some African elites the enticements of becoming a "friend" of China may be too good to pass up, others find Beijing's Sinocentric approach off-putting.

Taken together, the evidence suggests that while China has cultivated a large number of well-placed African elites and remains broadly popular among Africans, its favorability may be slipping somewhat, and, despite its anti-American messaging, perceptions of the United States appear to be more positive. Ultimately, it is unclear whether China's propaganda has mitigated the fall in favorable perceptions of China among Africans—a decline that has been less drastic in Africa than in most Western countries.

6

SECURITY STRATEGY AND INTERESTS

China's 2015 National Security Law underscores that the People's Liberation Army (PLA) engages in international military security cooperation, implements military support for United Nations peacekeeping operations, provides international aid and maritime escorts, and safeguards "overseas national interests," national sovereignty, security, territorial integrity, development interests, and world peace. The law also empowers the PLA to ensure that the natural resources and energy required for China's economic and social development are available in a sustained, dependable, and efficient manner. The law adds that the state guarantees food supply, quality, and security within China.[1]

An important amendment to China's 1997 National Defense Law took effect at the beginning of 2021. It spells out that China "will actively push for international military exchanges and cooperation" and "boost its national defense capabilities, including the capabilities to use them overseas for just causes."[2] S. D. Pradhan, India's former chair of the Joint Intelligence Committee, said the provision has three significant implications: it further strengthens Xi Jinping's hold over the armed forces; it gives Xi the authority to direct non-state-owned entities and individuals; and it allows

Xi to "coordinate more effectively the threat of use of force and wolf-warrior diplomacy to deter its adversaries."[3]

This chapter begins with an analysis of China's security strategy as it applies to Africa and distinguishes between its short-term and long-term goals in this domain. It underscores the significance for China of Africa's energy and mineral wealth and identifies Beijing's interest in deep seabed minerals in the western Indian Ocean. It reviews efforts by China to control the global trade in rare earth elements, and the larger role that Africa could play in this market. Looking to the future, the chapter highlights the potential importance of Africa for guaranteeing China's food security.

SECURITY STRATEGY

Africa is not a high priority in China's global security strategy, especially as compared to countries on its periphery and major Western military powers. As one analyst at the Shanghai Institute of International Studies noted, China has no clear military strategy for Africa, and the PLA neither sees Africa as especially important nor is anxious to engage there.[4] On the other hand, China does want to protect its personnel and interests in Africa, to have access to oil and minerals on the continent, to ensure the success of the BRI, and, looking forward, to project PLA military power to Africa's offshore waters and beyond. Nadège Rolland of the National Bureau of Asian Research concludes that "Beijing's emerging strategy aims at making the continent fit into a new subsystem comprising much of the 'global south' that China aspires to dominate."[5]

In 2014, at the fourth summit of the Conference on Interaction and Confidence-Building Measures in Asia, Xi Jinping articulated a concept of common, comprehensive, cooperative, and sustainable security. He defined common security as respecting and ensuring the security of every country and comprehensive security as upholding security in both traditional and nontraditional fields (for example, extremism and terrorism). Xi said cooperative security means promoting the security of both individual countries and the wider region through dialogue and cooperation. Finally, he defined sustainable security as the need for countries to focus on both development and security to realize durable security.[6]

Xi Jinping's speech on Asian security also linked security and development. He stated that "development is the foundation of security, and security the precondition of development."[7] At the same time, Xi Jinping acknowledged that development is not a panacea for solving intractable conflicts. In leaked documents about China's mass detentions of Muslim minorities in Xinjiang, he said: "We say that development is the top priority and the basis for achieving lasting security, and that's right. . . . But it would be wrong to believe that with development every problem solves itself."[8] Examples in Africa where development may fall short in solving the security problems are the civil war in South Sudan, the conflict in Sudan's Darfur region, and al-Shabaab's effort to topple the Somali government.

China's military strategy document in 2015 underscored "the CPC's absolute leadership over the military."[9] The paper outlined that China's armed forces will continue to develop nonaligned and nonconfrontational military-to-military relations with foreign partners and will work to continue friendly military ties with its African counterparts. To further these objectives, the document notes, China will hold dialogues, joint exercises, and exchanges with foreign militaries and strengthen cooperation in personnel training and the provision of materiel assistance, equipment, and technology. China's armed forces will gradually increase their participation in counter piracy, crisis management, international peacekeeping, and humanitarian assistance operations. The military strategy document is replete with references to development, peaceful development, and the linkage of security and development. It also addressed China's naval strategy (see chapter 9).[10]

In 2016 the People's Publishing House published the *Cadre Manual of the Holistic National Security Concept*, which, as Andrea Ghiselli of Fudan University has explained, began the process of dissemination of Xi's new security concept among CPC, PLA, and government officials.[11]

In 2018 Xi extended holistic security to Africa when he stated in his address at the opening session of the FOCAC summit in Beijing that

"China champions a new vision of security featuring common, comprehensive, cooperative and sustainable security."[12] The representatives of all fifty-three African countries attending the summit and China inked a final declaration that emphasized "the importance of advocating common, comprehensive, cooperative and sustainable security."[13]

China's 2019 white paper on national defense contains few references to Africa but does set forth principles that apply to the continent. While China says that it "will never threaten any other country or seek any sphere of influence," it states that one of the goals of its military policy is protecting overseas interests. China proposes to do this by providing more "public security goods" to the international community (including humanitarian assistance and disaster relief), participating in UN peacekeeping and anti-piracy operations, playing a constructive role in resolving political disputes, jointly maintaining the security of international sea passages, and responding to global threats of terrorism, cyber security, and major natural disasters. The white paper emphasizes that China is committed to "peaceful development" and will work with all countries to safeguard world peace and promote "common development."[14] China mixes economic, political, and security engagement in a way that downplays its military and strategic interests. This allows it to amplify its soft power while portraying its hard power as benign.[15]

At the opening of the 2022 Boao Forum for Asia Annual Conference, Xi announced a new Global Security Initiative, which is long on principles but lacking operational detail. It contained six commitments: common, comprehensive, cooperative, and sustainable security; respect for sovereignty and territorial integrity of all countries; abiding by the purposes and principles of the UN Charter; taking the security concerns of all countries seriously; peacefully resolving differences and disputes between countries through dialogue; and maintaining security in both traditional and non-traditional domains.[16] Although these are all long-standing principles of China's security policy, Chinese officials are taking this "new" initiative global, including across Africa.[17] China's mission to the African Union elaborating on what it means for Africa, stressed the importance of development.[18] At the eighth FOCAC ministerial follow-up meeting, the

African side welcomed the Global Security Initiative, noting that it "provides approaches and pathways for the world to address challenges in security, development and governance."[19]

The analysis of military strategy by Chinese academics tends to mirror official statements, albeit with useful nuances and detail. Wang Xuejun of Zhejiang Normal University argues that China's security approach toward Africa prioritizes development and the maintenance of internal stability, a concept he calls "developmental peace." This concept consists of four parts: promoting stability through peace, subordinating democratic political reform to national stability, strengthening the power of the state in the target country while weakening social forces, and safeguarding sovereignty and self-reliance. The policy thus emphasizes African ownership of, and sovereignty over, conflict management and postconflict reconstruction. It insists that economic development is the most important precondition for sustainable internal peace. It opposes coercive, external means for achieving peace and emphasizes cooperation with African governments and the African Union while avoiding interaction with civil society organizations. Wang says China's policy will become more flexible, creative, and constructive and assume greater initiative.[20]

Non-Chinese analyses of China's global military strategy and policy toward Africa, by contrast, often have different interpretations. For instance, the U.S. Defense Department has concluded that China is leveraging its economic, diplomatic, and military influence to establish preeminence and expand its international influence. This view posits the BRI as a driver of overseas military basing, such as has already occurred in Djibouti, because of a perceived need to provide security for BRI projects. In the next three decades, Pentagon planners contend, China will focus on becoming a powerful and prosperous country equipped with a world-class military.[21] In pursuit of this objective, Xi Jinping has directed the entire Chinese system—civilian and military—to pursue simultaneous economic and military advancement. Wherever Chinese companies and individuals operate overseas, they are expected to collect sensitive technology to enhance Chinese military capabilities.[22] Interoperability between the PLA and Chinese companies is central to China's concept of security and power projection.[23]

The U.S. Defense Intelligence Agency (DIA) has offered a more detailed analysis. In a study in 2019 it pointed out that China's 2015 military strategy paper was the first time Beijing publicly clarified the PLA's role in protecting China's evolving national security interests. The DIA report described the PLA as a "party army" that exists to guarantee the CPC's survival. Turning to external defense relations, the analysis emphasized that "the PLA engages with foreign militaries to demonstrate its growing capabilities; improve its tactics, techniques, and procedures; enhance China's image abroad, and further China's diplomatic objectives." It likewise stresses that China is developing new military capabilities that will enhance its ability to project power, including in Africa. These efforts include the production of large transport aircraft, building an aircraft carrier force, expanding submarine patrols, engaging in global humanitarian missions, contributing troops to UN peacekeeping operations, continuing antipiracy engagement in the Gulf of Aden, establishing overseas military bases, and increasing arms sales.[24]

Xi Jinping has made clear his desire to elevate China's role in the world. Gordon Barrass, who worked on China in the UK diplomatic service, and Nigel Inkster, who served with the British Secret Intelligence Service, argue that China intends to be a truly global power, as exemplified by Xi's concept of "a new model of great-power relations."[25] Xi uses terms such as "national rejuvenation" and "Chinese Dream" to describe a mid-twenty-first-century China that is powerful, prosperous, and harmonious. This construct includes a nimble and reorganized PLA that effectively projects power in the region and overseas. Some African states have made this evolution easier by encouraging China to deepen its security engagement in the region.[26] This goal is tied to the need to protect growing Chinese interests and more personnel living and working in Africa. It has led to debates about China's long-standing policy of nonintervention, rejection of military alliances, and, until Djibouti, unwillingness to establish military bases outside China.[27] Today, however, Chinese experts no longer dismiss the possibility of overseas military operations.[28]

Other analysts insist that, with the exception of UN peacekeeping operations, China has no interest in establishing global alliances, sustaining a far-flung military presence, or sending troops thousands of miles from its borders. The situation is different in the Indo-Pacific region, however, where China aspires to become the unchallenged political, economic, and military hegemon. China is purposely leaving the military dimensions of the BRI ambiguous, although it is probably not a prelude to global American-style military bases and presence. China may, however, seek to strengthen its position in more distant regions, including Africa, so as to deny the United States military access or diminish American influence.[29]

It is important to distinguish between China's long-term goal of global power projection and its more restrained short-term capabilities. Timothy Heath of the RAND Corporation, in a study of China's overseas security, has argued that while the PLA is increasing its international presence, its capability so far remains modest and limited to "other than war" missions to protect its interests outside China. He adds that China has ambitions to develop a "limited power projection" capability involving a small number of forces that can exert influence in Asia and as far afield as Africa. The PLA is increasing its ability to transport and operate troops in other countries, but for the near future its ability to conduct "other than war" missions will remain limited.[30]

Heath believes that China may accept a higher degree of disorder and risk in some countries where it is expanding its engagement and therefore rely heavily on non-PLA assets, such as funding for host country security protection and hiring of commercial security companies. China desires to enhance security while minimizing its military commitments overseas. Thus the PLA may send marines to Africa to guard key assets and installations. Special forces from the PLA and People's Armed Police may participate in combat operations against terrorist threats in collaboration with host country armed forces. The PLA Air Force will certainly expand the inventory of its heavy transport planes and aerial refueling tankers for security contingencies. As it does so, it will also require access to air bases in Africa. The PLA Navy (PLAN) may increase the number of amphibious vessels, replenishment ships, and aircraft carriers to assist with sea-lane protection and other missions.[31]

According to Obert Hodzi, a Zimbabwean scholar at the University of Liverpool, China "camouflages its military power in non-threatening ways," such as providing troops for UN peacekeeping operations in Africa. Beijing routinely packages its military activities by forging partnerships that replace confrontation with what it touts as a new type of international relations that emphasize "win-win" cooperation. Consequently, Hodzi argues, African countries often prefer China's security norms and principles such as noninterference and respect for state sovereignty, which effectively limits Western influence in many African countries.[32] Of course, China's significant economic engagement and financing of projects in Africa also affects the thinking of African leaders on security issues.

There is another essential element of Chinese security strategy that may be playing out in Africa. Graham Allison of Harvard University suggests that China traditionally seeks to improve its strategic position through well-designed incremental moves. He draws on the work of David Lai at the U.S. Army War College, who explains this approach by comparing the Western game of chess with its popular Chinese equivalent, *weiqi* (called "Go" in English). Chess players seek to dominate the center of the board and conquer the opponent. In Go, by contrast, players seek to surround the opponent. The Chinese strategist resists rushing prematurely toward victory and instead tries to build incremental advantage.[33] Ronak Gopaldas, a risk management expert in South Africa, notes that China has been able to make significant gains in Africa without generating widespread public outrage through this "salami-slicing" strategy. China engages in the slow accumulation of minor changes, which over time result in a substantial change in the strategic picture. China has employed this incremental strategy in the South China Sea, and there is evidence that it is doing so in Africa (see chapter 9).[34]

ENERGY SECURITY AND MINERALS

Chinese officials and most analysts in China tend to downplay the importance of energy and minerals in the China-Africa relationship. This is because doing so highlights Africa's role as a supplier of raw materials to a country that exports overwhelmingly finished products to the continent, thereby prompting unwanted allegations of neocolonialism and mercantilism. In 2018, 83 percent of all African exports to China were oil and minerals. After adding timber, the percentage jumped to 96 percent.[35] China's foreign direct investment in Africa, in turn, reinforces the argument. Between 2005 and 2017 about three quarters of China's foreign direct investment by dollar value in Sub-Saharan Africa went to the mineral and energy sectors.[36] That investment follows a clear governmental strategy; China's white paper on mineral resources in 2003 identified as a priority the need to import crude oil and certain minerals in order to guarantee "the sustained, rapid and healthy development of the Chinese economy."[37]

One of the issues driving China's security engagement in Africa is its need to access energy, crude oil, and a lengthy list of minerals and metals that are essential to China's industrial production.[38] In the past decade, rare earth elements have joined this discussion, albeit for different reasons. While these raw materials support China's wider economy, they also have significant implications for its security and, in many cases, have military applications. To be clear, China obtains and will continue to obtain most of its energy and mineral needs from domestic production and from countries other than those in Africa. However, significant percentages of these raw materials come from Africa. China depends heavily on these imports, especially African minerals, which are more important to China than African oil and natural gas.

Abdou Rahim Lema of Peking University writes that ensuring access to Africa's resources "plays a significant role in China's security thinking—though this factor is usually overemphasized to the extent that other equally important calculations are overlooked altogether."[39] Jing Gu of the Institute for Development Studies in the UK says that China's engagement in Rwanda and the DRC is driven primarily by its need for minerals such as cobalt and copper, and access to consumer markets.[40] An official in the Peace and Security Department of the African Union concurs that one of China's primary interests in Africa is access to minerals such as cobalt, tantalum, and rare earths.[41] And a member of Tanzania's parliament, when asked about China's engagement in the country, said Beijing wants Tanzania's resources.[42]

ENERGY SECURITY

In 2018 China imported 71 percent of its oil and 44 percent of its natural gas requirements. By 2035 it projects that imports will account for 85 percent of its oil and 46 percent of its natural gas. China satisfies growing domestic demand by importing oil and natural gas from the Persian Gulf, Africa, Russia, and Central Asia.[43] Its reliance on Africa for oil has actually been declining in recent years, falling from 22.2 percent of total imports in 2017 to 21.7 percent in 2018, then to 18.1 percent in 2019, and finally to roughly 15 percent in 2020.[44] In 2019 China's major African suppliers were Angola (9.5 percent of total imports), Republic of Congo (2.3 percent), and Libya (2 percent).[45] Nevertheless, Africa remains an important supplier because it helps to diversify China's sources of supply and permits Chinese oil companies to become global players and compete with the biggest international oil majors.[46] Thus China purchased Libyan oil even as conflict raged in that country between the national government based in Tripoli and the Libyan National Army forces led by General Khalifa Haftar, which control most of the production and export of oil, based in eastern Libya.[47]

Meanwhile, recent natural gas discoveries in Mozambique, Tanzania, Egypt, Senegal, and Mauritania suggest that Africa is likely to become a more important energy supplier to China. Africa accounted for half of the world's gas discoveries between 2011 and 2018.[48] As China moves away from coal as its major source of power, it is turning increasingly to liquid natural gas (LNG) and nuclear power.

China became a net importer of refined oil products in 1993 and a net importer of crude in 1996.[49] This has caused a growing focus among China's leaders on energy security; the country's three large state-owned oil companies—China National Petroleum Corporation (CNPC), China National Offshore Oil Corporation (CNOOC), and Sinopec—now operate in Africa, often in areas where their interests and personnel face significant threats.

In 1996 CNPC was the first Chinese company to invest in Africa, developing fields in Sudan discovered by Chevron but abandoned them due to civil strife in the 1980s. Over time, Sudan became a high-risk area usually avoided by the Western majors. CNPC controls 40 percent of Sudan's consortium, operates a refinery, and built the associated infrastructure. South Sudan, upon its independence from Sudan in 2011, inherited 75 percent of the oil fields where CNPC and Sinopec have significant interests. CNPC subsequently moved into neighboring Chad, where it operates fields together with a Swiss company, as well as Niger, where it runs the only operational oil field and a refinery in partnership with the central government. It also has a 20 percent stake in two natural gas projects in Mozambique.[50]

CNOOC's reserves in Africa constitute more than 2 percent of the company's total reserves and almost 5 percent of its daily global production. A CNOOC subsidiary owns 45 percent of the shares of one block in Nigeria and 20 and 18 percent, respectively, of two other blocks. It has partnered with Total and Tullow Oil to develop the Lake Albert basin deposit in Uganda, where it is also the operator. It holds stakes in several blocks in Senegal, Republic of Congo, Algeria, and Gabon. CNOOC plans to build a gas liquefaction plant in Mozambique and has contracted to buy much of the resulting LNG.[51]

In Angola, Sinopec established a fifty-fifty joint venture called Sonangol Sinopec International (SSI) with a private group based in Hong Kong, China Sonangol. SSI is a minority nonoperational partner with Angolan owners in several offshore blocks. POLY-GCL Petroleum, a joint venture between state-owned China POLY Group Corporation and privately owned, Hong Kong–based Golden Concord Group, is developing a $4 billion natural gas project in the Ogaden region of Ethiopia, with a production goal of three million tons per year. The project includes a pipeline to the Djiboutian coast and an export terminal, underscoring China's commitment to expanding imports of African LNG.[52]

South Africa, Niger, Namibia, and China each have about 5 percent of the world's developable uranium reserves and rank fifth, sixth, seventh and eighth in the world, respectively, in terms of proven reserves.[53] African countries account for about 14 percent of global uranium production. China obtains about one-third of its uranium supply domestically, one-third from Chinese equity in foreign mines, and one-third on the open market. Increasingly, China is looking to import uranium from Africa to meet its nuclear energy needs.[54] Nevertheless, it experienced early challenges: in 2007 the China National Nuclear Corporation (CNNC) obtained a 37 percent stake in Niger's Azelik uranium mine, but security, financial, and environmental problems soon undermined the project, and China stopped importing uranium from Niger in 2015.[55] By contrast, its experience in Namibia has been more positive. China has invested more than $2 billion in Namibia's Husab mine, and CNNC bought a 25 percent joint equity stake in the Langer Heinrich mine.[56] In 2019 CNNC purchased a 69 percent stake in Namibia's Rössing mine.[57]

MINERAL SECURITY

China's dependence on certain minerals and the importance of Africa as a supplier is a significant factor in the security relationship. At the beginning of this century, China's white paper on mineral resources identified the need to import large quantities of high-grade iron and copper, bauxite, chromite, manganese, and potash.[58] Subsequently, tantalum, platinum, lithium, and cobalt joined this list, as China greatly expanded manufacturing of certain products that had not been foreseen at the beginning of the century. African countries now account for more than 75 percent of global tantalum production, most of the world's cobalt production, 60 percent of platinum group production, 50 percent of manganese production, and 10 percent of copper production.[59]

Looking at the most strategic of these minerals, the importance of Africa as a supplier is clear. Columbite-tantalite, better known as coltan, is the naturally occurring metallic ore from which tantalum is extracted for capacitors in circuits of electronic devices. The defense, aviation, and medical technology industries also use tantalum. In 2019 China produced only 100 metric tons of tantalum, while African countries produced well over 1,800 metric tons. The overwhelming majority of African production went to China. Most African coltan originates in conflict zones in the DRC and Rwanda, where armed rebel groups control some of it. Consequently, the sale arrangements Chinese companies make to acquire coltan supplies are highly opaque.[60]

The Democratic Republic of Congo (DRC) has 51 percent of global cobalt reserves, as compared to China's 1 percent. In 2021 the DRC produced more than 70 percent of the world's cobalt output.[61] Morocco and South Africa are also among the top ten global producers. Chinese companies such as Zhejiang Huayou Cobalt purchase most African cobalt, reflecting China's interest in trying to control the supply chain. China's Export Import Bank financed the $3 billion Sicomines cobalt and copper mining project and $3 billion of Chinese-built infrastructure in the DRC as part of the deal. China Molybedenum is the largest stakeholder in the DRC's Tenke Fungurume cobalt and copper mine and, in 2020, acquired a 95 percent stake in the Kisanfu mine from U.S.-based Freeport-McMoRan. China Nonferrous Metal Mining Company has a 51 percent stake in the DRC's Deziwa cobalt and copper mine. All told, China has secured ownership over ten out of eighteen major mines in the DRC and now has a hand in more than half of the country's cobalt production. China controls about 85 percent of the global cobalt supply, which includes a major contract with Glencore, the largest cobalt producer. Cobalt is an essential component for batteries, including those used in electric cars, and China is a world leader in both production and technology associated with electric vehicles. Cobalt is also important in the construction of wind turbines and satellites.[62]

China has about 7 percent of the global manganese ore reserves and relies on imports for 80 percent of its needs. South Africa, Gabon, and Ghana are, respectively, the first, third, and sixth largest producers of manganese ore in the world. In 2017 China obtained 90 percent of its imported manganese ore from these three countries, with the remainder coming from Australia and Brazil. Manganese is an important alloy in steel production and used in zinc-carbon and alkaline batteries. It also shows promise for lithium-ion batteries. One of China's most recent investments has been lithium mines in Namibia.[63]

Industries in China requiring chrome ore are likewise reliant on imports. South Africa has the world's largest reserves of the mineral and provided 72 percent of China's imports in 2017. Zimbabwe and Madagascar have much smaller reserves. China's state-owned Sinosteel holds 50 percent ownership in a South African venture that has over seventy million tons of chrome ore reserves. Sinosteel is also investing in increased chrome ore production in Zimbabwe. Chrome is critical in the manufacture of stainless steel and jet engines.[64]

China is a significant importer of platinum, which is used for catalytic converters in vehicles, laboratory equipment, and electrodes. South Africa sits on 68 percent of global platinum reserves and in 2018 accounted for a quarter of global platinum exports. China's state-owned and private companies have made at least eight major equity and guaranteed market access agreements in platinum-group metals in South Africa. About 50 percent of the country's metal exports go to China, tying the sector closely to Chinese investment.[65]

China's reliance on imported bauxite has fluctuated between 40 and 60 percent in recent years. In 2019 Guinea supplied 44 percent of China's imported bauxite, while Ghana and Sierra Leone exported lesser amounts.[66] China's state-owned Société de Boké operates one of Guinea's largest bauxite mines. In 2017 Beijing announced a $20 billion infrastructure loan for Guinea over twenty years in exchange for concessions to the country's high-grade bauxite. So far, there has been little progress on this new infrastructure.[67] China negotiated a $2 billion infrastructure deal with Ghana for the right to mine bauxite in a forest reserve. Civil society groups, however, sued the government of Ghana to stop the project out of concern over damage to the environment, and the project remains deadlocked.[68]

China's copper ore reserves constitute only 4 percent of the global total; it relies heavily on imports. In 2017 China imported 55 percent of its copper ore from the world's two largest producers: Chile and Peru. Although the DRC and Zambia are the fourth and seventh largest producers of copper ore, respectively, they accounted for only about 16 percent of China's copper ore imports that year. Beijing, however, has invested heavily in DRC and Zambian copper mines, giving the impression that Africa is a more important source of supply for China than is actually the case.[69]

DEEP SEABED MINING

China is a leader in the race to explore and develop deep seabed mineral deposits. China has made funding for deep sea mining research a national security priority.[70] The other important players in this arena are India, Japan, South Korea, Germany, Russia, France, and the UK. The Jamaica-based International Seabed Authority (ISA), established in 1994 under the UN Convention on the Law of the Sea (UNCLOS), organizes, regulates, and controls all mineral-related activities in that part of the international seabed that lies outside the exclusive economic zones of individual countries. The ISA has the authority to grant contracts to countries to explore for polymetallic nodules, polymetallic sulfides, and cobalt-rich ferromanganese crusts in the deep seabed. As of 2022 it had issued thirty-one such contracts in the world's designated deep seabed zones. Chinese entities had secured five of them.[71]

While most of China's focus is on the Pacific zone, it has also been exploring the Southwest Indian Ridge, a 10,000-square-kilometer area just south of Madagascar and Mauritius in the Indian Ocean. In 2011 the China Ocean Mineral Resources Research and Development Association, which is part of the State Oceanic Administration, received one of China's five contracts to explore the Southwest Indian Ridge for polymetallic sulfides, with rights to develop ore deposits. Sulfides on the seabed typically contain considerable amounts of copper, zinc, gold, and silver. Although several countries have licenses in the central and northern Indian Ocean, China has the only one in the Southwest Indian Ridge.[72]

China has played a key role in the ISA since it joined in 1996 and is currently one of the organization's principal funding sources. (The United States has only observer status, because it believes the ISA could impinge on its economic and military sovereignty and it has never ratified UNCLOS.) To underscore its commitment to deep seabed mining, China passed the

2016 Deep Seabed Law and a year later issued regulations for the licensing of deep-sea mining operations. This was China's first law dealing with the exploration for and exploitation of deep seabed resources. The law complies with the principles set forth in UNCLOS.[73]

Chinese research vessels have been active in the Indian Ocean. In 2015 the deep-sea staffed *Jiaolong* submersible made a 118-day expedition with its mother ship to the region at the same time the *Dayang Yihao* explored the Southwest Indian Ridge. The following year the *Dayang Yihao* returned for a 216-day cruise and was joined by the *Xiang Yang Hong 10* research ship, which made additional visits to the Southwest Indian Ridge in 2017 and 2018.[74] In 2019 the Chinese Academy of Sciences conducted a 121-day research expedition in the Indian Ocean focused on hydrothermal vents using the newest deep-sea manned submersible, *Shenhai Yongshi*.[75] While the main driver of China's naval oceanography is the development of seabed resources, it has the additional purpose of supporting China's blue water naval capabilities and obtaining data that benefit the PLAN's submarine force.[76]

Deep seabed mining has not yet achieved economic viability, however. The cost of recovery of deep seabed minerals and the availability and price of land-based counterparts will determine its future. Nevertheless, China has positioned itself to take advantage of this situation once it arrives, and the Southwest Indian Ridge near African Indian Ocean island countries will be part of this important future economic opportunity.

RARE EARTH ELEMENTS

Rare earth elements are a special case, in that China dominates the market and African countries are just beginning to produce them. Hence, it is not a question of China relying on African supply, but whether China will try to extert influence over the nascent African market so that it can continue to control the global supply chain. Rare earth elements are a group of seventeen chemical elements that occur in the periodic table. The group includes yttrium and the fifteen lanthanide elements. Scandium is sometimes classified as a rare earth element. The elements are not actually rare, but they are expensive to mine because it is unusual to find them in sufficient concentrations for economical extraction. Rare earth elements are used as chemical catalysts, in ceramics and glass making, and in metallurgy and alloys. They are essential to national defense because they are used in the production of night-vision goggles, precision-guided missiles, communications equipment, GPS equipment, batteries, and defense electronics.[77]

China began producing significant quantities of rare earth oxides in the 1980s and became the world's leading producer in the 1990s. While China has only 36 percent of global rare earth reserves, it now controls about 60 percent of the global supply chain, down from 97 percent in 2010 when it restricted exports, prices peaked, and other countries began to return to production. But returning to production can take ten to fifteen years. The United States, for example, has one of the largest deposits in the world but still sources about 80 percent of its rare earths from China. So long as this situation continues, it provides Beijing with useful leverage, although the U.S. military could meet its requirements for rare earths even if China stopped their export to the United States.[78]

Namibia, South Africa, Kenya, Madagascar, Malawi, Mozambique, Tanzania, Zambia, Gabon, and Burundi have large deposits of high-grade, rare earth minerals. Most of these countries are experiencing an increasing debt burden and are seeking relief. China holds a significant percentage of the debt in several of these countries and is well positioned to obtain future rights to mining rare earths as part of debt relief negotiations.[79]

Chinese companies have been purchasing rare earth resources in several countries, including from the Baluba mine in Zambia.[80] In 2020 London-based Pensana Rare Earths signed an engineering, procurement, construction, and financing agreement with the China Great Wall Industry Corporation for the development of Pensana's Longonjo rare earths project in Angola.[81] Of thirteen additional rare earth mines in Africa, only two are currently producing: the Gakara mine in Burundi, operated by a German company, and the Glenover mine in South Africa. Three projects have failed, and eight are in the early stages of development.[82] Seeking an alternative to China for rare earth elements, the United States has contacted the management of Burundi's mine and a new operation in Malawi.[83] At this point, Africa is a minor producer of rare earth elements, and China's intentions remain unclear. Yet, because of the critical security implications of these raw materials, they merit continued attention.

FOOD SECURITY

While Africa's contribution to China's energy and mineral security has been significant for at least two decades, exporting food (other than seafood from offshore waters) to China has historically not been an important part of the relationship. Food security, however, is a top domestic and foreign policy priority for China, and agricultural cooperation has long been a mainstay of the China-Africa relationship.[84] Agricultural projects and technical assistance were tools in the competition with Taiwan for diplomatic recognition across Africa beginning in the late 1950s. China has used different agricultural cooperation approaches, some emphasizing food crops and others focusing on biofuels and cash crops such as tobacco. Some projects have succeeded, while others have failed.[85] As of 2016, China's State Council said it had assisted more than fifty African countries in implementing about five hundred agricultural programs, including completed projects and technical support and material supply in the areas of farming, food storage, agricultural machinery, farmland irrigation, and agro-processing.[86]

China's agricultural aid projects in Africa continue, but Beijing is now paying more attention to the role of trade and direct investment in agriculture as part of its food security strategy.[87] This has led to the leasing of land in Africa for both food production and cash crops. It has also resulted in often wildly inaccurate accounts of "land-grabbing" by Chinese companies. In 2007 the head of China's Export Import Bank, Li Ruogu, contributed to these charges when he urged Chinese farmers to move to Africa. Li stated: "There's no harm in allowing [Chinese] farmers to leave the country to become farm owners [in Africa]," adding that the bank would fully support this migration with investment.[88] This resulted in criticism from many Africans and then led Chinese officials to underscore the downsides of growing food in Africa for export to China. Beijing emphasized that China would continue to meet its food deficits by purchasing from major agricultural producers such as the United States.[89] The evidence so far suggests that China's long-term land leasing in Africa has been exceedingly modest, and there is no official plan to send Chinese farmers to Africa.[90]

China's newest agricultural focus in Africa is the development of Agricultural Technology Demonstration Centers (ATDCs) in twenty-four African countries. Their purpose is to transfer Chinese technology and methods of production through demonstrations and training to African farmers.[91] These centers combine a business operation with financial aid for the first three years, after which income from the centers should cover the costs. China provides $5–6 million in financing to build the ATDCs and keep them in operation for the initial three years. Individual Chinese companies or institutes manage the ATDCs, and each is paired with a Chinese province. The goal is to improve global food supply as well as to sell more Chinese-made agricultural equipment, which in turn contributes to both China's food security and its economy. The centers face numerous challenges, especially the difficulty of transferring China's agricultural technology to Africa. The ATDC model has had mixed results, and its success is not a certainty.[92] For example, one management expert described the ATDC in Mozambique, the first in Africa, as "a scattered mess."[93]

Since the mid-1970s African countries have faced a collective food trade deficit, which has grown rapidly this century. Thus it is unlikely that Africa, which relies primarily on subsistence agriculture, will soon become a stable exporter of food to China. The causes of Africa's persistent food deficits include low productivity, poor agricultural and trade infrastructure, low internal and external trade capacity, low investment in agricultural resources, domestic and foreign policy distortions, high population growth, and political instability.[94] African countries have also found it difficult to meet China's high standards and separate protocols for agricultural imports.[95] In theory, however, many of these problems can be ameliorated, and Africa has unused agricultural land that, climate change permitting, could be used for farming or herding.[96]

China exports food but has been a net food importer since 2003. The driving forces of China's food demand have, since the late 1980s, shifted from high population growth to rising income and urbanization, leading to major changes in diet and consumption. China's overall food self-sufficiency is projected to fall from 94.5 percent in 2015 to 91 percent in 2025.[97] About 40 percent of China's workforce is engaged in farming, most of it small-scale holdings, but agriculture accounts for less than 9 percent of GDP.[98] China is, however, feeding 18 percent of the world's population with only 9 percent of the planet's arable land.[99] China has modest goals to expand agricultural production acreage, but unless there are improvements in yields, they will be insufficient to keep pace with growing Chinese demand. Much of China's increased food production is due to excessive use of fertilizers and pesticides, which is causing land degradation and water pollution. The lack of additional water availability is also problematic.[100] As a result, China is looking increasingly at securing imported food and investing in overseas agricultural projects. In 2014 it issued a policy document that identified "moderate imports" as part of its food security strategy.[101]

China allocates 12 percent of its overseas agricultural investment for Africa but imports only 2 percent of its food from the continent.[102] Many African countries export modest quantities of a wide variety of food products to China. South Africa, for example, exports fruit, sugar, nuts, wine, and beef to China.[103] Chinese investments in food production in Africa have occurred in many countries and include a variety of crops, such as rice, oil palm, cassava, sugar cane, maize, peanuts, sesame, and fruit, as well as livestock. Most of the production is sold locally or on the international market and does not go to China because of high transport costs and inadequate infrastructure. In any event, China's stated policy is that any increase in global food supply in Africa or elsewhere contributes positively to China's food security.[104]

Seafood is the one commodity that is not only important to the Chinese diet but obtained in significant quantities in African waters. Documenting the quantity of seafood originating in African waters is impossible because African countries have limited ability to monitor fishing in their waters by foreign vessels, many of them illegal. The situation became sufficiently embarrassing that Beijing strengthened its offshore fisheries law and declared that it intends to abide by global agreements to reduce illegal fishing.[105] China has the world's largest fishing fleet, which includes about seventeen thousand distant-water vessels and accounts for more than 18 percent of global marine fishery production. More than five hundred vessels have Chinese owners, operators, or other Chinese interests that fly the flag of African nations with limited enforcement measures, and where fishing rights are often restricted to domestically registered vessels. The African countries that account for most of these Chinese-controlled, foreign-flagged vessels are Ghana (15 percent), Mauritania (14 percent), Côte d'Ivoire (7 percent), Morocco (5 percent), and Senegal (3 percent). China views the fishing industry strategically because it has a leading role in safeguarding its food security.[106] To meet growing demand for seafood, Beijing requires its fleet to send an estimated 60–65 percent of its catch back to Chinese markets.[107]

The waters off Africa in the Atlantic and Indian Oceans are prized zones for deep-water fishing fleets. China accounts for about 38 percent of global deep-water fishing, and an estimated 25–30 percent of it occurs in exclusive economic zones off Africa. China does sign fishing agreements with African countries, but they are opaque, and corruption is common.[108] In 2017 China provided Mozambique with $120 million in concessional loans to update the commercial fishing port in Beira. Almost immediately, there was an influx of Chinese industrial fishing vessels into the area, giving rise to charges that Mozambique's government had permitted China to devastate Mozambique's fishing industry.[109] In 2018 the president of Madagascar announced a ten-year investment deal with a Chinese consortium in exchange for fishing rights. The consortium reportedly promised $2.7 billion toward building fisheries infrastructure, although little activity of the sort seems to have occurred. Local fishing communities criticized the agreement at the time.[110] In 2020 six Chinese fishing trawlers entered South African waters without permission and were fined before they could leave.[111]

There is a long history of complaints about illegal fishing by Chinese trawlers off West Africa. In 2017 the governments of Senegal, Guinea, Sierra

Leone, and Guinea-Bissau seized Chinese vessels.[112] The situation involving Chinese fishing in Ghanaian waters is especially vexing. Chinese corporations control an estimated 90 percent of the trawlers operating in Ghanaian waters. In 2015 Chinese nationals captained more than 95 percent of trawlers licensed to fish in Ghanaian waters.[113] Ghanaian law prohibits joint ownership of fishing vessels, but trawlers linked to a Chinese state-owned company operate in Ghanaian waters. These vessels are registered as owned by Ghanaians in a successful effort to skirt the law.[114] In 2020 Ghana registered three more trawlers from China in this way, jeopardizing the sustainability of Ghanaian fisheries in the process.[115] Kofi Agbogah, an expert on Ghanaian fishery issues, argues that China's fleet has been operating illegally off the west coast of Africa for years using banned drift nets.[116] In 2019 Ghana slapped a $1 million fine on one of the Chinese trawlers.[117] In 2020 President Akufo-Addo pledged to end the illegal practice, known locally as *Saiko* and exercised mostly by Chinese industrial trawlers, of trans-shipping fish at sea.[118]

In 2020 six Chinese supertrawlers arrived in Monrovia, Liberia, after an apparent unsuccessful attempt to fish off the Mozambique coast. Each supertrawler can catch at least two thousand tons of fish annually. This is four thousand times the annual catch of a Liberian artisanal fisherman, who lands an average of five hundred kilograms using a traditional canoe. The supertrawlers compete unfairly for the same fish as local fishermen, who increasingly find themselves unable to earn a livelihood because of overfishing by the Chinese vessels.[119] As a result of pressure from local fishermen, the Liberian government subsequently refused to license the six Chinese supertrawlers.[120]

The waters off Mauritania are especially rich in fish. In 2010 the China-based Poly Hong Dong Fishery Company negotiated an agreement to provide Mauritania $100 million to construct an industrial complex in exchange for the right to fish in Mauritanian waters under favorable tax and trade conditions and with no restrictions on fishing methods for twenty-five years.[121] This deal subsequently resulted in a parliamentary investigation into its propriety.[122] In 2020 China's Export Import Bank provided an $87 million loan to construct a fishing harbor for local fishermen.[123]

Gambia, which relies heavily on fish in its diet, has experienced a different kind of problem. Most of the trawlers operating in Gambian waters are Chinese owned. More important, Chinese companies have established several fish meal factories in Gambia that are depleting the local fish stock, while exporting fish meal, much of it eventually reaching China.[124] Chinese fishing companies are also urging the construction of distant-water fishing bases in China to support their deep-water fishing activities in locations such as West Africa.[125]

While China now relies minimally on Africa for food security, this could change dramatically depending on China's future food production, the global impact of climate change, and the ability of African states to significantly increase their food production capacity. In the future, Africa could make a contribution to the food needs of China and other countries. China could also find itself in a food security situation where it decides to significantly expand its long-term land leases in Africa to produce food for itself, the African market, the world market, or all the above. Anna Woods of the New Zealand Ministry of Foreign Affairs and Trade argues that Beijing will not leave food security solely to the free market and multilateral liberal order. Rather, Chinese officials will engage with countries "that have the ability or the potential to grow the total global food supply and be of assistance to China."[126] Deborah Brautigam of Johns Hopkins University asked in her book in 2015 whether the Chinese have acquired large areas of farmland in Africa and if they plan to grow food in Africa that can be exported to China. Her carefully hedged response to both questions was, "No, or—at least—not yet."[127]

***

China's comprehensive security strategy in Africa is characterized by the link between security and development and driven by China's goal of protecting its nationals and economic interests. China makes every effort to avoid kinetic military activity in Africa and instead emphasizes military operations other than war. In its effort to become a global security power, however, China wants to expand its influence across the continent and simultaneously limit that of the West, especially the United States. This strategy complements China's BRI, Global Development Initiative, and Global Security Initiative, and the country's goal to extend its power well beyond Africa.

China's primary security interests in Africa are access to energy and, even more important, critical minerals such as cobalt, tantalum, platinum, lithium, and manganese. These are in short supply in China and essential to maintaining the country's industrial output. Deep seabed mining in the southwestern Indian Ocean is a longer-term interest, as is control over the rare earth supply chain as Africa becomes a more important source of supply. Finally, China is looking to global markets to guarantee food security. Africa is an important source of China's seafood but a minor source of land-based food. This situation could change with improved African agricultural policies, however, given that the continent has significant quantities of uncultivated land. This forward-thinking approach is emblematic of China's security interests in Africa.

7

PROTECTING INTERESTS AND MANAGING CONFLICT

China's 2015 National Security Law states that the government will take necessary measures to protect the security and interests "of Chinese citizens, organizations and bodies abroad."[1] This has since become a top priority under Xi Jinping and is supported by a Chinese domestic audience that has expressed concern about the increasing numbers of overseas Chinese who have been killed, kidnapped, and injured, often in Africa. Modernization of the military and development of expeditionary forces have emerged as key parts of Xi Jinping's strategy to protect China's overseas interests. More than his predecessors, Xi is staking the legitimacy of the CPC on a strong PLA that can defend Chinese nationals and interests at home and abroad.[2]

This chapter documents China's increasing interests and presence in Africa, and the new security challenges they have created. It describes attacks against Chinese nationals and the measures China is taking to counter them—or, at a minimum, to lessen their impact. This includes employing private security companies on the continent and taking steps to improve overall security in Africa. When its own efforts and those of local governments are insufficient, China has resorted to state action to facilitate the evacuation of its nationals. Concern over protection of Chinese nationals has also resulted in efforts by Beijing to play a more active role in conflict prevention, management, and mediation in Africa. Finally, attacks on Chinese nationals in Africa have encouraged China to support UN peacekeeping operations, including the deployment of Chinese combat forces.

ATTACKS AGAINST CHINESE NATIONALS AND INTERESTS

As the number of Chinese nationals living in, working in, and visiting Africa has increased over the years, so too have their security challenges. The fact that Chinese nationals and companies routinely have a presence in riskier locations in Africa such as Nigeria, Sudan, South Sudan, Somalia, and the Democratic Republic of Congo (DRC) is part of the problem.[3] Many Chinese companies and nationals, especially in earlier years, went to Africa with an inadequate understanding of the security situation there.[4] The Chinese communities in Africa include permanent or semipermanent residents (immigrants dating back decades, Chinese nationals married to Africans, long-term traders/entrepreneurs); temporary residents (official diplomatic and aid personnel, contract workers, Chinese company representatives); and short-term visitors (tourists, students, China-based businesspeople, government experts). China's Ministry of Commerce maintains a registry of more than 3,500 Chinese-owned companies in Africa. A 2018 study by McKinsey, however, estimates the figure at almost four times higher, with the vast majority being smaller, privately owned firms.[5] There is no reliable figure for the number of Chinese citizens in Africa. Prior to the outbreak of coronavirus, informed estimates ranged from 250,000 to two million.[6] COVID-19 has reduced the numbers, however. For example, Chinese contract laborers in Africa declined from over 250,000 at the end of 2015 to just over 100,000 at the end of 2020.[7]

Throughout this century Chinese nationals have experienced a persistent increase in the number of attacks in Africa, including theft, kidnapping, civil conflict, and terrorism. In most cases, except for crime and kidnapping, Chinese nationals have not been targeted per se but rather found themselves in the wrong place at the wrong time. In response, China's Ministry of Foreign Affairs issues "Special Notices for Chinese Citizens Abroad" that include security warnings encompassing things like natural disasters, social unrest, terrorist attacks, crimes, labor disputes, economic interest conflicts, traffic accidents, and high-profile mass events with security risks. From 2008 through 2010 China issued 453 of these notices globally. Sub-Sahara Africa accounted for 27 percent of this total and represented the highest security risk region for Chinese abroad.[8]

Some of the earliest attacks occurred in Nigeria when the Movement for the Emancipation of the Niger Delta (MEND) targeted Chinese nationals because of China's support for the government's development of oil resources in the region. In 2006 the MEND warned the Chinese government and its oil companies to stay out of the Niger Delta. When they continued operations, the MEND or other rebel groups kidnapped more than twenty Chinese nationals working in the Delta, eventually releasing all of them after apparently receiving a ransom payment. In 2007 the Ogaden National Liberation Front (ONLF), which sought self-determination from Ethiopia, warned foreign companies to stay out of the Ogaden region. The ONLF attacked a heavily guarded Chinese exploration base, killing nine Chinese employed by a subsidiary of Sinopec in a shootout with Ethiopian troops. The same year, in Darfur, Sudan, the rebel Justice and Equality Movement (JEM) publicly condemned China's supply of weapons to the Sudanese government and threatened Chinese oil interests in neighboring South Kordofan region. In 2008 one of the Darfur rebel groups attacked a China National Petroleum Corporation (CNPC) oil operation, capturing nine Chinese employees—five of whom died during a subsequent rescue attempt. In all, CNPC reported five hundred security emergencies in Sudan between 2007 and 2009. In 2012, a year after South Sudan became independent, a rebel group kidnapped twenty-nine Chinese construction workers in neighboring Sudan but released them after ten days.[9]

In 2007 Tuareg rebels in Niger briefly kidnapped a Chinese uranium executive as a warning to China for disregarding the environment and signing an agreement with Niger's government. In 2008 renewed fighting led to the death of one Chinese national in the eastern DRC. The same year, two Chinese died, and four others were injured in Equatorial Guinea, when two hundred striking Chinese construction workers clashed with security forces in a labor dispute. China's 2009 crackdown on its Muslim Uighur minority in Xinjiang resulted in a threat by al-Qaeda in the Islamic Maghreb (AQIM) against Chinese workers in Algeria. AQIM then ambushed Algerian security forces escorting Chinese construction workers, killing twenty-four Algerian troops but no Chinese. In 2010 one Chinese mineworker died and a dozen were seriously injured in a riot targeting foreign mining practices in Zambia. In 2012 a rebel group in Cabinda, Angola, claimed it had conducted three attacks against Chinese nationals affiliated with CNPC. Chinese in Angola faced a different problem that year, when China sent a special police team from the Ministry of Public Security to investigate Chinese criminal gangs. The team arrested and extradited to China thirty-seven suspects accused of extortion, kidnapping, armed robbery, and running prostitution rings in the Chinese community in Angola.[10] Similarly, in Uganda, China dispatched a special security team that, collaborating with Ugandan officials, tracked down four of eight Chinese nationals accused of kidnapping, extortion, and cyberattacks.[11]

In Ghana, large numbers of Chinese competed with Ghanaian artisanal gold miners, resulting in conflict and in the expulsion of many Chinese from the country. To protect themselves, some Chinese migrants obtained firearms, sometimes illegally, which has exacerbated the security problem.[12] In 2014 the Boko Haram terrorist group kidnapped ten Chinese nationals and injured another from a construction camp in northern Cameroon. The kidnappers eventually released these individuals, likely because China paid a ransom. The same year, the outbreak of Ebola in Liberia, Sierra Leone, and Guinea forced several Chinese enterprises to shut down temporarily, resulting in huge losses.[13] In 2015 an al-Qaeda-linked group attacked a luxury hotel in Bamako, Mali, killing nineteen persons, including three visiting Chinese executives.[14] The same year, the al-Shabaab terrorist organization in Somalia detonated a bomb in Mogadishu outside one of the city's major hotels, killing a Chinese Embassy security officer and injuring three other Chinese staff members.[15]

Between 2012 and 2022 Chinese nationals in Nigeria experienced a new round of kidnappings, this time in the central part of the country. In one case, four died and the others were released after a ransom payment.[16] In 2018 three Chinese furniture factory workers in northern Nigeria were killed, probably by Boko Haram. This incident resulted in China pledging to provide Nigeria with funding for training and equipment to fight against Boko Haram.[17] Kidnappings of Chinese working with mining, road construction, and glass companies resumed in southern Nigeria in 2019 and have continued since. In 2021 several ransom-motivated kidnappings of Chinese nationals occurred in southwestern Nigeria.[18]

In 2018 local villagers in the Central African Republic killed three Chinese gold miners and injured three others after their boat capsized, drowning a prominent local guide. The villagers blamed the Chinese for his death.[19] Following anti-China statements by a Zambian opposition leader in 2018, there was looting of Chinese shops. Beijing complained to the government of Zambia, which responded that it would take measures to safeguard the Chinese community.[20] In 2020 an armed attack in the northeastern DRC killed three Chinese miners. The Chinese Embassy called on the Congolese government to take effective measures to protect Chinese nationals and repeatedly advised Chinese citizens against travel to this region.[21] A year later, however, the embassy reported the kidnapping of another five miners in the eastern DRC.[22]

Since 2019 the Somalia-based al-Shabaab terrorist group has on two occasions attacked Chinese road construction sites in neighboring Kenya, destroying Chinese equipment but causing no casualties. In 2022 an al-Shabaab attack on the Chinese camp resulted in the injury of a Chinese national.[23] In 2021 rebels in Ethiopia's Benishangul Gumuz region killed a Chinese national during an attack on Ethiopian security forces.[24]

Although the media have focused on the more dramatic attacks against Chinese nationals in Africa, a more frequent problem has been robberies that sometimes result in death, which local or Chinese papers rarely report. In South Africa alone, eleven Chinese died during robberies in 2013, and twelve were killed in the first nine months of 2014. In 2020 criminals brutally murdered a prominent Chinese couple in broad daylight in Johannesburg. This followed the killing by robbers of their two-year-old son twenty-two years earlier in South Africa.[25] African criminal gangs target Chinese traders because they tend to do business in cash. The Chinese community in Kenya experiences numerous vehicle robberies by armed criminals. Robberies, some resulting in murder, have targeted Chinese residents working for companies in the eastern DRC and Liberia.[26] Chinese industrial parks are also vulnerable because they concentrate wealth and foreign employees and are easy targets for protests. Some Ethiopian employees of Chinese companies even joined the protests at one China-sponsored industrial park.[27]

In 2019 and 2020 we worked with the Nairobi-based China House to conduct surveys of the Chinese communities in twelve countries (Zimbabwe, South Africa, Angola, Nigeria, Cameroon, DRC, Ethiopia, Tanzania, Sudan, Kenya, Algeria, and Egypt) to determine their security concerns. The 794 responses yielded surprisingly consistent results, along with a few surprises. Without exception, robbery and theft, either collectively or individually, led the list of concerns. In Nigeria, Tanzania, Cameroon, Egypt, Algeria, and the DRC, fear of disease came in second. Concerns about kidnapping, extortion, personal assault, and exposure to civil conflict or a breakdown of law and order ranked high in almost every country. Most communities cited terrorism as a concern, but it ranked low in all countries except Kenya and Egypt. In at least one of the twelve countries the survey identified minor concerns, including extortion by local police, traffic accidents, industrial accidents, fraud, corruption, Chinese gangs, piracy, sexual harassment, and human trafficking.[28]

In many of Africa's fifty-four countries, the security environment and economic situation are constantly changing, which affects the degree to which Chinese nationals living in or visiting the continent face security threats. A country such as Botswana that is politically stable, is doing well economically, and has a low unemployment rate poses a much lower risk for the Chinese community than a country like South Africa, with its high unemployment rate, or the DRC, which is politically unstable. Highly authoritarian African governments such as Algeria may be more willing to crack down on local nationals who threaten or attack the Chinese community. Although it is difficult to generalize about the security situation facing Chinese nationals across Africa, we find that larger and wealthier Chinese communities tend to face more threats and attacks.

THREATS TO CHINESE NATIONALS AND INTERESTS

Amid growing security threats to Chinese nationals and interests in Africa, China has turned its attention to mitigating the challenge. Historically, China's policy has been (and theoretically continues to be) that African governments have the responsibility to protect Chinese nationals and interests in their respective countries.[29] As a result, China initially assumed that local security forces could protect Chinese personnel and investments.[30] It has concluded, however, that host government protection is often lacking due to security lapses, disinterest, or insufficient resources and determined that additional measures were needed.[31] China was initially slow to fill the void left by inadequate African security. Over time, however, Chinese citizens used social media to push the government to do more to protect them outside China, including in Africa.[32]

A turning point took place in 2011, when China evacuated almost thirty-six thousand nationals from Libya following the collapse of the government in Tripoli. The following year the kidnapping in Sudan of twenty-nine Chinese road construction workers drew outrage in China.[33] In response, President Hu Jintao identified the protection of nationals overseas as one of three new diplomatic priorities in his report to the Eighteenth Party Congress.[34] Then, in 2013, Premier Wen Jiabao declared protecting China's overseas interests to be one of the top priorities of the country's leadership.[35] Thereafter, Beijing began a major review of its policies and institutions with the goal of more effectively protecting its interests globally.[36] These priorities have subsequently become part of Chinese pop culture. One of China's highest-grossing movies of all time, *Wolf Warrior II* (2017), is a nationalistic action film in which an exiled elite Chinese soldier works in a fictional African country where a rebel army, backed by Western mercenaries, attempts to seize power. The hero defeats the mercenaries and leads African and Chinese civilians to safety in front of the Chinese Embassy. The film ends with the image of a Chinese passport and the words, "Don't give up if you run into danger abroad. Please remember, a strong motherland will always have your back!"[37]

China's authorities are taking steps to improve protection. They are urging nationals and companies to exercise more caution when deciding how and where to engage in Africa. While the government's decision-making process on political and security risk assessment remains opaque, it has become a more frequent topic of discussion, especially following the creation of the Belt and Road Initiative (BRI).[38] The state-owned CNPC, for example, invested in oil fields in high-risk locations, including Sudan and South Sudan. Political instability in both countries helped convince CNPC to alter its strategy by diversifying its international projects away from high-risk areas. CNPC did not abandon conflict-affected regions, rather it sought to balance the risk by investing more in stable countries.[39]

Nevertheless, China is still struggling to find the best way to protect its interests in Africa. Chinese social media users have called for a strong military that can deter overseas aggression.[40] CNPC suggested that the PLA follow Chinese companies abroad and respond directly to the kidnapping of Chinese workers.[41] Chinese leaders, however, remain reluctant to make this kind of military commitment.[42] Instead, China is working to improve the security and military capabilities of African countries in the belief that this will enhance its own security.[43] In 2012 China's noncombat troops assigned to the UN peacekeeping operation in Darfur asked to join the search for twenty-nine kidnapped Chinese road construction employees, but the UN commander did not allow them to leave their posts.[44] China's assignment of combat troops to UN peacekeeping operations in Mali and South Sudan positioned personnel in regions where they could theoretically protect Chinese civilians. In 2013 China assigned Chinese combat troops to the UN peacekeeping operation in northern Mali; the mission supported stability in both Mali and neighboring Algeria, where ninety thousand Chinese citizens then lived and worked.[45] In the case of South Sudan, China convinced the UN to include authorization for peacekeepers to deter violence against "foreign civilians" [read Chinese] in areas of high risk, including "oil installations" in the peacekeeping mandate.[46]

There is a growing realization that Chinese companies, at least the larger ones, must rely more heavily on their own resources for security.[47] Consequently, the government, Chinese companies, and individuals have been pursuing diverse ways to improve security. For example, in 2018 China held a four-week training seminar for Kenyan police officers charged with providing security for the Chinese-financed, built, and managed railway between Mombasa and Nairobi.[48] In 2021 China offered to send criminal investigation experts to Nigeria to help address the country's security problems.[49] Large Chinese companies like CNPC are trying to improve their relations with local government and security officials, community leaders, opposition political groups, and religious leaders to enhance protection for their employees.[50] Some Chinese companies are also employing more Africans in order to reduce the security exposure of Chinese nationals.[51]

Chinese communities in places like South Africa, which has the largest indigenous Chinese community in Africa, are taking matters into their own hands. Pervasive crime in South Africa resulted in the deaths of approximately twenty Chinese each year between 2004 and 2014. This led to the establishment of Chinese Community and Police Cooperation Centers to serve as a bridge between the South African police, the Chinese community, and the Chinese Embassy in the country. There are fourteen such nonprofit centers established with the help of the government of China. They have no law enforcement authority but serve as a place to report and investigate crimes, teach basic Mandarin to South African police, and teach English to members of the Chinese community.[52] The China House survey of 113 members of the Chinese community in South Africa in 2019 determined that 80 percent of respondents were concerned about their security, and most believed they had to take control of their own safety because they could not depend on South African police. About 20 percent of the respondents were Chinese students who were less concerned about security issues because they were affiliated with a school or university that looked after them.⁵³ In neighboring Angola, Chinese companies hired local military veterans to patrol parts of Luanda frequented by Chinese nationals.⁵⁴

In 2018 Chinese companies in Uganda threatened to leave the country unless security improved and robberies targeting the Chinese community declined. President Yoweri Museveni met with 120 members of the community and announced Uganda would increase military patrols around the Chinese industrial parks, install CCTV cameras, and establish a new civilian militia known as Local Defense Units.⁵⁵ In especially dangerous mining areas of the DRC, where large numbers of Chinese are working, the local military and police carry weapons to protect mining operations. A Chinese financial manager for Chinese mining companies in the DRC insisted, however, that good relations with local employees offer the best security.⁵⁶

China's Ministry of Foreign Affairs is taking steps to improve embassy outreach to Chinese communities in Africa and to coordinate more effectively in Beijing when there are threats or attacks. To this end, the Ministry of Foreign Affairs and Ministry of Commerce established an emergency response mechanism to deal with attacks on Chinese nationals in foreign countries. China used this mechanism, for example, during an attack on a Sinopec oil production project in Ethiopia, the evacuation of Chinese from Libya, and crimes against Chinese nationals in South Africa.⁵⁷ Chinese embassies are working to improve consular services, the issuance of travel warnings, and registration of their nationals living overseas. The Ministry of Commerce has issued guidelines to companies for providing improved security protection. China's Ministry of Public Security, which traditionally operated only internally, now has a modest network of attachés, placed in Chinese embassies, who are responsible for protecting Chinese nationals against crimes committed by other Chinese.⁵⁸ China is also strengthening its ability to take legal action against Chinese criminals overseas; as of 2022 it had signed extradition treaties with Algeria, Tunisia, Morocco, South Africa, Namibia, Angola, Lesotho, and Ethiopia.⁵⁹

China has experienced a considerable number of kidnappings of its nationals in Africa and has often paid ransoms to secure their release. In

2009 Somali pirates said they released a Chinese coal ship owned by a subsidiary of China Ocean Shipping and its Chinese crew after a helicopter dropped a $4 million ransom payment on the ship's deck.[60] Quoting a senior Chinese diplomat, Jonas Parello-Plesner and Mathieu Duchâtel wrote, "There is not complete ban on ransoms, we judge on a case-by-case basis. We see ransoms as last resort. We do not want to encourage rebels." Instead of a financial payment, the Chinese diplomat said China proposes development and infrastructure packages in bargaining for the release of hostages, as apparently happened with the kidnapped Chinese road construction workers in Sudan in 2012. Parello-Plesner and Duchâtel concluded that state-owned enterprises are more likely to pay a monetary ransom than government agencies.[61]

Chinese communities in Africa differ widely in their views about whether China's embassies and the host African governments are helpful in mitigating security concerns. In the 2019 China House survey, 60 percent of respondents in Kenya said the Chinese Embassy was helpful, holding regular informational workshops, participating actively with the Chinese Chamber of Commerce and Chinese companies, and providing early warnings of potential threats. By contrast, nearly 70 percent of those surveyed said the Kenyan government was not helpful and complained that local police and government officials were primarily responsible for extorting them.[62] The Chinese Embassy in Angola also received praise for meeting regularly with the local Chinese community and raising their security concerns with the Angola's Ministry of Interior.[63]

The 2019 survey we developed with China House revealed negative reactions in several other countries. In Ethiopia, for example, only 21 percent of respondents said the Chinese Embassy was responsive to their security concerns, while 38 percent said it was not. The others polled expressed a neutral view. The Ethiopian government fared less well in terms of public opinion, with 14 percent reporting a helpful response, 36 percent unhelpful, and 50 percent neutral.[64] In Nigeria, just 22 percent had a positive view of the assistance rendered by the Chinese Embassy and Consulate on security, while 69 percent held a negative one. The Chinese community's views on help from the Nigerian government were 89 percent negative and only 2 percent positive.[65] In Sudan, which had one of the smallest numbers of respondents (seventeen) in the twelve-country survey, 43 percent said the Chinese Embassy was helpful, and only 21 percent thought it was not; 67 percent reported the government of Sudan was not helpful, and no respondent had a positive reponse.[66]

PRIVATE SECURITY COMPANIES

The most common technique, other than precautionary measures, used by Chinese companies, communities, and individuals to improve security is the hiring of a private security company (PSC). The overwhelming majority of Chinese companies in Africa employ the services of such a firm.[67] Local and international, mostly European, companies have existed in Africa for decades, mainly to prevent theft at homes and places of business. As the variety of security threats has expanded over the years, clients have increasingly called on PSCs to prevent armed attacks by dissident groups, terrorists, robbers, and pirates and to obtain the release of hostages. Only about twenty of China's five thousand PSCs are operating overseas, yet their personnel are ill-equipped to deal with armed threats because China does not allow them to carry guns except in rare circumstances. There are exceptions; for instance, the Chinese shipping company COSCO received permission to use armed Hua Xin Zhong An Group security teams on Chinese-flagged vessels to ward off Somali pirates. Many African countries also do not permit PSCs to carry arms. Others, such as South Africa, allow local security personnel to do so but do not extend the privilege to foreigners.[68]

Chinese PSCs are expanding in Africa.[69] According to Chinese law they must be either wholly owned or majority-owned state enterprises; that is, at least 51 percent of their registered capital must be government-owned.[70] Because they lack authorization to carry guns, however, these firms tend to serve in managerial and advisory roles and collaborate with host government security personnel, local PSCs, and other international PSCs that are sometimes permitted to carry weapons. Many of the Chinese employees are veterans of the PLA or the People's Armed Police (PAP).[71] Yet China wants to avoid a PSC model like Russia's mercenary Wagner Group or the American Blackwater security firm, which private investors purchased and renamed. Chinese PSCs operate with Beijing's tacit support and encouragement and have links to the CPC because so many employees are PLA veterans. The advantages of Chinese PSCs are their ability to communicate effectively with Chinese nationals, to understand Chinese culture, to keep secrets, and to minimize costs. On the other hand, Chinese personnel often do not have fluency in languages common to Africa, tend to have little understanding of African culture, and have minimal combat experience. Chinese PSC procedures and tactics for providing security vary enormously from company to company, and from country to country.[72]

Several Chinese PSCs are active in Africa. Beijing DeWe Security Services, founded in 2011 by former employees of the Ministry of Public Security, is one of the most engaged on the continent. It focuses on advising, training, and overseeing site security management. CNPC hired DeWe to provide security for its oil operations in Sudan and South Sudan. The head of DeWe's Juba office and a PLA veteran explained that CNPC called on the company in 2016 to extricate 330 Chinese nationals stranded in Juba during factional fighting. Because DeWe's Chinese staff does not carry weapons, it led teams of armed South Sudanese in those missions. Another Chinese firm, Poly-GCL Petroleum Group Holdings, hired DeWe to manage security at its $4 billion LNG project in the Ogaden region of Ethiopia. China Road and Bridge Corporation employed DeWe to provide security during construction of the Mombasa to Nairobi railway in Kenya. As part of this effort, DeWe created a public safety commission in collaboration with Kenyan armed police and local security guards that may serve as a model for Chinese security efforts elsewhere. DeWe has also expanded its business into Cameroon, Chad, the DRC, Djibouti, Gabon, and Nigeria.[73]

One of the most intriguing PSCs is Frontier Services Group (FSG), founded in 2014 in Hong Kong by former U.S. Navy SEAL Eric Prince of Blackwater fame. The powerful state-owned China International Trust and

Investment Corporation (CITIC) subsequently purchased a 26 percent stake in FSG, exceeding Prince's 9 percent share. This forced Prince to step down as chairperson, but he remains one of the firm's three deputy chairpersons. One of the others is Luo Ning, a CITIC executive and graduate of the PLA Institute of Communication Command. Chang Zhenming, chairperson of CITIC, is head of the FSG board. FSG, which now has headquarters in both Hong Kong and Beijing, focuses on logistics, security, training, investments, and intelligence. It has built training centers in Yunnan and Xinjiang, which raises questions about its possible role in the repression of ethnic Uighurs. FSG is active in Africa, with offices in Kenya and South Africa. It has provided security in a Somali free zone, run air ambulances out of Kenya following terrorist attacks, repatriated the bodies of three Chinese executives killed in a hotel bombing in Mali, and invested in companies ranging from a bauxite mine in Guinea to a copper mine in the DRC. It also operates a logistic unit in South Africa. FSG employees should have at least five years of military experience or more than three years of experience in law enforcement. FSG trains candidates at Beijing's International Security Defense College, in which FSG has a 25 percent stake. Although FSG is different from Blackwater, Prince's role has resulted in vigorous debate in China regarding his Blackwater background and whether it influences the FSG model.[74]

The China Overseas Security Group (COSG), incorporated in Hong Kong in 2015 with its headquarters in Beijing, has assigned responsibility for its overseas work to Zhongjie Security Group Co. It has offices in Mozambique and South Africa and has provided security consulting and risk assessment services for Chinese companies in Nigeria and Kenya. In recent years COSG has also conducted field visits in Zambia, Djibouti, Ethiopia, and Somalia with the goal of opening branches in those countries.[75] Veterans Security Services Security Group, whose overseas clients are primarily state-owned companies such as PetroChina, is an especially opaque organization that has operated in both Sudan and South Sudan.[76] The Beijing-based Ding Tai An Yuan Security Technology Research Institute recruits from former special forces soldiers. It has been doing business in Nigeria for about fifteen years.[77]

PROTECTING INTERESTS AND MANAGING CONFLICT

China Security Technology Group (CSTG), incorporated in Hong Kong in 2016, has branches or subsidiaries in Kenya, Algeria, Mozambique, Nigeria, Ethiopia, and Angola to protect Chinese enterprises. In 2018 CSTG signed an MOU with Infinity Security, one of the largest security companies in Nigeria.[78] The following year it signed an agreement with another Nigerian security company, Perceival Security and Safety Agencies.[79] In Nigeria, CSTG has established a team composed primarily of retired military officers with experience in peacekeeping operations. The company works closely with the Chinese Embassy.[80]

In 2004 PLA veterans established Hua Xin Zhong An, a Beijing-based company specializing in maritime security. Many of its employees are ex-marine or navy officers with antipiracy experience in the Gulf of Aden. Core services include armed maritime security, executive protection, static site security, security training, risk assessment, and security technology integration.[81] Another company that specializes in maritime security is Hanwei International Security Services Co., which was registered in China in 2014. Its personnel come from China's special forces and have participated in Gulf of Aden escorts and the evacuation of Chinese nationals from Libya. It operates through subsidiaries in Nigeria and South Africa.[82] Hua-Yanan (Beijing) Security Services Co. has conducted escort missions for Chinese merchant ships in the Indian Ocean. It draws on retired cadets from the Marine Corps, Army Special Forces and Reconnaissance Units, and PAP, most of whom are CPC members.[83] The "Sea Guard" of the Zhongjun Hong Security Group hires veterans of the PAP and special operations forces. The company escorts ships in the Gulf of Guinea and Indian Ocean.[84]

Chinese companies also join with international and African security companies. China Overseas Security Services (COSS) is a Sino-British joint venture providing integrated security risk management services for companies operating in high-risk environments. At the height of the Somali piracy crisis, it designed security solutions for ships in the Gulf of Aden that did not require armed personnel. In 2011 a multinational news organization hired COSS to transport one of its journalists during the civil war in Libya. In 2013 COSS managed security for a construction firm building a European embassy in Mogadishu, Somalia.[85]

In 2014 China's Shandong Huawei Security Group and South Africa's Raid Private Security created a joint venture called HW Raid Security to provide security services for Chinese businesses and the Chinese community in South Africa. Raid Private Security had the necessary security skills and resources but lacked Chinese cultural understanding and language skills. The two sides agreed to provide each other cross-language and cultural training, services that the African firm hopes to expand to Chinese companies operating outside South Africa.[86] CNPC uses a different security model in Niger where the country's military is responsible for security in the CNPC's oil fields and outside its oil refinery at Zinder. Inside the refinery, meanwhile, a Chinese team assisted by South African private security guards is responsible for security.[87]

These efforts to protect Chinese interests and nationals in Africa have caused some problems for China. In 2017 Zambia commissioned eight Chinese nationals as part-time reservists wearing Zambian uniforms to support local police officers and serve as liaisons to the country's Chinese community. This unusual arrangement prompted widespread Zambian anger, however, and authorities ended it hours after its unveiling.[88] Then, in 2018, two Chinese security employees opened fire on thieves in Zimbabwe, accidentally injuring an innocent bystander, the son of a member of parliament. After the arrest of the two Chinese, it was learned authorities had asked them to leave Zimbabwe a year earlier, following another shooting incident. Both cases resulted in negative publicity and raised questions concerning authorization of the Chinese to carry guns.[89] These are the kinds of problems that Beijing wants its PSCs to avoid.[90]

EMERGENCY EVACUATION OF CHINESE NATIONALS

Once the security situation in a country deteriorates to the extent that Chinese nationals are endangered, Beijing has helped or even taken full responsibility for their safety and, when necessary, their evacuation. As

Peter Connolly, director of the Australian Army Research Centre, explains, evacuations are China's "response of a rising power needing to protect its people and interests overseas as its influence expands. It could also be interpreted as a justification for the projection of power to underwrite China's growing stake in world affairs."[91] Some evacuations require substantial resources, military and civilian, while Chinese companies conduct others with little if any governmental support.

China's first evacuation in Africa took place in 1991 during a civil war in Somalia, when the PLAN did not have the ability to remove Chinese Embassy personnel from Mogadishu on short notice. Consequently, China diverted a cargo ship, the *MV Yongmen*, and hired tugboats and a fishing vessel to evacuate 143 Chinese nationals to Mombasa, Kenya.[92] In 1998 Beijing facilitated the evacuation of Chinese business people and part of its embassy staff from Eritrea following conflict between that country and neighboring Ethiopia.[93] In 2008 heavy fighting broke out near Chad's capital, N'Djamena, between government troops and a rebel force, and China's Ministry of Foreign Affairs initiated an emergency response mechanism to organize the evacuation of Chinese nationals. The Chinese Embassy in N'Djamena then evacuated 212 persons to neighboring Cameroon. In addition to embassy staff, the evacuees included employees of PetroChina, CGC Overseas Construction, ZTE, and Huawei.[94]

The Arab Spring in February 2011 presented huge challenges for the Chinese communities and embassies in Egypt and especially Libya. Violent protests in Egypt caused the Chinese government to organize eight charter commercial flights to repatriate 1,848 Chinese nationals, including some from Hong Kong, Macao, and Taiwan. To underscore the importance that China attached to the evacuation, the CPC Central Committee member and state councilor Dai Bingguo coordinated the operation.[95]

The evacuation from Libya was China's largest, and the first to make use of the PLAN and the PLA Air Force. Prior to the evacuation, the Chinese Embassy in Tripoli had registered about six thousand Chinese workers in the country and was consequently surprised to learn there were seventy-five Chinese companies implementing fifty projects valued at $20 billion and about thirty-six thousand Chinese employees present in Libya.

When antigovernment protests led to looting of Chinese enterprises and dozens of serious injuries, Beijing created an emergency headquarters led by Vice Premier Zhang Dejiang, a Politburo member, to organize the evacuation. In a whole of government effort, China evacuated 35,860 nationals over twelve days using seventy-four civilian aircraft, fourteen commercial ships, and about one hundred buses that picked up evacuees from Libya's border with Egypt. Commercial aircraft transported Chinese nationals evacuated by land and sea from nearby countries back to China. The PLA Air Force sent four Il-76 transport aircraft to Libya, which took 1,655 people to Khartoum, Sudan. From there, most returned to China by commercial flights. The PLAN diverted a frigate from its antipiracy escort mission in the Gulf of Aden. Although symbolic, the navy's engagement demonstrated China's commitment to protecting its nationals living and working overseas. Beijing covered the entire $152 million cost of the operation.[96]

As the security situation improved in Libya, some Chinese returned to the country, only to encounter more political turmoil in 2014, necessitating evacuation anew. About a thousand Chinese left between May and August 2014, while another eleven hundred remained in the country. China called on this remaining group to depart, and the Chinese Embassy organized outbound transport, including chartered buses that took evacuees from Tripoli to neighboring Tunisia. The PLA did not participate in this evacuation.[97]

At the end of 2012 China launched its emergency response mechanism when the security situation deteriorated in the Central African Republic. The Chinese Embassy in Bangui coordinated the evacuation of an unspecified number of its nationals to neighboring Cameroon, from where chartered planes took them back to China.[98] In 2018, after a mob killed three Chinese nationals in southwestern Central African Republic, local government security forces escorted sixty-three Chinese nationals to safety in Cameroon.[99]

South Sudan, because of the substantial number of oil company employees in the country and the civil war that has continued sporadically since 2013, has been a challenge for China. At the end of 2013 CNPC arranged for an evacuation of more than 300 personnel from northern oil fields to

South Sudan's capital of Juba and then to Nairobi, Kenya.[100] Subsequently, in 2015, CNPC evacuated another 400 workers, flying them back to China.[101] In 2016 factional fighting broke out in Juba, resulting in the evacuation of 331 employees of China's state-owned companies by chartered flight to Nairobi.[102] Several days later, seventeen Chinese embassy staff, twelve members of a medical team, and twenty more company employees boarded a charter flight for Uganda.[103] As security in the north of the country also became problematic, CNPC evacuated 191 of its employees and another 157 persons working with other Chinese organizations.[104]

In 2014 the outbreak of Ebola in West Africa caused huge losses for Chinese companies and led to evacuations. China Energy Group's iron ore project in Sierra Leone, Chongqing Foreign Construction Group's highway project in Liberia, and China Harbor Engineering Company's iron ore project in Guinea all terminated operations and evacuated their respective employees.[105] Before the outbreak, an estimated twenty thousand Chinese nationals resided in the affected region. Within three months, that number had dropped by half. Chinese embassies assisted the evacuation, but it was the companies themselves that took primary responsibility.[106]

The most extensive evacuation involving the PLAN occurred in 2015 from Yemen, across the Red Sea from Africa, as the security situation there deteriorated. The operation included all three vessels attached to China's Gulf of Aden antipiracy effort and the use of its military base in Djibouti to support the evacuation. The PLA had primary responsibility for the evacuation. In all, the PLAN transported 621 Chinese nationals and 279 foreign citizens from fifteen countries.[107] One frigate picked up evacuees at Aden, and a second rescued an even larger group from al-Hudaydah on the Red Sea and moved them to Djibouti. From there, the Chinese nationals went to Addis Ababa and then returned to China by commercial aircraft.[108] In 2018 the PLAN assisted the filmmakers of *Operation Red Sea*, a highly popular nationalistic film that depicted an action-packed fictional account of what was, in fact, a violence-free evacuation from Yemen. Chinese naval expert Li Jie commented that such films seek to "generate pride in the nation."[109] The Ministry of Foreign Affairs pointed out that the operation also evacuated non-Chinese nationals.[110]

China's most recent evacuation in Africa occurred in northern Ethiopia when civil war broke out in 2020 between central government forces and regional Tigrayan forces. The Chinese Embassy in Addis Ababa helped state-owned companies in Tigray Region evacuate about six hundred nationals by road to the capital.[111]

One of the lessons from these evacuations, especially the Libyan operation in 2011, is that sending personnel overseas creates a responsibility to protect them. In 2012 the Ministry of Commerce began requiring state-owned companies to make a "risk deposit" of at least $482,000 in a Chinese bank to cover expenses for emergency evacuations and repatriation. The Libyan experience also underscored the importance of interagency coordination and led China to create an ad hoc task force on evacuations headed at the level of the CPC Politburo.[112] The Libyan crisis uncovered shortcomings in providing early warning information and revealed that the Chinese Embassy in Tripoli did not know how many Chinese passport holders were in the country. On the other hand, the evacuation demonstrated Beijing's ability to respond to emergencies far from its borders, and the PLAN's flexibility in African waters, while underscoring the need for more port access, increased funding for long-range military capabilities, and resources and training for operating in a nonpermissive environment.[113] Even though evacuations of Chinese nationals have become more frequent, China has yet to conduct an operation from a zone controlled by hostile nonstate forces.[114]

PREVENTING, MANAGING, AND MEDIATING CONFLICT

When it comes to conflict prevention and management, China's approach emphasizes national unity and territorial integrity, prioritizes negotiations to resolve problems peacefully and opposes the use of outside pressure to settle disputes. To protect its expanding interests in Africa, China has become more willing to engage in conflict resolution, mediation, and postconflict reconstruction.[115] This increasing engagement, however, often looks different from the more robust efforts of Western countries. China puts a premium on UN efforts to prevent conflict and often seeks UN approval when it decides to play such a role. Beijing's focus on development and ending poverty is also reflected in its approach to conflict management.[116] While China professes an interest in conflict prevention, it has not yet prioritized the concept in Africa and has had little experience in developing early warning systems for potential crises and conflicts.[117]

Here, the meaning behind the terminology is important. China's definition of mediation—"an effort by a third party to encourage parties to a dispute to voluntarily reach an agreement to resolve their dispute"[118]—sounds similar to one used by the U.S. Department of Justice, which stresses "an informal voluntary process that is unbinding unless agreement is reached by both parties."[119] But China's history of nonintervention and its emphasis on the preservation of sovereignty have strongly influenced the way it engages in conflict management and mediates disputes.[120] With very few exceptions, Chinese mediators in Africa have been exceedingly reluctant to use political and economic leverage even when they have it. And when China's attempts to end a conflict have failed, Beijing has been happy to let others take responsibility.

Wu Xiaohui and Cheng Qian of Harvard University have researched China's approach to mediation. They argue that China's diplomatic mediation is part of the nation's pursuit of harmony, which reflects a fundamental assumption that people, being ess good in nature, can live together peacefully. This belief led to former president Hu Jintao's "Harmonious World" concept, which seeks to achieve stability and face-saving reconciliation through mutual compromise. Unlike Western mediation, which Wu and Cheng contend emphasizes a search for truth, the Chinese approach is more concerned with creating and sustaining harmony, even if only at a superficial level. Chinese mediators are flexible; there is no right or wrong, only workable and unworkable solutions. China selects mediators based on their authority, seniority, and whether they enjoy good relations with the disputants; their professional background is less important.[121]

China's engagement in Sudan's Darfur region was the most energetic example of its mediation in Africa, one that some have argued constituted interference in Sudan's internal affairs. This was the result of a confluence of factors: harsh Western criticism of ethnic cleansing in Darfur by Sudan's government in the period before the Beijing Olympics of 2008, China's extensive oil interests in Sudan, and its initial acceptance of Khartoum's policy in Darfur.[122] China feared that some Western countries might boycott the Olympics and decided to use its leverage to convince Sudan to accept a joint African Union–UN peacekeeping force, which Sudan opposed. When Sudanese president Omar al-Bashir visited Beijing in 2006, Hu Jintao publicly urged him to "strengthen dialogue" with all concerned parties. In 2007, during a visit to Khartoum, Hu leaned hard on al-Bashir to accept the peacekeeping force, a request to which al-Bashir acquiesced. China argued that it had used its constructive, positive influence to convince Sudan to accept the peacekeeping force and appointed Liu Giujin, a former ambassador to South Africa, as its special envoy to Africa to oversee China's efforts to end the conflict in Darfur. Liu returned to encouraging political dialogue and opposed sanctions and pressure against Sudan.[123]

Once the Olympics were over, Liu focused on the upcoming independence in 2011 of South Sudan from Sudan. About 75 percent of Sudan's oil fields in which China had a 40 percent interest were situated in South Sudan. Only 25 percent remained in Sudan, although all the infrastructure for exporting oil, most of which went to China, was in Sudan. With the looming conflict between Sudan and South Sudan and the likely disruption of oil production, Liu shuttled between Khartoum and Juba to encourage dialogue and the continuing flow of oil.[124] Serious differences between Sudan and South Sudan regarding the use of the former's oil pipeline infrastructure contributed to conflict along their new border. The international community, including China, was unable to resolve the differences, and South Sudan's oil exports dropped significantly, at one point stopping entirely.

In 2019 the collapse of the al-Bashir government in Khartoum following widespread street protests provided another opportunity for China to mediate, this time between the military and the civilian protesters. China chose not to get involved, however, because of its close relations with al-Bashir and the military, its lack of experience in resolving internal conflicts, and Sudan's diminishing importance as an oil producer. An American diplomat in Khartoum said China was not an active player in solving the crisis and seemed focused on getting oil flowing again.[125] A State Department official similarly noted that China was following a "wait and see" policy and was mostly interested in oil.[126] Nor did China demonstrate much interest in the African Union's effort to mediate the conflict between Sudan's military and assorted protest groups, possibly because neighboring Egypt and Ethiopia had different approaches to Sudan's political transition, and China wanted to maintain good relations with both countries.[127]

In the meantime, in late 2013 civil war erupted in South Sudan based on a conflict between the president and vice president and their respective ethnic groups. China's ambassador to Ethiopia quickly convened a clandestine meeting in Addis Ababa with representatives of the rebel forces. This may have been an effort to obtain information on developments in South Sudan, rather than an attempt at mediation.[128] Foreign Minister Wang Yi said, however, that he was willing to mediate between the warring sides.[129] Then, early in 2014, Wang met with representatives of both factions in Addis Ababa and later in the year met in Beijing with the Foreign Affairs Committee of the opposition faction.[130] At the beginning of 2015, Wang visited Juba and again urged reconciliation between the warring groups.[131] The breakaway faction did not see China as a legitimate peace broker because it continued to arm South Sudan's military, its opponent in this dispute. The rebels said China was only trying to protect its oil interests.[132]

Probably realizing its tenuous position vis-à-vis the rebels, China stepped back into a supporting role. Zhong Jianhua, China's new special envoy for Africa and lead mediator on South Sudan, commented in late 2015 that China fully supported the efforts of the Intergovernmental Authority on Development to make peace in South Sudan.[133] A host of officials subsequently emphasized China's reluctance to mediate the conflict in South Sudan. A senior UN official involved with the issue commented that China had no desire to use its leverage there.[134] A senior Sudanese official said China was not playing a role in the South Sudan peace process.[135] In 2021 China's permanent representative to the United Nations, Zhang Jun, urged all armed factions to join the 2018 peace agreement and called on the international community to lift sanctions on South Sudan.[136]

Hend Elmahly Mahhoud Sultan of the Shanghai International Studies University and Degang Sun of Fudan University concluded that China tried to bring Sudan and South Sudan to the negotiating table and reach a peaceful solution by using Beijing's economic influence, its role in the United Nations, and development and military aid. China's goal was to protect its interests in both countries and adhere to the basic principles of noninterference. They described this concept as "creative mediation diplomacy" and suggested China will pursue it elsewhere.[137]

In 2008 China's $9.25 billion deal for copper and cobalt with the DRC emboldened President Laurent Kabila to take stronger action against Rwandan-backed militia leader Laurent Nkunda, who accused China of offering contracts to the DRC that are detrimental to the Congolese people. With Chinese interests threatened, Liu Guijin went to Kinshasa and Kigali to engage in direct mediation between Rwanda and the DRC. He called on both sides to cooperate and insisted in Kigali that Nkunda stop his criticism of China. This intervention convinced the government of Rwanda to withdraw its support of Nkunda but did not end conflict in the eastern DRC.[138]

Chad and China restored diplomatic relations in 2006, followed a year later by an oil deal with CNPC. Chadian President Idriss Déby demanded in return that China pressure Sudan to stop supporting Chadian rebel groups operating from its territory. In 2008 Sudan-backed rebels tried to topple Déby. Liu Guijin insisted that China would not become involved in mediating a proxy conflict between Khartoum and N'Djamena, although he urged both parties to establish friendly relations. Unlike the situation in the DRC, China opted not to become involved, suggesting there are limits to its engagement even where access to oil or minerals is important, although it had greater economic interests in Sudan than it did in Chad.[139]

In 2011, following the visit to Beijing of Mahmoud Jibril, head of Libya's Executive Committee of the ruling National Transitional Council (NTC), China initiated limited intercession between the Muammar al-Qaddafi government and the NTC.[140] Although China was importing oil from Libya, it was unwilling to help resolve the Libyan conflict.[141] The advance of Islamic insurgent groups into Mali, where China's interests are minimal (although considerably greater in neighboring Algeria), is another case of Beijing remaining aloof from conflict resolution. Consequently, China's Foreign Ministry supported the efforts of the African Union, Economic Community of West African States, and regional countries to mediate the crisis (see chapter 3).[142] China has never offered to engage actively in the peace process in war-ravaged Somalia, where it has few interests, but has made modest financial contributions to the African Union to assist with mediation efforts there. It has also avoided any involvement in mediation of the Western Sahara dispute, which pits Morocco against Algeria. China has good relations with both countries and does not want to put itself in the position of alienating either.[143]

There are at least two occasions where China offered to mediate disputes in Africa, but nothing came of either initiative. In 2017 China's ambassador to the African Union said Beijing was ready to help with mediation of the Eritrea-Djibouti border dispute, if requested to do so.[144] The interest was understandable; China had just opened a military base in Djibouti and had reason to seek an end to the conflict. In 2018 China said it would consider mediating the long-standing border dispute between Ethiopia and Eritrea and was ready to work closely with both countries.[145] In that case, however, the United Arab Emirates and Saudi Arabia stepped in, rendering China's offer moot. An official in the African Union's Peace and Security Department opined that it is unclear if China wants to broker peace deals or just give the appearance of doing so.[146]

Beginning in 2020, China had an opportunity to mediate an end to the civil war between Ethiopia's central government and the regional authority in Tigray. In spite of substantial interests in Ethiopia, however, Beijing chose to sit on the sidelines.[147] In 2022 China named a special envoy for the Horn of Africa, Xue Bing, to assist the Ethiopian and regional peace processes.[148] Xue's first effort was a much-hyped regional peace conference in Addis Ababa where he said Beijing was willing to act as a mediator to resolve disputes. At the end of the conference, he stated that the discussions with African leaders "did not touch upon the mediation efforts and nobody raised this issue."[149] An informed Ethiopian commented that the peace conference had no substantive value because China lacks mediation experience and has little understanding of the complex issues facing countries in the region. He acknowledged China's important economic role but suggested the peace conference was simply Beijing's attempt to "be relevant" in regional political matters.[150]

On those occasions when China has played a meaningful, if limited, role in conflict management or mediation, it always involved access to oil or minerals and protecting its economic interests.[151] On the other hand, there are cases where China had resource interests but nonetheless chose not to engage. In situations where China's interests are minimal, it has avoided direct involvement but has often been willing to support rhetorically and financially the efforts of other parties. While the FOCAC action plans since the 2012 summit have expressed African appreciation for China's mediation, in practice Beijing has been more willing to talk peace than to participate substantively in achieving it.[152] Even in the case of Sudan, where China's role was most robust, Beijing was unwilling to use its arms sales as leverage to pressure Khartoum to resolve conflicts with South Sudan or in Darfur.[153]

UN PEACEKEEPING OPERATIONS

China's policy on UN peacekeeping has shifted dramatically since the 1970s, when it opposed the concept based on strong adherence to the principles of state sovereignty and nonintervention. In the 1980s and 1990s China gradually expanded reactive participation that took account of its own economic development-oriented reform and "opening up" strategy. The Tiananmen Square crackdown in 1989 resulted in concerns about the international reaction and precipitated a need to reach out globally to reinforce a positive image of China. Taking an active role in UN peacekeeping operations was one way to achieve this goal. In the twenty-first century, China has increasingly participated in UN peacekeeping to demonstrate that it is a responsible power, to strengthen the UN, and to share common concerns for peace and security. Beijing also realized that participation in peacekeeping helped to project an image of it as a nonthreatening power. He Yin of the China Peacekeeping Police Training Center argues that China's support for UN peacekeeping benefits both China's peaceful rise strategy and global security governance, to which Beijing now contributes its own ideas and doctrine.[154]

China's first engagement in UN peacekeeping in Africa occurred from 1989 to 1990, when it sent twenty personnel to help monitor elections in Namibia.[155] Its second commitment began in 1991 in the Western Sahara, where China continues to assign about a dozen military personnel to help monitor the cease-fire between Morocco and the POLISARIO Front. China has usually eschewed leadership positions in UN peacekeeping operations. Nevertheless, in 2007 PLA Major General Zhao Jingman became the first Chinese officer to head a UN peacekeeping operation when he took command of the Western Sahara mission. A second Chinese officer served as the Western Sahara force commander from 2016 to 2019. During the 1990s China assigned small numbers of personnel to UN operations in Mozambique, Liberia, and Sierra Leone. Early in the twenty-first century China ramped up its support for UN operations in Africa, sending large troop contingents to the DRC, Liberia, Sudan, South Sudan, and Mali and small numbers of experts and observers to Eritrea, Côte d'Ivoire, and Burundi (see tables 7.1 and 7.2).[156]

Chinese officials frequently point out that China assigns more personnel to UN peacekeeping missions in Africa than do all other permanent members of the UN Security Council combined. While this is true, France and the United States assign far more soldiers to African operations that are not UN peacekeeping missions. China provides a small percentage of all peacekeepers serving in Africa during any given year, and far fewer than countries such as India, Bangladesh, Ethiopia, and Rwanda. As of mid-2022 Chinese peacekeepers accounted for 6 percent of the force in South Sudan, 1 percent in the DRC, and 2 percent in Abyei, Mali, and the Western Sahara. Between 2010 and the end of 2020, China's total contribution of troops, police, experts, and staff to missions in Africa ranged from a low of 1,520 at the end of 2012 to a high of 2,620 at the end of 2015. In 2016 China began drawing down its large contribution to the UN mission in

TABLE 7.1 China's completed UN peacekeeping participation in Africa as of 2022

UN MISSION (ACRONYM)	DATES CHINA PARTICIPATED	CHINESE PERSONNEL
Namibia (UNTAG)	April 1989–March 1990	20 observers
Mozambique (ONUMOZ)	June 1993–December 1994	20 observers
Liberia (UNOMIL)	November 1993–September 1997	33 observers
Sierra Leone (UNOMSIL)	August 1998–October 1999	"Few" observers
Sierra Leone (UNAMSIL)	October 1999–December 2005	37 observers
Ethiopia/Eritrea (UNMEE)	October 2000–August 2008	49 observers
DR Congo (MONUC)	April 2001–June 2010	2,296 troops/observers
Liberia (UNMIL)	October 2003–December 2017	10,440 troops/staff
Côte d'Ivoire (UNOCI)	April 2004–February 2017	79 observers
Burundi (ONUB)	June 2004–September 2006	6 observers
Sudan (UNMIS)	April 2005–July 2011	3,615 troops/observers
Sierra Leone (UNIOSIL)	February 2007–February 2008	1 staff
Darfur, Sudan (UNAMID)	November 2007–June 2021	5,000 troops/staff
Central African Republic (MINUSCA)	January–December 2020	2 staff

Sources: United Nations, https://peacekeeping.un.org; China State Council, https://english.www.gov.cn/.

TABLE 7.2 China's ongoing participation in UN peacekeeping in Africa as of 2022

UN MISSION (ACRONYM)	START DATE	PERSONNEL ENGAGED
Western Sahara (MINURSO)	September 1991	11 experts
DRC (MONUSCO)	July 2010	233 troops/experts/staff
South Sudan (UNMISS)	July 2011	1,062 troops/police/experts
Mali (MINUSMA)	October 2013	421 troops/staff
Abyei Sudan border (UNISFA)	May 2021	87 troops/staff

Source: United Nations, https://peacekeeping.un.org.

Liberia, which ended in 2018. The buildup of Chinese troops in South Sudan partially offset the drawdown from Liberia. The UN terminated the mandate of the hybrid AU/UN mission in Darfur on December 31, 2020, and all troop-contributing countries, including China, removed their forces.[157]

Since 2015, on December 31 of each year, China averaged about 2,100 personnel in UN peacekeeping missions in Africa. China assigns more than half of its total force in Africa to the mission in South Sudan but also has deployments to missions in Mali and the DRC. It sends less than 100 troops to Abyei along the Sudan–South Sudan border and about a dozen experts to the Western Sahara. As of December 2022, China's peacekeeping personnel contribution in Africa consisted of 1,732 soldiers, 31 staff, and 20 experts.[158]

The composition of China's participation in UN peacekeeping operations in Africa has evolved significantly over the years. In the 1990s it consisted entirely of small deployments of observers. In 2003 China sent its first PLA troop contingent to the DRC, where it joined Chinese observers who had arrived two years earlier. Larger numbers of forces soon followed to Liberia, and then to Sudan. All the early PLA units were engineering, medical, and logistical in nature. In 2012 China dispatched its first combat unit, a PLA infantry platoon, to South Sudan to protect PLA engineers and medical personnel there. The move underscored that China had to protect its peacekeepers in dangerous situations.[159]

In 2013 China sent engineering and medical troops to Mali and included 170 personnel from the People's Armed Police (PAP) to protect the UN military camp at Gao.[160] In 2015 China sent a combat battalion of 700 troops to join 350 noncombat Chinese forces in the UN's Chapter VII South Sudan operation. China deployed these troops to protect noncombat personnel and civilians as well as other UN peacekeepers; their purpose was not to engage in combat against warring parties. The UN assigned the combat battalion to the capital of Juba, far from the oil fields where CNPC operates.[161] In 2017 China sent four Mi-171 helicopters and a 140-strong unit to Sudan to conduct aerial patrols and transport personnel and cargo in the Darfur region.[162]

PROTECTING INTERESTS AND MANAGING CONFLICT

The UN mission in Mali is China's most recent large-scale peacekeeping commitment in Africa. The conflict in Mali has strong overtones of terrorism, given the involvement of groups such as al-Qaeda in the Islamic Maghreb. China acknowledged the need for regional stability and concerns about terrorism. The Chinese media, for its part, reported China's participation as an effort to improve the country's image as a responsible big power. China's engagement in Mali represents a comprehensive security approach to peacekeeping in Africa and, because China has few interests in Mali, helps deflect accusations that China is a neocolonialist power in Africa. UN reports of China's performance have been positive, especially the medical services it has provided to the local population. Other reports have been more critical, noting that China's peacekeepers are risk averse and rarely venture beyond their base. Some reports have criticized Chinese peacekeepers for having little contact with the local population and relying on interpreters because few speak French or English. China's focus on development as the backbone of security has also experienced serious limitations in the country. Mali has been an important experiment for the PLA because its combat unit provided force protection for a regional UN camp in an environment of terrorist activity. This has not been without its risks, however: in 2016 a terrorist attack on the base resulted in the death of one Chinese peacekeeper and injury of four others.[163]

China's largest and best-equipped peacekeeping commitment is in South Sudan. The UN mandate for South Sudan allows Chinese troops to protect Chinese civilians and commercial assets. China has engineering and medical units in Wau in Western Bahr el Ghazal province, and two engineering units in Warrap province. The engineering and medical units collaborate to build and renovate hospitals and engage in a variety of humanitarian projects. The infantry battalion in Juba has armored personnel carriers, antitank rockets, and unmanned drones. In addition to its force protection responsibilities, it supports humanitarian activities, suggesting that all Chinese peacekeeping units receive such training. China imports about two-thirds of South Sudan's oil production and has invested heavily in its oil infrastructure. The deployment of PLA combat units exposes them to more dangerous operations. In 2016, for instance, an artillery shell hit a

Chinese armored vehicle, killing two Chinese peacekeepers and injuring four others.[164]

In 2015 Xi Jinping announced that China would establish a peacekeeping standby force of eight thousand troops for UN operations. The troops can be dispatched on short notice, are not dedicated to Africa, and are available for global deployment.[165] China selected the first three hundred members from the PAP, and fifty-six of them had previously served in peacekeeping missions in Haiti, South Sudan, and Liberia.[166] Two years later China announced it had designated eight thousand troops to "conduct task-specific and adaptive training" in accordance with UN training standards.[167] In 2018 it said the standby force was ready for deployment.[168] The following year, China's permanent representative to the UN commented that the eight thousand troops and two standby peacekeeping police contingents "can be put into operation at any time."[169] As of 2022, however, the standby force has yet to be deployed to Africa or anywhere else, and the number of China's peacekeepers serving in Africa has actually declined since Xi Jinping's announcement in 2015.

China's growing personnel contributions since the 1990s to UN peacekeeping operations have been matched by increasing financial commitments. China began paying peacekeeping dues in 1982.[170] Throughout the 1990s it contributed less than 1 percent to the UN peacekeeping budget; it increased its allocation to 1.5 percent in 2000 and to 3 percent in 2008.[171] By 2016 China's contribution reached more than 10 percent of the budget and jumped to more than 15 percent in 2019, the second largest commitment after the United States.[172]

China benefits by participating in UN peacekeeping operations. Protection of economic interests and access to natural resources are key factors in some of China's largest peacekeeping commitments in Africa but not all of them.[173] China made major personnel contributions to the UN operations in Liberia, DRC, Sudan, South Sudan, and Mali. It has extensive mineral interests in the DRC and has or once had large oil investments in Sudan and South Sudan, suggesting that China's decision to support those UN peacekeeping operations was not coincidental. On the other hand, China's economic interests in Liberia and Mali are minimal and do not explain its large peacekeeping commitment in those countries. China also seeks regional stability to protect its wider investments. Its implementation of large infrastructure projects in Algeria may have contributed to its decision to support the operation in neighboring Mali. Likewise, Chinese investments in West Africa were a factor in its large commitment in Liberia.[174] The huge economic losses that China experienced in Libya and Sudan underscored the utility of participating in peacekeeping operations to stabilize situations where it has large investments.[175]

Gaining military experience, testing equipment in harsh environments, interacting with foreign military forces, improving foreign language skills, and learning more about African countries and cultures directly benefit the PLA, even as the United Nations reimburses China for its participation. All these engagements occur far from China, permitting the PLA to gain distant operational experience, assess military doctrine, and better understand the methods of foreign military forces. The PLA learns about operational logistics, multinational operations, combat, and unusual medical, de-mining, and civil engineering challenges. Each peacekeeping operation presents a unique situation and new learning opportunities. The PLA adds to its knowledge of ports of debarkation, lines of communication, lines of operation, operational intelligence, local atmospherics, and modus operandi.[176]

China also envisages a longer-term benefit from participation in UN peacekeeping. It improves China's image, demonstrates a willingness to be a responsible major power, and promotes China's peaceful development. China is keen to be perceived as a peace-loving nation and believes its support for UN peacekeeping furthers this goal. UN peacekeeping mandates provide China with legitimacy to send forces overseas and allow Beijing to work with other major powers on security issues. China desires a larger leadership role in global peacekeeping and the ability to impact military doctrine and a greater respect for state sovereignty. It also seeks to use UN peacekeeping to reshape Africa's security architecture and more effectively protect its interests and nationals on the continent.[177] An online survey of Chinese nationals found high levels of support for China's engagement in peacekeeping activities, which the respondents said provided positive benefits to China's international reputation.[178]

* * *

The combination of China's growing physical presence and continuing engagement in risky African regions has put more Chinese nationals in the wrong place at the wrong time and even made them targets for rebel and terrorist groups. Despite China's traditional policy of noninterventionism, Beijing has concluded, sometimes in response to domestic pressure, that it must do more to protect its nationals visiting, living, and working in Africa. China's embassies in Africa are often unable to prevent or even foresee these incidents. As a result, Chinese companies and other organizations have turned to private security companies for protection. Yet even these companies do not have the capacity to respond to major or particularly violent events. The last resort is the evacuation of Chinese nationals, which sometimes requires PLA help.

In some cases, China's participation in UN peacekeeping operations offers another venue for protecting Chinese nationals. China perceives any stability achieved by these operations as in its own interests, both by making a location safer for Chinese nationals and by projecting a positive image of China as contributing to African peace and development. China is also trying to improve its ability to prevent, manage, and mediate conflict in Africa, although that effort remains a work in progress. China is reluctant to get involved in conflict situations involving two or more countries, especially when it might jeopardize its interests in those places. When Beijing does try to mediate, it emphasizes dialogue, development, and compromise; it is reluctant to use force and generally eschews the application of political and economic leverage even in situations where it has one or both.

8

SECURITY DIPLOMACY

China employs a wide range of tools in conducting its security diplomacy in Africa. They include two recently established security forums: the China-Africa Defense and Security Forum and the China-Africa Peace and Security Forum. Another such tool, military exchange visits, ranks as among the oldest and most reliable methods of China-Africa military-to-military engagement—and one that continues to be an important feature of security diplomacy. Yet there are surprisingly few military attachés assigned to Chinese embassies in Africa, especially as compared to the larger number of African military attachés in Beijing. Arms transfers, mostly sales, are another long-standing way of linking China to Africa's security forces.

Training of, and exercises with, African military and police forces were increasing in frequency prior to the outbreak of COVID-19 early in 2020. Chinese construction companies have built military and police facilities in half a dozen African countries, but nothing significant in others. At the same time, the PLA is ramping up its humanitarian assistance, especially during the coronavirus pandemic, but remains a minor player in disaster relief in Africa. By contrast, China has increased its counterterrorism cooperation and intelligence sharing with African countries as well, although the latter remains difficult to document.

SECURITY FORUMS

China recently launched two new security forums for senior African officials. The first is the China-Africa Defense and Security Forum, established in 2018. The second is the China-Africa Peace and Security Forum, which first met in 2019. Although China implied these forums would become regularly held events, so far there has only been a second session for the Peace and Security Forum. The coronavirus pandemic may have disrupted plans for follow-up meetings. These gatherings represent a significant expansion of China's interaction with senior African security leaders but seem to emphasize form over substance.

CHINA-AFRICA DEFENSE AND SECURITY FORUM

Hosted by China's Ministry of National Defense, the China-Africa Defense and Security Forum began in Beijing and included visits to military installations and arms factories over a two-week period. There were discussions on China-Africa defense and security cooperation and the security situation in Africa. Representatives from fifty African defense departments or military branches and the African Union, including twelve chiefs or deputy chiefs of general staff, attended the forum, making it the largest and most senior gathering ever of Chinese and African defense and security personnel. The forum opened with a two-day conference at the PLA's International College of Defense Studies in Beijing.[1] The agenda included topics such as protecting Chinese interests in Africa and improving Africa's response to crises.[2]

At the forum, China announced it will provide "comprehensive support" for African countries' antipiracy and counterterrorism efforts, including the provision of technologies, equipment, personnel, and strategic advice.³ PLA Major General Hu Changming, director of the Office for International Military Cooperation of the Central Military Commission (CMC) of the Communist Party of China (CPC), said the gathering advanced Xi Jinping's concept of a Community of Shared Future for Mankind. The deputy director of China's State Administration for Science, Technology and Industry for National Defense explained that China had established defense industry ties with forty-five African countries and was looking to expand opportunities for collaboration across military and dual-use technologies. The overtures were well-received; Sierra Leone's chief of defense staff, for instance, used the occasion to urge China to continue to provide African armies with advanced military courses.⁴

African military officials seem unclear about the future of the forum, however. One analyst who discussed the issue with participants at South Africa's biannual Africa Aerospace and Defence Trade Show suggested it might become an "administrative alliance" in which China brings together military elites and subjects them to personal lobbying, military aid, and cooperation and training programs. The forum also appeared designed to promote Chinese arms sales to Africa. Another goal is to increase military access in Africa, including the possibility of establishing additional Chinese military facilities on the continent.⁵ An American analyst described the forum more strategically as a "potential launchpad for China's defense relations to regions beyond Africa" and a mechanism to organize policy-level training for African Union officials and personnel from individual African countries.⁶ A representative from Gambia's armed forces, meanwhile, said his country wants China to provide partnership, support, expertise, technical capability, capacity building, and infrastructure so that Gambia can take care of its own security.⁷

CHINA-AFRICA PEACE AND SECURITY FORUM

The weeklong China-Africa Peace and Security Forum, which was hosted by China's Ministry of National Defense in 2019, brought one hundred representatives, including fifteen defense ministers and chiefs of staff, from fifty African countries and the African Union to Beijing. China arranged visits with army, navy, and air force units and a session in Shanghai. Major General Song Yanchao, deputy director of the Office for International Military Cooperation of the CMC, was one of the hosts for the group. A recurrent theme during the forum, which appeared to be an appendage of FOCAC, was Xi Jinping's Community of Shared Future for Mankind. There was likewise overlap with the China-Africa Defense and Security Forum that took place a year earlier, although this event attracted more African civilians in the security sector.[8]

State Councilor and Minister of National Defense Wei Fenghe addressed the forum, calling on China and Africa to "contribute to the development of China-Africa comprehensive strategic cooperative partnership and an even closer China-Africa community with a shared future."[9] PLA Major General Xu Hui, dean of the International College of Defense Studies at the PLA's National Defense University (NDU), said the significance of the forum "lies in the gathering of senior Chinese and African representatives to jointly diagnose security issues faced by Africa, share their governing experience and wisdom, and then take targeted and suitable measures."[10] The Chinese side used the forum to highlight the benefits of military cooperation and to encourage senior African security personnel to accept China's approach to comprehensive security.

This goal seemed to resonate with the African Union commissioner for peace and security, Smail Chergui, who said the forum provides a platform to discuss a comprehensive framework to enhance China's support for peace and security in Africa. He concluded that the gathering would solidify the China-Africa strategic partnership "based on shared values and mutual respect."[11] All African participants who commented publicly on the forum expressed positive platitudes, with several emphasizing appreciation for China's past military assistance. There was skepticism regarding the event among Africans, however. For instance, Ovigwe Eguegu, a geopolitical analyst based in Nigeria, questioned whether this forum "will produce peace in Africa or just papers for Africa and receipts for China."[12]

In 2022 China held a one-day online version of the forum for senior defense officials from forty-eight African states. It included a separate session on military medicine, also by video link, that emphasized cooperation on fighting the COVID-19 pandemic. Wei Fenghe gave the keynote address, and Xi Jinping sent a letter promoting the Global Security Initiative (see chapter 7). Xi emphasized that "China is ready to work with African friends in upholding the concept of common, comprehensive, cooperative and sustainable security."[13]

MILITARY EXCHANGE VISITS

China attaches high priority to military-to-military exchanges, which improve the transmission of information, allow China to gather knowledge about foreign military technologies, doctrine, and strategy, increase relationships, and provide an opportunity for Beijing to promote the sale of Chinese weapons.[14] China perceives military personnel as more effective interlocutors on security issues than their civilian counterparts. Because of its more advanced armed forces, South Africa is a special case in this regard. For example, in 2019 a high-level delegation from the PLA's National University of Defense Science and Technology visited South Africa's Naval College, its National War College, and the country's arms manufacturer, Armscor. This was the second visit in two years aimed at exploring cooperation on mutual training and joint research between South Africa and China.[15] The same year, forty-five young African military officers toured China's defense industry, military academies, and an airbase in Tianjin as part of a weeklong visit.[16] The heads of the Egyptian, Nigerian, and South African military academies participated in a six-day symposium at the PLA Ground Force Engineering University in Nanjing.[17] The NDU, meanwhile, is strengthening cooperation with military academies around the world and has official ties with counterpart institutions in Mozambique and Egypt.[18]

Between 1998 and 2010 China nearly quadrupled the annual frequency of global high-level military exchanges, as compared to the preceding twenty years. Between 2003 and 2016, 259 PLA senior-level meetings with African counterparts took place—about 12 percent of China's global total. China hosted 158 of the meetings, while 101 took place abroad, mostly in

Africa. Military personnel from Egypt participated in 32 of the meetings, those from South Africa in 25, from Tanzania in 24, and from Namibia, Sudan, and Zambia in 14. Personnel from Zimbabwe and Mozambique participated in 12, from Angola and Kenya in 10, from Tunisia in 9, from Djibouti, Uganda, and Ethiopia in 8, and from Algeria, Morocco, Togo, and Republic of Congo in 6. Other African countries participated in 5 or less.[19] For some participants, the connections built during these exchanges develop into a personal relationships; for example, Ghana's deputy minister of defense was a regular visitor to China prior to COVID-19.[20]

High-level military exchange visits from 2000 to 2022 with Tanzania offer an example of this kind of security diplomacy. As one of China's most important military partners in Africa, Tanzania has more high-level exchange visits than most other African countries:[21]

- 2001—A senior PLA delegation led by General Fu Quanyou, a CMC member and chief of the PLA General Staff, visited Tanzania and met with the president.
- 2002—A senior Tanzanian People's Defense Force (TPDF) delegation led by TPDF chief General George Waitara visited China and met with the minister of national defense.
- 2003—The Tanzanian minister of defense visited China and met with Vice Premier Huang Ju, a member of the Standing Committee of the CPC Politburo.
- 2004—A senior delegation led by the TPDF chief of staff visited China and met with the PLA deputy chief of the general staff.
- 2005—A senior Chinese delegation led by the minister of national defense visited Tanzania and met with the country's president. A senior TPDF delegation led by General Waitara visited China and met with the minister of national defense.
- 2007—A senior TPDF delegation led by the chief of military staff visited China and met with the PLA deputy chief of the general staff.
- 2008—A senior TPDF delegation led by the chief of military staff visited China and met with the PLA deputy chief of the general staff.

- 2009—The Tanzanian minister of defense visited China and met with the minister of national defense and the vice chairperson of the CMC.
- 2010—The Tanzanian minister of defense and national service visited China and met with the PLA chief of the general staff.
- 2013—The Tanzanian minister of defense and national service visited China and met with the vice chairperson of the CMC. The director and deputy director of the foreign affairs office of China's Ministry of National Defense accompanied the PLAN's fifteenth escort fleet to Tanzania.
- 2014—China's minister of national defense visited Tanzania and met with the president.
- 2016—China's vice chairperson of the CMC visited Tanzania and met with the president.
- 2017—The Tanzanian Air Force commander visited China and met with the PLA Air Force commander.
- 2018—The TPDF chief of defense forces visited China and met with the minister of national defense.
- 2022—China's minister of national defense and Tanzania's minister for defense and national service held a video meeting.

Changes in the Chinese government's travel policies in recent years have affected exchanges. Senior PLA visits overseas peaked in 2010 and have decreased significantly since. Before 2010 there was approximate parity between visits abroad by PLA personnel and visits hosted in China. Since then and before COVID-19, as we saw with party-to-party exchanges (see chapter 4), senior PLA officers have travelled less overseas to visit foreign counterparts, while foreign military officers and defense officials have visited China more often. This trend reflects tighter travel restrictions as part of China's anticorruption campaign and greater demands on senior PLA officers due to military reform efforts and has been exacerbated by COVID-19.[22] China also engages with senior African security chiefs at less than half the rate of the United States.[23]

China's Ministry of Public Security oversees the country's police service and domestic security services. Increasingly, the ministry is engaging with foreign countries. It organized eleven bilateral police diplomacy meetings with African countries between 1997 and 2020. Africa accounted for about 10 percent of China's global police meetings. Counterterrorism was the most discussed topic. Other issues included transnational crime, drug trafficking, law enforcement cooperation, and border security.[24]

MILITARY ATTACHÉS

Like other countries, China assigns defense attachés to its embassies around the world. The Ministry of National Defense has primary responsibility for China's defense attachés. It guides and controls the military's external work as well as the activities of foreign military attachés assigned to China.[25] China manages its day-to-day overseas military diplomacy using PLA officers assigned as military attachés at embassies in at least 110 countries worldwide. These individuals serve as military advisers to the ambassador, assist the Ministry of Foreign Affairs, support PLA foreign policy objectives, and perform duties tied to PLA military and security cooperation, including counterpart exchanges with host-nation and third-country personnel. Military attachés also conduct clandestine and overt intelligence collection on foreign military command structures, unit formations, and operational training.[26] The majority of China's military attachés are army officers, most of whom are career intelligence officers.[27]

Tracking China's defense attaché offices in Africa is a challenge. While a few Chinese embassies include them as staff members on their websites, most do not. China does not have a military attaché in many African countries. Using open-source information, a study in 2007 identified at least fourteen Chinese military attaché offices, situated in Algeria, the Democratic Republic of Congo, Egypt, Ethiopia, Liberia, Libya, Morocco, Mozambique, Namibia, Nigeria, Sudan, Tunisia, Zambia, and Zimbabwe. China also assigns some of these attachés on a nonresident basis to neighboring countries.[28] A subsequent survey of Chinese embassy websites and the media demonstrated that China maintained military attachés in all these countries except Libya.

By 2022 China had increased its defense attaché offices in Africa to at least twenty-three, adding representation in Angola, Cameroon, Republic of Congo, Djibouti, Gabon, Kenya, Madagascar, Mali, South Africa, and South Sudan.[29] In Tanzania, China has a special military-to-military arrangement, but not a formal defense attaché office. China has a military attaché in every country where it participates in a UN peacekeeping operation: South Sudan, DRC, Mali, and the Sudan/South Sudan border. Although China's contribution to the Western Sahara peacekeeping operation is small, it nonetheless has defense attachés at its embassies in both Morocco and Algeria. Except for Ethiopia, Zambia, Zimbabwe, Mali, and South Sudan, all the countries where China has an attaché also have a coastline, underscoring the role of an attaché in assisting with PLAN ship visits in port cities. Overall, however, the number of defense attaché offices that China has in Africa is surprisingly low, given the volume of arms sales to the continent, the robust nature of the military exchange program, and, until the coronavirus pandemic, the growing number of PLAN port calls to African countries.

African defense attachés in Beijing are much more numerous than their Chinese counterparts in Africa. In 1988 there were only nine African defense attachés in Beijing: those of Algeria, Republic of Congo, DRC, Egypt, Somalia, Sudan, Tanzania, Zambia, and Zimbabwe. By 1998, however, the number had increased to thirteen, as Guinea, Côte d'Ivoire, Kenya, Mali, and Nigeria joined the group but the DRC closed its attaché office. In 2010 twenty-eight African countries had a defense attaché in Beijing.[30] As of 2018 the number of African defense attaché offices in Beijing reached thirty-five. Those countries establishing offices between 1998 and 2018 included Angola, Benin, Botswana, Burundi, Cameroon, Central African Republic, Chad, Equatorial Guinea, Ethiopia, Gabon, Ghana, Libya, Malawi, Morocco, Mozambique, Namibia, Niger, Senegal, Sierra Leone, South Sudan, Tunisia, and Uganda. The overwhelming majority of attachés came from the army at the rank of colonel or brigadier general.[31] Among their primary functions is to assist in arms transfers to their respective countries and arrange schedules for visiting military personnel.[32]

ARMS TRANSFERS

Arms transfers have been an important part of the China-Africa relationship dating back to the 1960s, when China provided small quantities of arms (usually free of charge) to liberation movements, left-wing governments, and occasionally to rebel groups trying to topple established conservative governments. China has continued such donations, which tend to range in value from $1 million to $10 million.[33] One study found that forty-seven African states received small quantities of donated military supplies between 2000 and 2020.[34] The Ministry of Public Security transferred police vehicles, bulletproof vests, night vision devices, uniforms, gas masks, and computers to police forces in ten African countries between 2006 and 2021.[35] By the 1990s, most of the transfers constituted sales and had increased significantly in volume and dollar value.[36]

During the twenty-first century, most arms transfers from all countries have gone to North Africa, where Russia and, until recently, the United States were the two leading suppliers. China has typically ranked as the third most important source of arms to Africa. In Sub-Sahara Africa, Russia and China have switched back and forth as the largest suppliers of conventional weapons.

Measuring the quantity and dollar value of arms transfers is difficult because China is often not transparent when it exports small arms and light weapons (SALW). However, information on China's transfer of conventional weapons is more detailed. The United Nations defines small arms as those weapons designed for personal use, such as an assault rifle; light weapons, by contrast, are those designed for use by several persons serving as a crew, such as heavy machine guns and portable launchers of anti-aircraft missile systems.[37] SALW involve much smaller dollar values than do conventional weapons, which are defined by the Stockholm International

Peace Research Institute (SIPRI) as including aircraft, armored vehicles, tanks, artillery above 100 millimeters in caliber, radars, sonars, air defense missile systems, torpedoes, bombs, ships with 100-ton displacement or more, gun or missile-armed turrets, reconnaissance satellites, air refueling systems, and engines for combat-capable aircraft, combat ships, and armored vehicles.[38] Conventional weapons normally remain under the permanent control of recipient governments. SALW, by contrast, often find their way into the hands of rebel and terrorist groups.

China's arms industry consists of ten major state-owned arms companies and one research institute. Most companies are diversified and offer products for both military and nonmilitary markets. Those most relevant to the transfer of weapons to African countries include the Aviation Industry Corporation of China (AVIC), China's largest aircraft producer; China Aerospace Science and Technology Corporation (CASC), which manufactures missiles, space systems, and unmanned aerial vehicles; China North Industries Group Corporation (NORINCO) and China South Industries Group Corporation (CSGC), both leading makers of land systems; and China Shipbuilding Industry Corporation (CSIC) and China State Shipbuilding Corporation (CSSC), which are major shipbuilding companies.[39]

CONVENTIONAL WEAPONS

Turning first to conventional weapons, Chinese arms exports to Africa were 122 percent higher in 2012–2016 than they were in 2007–2011. Between 2012 and 2016, Russia accounted for 35 percent of all arms shipments to Africa, followed by China at 17 percent. Between them, Algeria and Morocco received 61 percent of all arms imported by African countries during this period; by contrast, all Sub-Sahara Africa received only 35 percent. China accounted for 27 percent of the arms to Sub-Sahara Africa, while Russia came in second at 19 percent.[40] From 2017 to 2021, Russia was responsible for 44 percent of all conventional weapons transferred to Africa; the United States, 17 percent (mainly to Egypt and Morocco); and China, 10 percent. Algeria alone accounted for 44 percent of total African arms imports

SECURITY DIPLOMACY

during this period. Arms imports by Sub-Sahara Africa during 2017–2021 were 35 percent lower than in 2012–2016.[41]

In recent years, Chinese arms sales have declined as a percentage of conventional weapons transferred to Africa, although in Sub-Saharan Africa China remains second only to Russia. From 2010 through 2021, transfers from China to Africa also declined in dollar value. During those years, China transferred on average about $300 million worth of arms annually, ranging from a high of $692 million in 2016 to a low of $91 million in 2019, with small upticks in 2020 and 2021 (see figure 8.1).[42] To some extent, this is due to decreased arms purchases by Sub-Sahara African states from all suppliers. That, however, does not explain the percentage drop in Chinese transfers, and it comes after China expanded its sales efforts aimed at Africa. China traditionally has had the largest contingent of foreign exhibitors at the Africa Aerospace and Defence Trade Show in South Africa, Africa's most important arms exhibit. In 2018 the State Administration of Science, Technology, and Industry for National Defense and six Chinese

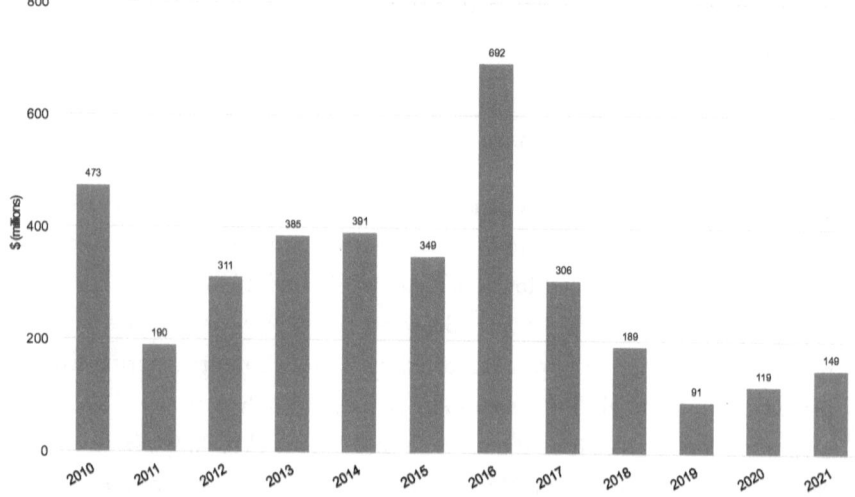

FIGURE 8.1 China's conventional arms transfers to Africa by year, 2010–2021. Source: SIPRI arms transfers database, https://www.sipri.org/databases/armstransfers.

SECURITY DIPLOMACY

arms companies offered a variety of missiles, vessels, aircraft, unmanned aerial vehicles (UAVs), radars, and ground force equipment to fulfill African security needs. Chinese firms are also among the largest exhibitors at the International Defense Exhibition in the United Arab Emirates and the Eurosatory international arms exhibition in France, both of which attract African buyers.[43]

Transfers of conventional arms to individual African countries (see figure 8.2) from 2010 through 2021 offer a few surprises. Algeria imported $1.025 billion worth of arms from China and was the continent's largest recipient. Morocco was China's second largest customer, at $478 million in imports. Nigeria imported $413 million of Chinese weapons, ranking third, commensurate with its status as the most populous country in Africa, the one with the continent's largest GDP, and facing a serious terrorist threat. Tanzania has the longest sustained military-to-military relationship with Beijing and ranked fourth at $371 million. Sudan, which also has a longstanding military relationship with China, occupied the fifth position, with $254 million in imports. Close partners Angola and Ethiopia were at

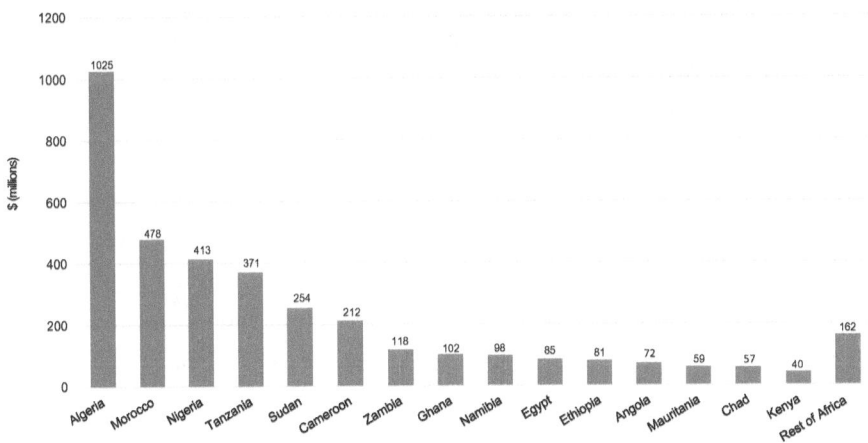

FIGURE 8.2 China's conventional arms transfers to Africa by country, 2010–2021. Source: SIPRI arms transfers database, https://www.sipri.org/databases/armstransfers.

the low end of the fifteen-country ranking during this twelve-year period. Even more surprising, the SIPRI database for this period showed no transfer of conventional arms to Zimbabwe, although Harare received an unknown quantity of SALW. Zimbabwe has historically been a modest importer of conventional weapons, but between 1980 and 2009 China was the single largest supplier, with more than one-third of total transfers.[44]

TRANSFERS TO NORTH AFRICA AND THE SAHEL

Africa obtains a wide variety of conventional weaponry from China. North African countries, however, order more sophisticated and expensive equipment. Between 2010 and 2019, China delivered to Algeria three C28A-class guided missile corvettes, fifty PLZ-45 155-mm self-propelled howitzers, fifty antiship missiles, eighteen 155-mm towed guns, fifty FM-90 SAMs for the corvettes, eighteen SR-5 self-propelled multiple rocket launchers, ten UAVs, and twenty-eight mortars. In 2022 Algeria ordered five CH-5 reconnaissance and strike drones from China.[45] Nevertheless, China's ambiguous policy regarding Algeria's conflict with Morocco over Western Sahara has constrained its security relations with Algiers.[46]

China has transferred twelve self-propelled multiple rocket launchers, fifty-four tanks, six Sky Shield air defense systems, seventy-five air-to-air missiles for the Sky Shields, and fifty antitank missiles to Morocco. In 2020 Morocco purchased additional multiple rocket launchers from China. In 2022 it acquired an undetermined number of Wing Loong II medium-altitude, long-endurance unmanned UAVs. Egypt received eighteen unarmed UAVs, forty-two armed UAVs, forty K-8 trainer/combat aircraft, and three hundred antitank missiles.[47] Chinese armed, Wing Loong II UAVs and missiles have found their way into Libya's internal conflict via the United Arab Emirates, which supports the western-based Libyan National Army (LNA) against the UN-recognized government in Tripoli.[48] Between April 2018 and November 2019, the LNA carried out more than eight hundred strikes using these UAVs, providing China with the ability to battle test its equipment without the risk of military or diplomatic repercussions.[49] In 2020 a UAE-provided Wing Loong II drone equipped with a Chinese Blue Arrow 7 missile hit a Libyan military academy, killing twenty-six cadets and wounding many others.⁵⁰

Chinese transfers to Mauritania in recent years have consisted entirely of navy vessels. In 2016 the Mauritanian Navy commissioned two new offshore patrol craft to help prevent illegal fishing, piracy, and trafficking. Mauritania purchased the vessels for $42 million, using government bonds.⁵¹ In 2019 the Mauritanian Navy took possession of a small landing ship built by China's Wuchang Shipbuilding Industry Group, which is affiliated with CSSC.⁵² China has extensive fishing rights in Mauritanian waters but competes with others, hence it is in Beijing's interest to minimize illegal fishing there.⁵³

TRANSFERS TO EAST AFRICA

Tanzania's long-standing reliance on Chinese military hardware is evident in its acquisitions from 2010 through 2019. During that decade, it received fifty-four tanks, twenty fighter/trainer aircraft, ten armored personnel carriers, twelve self-propelled multiple rocket launchers, one SAM system, fifty portable SAMs, air search radar, ten self-propelled mortars, five armored fighting vehicles, two patrol craft, and twelve armed patrol vehicles.⁵⁴ An overwhelming amount of the TPDF's armor and artillery is Chinese made. China has equipped the Tanzanian Air Force with both fighter and transport aircraft. Half of the navy's patrol and coastal craft are of Chinese origin.⁵⁵

Ethiopia has received thirty armored personnel carriers, one SAM system, seventy-five air-to-air missiles for the SAM system, ten surface-to-surface missiles, and eight multiple rocket launchers. Between 2010 and 2019, China transferred nine armed Panther helicopters to Kenya; it also exported sixty armored personnel carriers to the police force.⁵⁶ Wing Loong 1 drones began appearing in 2021 to aid in the central government's war against Tigrayan rebels.⁵⁷ In 2022 China donated an undetermined number of military vehicles and engineering equipment to the Kenyan Defense Forces.⁵⁸ And it donated $5 million worth of military trucks, ambulances, and landmine detectors to the Somali National Army.⁵⁹

Sudan, which periodically faced UN arms sanctions, is a long-standing consumer of Chinese weapons. China's first reported arms sale to Sudan occurred in the late 1980s, financed by Iran. China subsequently provided engineers to help Sudan build its own arms manufacturing industry, which is now one of the largest in Africa.[60] Between 2010 and 2019, Sudan received parts for fifty infantry fighting vehicles assembled in Sudan, fifty tanks, 450 antitank missiles, six self-propelled multiple rocket launchers, ten UAVs, two mobile SAM systems, one hundred portable SAMs, six FTC-2000 trainer/combat aircraft, and forty air-to-air missiles.[61] In 2018 Sudan was the first known export customer to receive the FTC-2000 aircraft from Guizhou Aircraft Industries Corporation.[62] In 2022 it began talks for the acquisition of Chinese J-10C fighter jets, perhaps the most capable fighter on the African continent.[63]

TRANSFERS TO WEST AND CENTRAL AFRICA

Nigeria, another major recipient of Chinese arms, purchased fifteen F-7M fighter aircraft, twenty air-to-air missiles, two offshore patrol vessels, one patrol craft, several hundred armored personnel carriers, thirty air-to-surface missiles, and five armed UAVs.[64] In 2020 China sent sixteen technicians to Nigeria to reactivate the F-7s.[65] The same year, in an effort to aid its fight against Boko Haram terrorists, Nigeria took possession of tanks, self-propelled howitzers, and wheeled tank destroyers built to specification by NORINCO as part of a $152 million contract.[66] In 2021 the Nigerian Army began deploying the tanks against Boko Haram.[67] It has also used the armed drones against the extremist group.[68] In 2020 Nigeria received a pair of Wing Loong II UAVs.[69]

China's transfer of conventional weapons to Ghana include a combination of small grants, loans, and purchases dating back to 2001. In 2004 China offered military assistance grants to purchase vehicles for the Ghana Armed Forces (GAF). In 2008 Ghana signed agreements with China for $160 million to equip the GAF and enhance Ghana's peacekeeping capabilities. Poly Technologies Incorporated (PTI) established an office in Accra to support improvements to maritime security; in 2011 Ghana purchased two forty-six-meter patrol boats from PTI to modernize the navy and combat piracy.⁷⁰ Other transfers between 2010 and 2019 included two more patrol boats, fifty-eight armored personnel carriers, four armored ambulances, twenty-four infantry fighting vehicles, four Panther helicopters, and one hundred portable SAMs.⁷¹

From 2010 through 2021, Cameroon was the sixth largest recipient of Chinese weapons. Imports included two transport aircraft, fifty portable SAMs, twelve anti-aircraft guns, two armored personnel carriers, eighteen infantry fighting vehicles, fifteen fire control radars, twelve armored fire support vehicles, and two patrol craft.⁷² In 2018 China and Cameroon signed a military assistance agreement that included $8 million, presumably grants, for the acquisition of military equipment.⁷³

TRANSFERS TO SOUTHERN AFRICA

From 2010 through 2019, China sold Zambia eight K-8 trainer/combat aircraft, six L-15 trainer/combat aircraft (about $35 million each), seven helicopters, fifty guided bombs for the L-15s, forty air-to-air missiles, and fifty air-to-surface missiles for the L-15s.⁷⁴ Zambia is a loyal AVIC customer. Between 2000 and 2017, China's Export Import Bank made available $1.5 billion in loans globally for military procurement. About $600 million of this amount went to Zambia. Every aircraft purchased by the Zambian Air Force received financial support in the form of Export Import Bank loans or AVIC's supplier credits. As of 2019 China was the source of 44 percent of the Zambian Air Force's 108 aircraft. The availability of financing and limited maintenance cost of the aircraft were deciding factors in the purchase.⁷⁵

Namibia received two Panther helicopters, one offshore patrol vessel, ten infantry fighting vehicles, and two secondhand but modernized submarine chasers, which were donated by the PLA.⁷⁶ Upon delivery of the submarine chasers at Walvis Bay in 2017, Namibian president Hage Geingob "thanked China for being an all-weather friend, adding that it is better to have one loyal friend than a hundred fair-weather friends."⁷⁷ In 2017 the U.S. Treasury Department forced Namibia to recall $12 million that it had transferred to PTI for arms, ammunition, and aircraft parts because the firm ignored international sanctions and sold weapons to Iran, North Korea, and Syria. PTI frequently wins Namibian military procurement contracts; Namibia's prosecutor general accused it of bribing senior military officers.[78]

Angola has traditionally relied on Russia for military hardware but has turned to China since 2015, receiving forty-five diesel engines for armored personnel carriers, ten armored fire support vehicles, five armored personnel carriers, and two MA60 transport aircraft. By the end of 2020, China had delivered twelve K-8W trainer/combat aircraft.[79] China National Aero-Technology Import and Export Corporation also trained Angolan pilots for the K-8Ws and announced it would supply two more MA60 transport aircraft.[80]

SMALL ARMS AND LIGHT WEAPONS

Many countries export enormous quantities of SALW. Some, including the United States, usually report the transfers to UN Comtrade. Others, including China and Russia, usually do not.[81] In addition, SALW are widely available from manufacturers on the international arms market; it is often impossible to determine how they reached these markets and made their way to Africa, especially to the continent's conflict zones. During the Cold War, the Soviet Union probably accounted for the single largest quantity of SALW transfers to African governments. It is impossible to say which country is the leading source. From 2013 to 2015, of those countries that reported transfers to UN Comtrade, France was the largest exporter of SALW to Sub-Sahara African governments, and the United States was the second largest.[82] By contrast, there is minimal documentation of China's SALW exports. Nevertheless, because of low cost, improving quality, and a willingness to transfer arms to countries under Western sanctions, Chinese arms manufacturers have a significant market share. But the fact that so many nations now export SALW to Africa underscores the need to exercise care before ascribing percentages to China or any other country. A study commissioned by the Small Arms Survey covering 2013–2015 concluded only that China was an "important" source of SALW for Africa.[83]

China has a good record of submitting annual reports to the UN Register of Conventional Arms (UNROCA), which also collects information on SALW. However, China usually does not include information on SALW in these reports.[84] In theory, China supports the UN Program of Action (POA) to Prevent, Combat, and Eradicate the Illicit Trade in SALW, but China's SALW transfer control system lacks clarity regarding licensing and navigating export licenses and national brokering controls. Nor do China's POA reports provide detailed information in response to requests for clarification filed by UN panels of experts about Chinese SALW found in destinations subject to UN arms embargoes.[85] Moreover, China has not ratified the UN Arms Trade Treaty (ATT), which also deals with SALW. Chinese arms exporters argue that they do not want to accept additional international scrutiny, and China is reluctant to meet the human rights criteria outlined in the ATT. As of 2022, almost half of all African states had signed and ratified the ATT.[86]

China's SALW transfer control system likewise lacks transparency. China's regulations do not cover the monitoring of transportation once SALW shipments leave Chinese territory, and there are no specific regulations regarding transit. Once China approves a shipment and it leaves the country, it falls outside the area of arms export regulations. The PLA has historically played a significant role in SALW exports, but the creation of the State Administration for Science, Technology and Industry for National Defense, the rise of powerful state-owned enterprises, and reforms prohibiting the military from conducting economic activities have diminished this role. China has not made public the operating licenses of state-owned arms exporters and the extent of its regulation of their export catalogs is not clear.[87]

China's official position is that SALW should not be transferred to unauthorized nonstate actors, although there is considerable evidence that this is in fact happening. In many cases, it is the African states that transferred the imported weapons to nonstate actors.[88] For its part, China argues that it is the responsibility of recipient governments to prevent SALW from falling into nefarious hands.[89] Wu Haitao, China's deputy permanent representative to the UN, commented that his government consistently opposes the illicit trade of SALW and cooperates internationally to stop it. He added that receiving governments "bear the primary responsibility for combating the illicit trade of SALWs and they should establish and improve laws and regulations and strengthen their enforcement."[90]

Most African government reports submitted to UNROCA fail to report their acquisition of SALW, although a few have documented arms received from China and other countries. In 2015 Liberia reported that it imported 560 rifles from China. In 2016 Sierra Leone's report said it received 235 pistols, 1,000 assault rifles, and 1,050 light machine guns from China.[91] In 2011 the press reported that the Zimbabwe Defense Force had received 20,000 AK-47 assault rifles from China.[92] In 2018 Namibia acknowledged that it acquired FN-6 MANPADS from China.[93] The Ghana Armed Forces once used Chinese AK-47s but decided to switch to the more accurate American M-16s.[94] In 2020 Algeria was the first export customer for NORINCO's new HJ-12 guided antitank missile.[95] It is, however, exceedingly difficult to document China's SALW transfers to African countries when relying solely on open source information.

While arms confiscated in African conflict zones originate in many nations, increasingly those from China are fueling conflicts in Sudan, South Sudan, the DRC, and Somalia.[96] In the case of Sudan and South Sudan, China has transferred SALW to governments that are party to an active conflict. In other conflicts, the arms may have been purchased on the international arms market or transferred to renegade groups by neighboring governments that received them legally from China. For example, Chinese-produced FN-6 MANPADS appeared in the hands of insurgent groups in Chad; they likely came from the government of Sudan, which at the time was the only known Sub-Sahara Africa recipient of these weapons.[97]

The Small Arms Survey concluded that between 2001 and 2012, China accounted for 58 percent of Sudan's reported imports of SALW, ammunition, and conventional weapons. The most ubiquitous of all Chinese SALW in Sudan was small-caliber ammunition. A variety of Chinese SALW has appeared in Sudan throughout this century, including in the Darfur conflict zone. The items include NORINCO's QLZ87 35-mm automatic grenade launchers, ammunition for RPG7s, Red Arrow-8 antitank guided missiles, and long-range 302-mm Weishi rockets. In addition, Sudan's Military Industrial Corporation (MIC) produces machine guns and an assault rifle that look identical to those manufactured in China. Whether the MIC, under license from China, manufactures the weapons in Khartoum or receives the parts and assembles them is unclear. Sudanese-manufactured mortar rounds often contain Chinese fuses and Bulgarian ignition charges.[98]

Prior to the independence of South Sudan in 2011 (and possibly after independence), the government in Khartoum transferred SALW to rebel groups that opposed the ruling Sudan People's Liberation Army (SPLA). The Small Arms Survey identified a significant quantity of Chinese-manufactured SALW and ammunition that made its way into South Sudan and became part of the conflict between the Khartoum-based government in the North and the SPLA in the South. Khartoum-backed rebels in the South opposed to the SPLA received Chinese-manufactured CQ rifles, Type 56-1 assault rifles, and Type-69 rockets. The Sudan Armed Forces used Chinese-manufactured SALW against the SPLA, including Red Arrow-8 antitank guided missiles and WS-1 long-range rockets.[99]

NORINCO's delivery of small arms to South Sudan during the initial stages of a civil war in 2014 provides one of the best-documented cases of Chinese SALW reaching an African conflict zone. The Hong Kong–based ship, the *Feng Huang Song*, arrived in Mombasa, Kenya, with more than one thousand tons of weapons, valued at almost $21 million. The shipment, which was not reported to UN Comtrade, then went overland to South Sudan. It included 100 antitank guided missile-launching and guidance systems and 1,200 rounds, 9,574 automatic rifles, 2,394 40-mm grenade launchers, twenty million rounds of 7.62 x 39 mm ammunition, 319 machine guns, two million rounds of 7.62 x 54 mm ammunition, 660 pistols, two million rounds of 9 x 19 mm ammunition, and 40,000 rounds of antitank rockets. China authorized this delivery to South Sudan's Ministry of Defense in 2011 and 2013, before the outbreak of civil war, but it arrived during the conflict. International pressure forced NORINCO to suspend delivery of the remaining $18 million of the contract. No sanctions were in effect on South Sudan at the time.[100]

SECURITY DIPLOMACY

An employee of a competing Chinese arms manufacturer commented he was not surprised by the botched NORINCO delivery. He explained there is little communication between state-owned arms exporters and the Ministry of Foreign Affairs and Chinese embassies. A similar problem occurred in 2008, when China tried to deliver SALW to Zimbabwe in the aftermath of a hotly disputed election.[101] Conflict Armament Research determined as of 2018 that China accounted for 37 percent of the weapons and more than 99 percent of the ammunition that it inspected in South Sudan. It found no indication, however, that Chinese weapons or ammunition reached South Sudan's army after May 2014.[102]

ADVANTAGES AND DISADVANTAGES OF CHINESE WEAPONS

China sometimes makes arms transfers more attractive by including them in package deals that encompass loans, grants, infrastructure projects, and access to natural resources. In 2018, for example, China gave Ghana's Ministry of Defense a $7.5 million cash grant.[103] Between 2003 and 2017, China provided financing of at least $1.44 billion for African countries to purchase aircraft, military hardware, and naval vessels.[104] Chinese weapons are usually less expensive than comparable Western counterparts and sometimes even those from low-cost competitors, such as Russia, and have fewer end use restrictions. Additionally, Chinese companies often offer flexible payment options and short delivery timelines.

Reports on the quality of the weapons vary widely. Western experts tend to emphasize their poor quality, but others suggest their quality is adequate and constantly improving.[105] A senior Ethiopian officer observed that some of the weapons, such as mortars, are more appropriate for harsh African environmental conditions and require less maintenance.[106] A Ghanaian military officer, by contrast, complained about the poor quality of eight coastal patrol craft that his country had purchased from China and one aircraft that it subsequently replaced with another from Brazil.[107] Nigerian and Ghanaian personnel have criticized the low quality of Chinese aircraft as well.¹⁰⁸ On the other hand, Ghana's minister of defense Dominic Nitiwul reportedly likes Chinese military equipment.¹⁰⁹

MILITARY AND POLICE TRAINING AND EXERCISES

Senior PLA generals consider professional military education a priority for China's security assistance program.¹¹⁰ Consequently, military and police training and, to a lesser extent, exercises have become an increasingly important part of the China-Africa security cooperation program, although COVID-19 has significantly reduced their frequency. This is one of the most productive areas for the PLA and the PAP to develop close personal relationships with African counterparts, especially when they combine training with arms transfers.

MILITARY TRAINING

More than twenty Chinese military academies and training institutions offer foreign military training programs, and hundreds of Africans have participated in them.¹¹¹ China also trains Africans at its two peacekeeping training facilities and sends military trainers to Africa, sometimes in connection with transfers of military equipment.¹¹² Since 1956 the NDU alone has trained more than ten thousand senior command officers from 160 countries, mostly developing countries.¹¹³ In the 1960s and 1970s, most of the Africans trained in China were members of liberation movements committed to ending European colonialism. Seven African heads of state received military training in China: Robert Mugabe of Zimbabwe, Isaias Afwerki of Eritrea, Sam Nujoma of Namibia, Samora Machel and Joaquim Chissano of Mozambique, and Laurent-Désiré Kabila and Joseph Kabila of the DRC. Until the coronavirus pandemic, China trained up to four thousand foreign military personnel each year, and about 60 percent of them were African.¹¹⁴

Absolute CPC control over the military is one of the pillars of China's governance model. As such, China's military training programs include the principle of party control. Most African military students train at the regional academies for cadets and junior officers and the command and staff colleges for midcareer officers. African students also receive instruction at the PLA's ideological colleges, such as Pudong Cadres College, Nanjing Political College, and Kunming National Cadres Academy. These political schools provide training on the way the CPC exercises control over the military through the political commissar system. Angola, Algeria, Cape Verde, Ethiopia, Eritrea, Guinea-Bissau, Mauritania, Mozambique, Rwanda, South Sudan, Tanzania, and Zimbabwe have all adopted a form of the political commissar system.[115] Most of these governments, however, have authoritarian political systems that are predisposed to control the military with political commissars. Consequently, military training in China may not have been the determining factor.

Cadets and junior officers from African countries usually attend China's regional academies, such as the Nanjing Military Academy, Dalian Naval Academy, and the PLA Air Force Aviation University in Changchun. The command and staff colleges, including the Army Command College in Nanjing and the Command and Staff Colleges of the PLA's service branches, train midcareer officers. Nanjing has trained more African noncommissioned, junior, and middle-grade officers than any other school in the world. Mozambique alone has graduated ninety-seven military leaders from the Army Command College in Nanjing. More than three hundred senior officers, just under 60 percent from Africa, train annually at the NDU, National University of Defense Technology, and the International College for Defense Studies and National Security. China's system combines military and technical subjects with ideological and political training.[116]

The NDU courses for foreigners usually attract officers at the rank of colonel. The proportion of courses dealing with traditional security is declining, while those concerning counterterrorism, natural disasters, climate change, international financial crises, and other nontraditional security challenges are on the rise. Field trips to air force and navy installations are common, in addition to exposure to modern information technology.

African officers who bring special expertise to the classroom, such as peacekeeping in Africa, often share their experiences. Attendees receive three free meals daily and a monthly stipend of about $280.[117]

The College of Defense Studies (CDS), a component of the NDU, is the primary institution for graduate-level international military education in China. In 2012 CDS began awarding war college master's degrees to foreign students, who receive training separate from Chinese students at a satellite campus in northern Beijing, possibly because of language differences. The CDS offers courses in English, French, Russian, Spanish, and Chinese. The separation of Africans and Chinese, however, limits efforts to build relationships between PLA and foreign officers. The curriculum instills respect for China and introduces students to Chinese strategic culture through classics such as Sun Tzu's *The Art of War*. The China studies course promotes the concept of peaceful development and explains the "China Dream" (see chapter 1). A senior African officer who attended the CDS course said it emphasized postcolonial grievances and underscored that the West, especially the United States, continues to subjugate Africa by controlling means of production and exploiting African labor.[118]

China offers short-term military training at several of its academies. In 2018, for example, thirty-one military academy cadets from eleven countries, including Egypt and South Africa, attended the weeklong international cadets' course at the PLA Army Engineering University in Nanjing, Jiangsu. Joined by seventy-three Chinese cadets from eleven Chinese PLA academies, its goal was to explain China and the PLA to the visitors. The program included shooting practice, obstacle courses, field training, simulations of UN peacekeeping operations, and courses on traditional Chinese culture. The Chinese cadets had an opportunity to learn about other countries' strengths and weaknesses.[119] After Burkina Faso switched diplomatic recognition from Taipei to Beijing in 2018, China offered it seventy-two scholarships for training at its military schools.[120]

In 2019 the International Military Education Exchange Center of the Army Command College in Nanjing hosted 146 officers from seventy-seven countries. In all, it has trained about 4,000 middle and senior command officers and government officials from 118 countries in recent decades. The programs vary in length between six months and a year. Courses focus on coordinated tactics, counterterrorism, battlefield intelligence collection, and the operational system of China's military. A participant from Cameroon concluded that his country needed to update its doctrine and technology. An officer from Gambia commented favorably that China's army is becoming more transparent.[121] China also offers courses based on language groupings. It has hosted workshops for heads of military academies from English-speaking African countries, for directors of military hospitals from French-speaking African countries, and for intermediate and senior officers from Portuguese-speaking African countries.[122]

As of 2012, about four hundred Nigerian Armed Forces personnel had participated in training in China. A navy captain who attended the defense and strategic studies course at NDU commented that the language barrier was a challenge, particularly at the operational/tactical levels, where there were misunderstandings concerning the operation and maintenance of systems and equipment. The officer added that training tends to be one-way, with Nigerians training in China, while Nigeria does not reciprocate even though it has a peacekeeping training center that might be useful to Chinese soldiers. Nor has Nigeria always made full use of training opportunities in China; as of 2012, Nigeria had filled only twenty-eight of the forty-four positions offered in one program.[123]

Since it opened in 2009, China has trained more than 1,500 international peacekeepers from dozens of countries at the PLA Peacekeeping Training Center in Huairou, Beijing.[124] In 2016 China held its first joint training course with the UN Peacekeeping Department. Senior peacekeeping experts from seventeen countries trained peacekeeping commanders and soldiers on peacekeeping leadership, legal frameworks, civilian protection, and logistical support.[125] The focus is on training for UN peacekeeping operations globally. There has been surprisingly little effort by Beijing to publicize positive coverage of foreign training at the Peacekeeping Training Center. There may be practical reasons for this, such as limited training capacity, the need to focus on training Chinese peacekeepers, and, therefore, a policy that does not encourage requests from foreign governments for peacekeeping training.

SECURITY DIPLOMACY

China's training of African military personnel usually occurs within China. Ethiopia signed a military cooperation agreement with China in 2005 for training, exchange of technologies, and joint peacekeeping missions, and Ethiopian field-grade officers routinely receive training in China. A Western military attaché in Addis Ababa described the program as a "conveyer belt" between Ethiopia and China.[126] Djibouti has similarly turned to China for small-arms training and artillery repair.[127] China began training Tanzanian pilots in the early 1970s and has supported air force training for the country ever since.[128] Tanzania annually sends a significant number of officers and noncommissioned officers for training to various institutions in China. The TPDF hosts about twelve Chinese instructors, who teach at the junior staff college in Dar es Salaam.[129] In 2019 fifty-seven officers and soldiers from China's Eastern Theater Command joined counterparts in Tanzania for a twenty-five-day military training program called "Sincere Partners." The joint training covered command post exercises, explosive operations, light weapons shooting, and search of residential areas.[130] The PLA trained an engineering unit in Liberia and has trained presidential guard units in several African countries.[131] Beijing has also created Chinese language programs for African military personnel in cooperation with its Confucius Institutes in Sudan and the DRC.[132]

China's military training program with South Africa is surprisingly small in view of the strong relationship between the African National Congress and the CPC (see chapter 4). This is due in part to the fact that South Africa manufactures most of its own military hardware.[133] The PLA sent a training and advisory team to the Zimbabwe Staff College, which instructed soldiers and civilians from Botswana, Namibia, Zambia, Tanzania, Malawi, and Lesotho.[134] China's training of Namibian military personnel began during the country's independence struggle and continues today.[135] Senior Sudanese Army officers have trained at the NDU, while those from South Sudan trained at the Shijiazhuang Army Command College.[136] Six Chinese drill instructors sent to Rwanda trained almost two thousand soldiers and police for military parades.[137] China is providing military training and Mandarin language instruction for soldiers from the Comoro Islands.[138]

African officers who have studied in both the United States and China reported that training in China is particularly strong for noncommissioned, junior, and midlevel officers and in technical subjects such as engineering, geography, technology, and mechanics. China focuses on training African soldiers in basic skills for their branch or support function, such as infantry, artillery, and armor. Political commissars earmarked for leadership undergo additional training at the PLA Nanjing Political College in Jiangsu. Senior officers attend the CPC Central Party School in Beijing. The PLA also sends instructors to political and ideological schools across Africa.[139]

China links military training to arms transfers. In 1991 China delivered a variety of military equipment to Sudan, including high-altitude bombs. China then sent a team to instruct Sudanese pilots and aircrews in high-altitude bombing.[140] In 2008 China provided training for Sudanese pilots on Chinese A5 Fantan fighter aircraft.[141] The two submarine chasers donated by the PLA to the Namibian Navy also came with a training package.[142] AVIC has established an aviation training center in Kenya to support African sales of the Y-12 military trainer aircraft.[143] In 2007 Rwanda sent twenty officers to China for training following the country's acquisition of large-caliber artillery.[144] In 2011 China donated a variety of SALW to Sierra Leone and then sent a six-man team to train its military personnel.[145] In 2020 Nigeria purchased a large package of military equipment from China and then arranged to have the PLA train some of its personnel.[146] Nigeria ordered CH-3 armed UAVs from China and identified about seventy personnel for training in China on the operation and maintenance of those systems.[147]

POLICE TRAINING

Training of African police has become a higher priority as China emphasizes its role in UN peacekeeping and increases the number of PAP that it assigns to UN operations in Africa.[148] In 2000 it established what is now called the China Peacekeeping Police Training Center in Langfang City.[149] The PAP now reports to the CMC, which puts it directly under the control of Xi Jinping. In 2016 China's Ministry of Public Security and the UN collaborated for the first time on a two-week training program in China for seventeen senior police officers from Angola, Djibouti, Kenya, Liberia, Namibia, Tanzania, Uganda, Zambia, and Zimbabwe. The training was a response to Xi Jinping's announcement a year earlier that China would train two thousand foreign peacekeepers over the next five years.[150]

China also has about twenty-five police colleges and universities nationwide. The Beijing People's Police College has held training programs for police officers from at least twenty countries. While African police officers have visited the college, it is not clear if Africans have been trained there. Zhejiang Police College in Hangzhou, one of the few police universities permitted to award a bachelor's degree to international students, has attracted African students.[151] As of 2020, Shandong Police College in Jinan had arranged training for police delegations from eighty-seven countries. In 2019 Rwanda sent a twenty-five-member delegation to the college, which included police officers, for a three-week course in law enforcement.[152]

Under Xi Jinping, the Ministry of Public Security has increased training of foreign police forces. It provided seventy-seven training sessions from 2004 to 2021, most of them recently; twenty-seven, or about 35 percent, were for African police forces. Training included riot control tactics, Internet and cyber control, management of public opinion online, and securing stability.[153] A more recent development has been China's effort to improve African policing capabilities so they can more effectively protect Chinese nationals living and working in Africa (see chapter 7).

Beginning in 2013, China's Ministry of Public Security invited three to four groups of about eighty South African Police Service officers to China for monthlong training in criminal investigation, community policing, and kung fu.[154] Following the closure of the UN peacekeeping mission in Liberia and the departure of the Chinese police unit there, China pledged to send special teams to train the Liberian National Police with the goal of improving security for Chinese citizens.[155] Similarly, China assigned a team to train Uganda's police force in criminal investigations, crime intelligence, and cybercrime, including an investigation of the murder of two Chinese nationals.[156] Kenya sent twenty-nine railway police officers to Beijing for training on security, investigations, and evidence collection to improve security on the Chinese-built and managed railway between Mombasa and Nairobi.[157] Namibia routinely sends police officers to China for training programs. Beijing pays the costs, and Namibia has been pleased with the results.[158]

MILITARY EXERCISES

In 2002 the PLA began conducting exercises with counterparts from other countries. Just over half of those drills through 2018 involved military operations other than war (MOOTW). Most of the others were antipiracy or antiterrorism exercises aimed at combatting nonstate actors.[159] In 2009 China held its first African exercise in Gabon, a humanitarian and medical training practice named Operation Peace Angel.[160] Although exercises with African military units increased until the outbreak of COVID-19, they remained infrequent and limited in scope. They often occur in connection with PLAN ship visits to African ports following antipiracy escort duty in the Gulf of Aden (see chapter 9). In 2014 Chinese navy ships conducted antipiracy drills with the Nigerian Navy and Cameroonian Navy in the Gulf of Guinea.[161] The same year China and Tanzania conducted their first naval training exercise, which lasted one month.[162] In 2015 the PLAN frigate *Yiyang* and the Egyptian frigate *Toshka* conducted basic maneuver drills during a visit to Alexandria.[163]

From 2003 through 2016, China held three military exercises with Egypt, two each with South Africa, Angola, Nigeria, and Zimbabwe, and one apiece with Tanzania, Namibia, Gabon, Cameroon, and Ghana.[164] In 2018 PLAN ships held exercises with navies from Cameroon, Ghana, Gabon, and Nigeria, while PLA medical units worked with counterparts in Ethiopia, Sierra Leone, Sudan, and Zambia to develop their combat casualty care capabilities.[165] From 2014 to 2018, the PLA conducted twenty-one exercises with eleven African militaries, but this constituted only 8 percent of China's total international exercises.[166] Notably, however, China does not participate in or offer anything comparable to AFRICOM's annual Flintlock exercises, which bring together special forces from West African and international militaries.[167]

SECURITY DIPLOMACY

CONSTRUCTION OF MILITARY AND POLICE FACILITIES

Chinese companies have built a significant amount of the military and police infrastructure in several African countries and at least one project in most others. China has concentrated its military and police construction in Ghana, Namibia, Tanzania, Uganda, and Zambia. Although Chinese companies have built civilian government infrastructure throughout Africa, they have limited military and police facilities almost entirely to Anglophone Africa. There is no obvious explanation for this phenomenon, however, and it may be coincidental. China usually does not publish the terms of the contracts, although Beijing has provided loan financing for many of them and grants for a few.[168] Presumably, recipient governments fund or obtain financing for the remainder. Whatever the funding arrangement, these construction projects enhance China's access to African military, civilian defense, and police personnel.

In 2004 China provided a $3.8 million loan to build the Burma Camp military/police barracks in Accra. Two years later, China constructed additional facilities at the complex. In 2008 Ghana received a $7.5 million grant from China to build a new Ministry of National Defense headquarters at Burma Camp. China then won a $6 billion contract to build Ghana's largest hydropower dam.[169] In 2019 Ghana signed a $100 million contract with Chinese companies to construct military housing in Takoradi, Tamale, and Sunyani, along with housing, teaching, and administration facilities for the military academy in Accra.[170] In 2019 Namibian president Hage Geingob opened the Chinese-funded and built Command and Staff College in Okahandja.[171] The same year China Jiangxi International built a $38 million military base in northern Namibia at Ondangwa.[172] Chinese companies constructed the police and prison training college and national police headquarters in Windhoek, the Oshikoto police regional headquarters and the police station in Omuthiya, and the police station in Otjomuise.[173]

In the early 1970s China helped Tanzania complete its major air base at Ngerengere and constructed the naval base in Dar es Salaam.[174] In 2013

SECURITY DIPLOMACY

China provided $68.5 million to finance reconstruction of the Ngerengere base.[175] China built the Tanzanian Military Academy, as well as the Ministry of Defense and National Service, and contracted with the Shanghai Construction Group to build twelve thousand housing units, financed by a $550 million loan from China's Export Import Bank. In 2018 President John Magafuli opened the Chinese-built TPDF training center in Bagamoyo District.[176] Chinese firms also constructed Tanzania's defense headquarters and the National Defense College in Dar es Salaam.[177]

China built Uganda's Defense Ministry headquarters and the Uganda People's Defense Forces (UPDF) headquarters in Bombo, the Senior Command and Staff College in Jinja, and the UPDF National Referral Hospital in Kampala. Chinese companies also constructed the UPDF barracks in Kakiri and Lunyo.[178] In 2021 Kenya and China broke ground for the National Research and Referral Hospital at the Kenya Defence Forces.[179] China has funded and built housing for the Zambian military and police in Lusaka, Kabwe, and Mufulira. The Anhui Foreign Economic Construction company built the National Defense College in Zimbabwe, financed by a $107 million Chinese loan.[180] Other Chinese-financed and built military and police construction projects in Africa include the Republican Guard barracks in Algeria, the police headquarters in Gambia, the Camp Tubman military barracks in Liberia, military housing in Mozambique, the army headquarters and police headquarters in Sierra Leone, and a medical laboratory for Ethiopia's Defense Referral Hospital.[181]

Joshua Meservey of the Heritage Foundation has suggested that government buildings constructed by Chinese state-owned companies across the continent leave African governments open to Chinese spying. He points out that Chinese companies are legally obligated to help the CPC gather intelligence, and constructing government buildings gives them the opportunity to do so.[182] China's National Intelligence Law does state that "any organization or citizen shall support, assist and cooperate with the state intelligence."[183] As yet, however, no African government has publicly acknowledged that China has installed surveillance equipment in any Chinese-built military structure.

SECURITY DIPLOMACY

HUMANITARIAN ASSISTANCE, DISASTER RELIEF, AND DE-MINING AID

China likes to publicize the civilian and military humanitarian assistance and disaster relief (HADR) that it provides to other countries. China's military strategy white papers routinely cite the importance of HADR.[184] The primary goals of HADR programs are to demonstrate that China is a responsible great power and to enhance the operational capabilities of the PLA.[185] In the case of Africa, however, the PLA's contribution has been exceedingly modest compared to that of civilian ministries and the PLA's response to disasters in Asia.[186] One of the more visible PLA HADR programs has been visits to African ports by the navy's *Peace Ark* hospital ship (see chapter 9).

In 2001 the Beijing Military Engineering Department established the China International Search and Rescue (CISAR) team, which consisted of administrators and technical experts from the China Earthquake Administration, the thirty-eighth division of the military search and rescue corps, and medical teams from the China Armed Police General Hospital. Its first and only use in Africa occurred in Algeria in 2003, following a major earthquake. In 2018, after China created the new Ministry of Emergency Management, the China Search and Rescue team replaced CISAR and was staffed entirely by ministry personnel, apparently all civilians. Its first international mission was to cyclone-devastated Mozambique.[187] The PLA's longest HADR commitment in Africa has been the military medical teams it has sent since 1984 to Zambia on a one-year rotational basis. As of 2019, China assigned a total of 277 military doctors to the general hospital of the Zambian Defense Force in Lusaka.[188]

In 2014 and 2015 the PLA deployed 524 medical staff in seven groups on a rotational basis to combat the Ebola virus in Liberia, Sierra Leone, Guinea, and Guinea-Bissau.[189] This was the PLA's most significant HADR intervention in Africa, and its largest ever medical assistance mission overseas. The PLA contingent was part of a larger Chinese civilian medical effort in

West Africa and eventually totaled 1,200 personnel. Most of the PLA team sent to Liberia, where it set up a hundred-bed Ebola treatment unit, came from the Third Military Medical University in Chongqing.[190] The PLA also deployed three rotating medical teams to Freetown, Sierra Leone, to assist with infection prevention and control, clinical care, and health promotion and training.[191] The PLA constructed the hospital in Liberia in one month and converted in one week a small general hospital in Sierra Leone to one specializing in infectious diseases.[192]

China has significant investments in West Africa, and more than twenty thousand Chinese nationals live and work in the region. Through the PLA's efforts to improve its HADR capability, it has learned more about military diplomacy. China also responded to a request from the United States to cooperate in containing the Ebola outbreak.[193] It was in Beijing's interest to mitigate the impact of this highly contagious disease. China's contribution was both welcome and successful, but it was not without challenges. Chinese military doctors and nurses struggled with the language barrier and cultural differences. The PLA units had little or no experience outside China in practicing clinical or public health services, hospital construction, foreign staff training, long-term overseas logistical support, or cooperating with other foreign medical units.[194]

The PLA periodically makes small donations of medicine, food, school supplies, and tents to countries in Africa. In 2011, for example, it made a $4.5 million donation of medicine, food, and tents to Tunisia and $7.7 million to Libya as both countries faced internal turmoil.[195] In 2017 the PLA base in Djibouti donated medical equipment and supplies to the Djiboutian military police.[196]

In 2020 the PLA ramped up its HADR activities to combat COVID-19 as part of China's strategic health diplomacy. In Africa, the PLA contribution to COVID-19 diplomacy is a small component of the much larger program led by Chinese state-owned companies, government ministries, Jack Ma, and Alibaba.[197] The PLA delivered protective equipment and 300,000 doses of vaccine to the South African National Defense Force (SANDF) and then organized a video conference between PLA medical experts and SANDF counterparts to share experiences for treating

COVID-19 patients.¹⁹⁸ China's defense attaché in South Africa handed over a second consignment of personal protective equipment to the SANDF.¹⁹⁹ The PLA also donated sixty-two thousand masks, nineteen thousand items of personal protective equipment, and other medical supplies to the Zimbabwe Defense Forces.²⁰⁰ China's Ministry of National Defense, meanwhile, shipped COVID-19 medical supplies to the Ministry of National Defense in the Republic of Congo, and the PLA sent $290,000 worth of protective gear and supplies to the Rwanda Defense Force.²⁰¹ The PLA also delivered COVID-19 vaccine to the Republic of Congo, Equatorial Guinea, Guinea, and Tunisia.²⁰²

PLA medical units and, on rarer occasion, engineering companies attached to UN peacekeeping missions in Africa engage in HADR activities. The primary task of the medical units is to provide care for UN peacekeepers, but they also work with local hospitals and communities.²⁰³ Jung Jae Kwon of the Massachusetts Institute of Technology offers four reasons why the PLA encourages medical and engineering units to engage in HADR projects. First, it improves China's image in the country. Second, it is an overseas extension of China's domestic model of civil-military relations. Third, it demonstrates a fundamentally different approach to peacekeeping and underscores the concept of "developmental peace." Finally, it sends a message to China's domestic audience that is intended to build support for its peacekeeping commitments overseas.²⁰⁴ These HADR contributions appear to be achieving the results desired by China, but they raise questions about UN operational control over peacekeeping missions and their intended purpose.²⁰⁵

There are numerous examples of HADR by PLA medical units assigned to UN peacekeeping operations in the DRC, Liberia, South Sudan, and Mali and a few by engineering units in the DRC and Sudan. In Mali, for example, Chinese medics have provided medical services to the local population and donated medical supplies to international aid organizations and school supplies and soccer balls to nearby schools. In the DRC, the Chinese peacekeepers developed a close relationship with SOS Children's Village and donated appliances, food, clothing, and medicine. The PLA engineering unit in Sudan renovated an elementary school in Nyala, built a playground, and donated school and athletic supplies. PLA forces in Liberia donated medical, school, and athletic supplies to a variety of organizations and taught first aid, martial arts, calligraphy, and Chinese in several schools. The medical unit in South Sudan forged a close relationship with a nursing school in Wau, and the relevant engineering company helped with the renovation of hospitals and the nursing college.[206]

Another area of PLA HADR engagement is mine clearance, to which China attaches considerable importance.[207] China actively supports and participates in international demining efforts but, like the United States, has not signed the Ottawa Landmine Convention.[208] The African Union and most African states, by contrast, strongly support the Landmine Convention. Although China's demining assistance to any single country in Africa has been modest, Beijing has aided a wide range of them. China donated demining equipment to Ethiopia, Mozambique, Burundi, Rwanda, Angola, Namibia, Egypt, Guinea-Bissau, Chad, and Eritrea. It has trained personnel from Angola, Eritrea, Rwanda, Mozambique, Chad, Burundi, Guinea-Bissau, Egypt, Sudan, and South Sudan. A PLA team from the Lanzhou Military Area Command conducted landmine detection in the DRC as part of the UN peacekeeping operation.[209] As of 2017, China had trained two hundred Africans from fourteen countries on de-mining.[210] Nearly all this activity took place in the late 1990s and the first ten years of this century.

COUNTERTERRORISM COOPERATION AND INTELLIGENCE SHARING

China's position is that combatting terrorism must deal with its root causes, including the eradication of poverty. Although it agrees that the use of force may be necessary, it argues that relying on the military is often counterproductive. In recent years China's response to global terrorism has been guided by terrorist attacks in China and its insistence that the Muslim Uighur community in Xinjiang is a hotbed of domestic terrorism with links outside China (see chapter 2). Consequently, China's counterterrorism strategy has shifted from generic concerns about international terrorism to its Muslim population's alleged international ties, and the protection of Chinese nationals abroad.[211]

China's 2015 counterterrorism law permits relevant departments of the State Council to engage in counterterrorism policy dialogues and exchanges of intelligence information, enforcement cooperation, and international financial monitoring with foreign nations and international organizations. The State Council may assign personnel outside the country on counterterror missions. The PLA and the PAP also have the authority to send staff outside of China on counterterrorism missions as approved by the CMC.[212] The PAP may be emerging as the partner of choice to assist foreign governments with counterterrorist operations.[213]

Beijing's counterterrorism diplomacy prioritizes bilateral exchanges but also utilizes multilateral organizations. A founding member of the Global Counterterrorism Forum, in 2013 China announced its intention to increase involvement in the forum's working groups on the Horn of Africa and the Sahel. Its international counterterrorism cooperation includes repatriating to China individuals suspected of terrorism and protecting the security of its diaspora population. International collaboration has focused on its neighbors, Central Asia, South Asia, and Southeast Asia. Africa has been a low priority in this regard, and counterterrorism has only recently become a significant part of the security relationship. Between 2002 and 2015, for example, China held thirty-eight counterterrorism exercises with other countries, and not one of them with an African nation.[214] Counterterrorism is not part of China's military assistance; Beijing treats the issue separately.[215]

Every FOCAC action plan since 2003 has included a pledge, or at least a reference, to strengthening counterterrorism cooperation, although in the early years there was little collaboration in this arena. The most recent action plan for 2022–2024 pledged stronger "collaboration and coordination of actions in cracking down on international terrorist organizations."[216] Growing concerns about terrorism in Africa, potential harm to Chinese nationals and interests there, and the inability of African security forces to protect foreigners all caused China to pay more attention to the problem. China's dialogue on this topic with Arab states is even more explicit. Its Arab policy paper in 2016 stated that China "believes that counterterrorism needs comprehensive measures to address both the symptoms and root causes," and "China is ready to strengthen anti-terrorism exchanges and cooperation with Arab countries to establish a long-term cooperation mechanism."[217]

In Africa, China has focused its counterterrorism cooperation on North Africa, especially Algeria and Egypt. This is understandable, as China had a narrow escape in Algeria. In 2009 the Algeria-based al-Qaeda in the Islamic Maghreb (AQIM) threatened attacks against Chinese nationals and interests following Uighur protests and deaths in Xinjiang. AQIM then attacked an Algerian convoy protecting a group of Chinese engineers, killing twenty-four Algerian paramilitary police officers. Two al-Qaeda-affiliated websites subsequently called for the killing of Chinese nationals working in Algeria.[218] Although AQIM has since ended its public threats against Chinese interests in Algeria, it did attack Chinese peacekeepers in nearby Mali.[219] In 2016 a special representative from China's Ministry of Foreign Affairs visited Algeria and pledged to strengthen bilateral cooperation in the fight against terrorism.[220] Later that year one of China's assistant foreign ministers led a delegation to Algiers for the first ever China-Algeria counterterrorism and security consultation, where the protection of Chinese nationals, institutions, and projects was discussed.[221]

During a visit by Xi Jinping to Egypt in 2016, the foreign ministers of China and Egypt signed a five-year program to jointly combat terrorism and extremism, with extensive cooperation in information exchange, evidence collection, and arrest and the repatriation of suspects. The two countries also vowed to strengthen cooperation in capturing and punishing members of terrorist organizations and stemming the financial sources of terrorism.[222] Egypt subsequently participated in the inaugural session of the Great Wall Counter-Terrorism International Forum in Beijing.[223] China and Egypt reiterated their collaboration on counterterrorism during President Abdel-Fattah al-Sissi's visit to Beijing in 2018.[224] In 2020, during a visit to Cairo, Foreign Minister Wang Yi stressed that the issue of Xinjiang is solely an internal affair and most Islamic countries, including Egypt, are not deceived by "Western lies" on this issue (see chapter 2).[225]

In 2017 at China's behest Egyptian security forces detained more than a hundred Uighurs in the country. Many were students at Cairo's al-Azhar University. Before authorities could detain others, they fled to Turkey, which sympathizes with the Uighurs because of their Turkic ethnic background. Reports that Egypt deported twelve Uighurs to China appear to be inaccurate. Rather, authorities apparently put the Uighurs on a plane for China that stopped in Istanbul, where they disembarked.[226]

China's counterterror relationship with Morocco is less developed than the one with Algeria or Egypt. During a visit to Morocco by Foreign Minister Wang Yi in 2014, a Chinese press release said Morocco condemns recent violent terrorist attacks in China and is determined to work with China to combat all forms of terrorism.[227] In 2019 a Uighur living in exile in Turkey transited Casablanca en route to Germany. After three days of detention, he returned safely to Istanbul, having faced possible deportation to China.[228] In 2021 Moroccan authorities arrested a Uighur involved in documenting crimes in Xinjiang and accused by Beijing of being a member of the "terrorist" East Turkestan Islamic Movement. A Moroccan court agreed to extradite the subject to China, although an outcry from human rights groups held up the extradition.[229]

In Sub-Sahara Africa, Mali has been a focus of China's counterterrorism efforts for three reasons. Following the breakdown of authority in Libya, Mali's northern neighbor, terrorist groups became active and destabilized the area, leading to the establishment of a UN peacekeeping mission in Mali. China agreed to contribute troops, putting them in harm's way. In 2015 three senior executives with the China Railway Construction Corporation died during an AQIM attack on the Radisson Blu hotel in Bamako, Mali. The day after the attack, Chinese peacekeepers organized an emergency antiterrorism exercise.[230] In 2016 an attack on the UN peacekeeping camp killed a Chinese peacekeeper and injured four others.[231] China vowed to remain part of the peacekeeping operation and sent a task force made up of military and Foreign Ministry personnel to evaluate the protection of Chinese peacekeepers.[232] A senior Malian military officer commented that he was unaware, despite rumors, of any Uighur involvement in the armed groups opposing UN peacekeepers in the country.[233] In 2020, after Nigeria signed an agreement with China for military equipment, the two signed an MOU on combatting terrorism.[234]

China has emphasized its desire to cooperate on counterterrorism with Kenya, which has troops in Somalia combatting al-Shabaab. Premier Li Keqiang, during a visit to Nairobi in 2014, said the two countries reaffirmed their commitment to oppose terrorism and to cooperate closely in promoting international counterterrorism initiatives.[235] In 2015 the al-Qaeda-affiliated al-Shabaab terrorist group conducted a bombing in Mogadishu, Somalia, that killed a security officer at China's embassy.[236] In 2020, underscoring the regional threat, a al-Shabaab-aligned cleric in Somalia announced that COVID-19 affected only the enemies of Islam, specifically referring to China, which he said was being punished for its persecution of the Uighurs.[237] This was a rare criticism of China by Africans for its mistreatment of the Uighur population.

Because of its sensitive nature, there is little information on China's intelligence cooperation with African countries. Due to China's increased concern about terrorism, however, it has become a more important part of the China-Africa strategic relationship.[238] The past three FOCAC action plans and China's 2016 Arab policy paper have mentioned strengthening intelligence information exchange on security issues generally and specifically on combatting terrorism. Likewise, the African Union endorsed intelligence cooperation with China.[239] Increasingly, China is emphasizing the need for intelligence cooperation in its bilateral discussions. In 2014, during a visit to Nigeria, Premier Li Keqiang promised that China will make any useful information acquired by its satellites and intelligence services available to Nigeria's security services.[240] During that same visit to Africa, Li Keqiang proposed in Ethiopia the 461 Framework to promote China-Africa cooperation, including a project to strengthen cooperation in personnel training, intelligence sharing, and joint exercises and training.[241]

* * *

China ties its security diplomacy to the transfer (mostly sales) of conventional weapons and SALW to Africa. The arms connection is, in turn, linked to military exchange visits, new security forums, the use of military attachés, and bilateral military and police training and exercises. All are tools for enhancing security collaboration and arms sales. China's transfer of arms to African countries has been essential to the development of several military organizations, especially in countries that have faced Western sanctions. China's weapons are reliable and often cheaper than those from any other source. Because China has become a growing source of weapons, however, they are showing up more frequently in African conflict zones. Beijing has increased its military and police training programs, most of which take place in China. Africans speak positively about these programs, although language differences continue to pose a challenge.

China has become a major source of funding and serves as the contractor for numerous military and police facilities, giving Beijing another opportunity for contact with African security forces. It also raises the possibility of placing surveillance devices in the structures, although no African government has ever complained, at least publicly, that China has done so. In recent years China has emphasized military cooperation in the areas of humanitarian assistance and disaster relief. There has also been more Chinese support for Africa's counterterrorism programs and a greater willingness to share intelligence. All these programs allow Chinese officials to increase their personal interaction with African counterparts.

9

MARITIME SECURITY

China's naval interest in African waters began in the western Indian Ocean, the Gulf of Aden, and the Red Sea and has expanded into the Mediterranean and Africa's Atlantic coast. As the PLA Navy (PLAN) engages in the Indian Ocean, it encounters the Indian and U.S. navies and growing concerns from others. Increased PLAN deployments in African waters, especially in support of the antipiracy operation in the Gulf of Aden, convinced China that it must develop facilities to replenish supplies and provide rest for ship crews. This led to a search for regional ports and more permanent support arrangements to dock and/or service PLAN vessels. China has engaged in port financing, construction, and management along the northern rim of the Indian Ocean and around Africa, efforts that were catalyzed by Xi Jinping's Belt and Road Initiative (BRI) and subsequent Global Security Initiative.

After reviewing the competing security interests in the western Indian Ocean by the major naval powers, this chapter examines China's maritime interests and naval strategy in African waters. It discusses China's counterpiracy operations, especially in the Gulf of Aden, which was ostensibly the reason for expanding the navy's reach into the region. This leads to an analysis of Chinese companies' successful efforts to finance, construct, and manage ports in Africa. Until the onset of the coronavirus pandemic, this effort contributed to a major increase in naval port calls in Africa supported by China's global efforts to expand its merchant fleet. The chapter concludes with a discussion of China's first overseas military base, in Djibouti, and the prospect for the establishment of additional bases or dual-use facilities in African waters.

COMPETING SECURITY INTERESTS IN THE WESTERN INDIAN OCEAN

China's naval strategy over the short and medium term, as it pertains to Africa, focuses on the western Indian Ocean, which includes African island nations (Madagascar, Mauritius, Comoro Islands, and the Seychelles), Africa's Indian Ocean littoral states, the Gulf of Aden, and the Red Sea. An analysis of China's maritime strategy in the western Indian Ocean and African territorial waters of the Atlantic and Mediterranean requires an understanding of the interests and concerns of the principal naval powers active there. Over the longer term, China's naval expansion will turn increasingly to waters off Africa in the Mediterranean and the Atlantic. Piracy in the Gulf of Aden initially stimulated China's naval interest in the western Indian Ocean, which took on added significance after 2013 when Xi Jinping unveiled the BRI, including the Maritime Silk Road and more recently the Global Security Initiative.[1] Both of these initiatives have raised concerns in India, whose security is closely tied to the Indian Ocean, as well as in the major Asian shipping nations that rely on the same sea lines of communication (SLOCs). It is also of concern to the principal naval power in the Indian Ocean, the United States. European countries, especially France and the UK, likewise have a strong interest in freedom of navigation from the Suez Canal to the Persian Gulf.

Since the withdrawal of the European navies in the 1970s, the United States has been the primary guarantor of freedom of navigation in the

Indian Ocean and remains the most important security partner for many states in the region.[2] In the Indian Ocean region, the United States has the most powerful navy, which counters terrorism, deters piracy, and supports the U.S. military presence in Iraq, the Gulf States, Somalia, and Djibouti. The monitoring of China's naval expansion in the Indian Ocean has added to its responsibilities. In 2017 the United States revived a multilateral partnership initiated in 2004 with India, Japan, and Australia aimed at a "Free and Open Indo-Pacific" region that China does not dominate. Known as the Quadrilateral Security Dialogue or "Quad," the members are expanding the concept, which secures the naval interests and presence of the United States, India, and Japan in the western Indian Ocean.[3] Beijing accuses the United States of following a "containment" strategy in the Indo-Pacific region aimed at limiting China's economic growth and military options in order to preserve its own hegemonic status.[4]

American military and naval power focus on the Persian Gulf region, but U.S. ships also pass routinely through the western Indian Ocean and visit African ports. Bahrain hosts two U.S. air bases, the U.S. Naval Forces Central Command, and the U.S. Fifth Fleet. The largest U.S. air base in the Middle East is in Qatar; the United States has another in the United Arab Emirates, and forces stationed at two of its ports. Kuwait hosts an estimated fifteen thousand U.S. personnel at an air base and three military camps. The United States has an agreement with Oman to use the ports of Salah and Duqm and for the air force to use various bases. U.S. military facilities in East Africa have a counterterrorism emphasis. The U.S. base in Djibouti supports about four thousand personnel. Several hundred more use a forward operating base near Lamu in Kenya, including special forces operators in Somalia.[5] The United States has a major air and naval support facility in the middle of the Indian Ocean at Diego Garcia, which can accommodate an aircraft carrier and host B-1B bombers.[6]

India has the most to lose from a growing Chinese naval presence in the Indian Ocean and sees China as its major adversary. All of India's seaborne traffic must pass through the Indian Ocean. More than 90 percent of India's international trade by volume, 68 percent by value, and 90 percent of its oil imports rely on Indian Ocean SLOCs.[7] At least 75 percent of India's oil imports pass through the Gulf of Aden.⁸ A common theme of Indian military analysts is the fear of Chinese "encirclement" due to their country's lengthy and troubled border with China to the north; contentious relations with nuclear-armed and China-aligned Pakistan to the west; China-friendly Myanmar to the east; and now expanding Chinese naval power in the Indian Ocean to the south.⁹ Colonel Saji Abraham of the Indian Army has written: "China's deeds are clearly aimed at the strategic encirclement of India in order to marginalise India in Asia and tie it down to the Indian sub-continent."¹⁰ India's ambassador to China in 2017–2018, Gautam Bambawale, commented that "there has been a sea change in India about how we look at geopolitics and how we look at China," and a harder attitude toward China will likely shape Indian policies for years.¹¹

A corollary of this strategy is the "string of pearls" argument coined by U.S. consulting firm Booz Allen Hamilton in 2005 as part of a Pentagon study. It posits that China is developing a series of ports and military access points from the Strait of Malacca along the northern rim of the Indian Ocean to the Red Sea. Many Indian analysts see this as part of China's strategy to box in India in its subregion.¹² India perceives China's military base in Djibouti and its guaranteed access to Gwadar in Pakistan as being designed potentially to sever Indian energy supplies from East and West Africa and the Persian Gulf.¹³ China, for its part, denies the validity of this encirclement theory and the string of pearls argument.¹⁴ Nevertheless, India is responding with a strategy that emphasizes improving naval support facilities in the Andaman and Nicobar Islands in the eastern Indian Ocean and increased collaboration with Africa's Indian Ocean island countries in the west, combined with closer ties to the Australian, French, and U.S. navies.¹⁵

Sea control is the central concept around which the Indian Navy is structured. India has the most ships and submarines in the Indian Ocean: about 150, with another fifty under construction. Most, however, are for coastal protection.¹⁶ India has one aircraft carrier, and a second that is being prepared for commissioning.¹⁷ China's naval presence in the Indian Ocean is a significant driver of India's strategic naval planning especially since 2017, when China established its first overseas military base in Djibouti. China is also dependent on the SLOCs that pass through the Indian Ocean, an area where India enjoys the advantage of proximity. India must balance concerns about Beijing's intentions with the fact that China is its largest trading partner, and that both countries belong to the BRICS (see chapter 3). India is also a member of the China-led Asian Infrastructure Investment Bank and the Shanghai Cooperation Organization.[18]

To monitor PLAN activities in the Indian Ocean, India has established naval surveillance facilities in Madagascar and Mauritius and launched a military satellite to improve communication with ships far offshore. India has increased the number of calls at ports along the Indian Ocean rim and has secured access rights from the United States to the military facility on Diego Garcia, the port of Duqm from Oman, and Réunion from France. India has stationed military personnel in the Seychelles, Mauritius, and the Maldives to train local troops in the use of patrol planes, helicopters, and boats supplied to those countries.[19] In 2015 India and the Seychelles agreed to develop a joint military facility on Assumption Island. The Seychelles' opposition party opposed the project and prevented its implementation. It then won the election in 2020 and has reopened discussions with India, but prefers to balance its relations between India and China.[20] India has also developed a close military relationship with Mozambique, providing training to the navy and intelligence service and antipiracy patrols in the Mozambique Channel.[21] India has defense cooperation agreements with Kenya, Mozambique, South Africa, Mauritius, and Seychelles.[22] India has stepped up naval cooperation, including joint exercises, with the United States, France, Japan, and other major seafaring countries wary of China.[23]

While Japan is primarily concerned about China's presence in the East China Sea, it is also closely monitoring China's growing influence in the Indian Ocean, where the SLOCs are "vitally important" for Japan.[24] Tokyo sees the Indian Ocean as a highway for trade with Europe, Africa, and the Middle East, and central to its concept of a "Free and Open Indo-Pacific." Japan is deeply concerned with Indian Ocean security, especially the choke points at the Strait of Malacca in the east and the Red Sea in the west.[25] Japan imports 90 percent of its energy across the Indian Ocean.[26] In 2009 Japan began deploying two destroyers to the counterpiracy operation in the

Gulf of Aden and subsequently assigned two maritime patrol aircraft to the mission.[27] In 2011 Japan opened its first overseas military base since World War II in Djibouti, in part to counter the influence of China. In 2016 Japan expanded its Djibouti base, which hosts about two hundred military personnel.[28]

Since the end of World War II, Japan has not had a significant presence in the Indian Ocean. Consequently, Tokyo aligned its interests with those of the United States in Djibouti and is working hard to improve its military relations with India. There are now regular Japan-India defense minister meetings, joint staff talks, and exercises between the militaries and coast guards of the two countries.[29] In 2020 Japan and India signed an Acquisition and Cross-Servicing Agreement that permits the use of each other's bases for logistical support. In the Indian Ocean region, this gives India access to Japan's facility in Djibouti and Japan access to Indian installations on the Andaman and Nicobar Islands near the Strait of Malacca.[30]

Many European countries are dependent on the Suez Canal, Red Sea, Gulf of Aden, and Persian Gulf for transit of their energy supplies. Nearly all rely on western Indian Ocean SLOCs for their trade with Asia. The UK has a military presence in Kenya, an air base in Qatar, a naval logistics support base in Oman, and a naval base in Bahrain.[31] France has a military base in Djibouti, which allows it to send nuclear attack submarines into the Indian Ocean. The base has a squadron of combat fighters and a special forces detachment and hosts Spanish and German troops. France has permanent military forces at its overseas territories on Réunion and Mayotte totaling 1,600 military personnel, as well as two frigates and smaller naval vessels and aircraft. France also has 650 personnel at naval and army bases in the UAE.[32]

CHINA'S MARITIME INTERESTS AND NAVAL STRATEGY IN AFRICAN WATERS

From a military and defense perspective, the Pacific is more important to China than the Indian Ocean. Yet the Indian Ocean is critical to China's economic, especially energy security.[33] The BRI has increased the significance of the Indian Ocean and Africa's Mediterranean coast. Even Africa's Atlantic coast is attracting more attention because of China's energy imports from the region and fishing activity in West African exclusive economic zones. About 40 percent of China's foreign trade and more than 80 percent of its oil imports pass through the Indian Ocean.[34] China sends $1 trillion of goods annually through the Red Sea alone.[35] About 18 percent of China's imported oil and enormous quantities of strategic minerals come from African countries. As China's demand for fish increases, African waters in both the Indian Ocean and the Atlantic have become more important to Beijing.[36] China is also looking to the future exploitation of deep seabed minerals in the southwestern Indian Ocean (see chapter 6).

China's maritime interests include protecting Chinese-flagged vessels and crews in the waters off Africa. The PLAN also contributes to the protection of Chinese investments and personnel in Africa and the Middle East and, if necessary, the evacuation of Chinese nationals (see chapter 7). China wants to develop the economies of its partners and encourage political stability in volatile and sometimes chaotic regions in order to help advance its own economic interests and protect its nationals living and working there.[37] The navy attaches growing importance to long-range SLOC protection and general naval presence capabilities.[38] Li Jiacheng of Liaoning University has concluded: "As its primary interest in the Indian Ocean is to ensure free and safe trade routes, including the crucial energy transport routes, China has no other choice but to build a blue-water navy that can support its expanding role in the region (specifically anti-piracy missions) and make sure that its trade routes, in particular the safe and free passage through the Strait of Malacca, are not subject to the caprice of any dominant power."[39]

China periodically issues defense strategy white papers that offer insights into its global maritime strategy. Its white paper in 2015, for instance, stated that the PLAN "will gradually shift its focus from 'offshore waters defense' (近海防御) to the combination of 'offshore waters defense' with 'open seas protection' (外海保护), and build a combined multifunctional and efficient marine combat force structure." The document lays out that China must move away from the traditional view that land is more important than the sea and develop a modern maritime force commensurate with its national security that includes protection of "the security of strategic SLOCs and overseas interests" to build itself into a "maritime power."[40] The white paper does not define "open seas" (外海), however, and previous white papers have used the term "far seas" (远海), which also remains undefined but is used in similar fashion. You Ji of the University of Macau defines "far seas" as "China's eighteen thousand nautical miles of SLOCs from Western Africa through the Indian Ocean, the Malacca Strait, and the South China Sea to the Chinese ports in Guangzhou and Shanghai."[41]

According to Wu Zhengyu of Renmin University, China's 2015 white paper reflected a shift in naval strategy as a response to the BRI. The Maritime Silk Road underscores the paramount importance of economic development for China and the inherent advantages of sea over land routes. The resultant shift in naval strategy reflected the effort to ensure the safety, security, and success of the BRI in the Indian Ocean region and beyond as Beijing extended the initiative into northern and southern Africa. The "open seas protection" cited in the white paper has resulted in an extensive naval building program and highlighted China's weakness in not having overseas naval bases or support facilities, hence the base in Djibouti. Wu Zhengyu added that the new naval strategy is likely to push China to reconsider its "doctrinaire adherence to the principle of noninterference."[42]

The reports of the Eighteenth and Nineteenth Party Congresses of the CPC in 2012 and 2017, respectively, prioritized China's development of maritime capabilities. Both stated that it is a national goal of China to become a "strong maritime power," which means being able to "resolutely safeguard China's maritime rights and interests."[43] An article in 2017 in *Contemporary World*, a journal published by the International Department of the CPC, advocated building a "China-Indian Ocean economic circle" to promote synergistic development from the Middle East to China before "outside powers" were able to do so.[44] Feng Chuanlu of the Yunnan University of Finance and Economics has said that China's growing influence in the Indian Ocean is not a case of strategic overreach, but an inevitable development as China's interests expand globally.[45]

MARITIME SECURITY

In 2017 China published its "Vision for Maritime Cooperation Under the Belt and Road Initiative," which urged countries to build safe and efficient maritime transport channels. It called for a China-Indian Ocean-Africa-Mediterranean Sea Blue Economic Passage (中国-印度洋-非洲-地中海 蓝色经济通道).[46] China's unclassified maritime strategy documents tend to be general in nature, and there remains no official document that lays out a comprehensive Indian Ocean strategy. In fact, the first *Annual Report on the Development of the Indian Ocean Region* (better known as the *Blue Book*), produced in 2013 by the government-affiliated Chinese Academy of Social Sciences, stated explicitly that China did not have an Indian Ocean strategy. While the *Blue Book* does not represent official policy, it advocated for China to deepen its economic engagement with Indian Ocean littoral states, stressing that commercial rather than military objectives drive Beijing's interests. It warned that the Indian Ocean region may turn from a zone of cooperation and peace into an "ocean of conflict and trouble."[47]

An article in 2016 in the Chinese-language *Naval Affairs*, a journal for internal governmental distribution, authored by two PLAN officers discussed China's "far seas" naval strategy. According to them, PLA goals in the far seas include fostering closer ties with foreign militaries, rescuing Chinese living abroad, and overseeing the transfer of Chinese assets abroad. The authors argued that the PLA should also be able to "exploit contradictions between the United States and other countries" and take advantage of its tendency as the global hegemon to be distracted by issues such as terrorism. They urged the navy to seek an "asymmetrical balance of power" in the far seas, which includes an emphasis on more aircraft carriers, nuclear-powered ballistic-missile submarines, and amphibious assault ships. While the article is not a formal statement of Chinese naval strategy, it nonetheless offers insights into how navy strategists are thinking of implementing Xi Jinping's ambitions for a world-class navy.[48]

Mike Chia-Yu Huang of Sun Yat-Sen University has laid out the evolution of China's Indian Ocean strategy. He argues that it began with former President Hu Jintao's concern about the Strait of Malacca chokepoint and China's 2004 defense white paper, which extended the range of the PLAN's offshore operations. Although at first Hu Jintao did not want to appear too assertive in the Indian Ocean, beginning in 2008 the PLAN's antipiracy operation in the Gulf of Aden afforded the opportunity to increase deployments in the region without threatening other naval powers. It touched off a heated debate, however, among Chinese strategists concerning the need to construct military bases in the Indian Ocean. Thereafter, Xi Jinping's announcement in 2013 of the BRI and Maritime Silk Road marked a new phase aimed at restoring the former glory of China's maritime achievements as well as strengthening its trade relations. The 2015 white paper explained the need for "open seas protection" and construction of overseas military installations.[49]

Other Chinese strategists proposed a Chinese Atlantic maritime strategy. A 2016 article in *Ocean Development and Management*, the official Chinese-language publication of the State Oceanic Administration, argued that the PLAN must enter the Atlantic to break the American maritime blockade and develop China's maritime "external line," albeit primarily for commercial purposes. They observed that the Atlantic is the endpoint of the Maritime Silk Road and noted the enormous potential for increased trade with countries on Africa's and Latin America's Atlantic coasts.[50] Ryan Martinson of the U.S. Naval War College has argued that China is preparing for future operations in the South Atlantic, noting that it has had ships there every year since 2014. China, according to Martinson, has also increased the number of navy visits to ports along the West African coast. A major obstacle in this regard, however, is the fact that China has no shore-based infrastructure to support operations in the South Atlantic or off Africa's Atlantic coast.[51]

It is difficult to speak of a "Mediterranean strategy" in a Chinese context, as Chinese officials and analysts rarely use the term; they refer to southern Europe and northern Africa. Most of China's maritime cooperation in the Mediterranean has been with Greece, although it has considerable interaction with North African countries in the context of FOCAC and CASCF (see chapter 3). China has comprehensive maritime cooperation partnerships with Greece, Italy, Spain, Portugal, Cyprus, and Malta.[52] Beijing has paid less attention to the North African maritime domain, but it has increased navy port calls and is engaged in the development of North African ports.

Non-Chinese analysts are more concerned about China's naval strategy. Writing in 2016, Gurpreet S. Khurana of India's National Maritime Foundation said China was seeking access facilities in the Indian Ocean. Until the PLAN can establish carrier-based sea control in the Indian Ocean, however, it will likely deploy its nuclear attack submarines as part of its deterrence-by-punishment strategy. China may also establish an Indian Ocean fleet in a decade or so, after it has adequate numbers of long-range vessels and can insure sustainability in the Indian Ocean. Khurana believes that China will resort to a combination of access facilities and sea-basing, rather than developing full-fledged military bases, which will come later.[53]

In 2016 retired U.S. rear admiral Michael McDevitt conducted a major study of China's maritime goals. He explained that, for China, *far seas* mean regions well outside the first island chain (referred to as *near seas*) and includes SLOCs in the Indian Ocean. Operationally, the distinction between near seas and far seas is the difference between defending China proper from attacks and protecting Chinese interests and sea lanes abroad. He pointed out that Chinese writings on maritime power often state that China must achieve naval superiority in its near seas while increasingly improving its far seas capability. The deployment of both conventional and nuclear-powered submarines in the Indian Ocean reflects an effort to determine their contribution to defending key SLOCs from wartime interdiction. McDevitt argued that Xi Jinping has embraced maritime power as an essential element of the "Chinese Dream" and it will remain a national objective throughout his rule (see chapter 1).[54]

David Brewster of Australian National University set forth three scenarios, which are not mutually exclusive, for China's Indian Ocean strategy. The first is a limited Chinese naval presence with an emphasis on military operations other than war, such as countering piracy. The second strategy revolves around the ability to conduct limited sea-denial operations by relying heavily on submarines. The third is sea control, whereby China tries to achieve naval predominance in the Indian Ocean to protect its SLOCs. Brewster concluded that while Chinese naval planners are inclined to pursue the sea control strategy, there are stronger arguments favoring sea denial because of the prohibitive cost and strategic disadvantages of sea control.[55]

Drawing on Chinese sources, Andrew S. Erickson of the U.S. Naval War College has argued that Chinese naval strategists envision a significant outward extension of China's maritime interests, capabilities, and forces. The authoritative doctrinal text *The Science of Military Strategy* (2013) called for establishment of a Chinese "arc-shaped strategic zone that covers the western Pacific Ocean and northern Indian Ocean" termed the "two oceans region/area" (两海区). Erickson concluded that "China is enacting a maritime theater concept that provides a focus for the PLAN extending across the Indo-Pacific and beyond."[56] Increasingly, this strategy will also require power-projection capabilities for the PLA Air Force and PLA Naval Air Force to support MOOTW, emergency evacuations, UN peacekeeping missions, humanitarian assistance and disaster missions, and limited military tasks.[57]

To implement its naval strategy, whatever direction it takes, China is engaged in a major expansion of naval capabilities.[58] As of 2019, the PLAN had an inventory of 335 surface combatants, submarines, amphibious ships, patrol craft, and specialized units. The U.S. Office of Naval Intelligence believes that China will have 400 battle force ships by 2025 and 425 by 2030.[59] China's inventory includes three aircraft carriers (two with antiquated ski lift launch technology and a third with an electromagnetic catapult for launching aircraft that will not be battle ready until 2027), thirty-three destroyers, fifty-four frigates, fifty-nine amphibious ships, and sixty submarines, six of which are nuclear attack and four nuclear-powered ballistic missile submarines.[60]

The PLAN's recent ship acquisitions demonstrate a growing emphasis on craft that are multimission capable and large enough to sustain open seas protection operations. In particular, these are the aircraft carriers, amphibious ships, and nuclear- powered submarines.[61] The navy has also emphasized the need for replenishment ships in order to minimize the acquisition of naval bases and support facilities.[62] The regional antipiracy operation underscored the need for more supply ships and their limitations.[63] Although China's naval modernization effort has substantially improved its capabilities, the PLAN has weaknesses in conducting joint operations with other parts of China's military, as well as in antisubmarine warfare, long-range targeting, and a lack of combat experience.[64]

There have been other important indicators of China's longer-term maritime goals as well. In 2013 the PLAN began deploying submarines to the Indian Ocean, and despite COVID-19 it has continued to conduct two deployments annually, including nuclear-powered attack submarines.[65] In 2017 a formation consisting of a destroyer, a guided-missile frigate, and a supply ship conducted a live-fire drill in the western Indian Ocean. The reason given was to conduct strikes against unidentified "enemy" surface ships.[66] The drill took place as China and India engaged in a border dispute encompassing Tibet's Chumbi valley to the north, Bhutan's Ha valley to the east, and India's Sikkim state to the west. This led to speculation that the perceived "enemy" was India. A Shanghai-based military affairs commentator said the drill was a sign that Beijing would act if Chinese vessels were blocked from traveling through the Indian Ocean.[67]

Another indicator of China's focus on far seas operational capacity is the rapid expansion of the PLAN Marine Corps (PLANMC). Until 2017 it consisted of two brigades, about twelve thousand personnel and was limited to defense of South China Sea outposts. By late 2021 the PLANMC had expanded to six brigades each with six thousand marines, two supporting brigades, one aviation and one of special operations forces. The goal is to reach one hundred thousand personnel, operating much like the U.S. Marine Corps.[68] Its mission now includes expeditionary operations well beyond China's borders. It has participated in the PLAN's Gulf of Aden antipiracy missions and has a contingent stationed at China's base in Djibouti. It will become the core of the PLA's future expeditionary force.[69] China has also launched its first two amphibious assault ships, which can accommodate up to nine hundred troops and carry up to thirty helicopters. These vessels have a range of ten thousand nautical miles.[70]

This analysis suggests that the PLAN has a modest but growing presence in the Indian Ocean and at any given time has six to eight warships there.[71] It likewise has an exceedingly limited capacity in the Mediterranean and in the waters off Africa's Atlantic coast. Under Xi Jinping there is a commitment to build the navy into a global maritime force capable of operating far from China's shore, complete with the necessary supporting infrastructure. The time it takes Beijing to achieve this goal will depend on a combination of factors, among them the availability of domestic financial resources to add ships for a "far seas" navy and the willingness of countries around the world to host additional Chinese naval support facilities and bases. Africa's geography positions it to play a role in the next stage of the PLAN's expansion.

COUNTERPIRACY OPERATIONS

Somali piracy became a severe problem in 2005 and provided China with the opportunity it needed to extend its naval power far from its shores in a nonthreatening manner. Beijing received praise for its contribution to the international antipiracy effort and mitigated domestic criticism once pirates attacked Chinese crews and ships in what constituted a major threat to commercial shipping on one of the world's most important SLOCs. Somali pirate activity focused initially on the waters off Somalia and in the strategic Gulf of Aden, the sea lane that funnels shipping through the Red Sea and Suez Canal. Piracy subsequently expanded into the Red Sea and to the east and south in the western Indian Ocean. Nearly all the pirate activity involved seizing ships and crews for ransom.

In 2007 Somali pirates captured a Taiwanese fishing vessel with twelve Chinese crew members aboard; they were released after a ransom payment. The same year pirates seized two South Korean vessels with ten Chinese crew members. Then, in 2008, pirates attacked 7 of the 1,265 Chinese commercial vessels passing through the Gulf of Aden and captured a Chinese fishing vessel off the coast of Kenya with fifteen Chinese crew aboard. In 2009 another five Chinese crewmembers fell victim following the seizure of a Taiwanese fishing vessel. After the pirates captured a Chinese bulk carrier, the *De Xin Hai*, with twenty-five Chinese sailors, the pirates claimed they collected $3.5 million in ransom before releasing the vessel. In 2010 the pirates hijacked a St. Vincent and Grenadine cargo ship with twenty-three Chinese crew, a Singapore vessel with seventeen Chinese sailors, and a Panama-flagged ship staffed by a Chinese crew of twenty-nine. In 2011 Somali pirates seized another Chinese ship and twenty-four Chinese crew members.[72]

These incidents spurred the Chinese government into action. In December 2008, at a meeting of the UN Security Council, deputy minister of foreign affairs He Yafei proposed a coordinated UN response to piracy that included political, military, and economic components, respect for state sovereignty and international law, and capacity building in Somalia.[73] Before the end of the month, China had dispatched two destroyers and a supply ship that arrived in the Gulf of Aden in early January 2009. The ships included a special forces team from the PLANMC and attack helicopters. PLAN vessels operated independently of the multinational task forces and initially only escorted Chinese commercial ships. After the navy failed to prevent the seizure of the *De Xin Hai*, China saw the importance of cooperative rescue operations and began to coordinate its efforts with other nations. China took particular satisfaction in protecting ships from Taiwan, Hong Kong, and Macau.[74]

Somali piracy in the Gulf of Aden and surrounding waters reached a peak in 2010, when pirates attacked almost two hundred vessels and captured fifty, remaining a serious threat to international shipping until 2013. After 2012 no successful attacks occurred until 2017.[75] Improved practices by commercial vessels, armed teams on ships, and the international antipiracy naval effort ended the pirate threat. Nevertheless, China continued to deploy ships to the Gulf of Aden and used piracy to justify establishing a military base, or what Beijing calls a "logistics support base" (后勤基地) in Djibouti. China says it will continue to send warships to the Gulf of Aden and waters off Somalia indefinitely to combat piracy.[76]

Since 2008 the composition of China's task forces has remained remarkably consistent, usually encompassing two frigates and a supply ship. In terms of equipment, the missions added Z-9C helicopters that improved situational awareness and are better suited to assisting special operations forces in counterpiracy operations. About seventy PLANMC personnel accompany each task force. As the piracy threat diminished, ships sent to the Gulf of Aden engaged increasingly in goodwill visits to ports in African and Indian Ocean waters.[77]

The most surprising change has been the occasional addition since 2014 of submarines, including nuclear-powered ones, to the task force. As submarines are not suited to antipiracy operations, the purpose is to provide far seas experience in a nonthreatening manner for China's submarine force.[78] By mid-2022, forty-one PLAN task forces consisting of well over one hundred ships had participated in the antipiracy operation in the Gulf of Aden and reportedly protected more than seven thousand Chinese and foreign ships.[79]

While the task forces continue their antipiracy duties, over time they have assumed other functions. The counterpiracy operation enabled the navy to improve its strategy in the Indian Ocean and the far seas. The PLAN now has a much better understanding of the logistical support required for operating far from its shores. It has demonstrated that it can project power well beyond China. Its crews are developing naval skills in a harsh operational environment that provides unique opportunities to improve their combat readiness. The task forces have trained a generation of officers and sailors.

The navy increasingly has focused on protecting Chinese interests, as evidenced by its engagement in the evacuation of Chinese nationals from Libya in 2011 and Yemen in 2015 (see chapter 7). The task force deployments also permit China to improve its international image and support its diplomacy.[80] In the context of the antipiracy operation in the Gulf of Aden, the navy's ability to improve its training and tactics is benign. But in the context of its more aggressive actions in the East and South China Seas and a rapidly expanding naval force, it appears more destabilizing to Western countries, India, and Japan.[81]

PLAN ships have conducted joint escorts with their Russian counterparts, conducted antipiracy exercises with ships from the Republic of Korea and Pakistan, and coordinated with the European Union's Operation Atalanta naval task force off Somalia to protect ships carrying supplies for the

World Food Program. In 2013 the PLAN conducted a two-day joint counter-piracy exercise with a U.S. Navy vessel, landing helicopters on each other's ships.[82] China was active in the international Contact Group on Piracy off the Coast of Somalia. More significantly, it joined the Shared Awareness and Deconfliction organization, a Bahrain-based group that coordinates antipiracy military efforts at the tactical and operational levels.[83]

The Gulf of Guinea is Africa's most serious piracy challenge. Unlike Somali piracy, the attacks there did not begin with the seizure of ships and crews for ransom. Rather, heavily armed criminal gangs attacked commercial vessels in harbors or close to shore to steal cash from the crew and valuable cargo from the ship. From 2014 to 2016 there were more than forty attacks annually. Since 2019 the Gulf of Guinea has experienced an unprecedented rise in crew kidnappings, accounting in 2020 for 95 percent of the 135 global totals.[84] The attacks have become more like the Somali pattern, although the pirates do not have ungoverned spaces where they can detain hijacked ships.

Chinese ships and crew have been victims of these attacks. In 2019 pirates seized four Chinese crew members from fishing vessels in Libreville, Gabon's harbor, and held them hostage in Nigeria until they were rescued.[85] In 2020 pirates successfully attacked a Chinese cargo ship, which was subsequently found drifting off Lagos, Nigeria.[86] Pirates seized a Chinese fishing trawler with eight Chinese crew in Côte d'Ivoire's exclusive economic zone; the Nigerian Navy Special Boat Service interdicted the vessel and arrested the pirates.[87] Pirates abducted five Chinese sailors from a Singapore-flagged cargo ship in Nigerian waters and held them for ransom.[88] Also in 2020, pirates kidnapped fourteen Chinese crewmembers off São Tomé from a Liberian-flagged and Chinese-owned heavy lift ship.[89] In 2021 pirates freed six Chinese nationals kidnapped from a fishing boat off Gabon after paying a $300,000 ransom.[90]

China has had limited success in the Gulf of Guinea preventing attacks against its ships and crew. International collaboration has not been effective. Since 2014 China has been conducting counterpiracy drills with and assisting individual countries in West Africa.[91] China, for example, provided Ghana with military equipment to enhance maritime security, while Ghana's navy agreed to help Chinese vessels combat piracy in the Gulf of Guinea.[92]

MARITIME SECURITY

According to the 2019–2021 FOCAC Action Plan, the African side encouraged China "to do more to support Africa's anti-piracy efforts in the Gulf of Guinea."[93] In 2022 China hosted a virtual symposium on the security situation in the Gulf of Guinea for the PLAN and relevant African navies in the region.[94]

AFRICAN PORT DEVELOPMENT AND NAVAL ACCESS

Chinese state-owned companies are the principal builders of ports on African coastlines and along the northern rim of the Indian Ocean. Chinese state-controlled banks are an important funding source for port construction. Most significantly, Chinese companies operate and hold equity investments in an increasing number of these ports. Chinese port construction usually has a commercial purpose, but it also has important security implications. State-owned institutions responsible for these projects have close ties to the CPC, which sometimes instructs them to pursue an equity investment. From a security perspective, China is most interested in port development that will help ensure access for its naval vessels and lead to more formal arrangements, which allow for resupply and ship repairs. The Chinese-built port of Hambantota in Sri Lanka is one example. China Merchants Port Holdings, the Hong Kong–based subsidiary of state-owned Merchants Group, has a 70 percent stake in the port pursuant to a ninety-nine-year lease. In 2017 the state-owned China Overseas Port Holding Company took over management of the Chinese-financed Gwadar port on Pakistan's Arabian Sea coast for a period of forty years. The PLAN routinely berths ships at Gwadar, effectively making it a naval support facility that helps sustain deployments into the Indian Ocean and beyond—and will continue to do so at least until 2057.[95]

China is working to gain control over, or at least influence, key parts of the global maritime transportation system. It has been successful in doing so in Africa and along the northern rim of the Indian Ocean. Direct investment in ports and their operating companies aided this goal.[96] The CPC expects that Chinese companies and their network of ports will advance China's "core interests" (see chapter 1). China's aforementioned *Blue Book* noted that investment in ports and other assets should be considered in the context of "strategic support states."[97] Similarly, China's BRI vision statement of 2015 urges that it "push forward port infrastructure construction" and "advance port cooperation."[98] This strategy potentially gives China considerable leverage in using ports for security purposes.

China seeks to create dual-use ports so that it can avoid, at least for the time being, the need to create a string of costly military bases. Some analysts have termed this the "places not bases" strategy.[99] These ports would not necessarily house military weapons and platforms, but rather preposition dual-use goods such as petroleum, lubricants, food, and water.[100] Xue Guifang of the Shanghai Jiao Tong University has argued that China is not motivated to replicate the Djibouti base model, but instead favors a commercial or dual-use one, which has the potential to serve military functions.[101] Similarly, China's internal *Global Military* journal stated that China should negotiate with countries in the Indian Ocean region to secure reliable supply locations for the PLAN.[102] Chinese security analysts describe port investments as discreetly enabling China to enhance its military presence.[103]

Daniel Russel and Blake Berger of the Asia Society argue that China is developing ports with a dual-use functionality along the Maritime Silk Road. The National Development and Reform Commission's Five-Year Plan calls for the construction of "strategic strongpoints" (战略支点) capable of offering logistical support for Chinese vessels to create an "advantageous external environment for China." At the low end commercial ports support China's military by servicing civilian ships that replenish PLAN vessels in the open sea. Navy ships may also be able to dock for resupply. At the high end the Djibouti base serves as a PLAN logistics facility.[104]

Isaac Kardon of the U.S. Naval War College explains that, because it lacks overseas bases, the PLAN must rely on commercial access points beyond China's first island chain. Consequently, it procures fuel and supplies at hundreds of ports around the world. While many other navies operate similarly, the PLAN is unique in that it accesses a large and growing number of ports partially owned and operated by Chinese companies. As of early 2023 Chinese firms built, financed, invested in, or operated one or more terminals at sixty-one port facilities in thirty African countries.[105]

Since 2012 Chinese scholars have suggested that China is pursuing a strategy to expand its presence in the Indian Ocean by creating a network of ports for replenishing PLAN vessels. These are not bases in the Western context, but "strategic pivots" (战略枢纽) aimed at mitigating concerns over China's growing naval strength and reach. According to Mike Chia-Yu Huang this network has three features. First, the pivots accommodate China's historical principle of not building foreign naval bases. Second, they address China's preoccupation with freedom of passage through the Strait of Malacca, create the ability to replenish PLAN ships engaged in the counterpiracy mission in the Gulf of Aden, and support other noncombat missions. Third, development of these "supportive facilities" (保障设施) has significant political and economic goals in addition to supporting the navy.[106] Writing in 2014, before the opening of the Djibouti base, Zhou Bo, a frequent spokesperson on Chinese naval issues, said "access, rather than bases, is what the Chinese Navy is really interested in in the Indian Ocean."[107]

China replicated the Gwadar model in Piraeus, Greece, where state-owned China COSCO Shipping Corporation has a 67 percent stake in the port and 100 percent ownership of container terminals.[108] During missions to the Mediterranean, PLAN ships call routinely at Piraeus.[109] China significantly expanded its port strategy in Djibouti, where China Merchants Port Holdings (CMPorts) has a 23.5 percent stake in the port management company of the Doraleh Container Terminal and in 2018 won the concession to manage the port.[110] The state-owned China Civil Engineering Construction Corporation and China State Construction Engineering Corporation then built a multipurpose cargo facility next door.[111] In 2020 China Merchants Group signed a $350 million investment deal as part of a $3 billion project to modernize and add facilities to the port of Djibouti.[112]

The Washington-based Center for Strategic and International Studies looked at forty-six ports in Sub-Sahara Africa that have financial, construction, and/or operational involvement by Chinese companies and banks. The study concluded that China pursued most of the projects for commercial gain and acknowledged that, while they may contribute to the economic growth of African countries, China intends to use them to advance its strategic objectives.[113]

Several of the port projects merit special attention because of their inherent importance or potential for dual use by the PLAN. In 2013 CMPorts signed a framework agreement with Tanzania to build the largest deepwater port in Africa at Bagamoyo, a small town forty-five miles north of the capital, Dar es Salaam. The $10 billion project included construction of a railway and special economic zone. After initial progress, port construction stalled in 2018. The project restarted and then ran into trouble again in mid-2019, when President John Magufuli stated the contract conditions were "exploitative and awkward" and could "only be accepted by mad people." CMPorts originally negotiated a ninety-nine-year lease; Tanzania subsequently said it is willing to offer a thirty-three-year lease—take it or leave it.[114] In 2021 Tanzania and China resumed discussions on the project under Tanzania's new president, but they had yet to reach an agreement.[115]

China has long and deep military ties with Tanzania. A port of this magnitude, if China builds it, could be invaluable to the PLAN. But even as the Bagamoyo port negotiations remain deadlocked, China Harbor Engineering Company (CHEC) is upgrading the World Bank–funded port of Dar es Salaam.[116] The privately owned and Hong Kong–based CK Hutchison Port Holdings owns 70 percent of Dar es Salaam's container port operating company.[117] The China Railway Construction Engineering Group and China Railway Major Bridge Engineering Group are building a multipurpose terminal at Mtwara on Tanzania's southern coast.[118]

In 2015 the China Communications Construction Company (CCCC) won the $449 million contract to construct the first three berths of the projected thirty-two-berth Lamu Port in Kenya as part of the massive Lamu Port-South Sudan-Ethiopia-Transport (LAPSSET) Corridor that will connect landlocked South Sudan and Ethiopia to the Indian Ocean coast. Although the project is behind schedule and of questionable economic viability, CCCC has completed the first three berths.¹¹⁹ The company is also constructing the $385 million Kipevu Oil Terminal at the Port of Mombasa, funded by the Kenya Ports Authority.¹²⁰

In 2019 Namibia inaugurated a $400 million container terminal in Walvis Bay built by CHEC.¹²¹ Windhoek envisages that the port, which has a separate Chinese-built fuel depot, will serve as a gateway to southern Africa. In 2014 the Namibian press reported that discussions were underway at the highest levels between the Namibian government and China about locating a PLAN base at Walvis Bay.¹²² While the rumors about a base persist, encouraged by construction of the fuel depot, there is no evidence so far that a naval base is moving forward there. China's ambassador to Namibia said there is no thought of turning the Walvis Bay commercial port into a military facility.¹²³ A senior Namibian police official added that the United States had also inquired about basing ships at Walvis Bay but that Namibia turned down the request and would do the same for Beijing.¹²⁴ An opposition member of Namibia's parliament charged in 2020 that China had more than 3,500 military personnel stationed at its satellite tracking station in Swakopmund, Walvis Bay, and Henties Bay. Namibia's minister of defense quickly denied the report but declined to say how many Chinese military personnel are in fact present (see chapter 10).¹²⁵

Further up the Atlantic coast, Angola has been a focus of Chinese port construction. Angola unveiled plans in 2007 for construction of a port at Caio in Angola's northern enclave of Cabinda. China's Export-Import Bank provided $600 million in financing, and the China Road and Bridge Corporation began construction in 2015 and then stopped in 2017 because of payment issues; it resumed once more in 2020. China Road and Bridge Corporation also received the contract to build a port at Barra do Dande near Luanda, the capital, but that project became embroiled in Angolan politics and stalled. In 2013 CHEC gave a facelift to Angola's port of Lobito, which two Chinese companies now manage.¹²⁶ Angola is the largest African supplier of oil to China and as a result has received more Chinese financing than any other country on the continent. China's involvement in three of Angola's ports makes them prime candidates for dual use by the PLAN, although two of the projects remain unfinished.

The China Export-Import Bank financed 85 percent of the deep-water port at Kribi, Cameroon. CHEC built the first two stages and has 20 percent equity in the project. In 2016 a consortium led by France's Bolloré Ports, which included CHEC, received a twenty-five-year contract to operate the container terminal.[127]

Chinese companies have been involved in three Nigerian ports. CMPorts holds 28.5 percent and the China Africa Development Fund 19 percent, respectively, of the Tin-Can Island Container Terminal.[128] CHEC and the China Development Bank are funding the deep-sea port at Lekki. CHEC is doing the construction on a finance-build-operate basis with a forty-five year concession agreement. The firm holds 52.5 percent of the shares, with the remainder held by a Singaporean conglomerate.[129] In addition, the China Communications Construction Company has acquired a majority $233 million stake in the Lekki Port Enterprise Ltd., a deep-sea freight transportation firm.[130] Bolloré Ports and PowerChina International Group won the tender to build and operate the deep-sea port at Akwa Ibom for fifty years.[131]

CMPorts holds 50 percent of the shares in the Lomé Container Terminal and 12.25 percent of the Terra terminal financed by China's Export-Import Bank at Abidjan, Côte d'Ivoire.[132] A consortium of three companies, including China Hongqiao Group Limited, a Chinese aluminum producer, have 90 percent of the shares of the Boke bauxite operation, including the port, in Guinea. The other shareholders are based in Singapore and Guinea. The Yantai Port Group Company, which operates a terminal port in China, controls the remaining 10 percent.[133] Yantai also controls 50 percent of the shares of the Boffa bauxite terminal in Guinea.[134]

In the 1980s China built the original port in Nouakchott, Mauritania's capital, and a small port at Nouadhibou in the country's north.[135] Beijing subsequently provided patrol boats to the Mauritanian Navy and signed fishing agreements with the government. In 2009 China agreed to triple the capacity of the Nouakchott port.[136] In 2016 Mauritania awarded a $325 million contract to China's Poly Technologies to build a large military and commercial port at N'Diago on the bank of the Senegal River.[137] There are concerns, however, about its economic viability.[138] In 2020 China's Export-Import Bank extended an $87 million loan for construction of a fishing harbor north of Nouakchott.[139] Because of its large size, dual military/commercial function, and questionable economic prospects, the N'Diago port appears to be a good prospect for eventual use by the PLAN.

Turning to the Mediterranean, all the continent's major ports are located on the European side, save for Morocco's modern Tanger Med port on the Strait of Gibraltar and three Egyptian ports. CMPorts has a 48.75 percent share in Somaport at Casablanca, and a 19.6 percent share in Tanger Med.[140] Algeria is the location of a huge Chinese port project, albeit one that has suffered serious setbacks. In 2016 China announced it would construct the $3.3 billion deep water container port near Cherchell, about fifty miles west of Algiers. CHEC and China State Construction Engineering Corporation planned to complete the project in seven years, after which Shanghai Ports Group would manage the port's twenty-three docks. China was to have 49 percent ownership of the operating company and the Algerian Ports Authority 51 percent. The African Development Bank and a consortium of Chinese banks reportedly agreed to fund the project.[141] The project then went silent. In 2020 an Algerian government spokesperson said that after the COVID-19 crisis ends, "the project will be considered."[142] As of early 2023, in spite of claims that construction began in 2021, there has been no evidence of actual construction activity.[143]

China has major port and warehousing interests on Egypt's Mediterranean coast and in the Suez Canal Zone. CK Hutchison operates Egypt's two main commercial ports on the Mediterranean—Alexandria and El-Dekheila—and holds 80.3 percent of the shares in each.[144] In recent years CHEC completed the $219 million quay at the northern end of the Canal and a $1 billion quay at the southern end, followed by construction of a $416 million cargo terminal.[145] In 2019 CK Hutchison signed an agreement with the Egyptian Navy to establish and own a container terminal able to handle one million containers annually at the port of Abu Qir near Alexandria as part of a thirty-eight-year concession.[146] In 2020 CHEC completed a $520 million terminal basin at Sokhna Port south of the Suez Canal. China has become the biggest investor in the Suez Canal Area Development Project. China's Tianjin Economic-Technological Development Area (TEDA)

Group established a joint Suez Economic and Trade Cooperation Zone in the Ain Sokhna district of the Suez Canal corridor. Industries are now beginning to locate there.[147] COSCO then agreed to build a bonded logistics park in the zone to serve as a major international service provider.[148] COSCO holds a 20 percent stake in the Suez Canal Container Company located in Port Said, and a 20 percent stake in the Damietta container port in the Mediterranean.[149]

In 2011 China's minister of national defense, Liang Guanglie, visited the Seychelles and met with President James Michel. During the visit, the African country's minister of foreign affairs announced that "we have invited the Chinese government to set up a military presence on Mahe to fight the pirate attacks that the Seychelles face on a regular basis."[150] Beijing apparently turned down the offer, but said it will consider refueling and resupplying in the Seychelles.[151] Whatever was offered, it has not resulted in a naval facility and may have been rendered obsolete by the sharp decline in pirate attacks. India, which has a stronger relationship with the Seychelles than China, did negotiate a joint naval base agreement. This, however, has failed to materialize because of opposition by one of the Seychelles's main political parties. Nevertheless, China has routinely obtained access for PLAN vessels at Port Victoria in the Seychelles. In 2016 General Wang Guanzhong, deputy chief of the Joint Staff Department at the CMC, visited the Seychelles to expand military cooperation. Then-president Danny Faure told General Wang that the country welcomed more PLAN ship visits for replenishing, which underscores their "excellent relationship."[152]

Chinese state-owned companies have acquired equity in an increasing number of African ports. Table 9.1 shows publicly available shareholdings by Chinese companies. While partial ownership does not guarantee PLAN access, it increases the likelihood. Some of the ports in which Chinese companies have shares are not well suited to host naval vessels. The degree to which the Chinese company controls port operations, the physical capacity of the port to supply naval vessels, the conditions of the concession, and China's broader relationship with the host government play a key role in their potential use by the PLAN.[153]

TABLE 9.1 Chinese companies' investment in African ports as of 2022

LOCATION	CHINESE COMPANY	EQUITY SHARES (PERCENT)
Dar es Salaam, Tanzania	Hutchison	70%
Kribi, Cameroon	CHEC	20%
Abidjan, Côte d'Ivoire	CMPorts	12.25%
Boke, Guinea	China Hongqiao Group (with two non-Chinese partners)	90%
	Yantai Port Group	10%
Boffa, Guinea	Yantai Port Group	50%
Tin-Can Island, Nigeria	CMPorts	28.5%
	China Africa Development Fund	19%
Lekki, Nigeria	CHEC	52.5%
Lomé, Togo	CMPorts	50%
Alexandria, Egypt	Hutchison	80.3%
El Dekheila, Egypt	Hutchison	80.3%
Port Said, Egypt (Suez Canal Container Terminal)	COSCO	20%
Abu Kir, Egypt	Hutchison	100%
Damietta, Egypt	COSCO	20%
Casablanca, Morocco	CMPorts	48.75%
Tanger-Med, Morocco	CMPorts	19.6%

Source: Compiled from shipping company and press accounts.

A 2020 study by *Janes* concluded that China would rely primarily on overseas military logistics support from commercial facilities in the Indian Ocean region, Red Sea, and Africa until about 2030. As its expeditionary capabilities improve—including the introduction of new naval surface combatants, amphibious warfare ships, anti-submarine warfare capabilities, aircraft carriers, and strategic airlift and tanker fleets—China may pursue more formal military bases with prepositioned offensive capabilities and weapons. China may also seek access arrangements with countries in West Africa.¹⁵⁴

PORT CALLS, NAVAL EXERCISES, AND *PEACE ARK* DIPLOMACY

PLAN port calls are linked to the preceding discussion on port development and access in that Chinese state-owned companies financed, built, invested in, and/or currently operate many of the ports visited by PLAN ships. Some of the ports frequented by such vessels, however, have no financial or management connection with China. This section identifies where PLAN ships have called in Africa, and which African navies have held exercises with the PLAN. As of 2022, South Africa is the only African country to send a naval vessel to China. In 2008 the *SAS Spioenkop*, a frigate, called at Shanghai to mark the tenth anniversary of diplomatic relations between the two countries.¹⁵⁵

The first PLAN port calls in Africa took place in 2000, when a guided missile destroyer and a supply ship visited Tanzania and South Africa. In 2002 the commander of the North China Sea Fleet accompanied a guided missile destroyer and a supply ship on the PLAN's first world cruise. After passing through the Suez Canal, the ships called at Alexandria, Egypt. Eight years passed until the next PLAN vessels visited Africa; a guided missile frigate, part of China's antipiracy effort in the Gulf of Aden, made a port call at Djibouti in 2010 to replenish. This began a sharp increase in calls at Djibouti by ships assigned to the antipiracy patrol. It also started a pattern of PLAN vessels completing their duty in the Gulf of Aden and then making port calls in African waters. In 2011, for example, the navy's two frigates finished their antipiracy rotation and then called at South Africa, Tanzania, and the Seychelles before returning to China.¹⁵⁶

Table 9.2 is a list of China's naval ship visits to African countries through 2022. It includes port calls by warships, the hospital ship *Peace Ark*, and the PLA oceanographic research ship *Zhu Kezhen*. More than

MARITIME SECURITY

TABLE 9.2 China's naval ship visits to African countries, 2000–2022

COUNTRY	YEAR	# VISITS
Djibouti	2000 until January 2020	108
South Africa	2000, 2011, 2014, 2015, 2016, 2017, 2018(2), 2019	9
Tanzania	2000, 2011, 2013, 2016, 2017(2)	6
Egypt	2002, 2010, 2015, 2019	4
Seychelles	2010, 2011, 2013, 2017	4
Kenya	2010, 2014, 2019	3
Mozambique	2012, 2017, 2019	3
Algeria	2013, 2018	2
Angola	2014, 2017	2
Cameroon	2014, 2018	2
Gabon	2017, 2018	2
Morocco	2013, 2018	2
Nigeria	2014, 2018	2
Tunisia	2014, 2018	2
Congo Republic	2017	1
Côte d'Ivoire	2014	1
Ghana	2018	1
Madagascar	2017	1
Mauritius	2015	1
Namibia	2014	1
Senegal	2014	1
Sierra Leone	2017	1
Sudan	2015	1

Source: Compiled from scholarly and press accounts.

two-thirds of the visits were at Djibouti, nearly all of them for replenishment in connection with the antipiracy operation in the Gulf of Aden. The South African ports of Cape Town and Durban received nine visits, followed by Dar es Salaam, Tanzania with six, and Alexandria, Egypt, and Port Victoria, Seychelles, with four each. Coastal countries that have not yet received PLAN visits are those locked in conflict, such as Somalia and Libya, several small island nations, and a half dozen others in West Africa. Notable for not yet having received a visit are Mauritania, Guinea, Liberia, and Eritrea. Except for visits to Djibouti, port calls ended at

African ports with the onset of COVID-19 and did not resume until February 2023.¹⁵⁷

Replenishment port calls normally last two to five days, during which the ship takes on fuel, water, and food. The Chinese ambassador and military attaché usually meet the crew, which does not interact with the host country navy or open the ship to visitors. "Friendly visit" calls have broader soft power and diplomatic goals. These usually last two to four days and involve meetings with the Chinese ambassador and embassy staff as well as host country government and naval officials. The local Chinese community routinely appears for the arrival and departure of the ship, which is open to the public. Crew members often engage in sports events with host navy personnel. Since 2012 and until the beginning of the coronavirus pandemic, the PLAN was expanding the number of friendly visits by its ships to ports beyond Djibouti.¹⁵⁸

Exercises with African navies have become an increasingly important component of the PLAN's "friendly visits." Most African navies are small and resemble a coast guard; the exercises are usually basic. In 2014, for example, after three Chinese ships completed their antipiracy duties in the Gulf of Aden, they held an exercise off Walvis Bay with a Namibian ship that focused on formation movement, communication, and rescue operations.¹⁵⁹ The same task force then conducted an antipiracy drill in the Gulf of Guinea with the Nigerian Navy, which emphasized ship defense, taskforce maneuvering, and replenishment under sail.¹⁶⁰ In 2018 the ships called at Ghana, Cameroon, and Gabon, holding a naval exercise with the Ghanaian Navy that involved maritime formation movement drills and ship-to-ship communication.¹⁶¹ One of the PLAN ships participated in an antipiracy drill in the Gulf of Guinea with twelve Nigerian vessels and one each from Cameroon, Ghana, Togo, France, and Portugal.¹⁶² In 2019 a guided missile destroyer conducted an exercise with an Egyptian ship in the waters off Alexandria. It included formation alternation, flashing light signaling, helicopter deck landing, fast roping by special operations soldiers, and search and seizure operations.¹⁶³

In 2014 the PLAN held a month-long exercise called "Transcend-2014" at Kigamboni Naval Base involving a hundred officers and sailors from the

South Sea Fleet and the Tanzanian Marine Corps. The drills focused on marine tactics, antipiracy, and counterterrorism exercises. The scenario required that the marines rescue civilians held hostage on a small island after a terrorist hijacking.[164] Subsequently, in 2019, a PLAN frigate joined a Russian fleet tanker and South African frigate at Cape Town for a trinational exercise in safe navigation and maritime economic security. This was the first time that the South African Navy exercised jointly with the Russian and Chinese navies. A second trinational exercise took place off the South African coast in February 2023.[165]

The PLAN's hospital ship, *Peace Ark*, has been active in African waters since 2010, when it made its maiden overseas deployment to Djibouti, Kenya, Tanzania, and the Seychelles. In 2017 it returned to Djibouti, Sierra Leone, Gabon, Republic of Congo, Angola, Mozambique, and Tanzania.[166] The *Peace Ark* is part of China's charm offensive to counter the perception that its increase in naval power is a threat to others.[167] Recalling Hu Jintao's concept of a harmonious world, PLA Major General Bao Yuping, commander of the *Peace Ark*, said the mission of the ship is "to reflect the theory of harmonious world and harmonious sea."[168] *Peace Ark* deployments are intended to enhance China's soft power, increase economic opportunities, and gain access to foreign naval facilities that might not be open to warships.[169] The ship has 115 doctors and nurses, most of them from the PLA Naval Medical University and Navy General Hospital.[170] During its "Harmonious Mission" to Africa in 2017, the ship's personnel provided medical treatment for 7,508 Congolese, 9,881 Mozambiquans, and 6,421 Tanzanians. In Djibouti, it provided services to Chinese soldiers and contractors at the military base and 7,841 Djiboutians.[171]

SHIP BUILDING AND MERCHANT FLEET

For most countries, there would be little reason to include a section on ship building and the merchant fleet in a book that focuses on strategic engagement. China is an exception, however, because its merchant fleet and ship building are closely linked to the military. The implications of this play out globally, including in African waters. China mobilizes commercial vessels in support of its security needs and requires that all container, roll-on/roll-off, multipurpose, bulk carrier, and break-bulk vessels be built to military standards. A law in 2016 created a legal framework for the use of civilian assets to support military logistics operations and requires all Chinese industries that conduct international transportation to supplement Chinese military vessels as needed.[172] COSCO and CMPorts container and roll-on/roll-off vessels have participated in military-civilian exercises, including the transport of live ammunition.[173] COSCO in particular has a close relationship with Chinese political and military leaders.[174]

In 2006, as part of its eleventh five-year plan, China identified shipbuilding as a "strategic industry." In 2009 the State Council adopted the *Plan on the Adjustment and Revitalization of the Shipbuilding Industry*.[175] China views shipbuilding strategically rather than commercially and in 2010 became the world's largest merchant shipbuilder. Hundreds of private shipyards began competing with state-owned companies, which led to excessive production, bankruptcies, and closure of some private yards. By 2014 the China State Shipbuilding Corporation (CSSC), China Shipbuilding Industry Corporation (CSIC), and other government-backed companies won three-quarters of all Chinese orders. Beijing has backed these builders and encouraged civil-military integration, including combining military with civilian technology. China's shipbuilding plan of 2013 calls for its military shipbuilding industry to be rooted in civilian shipbuilding, to rely on civilian projects, and to use civilian industry to overcome military industry bottlenecks.[176]

CSSC and CSIC dominate commercial shipbuilding and have become major military ship manufacturers. They are responsible for three quarters of China's shipbuilding production and have built all domestically contracted vessels for the PLAN. As of 2023, six Chinese shipyards account for most of China's production; CSIC and CSSC control half of them. Each shipyard produces commercial and military vessels. Jiangnan shipyard, the largest one located near Shanghai, builds commercial ships as well as the PLAN's most sophisticated surface combatants. The navy is building its third aircraft carrier there.[177] Despite China's shipbuilding success, its shipyards suffered from financial, technological, and managerial problems such as poor cost control, inadequate control over the production process, and out-of-date equipment and technology.[178]

By any measure, China's merchant fleet, including Hong Kong's fleet, ranks at or near the top. Based on the number of ships owned by and registered in China and Hong Kong (flying Chinese and Hong Kong flags), China is first. Based on the number of ships owned by and registered in China and Hong Kong, in addition to those owned by China and Hong Kong and registered in another country (flying the other country's flag), China is still the first. If the measure is gross tonnage, Chinese-owned ships rank third behind Greece and Japan. Based on deadweight tonnage, Hong Kong ranks fourth in the world and China eighth. China and Hong Kong together rank second globally after Panama. In 2018 China's COSCO acquired Hong Kong's Orient Overseas International, making it the world's third largest container fleet. Chinese shipping lines deliver more containers than any other country.[179]

The PLAN's effort to counter piracy in the Gulf of Aden underscored the importance it attaches to protecting China's merchant fleet, which is becoming more integrated into routine naval operations. China, for example, used elements of its merchant fleet to evacuate almost thirty-six thousand Chinese from Libya in 2011 (see chapter 7). Beijing is trying to ensure that Chinese-owned merchant ships it might call on for emergency purposes fly the Chinese flag. Retrofitted merchant ships or those recently built to military specifications tend to be small or medium-size vessels because they are cheaper and can operate in more circumscribed ports and harbors.[180]

MILITARY BASES

The size of the Indian Ocean and its distance from China mean that access to naval and air bases or logistics facilities will be important to any sustained Chinese presence in the region.[181] In 2017 China opened its first and, so far, only military base beyond its borders in Djibouti. This was a controversial and dramatic change for a government that has consistently stated that it will not have military bases outside the country. To that end, China insists that the Djibouti facility is a "logistics support base" and that it still has no overseas military bases. When asked during a visit to India in 2012 if China will require in the future a permanent military facility for its ships in the Indian Ocean region, China's minister of national defense responded ambiguously, noting the need for crews to rest and resupply at ports in other countries, adding "such logistic supply activities do not have any connection with establishing military bases overseas."[182]

A Chinese researcher we spoke with explained that, because of China's long-standing "principle of no foreign military bases" and the reluctance of the CPC to break with the past, it is necessary to call any overseas military facility something other than a military base.[183] Even within China, there apparently was no unanimity regarding the need to avoid the "military base" terminology. A professor at Shanghai Normal University commented that the Ministry of Foreign Affairs did not object to calling Djibouti a military base, but the Ministry of National Defense insisted there should be no break with the principle of no foreign military bases.[184]

Well before the opening of the Djibouti facility, a vigorous debate took place among Chinese strategists regarding the need for overseas bases in the Indian Ocean region.[185] In a 2009 poll, 90 percent of almost nineteen thousand Chinese surveyed responded affirmatively to a question regarding whether China should establish overseas military bases.[186] In 2010 Shen Dingli of Fudan University wrote: "The real threat to us is not posed by the pirates but by the countries which block our trade route. . . . So we need to set up our own blue-water navy and to rely on the overseas military bases to cut the supply costs. . . . Setting up overseas military bases is not an idea we have to shun; on the contrary, it is our right."[187] In 2013 Beijing's *Science of Military Strategy* stated that China "must build overseas strategic strong points that depend on the homeland, radiate into the surrounding areas, and move toward the two oceans [Pacific Ocean and Indian Ocean]."[188] That year the PLA National Defense University submitted a research report to the Central Military Commission recommending that China build a military base in Djibouti. Xi Jinping approved the report, and Djibouti eventually became the location of China's first overseas military base.[189]

China's presence in Djibouti is far from unique. France has had a military base there since the colonial period and now includes small German and Spanish military contingents. The United States began developing its facility there in 2001 and now hosts UK military personnel. Japan opened a small military base in 2011, followed by an even smaller Italian base. Beginning in 2013, China started to transfer weapons to Djibouti, exchanged senior military delegations, and arranged training programs for Djiboutian military personnel in China.[190] In 2014 the United States successfully pressured Djibouti to refuse a Russian request for a base but, unbeknownst to Washington, Djibouti was simultaneously in discussion with China for one, which it accepted in 2015. China now has a ten-year lease, renewable for another ten, for which it pays Djibouti $20 million annually. This compares with $58 million annually for the larger American base.[191] Djibouti was a logical choice for a basing location because it was hard to fault China when so many other countries already had a base there.[192]

China's base occupies ninety acres, adjacent to the Chinese-built Doraleh Multipurpose Port. The base has a heliport with a 1,300-foot runway, a control tower, a large hangar, and seven smaller ones for helicopters. There is no airstrip for fixed-wing aircraft, but there are ground control systems for UAVs. The base has a 1,120-foot pier that can accommodate an aircraft carrier, assault carrier, or other large warship. It could easily receive four of China's nuclear-powered attack submarines. There are ship repair facilities and housing for up to ten thousand personnel, although the number currently deployed is much lower (estimates range from one to two thousand).[193] A PLANMC mechanized infantry company operates the base. China has also deployed wheeled armored combat vehicles, which are more effective for land-based than amphibious operations.[194] In 2017 Chinese television covered the PLANMC's first live-fire exercise in Djibouti, which involved several wheeled tank destroyers and wheeled infantry fighting vehicles.[195] The following year the PLA held a live-fire counterterrorism exercise.[196] Notably, these drills have nothing to do with combatting piracy, the original rationale for establishing a base in Djibouti.[197]

MARITIME SECURITY

China has insured its close relationship with the government of Djibouti by becoming the largest financier of infrastructure projects in the country. It provided $1.16 billion in loans for three large-scale projects built by Chinese state-owned companies: the Doraleh Multipurpose Port, the Djibouti section of the standard-gauge Addis Ababa–Djibouti railway, and the Ethiopia-Djibouti water pipeline.[198] China has also financed, usually through the Export-Import Bank, and built several smaller projects.[199] These loans, in turn, have contributed significantly to a debt crisis in Djibouti that the two countries are working to resolve. This financing has had the effect of tilting Djibouti toward Beijing. In 2016 the country's foreign minister said, "We don't want the Americans to leave but the Chinese invest billions of dollars in our infrastructure; that's what the Americans are not doing."[200]

The base provides logistics for PLAN ships taking part in the antipiracy mission in the Gulf of Aden. Personnel and equipment at the base are available to support evacuations of Chinese nationals and HADR operations in the region. The base facilitates China's contributions to UN peacekeeping missions in Africa and the Middle East.[201] When the base opened and faced criticism in some quarters, the official Xinhua news agency claimed that "the base has not been established for China's strategic deployment of military forces, but for implementing the country's escorting, peace-keeping and humanitarian aid missions in Africa and West Asia."[202]

While China's stated justifications for the base are valid, they do not tell the whole story. As demonstrated by the live-fire exercises and the passage of a counterterrorism law in 2015, which provides legal grounds for the PLA and PAP to conduct counterterrorism operations overseas, Djibouti would likely play a significant role in any operation in the region (see chapter 8). Additionally, all the military bases in Djibouti, including China's, collect intelligence on the other foreign military operations in the country and the security situation throughout the region. PLAN ships for the antipiracy operation are not focused exclusively on protecting SLOCS in the Gulf of Aden; they are available for duty from the Mediterranean to the Indian Ocean, especially to ensure energy security.[203] Djibouti offers a unique ability to test and train troops in a harsh environment, learn the strengths and weaknesses of Chinese-manufactured equipment, gain experience in far seas operations, learn from other military forces, and evaluate new naval platforms.[204] Most important, the Djibouti base signals a turning point in the expansion of PLA operations in the Indian Ocean and beyond that increases China's ability to project power over the next decade.[205]

Since China has opened its first military base and altered its principle of "no foreign military bases," many believe that additional military facilities are likely to follow. The question is when, where, and whether future sites will constitute fully developed bases, dual-use facilities, or just replenishment points as discussed earlier. An article by professors at the PLAN's Dalian Naval Academy in 2014 framed overseas bases as necessary for SLOC protection and argued that they will support distant sea operations, strengthen bilateral relations, and influence regional strategic balance.[206] Liu Jiasheng, chief of staff of the CMC's Transport and Projection Bureau, contended in *The Science of Military Strategy* in 2015 that the PLA will, over the long term, primarily focus on global power projection. It will rely on China's overseas bases and air and space multidimensional projection systems to meet the rapid reaction requirements of transportation projection capabilities in the event of war anywhere in the world.[207]

In 2016 *China Military Online* stated that "the PLA must protect China's interests anywhere in the world. Overseas military bases will provide cutting-edge support for China to guard its growing overseas interests." The article reported that a PLAN commander said that "Djibouti will provide China with experience of building overseas military bases. China has not had any such bases before. Djibouti is just the first step."[208] The same year, PLAN Admiral Sun Jianguo said that Xi Jinping instructed the PLA to "steadily advance overseas base construction."[209] In 2017 a researcher at the Shanghai Institutes for International Studies said China is considering additional overseas military facilities.[210] In 2018 Victor Zhikai Gao of the China National Association of International Studies said he would not be surprised if in the near future China establishes another military base, probably in West Africa.[211] In 2019, during an interview on Chinese television, Li Chunpang, political commissar at the Djibouti base, said: "We will be gradually moving from depending on dispatching supply vessels to setting up overseas bases."[212] Even China's National Defense white paper in 2019 stated that "to address deficiencies in overseas operations and support, it builds far seas forces, develops overseas logistical facilities, and enhances capabilities in accomplishing diversified military tasks."[213]

Washington is convinced that Beijing plans to expand the number of overseas bases. In his 2018 congressional testimony, AFRICOM commander Thomas Waldhauser said: "There are some indications of [China] looking for additional facilities, specifically on the eastern coast. . . . So Djibouti happens to be the first. There will be more."[214] Commenting on China's military base in Djibouti, a subsequent U.S. Department of Defense report concluded that "China will seek to establish additional military bases in countries with which it has a longstanding friendly relationship and similar strategic interests."[215] In 2021 Waldhauser's successor, General Stephen Townsend, commented that China has approached countries on Africa's Atlantic coast from Mauritania to Namibia with the goal of establishing a naval facility. Townsend said, "They're looking for a place where they can rearm and repair warships. That becomes militarily useful in conflict."[216] Townsend subsequently said China approached Equatorial Guinea about the possibility of locating a base there. The United States then sent two delegations to the country to dissuade the government from approving such a base.[217] In 2022 AFRICOM's director of intelligence analysis said, "Silence and apathy will ensure a Chinese base in West Africa becomes a matter of when, not if."[218]

Many analysts believe that China will establish additional bases in Africa. In 2014 the PLAN's Naval Research Institute recommended that China build "replenishment and logistics points" at key ports in the Bay of Bengal; Dar es Salaam, Tanzania; Djibouti; Gwadar, Pakistan; Hambantota, Sri Lanka; Sittwe, Myanmar; and the Seychelles.[219] The discussion has since expanded in Chinese academic and military circles about possible locations in the Indian Ocean for additional Chinese bases.[220] Some have speculated that the Comoro Islands and Madagascar are likely future basing sites.[221]

In 2020 *Janes* did an analysis of locations that China might select for future military bases. The criteria used were the host country's geostrategic value, presence of major BRI infrastructure investments, debt to China, history of replenishment port calls, the host government's past support for a Chinese security presence, its willingness to host a foreign military base, and open-source reporting on a basing offer to China or a basing request from China.

The study concluded that there are eighteen such potential locations in Indian Ocean and African waters, of which African ports accounted for six: Luanda, Angola; Mombasa, Kenya; Walvis Bay, Namibia; Lekki, Nigeria; Port Victoria, Seychelles; and Dar es Salaam, Tanzania.[222] The U.S. Department of Defense concluded in 2022 that China "has likely considered" military logistics facilities in Kenya, the Seychelles, Equatorial Guinea, Tanzania, and Angola and already made overtures to Namibia.[223] In a research report in 2022, the RAND Corporation assessed the desirability and feasibility globally of PLA basing and access locations. There were no African countries that met the high desirability criteria, but Djibouti and Equatorial Guinea qualified as medium desirability and high feasibility. Angola, Gabon, Kenya, Morocco, and Tanzania met RAND's criteria for medium desirability and medium feasibility.[224]

***

China's maritime strategy in African territorial waters and the western Indian Ocean is primarily focused on trade. With such a significant percentage of China's maritime commerce passing through the Indian Ocean and Red Sea and the importance of this region to the BRI, China can easily justify an increased naval presence there. Official reports and statements make clear that China intends to become a global maritime power, and that access to the Indian Ocean and African waters is essential for achieving that objective. A key step in reaching both goals has been China's active engagement in the antipiracy operation in the Gulf of Aden, which increased its security cooperation with regional countries and navies. China is not only providing more protection for its ships and crews but can more effectively evacuate Chinese nationals in harm's way, gain valuable experience for PLAN personnel, and evaluate its equipment under difficult operating conditions.

Chinese support for African port development has been a major factor as of 2023 in expanding its influence and gaining access for PLAN vessels. This has included a notable increase in equity investments in African ports. PLAN port calls rose dramatically after 2010, and exercises with African navies also increased. Some of these ports are dual-use facilities, where PLAN ships have guaranteed access and permanent support infrastructure. China is a major shipbuilder and has one of the largest merchant fleets in the world, which also contributes to its desire to expand its access and influence in African waters. While, as of 2023, China has only one overseas military base, its experts and officials have sent strong signals there will be more and that African ports are prime candidates.

10

TECHNOLOGY AND INFORMATION SECURITY

The issues discussed in this chapter are subject to article 7 of China's National Intelligence Law, which states that "any organization or citizen shall support, assist and cooperate with the state intelligence work in accordance with the law, and keep the secrets of the national intelligence work known to the public." Article 14 adds that state intelligence "may require relevant organs, organizations and citizens to provide necessary support, assistance and cooperation."¹ Gu Bin of the Beijing Foreign Studies University argues that Western concerns about article 7 and the Communist Party of China's (CPC) control over Chinese companies and individuals reflect a misunderstanding of Chinese law, which does not authorize preemptive spying; national intelligence must be defensive in nature.² Nevertheless, he says the government expects companies and citizens to support intelligence activities. The question is when and how the spying begins.³ The 2016 cybersecurity law, the 2017 national intelligence law, and the 2021 data security law obligate firms to cooperate with state security organs when requested; there are no legal or administrative means to decline requests.⁴

This chapter covers topics that existing literature infrequently discusses, in part because China's engagement with Africa on them is both relatively recent and sensitive, making it difficult to develop reliable information. Yet as China expands its outreach and seeks new ways to turn a profit from its engagement with African countries, technology and information security have become an increasingly important part of China's comprehensive security strategy and effort to draw African countries into its broader security network. We examine China's modest but growing nuclear, space, and satellite cooperation with African states; its extensive collaboration on information technology equipment and networks; sales and programs in artificial intelligence (AI) and surveillance technology; and cybersecurity.

China's nuclear cooperation with Africa has encountered intense competition from other countries, especially Russia. China has been successful in launching satellites for African countries but still lags behind Russia, France, and the United States in this area. Space tracking facilities in Kenya and Namibia, however, have assisted China's own satellite program. Chinese companies, meanwhile, have become the dominant player in the information technology field. Huawei and ZTE equipment has been installed throughout Africa, and Chinese brands unknown in the West are popular among Africans. Chinese companies are major suppliers and technology providers. China's extensive engagement in Africa's IT sector has led, in turn, to credible reports of Chinese cyberintrusion into African systems.

NUCLEAR COOPERATION

Nuclear cooperation and investments are a recent but growing component of China's strategic interaction with African states.[5] About thirty African countries (especially Niger, Namibia, and South Africa) hold an estimated 20 percent of the world's uranium reserves. An increasing number of African countries are looking at the possibility of developing nuclear energy for power, desalination, and research. Russia leads this competition in Africa, but China is strategically positioned to become a player as well and is working hard to win contracts and supply expertise and services.[6]

China's 2016 Arab policy paper, which also pertains to Arab League member countries in Africa, called for strengthening "China-Arab cooperation on the design and construction of nuclear power plants and nuclear technology training."[7] The China National Nuclear Corporation (CNNC) stated in 2018 that it attaches "great importance" to cooperation with Africa in uranium resources, nuclear technology applications, human resources, and nuclear power plants.[8] The FOCAC action plan for 2022–2024 committed both sides "to deepen mutually beneficial cooperation between China and Africa in such areas as nuclear science research, nuclear personnel training, nuclear technology application and nuclear power project development."[9]

The development of nuclear energy for any purpose in Africa has been a slow process. Most agreements signed with China and other countries have had limited tangible results—at least so far. Nevertheless, the increasing pace of Chinese activity reflects real interest from the Chinese government in expanding its engagement with Africa on nuclear cooperation.

South Africa is the only African country with an operating nuclear power plant; it has been producing power since 1984 without Chinese assistance.[10] Over the past decade, however, China has made inroads into South Africa's nuclear sector. In 2010 China General Nuclear Power Corporation (CGN) established an office in Johannesburg. Then, in 2014, South Africa signed a nuclear energy cooperation agreement with CNNC that initiated a preparatory phase for utilization of Chinese nuclear technology. CNNC signed three additional agreements with South Africa's state-owned Nuclear Energy Corporation SOC Limited (NECSA) to establish a cooperative partnership supporting South Africa's nuclear industry. These agreements were with China's State Nuclear Power Technology Corporation (SNPTC), the Industrial and Commercial Bank of China, and South Africa's Standard Bank, to finance new nuclear plants, and between NECSA and SNPTC, to train South African nuclear professional staff. In 2015 NECSA signed a skills-development and training agreement with SNPTC and CGN, which China funded up to 95 percent.[11]

Egypt has considered developing nuclear energy since the 1960s and is planning, with Russian assistance, to build four large nuclear power reactors with significant desalination capacity. Egypt's collaboration with Russia is in an advanced stage. By contrast, China's only nuclear involvement with Egypt is an agreement in 2015 between the CNNC and Egypt's Nuclear Power Plants Authority to enhance cooperation and to "become an official partner" in Egypt's nuclear project.[12] The state-owned China Zhongyuan Engineering Corporation (CZEC), the overseas nuclear power project platform of CNNC, maintains an office in Egypt.[13]

In 2017 the CNNC signed a cooperation agreement with Tunisia's National Centre of Nuclear Sciences and Technology.[14] In 2019 the Tunisian Association of Nuclear Sciences and Techniques, a nonprofit organization representing nuclear engineers, signed an agreement with CZEC for collaboration on nuclear training and research between the two organizations. The protocol covers the production of electricity using nuclear energy, nuclear medicine, training of engineers, and the exchange of nuclear expertise.[15]

In the 1980s CZEC built the Birine Nuclear Research Center in Algeria, marking the first export of China's civilian nuclear technology.[16] Algeria has operated a Chinese heavy water reactor supplied by CNNC at Birine that began operation in 1992 and CZEC refurbished in 2016–2019. Algeria uses it for scientific, research, medical isotope production, hot-cell laboratories, waste storage, and other civil purposes.[17] In 2015 the CNNC and the Algerian Atomic Energy Commission signed an agreement to cooperate on nuclear energy, research reactors, nuclear safety, nuclear technology, and water desalination. The following year, Algeria reached a preliminary agreement with CNNC concerning the building of a nuclear research center, the Hualong One reactor, the ACP100 small reactor, and renewable energy projects. Russia's Rosatom appears, however, to have the inside track on developing nuclear power in Algeria. Neighboring Morocco has completed a preproject study with China for potable water desalination at Tan-Tan on the Atlantic coast using a 10 MWt heating reactor.[18]

In 2012 China began negotiations with Sudan on a nuclear power project as part of a strategic partnership between the two countries.[19] In 2016 CNNC signed a framework agreement with Sudan for the construction of one or two 600 MWe nuclear power reactors, as well as the formulation of a ten-year nuclear cooperation roadmap.[20] In 2019 the director of Sudan's Geological Research Organization said that his country will partner with CNNC for enrichment of the country's uranium.[21] Nevertheless, Sudan is another case where nuclear cooperation with China is progressing slowly and faces stiff competition from Russia.

In 2015 Kenya's nuclear power agency signed an agreement with CGN to study the building of a Hualong One reactor. The agreement enabled Kenya to obtain expertise on nuclear development from China by way of skills training, technical support in areas such as site selection for Kenya's nuclear power plants, and feasibility studies. Kenya subsequently conducted a technology assessment and signed an additional agreement with CGN in 2017.[22] In 2019 Kenya's Nuclear Power and Energy Agency contracted with CNNC to determine the most suitable location for the country's first nuclear power plant, which the Chinese conglomerate planned to design and build. In preparation for the nuclear project, twenty-nine Kenyan scientists were trained at Russian and Chinese universities.

In 2017, a year after signing an agreement with Russia's Rosatom, Uganda signed a similar nuclear energy cooperation agreement with China Central Plains Foreign Engineering Company and China Nuclear Manufacturing Group, as well as a draft agreement with CNNC. In 2018 it signed another agreement with CNNC on the peaceful use of nuclear energy. In 2019, however, Uganda decided to work with Rosatom to develop its nuclear power program. A senior Ugandan official, explaining the decision, complained that China was trying to hurry the negotiations by lobbying at the highest political level, which irritated expert personnel.[23]

In 2004 Nigeria's Ahmadu Bello University commissioned the country's first research reactor, a 30 KW Chinese Miniature Neutron Source Reactor used for scientific research. In 2018 China, Norway, the United Kingdom, and the United States converted the reactor from highly enriched uranium to low enriched uranium fuel. A Russian aircraft removed the highly enriched uranium to China. A CNNC official noted that this joint project demonstrated a commitment to the peaceful uses of nuclear energy.[24] Subsequently, in 2018 CNNC signed a MOU on nuclear energy cooperation with the Nigeria Atomic Energy Commission. The chairperson of the commission said Nigeria hopes to cooperate with CNNC in nuclear power, nuclear technology application, and human resources training.[25]

In 1995 the China Institute of Atomic Energy designed and built a highly enriched uranium research reactor for Ghana's Atomic Energy Commission. In 2014 the International Atomic Energy Agency supervised a project involving China, the United States, Russia, and India to convert the reactor to low enriched uranium—a process they completed in 2017. This complex project resulted in close collaboration between American and Chinese nuclear scientists. In 2018 Ghana and China signed an agreement for cooperation on the peaceful use of nuclear energy. During a ceremony in 2019 celebrating the inauguration of the research reactor, Ghana's vice president thanked Beijing for its support in the field of nuclear energy and pledged that his country would strengthen its cooperation with China, the United States, Russia, India, and other parties to ensure the safe and peaceful development of nuclear energy.[26]

Namibia holds about 7 percent of the world's uranium reserves, in which China has a major investment (see chapter 6). At one time, Namibia had proposed to supply its electricity needs from nuclear power by 2018.[27] In 2017 Chinese-owned and Namibia-based Swapko Uranium submitted a proposal to build a small nuclear power plant in the African nation.[28] In spite of its large uranium reserves, however, Namibia has not pursued the nuclear power option.

SPACE AND SATELLITE COOPERATION

One of the priorities for cooperation in China's vision statement for the BRI is to "improve spatial (satellite) information passageways."[29] The FOCAC action plan for 2022–2024 commits China to using space technology to enhance cooperation with African countries and to establish centers for China-Africa cooperation on satellite remote sensing application.[30] China has raised the importance of space exploration and includes it as part of the Chinese Dream (see chapter 1). China's space program is designed to contribute to Chinese nationalism, prestige, and military power. The PLA leads this effort, which is intended to make China a world leader in space exploration. The program is attracting developing countries by launching satellites at reduced rates, often financed by Chinese policy loans.[31]

Nigerian space scientist Temidayo Oniosun commented that the African space industry is growing rapidly, reached a value of almost $20 billion in 2021, and will increase to $23 billion by 2026.[32] African countries are increasingly turning to China for satellite launches and specialized training, opening another field for building comprehensive security relationships. Since 2016 China has signed forty-six space cooperation agreements or MOUs with nineteen countries and regions, including a half dozen in Africa.[33] The China National Space Administration initiated an aerospace student exchange between China and African countries as part of the Hyperspace Opportunity for Pioneering Education program.[34] In 2022 China's mission to the AU in Addis Ababa arranged via video link for students from eight African countries to meet with three Chinese astronauts.[35] Michael Chase of the RAND Corporation concluded that Beijing seems to view space as important both in terms of expanding Chinese influence within the context of the BRI and because it supports "China's pursuit of economic and security interests more generally."[36]

As of 2021, Russia had launched thirteen satellites for African countries, followed by France with ten, the United States with eight, and China with six.[37] Russia has been more cost competitive than China in this arena and offered better insurance guarantees.[38] China has launched two satellites apiece for Nigeria and Ethiopia and one each for Algeria and Sudan (see table 10.1). China is pursuing space cooperation with Africa in a variety of ways, such as collaboration in the context of the BRI, the BRICS, the China-Brazil Earth Resource Satellite for Africa Program, the Arab Satellite Communications Organization, the China-Arab States BeiDou Global Satellite Navigation System (BDS), and the international Disaster Monitoring Constellation.[39] BeiDou, an alternative to the U.S.-controlled Global Positioning System (GPS), has the potential to challenge American technological dominance, and increase China's leverage over other countries.[40] In 2021 representatives from fifty African nations attended the first

TABLE 10.1 China's launch of African satellites as of 2022

COUNTRY	YEAR	NAME, TYPE, OR PURPOSE	FUNDING SOURCE
Nigeria	2007	Communications	China Ex-Im Bank loan
Nigeria	2011	Communications	Insurance payment
Algeria	2017	Geostationary communications	Algerian Space Agency
Sudan	2019	Remote sensing	China Ex-Im Bank loan
Ethiopia	2019	Remote sensing	75% grant from China
Ethiopia	2020	Remote sensing	Cofunded by China and Ethiopia
Egypt	2022	Remote sensing	Grant from China
Nigeria	unknown	Communications (two)	China Ex-Im Bank equity deal

Source: Compiled from press accounts.

China-Africa BeiDou System Cooperation Forum in Beijing, which promoted BeiDou-based services.[41]

China initially focused more of its space effort on the Arab countries, including North Africa, than on Sub-Sahara African countries, probably because those nations are more integral to the BRI and have greater capacity to purchase and launch satellites. China's Arab policy paper in 2016 thus highlighted space cooperation and called for adopting the BDS in Arab countries, exploring joint projects in space technology and satellites, and promoting exchanges and cooperation on manned spaceflight.[42] The BDS is now being implemented in Tunisia (the location of the BDS Center), Algeria, and Sudan in areas such as precision agriculture, telecommunications, maritime monitoring, and disaster relief. The chairperson of the Chinese Satellite Navigation Committee has called for a joint China-Arab "Space Silk Road."[43]

In 2016 China provided a grant of $23 million to Egypt's space program. Grants of $45 million and $72 million followed in 2018 and 2019, respectively.[44] These grants led to the design of Egypt-Sat-2, a remote-sensing satellite that China has agreed to launch. China is also cooperating with the Egyptian Space Agency to develop the Assembly and Integration Testing Centre in Egypt's Space City.[45]

In 2007 Algeria and China signed a MOU to cooperate in outer space. In 2016 China signed a space cooperation agreement and established a space cooperation mechanism with Algeria.[46] China is not Algeria's primary space partner, however; the country also has space cooperation agreements with Argentina, France, India, Russia, Syria, Ukraine, the United Kingdom, and the United States. In 2013 the Algerian Space Agency purchased from the China Great Wall Industry Corporation a geostationary communications satellite. In 2017 China launched the satellite, and the Algerian Space Agency assumed control of in-orbit operation, management, and applications from ground stations in Algeria. It currently provides broadcasting, emergency communications, remote education, and satellite broadband.[47]

In 2017 the South African National Space Agency (SANSA) joined the BRICS space program, which includes the China National Space Administration.[48] In 2021 SANSA signed a MOU with the China Satellite Network Office for collaboration in satellite navigation, strengthening exchanges, and cooperation on satellite navigation technologies.[49] China also built a satellite data receiving station in South Africa.[50]

Nigeria has Africa's most developed satellite relationship with China. In 2006 Nigeria signed an agreement with China's Export-Import Bank for $200 million in preferential buyer's credit to help fund its first communications satellite. Nigerian scientists and engineers subsequently received training and participated in satellite design and construction in China. The first satellite, built by the China Great Wall Industry Corporation, launched in 2007 but failed the following year due to problems with its solar arrays. China successfully launched a replacement in 2011. Nigeria has an agreement with China for seven hundred government-funded scholarships and technical training for a thousand space engineers. As of mid-2019, five hundred Nigerian students had taken advantage of the program.[51] In 2018 Nigeria signed a $550 million deal for two communications satellites, with financing provided by China's Export-Import Bank. Beijing received an undetermined equity stake in NigComSat, a company owned by the Nigerian government and responsible for managing satellite communications.[52]

In 2019 China launched Sudan's first satellite from the Taiyuan Satellite Launch Center in Shanxi province. Shenzhen Aerospace Oriental Red Sea Satellite Co. developed and built the vehicle. Financed by China's Export-Import Bank, it develops data on topographic mapping and natural resources for developmental planning, exploration of natural resources, environmental monitoring, agricultural monitoring, and yield estimation in addition to "public security (intelligence) and defense applications."[53]

In 2019 China launched a multispectral remote-sensing microsatellite for Ethiopia from the Taiyuan Satellite Launch Center. Beijing provided grant funding for 75 percent of the $8 million project. The China Academy of Space Technology developed the satellite in partnership with Ethiopian engineers. China financed the training of twenty-one Ethiopian engineers in China as well as the cost of the microsatellite, while the Ethiopian government funded the construction of the ground station facilities near Addis Ababa. Ethiopia uses the satellite for mining, environmental protection, weather forecasting, crop monitoring, and earth observatory purposes.[54] In 2020 China launched a second remote-sensing satellite for Ethiopia to monitor floods and disasters.[55]

African countries have helped China's space program. China and Namibia jointly control the China Telemetry, Tracking, and Command Station established in 2001 at Swakopmund, located north of Walvis Bay. The station, which tracks China's satellites and space missions, helps account for China's elevation of Namibia to a comprehensive strategic partner.[56] China's ambassador to Namibia has said that the tracking station in Swakopmund "links Namibia and China together for the peaceful use of space" and noted that Namibian officials "honour and cherish this support system."[57] The station has allowed Namibian military personnel to participate in the Chinese space program, to train more Namibian engineering and science students in space science, and to enable Namibia to expand its remote sensing and earth observation capabilities. The Namibian Defense Force participates in the operation of Chinese space missions as they launch and return to Earth.⁵⁸ China has agreed to construct a satellite digital-receiving ground station on the outskirts of Windhoek.⁵⁹ During Chinese space launches, one of the PLAN's space-tracking ships frequently appears in Walvis Bay.⁶⁰

Chinese technicians used the Italian-built San Marco tracking station near Malindi in Kenya for China's first crewed space mission, Shenzhou-5, in 2003 and its second mission, Shenzhou-6, in 2005. China operated its own domestic voice and data links with its mission control center.⁶¹ In 2018 China offered to partner with Kenya to upgrade and renovate the San Marco facility, which Kenya expects to take full ownership of from Italy.⁶² The following year an engineer at the Kenya Space Agency said, "We are keen to partner with China."⁶³ The American National Aeronautics and Space Administration has complained to Kenya that this is an effort by China to take a leading position in the economic and military use of outer space, concerns that may have stalled the China-Kenya partnership.⁶⁴

INFORMATION TECHNOLOGY STRATEGY

China is working hard throughout Africa to win IT contracts, establish networks, and, if possible, to control those networks. It is doing so through commercial sales of IT equipment and services, equity investments in African IT companies, government financing of major IT systems, aid and training programs, and standards setting. Profit, geopolitical, and security considerations are driving the effort, which has had considerable success. While China's IT program began years ago in Africa primarily for commercial reasons, the "Digital Silk Road" (数字丝路), announced by Xi Jinping in 2017, has elevated China's political, security, and strategic interests.⁶⁵ Western countries, especially the United States, developed and control global core IT infrastructure. While the West views the current network domain as neutral, China sees it as "network hegemony" (网络霸权) imposed by Washington and its allies. The PLA's influential Academy of Military Sciences publication, *The Science of Military Strategy*, makes clear that China intends to mobilize its IT industry as a component of national power.⁶⁶ By 2021 China was working with Russia to topple the existing Internet governance structure and replace it with an International Telecommunications Union–run system that the two countries hoped to dominate.⁶⁷ The CPC envisages that China will lead this new international digital order.⁶⁸

Alina Polyakova and Chris Meserole of the Brookings Institution concluded that, "for Beijing, exporting its information technology is not only about securing important new sources of revenue and data, but also generating greater strategic leverage vis-à-vis the West."⁶⁹ The evidence bears out this contention. In 2017 a leading CPC journal, *Qiushi*, published an article stating that the purpose of strengthening international information technology and cybersecurity exchanges and cooperation is "to push China's proposition of Internet governance toward becoming an international consensus."⁷⁰ China wants to replace the existing technological architecture that supports the Internet with a new protocol created by Huawei.⁷¹ Beijing believes this effort, sometimes called cybersovereignty, is critical for China to maintain its core values and control the narrative about the nation and the party.⁷² Adam Segal of the Council on Foreign Relations observes that China "will work to subvert and diminish the idea of a free and open internet, replace it with its own views on cyber sovereignty, and strengthen institutions and processes that accord with a more state-centric view of cyber governance."⁷³

The 2015 BRI Vision statement explicitly calls for the construction of cross-border optical cables and other trunk line networks, international communications connectivity, and the creation of an Information Silk Road, also known as the Digital Silk Road. It adds that China should build transcontinental submarine optical cables and improve satellite information passageways to expand information exchanges and cooperation.⁷⁴ China recognizes the increasing importance of e-commerce and mobile payments in Africa. Its director general for African affairs in the Ministry of Foreign Affairs has urged Chinese companies to "blaze new trails in the digital economy" to advance BRI cooperation.⁷⁵ China's "International

Strategy of Cooperation on Cyberspace" states that it will work with other countries to strengthen global information infrastructure and connectivity to share "development opportunities."[76]

One of the goals is to encourage the globalization of Chinese technical standards that advantage Chinese companies while another is to create new legal and governance frameworks that align with Chinese preferences. China is seeking to lead in the creation of technical standards for a range of emerging industries from ultra-high voltage (UHV) transmission (power transmission lines operating at more than 800,000 volts) to the Internet of Things, and quantum communications.[77] It advances this agenda through its China Standards 2035 Plan, an ambitious effort by Beijing and leading technology companies to set global standards for new technology.[78] The primary companies for implementing this program are tech giants Huawei and ZTE. As of 2021 Huawei was the world leader in market share of telecommunications equipment at 29 percent, while ZTE ranked fourth at 11 percent.[79] Chinese companies are building communications systems for African armed forces and security agencies. This gives China and its companies access to key African security personnel and IT systems. The relationship then opens the door to sensitive information and even the recruitment of African personnel as intelligence sources.[80]

China has increasingly become the supplier of choice for illiberal governments seeking to obtain greater control over information transmission, including those in Africa.[81] A 2020 report by the Democratic Party staff of the U.S. Senate Committee on Foreign Relations concluded that China's growing digital influence "enables China to promote an alternative model for the digital domain based on state control." Even more important, China advances surveillance and censorship by providing countries with social-control systems that run on exported digital technologies.[82] This is not surprising in light of the influence and reach of the CPC into China's state-owned and private companies. Chinese IT companies have an especially high number of CPC committees as compared to other kinds of companies. The International Cyber Policy Centre at the Australian Strategic Policy Institute has mapped China's major IT companies and concluded that Alibaba has about two hundred CPC branches, Tencent has eighty-nine, and Huawei boasts more than three hundred.[83]

The CPC understands the threat to its hold on power posed by an open Internet, as well as the opportunity that dominance over global cyberspace simultaneously offers to extending this control.[84] *Qiushi* published an important article in 2017 outlining Xi Jinping's strategic thinking on "building China into a national power in cyberspace." China's strategy for doing so calls for a series of steps, including increasing the country's "role in building, governing and operating the Internet globally." Drawing on Xi Jinping's "Four Principles and the Five Propositions" (四项原则和五点主张), the article explains that cyberspace has become a new field of competition for global governance, and Beijing must comprehensively strengthen international exchanges and cooperation in cyberspace so that China's concept of the Internet becomes an international consensus. It also calls for the integration of cyberspace military and civilian systems and policies.[85]

The China model of digital authoritarianism is spreading beyond China's borders. The use of technology for repression, censorship, Internet shutdowns, and the targeting of bloggers, journalists, and human rights activists is becoming standard practice for nondemocratic governments.[86] China's Great Firewall is catching on in several African countries, although these governments do not have the experience or human resources capacity to do it as effectively as China does. A team of academics from four universities in the United States and Canada determined in 2020 that Chinese authorities blocked more than 300,000 domains in China.[87] In 2019 at least fourteen African countries shut down the Internet; Algeria, Ethiopia, Benin, and Sudan each did so more than once.[88] Increasingly, the more authoritarian African governments are using Chinese equipment to monitor and to control social media and the Internet. In some cases, China is aiding and abetting this practice, although African governments rarely acknowledge this fact. Cybersecurity laws in Tanzania and Uganda closely resemble China's laws. Chinese companies were responsible for building the Internet system in Ethiopia, where government controls over social media are also similar to those used in China.[89]

INFORMATION TECHNOLOGY INFRASTRUCTURE

Both Huawei and ZTE are well established in Africa. Huawei has branch offices in Algeria, Egypt, Morocco, Tunisia, Ethiopia, Nigeria, and South Africa.[90] The company has likewise established training centers in Angola, the DRC, Egypt, Kenya, Morocco, Nigeria, and South Africa and has sponsored programs throughout Africa. It claims to provide training for twelve thousand African students annually.[91] As of 2020 Huawei had worked on projects in at least twenty-three African countries, where China had provided fifty-seven loans totaling $4.7 billion to government borrowers and SOEs.[92] It has built at least fifty 3G networks in thirty-six African countries and implemented 70 percent of the continent's 4G networks. Huawei, ZTE, and other Chinese companies engage in everything from constructing undersea Internet cables and national data networks to selling millions of mobile phones to Africans. Chinese technology provides the backbone of network infrastructure in several African countries, and Chinese companies are the major builders of the infrastructure, including 5G, for next-generation technologies across Africa. Other large Chinese IT companies with operations in Africa include Alibaba, Baidu, China Electronics Technology Group, China Mobile, China Telecom, China Unicom, Hikvision, and Tencent.[93]

Chinese IT products have done well in Africa for a variety of reasons. Companies such as Huawei and ZTE have targeted the African market and developed reputations for producing low cost, high-quality goods. Huawei's prices are 5–15 percent lower than those of its major international competitors Ericcson and Nokia. ZTE prices are 30–40 lower than those its European competitors offer. The larger companies have the full backing of China's government, work closely with African governments, and often find financing for major IT projects through institutions such as the China Export-Import Bank. China's financing does not attach overt political conditions, other than a requirement to recognize Beijing and not Taipei and not to publicly contradict China's "core interests" (see chapters 1 and 2).

Chinese companies have focused on building the initial core network in numerous countries, which makes it easier to win subsequent contracts. They often enjoy a monopoly on spare parts delivery and after sales service. They are quick to establish regional offices and training facilities and to support local network operators. The companies have a good reputation for customer support.[94]

Even smaller, private Chinese IT companies are doing well in Africa. For instance, Transsion Holdings, established in Shenzhen in 2006, is now the largest provider of cell phones in Africa. In the third quarter of 2021, Transsion was responsible for 47 percent of all smartphone sales in Africa.[95] It has explicitly adapted phones for the African market by keeping prices low, offering good quality and longer battery life, manufacturing some of its phones in Ethiopia, and supporting African languages in its systems. It sells under the Techno, itel, and Infinix brand names. While it receives official financing, unlike Huawei and ZTE, Transsion has so far avoided close association with the government of China.[96]

China supports its IT objectives in Africa with an assistance program that aided forty-four countries between 2000 and 2014. China is positioning itself to dominate IT throughout the continent; however, the sector makes up only a small portion of total Chinese aid to Africa. One study found that 70 percent of the aid in question involved technical assistance, monetary grants, in-kind grants, and scholarships. The remaining amount consisted of export credits, loans, loan guarantees, and supplier credits. Three countries—Nigeria, Ethiopia, and Zimbabwe—received 50 percent of the total IT aid for Africa, and ten countries accounted for 80 percent of the total. Huawei and ZTE were the top implementing companies, and the largest funding sources were Huawei, ZTE, and China Export-Import Bank. Beijing's assistance has not been a prerequisite for market entry or success, however, and Chinese IT companies have entered Africa with or without state support.[97]

Chinese companies have also built submarine cable systems in Africa. In 2009 Huawei Marine Networks delivered the Hannibal submarine cable communications system for Tunisie Telecom across the Mediterranean to Italy.[98] In 2013 Huawei Marine Networks completed the Silphium submarine cable system from Libya to Greece.[99] In 2015 Huawei upgraded the

West African Cable System, which runs along the entire western coast of Europe and Africa from the UK to South Africa. In 2019 Huawei and China Unicom completed the South Atlantic Inter Link between Brazil and Cameroon, which carries more than 95 percent of international communications traffic.[100]

In 2018 Huawei Marine Networks signed a joint venture with a UK-based submarine communications firm to build a submarine high-speed Internet cable system stretching from Pakistan to France. The goal was to construct it jointly with the Peace Cable International Network, a subsidiary of Chinese fiber optic manufacturer Hengtong Group. Specialists saw this project as a strategic move to circumvent international telecommunications consortiums dominated by Western and Indian companies.[101] Reacting to Western concerns about Huawei's potential for monitoring communications traffic, Huawei sold its 51 percent stake in the submarine cable company to Hengtong. Huawei is, however, the third largest shareholder in Hengtong. The 9,300-mile cable is moving forward with African landing points in Seychelles, Kenya, Somalia, Djibouti, and Egypt.[102] In 2020 China Mobile International joined an international consortium to build 2Africa, one of the largest submarine cables in the world linking West and East Africa with Europe and the Middle East. The 23,000-mile-long cable will have twenty-one landing points in sixteen African countries.[103]

China focused its IT engagement on African countries based on their large market size, strategic location, and receptivity to the China development model. Ethiopia meets all three of these criteria. The presence of the African Union in Addis Ababa gives the country strategic importance, and the then ruling Ethiopian People's Revolutionary Democratic Front was receptive to China's development model and governmental control over communications. Ethiopia decided to sacrifice easy access to information for internal political control and security. Consequently, China provided Ethiopia its largest telecommunications loan in Africa: $1.9 billion in 2006 for ZTE to overhaul its telecommunication system and expand mobile service and Internet connectivity while keeping Ethio Telecom as the only provider. ZTE and Huawei subsequently signed two separate agreements for $800 million each, suggesting a measure of competition among Chinese firms. China helped Ethiopia achieve a tightly controlled but developmentally oriented national information system.[104] Ethio Telecom relies on telecommunications infrastructure, including 5G, supplied by ZTE and Huawei.[105] Ethiopia's cybersecurity law mimics China's laws. One study concluded that "use of Chinese ICT in Ethiopia leads to strengthened control of the Ethiopian government over its citizens."[106]

Kenya is another country of IT focus for China. Huawei, which entered Kenya in 1998, and ZTE, together with the French company Sagem, built the first National Optic Fiber Backbone Infrastructure expansion, bringing fiber to the main urban centers and allowing the regional delivery of e-government projects. In 2012 the China Export Import Bank provided a $71 million loan to extend this system to thirty-six administrative district centers across Kenya. China supported the expansion of government-led initiatives aimed at extending Internet connectivity and improving e-government services. In Kenya, however, the Internet remained more open than it did in Ethiopia.[107] Huawei is consolidating its position in Kenya by providing online training for hundreds of government employees on IT trends, smart cities, Internet of Things, and cybersecurity.[108] In 2022 Huawei announced it will roll out 43,000 kilometers of fiber cable across Kenya to improve Internet connectivity.[109] Kenya's Communications Authority also signed a 5G technical cooperation agreement with Huawei.[110]

China pursued a similar approach in Ghana, where the Export-Import Bank provided $180 million in two concessionary loans to connect the country by fiber optics and WiMAX technology. Remote areas relied on satellites and leased terrestrial circuits. A national data center in the president's office coordinated communications and offered secure data storage facilities. Huawei provided technical guidance, but Ghana's National Information Technology Agency supervised its implementation. Vodafone became the owner and manager of the IT infrastructure, and other donors, including the Danish government, provided funding for extending the project to remote areas.[111]

In 2021 Senegal commissioned the construction of a new $18 million national data center financed by China and built by Huawei, which will also provide equipment and technical support. Senegal previously stored most of its information in the United States and Asia; the planned data center will allow it to store all information domestically, theoretically strengthening the country's digital sovereignty.[112] Similarly, in 2022 Malawi launched a national data center built by Huawei that will host all government-wide systems.[113]

Nearly every major Chinese IT company has an office in South Africa, the most developed country in Africa. Huawei entered the South African market in 1998. Twenty years later, China Unicom opened its first African operation center in Johannesburg.[114] Also in 2018, China Mobile International opened an office in Durban. The company signed a MOU for strategic alliance with MTN South Africa and said its goal is to use South Africa as a gateway to the rest of Africa.[115] ZTE has partnered with MTN South Africa on an ultra-high-speed 5G network. Rival Telkom launched its 5G Internet network with technology from Huawei.[116] South African wireless carrier Rain launched Africa's first stand-alone 5G network, featuring Huawei equipment.[117] Vodacom South Africa is partnering with China's Alipay, a subsidiary of Alibaba, for the South African market. Customers and merchants transact business on a platform operated by Vodacom Financial Services, with Alipay as the technology provider.[118] Vodacom, MTN, and Rain use Huawei 5G equipment and say they intend to continue relying on Huawei.[119] Dismissing Washington's effort to ban Huawei equipment as jealousy, South African president Cyril Ramaphosa responded that "we support a company [Huawei] that is going to take our country and indeed the world to better technologies and that is the 5G."[120]

Zambia is spending $1 billion on Chinese-made telecommunications, broadcasting, and surveillance technology. China financed and built most of the digital infrastructure in Zambia. TopStar Communications Company, a 60–40 venture between Beijing-based StarTimes Group and Zambia's state-owned broadcaster, is migrating Zambia's analog TV to digital. China's Export Import Bank provided almost half of the $282 million for the project, which some Zambians have described as excessively expensive. The Zambian government argues the project is expensive because it includes eight new studios, broadcasting vans, and trips to China to train hundreds of government journalists.[121] Huawei received a $13.5 million contract to erect telecom towers that fell well short of the specified range. Although Huawei eventually fixed the problem, it demonstrated an initial lack of attention to quality.[122] Undeterred, Zambia continues to source most of its IT equipment from China. In 2020 MTN Zambia awarded ZTE the contract to build the fiber connection to the Namibian border.[123]

Zimbabwe is developing one of the more problematic IT relationships with China, especially its facial recognition program. Huawei established a joint venture with state-owned landline operator TelOne and invested directly in mobile operator NetOne. The Chinese firm Inspur created a joint venture with TelOne for Zimbabwe's first computer and laptop assembly plant.[124] In 2019 China and Zimbabwe signed a comprehensive MOU on information communication technology. It included the development of fiber optic backbone networks, mobile broadband and Internet connectivity, international land and submarine cables, voice and data services, and manufacturing and assembly factories. It envisaged cooperation in big data, artificial intelligence, cloud computing, data-center technology, software application and product development, faster mobile and Internet-based applications for smart cities, and the utilization and management of satellite radio spectrum. Zimbabwe's official in charge of information communication technology said that Chinese companies such as Huawei and ZTE have played a "critical role" in transforming Zimbabwe's IT sector.[125]

Chinese IT companies have also been active in North Africa. In Morocco, Huawei has established a logistics center at Tangier Med Port, provides communications technology for the national railway system, and offers equipment for telecommunications systems across the country. Huawei will play a key role in Digital Silk Road projects in Morocco.[126] In Tunisia, Huawei has trained over a thousand Tunisian IT professionals and established a talent center, a service resource center, and an academy to serve as a regional educational hub. In 2012 Algeria banned Huawei and ZTE for two years following a $10 million bribery scandal involving two ZTE employees, one Huawei employee, and one official from Algeria Telecom. In 2018 Huawei signed a memorandum with Telecom Egypt to establish a $5 million data center for a cloud computing network as part of its mission to develop one of the five largest cloud networks in the world. Huawei has trained over five thousand Egyptian IT personnel, and the company built the first "open laboratory" in Cairo and four centers for training and IT smart city solutions.[127]

ARTIFICIAL INTELLIGENCE AND SURVEILLANCE TECHNOLOGY

There is no widely accepted definition of AI. In its simplest form, however, it combines computer science and robust datasets to enable problem-solving.[128] It is a mixture of multiple research fields, each with its own goal, methods, and applicable situations.[129] AI is becoming increasingly ubiquitous in Africa, as is surveillance technology, which Chinese equipment and funding often support. However, European, North American, and Israeli companies also sell surveillance equipment and technology to African governments.[130] Surveillance technology is supported by AI software capable of processing large amounts of data and extracting trends, for example, using facial recognition technology to quickly identify someone in a large database.[131] On one hand, Chinese facial recognition technology and "smart city" or "safe city" surveillance programs come with worrisome implications. The increased capability of governments to monitor citizens can lead to abuses of democratic norms and practices.[132] On the other hand, Chinese drones operated by AI are improving agriculture, traffic management control, and mobile payment systems in African countries.

This section focuses on China's surveillance programs in Africa that have security implications. Huawei is the leading vender of advanced surveillance systems; as of 2019, it had provided surveillance technology to thirteen African countries.[133] Hikvision, Huawei, Dahua Technology, and ZTE are the largest exporters of smart city and surveillance equipment.[134] China's major AI companies are CloudWalk Technology, SenseTime, Megvii Technology, and Yitu Technology. CloudWalk focuses on smart transportation, finance, governance, and business. SenseTime is an AI startup specializing in systems that analyze faces and images on an enormous scale. Megvii and SenseTime products are among the most powerful facial recognition systems in the world. Shanghai-based Yitu also has a facial scan platform that can identify a person from a database of two billion people in a matter of seconds.[135]

China aims to overtake the West in AI research and development by 2025 and become the world leader by 2030. China's focus on surveillance, weak privacy laws, and extensive databases have allowed it to improve its AI.[136] China sees leadership in AI technology as essential to achieving economic and military power as part of its comprehensive security strategy. The CPC's model of digital authoritarianism uses its technology to suppress dissent and build support.[137] In the spirit of the CPC's Eighteenth National Congress, the State Council's New Generation of Artificial Intelligence Development Plan lays out a detailed program for taking the global lead in AI. This includes embedding AI in national defense, encouraging foreign AI companies and research institutions to establish research and development centers in China, and promoting AI along the BRI.[138]

Both Made in China 2025, which promotes AI and robotics manufacturing, and the New Generation of Artificial Intelligence Development Plan are receiving sustained attention from China's leadership, including Xi Jinping.[139] Another part of this effort is the previously mentioned China Standards 2035, which intends to set global standards for AI.[140] While China says it is committed to active participation in the global governance of AI, it seeks to do so in a leadership role.[141] Beijing is driving AI surveillance technology through programs subsidized by the Digital Silk Road and exporting its policy of authoritarian cybercontrols.[142] The 2019–2021 FOCAC action plan committed China to assist African countries in the development of AI and quantum computing.[143] U.S. Department of Defense analyst Jonah Victor finds that becoming the leading provider of surveillance systems in Africa is an official part of China's strategy.[144]

A Freedom House study in 2018 determined that Chinese companies provided intelligent monitoring systems and facial recognition technology to Kenya, Rwanda, Zambia, and Zimbabwe.[145] At least sixteen African countries have safe city agreements with Huawei.[146] China's export of technology infrastructure and equipment has been used for politically motivated surveillance and repression in countries such as Uganda and Zambia. While improved surveillance may enhance public safety, it can also contribute to targeted repression of political opponents.[147] China provides AI to authoritarian African governments and those with poor human rights records. Less than 20 percent of African countries have signed progressive legal frameworks like the AU Convention on Cybersecurity and Personal Data Protection.[148] A study published by the International Cyber Policy Centre in Australia concluded that "the 'China model' of digitally enabled authoritarianism is spreading well beyond China's borders," including to countries like Zimbabwe.[149]

Zimbabwe is the African country cited most often as using surveillance technology for nefarious purposes. China, Russia, and Iran have helped Zimbabwe set up a sophisticated surveillance system for its state telecommunications provider. Zimbabwe's former intelligence minister stated that "we just see things through our system. So, no one can hide from us, in this country."[150] Zimbabwe has signed multiple agreements with Chinese companies for physical surveillance systems, including a highly controversial national facial recognition system provided by CloudWalk, which provides facial recognition for smart financial service networks as well as security applications at airports, railway, and bus stations. CloudWalk is using its facial recognition experience in Zimbabwe to recalibrate its technology through three-dimensional light to recognize darker skin tones.[151] This permits CloudWalk to develop and refine its databases with different ethnicities and demographics while Zimbabwe receives innovative technology to monitor its population.[152] Some Zimbabweans are concerned that their government is using technology to control people's freedoms.[153]

Zimbabwe is also working with Hikvision, which provides surveillance cameras for police and traffic control systems, to develop indigenous facial recognition technology. In 2018 Zimbabwe signed a MOU with Hikvision to implement a smart city program in Mutare, which included the donation of facial recognition terminals equipped with deep-learning AI systems.[154] China and Chinese companies have inspired Zimbabwe's cybersecurity legislation and have provided the financing, equipment, and training to implement a comprehensive surveillance system.[155]

Zambia is spending $1 billion on Chinese telecommunications, broadcasting, and surveillance technology. ZTE installed cameras in public spaces in Lusaka as part of a $210 million safe-city project designed to increase policing ability. Although Zambian officials deny the technology is being used for political purposes, some believe otherwise. Gregory Chifire, the director of an anticorruption organization who fled Zambia, said that "We have sold ourselves to the Chinese," adding that "people's freedom to express themselves—their freedom of thought, their freedom of speech—is shrinking by the day."[156]

Other countries in southern Africa are looking to China for help with AI. Huawei provides free AI training in China for South African students, although the program moved online in 2020 due to COVID-19. The course includes modules on 5G, cloud computing, and the "Internet of Things." The goal is to train South African students "to design, develop, and innovate AI products and solutions."[157] Namibia, a democratic country, is heavily dependent on Huawei equipment and denies accusations it is trying to monitor domestic critics.[158] In 2017 China's big data and AI provider, Percent Corporation, built a system for information visualization and data analysis for the Angolan government.[159] China financed Angola's Center for Public Security, which facilitates the exchange of information between the police and security agencies throughout the country. The project includes seven hundred cameras in Luanda, the capital, and is expanding to sixteen other provinces to identify individuals and monitor public spaces. China trained forty-five personnel in China and another six hundred locally in GPS, closed circuit television camera (CCTV) operations, criminal analysis, and the maintenance of hardware and software.[160]

Ethiopia is another country that relies on Chinese telecommunications equipment. Ethiopia's extensive governmental control of its telecom sector has eroded freedom of expression and association. Technology provided by China facilitates government monitoring of private citizens and organizations and opposition elements. Arrests, detentions, and interrogations are linked to the government's surveillance program.¹⁶¹ Ethiopia has also purchased monitoring equipment from European and Israeli commercial sources to enhance its surveillance capacity. This equipment, which logs keystrokes and passwords and can turn on webcams and microphones by stealth, runs on Chinese IT systems.¹⁶²

Huawei installed a $126 million CCTV project for Uganda's police force, ostensibly to fight crime. Opposition political leaders fear the police may use the cameras, which have facial recognition technology, to target demonstrators. The leader of one opposition party complained that "the CCTV project is just a tool to track us, hunt us and persecute us."¹⁶³ In 2017 Uganda's state minister for privatization and investment signed a preliminary agreement with the China National Electronics Import and Export Corporation to supply a "comprehensive cyber-security solution," enabling the Uganda Communications Commission, the police, and the Ministry of Internal Affairs "to guard against cyber criminals."¹⁶⁴

Nairobi's high crime rate made the city a strong candidate for Chinese surveillance technology. Huawei installed 116 long-term evolution base stations, 1,800 cameras, 200 traffic surveillance systems, and 2 data centers. Stores across Nairobi use Hikvision's cloud-based video management system. Dahua Technology earns more than $10 million annually in Kenya supplying surveillance equipment for public spaces. Nairobi's senior superintendent of police said that "anybody who does anything is being watched."¹⁶⁵ Bulelani Jili of Harvard University writes that "even in the context of a democratic government like Kenya's, bolstering state surveillance capacity without robust checks and balances renders citizens more vulnerable to the misuse of digital tools."¹⁶⁶

Amy Hawkins of the *Economist* believes that Tanzania is following the Chinese legal model of information management. She explains that Tanzanian law prohibits the use of "false content" while Chinese law bans "making falsehoods." Tanzania does not allow "content that causes annoyance," and China prohibits content that "destroys the order of society." Tanzania justifies its law to crack down on "moral decadence," while China bans "decadent" material from social media.¹⁶⁷

TECHNOLOGY AND INFORMATION SECURITY

In 2010 Nigeria signed a $470 million loan agreement with China's Export Import Bank for ZTE to install two thousand solar-powered CCTV cameras in Abuja and Lagos, a microwave network, thirty-seven emergency response systems, thirty-eight video conference subsystems, and thirty-seven e-police systems to improve antiterror monitoring. Six years later the system was not functioning and had been mothballed.[168] In 2022 Nigeria signed an agreement with Huawei for a system at the country's land borders to establish 24/7 satellite-based electronic surveillance.[169]

In 2016 China's Export Import Bank provided Côte d'Ivoire a $56 million loan to develop a video surveillance platform for Abidjan.[170] Ghana's National Security is installing seven thousand CCTV cameras to combat crime in a project that is believed to be facilitated by Huawei.[171] In 2021 Burkina Faso announced a $94 million program by Huawei and the China International Telecommunication Construction Corporation to install nine hundred surveillance cameras in two major cities to fight crime and improve internal security.[172]

Chinese companies are installing surveillance technology in Egypt, where Huawei expects to debut North Africa's first cloud computing network. Hikvision provides CCTV cameras for buses in Egypt's Suez Canal zone. Civil society watchdogs are critical of Egypt for its surveillance of activists and dissidents; Egypt has weakened protections for privacy and free expression. Cairo has helped China identify and detain Uighur Chinese (see chapter 2).[173]

Huawei is installing four thousand CCTV cameras in Mauritius, prompting opposition politicians to fear an increase in monitoring and surveillance. Former Mauritian deputy prime minister and leader of the opposition in the National Assembly Xavier-Luc Duval said, "It's really Big Brother. They'll be able to spy on all political opponents and control all the political activity. The potential for misuse is enormous."[174] In 2017 China helped Cape Verde develop a safe city project in Praia, the capital. The government subsequently hired Huawei to expand the video surveillance system throughout the country, with the goal of making Cape Verde a more secure tourist destination.[175]

TECHNOLOGY AND INFORMATION SECURITY

CYBERSECURITY

The United States has taken the lead in suggesting that Chinese IT equipment creates vulnerabilities and opens the door to abuses. While these warnings have resonated in parts of the world, they have had minimal impact in Africa, where Chinese equipment leads the way, and some countries even emulate Chinese cyberpolicies. Nevertheless, some Africans have expressed concerns, and several credible reports of cyberabuse involving Chinese-installed communications system or even China itself have emerged. For its part, China says it will actively support Africa's efforts to build cybersecurity capacity through seminars and training.[176]

China requires its citizens and companies to support its intelligence services. China's National Intelligence Law gives the state wide latitude to take whatever measures are necessary to conduct intelligence work. Article 17 authorizes the state to "legally requisition the means of transport, communication tools, sites and buildings of relevant organs, organizations and individuals." Chinese telecommunications companies cannot legally refuse to provide information requested by Chinese intelligence agencies.[177] U.S. senators Tom Cotton of Arkansas and Jon Cornyn of Texas, both members of the Senate Select Committee on Intelligence, have explained "If Huawei is directed by Chinese military or intelligence officials to compromise a foreign country's 5G network, it will comply."[178]

In 2019 American intelligence operatives shared with their counterparts in the United Kingdom evidence that Huawei has taken money from the PLA, China's National Security Commission, and a third branch of the Chinese state intelligence network.[179] Christopher Krebs, former head of the U.S. Department of Homeland Security's Cyber and Infrastructure Security Agency, emphasized that the threat is not limited to Huawei. It includes China Mobile, China Telecom, and China Unicom. These "companies are required to provide the government with access to all the data they collect."[180]

The U.S. campaign against Chinese equipment has focused on Huawei and especially its 5G system, which, as noted, has been widely accepted in

Africa. Supported by greater bandwidth, faster speeds, and the ability to transmit more data, faster, and with a quicker response time, 5G has far-reaching commercial and military applications. Chinese-led 5G infrastructure provides Beijing with the possibility for widespread data collection, including the ability to clandestinely collect privileged information from billions of people.[181] Whoever controls the networks can access the information flow, which drives the U.S. argument that China could insert a "back door" into the network that allows Chinese security services to intercept sensitive communications. The close ties between Chinese IT companies and the CPC underscore Washington's concerns.[182]

In 2019 the then principal deputy director of U.S. National Intelligence, Sue Gordon, outlined that the danger lies not just in the hardware Huawei and other Chinese IT companies provide, but in the software, such as the code used in routine security updates.[183] One company that has come under fire for code vulnerability is Hikvision, in which the government of China has a controlling share. The U.S. government prohibits the purchase and use of telecoms and surveillance technology from Hikvision, among other Chinese companies.[184] Kai von Carnap of the Mercator Institute for China Studies points out that blockchain technology, which allows fast, secure, and immutable data management through clever cryptology and distributed computing, is available on Chinese systems. He argues that it has the potential to provide the CPC with substantial amounts of personal and company data originating outside China.[185]

China's officials and representatives of IT companies vehemently deny that Chinese equipment has been co-opted for spying purposes. They insist that China's critics have not presented any evidence of abuse and that it is not in the company's interest to do so.[186] Vincent Pang, a senior Huawei manager, said that his company has a strong incentive not to spy on its customers. If a back door were ever discovered, he posits, "It would destroy our markets."[187] The UK set up a lab, paid for by Huawei but run by the British, that over eight years of evaluating Huawei equipment has not yet found a back door. On the other hand, the lab concluded that code included in Huawei's products is a "buggy, spaghettified mess" that can be as useful to hackers as any back door.[188]

TECHNOLOGY AND INFORMATION SECURITY

In January 2018 *Le Monde* published a detailed report based on internal AU sources of a major cyberbreach at the AU headquarters in Addis Ababa, which China built in 2012 free of charge at a cost of $200 million. In 2017 the AU's small IT staff discovered that its Huawei servers were unusually busy each night between midnight and 2:00 a.m., when AU offices were empty. The IT staff determined that Chinese technicians in Shanghai were downloading secret AU communications. It is possible this had been going on for the previous five years. China's mission to the AU did not respond to requests for comment from *Le Monde* prior to publication of the story.[189]

In February 2018 AU chairman Moussa Faki, following a meeting with Foreign Minister Wang Yi in Beijing, said that the allegations of Chinese spying are "all lies." Flanked by Wang, Faki added the AU would open a new office in Beijing with support from China. Faki insisted that "no maneuvers could distract and divert us from our mission" of strengthening relations with China. Wang predictably responded that China was "selflessly" helping Africa to develop while some powers are not interested in Africa's development.[190] Rwandan president Paul Kagame, AU chairperson at the time of the *Le Monde* article, downplayed the incident and said he knew nothing about it. He added, in any event, nothing is done at the AU that we would not like people to know about, and he was not "worried about being spied on in this building."[191] Following the breach discovered in 2017, however, *Le Monde* reported that the AU acquired its own servers and declined China's offer to configure them. It also began encrypting all electronic communications and stopped transmitting them through Ethio Telecom, the Ethiopian government communications monopoly that relies on Chinese equipment.[192]

Undeterred by this cybersecurity debacle, the deputy chairperson of the AU Commission, Thomas Kwesi Quartey, and Huawei's vice president for North Africa, Philippe Wang, signed a MOU in June 2019 to consolidate IT cooperation. The agreement covered broadband, the "Internet of Things," cloud computing, 5G, artificial intelligence, and the training of Africans. Wang commented at the signing that collaboration between the AU and Huawei demonstrates the AU's continuing trust in the company. He said this agreement should end "the rumors of data leakage from AU by Huawei equipment, as AU has totally audited their IT system for the whole organization, and nothing corroborates what was said in media reports one year ago."[193] A Western embassy officer who follows AU matters explained that, after the bugging episode, the AU began to diversify its cybersecurity ties away from Chinese companies, including with America's Qualcom. The AU drafted a model Convention on Cybersecurity and Personal Data, but only thirteen countries have ratified it so far.[194]

In 2019 an investigation by the *Wall Street Journal* uncovered two cases in Africa where Huawei technicians helped Ugandan and Zambian security personnel intercept encrypted communications and social media interactions of the political opposition. The investigation did not find that Huawei executives in China knew of, directed, or approved these activities. Nor did it determine there was something unique about Huawei's technology that enabled these intercepts. It did, however, find that there was compelling evidence that Huawei employees played a direct role in Ugandan and Zambian government efforts to intercept the private communications of political opponents.[195]

In 2020 the AU experienced another cyberattack, this time by a group called "Bronze President" that specialists from Dell Technologies found with high confidence is based in China and with moderate confidence was sponsored by the government of China.[196] Reuters received access to a five-page internal AU memo that documented the breach. A tip from Japan's Computer Emergency Response Team in January 2020 alerted the AU to unusual traffic between its network and a domain associated with Bronze President. The AU's information technology team traced the suspicious traffic to a set of servers in the basement of the AU's Building C, part of an older complex across the road from the new Chinese-built conference center. The hackers stole footage from the AU's security cameras that covered offices, parking areas, corridors, and meeting rooms.[197]

The Chinese mission to the AU responded in an email that "the AU side has not mentioned being hacked on any occasion" and that Africa and China are "good friends, partners and brothers." The email added "we never interfere in Africa's internal affairs and wouldn't do anything that harms the

TECHNOLOGY AND INFORMATION SECURITY

interests of the African side." A former AU staff member said that an official protest over the spying is unlikely because China plays a critical role in funding the organization. He added that, like the security breach reported by *Le Monde* in 2018, the incident would be swept under the rug; "attacking the Chinese for us, it's a very bad idea."[198]

U.S. warnings and credible reports about the security risks of Chinese IT equipment, personnel, and construction have mostly fallen on deaf ears in Africa. A senior official in Ghana's Ministry of Foreign Affairs noted that China built the ministry's headquarters but expressed no concern about bugging because "we trust our ICT people."[199] Kenya's cabinet secretary for ICT, Joe Mucheru, said U.S. pressure to avoid Huawei equipment in its networks is politically motivated and not based on evidence showing it would enable Chinese spying.[200] On the other hand, a senior officer at Ghana's Armed Forces Command and Staff College said there was concern about bugging after China constructed the Ministry of Defense headquarters, warning "we must be careful" and assume it happens.[201] Arthur Gwagwa, a Zimbabwean cybersecurity expert at Utrecht University, added that "some of the vulnerabilities in the Chinese equipment are intentional, they are introduced for malicious purposes."[202]

Ultimately, however, the lower prices and financing offered by Chinese companies remain attractive, and Chinese IT products have become so deeply embedded in African networks that it would be expensive and disruptive to switch to Western companies and equipment.[203] There is also a sense of fatalism that whether the technology is French, Russian, or Chinese, no one is fully protected, and no African country can adequately safeguard its systems without outside help.[204] Cybersecurity is seen as a luxury, not a necessity, in many African countries.[205] A survey conducted by the AU Commission concluded that only eight African countries have a national strategy on cybersecurity, thirteen have a Computer Emergency Response Team or Computer Security Incident Response Team, fourteen have data protection laws, and eleven have cybercrime laws.[206] It is not surprising that the deputy CEO for Huawei South Africa commented that the U.S. ban on Huawei "has had no substantial effect on our local operations."[207]

TECHNOLOGY AND INFORMATION SECURITY

* * *

China's increasing engagement in technological and informational security reflects a desire to extend its influence in Africa and to become the global leader in these emerging fields. Beijing continues to face competition from Western countries and Russia in the areas of nuclear, space, and satellite development. Meanwhile, it has become a leader in information technology and AI in Africa. In some cases, Chinese firms have tailored their IT products, such as smartphones, to the African market. In others, the lower cost of Chinese products and greater willingness to provide financing have overwhelmed the competition.

Technological and informational security cooperation with African countries benefits China. These collaborations provide opportunities, especially through training, for China to expand its relationships with Africans. Chinese facial recognition companies use Africans to improve their technology for more effective identification of darker skin tones. China's satellite launches use tracking facilities in Namibia. Its ubiquitous communications equipment, systems, and personnel in Africa provide an excellent opportunity, even when overt, to collect valuable information that assists China's economic, political, and security interests in Africa. China is competing in all these areas as part of its comprehensive security strategy and strategic engagement with Africa.

11
PROJECTING TRENDS IN CHINA-AFRICA STRATEGIC RELATIONS

The preceding chapters document and analyze the rapidly expanding scope and scale of China's strategic relations with Africa across the breadth of political and security-related topics—from diplomacy and propaganda to arms sales and space cooperation. Based on our research, two decades of systematic data, and hundreds of surveys and in-person interviews, we found that Africa has steadily risen in Beijing's strategic calculus, and that Chinese interlocutors have created partnerships with more African elites across a broader range of political and security sectors than ever before. Simply put, prior to COVID-19, China's purposeful, well-funded campaign to build "win-win" relationships was having an unprecedented influence on its African counterparts.

Here, in the final chapter, we offer nine findings and emerging trends that we believe will continue to shape Sino-African strategic relations for the foreseeable future. Of course, as COVID-19 and climate change demonstrate, predicting the future is always fraught with uncertainty. Past performance, as the usual disclaimer warns, is no guarantee of future results. Despite the uncertainties, however, we forge ahead in an effort to shed light on the future of China-Africa strategic relations.

PROJECTING TRENDS IN CHINA-AFRICA RELATIONS

1. CHINA'S STRATEGIC RELATIONS WITH AFRICA WILL REBOUND

Throughout this book we have documented both the expansion of China-Africa political and security relations prior to COVID-19 and their precipitous contraction following the onset of the pandemic. Beginning with the virus's outbreak and continuing throughout 2022, many indicators in the strategic relationship—from the number of port calls to media exchanges—have stagnated, declined, or even collapsed entirely. In 2020 fears of COVID-19 led to a rise of anti-Chinese racism in Africa, which was stoked by widely shared videos of African residents sleeping in the streets after local Chinese authorities evicted them from their homes. For three years, large Chinese cities (including Shanghai, Xian, and Chengdu) endured weeks of unprecedented lockdowns. Many foreigners left, among them tens of thousands of African students and businesspersons, who as of January 2023 remained unable to return to China due to COVID-19.

In January 2023, China ended its "zero-COVID" policies and reopened its borders, prompting a revival of person-to-person exchanges. During the pandemic Beijing had shifted from in-person meetings to virtual online exchanges. In August 2022, for instance, China hosted the fifth Forum on China-Africa Media Cooperation in Beijing, with nearly all the African participants (representing more than forty countries) attending virtually.[1] Given China's prioritization of Africa and the Global South more broadly, we predict that, now that the country has reopened, China-Africa strategic relations will return to pre-COVID levels within two to three years.

2. CHINA WILL CONSOLIDATE ITS MULTITIER NETWORK OF RELATIONSHIPS WITH AFRICAN POLITICAL AND SECURITY ELITES

China-Africa strategic relations not only traverse multiple sectors (e.g., political, media, education, military, police, and technology) but also span four distinct yet overlapping levels of international engagement: bilateral, global, regional, and subregional (see figure 1.1). As one senior Chinese diplomat explained, Beijing's strategic relations involve "multi-centric, multi-layered and multi-pivotal subnetworks of regional and international cooperation that are interconnected and interwoven."[2] By building interlocking and mutually reinforcing relationships, China has created a dense and durable network of ties with Africans that advance its influence and interests simultaneously across all four levels.

Chinese interlocutors build relationships with Africans on each level, but bilateral ties remain the foundation of Beijing's approach. Each year since 1991, the Chinese foreign minister's first overseas trip has been to Africa. In 2020 Wang Yi visited Egypt, Djibouti, Eritrea, Burundi, and Zimbabwe; in 2021 he visited Nigeria, the Democratic Republic of Congo, Botswana, Tanzania, and Seychelles; in 2022 it was Eritrea, Kenya, and Comoros; and in 2023 it was Ethiopia, Gabon, Angola, Benin, and Egypt. The Foreign Ministry describes these trips as "a sign of how highly Beijing regards its ties to the region."[3]

Beijing underwrites various types of bilateral strategic engagements, including diplomatic meetings, party-to-party exchanges, military-to-military dialogues, training sessions for African journalists, and educational and cultural programs. These interactions are flexible and are adapted in accordance with the African partner's domestic political constraints. For instance, in a tightly controlled autocracy, like Ethiopia under the Ethiopian People's Revolutionary Democratic Front until 2019, the Communist Party of China (CPC) confined its relations entirely to the ruling party. In an electoral democracy like Ghana, by contrast, Beijing maintains ties and provides material support to both the ruling party and the opposition—an approach that allows it to manage political power transitions. In South Africa, the CPC leverages its partnership with a smaller coalition partner, the South African Communist Party, to help maintain close relations with the ruling African National Congress.

African regional and subregional organizations have also become venues for China to find and cultivate new partners. The most important of these are the African Union and the Forum on China-Africa Cooperation (FOCAC), which China created in 2000 to coordinate and pursue its continent-wide initiatives. Meanwhile, at the subregional level, China also seeks to advance its strategic interests by building relations with African organizations (e.g., ECOWAS, SADC, COMESA)—which, taken together, now constitute a distinct tier of China-Africa strategic relations. Working through FOCAC and existing African subregional institutions allows Beijing to exercise and strengthen its relationships with well-placed African partners while monitoring and discouraging collective action against its interests.

On the global level, at the United Nations, the World Trade Organization, and other international institutions, China has supported African initiatives and friendly African countries facing criticism from the West for human rights abuses. Beijing regularly affirms its "UN-centered diplomacy," calls on all states to observe the UN Charter, and contributes more peacekeepers than any other UN Security Council permanent member. Still, China opposes any perceived impingement on its sovereignty by an international organization. In 2016, for instance, it condemned the UN Permanent Court of Arbitration after it ruled against China's territorial claims in the South China Sea. And in 2022 China lambasted a UN Human Rights Council report as "wholly illegal and invalid" after it found evidence of torture, sexual assault, and forced labor in Xinjiang.[4] On these and other occasions when UN findings have run contrary to Chinese interests, Beijing has sought and obtained the support of dozens of African countries.

By building relationships with African officials, party cadres, military leaders, and social elites across all four levels, Chinese interlocutors advance the notion that their country is the leader of a like-minded group of developing states seeking "south-south" cooperation to achieve a more fair and "democratic" world order. Thus, as the U.S.-China relationship grows increasingly contentious, we predict that Beijing will increasingly seek to harness the collective normative power of African and other developing countries to constrain the capability of the United States and its allies to act against Beijing's interests.[5] Under the banners of "sovereignty" and "autonomy," Chinese officials and propagandists will continue to build and consolidate relations with Africans across all four levels of engagement, with an eye toward shielding China from international scrutiny and countering American "hegemony."

3. CHINA OFFERS AFRICAN COUNTRIES AN ALTERNATIVE MODEL OF POLITICAL GOVERNANCE

Chinese officials, cadres and propagandists have long been antagonistic toward liberal democracy, which they blame for political instability in African countries. Beginning in the 1970s, China adopted a largely nonideological approach to building relations in Africa—a strategy that endured until the end of the Hu Jintao era (covered in our first book) in 2012. Under Xi Jinping, however, a gradual evolution has taken place in outreach, such that Chinese officials have gone from merely disparaging liberal democracy to offering China's political system as a *better* model of political governance for African and other developing countries. Today, China seeks not only to improve the perceptions of African elites and "debunk misconceptions" about its rise, but also to persuade Africans that its illiberal politics and state-driven development strategy are *superior* to liberal democracy and the rule of law.

The notion that China's autocratic political system has been the essential ingredient in its economic rise is a central element in Beijing's messaging to Africans. Unlike Western liberal democracy, China's socialist system claims it "brings people together in order to pool wisdom" and creates consensus for the benefit of the majority of society.[6] This model of centralized political control is distinct from the Mao era in that it appeals to established African elites, not revolutionaries or the working classes. For China, the adulation of African leaders lionizes its national socialist political model and furthers its image as a benign and trustworthy actor, one whose presence is good for the continent. For many leaders in Africa and other developing regions—having witnessed the failure of neoliberal growth policies advocated by the World Bank and the IMF in the 1990s and 2000s—the siren song of rapid economic growth without giving up political control is irresistible.

In return for financial and material support, China's African partners are asked to provide rhetorical and diplomatic support for China's political system, its revanchist territorial claims, and its alternative conceptions of "democracy" and "human rights." In this way, the Chinese side uses tangible benefits to incentivize its African partners to monetize their political compliance by affirming that China's political system is superior to that of the United States.

Some researchers argue that China is merely seeking to legitimize, not spread, its political system. However, we believe this argument creates a distinction without a difference because, as Oscar Wilde famously wrote, "Imitation is the sincerest form of flattery." By publicly lauding and studying the CPC's governance methods and techniques, African leaders can ingratiate themselves with Beijing. Still, rhetoric notwithstanding, it remains unclear what, if any, aspects of China's political system can actually be successfully replicated in African countries. Volatility among longstanding African political partners like the ANC and now defunct EPRDF not only presents challenges for Chinese interests in South Africa and Ethiopia, respectively, but also forces Beijing to confront hard questions about the applicability of its governance model to African conditions.

While China is not responsible for the political and security crises of its African partners, we found that the type of reciprocal relationships that Beijing cultivates do facilitate corrupt and nontransparent dealings with African elites, which in turn create tensions and contradictions. This is because, while many African partners undoubtedly benefit from their relationships with Beijing, those benefits often serve their own personal, rather than the national, interest. By blurring the lines between the personal interests of African political leaders and those of their countries,

Chinese partners create space for corrupt side deals—a hallmark of elite capture. This conflation of personal and national interests has led some analysts to overestimate the agency possessed by African policy makers in their negotiations with China.

4. CHINA WILL EXPAND POLITICAL AND SECURITY EXCHANGES AND TRAINING PROGRAMS FOR AFRICANS

Over the past decade, Beijing has funded a growing number of meetings and trainings for African political and military elites in China. "The CPC is ready to make more friends across the world," Xi Jinping told the assembled guests at the CPC in Dialogue with World Political Parties in 2017.[7] Chinese interlocutors use these exchanges to build more and closer ties with current and future African leaders and improve their understanding of local developments. Beijing hosts and trains officials from African governments across the ideological spectrum, from liberal democracies to autocracies, rightist to leftist, Islamist to secular. Rather than ideological affinity, China prizes reliable African political and security partners both across the aforementioned four levels as well as vertically, within each successive generation of elites. The better China's relationships are in a particular country, the greater its capacity to pursue and defend its interests there.

In addition to the traditional diplomacy conducted by top leaders and the Ministry of Foreign Affairs and other state organs, the International Department of the Central Committee of the CPC (ID-CPC) is tasked with building relations with political parties. While the ID-CPC has expanded its hosting and training of political parties throughout the developing world, our data reveals that in the years leading up to the COVID-19 pandemic there was a rapid increase in the number and frequency of exchanges with African political parties. Although some of these meetings have continued online, given the advantages that in-person hosting affords, we believe Beijing will return to sponsoring both large and small gatherings as COVID-19 travel policies permit.

The ID-CPC offers both short- and longer-term bilateral and multilateral cadre training programs, which are sometimes done in collaboration with the Party School of the CPC Central Committee, a provincial-level institution, and/or a university. The Chinese side sets the agenda and coordinates and closely monitors guest interactions. When Africans visit China, Chinese hosts are generous and project modesty by using terms such as "brotherhood" and "equality" and meeting African leaders at or above their rank. By feting African visitors, the Chinese side seeks to identify and cultivate enduring and reliable partners that will support its territorial claims and legitimize its political system. Positive perceptions acquired by African political leaders in China help advance the country's image as a defender of African stability and development.

Military-to-military exchanges and trainings are another component of China's strategic relations with African countries. The PLA exchanged high-level delegations with African militaries regularly until the outbreak of COVID-19. In 2018 and again in 2019, China hosted its first large, high-level, multilateral forums for senior African security personnel and was in the midst of expanding training and exercises between Chinese and African soldiers and police when the pandemic began. In a number of African countries, including Ghana, Namibia, Tanzania, Uganda, and Zambia, China has also built military and police infrastructure, such as barracks, training facilities, military bases, and military/police headquarters. As the effects of COVID-19 abate, we expect China's bilateral and multilateral military diplomacy and training of African forces will emerge as an even more important complement to Sino-African strategic relations.

5. CHINA WILL INCREASINGLY TURN TO AFRICA FOR FOOD, FUEL, AND MINERALS

Since China's "going out" strategy was launched in the late 1990s, distinctions between external vs. internal security and traditional vs. nontraditional threats have largely disappeared from Chinese strategic thinking.[8] In his keynote address to the FOCAC summit in Beijing in 2018, Xi applied this enlarged "comprehensive security" concept directly to China-Africa relations.[9] According to Shu Zhan, China's former ambassador to Eritrea and Rwanda, for Africa "comprehensive security means providing security in both traditional and non-traditional fields, which are more and more interwoven." He identified a list of what he called "non-traditional security threats," which included "food security, energy and resource security."[10]

Although food and energy security have long been top priorities for China, in 2022 they became acute concerns as China experienced the worst drought since its establishment in 1949. Crops baked to a crisp in the fields amid weeks of 104-degree heat, which dried up rivers and cut hydropower production in half. Although Africa is a net food importer, some countries do export agricultural products, and the continent has uncultivated and undercultivated lands. While African food exports to China have been modest, they are likely to grow over time, as will Chinese investments in the African agricultural sector and imports of food products. We do not, however, predict an influx of Chinese farmers into Africa.

African waters are already an important source of seafood for China, a trend we expect will continue apace with consumer demand and the depletion of fish stocks in Asian waters. As in mining and small trading, however, we predict that Chinese nationals moving into the fishing sectors of African countries will displace increasing numbers of local fishers. Indeed, in both West and East African waters, traditional fishers have already seen their catches shrink due to the activities of Chinese trawlers.

Energy security remains among China's primary interests in Africa, yet the country has become less reliant on African oil—which fell from about 22 percent of total petroleum imports in 2017 to 18 percent in 2019, to 11 percent in 2021. In 2021 and 2022 China imported a small percentage of its LNG from African countries. But if China intends to reach its stated long-term goal of carbon neutrality by 2060, then its energy mix must eventually evolve in favor of more natural gas imports from, among other regions, Africa.

African minerals (e.g., cobalt, manganese, chrome ore, tantalum, lithium, and platinum) are also likely to become increasingly sought-after strategic commodities for China. Such resources are essential to meet the needs of the country's military and space sectors, as well as to ensure China will remain a global leader in the manufacture of high-end "green" products, such as electric vehicles, solar panels, and wind turbines. About 70 percent of the world's cobalt, for instance, is mined in the Democratic Republic of Congo. We predict that China's firms will also seek more opportunities to extract rare earth elements in African countries and expand deep seabed mining activities in the western Indian Ocean.

6. CHINA'S "NONINTERFERENCE PRINCIPLE" IS EVOLVING

The principle of noninterference in the internal affairs of other countries has long been a hallmark of Chinese foreign policy, with the corollary being that others must not involve themselves in issues that China views as its own domestic affairs. Beijing's original noninterference principle has long been well-received among African governments because, as small countries, they naturally fear outside impingements on their autonomy. The brutal legacy of European colonialism in Africa also makes these countries particularly sensitive to Western interference. Moreover, for both China and its more authoritarian African partners, support for noninterference is motivated by a desire to ward off international condemnation, sanctions, and intervention related to their repressive domestic policies.

Over the past decade or so, as Chinese policy makers have responded to political and security challenges in African countries, Beijing's conception of noninterference has been expanded to address threats to Chinese nationals and property.

The number of Chinese nationals and firms in Africa rose steadily prior to COVID-19. But as their presence in African countries has grown, so too have their security challenges. Attacks range from targeted kidnappings to terrorist incidents when Chinese people were simply in the wrong place at the wrong time. Robberies and killings by criminal gangs have become all too common. In response, Chinese companies, particularly those extracting resources in unstable areas, hire off-duty security personnel from African governments or foreign security firms to protect their operations.

But as the demand for security has risen, so has the pressure on Beijing. China's security forces are working with and training local police to protect larger Chinese communities in South Africa. China is also improving preproject risk assessment and local communications, creating embassy databases of its nationals, and delivering more timely security warnings to local Chinese communities. When these efforts have proven inadequate, however, Beijing has turned to more proactive measures that go beyond its previous conceptions of noninterference. For instance, private Chinese security firms are increasingly active in some African countries—although they remain constrained by Beijing's official prohibition on Chinese nationals carrying firearms.

In South Sudan, where many Chinese work in the oil sector, Beijing agreed to contribute a combat battalion of peacekeepers, but only after the UN expanded the mission's mandate to include the protection of foreigners. When all else has failed, China has had to evacuate its nationals from Somalia, Chad, Central African Republic, South Sudan, Sierra Leone, Guinea, and Ethiopia. Most significantly, during the Libyan civil war in 2011, Beijing evacuated nearly thirty-six thousand Chinese nationals and incurred billions of dollars in losses. Such incidents have catalyzed the view that China should build the capacity to safeguard its nationals and property in Africa.

The most readily observable change to China's noninterference principle and evidence of its growing security presence on the continent has been the country's establishment of a naval base in Djibouti in 2017. Beijing, which had long eschewed overseas bases, changed its position and established its first base in Africa to support the PLA naval antipiracy task force in the Gulf of Aden, which was created in 2009 to thwart Somali pirate attacks on Chinese and other foreign ships. The base also supports China's UN peacekeepers, trains PLA personnel, tests military equipment, and is prepared to support the large-scale evacuation of Chinese nationals. For Djibouti, however, which was already home to several foreign military bases, including a large U.S. facility, China's new base is primarily a way to attract infrastructure financing and collect rental income.

China's noninterference principle is also evolving in response to political considerations in Africa. This evolution began in 2006, when China, under pressure from Western governments and with an eye toward the summer Olympic Games in Beijing in 2008, altered its position on the conflict in Sudan's Darfur region. In 2007 President Hu Jintao visited Sudan and pressed President Omar al-Bashir to come to an agreement with the UN. After the meeting, Bashir grudgingly accepted the UN-AU peacekeeping mission in Darfur. China "never twists arms," but Sudan "got the message," China's ambassador to the United Nations explained at the time.[11]

The Libya crisis in 2011 produced another, albeit somewhat confusing, evolution of the noninterference principle. Under pressure from the African Union and the Arab League, Beijing supported the UN Security Council resolution that imposed an arms embargo, travel ban, and asset freeze on Mu'ammar al-Qadhafi and referred him to the International Criminal Court. Three weeks later, however, Chinese leaders abstained from voting on a UN resolution that authorized a no-fly zone, although they knew that Western countries intended to use it to push for regime change in Tripoli. In this way, China tacitly supported the multilateral intervention, even going so far as to recognize the Libyan opposition while al-Qadhafi was still in power.

Another adaptation came in 2017, when Zimbabwe's former vice president Emmerson Mnangagwa, who was wanted in Harare on murder and money laundering charges, took refuge in China after his longtime ally (and China's longtime partner), President Robert Mugabe, removed him from office. Zimbabwe's Defense Forces commander Constantino Chiwenga was visiting China at the time and met with Defense Minister Chang Wanquan, who reportedly assured him that China would not object if he removed Mugabe and took temporary control of the country. In November Chiwenga and the army orchestrated Mugabe's removal and arranged for the return from China of Mnangagwa, who subsequently became president.[12]

China's offers to mediate disputes in South Sudan, between Ethiopia and Eritrea, and the Eritrea-Djibouti border dispute showcase still another evolution of its noninterference principle. Yet peacebuilding remains a double-edged sword. If successful, it can serve to underscore Beijing's leadership and commitment to African security and stability. It could also, however, entangle China in local conflicts, or tie its interests and credibility to the success of any deals that it brokers. Ultimately, while Beijing did help mediate the South Sudan conflict, it did not help resolve the other two.

Rather than jettison its noninterference policy entirely, we expect that Beijing will continue to reference it even while ad hoc changes are made in response to threats to Chinese nationals and property, and emerging political and security challenges in African countries. Where and when its interests are affected, China will become increasingly proactive and assertive. But if they are not impacted, China is likely to keep a low profile. Thus changes in China's nonintervention principle will be made as needed, and primarily in response to strategic concerns in African countries.

7. CHINA NAVAL POWER PROJECTION AROUND AFRICA IS GROWING

China has stated its intention to build a navy with global reach, and doing so requires port facilities and docking agreements around the world, including along the African coast. Perhaps not surprisingly, then, we found that prior to COVID-19, China's increased attention to African ports coincided with a rapid increase in PLA Navy port calls around the continent, but primarily at Djibouti. Between 2010 and 2022, PLA Navy ships made 160 port calls in Africa—far more than the U.S. Navy (see table 9.2). Since the pandemic began, however, except for the Djibouti base, port calls have been paused, even as Beijing continues to increase its financing, construction, expansion, and management of African ports and storage facilities. Although COVID-19 interrupted their growth trend, port calls resumed again in February 2023 and we predict that they will gradually return to and then exceed prepandemic levels in terms of frequency, ship size, and the number of ships per visit.

While it remains unclear whether the PLA will establish additional naval bases in African ports, China is in the process of creating the physical port infrastructure its navy needs to expand its capabilities and project power further than ever before. In some countries, like in Togo and Nigeria, Chinese companies have won contracts to manage existing ports. In others, like Namibia and Mauritania, they have financed or built them. Chinese investors have also acquired equity stakes in strategic ports in African countries, including Egypt, Morocco, Tanzania, Cameroon, and Nigeria. Those investments that are above 50 percent equity give China a controlling interest in the port, including a say in which ships can and cannot dock there. China's deepening involvement in African ports raises questions about its intentions. In some cases these port deals appear to be largely profit-driven enterprises, while in others there is also a security dimension.

8. CHINA-AFRICA TECHNOLOGY AND INFORMATION SECURITY COOPERATION ARE EXPANDING

Although China's arms industry continues to export both small and big-ticket weapons systems to a range of African buyers, sales peaked in 2016 and have declined sharply since (see figures 8.1 and 8.2). It is hard to know precisely why African purchases of Chinese-made conventional arms have slowed, but the main reasons appear to be a reduction in total African arms purchases and growing competition from Russian suppliers. These and other trends suggest that while Chinese arms sales to Africa will continue, they are unlikely to return to pre-2016 levels any time soon. That said, over time we expect that sales of more expensive equipment, such as aircraft, will gradually, albeit slowly, increase the dollar value of China's sales to African militaries.

China is determined to have a dominant role in setting international standards. As Chinese firms have become the world leaders in technology

PROJECTING TRENDS IN CHINA-AFRICA RELATIONS

products, services, and logistics, they have increasingly sought to collaborate with African governments and companies. In recent years, China has emphasized cooperation with African countries in the fields of nuclear, space, information technology equipment, artificial intelligence, surveillance technology, and cybersecurity.

Chinese firms have been especially successful in the information technology sector, where their equipment and services sales exceed those of all other countries. China's two national champions—Huawei and ZTE—have accomplished this thanks to attractive pricing and easy financing. Meanwhile, several less well-known Chinese companies design technology products and software specifically for the African market. Chinese satellite TV providers like StarTimes, for instance, are gaining market share by providing low-cost content to viewers in numerous African countries. The demand for affordable telecommunications services, equipment, and content has grown rapidly in Africa, and we predict that Chinese firms will remain leaders in these areas. Some sectors, like telecommunications, e-commerce, and phone applications, actually benefited from Africans spending more time and money online during the pandemic.

Perhaps the most controversial areas of technological collaboration are artificial intelligence, surveillance technology, and cybersecurity. While these technologies can be used for benign purposes, like improving traffic flow and agricultural production, they also can be deployed to monitor and repress the citizens of African countries and can open the door for China to exploit the systemic vulnerabilities of local networks. The United States has discouraged African countries from purchasing Huawei equipment due to such concerns, and on at least two occasions Beijing was found to have surveilled the African Union headquarters. Yet neither Washington's entreaties nor Beijing's intrusions have slowed China's expansion into the African telecommunications and information technology sectors. Instead, African governments have rationalized China's activities, arguing that other countries are doing the same, and pointing to the prohibitive costs of other options. If such incidents become common, however, then we expect that African countries with sufficient resources will quietly search for non-Chinese suppliers.

9. CHINA WILL INVEST MORE IN AFRICA-FOCUSED PROPAGANDA TO BOLSTER ITS IMAGE AND BUILD RELATIONSHIPS WITH INFLUENTIAL AFRICANS

Over the last decade, perceptions of China among Africans have been broadly positive. A Pew survey in 2015 that looked at favorable/unfavorable views of China in nine African countries put China's average favorable rating at about 70 percent.[13] In 2019 another Pew survey found that people in Tunisia, Nigeria, Kenya, and South Africa had more favorable views of China than people in Europe, Asia, and North America.[14] Amid this generally positive picture, there are indications that, even before COVID-19, trends in some African nations had begun shifting downward. For instance, between 2013 and 2019 China's favorability fell from 76 percent to 70 percent in Nigeria, 78 percent to 58 percent in Kenya, and 48 percent to 46 percent in South Africa.[15] These declines are consistent with trends in other developing regions.[16]

During our fieldwork in Africa, we heard many reasons for rising anti-Chinese sentiment, including the "capture" of African elites, illegal fishing and mining by Chinese nationals, Chinese firms' disregard for the environment and wildlife, nontransparent commercial debt held by Chinese banks, poor-quality Chinese imports, and the illicit practices of Chinese firms, such as tax evasion, poor treatment of African workers, and illegal currency repatriation. In addition to COVID-19, another driver of negative sentiments was the viral spread of various videos on social media showing Chinese bosses mistreating and sometimes beating African workers. Although each such incident did not affect the official China-Africa relationship, taken together they have contributed to the proliferation of grassroots anti-Chinese narratives.

To bolster its image, China is working to develop a compelling narrative and strengthening its capacity to reach African audiences. "We should increase China's soft power, give a good Chinese narrative and better communicate China's messages to the world," Xi Jinping has instructed.[17] To this end, China's "Africa-focused propaganda" is best understood as a subset of its "foreign-focused propaganda" work, which includes the media, educational, and cultural sectors. China's "big four" official propaganda outlets (*China Daily*, CGTN, China Radio International, and Xinhua) aim to improve African perceptions of China and cultivate relations with influential African partners who are brought on air to express pro-China sentiments. Chinese propaganda emphasizes positive changes in African societies, which, whenever possible, are attributed to cooperation with, or learning from, China. But while positive messaging is the most readily observable goal of China's state media outlets, they continue to draw low levels of African viewership, and there remains little overlap between the dominant themes in China's coverage and coverage in mainstream African media. Going forward, we expect that, despite their abundant resources, the CPC's tight controls on information flows and messaging will further constrain the coverage of its Africa-focused propaganda outlets in ways that make it unlikely they will emerge as news leaders in Africa.

Nevertheless, China's Africa-focused media, educational, and cultural propaganda programs have successfully cultivated a group of influential African interlocutors who help promote the country's image and interests. Of course, not every engagement created through China's Africa-focused propaganda programs can yield a reliable, long-term partnership. But Beijing's growing expenditures on them prior to the onset of COVID-19, and the positive reactions we heard from African participants, suggest that they have been at least somewhat effective. As such, we expect that Beijing will gradually reinvigorate and expand its Africa-focused education and cultural propaganda programs.

LOOKING AHEAD

From when Xi Jinping took power until the outbreak of COVID-19, China expended vast economic and human resources to build its strategic relations with Africans in nearly all areas. Officials from China's government, party, and military maintain long-standing personal and institutional relationships with their African counterparts and before the pandemic were interacting with them regularly at bilateral, global, regional, and subregional venues. Beijing had also stepped up its propaganda programs, scaled up training for African political parties, armies, and police forces, invested in African ports, and improved its capability to dispatch and maintain forces on the continent via its military base in Djibouti.

Although COVID-19 interrupted many areas of Sino-African strategic engagement, China maintained interaction with its partners by organizing virtual events and providing material support (e.g., face masks) that required minimal face-to-face contact. We predict that China-Africa political and security engagement will regain its pre-COVID-19 momentum. Moreover, given the extent and speed of China's strategic relations with Africa, we expect to see elements of this approach replicated throughout the Global South.

APPENDIX

CHINA'S ESTABLISHMENT OF DIPLOMATIC RELATIONS WITH AFRICAN COUNTRIES

COUNTRY	INITIAL DATE OF ESTABLISHMENT OF DIPLOMATIC RELATIONS	SUBSEQUENT CHANGES
Egypt	May 30, 1956	–
Morocco	November 1, 1958	–
Algeria	December 20, 1958	China recognized Algeria's provisional government on this date and Algeria's independent government in 1962.
Sudan	February 4, 1959	–
Guinea	October 14, 1959	–
Ghana	July 5, 1960	Following a military coup, Ghana closed the Chinese Embassy in 1966, charging that China supported former leader Kwame Nkrumah, who took exile in Guinea. Chinese personnel left in November. Ghana restored ties in January 1972.

(continued)

APPENDIX

COUNTRY	INITIAL DATE OF ESTABLISHMENT OF DIPLOMATIC RELATIONS	SUBSEQUENT CHANGES
Mali	October 25, 1960	–
Somalia	December 14, 1960	–
Democratic Republic of Congo	February 20, 1961	China recognized Congo's government headed by Antoine Gizenga. In September 1961, after Gizenga joined the Adula government, which recognized Taipei, Beijing suspended relations. China established relations with the Mobutu government in November 1972.
Tanzania	December 9, 1961	–
Uganda	October 18, 1962	–
Kenya	December 14, 1963	–
Burundi	December 21, 1963	Burundi severed ties with China in January 1965 following hostile Chinese activities in Burundi. Diplomatic relations were restored in October 1971.
Tunisia	January 10, 1964	Disagreement between the Tunisian government and Chinese Embassy in September 1967 resulted in Chinese suspension of relations. Bilateral relations were restored in 1971.
Congo, Brazzaville	February 22, 1964	–
Central African Republic	September 29, 1964	The CAR severed relations with China in January 1966 and recognized Taipei in 1968. Relations were restored in August 1976. The CAR again recognized Taipei in July 1991, and Beijing suspended relations. In January 1998 China and CAR resumed relations for a third time.
Zambia	October 29, 1964	–

APPENDIX

COUNTRY	INITIAL DATE OF ESTABLISHMENT OF DIPLOMATIC RELATIONS	SUBSEQUENT CHANGES
Benin	November 12, 1964	Benin severed relations with China in January 1966 and resumed relations with Taipei in April. China and Benin restored relations in December 1972.
Mauritania	July 19, 1965	–
Equatorial Guinea	October 15, 1970	–
Ethiopia	November 24, 1970	–
Nigeria	February 10, 1971	–
Cameroon	March 26, 1971	–
Sierra Leone	July 29, 1971	–
Rwanda	November 12, 1971	–
Senegal	December 7, 1971	China suspended ties in January 1996 when Senegal resumed relations with Taipei. Beijing and Senegal restored ties in October 2005.
Mauritius	April 15, 1972	–
Togo	September 19, 1972	–
Madagascar	November 6, 1972	–
Chad	November 28, 1972	China suspended relations in August 1997 when Chad recognized Taipei. Beijing and Chad restored ties in August 2006.
Burkina Faso	September 15, 1973	China suspended relations in February 1994 when Burkina Faso recognized Taipei. Ouagadougou reestablished relations with Beijing on May 26, 2018.
Guinea Bissau	March 15, 1974	China suspended relations in May 1990 when Guinea Bissau recognized Taipei. Beijing and Guinea Bissau restored relations in April 1998.

(continued)

APPENDIX

COUNTRY	INITIAL DATE OF ESTABLISHMENT OF DIPLOMATIC RELATIONS	SUBSEQUENT CHANGES
Gabon	April 20, 1974	–
Niger	July 20, 1974	China suspended relations in July 1992 when Niger recognized Taipei. Beijing and Niger restored ties in August 1996.
Gambia	December 14, 1974	China suspended relations in July 1995 when Gambia recognized Taipei. Banjul reestablished relations with Beijing on March 17, 2016.
Botswana	January 6, 1975	–
Mozambique	June 25, 1975	–
São Tomé and Principe	July 12, 1975	China suspended relations in July 1997 after São Tomé announced it would recognize Taipei. São Tomé reestablished relations with Beijing on December 26, 2016.
Comoro Islands	November 13, 1975	–
Cape Verde	April 25, 1976	–
Seychelles	June 30, 1976	–
Liberia	February 17, 1977	China suspended relations in October 1989 when Liberia recognized Taipei. Beijing and Liberia restored ties in August 1993. China again suspended ties in September 1997 when Liberia resumed relations with Taipei. Beijing and Liberia restored ties in October 2003.
Libya	August 9, 1978	–
Djibouti	January 8, 1979	–
Zimbabwe	April 18, 1980	–
Angola	January 12, 1983	–
Côte d'Ivoire	March 2, 1983	–

APPENDIX

COUNTRY	INITIAL DATE OF ESTABLISHMENT OF DIPLOMATIC RELATIONS	SUBSEQUENT CHANGES
Lesotho	April 30, 1983	China suspended relations in April 1990 when Lesotho recognized Taipei. Bilateral ties were restored in January 1994.
Namibia	March 22, 1990	–
Eritrea	May 24, 1993	–
South Africa	January 1, 1998	–
Malawi	December 28, 2007	–
South Sudan	July 9, 2011	–
Eswatini	–	Eswatini, formerly Swaziland, is the only African country that has never had diplomatic relations with Beijing. It has maintained diplomatic ties with Taipei since 1968.

Sources: Most of the data is from country fact sheets prepared by the PRC Ministry of Foreign Affairs and Xinhua press items. Also see Wei Liang-Tsai, *Peking Versus Taipei in Africa 1960–1978* (Taipei: Asia and World Institute, 1982), 26–27; Bruce D. Larkin, *China and Africa 1949–1970* (Berkeley: University of California Press, 1971), 66–67; George T. Yu, *China's African Policy: A Case Study of Tanzania* (New York: Praeger, 1975), 8; and Sithara Fernando, "Chronology of China-Africa Relations," *China Report* 43, no. 3 (July 2007): 363–73.

NOTES

1. LOCATING AFRICA IN CHINA'S GEOSTRATEGY

1. China State Council Information Office, "China's Peaceful Development," September 6, 2011.
2. Liu Yuejin, "论总体国家安全观的五个'总体'" [On the five components of the "Overall National Security Concept"], 人民论坛·学术前沿 [Frontiers], no. 11 (2014): 14–20; Liu Yuejin, "非传统的总体国家安全观" [Nontraditional concept of overall national security], *Journal of International Security Studies*, no. 6 (2014): 3–25.
3. Xiong Guangkai, 国际战略与新军事变革 [International strategy and revolution in military affairs] (Beijing: Qinghua University Press, 2003), 77.
4. Xi Jinping, "A Holistic View of National Security," in *Xi Jinping: The Governance of China* (Beijing: Foreign Languages Press, 2014), 221.
5. Central Institute of Party History and Literature, ed., 习近平关于总体国家安全观论述摘编 [Excerpts of Xi Jinping's discussions related to the comprehensive national security concept] (Beijing: Central Party Literature Press, 2018), 5, 215–23.
6. "'总体国家安全观干部读本'出版发行" [Publication of "The Cadre Manual of the Holistic Security Strategy" begins], Xinhua, April 16, 2016; Andrea Ghiselli, *Protecting China's Interests Overseas: Securitization and Foreign Policy* (Oxford: Oxford University Press, 2021), 37.
7. Feng Zhongping and Huang Jing, "China's Strategic Partnership Diplomacy: Engaging with a Changing World," European Strategic Partnerships Observatory, ESPO Working Paper no. 8, June 2014, 13.

1. LOCATING AFRICA IN CHINA'S GEOSTRATEGY

8. For example, see Xinhua, "Full Text of Chinese President Xi Jinping's Speech at Opening Ceremony of 2018 FOCAC Beijing Summit," September 3, 2018.
9. "十八大之后的中国外建新局面" [China's new foreign policy after the Eighteenth Party Congress], *Sina News*, January 9, 2014.
10. The phrase is a summary of Hu's comments during an August 29, 2004, meeting with Chinese diplomats. "中国走向'大外交'" [China moves toward "big power diplomacy"], *People's Daily*, February 8, 2011. See "The 10th Conference of Chinese Diplomatic Envoys Stationed Abroad Held in Beijing," *People's Daily*, August 30, 2004.
11. Chen Xiangyang, "中国推进大周边战略正当时" [The right time for China to advance a "greater periphery" strategy], China Foundation for International Studies, January 1, 2015.
12. He Yafei, "China's Major-Country Diplomacy Progresses on All Fronts," *China.org.cn*, March 23, 2016.
13. China State Council Information Office, *China's National Defense in the New Era*, July 24, 2019.
14. For the low-profile strategy, see Pang Guangqian, "'韬光养晦'绝非暗藏杀机(大势)" [Keeping a low profile is not a hidden danger], *Beijing huanqiu shibao*, September 21, 2006. For China's evolution toward a more proactive foreign policy, see Yan Xuetong, "From Keeping a Low Profile to Striving for Achievement," *Chinese Journal of International Politics* 7, no. 2 (2014): 153–84; David Shambaugh, *China Goes Global: The Partial Power* (New York: Oxford University Press, 2014); Elizabeth Economy and Michael Levi, *By All Means Necessary: How China's Resource Quest Is Changing the World* (Oxford: Oxford University Press, 2014).
15. Yan Xuetong, "China Must Not Overplay Its Strategic Hand," *Global Times*, September 8, 2017.
16. Xinhua, "习近平出席中央外事工作会议并发表重要讲话" [Xi Jinping chairs Central Conference on Work Relating to Foreign Affairs and delivers an important speech], November 29, 2014.
17. Joshua Eisenman and Eric Heginbotham, "Building a More 'Democratic' and 'Multipolar' World: China's Strategic Engagement with Developing Countries," *China Review* 19, no. 4 (November 2019): 63–64.
18. He Yafei, "China's Major-Country Diplomacy." Scholars have also described China's U.S.-focused "soft-balancing" strategy and its evolution toward a more confrontational attitude toward the United States. See Michael J. Mazarr, Timothy R. Heath, and Astrid Stuth Cevallos, *China and the International Order* (Santa Monica, Calif.: RAND Corporation, 2018); Zhou Weifeng, "Beyond Balancing: China's Approach Towards the Belt and Road Initiative," *Journal of Contemporary China* 27, no. 112 (2018): 487–501; Randall L. Schweller and Pu Xiaoyu, "After Unipolarity: China's Visions of International Order in an Era of U.S. Decline," *International Security* 36, no. 1 (September 2011).
19. Jin Xin and Lin Yongliang, "共同推动世界多极化深入发展" [Together promote the deepening of world multipolarity], *People's Daily*, February 15, 2019.
20. China State Council Information Office, *China's National Defense in the New Era*.
21. Eisenman and Heginbotham, "Building a More 'Democratic' and 'Multipolar' World."

1. LOCATING AFRICA IN CHINA'S GEOSTRATEGY

22. Lei Yu, "China's Expanding Security Involvement in Africa: A Pillar for 'China-Africa Community of Common Destiny,'" *Global Policy* 9, no. 4 (November 2018): 490.
23. Xinhua, "习近平：中国梦不是'霸权梦'" [Xi Jinping: The Chinese Dream is not a "hegemonic dream"], November 22, 2019; Xinhua, "走向人类命运共同体" [Moving toward the Community of Shared Future], November 24, 2019.
24. Astrid Nordin, *China's International Relations and Harmonious World: Time, Space and Multiplicity in World Politics* (Abingdon, UK: Routledge, 2016); David H. Shinn and Joshua Eisenman, *China and Africa: A Century of Engagement* (Philadelphia: University of Pennsylvania Press, 2012), 43–53; Chinese Communist Party, "和平与发展" [Peace and development], September 26, 2008; Liu Jianmei, "和平发展" [Peaceful development], *China News Service*, June 23, 2011; "习近平关于和平发展的大智慧" [The wisdom of Xi Jinping on peaceful development], *People's Daily Online*, August 8, 2017.
25. Nadège Rolland, "Beijing's Vision for a Reshaped International Order," *China Brief* 18, no. 3 (2018). Examples of top Chinese officials using the term include "习近平：共同构建人类命运共同体" [Xi Jinping: To jointly build a Community of Shared Future for Mankind], Xinhua, January 1, 2021; "汪洋：对外讲好中国故事，推动构建人类命运共同体" [Wang Yang: Tell the Chinese story well to the outside and promote the building of a Community of Shared Future for Mankind], *China News*, March 3, 2019; "李克强：中国愿为推动构建人类命运共同体不懈努力" [Li Keqiang: China is willing to make unremitting efforts to promote the building of a Community of Shared Future for Mankind], *People's Daily*, March 5, 2018.
26. Rolland, "Beijing's Vision."
27. Xi Jinping, "Secure a Decisive Victory in Building a Moderately Prosperous Society in All Respects and Strive for the Great Success of Socialism with Chinese Characteristics for a New Era," October 18, 2017, Nineteenth National Congress of the CPC, Beijing, China, transcript, Xinhua, 6.
28. Xinhua, "Xi Calls on World Political Parties to Build Community of Shared Future for Mankind," December 2, 2017.
29. "傅莹：携手构建人类命运共同体" [Fu Ying: Join hands to build a Community of Shared Future for Mankind], *Chinese Social Sciences Net*, May 16, 2017; "Xi Calls on World Political Parties."
30. Fu Ying, "China's Vision for the World: A Community of Shared Future," *Diplomat*, June 22, 2017; Jacob Mardell, "The 'Community of Common Destiny' in Xi Jinping's New era," *Diplomat*, October 25, 2017.
31. *China's National Defense in the New Era*, July 24, 2019, 10.
32. Xu Jin and Guo Chu, "命运共同体概念辨析" [Analysis of the Community of Shared Future for Mankind concept], Chinese Academy of Social Sciences, Institute of World Economics and Politics, 1–14.
33. The view that adherence "does not require participants' emotional dedication, only their physical participation," can be traced to the Maoist period. Wang Tuo, *The Cultural Revolution and Overacting: Dynamics Between Politics and Performance* (Lanham, Md.: Lexington Books, 2014).

1. LOCATING AFRICA IN CHINA'S GEOSTRATEGY

34. "习近平：永远做可靠朋友和真诚伙伴" [Xi Jinping: Always be a reliable friend and sincere partner], *People's Daily*, March 26, 2013.
35. Xinhua, "习近平：愿同非洲人民筑梦更加紧密的中非命运共同体" [Xi Jinping: Willing to build a closer China-Africa Community of Shared Future with the people of Africa], September 3, 2018.
36. China Ministry of Foreign Affairs, "FOCAC: Working toward even stronger China-Africa Community of Shared Future," July 1, 2019; Wu Chuanhua, "中非命运共同体：历史地位、典范作用与世界意义" [China-Africa Community of Shared Future: Historical status, exemplary role and world significance], *Xiya Feizhou* [West Asia and Africa] 2 (2020): 12–21.
37. He Yafei, "China's Major-Country Diplomacy."
38. Lina Benabdallah, "Power or Influence? Making Sense of China's Evolving Party-to-Party Diplomacy in Africa," *African Studies Quarterly* 19, no. 3–4 (October 2020): 102. For how traditional Confucian concepts of interpersonal relations or *guanxi* influence China's contemporary international relations, see Emilian Kavalski, "*Guanxi* or What Is the Chinese for Relational Theory of World Politics," *International Relations of the Asia-Pacific* 18, no. 3 (2018): 397–420.
39. Liu Hongwu, "命运共同体视域下中非共享知识体系的建构 [Construction of shared knowledge system between China and Africa from the perspective of Community of Shared Future]," *Xiya Feizhou* [West Asia and Africa] 5 (2018): 42–60; Zhang Ying and Pan Jingguo, "中非'命运共同体'的历史传承与现实含义" [The historical inheritance and practical implications of China-Africa "Community of Shared Future"], *Xiandai guoji guanxi* [Contemporary international relations] 7 (2017): 39–45; Long Xiaonong, "从'兄弟'到'命运共同体'：中国建构对非话语体系的理念与实践" [From "brothers" to "Community of Shared Future": The idea and practice of China's construction of African discourse system], *Xiandai chuanbo (Zhongguo Chuanmei Daxue xuebao)* [Modern communication (journal of Communication University of China)] 1 (March 2016): 75–81.
40. Daniel Nasaw, "China and Russia Veto Zimbabwe Sanctions," *Guardian*, July 11, 2008; Reuters, "Sudan's Bashir to Visit China Despite International Arrest Warrant," August 30, 2015.
41. "China Slams UN Report Alleging Litany of Rights Abuses in Xinjiang," *Channel News Asia*, September 1, 2022.
42. Ghiselli, *Protecting China's Interests Overseas*, 22.
43. Jiang Zemin, *Selected Works of Jiang Zemin*, vol. 2 (Beijing: Foreign Language Press, 2012), 201.
44. Yun Sun, "FOCAC 2021: China's Retrenchment from Africa?" Brookings, December 6, 2021.
45. China Ministry of Commerce, "以更大的战略定力构建中非命运共同体" [Use greater strategic determination to build China-Africa shared future], March 1, 2019; Xi Jinping, "Uphold the Tradition of Always Standing Together and Jointly Build a China-Africa Community of Shared Future in the New Era [Speech Transcript]," China Ministry of Foreign Affairs, November 29, 2021.

1. LOCATING AFRICA IN CHINA'S GEOSTRATEGY

46. "African Union Opens Chinese-Funded HQ in Ethiopia," *BBC*, January 28, 2012.
47. Xu Yi, "Feature: Overview of 1st China-Africa Peace and Security Forum," *China Military Online*, July 17, 2019.
48. ECOWAS, "ECOWAS Signs MOU with China for the Construction of the New ECOWAS Commission Headquarters," March 14, 2018; John Campbell, "China to Build New ECOWAS Headquarters in Abuja," Council on Foreign Relations, April 11, 2018.
49. Qin Yaqing, "A Relational Theory of World Politics," *International Studies Review* 18, no. 1 (2016): 44.
50. James P. Harrison, *Modern Chinese Nationalism* (New York: Hunter College of the City University of New York, 1969), 2.
51. Zhao Suisheng, "Rethinking the Chinese World Order: The Imperial Cycle and the Rise of China," *Journal of Contemporary China* 24, no. 96 (2015): 965.
52. Lucian Pye, *Asian Power and Politics: The Cultural Dimensions of Authority* (Cambridge, Mass.: Harvard University Press, 1985), 41.
53. James C. Hsiung, "A Re-appraisal of Abrahamic Values and Neorealist IR Theory: From a Confucian-Asian Perspective," in *China and International Relations: The Chinese View and the Contribution of Wang Gungwu*, ed. Zheng Yongnian (Abingdon, UK: Routledge, 2010), 17–42.
54. Zhao Suisheng, "Rethinking the Chinese World Order," 973.
55. Qin Yaqing, "The Possibility and Inevitability of a Chinese School of International Relations Theory," in *China Orders the World: Normative Soft Power and Foreign Policy*, ed. William A. Callahan and Elena Barabansteva (Washington, D.C.: Woodrow Wilson Center Press with Johns Hopkins University Press, 2011), 42–43.
56. Zhao Tingyang, "A Political World Philosophy in Terms of All-Under-Heaven (Tianxia)," *Diogenes* 56, no. 1 (2009): 5–18.
57. Florian Schneider, "Reconceptualising World Order: Chinese Political Thought and Its Challenge to International Relations Theory," *Review of International Studies* 40, no. 4 (2014): 683–703.
58. John Eperjesi, "Crouching Tiger, Hidden Dragon: Kung Fu Diplomacy and the Dream of Cultural China," *Asian Studies Review* 28, no. 1 (2004): 30.
59. Zhao Suisheng, "Rethinking the Chinese World Order," 963–64, 971.
60. Shaun Breslin, "China's Global Cultural Interactions," in *China and the World*, ed. David Shambaugh (Oxford: Oxford University Press, 2020), 142.
61. Hsiung, "A Re-appraisal of Abrahamic Values."
62. I. William Zartman and Jeffrey Z. Rubin, eds., "Symmetry and Asymmetry in Negotiation," in *Power and Negotiation* (Ann Arbor: University of Michigan Press, 2002), 273.
63. Ilaria Carrozza and Lina Benabdallah, "South–South Knowledge Production and Hegemony: Searching for Africa in Chinese Theories of IR," *International Studies Review* 24, no. 1 (2022): 7.
64. Chen Dongxiao, "China's "Host Diplomacy: Opportunities, Challenges and Undertakings," *China Institute of International Studies* 48 (2014): 12–31.
65. Kavalski, "*Guanxi* or What," 404.

1. LOCATING AFRICA IN CHINA'S GEOSTRATEGY

66. Benabdallah, "Power or Influence?" 103.
67. *Implications of China's Presence and Investment in Africa, Before the Subcommittee on Emerging Threats and Capabilities of the Committee on Armed Services United States Senate*, 105th Cong. 9 (2018), statement of Yun Sun, codirector, East Asia Program, and director of the China Program, Stimson Center.
68. These include Emmanuel John Hevi, *The Dragon's Embrace: The Chinese Communists in Africa* (New York: Praeger, 1966); John C. Cooley, *East Wind Over Africa: Red China's African Offensive* (New York: Walker, 1965); Sven Hamrell and Carl Gosta Widstrand, *The Soviet Bloc, China and Africa* (London: Scandinavian Institute of African Studies, 1964); Emmanuel John Hevi, *An African Student in China* (New York: Praeger, 1963).
69. Surveys of China's relations with the Third World in the 1970s include Michael Yahuda, *China's Role in World Affairs* (London: Croom Helm, 1978); Robert G. Sutter, *Chinese Foreign Policy After the Cultural Revolution, 1966–1977* (Boulder, Colo.: Westview Press, 1978); Richard Lowenthal, *Model or Ally? The Communist Powers and the Developing Countries* (New York: Oxford University Press, 1977); George T. Yu, "China and the Third World," *Asian Survey* 17, no. 11 (1977): 1036–48; Janos Horvath, *Chinese Technology Transfer to the Third World* (New York: Praeger, 1976); Alvin Z. Rubinstein, *Soviet and Chinese Influence in the Third World* (New York: Praeger, 1975); Shen-Yu Dai, *China, The Superpowers and the Third World* (Hong Kong: Chinese University of Hong Kong, 1974); King C. Chen, *The Foreign Policy of China* (Roseland, N.J.: East-West Who, 1972); Cecil Johnson, *Communist China and Latin America 1959–1967* (New York: Columbia University Press, 1970); Jerome Alan Cohen, *The Dynamics of China's Foreign Relations* (Cambridge, Mass.: Harvard University Press, 1970); Charles Neuhauser, *Third World Politics: China and the Afro-Asian People's Solidarity Organization 1957–1967* (Cambridge, Mass.: Harvard University Press, 1970).
70. Books on China's political and security relations with Africa in the 1970s include Martin Bailey, *Freedom Railway: China and the Tanzania-Zambia Link* (London: Rex Collings, 1976); Alan Hutchison, *China's African Revolution* (London: Hutchison, 1975); George T. Yu, *China's Africa Policy: A Study of Tanzania* (New York: Praeger, 1975); Warren Weinstein, ed., *Soviet and Chinese Aid to Africa* (New York: Praeger, 1975); Alaba Ogunsanwo, *China's Policy in Africa 1958–1971* (Cambridge: Cambridge University Press, 1974); Bruce D. Larkin, *China and Africa 1949–1970: The Foreign Policy of the People's Republic of China* (Berkeley: University of California Press, 1971).
71. Articles from the 1980s and 1990s include Ian Taylor, "China's Foreign Policy Towards Africa in the 1990s," *Journal of Modern African Studies* 36, no. 3 (1998): 443–60; Gerald Segal, "China and Africa," *Annals of the American Academy of Political and Social Science* 519, no. 1 (January 1992): 115–26; Lin Yung-lo, "Peking's Africa Policy in the 1980s," *Issues and Studies* 25, no. 4 (April 1989).
72. Academic books from this period include Samuel S. Kim, *The Third World in Chinese World Policy* (Princeton, N.J.: Princeton University, 1989); Lillian Craig Harris and Robert L. Worden, eds., *China and the Third World: Champion or Challenger?* (Dover, Mass.: Auburn House, 1986); Lillian Craig Harris, *China's Foreign Policy Toward the Third World*

1. LOCATING AFRICA IN CHINA'S GEOSTRATEGY

(New York: Praeger, 1985); G. W. Choudhury, *China in World Affairs: The Foreign Policy of the PRC Since 1970* (Boulder, Colo.: Westview Press, 1982); James C. Hsiung and Samuel S. Kim, *China in the Global Community* (New York: Praeger, 1980);

73. For the China-Africa literature between 2000 and 2012, see Shinn and Eisenman, *China and Africa*, 9–15.
74. Shinn and Eisenman, 9.
75. Edited books on China's relations in the developing world published since 2012 include Joshua Eisenman and Eric Heginbotham, eds., *China Steps Out: Beijing's Major Power Engagement with the Developing World* (New York: Routledge, 2018); Andrew Scobell et al., eds., *At the Dawn of Belt and Road: China in the Developing World* (Santa Monica, Calif.: RAND Corporation, 2018); Evelyn Goh, ed., *Rising China's Influence in Developing Asia* (New York: Oxford University Press, 2016); Carla Freeman, ed., *Handbook on China and Developing Countries* (Cheltenham, UK: Edward Elgar, 2015); Jan Wouters, Jean-Christophe Defraigne, and Matthieu Burnay, eds., *China, the European Union and the Developing World: A Triangular Relationship* (Cheltenham, UK: Edward Elgar, 2015).
76. Books touching on China-Africa strategic relations include Dawn C. Murphy, *China's Rise in the Global South: The Middle East, Africa, and Beijing's Alternative World Order* (Stanford, Calif.: Stanford University Press, 2022); Philani Mthembu and Faith Mabera, *Africa-China Cooperation: Towards an African Policy on China?* (Cham, Switz.: Palgrave Macmillan, 2021); Lina Benabdallah, *Shaping the Future of Power: Knowledge Production and Network-Building in China-Africa Relations* (Ann Arbor: University of Michigan Press, 2020); Emeka Umejei, *Chinese Media in Africa: Perception, Performance, and Paradox* (Lanham, Md.: Lexington Books, 2020); Olayiwola Abegunrin and Charity Manyeruke, *China's Power in Africa: A New Global Order* (Cham, Switz.: Palgrave Macmillan, 2019); Alexis Abodohoui, *Influence of Chinese Management Soft Power on African Skills Development* (Quebec City: Université Laval, 2019); Kenneth King, *China's Aid and Soft Power in Africa: The Case of Education and Training* (Rochester, N.Y.: James Currey, 2013). Edited books include Christof Hartmann and Nele Noesselt, eds., *China's New Role in African Politics: From Non-Intervention towards Stabilization?* (London: Routledge, 2021); Aleksandra W. Gadzala, ed., *Africa and China: How Africans and Their Governments Are Shaping Relations with China* (Lanham, Md.: Rowman & Littlefield, 2018); Chris Alden, Abiodun Alao, Zhang Chun, and Laura Barber, eds., *China and Africa: Building Peace and Security Cooperation on the Continent* (Cham, Switz.: Springer International, 2018); Zhao Suisheng, ed., *China in Africa Strategic Motives and Economic Interests* (London: Routledge, 2017).
77. Examples of country-specific books include Aaron Tesfaye, *China in Ethiopia: The Long-Term Perspective* (Albany: State University of New York Press, 2020); Ching Kwan Lee, *The Specter of Global China: Politics, Labor, and Foreign Investment in Africa* (Chicago: University of Chicago Press, 2017).
78. Keyword searches on China National Knowledge Infrastructure (CNKI) reveal that of the 570 articles published on China-Africa economic, political, and security relations between January 1, 2012, and July 22, 2021, 443 were on economic/political economy

1. LOCATING AFRICA IN CHINA'S GEOSTRATEGY

topics and 127 were on political/security topics. For articles on China-Africa political relations, see Anas Elochukwu and Austine Okere, "Africa's Perception of China: A Descriptive Discourse on its Determinants," *Journal of Chinese & African Studies* 2, no. 1 (2021): 23–36; Dani Madrid-Morales, "Who Set the Narrative? Assessing the Influence of Chinese Global Media on News Coverage of COVID-19 in 30 African Countries," *Global Media and China* 6, no. 2 (2021): 129–51; Benabdallah, "Power or Influence?"; Herman Wasserman, "China-Africa Media Relations: What We Know So Far," *Global Media and China* 3, no. 2 (2018): 108–12; Lina Benabdallah, "Explaining Attractiveness: Knowledge Production and Power Projection in China's Policy for Africa," *Journal of International Relations and Development* 22, no. 2 (2017): 495–514; Courage Mlambo, Audrey Kushamba, and More Blessing Simawu, "China-Africa Relations: What Lies Beneath?" *Chinese Economy* 49, no. 4 (2016): 257–76; Sven Grimm, "China–Africa Cooperation: Promises, Practice and Prospects," *Journal of Contemporary China* 23, no. 90 (2014): 993–1011; Giles Mohan and Ben Lampert, "Negotiating China: Reinserting African Agency Into China–Africa Relations," *African Affairs* 112, no. 446 (2013): 92–110; Jonathan Holslag, "China and Coups: Coping with Political Instability in Africa," *African Affairs* 110, no. 440 (July 2011). For articles on China-Africa security relations, see Andrea Ghiselli and Mordechai Chaziza, "China's Military Base in Djibouti," *Mideast Security and Policy Studies*, no. 153 (August 2018): 5–27; Lina Benabdallah, "China's Peace and Security Strategies in Africa: Building Capacity Is Building Peace?" *African Studies Quarterly* 16, no. 3-4 (December 2016): 17–34; Sara Van Hoeymissen, "Regional Organizations in China's Security Strategy for Africa: The Sense of Supporting 'African Solutions to African Problems,'" *Journal of Current Chinese Affairs* 40, no. 4 (2011): 91–118.

79. Alden et al., eds., *China and Africa*; Abegunrin and Manyeruke, *China's Power in Africa*; Daniel Large, *China and Africa: The New Era* (Oxford: Polity Press, 2021); Murphy, *China's Rise in the Global South*.
80. Hong Yu Liu, "Reflections on Conducting Fieldwork Under Digital Surveillance: Investigating Labour Politics in China's Tech Industry," *Journal of Contemporary Asia* 52, no. 1 (2022): 152–62.

2. BILATERAL AND GLOBAL RELATIONS

1. For our analysis of the recognition for competition by Beijing and Taipei, see David H. Shinn and Joshua Eisenman, *China and Africa: A Century of Engagement* (Philadelphia: University of Pennsylvania Press, 2012), 85–90.
2. Ghana Ministry of Information and Broadcasting, *Nkrumah's Subversion in Africa: Documentary Evidence of Nkrumah's Interference in the Affairs of Other African States* (Accra: Ministry of Information, 1966); *Nkrumah's Deception of Africa* (Accra: Ghana Ministry of Information, 1967).

2. BILATERAL AND GLOBAL RELATIONS

3. Shinn and Eisenman, *China and Africa*, 306.
4. Obert Hodzi, *The End of China's Non-Intervention Policy in Africa* (Cham, Switz.: Palgrave Macmillan, 2019), 104–6.
5. Oana Burcu and Eloïse Bertrand, "Explaining China's Latest Catch in Africa," *Diplomat*, January 16, 2019; "王毅同布基纳法索外长巴里举行会谈" [Wang Yi holds talks with Burkina Faso foreign minister Barry], Xinhua, January 5, 2019.
6. Based on Shinn's seven diplomatic assignments in Africa from 1967 to 1999 and numerous meetings with Chinese Embassy personnel in Africa during the twenty-first century.
7. Comment made by Michael Keating, UN Special Representative for Somalia, at the Atlantic Council in Washington, D.C., April 19, 2017.
8. Interview with Ismaïl Omar Guelleh in *Jeune Afrique*, April 4, 2017.
9. Presentation at the Center for Strategic and International Studies in Washington, D.C., March 25, 2019.
10. Conversation in Washington, D.C., with Shinn, January 18, 2018.
11. Shinn interview with senior Western diplomatic official, Addis Ababa, June 20, 2019.
12. Xinhua, "Xi Meets Ethiopian Prime Minister," April 24, 2019.
13. Feng Zhongping and Huang Jing, "China's Strategic Partnership Diplomacy: Engaging with a Changing World," European Strategic Partnerships Observatory, ESPO Working Paper no. 8, June 2014; David Cowhig, "China's Diplomacy: How Many Kinds of Major and Minor Partner 'Relations' Does China Have?" *David Cohig's Translation Blog*, April 7, 2017; Georg Strüver, "China's Partnership Diplomacy: International Alignment Based on Interests or Ideology," *Chinese Journal of International Politics* 10, no. 1 (2017): 34–39; Shinn/Eisenman interview with Zhang Yiming, China's ambassador in Namibia, Windhoek, June 7, 2018; Shinn/Eisenman interview with Tan Jian, China's ambassador in Ethiopia, Addis Ababa, June 13, 2018.
14. Shinn interview with Fathallah Oualalou, former Moroccan minister of economy and minister of finance, Rabat, December 20, 2018.
15. Joshua Meservey, "Government Buildings in Africa Are a Likely Vector for Chinese Spying," *Heritage Foundation Backgrounder*, no. 3476, May 20, 2020, 13–19. See also Meservey, "China's Palace Diplomacy in Africa," Heritage Foundation, June 29, 2020.
16. Martin Choi, "How a Presidential Palace in Burundi Fits in with China's Plans in Africa," *South China Morning Post*, February 20, 2019.
17. Agence France Presse, "China-Funded Sudan Palace to Replace Historic Building," September 10, 2014.
18. Jevans Nyabiage, "China-Africa Relations: Beijing's Financial Aid Leans Towards Grants, Away from Cheap Loans, White Paper Shows," *South China Morning Post*, January 18, 2021; China Ministry of Foreign Affairs, "Highway Joins List of China-Guinea Bissau Projects," January 27, 2021.
19. Gretinah Machingura and Tafara Mugwara, "China to Hand Over Completed New Parliament Building to Zimbabwe," Xinhua, June 30, 2022.
20. China's Embassy in Uganda, "Sino-Ugandan Relations," October 28, 2004.

2. BILATERAL AND GLOBAL RELATIONS

21. Johanna Jansson and Carine Kiala, "Patterns of Chinese Investment, Aid and Trade in Mozambique," Centre for Chinese Studies, October 2009, 6.
22. "China Constructs Ministry of Foreign Affairs Building at Tower Hill," AIDDATA.
23. China Ministry of Foreign Affairs, "Foreign Minister Wang Yi Pays Official Visit to Equatorial Guinea," January 15, 2015.
24. Eric Biegon, "China to Build Kenya's New Foreign Affairs HQ, Pledges Sustained Development Support," *Kenya Broadcasting Corporation*, May 14, 2021.
25. "PM Inaugurates African Leadership Excellence Academy," *Walta*, June 27, 2021.
26. Xinhua, "Tunisia, China Celebrate Handover of China-Aided Diplomatic Academy," April 29, 2022.
27. Joan Tilouine and Ghalia Kadiri, "A Addis-Abeba, le Siège de l'Union Africaine Espionné par Pékin," *Le Monde Afrique*, January 27, 2018.
28. Julia C. Strauss, "The Past in the Present: Historical and Rhetorical Lineages in China's Relations with Africa," *China Quarterly*, no. 199 (September 2009): 781–82.
29. Chen Dongxiao, "China's 'Host Diplomacy': Opportunities, Challenges and Undertakings," *China International Studies* 48 (September/October 2014).
30. For example, Steven C. Y. Kuo prepared a list of high-level visitors between China and Liberia. See Steven C. Y. Kuo, *Chinese Peace in Africa: From Peacekeeper to Peacemaker* (London: Routledge, 2020), 74. For major visits between Namibia and China, see Dietrich Remmert and Rakkel Andreas, "Risks and Rewards: Making Sense of Namibia-China Relations," Institute for Policy Research, Hanns Seidel Foundation, October 2019, 7–8.
31. Jevans Nyabiage, "Chinese Foreign Minister Wang Yi Looks to Boost Ties with Africa on Five-Nation New Year Tour," *South China Morning Post*, January 4, 2020.
32. Eleanor Albert, "China's Foreign Minister Revives Belt and Road on 5-Country Africa Tour," *Diplomat*, January 12, 2021; Chris Devonshire-Ellis, "China's Foreign Minister Wang Yi Visits Eritrea, Kenya and Comoros: Report and Analysis," *Silk Road Briefing*, January 10, 2022.
33. Development Reimagined, "Who Does China Prioritise? Our First Infographic Sheds Some Light," January 30, 2018.
34. Zhang Ying, "China's Diplomacy in Africa: Ideas and Practices," *China International Studies* 69 (March/April 2018): 33–34.
35. Shinn interview with well-informed Ethiopian, Washington, D.C., January 18, 2018.
36. "China's Top Legislator Visits Ethiopia to Boost Bilateral Ties," Xinhua, May 12, 2018; Shinn/Eisenman interview with editor of Ethiopian newspaper, Addis Ababa, June 12, 2018.
37. Shinn/Eisenman interview, Accra, June 22, 2018.
38. Abdur Rahman Alfa Shaban, "Handful of African Presidents Not Attending 2019 FOCAC Summit in China," *Africa News*, September 3, 2018.
39. Shinn/Eisenman interview, Addis Ababa, June 11, 2018.
40. Shinn and Eisenman, *China and Africa*, 40.
41. Shinn/Eisenman interview, Pretoria, June 5, 2018.

2. BILATERAL AND GLOBAL RELATIONS

42. David Shinn, "China and the Conflict in Darfur," *Brown Journal of World Affairs* 16, no. 1 (Fall/Winter 2009): 85.
43. Daniel Nasaw and Mark Rice-Oxley, "China and Russia Veto Zimbabwe Sanctions," *Guardian*, July 11, 2008.
44. Elor Nkereuwem, "Nontraditional Actors: China and Russia in African Peace Operations," Stimson Center Policy Brief, March 2017, 22–30.
45. Yiqin Fu, "Data Analysis: Who Votes with China, and Who Votes with the US and Europe at the UN?" June 10, 2018.
46. Ted Piccone, "China's Long Game on Human Rights at the United Nations," Brookings, September 2018, 8–13. Another study that focused on African countries in the UN Human Rights Council concluded that China has begun to demonstrate its influence, but its efforts have not yet won major African support. See Eduard Jordaan, "The African Group on the United Nations Human Rights Council: Shifting Geopolitics and the Liberal International Order," *African Affairs* 115, no. 460 (2016): 490–515.
47. Brett D. Schaefer, "How the U.S. Should Address Rising Chinese Influence at the United Nations," *Heritage Foundation Backgrounder*, no. 3431, August 20, 2019, 12.
48. Colum Lynch and Robbie Grammar, "Outfoxed and Outgunned: How China Routed the U.S. in a U.N. Agency," *Foreign Policy*, October 23, 2019.
49. Maurizio Guerrero, "As Kenya and Djibouti Fight Over a UN Security Council Seat, China Pops Up," *Pass Blue*, January 24, 2020.
50. Michael D. Swaine, "China's Assertive Behavior, Part One: On 'Core Interests,'" *China Leadership Monitor*, no. 34 (Winter 2011): 1–25.
51. "Chinese Defense Minister Vows to Promote Military Ties with Tanzania to New Height," *People's Daily*, June 16, 2011.
52. Shinn and Eisenman, *China and Africa*, 40.
53. "China Squeezes Only Country in Africa That Recognized Taiwan," *Swaziland News*, February 4, 2020; Emerson Lim and Ku Chuan, "Eswatini's Ties with Taiwan Firm Despite Pressure from China: MOFA," *Focus Taiwan*, February 3, 2020; "关于斯威士兰护照持有者办理签证的通知" [Notice on visa application for Swaziland passport holders], China Visa Application Service Center, January 15, 2020.
54. Carien Du Plessis, "China Turns the Screws on Eswatini," *Daily Maverick*, February 3, 2020.
55. See "List of TAITRA Overseas Offices" at Taiwan Trade, https://officeportal.taiwantrade.com/flash/big/unitList.jsp?lang=en_US.
56. Shinn and Eisenman, *China and Africa*, 87–88.
57. Matthew Strong, "Taiwan to Open Office in Lagos, Nigeria, on Jan. 5," *Taiwan News*, January 2, 2018.
58. Thomas J. Shattuck, "Taiwan Finds an Unexpected New Friend in Somaliland," Foreign Policy Research Institute, July 1, 2020; Jean-Pierre Cabestan, "The Somaliland Connection: Taiwan's Return to Africa?" *Diplomat*, September 2, 2021.
59. Abdur Rahman Alfa Shaban, "China Rejects Taiwan-Somaliland 'Bilateral, Diplomatic' Overtures," *Africa News*, July 2, 2020.

2. BILATERAL AND GLOBAL RELATIONS

60. Sarah Zheng and Kinling Lo, "How Taiwan Found a New African Friend in Somaliland," *South China Morning Post*, August 16, 2020.
61. Thomas J. Shattuck, "China-Taiwan Competition Over Somaliland and Implications for Small Countries," Foreign Policy Research Institute, August 28, 2020; Republic of China (Taiwan) Ministry of Foreign Affairs, "我國宣布將與索馬利蘭共和國互設代表處" [My country announced that it will establish mutual representative offices with the Republic of Somaliland], July 1, 2020.
62. China Ministry of Foreign Affairs, "Foreign Ministry Spokesperson Zhao Lijian's Regular Press Conference on August 19, 2020."
63. Shinn/Eisenman interview with Taipei liaison office staff, Pretoria, June 5, 2018.
64. Andrea Worden, "China Pushes 'Human Rights with Chinese Characteristics' at the UN," *Hong Kong Free Press*, October 14, 2017.
65. Xinhua, "China, on Behalf of 26 Countries, Criticizes U.S., Other Western Countries for Violating Human Rights," October 6, 2020.
66. Shinn and Eisenman, *China and Africa*, 93–96.
67. "Dalai Lama Denied South Africa Visa for Nobel Summit," *The Guardian*, September 4, 2014; Ross Anthony, "China, South Africa and the Dalai Lama: Costs and Benefits," Centre for Chinese Studies at Stellenbosch University, September 8, 2014.
68. Peter Fabricius, "China Reacts with Fury to Tibetan Leader's Visit to South Africa," *Daily Maverick*, February 9, 2018; Fabricius, "Sudden Recall of China's Ambassador to SA Raises Questions, Offers Few Answers," *Daily Maverick*, March 19, 2020.
69. Yangchen Dolma, "Tibetan President Meets Former President of South Africa," *Tibet Post International*, February 8, 2019.
70. Khonani Ontebetse, "Dalai Lama Visit Cancelled Following Khama/Masisi Clash?" *Sunday Standard*, August 13, 2017; Dikarabo Ramadubu, "Khama Blasts China," *Botswana Guardian*, August 17, 2017.
71. Shinn and Eisenman, *China and Africa*, 90–93.
72. Amnesty International, "Up to One Million Detained in China's Mass 'Re-education' Drive," September 2018.
73. Shinn interview with former senior Ethiopian official, Addis Ababa, June 20, 2019; Eisenman interview with current Egyptian official, Cairo, October 15, 2019.
74. Shinn interview with Abdalhak Bassou, Policy Center for the New South, Rabat, January 1, 2019.
75. Adam Lammon, "Why the Muslim Middle East Supports China's Xinjiang Crackdown," *National Interest*, October 24, 2020.
76. Resolution adopted in Abu Dhabi, UAE, at the Forty-sixth Session of the OIC Council of Foreign Ministers, March 1–2, 2019.
77. "OIC Independent Permanent Human Rights Commission Concludes Its 15th Regular Session Held in Jeddah from 21–25," April 25, 2019.
78. Shinn/Eisenman interview, Djibouti, June 14, 2018.
79. Nick Cumming-Bruce, "China Rebuked by 22 Nations Over Xinjiang Repression, *New York Times*, July 10, 2019.

2. BILATERAL AND GLOBAL RELATIONS

80. Tom Miles, "Saudi Arabia and Russia Among 37 States Backing China's Xinjiang Policy," Reuters, July 12, 2019; Xinhua, "外交部：国际社会对新疆发展自有公论" [Ministry of Foreign Affairs: 'The international community has its own opinions on Xinjiang's development'], July 29, 2019. The initial seventeen African countries were Algeria, Egypt, Sudan, South Sudan, Somalia, Eritrea, Comoros, Togo, Burkina Faso, Nigeria, Cameroon, Gabon, Republic of Congo, Democratic Republic of Congo, Burundi, Angola, and Zimbabwe. Subsequent signers included Uganda, Djibouti, Equatorial Guinea, Mozambique, and Zambia. Catherine Putz, "Which Countries Are for or Against China's Xinjiang Policies?" *Diplomat*, July 15, 2019; "China Seeks Support from Africa on Uighur Policy," *Daily Nation*, October 13, 2019.
81. Haisam Hassanein, "Arab States Give China a Pass on Uyghur Crackdown," Washington Institute for Near East Policy, August 26, 2019.
82. "China Seeks Support from Africa on Uighur Policy," *Daily Nation*, October 13, 2019.
83. Stéphanie Fillion, "China Flexes Its Economic Might More Openly at the UN on Human Rights," *Pass Blue*, November 17, 2019. The African signatories were Angola, Burkina Faso, Burundi, Cameroon, CAR, Chad, Comoros, Congo, DRC, Djibouti, Egypt, Equatorial Guinea, Eritrea, Gabon, Guinea, Guinea Bissau, Mauritania, Mozambique, Niger, Nigeria, Sierra Leone, South Sudan, Sudan, Tanzania, Togo, Uganda, Zambia, and Zimbabwe.
84. Catherine Putz, "2020 Edition: Which Countries Are for or Against China's Xinjiang Policies?" *Diplomat*, October 9, 2020. The twenty-one African countries that supported the October 2020 statement were Angola, Burundi, Cameroon, CAR, Comoros, Republic of Congo, Egypt, Equatorial Guinea, Eritrea, Gabon, Guinea, Guinea Bissau, Madagascar, Morocco, Mozambique, South Sudan, Sudan, Tanzania, Togo, Uganda, and Zimbabwe.
85. CGTN, "Zimbabwe's Ruling Party Hails China's Transparency Over Xinjiang," March 22, 2021.
86. Zhou Jin and Zhao Jia, "African Diplomats Blast Meddling Over Xinjiang," *China Daily*, March 16, 2021; Carine Kaneza Nantulya, "Why Are Some African Governments Shielding China Over Xinjiang?" Human Rights Watch, March 29, 2021.
87. Eric Olander, "China Launches Full-Scale Media Blitz in Africa to Counter Mounting U.S.-European Pressure on Xinjiang," China Africa Project, February 3, 2021.
88. "UN Human Rights Council 47: Joint Statement on the Human Rights Situation in Xinjiang," *GOV.UK*, June 22, 2021.
89. Simon Wiakanty, "Liberia: China 'Disappointed' with Liberia," *Daily Observer*, December 6, 2021.
90. Wang Jin, "Doha Declaration Comes Right on Time," *China.org.cn*, May 17, 2016.
91. Wang Wen and Chen Xiaochen, "Who Supports China in the South China Sea and Why," *Diplomat*, July 27, 2016; "South Africa Backs Chinese Stance on South China Sea Dispute," *thebricspost.com*, June 22, 2016; Dong Zhaohui, "African Countries Back China's Approach to South China Sea Dispute," *Chinamil.com.cn*, July 10, 2016; Lesotho Ministry of Foreign Affairs and International Relations, "Statement of the Kingdom of Lesotho on the Situation in the South China Sea," *Foreign.gov.ls*, May 24, 2016.

2. BILATERAL AND GLOBAL RELATIONS

92. Wang Wen and Chen Xiaochen, "Who Supports China in the South China Sea and Why," Chongyang Institute for Financial Studies at China's Renmin University, July 28, 2016.
93. Kristin Huang, "Why China Went on a Global Media Blitz Over the Hong Kong Protests—and Why It Probably Won't Work," *South China Morning Post*, September 10, 2019.
94. "Uganda Sides with China on Hong Kong Protests," *Observer*, October 4, 2019.
95. "Tanzanian Government Supports Chinese Government's Position on the Issue of Hong Kong," Embassy of China in Tanzania, October 4, 2019, http://tz.china-embassy.gov.cn/eng/.
96. "Tanzania: JPM to China—We're Together," *allafrica.com*, October 31, 2019.
97. Sharon Kavhu, "Namibia Reaffirms Its Full Support for the One-China Policy," *Southern Times*, January 20, 2020.
98. Chinese Ministry of Foreign Affairs, "Li Jie, Ambassador to Zambia, Takes a Joint Media Interview on the 55th Anniversary of the China-Zambia Diplomatic Relations," October 26, 2019.
99. Xinhua, "Visiting Chinese Senior Legislator Hails China-Liberia Ties," November 13, 2019.
100. "Ghana Pledges Support for China Over Hong Kong Crisis," *GhanaWeb.com*, October 16, 2019.
101. China Ministry of Foreign Affairs, "Xi Jinping Speaks with Burundian President Evariste Ndayishimiye on the Phone," March 29, 2021.
102. Dave Lawler, "The 53 Countries Supporting China's Crackdown on Hong Kong," *Axios*, July 3, 2020. The twenty-five African countries voting with China were Burundi, Cameroon, Central African Republic (CAR), Comoros, Republic of Congo, Djibouti, Egypt, Equatorial Guinea, Eritrea, Gabon, Gambia, Guinea, Guinea Bissau, Lesotho, Mauritania, Morocco, Mozambique, Niger, Sierra Leone, Somalia, South Sudan, Sudan, Togo, Zambia, and Zimbabwe.
103. "More than 70 Countries Voice Support for China's HK National Security Law at UNHRC," *Global Times*, July 3, 2020.
104. China Ministry of Foreign Affairs, Joint Statement of the Extraordinary China-Africa Summit on Solidarity Against COVID-19, June 17, 2020.
105. Shannon Tiezzi, "Which Countries Support China on Hong Kong's National Security Law," *Diplomat*, October 9, 2020. African signatories to the October 2020 Pakistani statement were Algeria, Angola, Burundi, Cameroon, CAR, Comoros, Republic of Congo, Djibouti, Egypt, Equatorial Guinea, Eritrea, Gabon, Gambia, Guinea, Guinea Bissau, Madagascar, Mauritania, Morocco, Mozambique, Niger, Somalia, South Sudan, Sudan, Tanzania, Togo, Uganda, and Zimbabwe.
106. Eric Olander, "Why Would Uganda Write a Letter to Support China's Position in Hong Kong?" *Chinafrica Project*, October 6, 2019.
107. Comment made at meeting attended by Shinn in Washington, D.C., November 13, 2019.

2. BILATERAL AND GLOBAL RELATIONS

108. For an African view of concerns about debt to China, see, for example, Abel Kinyondo, "Is China Recolonizing Africa? Some Views from Tanzania," *World Affairs*, Summer 2019, 147–54. For an analysis of China's role in African debt, see Alex Vines, Creon Butler, and Yu Jie, "The Response to Debt Distress in Africa and the Role of China," Chatham House research paper, December 2022.
109. Kinyondo, "Is China Recolonizing Africa?" 147–54.
110. Shinn/Eisenman interview, Accra, June 18, 2018.
111. Shinn/Eisenman interview with Emmanuel O. Akwetey, executive director, Institute for Democratic Governance, Accra, June 20, 2018, and with Kofi Attor, director for international affairs, National Democratic Congress, June 21, 2018.
112. Justina Crabtree, "Africa Needs to Know What It Wants from China, Expert Says. Here Are Two Key Issues," *CNBC*, April 25, 2018.
113. Carlos Lopes, "Reinserting African Agency Into Sino-Africa Relations," *Strategic Review for Southern Africa* 38, no. 1 (May 2016): 62.
114. Shinn/Eisenman interview, Addis Ababa, June 13, 2018.
115. Shinn/Eisenman interview with Lloyd G. Adu Amoah, director, Center for Asian Studies, University of Ghana, Accra, June 19, 2018.
116. Edwin Okoth, "SGR Pact with China a Risk to Kenyan Sovereignty, Assets," *Nation*, January 13, 2019.
117. Ulrikke Wethal, "Passive Hosts or Demanding Stakeholders? Understanding Mozambique's Negotiating Power in the Face of China," *Forum for Development Studies* 44, no. 3 (2017): 509–11.
118. Shinn/Eisenman interview with Philani Mthembu, executive director, Institute for Global Dialogue at the University of South Africa, Pretoria, June 5, 2018.
119. Ronald Chipaike and Matarutse H. Knowledge, "The Question of African Agency in International Relations," *Cogent Social Sciences* 4, no. 1 (2018): 9–10; for the role of nonstate actors in African agency, see Stacey Links, "Ascertaining Agency: Africa and the Belt and Road Initiative," in *Global Perspectives on China's Belt and Road Initiative*, ed. Florian Schneider (Amsterdam: Amsterdam University Press, 2021), 127–30.
120. Maddalena Procopio, "Kenyan Agency in Kenya-China Relations: Contestation, Cooperation and Passivity," in *New Directions in Africa-China Studies*, ed. Chris Alden and Daniel Large (London: Routledge, 2019), 177.
121. David H. Shinn, "The Environmental Impact of China's Investment in Africa," *Cornell International Law Journal* 49, no. 1 (Winter 2016): 46.
122. Peter Volberding and Jason Warner, "China and Uranium: Comparative Possibilities for Agency in Statecraft in Niger and Namibia," China Africa Research Initiative, Working Paper no. 011, March 2017, 22.
123. Yunnan Chen, "Laying the Tracks: The Political Economy of Railway Development in Ethiopia's Railway Sector and Implications for Technology Transfer," Boston University Global Development Policy Center, Working Paper no. 014, January 2021, 12.

2. BILATERAL AND GLOBAL RELATIONS

124. Frangton Chiyemura, "Contextualizing African Agency in Ethiopia-China Engagement in Wind Energy Infrastructure Financing and Development," Innovation Knowledge Development, Working Paper no. 88, October 2020, 24–25.
125. Arthur G. O. Mutambara, "Africa's Emerging China Strategy: How African States Need to Respond to China's Shifting Growth Model," in *Key Issues in Regional Integration: Volume 2*, ed. Ann Mugunga, COMESA (2013): 53.
126. Wenyuan Wu, "Beyond the 'Chinese Debt Trap,'" Lowy Institute, May 30, 2018; Paul Nantulya, "Reshaping African Agency in China-Africa Relations," Africa Center for Strategic Studies, March 2, 2021.
127. Jean-Pierre Cabestan, "African Agency and Chinese Power: The Case of Djibouti," South African Institute of International Affairs, Policy Insights no. 93, October 7, 2020, 14–15.
128. Jean-Pierre Cabestan, "Seychelles: How a Small Island State Is Navigating Through the Emerging Competition Between India and China," *Seychelles Research Journal* 3, no. 1 (February 2021): 72–73.
129. Derek McDougall and Pradeep Taneja, "Sino-Indian Competition in the Indian Ocean Island Countries: The Scope for Small State Agency," *Journal of the Indian Ocean Region* 16, no. 2 (2020): 138–40.
130. Folashade Soule, "Negotiating Local Business Practices with China in Benin," Carnegie Endowment for International Peace, April 2022.
131. Lucy Corkin, "Understanding Angolan Agency: The Luanda-Beijing Face-Off," in *Africa and China: How Africans and Their Governments Are Shaping Relations with China*, ed. Alexsandra W. Gadzala (Lanham, Md.: Rowman and Littlefield, 2015), 70–71; Ian Taylor, "The Good, the Bad, and the Ugly: Agency-as-Corruption and the Sino-Nigerian Relationship," in Gadzala, *Africa and China*, 28.
132. Chipaike and Knowledge, "The Question of African Agency," 9.
133. Ian Taylor, "The Good," 41.
134. Fantu Cheru and Arkebe Oqubay, "Catalysing China-Africa Ties for Africa's Structural Transformation: Lessons from Ethiopia," in *China-Africa and an Economic Transformation*, ed. Arkebe Oqubay and Justin Yifu Lin (Oxford: Oxford University Press, 2019), 284.
135. Maddalena Procopio, "Kenyan Agency," 179.
136. Cobus van Staden, Chris Alden, and Yu-Shan Wu, "Outlining African Agency Against the Background of the Belt and Road Initiative," *African Studies Quarterly* 19, no. 3/4 (October 2020): 126.
137. Yu-Shan Wu, Chris Alden, and Cobus van Staden, "Ties Between African Countries and China Are Complex. Understanding This Matters," *Conversation*, October 15, 2018.
138. Comments by Folashadé Soulé, University of Oxford, during online seminar hosted by the Center for African Studies at the University of Florida, February 12, 2021.
139. Wesley Ngwenya, "Does Africa Need China More than China Needs Africa?" *Lusaka Times*, June 7, 2020.
140. Hannah Ryder, "Can China-Africa Shift to Become Africa-China?" *African Business*, June 1, 2021.

141. Calestous Juma, "Afro-Chinese Cooperation: The Evolution of Diplomatic Agency," in Gadzala, *Africa and China*, 187–88.
142. Johanna Malm, "'China-Powered' African Agency and Its Limits: The Case of the DRC 2007–2019," South African Institute of International Affairs, November 2020, 5–7.
143. Kingsley Moghalu, "China, Africa and the World After COVID-19," *Premium Times*, May 19, 2020.
144. Ronak Gopaldas, "China's Post-Corona Future in Africa," *Africa Current Issues*, no. 23 (2020).
145. Nantulya, "Reshaping African Agency."

3. REGIONAL AND SUBREGIONAL RELATIONS

1. "Regional Economic Communities (RECs)," African Union, https://au.int/.
2. Jakub Jakóbowski, "Chinese-Led Regional Multilateralism in Central and Eastern Europe, Africa and Latin America: 16 + 1, FOCAC and CCF," *Journal of Contemporary China* 27, no. 113 (2018): 664; Ilaria Carrozza, "China's African Union Diplomacy: Challenges and Prospects for the Future," LSE Global South Unit Policy Brief no. 2, 2018.
3. Barney Walsh, "China's Pervasive yet Forgotten Regional Security Role in Africa," *Journal of Contemporary China* 28, no. 120 (2019): 974–75.
4. Walsh, 970.
5. Chinese sources argue that African leaders urged China to create FOCAC. Shen Xiaolei, Chinese Academy of Social Sciences, makes this argument. She cites a request by some African diplomats who in 1998 participated in a workshop at the China Foreign Affairs University and a proposal in 1999 by the assistant secretary-general of the Organization of African Unity during a meeting in Beijing with Vice Premier Li Lanqing. See "Inception, Development and Achievements of FOCAC," *Pacific Journal* 28, no. 3 (2020): 80–93. Whatever the case concerning the origin of FOCAC, China has remained in control of the process, and Beijing mostly sets the agenda and determines the outcome. Ian Taylor, "The Institutional Framework of Sino-African Relations," in *China-Africa and an Economic Transformation*, ed. Arkebe Oqubay and Justin Yifu Lin (Oxford: Oxford University Press, 2019), 118–19.
6. For a summary of China's financial commitments at the 2018 FOCAC, see Yun Sun, "China's 2018 Financial Commitments to Africa: Adjustment and Recalibration," Brookings, September 5, 2018; David Shinn, "Forum on China-Africa Cooperation Meets the Belt and Road," *East Asia Forum*, October 18, 2018. For Chinese work on this topic, see Xinhua, "中国扩大援非规模 提供50亿美元贷款和信贷" [China expands aid to Africa, provides US$5 billion in loans and credit], November 4, 2006; Xinhua, "习近平在2018年中非合作论坛北京峰会开幕式上的主旨讲话" [Keynote speech by Xi Jinping at the opening ceremony of the 2018 Beijing Summit of the Forum on China-Africa Cooperation], September 3, 2018.

3. REGIONAL AND SUBREGIONAL RELATIONS

7. Lucie Morangi, "China-Africa Successes Seen as Template for World," *China Daily*, June 8, 2018.
8. Ilaria Carrozza, "China's Multilateral Diplomacy in Africa: Constructing the Security-Development Nexus," in *New Perspectives on China's Relations with the World*, ed. Daniel Johanson, Jie Li, and Tsunghan Wu (E-International Relations Publishing, 2019), 145–53.
9. Li Anshan et al., "The Forum on China-Africa Cooperation: From a Sustainable Perspective," World Wide Fund for Nature, 2011, 31–32.
10. China Ministry of Foreign Affairs, "Forum on China-Africa Cooperation Dakar Action Plan (2022–2024)," November 30, 2021.
11. Abiodun Alao and Chris Alden, "Africa's Security Challenges and China's Evolving Approach to Africa's Peace and Security Architecture," in *China and Africa: Building Peace and Security Cooperation on the Continent*, ed. Chris Alden, Abiodun Alao, Zhang Chun, and Laura Barber (Cham, Switz.: Palgrave Macmillan, 2018), 32.
12. Cobus van Staden, Chris Alden, and Yu-Shan Wu, "In the Driver's Seat? African Agency and Chinese Power at FOCAC, the AU and the BRI," South African Institute of International Affairs, Occasional Paper 286, September 2018, 16–17.
13. Harsh V. Pant and Ava M. Haidar, "China's Expanding Military Footprint in Africa," Observer Research Foundation Issue Brief no. 195, September 2017, 5–6.
14. China Ministry of Foreign Affairs, "Forum on China-Africa Cooperation Beijing Action Plan (2019–2021)."
15. "Forum on China-Africa Cooperation Dakar Action Plan (2022–2024)"; Ma Tianjie and Tom Baxter, "China and Africa's Post-COVID Partnership: Key Takeaways from FOCAC8," *Panda Paw Dragon Claw*, December 6, 2021.
16. Shinn/Eisenman interview, Johannesburg, June 4, 2018.
17. Shinn/Eisenman interview, Addis Ababa, June 13, 2018.
18. Shinn/Eisenman interview, Accra, June 22, 2018.
19. Shinn interview, Johannesburg, August 26, 2015.
20. Clara Giffoni et al., "The China-Arab States Cooperation Forum (CASCF)," BRICS Policy Center, May 2016.
21. China Ministry of Foreign Affairs, "Action Plan of the China-Arab Cooperation Forum (2008–2010," June 18, 2008.
22. Mohammed Numan Jalal, "The China-Arab States Cooperation Forum: Achievements, Challenges and Prospects," *Journal of Middle Eastern and Islamic Studies (in Asia)* 8, no. 2 (2014): 6–7, 18.
23. Sun Degang, "China's Soft Military Presence in the Middle East," *Dirasat*, no. 30 (January 2018): 8.
24. Yao Kuangyi, "China-Arab States Cooperation Forum in the Last Decade," *Journal of Middle Eastern and Islamic Studies (in Asia)* 8, no. 4 (2014): 40.
25. China Ministry of Foreign Affairs, "The 7th Ministerial Meeting of the China-Arab States Cooperation Forum Concludes in Doha," May 12, 2016.

3. REGIONAL AND SUBREGIONAL RELATIONS

26. Laura Zhou, "China Pledges US$23 Billion in Loans and Aid to Arab States as It Boosts Ties in Middle East," *South China Morning Post*, July 10, 2018.
27. "Action Plan for China-Arab Cooperation Forum 2018–2020."
28. China Ministry of Foreign Affairs, "The 16th Senior Officials' Meeting of CASCF and the 5th Senior Official Level Strategic Political Dialogue of the CASCF Held in the UAE," June 19, 2019.
29. Xinhua, "Jordan Says Holding China-Arab States Cooperation Forum Shows Keenness to Boost Mutual Ties," July 7, 2020; China Ministry of Foreign Affairs, "China-Arab States Cooperation Forum Holds Ninth Ministerial Conference," July 6, 2020.
30. Lina Benabdallah, "China's Relations with Africa and the Arab World: Shared Trends, Different Priorities," South African Institute of International Affairs, Policy Insights 67 (November 2018): 6.
31. China State Council, "Action Plan on the Belt and Road Initiative," March 30, 2015.
32. Shinn/Eisenman interview, Shanghai, June 30, 2017.
33. Nadège Rolland, "A Concise Guide to the Belt and Road Initiative," National Bureau of Asian Research, April 11, 2019; Rolland, "China's Vision for a New World Order," National Bureau of Asian Research, Special Report no. 83, January 27, 2020, 40.
34. Paul Nantulya, "Implications for Africa from China's One Belt One Road Strategy," Africa Center for Strategic Studies, March 22, 2019. Steven C. Y. Kuo makes a similar argument in *Chinese Peace in Africa: From Peacekeeper to Peacemaker* (London: Routledge, 2020), 63.
35. John Lee, "China's Trojan Ports," *American Interest*, November 29, 2018. Also see Yu Xiaofeng, Wei Zhijiang, Fan Shouzheng, An Xiaoping, and Choi Sun Hee, "中国非传统安全研究报告" [China nontraditional security research report (2014–2015)], *Blue Book of Non-Traditional Security* (Beijing: Social Sciences Academic Press, 2015).
36. Ian Taylor and Tim Zajontz, "In a Fix: Africa's Place in the Belt and Road Initiative and the Reproduction of Dependency," *South African Journal of International Affairs* 27, no. 3 (2020): 227–95.
37. Umar Muhammad Gummi, Yang Rong, Asiya Mu'azu, and Chen Ding, "China-Africa Economic Ties: Where Agenda 2063 and Belt and Road Initiative Converged and Diverged?" *Modern Economy* 11, no. 5 (May 2020): 1029; Stacey Links, "Ascertaining Agency: Africa and the Belt and Road Initiative," in *Global Perspectives on China's Belt and Road Initiative*, ed. Florian Schneider (Amsterdam: Amsterdam University Press, 2021), 115, 120.
38. Xinhua, "China's Second Africa Policy Paper," December 5, 2015.
39. "Action Plan on the Belt and Road Initiative."
40. Center for Dialogue, Research, and Cooperation, "The Belt and Road Initiative: The Silk Route Economic Belt (SREB) and the 21st Century Maritime Silk Road (MSR)," Special Digest, May 2017, 5, 7.
41. China State Council, "Full Text of the Vision for Maritime Cooperation Under the Belt and Road Initiative," June 20, 2017; Mesafint Tarekegn Yalew and Guo Changgang,

3. REGIONAL AND SUBREGIONAL RELATIONS

"China's 'Belt and Road Initiative:' Implication for Land Locked Ethiopia," *Insight on Africa* 12, no. 2 (2020): 175–93.
42. China Ministry of Foreign Affairs, "Joint Communique of the Leaders Roundtable of the Belt and Road Forum for International Cooperation," May 16, 2017.
43. Luo Lin, "China Arab Economic and Trade Cooperation Under the Background of Belt and Road Initiatives," *People's Daily*, May 27, 2019.
44. Shannon Tiezzi, "Who Is (and Who Isn't) Attending China's 2nd Belt and Road Forum?" *Diplomat*, April 27, 2019. Also see "携手共建'一带一路'" [Work together to build "the Belt and Road Initiative"], Second Belt and Road Forum for International Cooperation, April 19, 2019.
45. China Ministry of Foreign Affairs, "Xi Jinping Met with Foreign Leaders Attending the Second Belt and Road Forum for International Cooperation," April 29, 2019.
46. China Ministry of Foreign Affairs, "List of Deliverables of the Second Belt and Road Forum for International Cooperation," April 27, 2019.
47. Shinn/Eisenman interview, Addis Ababa, June 11 and 13, 2018.
48. Jean-Marc F. Blanchard, "Problematic Prognostications About China's Maritime Silk Road Initiative (MSRI): Lessons from Africa and the Middle East," *Journal of Contemporary China* 29, no. 122 (2020): 172.
49. For analyses of the BRI in individual countries, see Tukumbi Lumumba-Kasongo, "China-Kenya Relations with a Focus on the Maritime Silk Road Initiative (MRI) within a Perspective of Broad China-Africa Relations," *African and Asian Studies* 18 no. 3 (2019): 257–87; Mohamed Fayez Farahat, "The One Belt One Road: A Framework for Egyptian-Chinese Strategic Partnership," in *ChinaMed Report 2019: China's New Role in the Wider Mediterranean Region*, ed. Enrico Fardella and Andrea Ghiselli (2019), 35–39; El Mostafa Rezrazi, "The Belt and Road Initiative: A View from Morocco," in *ChinaMed Report 2019*, 29–34.
50. Christoph Nedopil, "Countries of the Belt and Road Initiative," Green Finance & Development Center FISF Fudan University; China Ministry of Foreign Affairs, "Foreign Ministry Spokesperson Wang Wenbin's Regular Press Conference on December 18, 2020," December 18, 2020.
51. "Liberia Signs on to China's Belt and Road Initiative," *Nordic Africa News*, May 4, 2019. For the complete text of the China-Italy MOU, see Hussein Askary, "Italy and China Sign Groundbreaking MOU on Belt and Road Initiative," Belt and Road Institute in Sweden, https://brixsweden.org.
52. "Foreign Minister of China and Morocco Sign MOU on Belt and Road," *Infra News*, November 21, 2017; Rezrazi, "The Belt and Road Initiative," 33.
53. Plamen Tonchev, "The Belt and Road After COVID-19," *Diplomat*, April 7, 2020; Kingsley Moghalu, "China, Africa and the World After COVID-19," *Premium Times*, May 19, 2020. Also see Xinhua, "共战新冠疫情 共建'一带一路'" [Fight the coronavirus and build the Belt and Road Initiative], June 17, 2020.
54. Andreea Brînza, "What Happened to the Belt and Road Initiative?" *Diplomat*, September 6, 2022.

3. REGIONAL AND SUBREGIONAL RELATIONS

55. Andrew Scobell and Nathan Beauchamp-Mustafaga, "The Flag Lags but Follows: The PLA and China's Great Leap Outward," in *Chairman Xi Remakes the PLA: Assessing Chinese Military Reforms*, ed. Phillip C. Saunders et al. (Washington, D.C.: National Defense University Press, 2019), 183–87.
56. Zhengyu Wu, "Towards Naval Normalcy: 'Open Seas Protection' and Sino-US Maritime Relations," *Pacific Review* 32, no. 4 (2019): 676–77.
57. Alessandro Arduino, "China's Belt and Road Security: The Increasing Role of Insurance and Private Security Companies," in *Securing the Belt and Road Initiative: Risk Assessment, Private Security and Special Insurances Along the New Wave of Chinese Outbound Investments*, ed. Alessandro Arduino and Xue Gong (Singapore: Palgrave Macmillan, 2018), 54.
58. Richard Ghiasy, Fei Su, and Lora Saalman, *The 21st Century Maritime Silk Road: Security Implications and Ways Forward for the European Union* (Stockholm International Peace Research Institute, September 2018).
59. Muhammad Sabil Farooq, Yuan Tongkai, Zhu Jiangang, and Nazia Feroze, "Kenya and the 21st Century Maritime Silk Road: Implications for China-Africa Relations," *China Quarterly of International Strategic Studies* 4, no. 3 (2018): 417.
60. Philani Mthembu, "China's Belt & Road Initiative: How Can Africa Advance Its Strategic Priorities?" in *Africa and the World: Navigating Shifting Geopolitics*, ed. Francis Kornegay Jr. and Philani Mthembu (Johannesburg: Mapungubwe Institute for Strategic Reflection in Africa, 2019); Aleksi Ylönen, "The Dragon and the Horn: Reflections on China-Africa Strategic Relations," *Insight on Africa* 12, no. 2 (2020): 149–51.
61. U.S. Office of the Secretary of Defense, *Annual Report to Congress: Military and Security Developments Involving the People's Republic of China 2020* (Washington, D.C., 2020), 15; Daniel R. Russell and Blake H. Berger, *Weaponizing the Belt and Road Initiative* (New York: Asia Society Policy Institute, September 2020), 22.
62. See Permanent Secretariat of Forum for Economic and Trade Cooperation Between China and Portuguese-Speaking Countries (Forum Macao), https://forumchinaplp.org.mo.
63. China Ministry of Commerce, "The Extraordinary Ministerial Conference of the Forum for Economic and Trade Cooperation Between China and Portuguese-Speaking Countries Successfully Held in Macao," April 13, 2022.
64. Wang Chenxi, Hu Yao, and Qi Yue, "Macao Platform Boosts China-Portuguese Speaking Countries Trade, BRI Cooperation," Xinhua, December 16, 2019.
65. Carmen Amado Mendes, "Macau in China's Relations with the Lusophone World," *Revista Brasileira de Política Internacional* 57, special edition (2014): 236.
66. Eilo W. Y. Yu and Ming K. Chan, *China's Macao Transformed: Challenge and Development in the 21st Century* (Hong Kong: City University of Hong Kong Press, 2014), 344.
67. China Ministry of Foreign Affairs, "China's African Policy," January 2006; Xinhua, "China's Second Africa Policy Paper," December 4, 2015; Sara Van Hoeymissen, "Regional

3. REGIONAL AND SUBREGIONAL RELATIONS

Organizations in China's Security Strategy for Africa: The Sense of Supporting 'African Solutions to African Problems,'" *Journal of Current Chinese Affairs* 40, no. 4 (2011): 94.

68. Georg Lammich, "Stability Through Multilateral Cooperation: China and Regional Security in Africa," *African Conflict & Peacebuilding Review* 9, no. 1 (Spring 2019): 115.
69. Van Hoeymissen, "Regional Organizations in China's Security Strategy," 101.
70. Arthur G. O. Mutambara, "Africa's Emerging China Strategy: How African States Need to Respond to China's Shifting Growth Model," in *Key Issues in Regional Integration: Volume 2*, ed. Ann Mugunga, COMESA (2013), 55.
71. Charles Ukeje and Yonas Tariki, "Beyond Symbolism: China and the African Union in African Peace and Security," in Alden et al., *China and Africa Building Peace on the Continent*, 304–5.
72. African Union Commission, Meeting of the Task Force on Africa's Strategic Partnership with Emerging Powers: China, India and Brazil," Addis Ababa, September 11–13, 2006, 11–12. Francis Ikome, Institute for Global Dialogue in South Africa, elaborated on the role of the AU in the China-Africa relationship in "The Role and Place of the African Union in the Emerging China-Africa Partnership," in *Chinese and African Perspectives on China in Africa*, ed. Axel Harneit-Sievers, Stephen Marks, and Sanusha Naidu (Cape Town: Pambazuka Press, 2010), 201–12. In a Shinn/Eisenman meeting in Accra on June 19, 2018, the head of a Ghanaian think tank complained that the AU "has no backbone" and we only deal with it "because it is there." The bilateral relationship is the important one.
73. African Union Commission, "Meeting of the Task Force," 13.
74. Mutambara, "Africa's Emerging China Strategy," 55.
75. Nancy Muthoni Githaiga et al., "The Belt and Road Initiative: Opportunities and Risks for Africa's Connectivity," *China Quarterly of International Strategic Studies* 5, no. 1 (2019): 140.
76. Hellen Adogo, "The African Union Cannot Go to Beijing Without an Action Plan," *Daily Maverick*, March 7, 2022.
77. Ian Taylor, *The Forum on China-Africa Cooperation (FOCAC)* (London: Routledge, 2011), 77–78.
78. "African Union Opens Chinese-funded HQ in Ethiopia," *BBC*, January 28, 2012.
79. "The Fifth Ministerial Conference of the Forum on China-Africa Cooperation Beijing Action Plan (2013–2015)," FOCAC, July 23, 2012, http://www.focac.org/eng/. See also Lina Benabdallah and Daniel Large, "China and African Security," in *New Directions in Africa-China Studies*, ed. Chris Alden and Daniel Large (London: Routledge, 2019), 313–15.
80. China Ministry of Foreign Affairs, "Wang Yi and Chairman of the African Union Commission Moussa Faki Mahamat Hold China-AU Strategic Dialogue," February 8, 2018.
81. African Union, "Communique on the Meeting Between the Chairperson of the Commission and the President of the People's Republic of China," September 5, 2018. Also see Xinhua, "习近平会见非洲联盟委员会主席法基" [Xi Jinping meets with Chairman Faki of the African Union Commission], September 5, 2018.

3. REGIONAL AND SUBREGIONAL RELATIONS

82. Jevans Nyabiage, "After US Retreat, China Breaks Ground on Africa CDC Headquarters Project," *South China Morning Post*, December 16, 2020.
83. Dawit Yohannes, Yonas Tariku, and Dereje Seyoum, "Enhancing Multidimensional Peace Support Operations (PSOs) Capacities in Africa: Any Role for China?" Institute for Peace and Security Studies, Addis Ababa University, November 2016, 18.
84. Gisela Grieger, "China's Growing Role as a Security Actor in Africa," European Parliamentary Research Service, October 2019, 5–6; "FOCAC Beijing Action Plan (2019–2021)."
85. Alao and Alden, "Africa's Security Challenges," 32.
86. Statement by Ambassador Smail Chergui, African Union Commissioner for Peace and Security, Beijing, July 14, 2019.
87. Van Hoeymissen, "Regional Organizations in China's Security Strategy," 105–6.
88. Shinn/Eisenman interview, Djibouti, June 14, 2018.
89. Liselotte Odgaard, "China's Policy on Development and Security in East Africa," *Scientia Militaria: South African Journal of Military Studies*, 46, no. 2 (2018): 87.
90. "NEPAD/AU Development Agency," African Union, https://au.int/; Mzukisi Qobo and Garth le Pere, "Between Resource Extraction and Industrializing Africa," in *New Directions in Africa-China Studies*, 261; Emmanuel Nwakanma, "NEPAD and Africa's Development: A Critical Analysis," *Pan African Social Science Review* 13 (December 2016): 92, 98–99.
91. Zhang Ying, "China's Diplomacy in Africa: Ideas and Practices," *China International Studies* 69 (March/April 2018): 44–45.
92. Lammich, "Stability Through Multilateral Cooperation," 118.
93. Shinn/Eisenman interview with former African ambassador to China, Addis Ababa, June 13, 2018.
94. Shinn/Eisenman interview, Addis Ababa, June 11, 2018.
95. Shinn/Eisenman interview with head of South African think tank, Pretoria, June 5, 2018.
96. Shinn/Eisenman interview with Western press representative, Addis Ababa, June 13, 2018.
97. Ukeje and Tariki, "Beyond Symbolism," 306.
98. Shinn interview with Abdelhak Bassou, senior fellow, Policy Center for the New South, Rabat, January 1, 2019.
99. China Ministry of Foreign Affairs, "League of Arab States-LAS," November 15, 2000.
100. Xinhua, "President Hu and Arab League Leader Meet to Boost Ties," January 31, 2004.
101. Xinhua, "President Xi's Speech at Arab League Headquarters: Full Text," January 22, 2016; China Ministry of Foreign Affairs, "China's Arab Policy Paper," January 2016.
102. China-Arab States Cooperation Forum, "Declaration of Action on China-Arab States Cooperation under the Belt and Road Initiative," July 10, 2018.
103. Chinese Ministry of Foreign Affairs, "Chinese FM Meets with Arab League Chief," January 8, 2020.
104. "History and Treaty," Southern Africa Development Community, https://www.sadc.int/.

3. REGIONAL AND SUBREGIONAL RELATIONS

105. Sophie Desmidt, "Understanding the Southern African Development Community—Peace and Security: How to Fight Old and New Demons?" European Center for Development Policy Management, March 2017, 14–17.
106. "Chinese Government Pledges Continued Development Cooperation with SADC," SADC, November 28, 2019, https://www.sadc.int/.
107. "China to Help with SADC Regional Logistics Depot," *DefenceWeb*, September 7, 2018; Southern African Development Community, "SADC Executive Secretary Commends Botswana Government for Signing Agreement for Hosting the SADC Standby Force Regional Logistics Depot," October 21, 2021.
108. "Basic Information," ECOWAS, https://ecowas.int.
109. Shinn/Eisenman interview with head of a think tank, Accra, June 19, 2018.
110. "Ambassador Deng Boqing Presents Credentials to the President of ECOWAS Commission," Chinese Embassy in Nigeria, December 14, 2010, http://ng.china-embassy.gov.cn/eng/.
111. African Union Commission, "China & Africa: Assessing the Relationship on the Eve of the Fourth Forum on China Africa Co-operation (FOCAC IV)," *Bulletin of Fridays of the Commission* 3, no. 1 (January 2010): 31–32; Emmanuel Akyeampong, "China in West Africa's Regional Development and Security Plans," *Africa Development* 40, no. 4 (2015): 11.
112. ECOWAS, "ECOWAS Signs MOU with China's CGCOC on Development Projects," January 22, 2016.
113. Sophie Chapman, "New ECOWAS Headquarters to Be Built in Abuja," *Construction Global*, April 13, 2020; Xinhua, "A Glimpse Into China-Aided ECOWAS Headquarters Under Construction," December 17, 2022.
114. China Ministry of Foreign Affairs, "Assistant Foreign Minister Zhai Jun Meets with President of ECOWAS Commission Chambas," September 23, 2008.
115. Shinn/Eisenman interview with Emmanuel Akwetey, executive director, Institute for Democratic Governance, Accra, June 20, 2018.
116. Rodrigo Tavares, "The Participation of SADC and ECOWAS in Military Operations: The Weight of National Interests in Decision-Making," *African Studies Review* 54, no. 2 (September 2011): 147–58.
117. Oita Etyang and Simon Oswan Panyako, "China and Africa's Peace and Security Agenda: The Burgeoning Appetite," *Journal of African Conflicts and Peace Studies* 3, no. 1 (August 2016): 7; African Union Commission, "Meeting of the Task Force," 32.
118. Johan Tejpar and Adriana Lins de Albuquerque, "Challenges to Peace and Security in West Africa: The Role of ECOWAS," FOI Memo 5382, Swedish Defence Research Agency, August 2015.
119. Obert Hodzi, *The End of China's Non-Intervention Policy in Africa* (Cham, Switz.: Palgrave Macmillan, 2019), 155–56.
120. Tom Bayes, *China's Growing Security Role in Africa: Views from West Africa, Implications for Europe* (Berlin: Konrad-Adenauer-Stiftung, 2020), 56.

3. REGIONAL AND SUBREGIONAL RELATIONS

121. Hang Zhou and Katharina Seibel, "Maritime Insecurity in the Gulf of Guinea: A Greater Role for China?" *China Brief* 15, no. 1 (January 9, 2015): 17.
122. ECOWAS, "China Supports ECOWAS Standby Force with Military Equipment," March 24, 2016.
123. ECOWAS, "ECOWAS Commission President Task China on Regional Peace and Security, Receives $200,000 Capacity Building Grant," November 10, 2017.
124. Shinn/Eisenman interview with senior officials in Ghana's Foreign Ministry, Accra, June 22, 2018; "Nigeria, China, France, Portugal Navies Combat Piracy in Gulf of Guinea," *Hellenic Shipping News*, June 5, 2018.
125. "COMESA in Brief," COMESA, September 2018, 1–2, https://www.comesa.int.
126. "COMESA in Brief," 35–36.
127. "Governance, Peace & Security," COMESA, April 4, 2020, https://www.comesa.int.
128. "Governance, Peace and Security"; "Biennial Report 2016–2017," COMESA, 9, 105, 205; Matias Assefa, "COMESA's Trading with China: Patterns and Prospects," *International Journal of African Development* 1, no. 2 (Spring 2014): 31–34; David Shinn and Joshua Eisenman, *China and Africa: A Century of Engagement* (Philadelphia: University of Pennsylvania Press, 2012), 122–24.
129. Michael Chawe, "COMESA Defends Sino-Africa Relations," *East African*, July 10, 2018; China Ministry of Foreign Affairs, "Ambassador Li Jie Presents His Letter of Accreditation to H.E. Mr. Sindiso Ngwenya, Secretary-General of COMESA," July 13, 2018.
130. IGAD, https://igad.int.
131. Shinn/Eisenman interview with senior IGAD official, Djibouti, June 14, 2018.
132. Redie Bereketeab, "Regional Economic Communities and Peacebuilding: The IGAD Experience," *South African Journal of International Affairs* 26, no. 1 (2019): 142, 147.
133. Chris Alden, "Seeking Security in Africa: China's Evolving Approach to the African Peace and Security Architecture," *NOREF Report*, March 2014.
134. IGAD, https://igad.int; Xinhua, "East Africa Hails China's Win-win Approach," November 13, 2018.
135. Shinn/Eisenman interview, Addis Ababa, June 16, 2018.
136. Aly Verjee, "Explaining China's Involvement in the South Sudan Peace Process," Lowy Institute, December 22, 2016. Also see Xinhua, "'中国方案'助力南苏丹和平进程" ["China Plan" helps South Sudan's peace process], February 21, 2015.
137. China Ministry of Foreign Affairs, "Ambassador He Xiangdong Meets with IGAD Special Envoy for South Sudan," January 19, 2018.
138. Shannon Tiezzi, "China in South Sudan: Practical Responsibility," *Diplomat*, January 13, 2015; Xinhua, "Foreign Ministry Spokesperson Hong Lei's Regular Press Conference on January 12, 2015," January 12, 2015.
139. Obert Hodzi, "Strategy of 'Parallels': China in the South Sudanese Armed Conflict," *Note d'Actualité 14/16 Observatoire de la Chine*, January 2017.
140. East African Community, https://eac.int.

3. REGIONAL AND SUBREGIONAL RELATIONS

141. World Trade Organization, "Trade Policy Review: East African Community (EAC)," February 13, 2019, 12.
142. Samu Ngwenya and Abdou Rahim Lema, "China's Role in Regional Integration in Africa: The Case of East African Community," *Stanford International Policy Review* 5, no. 1 (2020).
143. "China Appoints Envoy to EAC," *New Times* (Rwanda), May 11, 2011; EAC, "EAC and China Sign Framework Agreement to Boost Trade, Investment," November 17, 2011.
144. Abdur Rahman Alfa Shaban, "China Donates $200,000 to EAC Towards Burundi Political Dialogue," *Africa News*, September 26, 2016.
145. "China Accredits Envoy to EAC Bloc," EAC press release, November 18, 2017.
146. "China Gifts EAC 12 Cars Worth US$400,000 for Capacity Building Programmes," EAC press release, November 6, 2019.
147. Camilla Elowson and Cecila Hull Wiklund, "ECCAS Capabilities in Peace and Security," Swedish Defense Research Agency, September 2011, 34–46; Nurettin Can and Abubakar Aliyu Maigari, "Economic Regionalism in Africa: A Study of ECCAS," paper delivered at International Conference on Management, Economics and Humanities, London, July 26–28, 2019, 90–100.
148. Angela Meyer, "Regional Conflict Management in Central Africa: From FOMUC to MICOPAX," *African Security*, no. 2 (2009): 162.
149. Xinhua, "China Hopes Central African Republic Will Have New Leaders Soon," January 13, 2014.
150. "CEN-SAD—The Community of Sahel-Saharan States," UN Economic Commission for Africa, https://www/uneca.org; "Community of Sahel Saharan States (CEN-SAD)," Small Arms Survey, https://www.smallarmssurvey.org. The members are Benin, Burkina Faso, Central African Republic, Chad, Comoros, Côte d'Ivoire, Djibouti, Egypt, Eritrea, Gambia, Ghana, Guinea, Guinea-Bissau, Kenya, Liberia, Libya, Mali, Mauritania, Morocco, Niger, Nigeria, São Tomé and Principe, Senegal, Sierra Leone, Somalia, Sudan, Togo, and Tunisia.
151. "Construction of CEN-SAD Regional Anti-terrorism Center in Cairo Completed," *Egypt Today*, June 24, 2018; Shaul Shay, "Egypt and the CEN-SAD Counterterrorism," International Institute for Counter-Terrorism, January 13, 2019.
152. Union du Maghreb Arabe, http://au.int/en/node/135?q=node/135; Daouda Cissé, "Globalisation and Sustainable Africa-China Trade: What Role Play the African Regional Organisations?" Nordic Africa Institute, 2015, 17–18; Institute for Security Studies, "Profile: Arab Maghreb Union (AMU)"; Yahia Hatim, "Arab Maghreb Union Secretary-General Calls for Reopening Borders," *Morocco World News*, December 5, 2019.
153. May Barth, "Regionalism in North Africa: The Arab Maghreb Union in 2019," Brussels International Center for Research and Human Rights, June 2019, 24; Walsh, "China's Pervasive yet Forgotten Security Role," 974.
154. Organization of Islamic Cooperation, http://oic-oci.org/home/?lan=en.
155. Ma Lirong and Hou Yuxiang, "Analysis on the Potential of Strategic Cooperation Between China and OIC Under the 'Silk Road Strategy' Framework," *Journal of Middle*

3. REGIONAL AND SUBREGIONAL RELATIONS

Eastern and Islamic Studies (in Asia) 9, no. 1 (2015): 22–53; China Ministry of Foreign Affairs, "Xi Jinping Meets with Secretary-General Iyad Ameen Madani of Organisation of Islamic Cooperation," January 20, 2016; Xinhua, "Xi Sends Congratulatory Message to 14th OIC Summit," June 1, 2019.
156. "China Lauds OIC's Resolution on Xinjiang," *News International*, March 5, 2019.
157. Yang Sheng, "China, Islamic World 'Standing Closer' as Chinese FM Attends OIC Meeting for First Time," *Global Times*, March 22, 2022.
158. Group of 77, http://g77.org/.
159. Satyabrata Pal, "The Group of 77 in a Changing World," *UN Chronicle*, August 2014.
160. Xinhua, "Chinese Envoy Calls for Common Efforts with G77 in Global Economic Governance," January 14, 2017.
161. "Members and Other Participants of NAM Movement," Indian Ministry of External Affairs, https://www.india.gov.in/website-ministry-external-affairs; "History and Evolution of Non-Aligned Movement," Indian Ministry of External Affairs, https://www.india.gov.in/website-ministry-external-affairs, August 22, 2012; Xinhua, "Basic Facts About Non-Aligned Movement," August 26, 2012.
162. Shinn and Eisenman, *China and Africa*, 33.
163. China Ministry of Foreign Affairs, "Hu Jintao Attends the Commemoration Events of the 50th Anniversary of Bandung Conference," April 24, 2005.
164. Xinhua, "Xi Raises Three-point Proposal on Carrying Forward Bandung Spirit," April 22, 2015.
165. China Ministry of Foreign Affairs, "Foreign Ministry Spokesperson Lu Kang's Regular Press Conference on September 20, 2016."
166. Xinhua, "Non-Aligned Movement Baku Summit Emphasizes Stronger Multilateral Cooperation," October 27, 2019; "18th Summit of Heads of State and Government of Non-Aligned Movement Gets Underway in Baku," *China Daily*, October 28, 2019.
167. "About IORA," IORA, https://iora.int/en; Wei Hong and Li Ciyuan, "Indian Ocean Rim Association: New Developments and China's Engagement," *China International Studies* 70 (2018): 153–54.
168. Wei Hong and Li Ciyuan, "Indian Ocean Rim Association," 160–64; China Ministry of Foreign Affairs, "Special Representative of the Chinese Government on African Affairs Xu Jinghu Attends IORA 17th Meeting of the Council of Ministers," October 20, 2017; China State Council, "Full Text of the Vision for Maritime Cooperation Under the Belt and Road Initiative," Xinhua, June 20, 2017.
169. Wei Hong and Li Ciyuan, "Indian Ocean Rim Association," 159–64; David Brewster, "Stronger Institutions Sorely Needed in the Indian Ocean," *East Asia Forum*, July 9, 2019; Angela Stanzel, "China's String of Ports in the Indian Ocean," *China Trends*, Institut Montaigne, June 25, 2019; Embassy of the People's Republic of China in the People's Republic of Bangladesh, "Ambassador Li Jiming Attends the 22nd IORA Council of Ministers Meeting," November 25, 2022.
170. Alyssa Ayres, "How the BRICS Got Here," Council on Foreign Relations, August 31, 2017; Hong Xiao, "New Bank Embraces Role in BRICS Growth," *China Daily*,

3. REGIONAL AND SUBREGIONAL RELATIONS

November 14, 2019; Shinn/Eisenman interview with Erwin Pon, head of the Chinese Association of Gauteng, Johannesburg, June 6, 2018; Shinn/Eisenman interview with Philani Mthembu, executive director of the Institute for Global Dialogue at UNISA, and Iqbal Jhazbhay, member of the ANC International Relations Subcommittee, Pretoria, June 5, 2018.

171. Pádraig Carmody, "The Geopolitics and Economics of BRICS' Resource and Market Access in Southern Africa: Aiding Development or Creating Dependency?" *Journal of Southern African Studies* 43, no. 5 (2017): 865, 875.

4. PARTY-TO-PARTY RELATIONS

1. For work on the International Department of the Central Committee of the CPC in Africa, see Dawn Murphy, *China's Rise in the Global South: The Middle East, Africa, and Beijing's Alternative World Order* (Stanford, Calif.: Stanford University Press, 2022); Jean-Pierre Cabestan, "Party-to-Party Relations and Political Training," in *NBR Special Report: Political Front Lines China's Pursuit of Influence in Africa*, (2022); Daniel Large, *China and Africa: The New Era* (Cambridge: Polity Press, 2021); Joshua Eisenman and David Shinn, "China's Strategy in Africa," in *China Steps Out: Beijing's Major Power Engagement with the Developing World*, ed. Joshua Eisenman and Eric Heginbotham (New York: Routledge, 2018); Christine Hackenesch and Julia Bader, "The Struggle for Minds and Influence: The Chinese Communist Party's Global Outreach," *International Studies Quarterly* 64, no. 3 (2020): 723–33.
2. ID-CPC, "Department Profile."
3. For case studies on the CPC's party-to-party relations in Zambia, Zimbabwe, and Sudan, see David Shinn and Joshua Eisenman, *China and Africa: A Century of Engagement* (Philadelphia: University of Pennsylvania Press, 2012), 72–82.
4. We were not always successful. In June 2018 we visited Namibia, where South-West African People's Organization cadres declined our meeting requests. We were, however, able to meet with the Chinese ambassador and a junior ID-CPC official who was resident in Windhoek.
5. Andrew J. Nathan and Andrew Scobell, *China's Search for Security* (New York: Columbia University Press, 2012), 38.
6. Xi Jinping, "中国共产党领导是中国特色社会主义最本质的特征" [Leadership of the Communist Party of China is the most essential characteristic of socialism with Chinese characteristics], *QS Theory*, July 15, 2020.
7. "Department Profile."
8. Jessica C. Teets, "The CCP Is Eating the State," *East Asia Forum*, April 4, 2018.
9. Li Cheng, "Xi Jinping's Inner Circle: Part 5 the Mishu Cluster II," *China Leadership Monitor* 47 (2015); Helena Legarda, "In Xi's China, the Center Takes Control of Foreign Affairs," *Diplomat*, 2018.

4. PARTY-TO-PARTY RELATIONS

10. Xi Jinping, "习近平在中非合作论坛约翰内斯堡峰会开幕式上的致辞（全文）" [Speech by Xi Jinping at the opening ceremony of the Johannesburg FOCAC summit], Xinhua, December 4, 2015.
11. Xi Jinping, "习近平: 决胜全面建成小康社会夺取新时代中国特色社会主义伟大胜利在中国共产党第十九次全国代表大会上的报告" [Xi Jinping: Securing a decisive victory in building a moderately prosperous society in all respects and securing the great victory of socialism with Chinese characteristics for a new era—report delivered at Nineteenth National Congress of the Communist Party of China], Xinhua, October 27, 2017.
12. Xi Jinping, "Working Together to Build a Better World—Keynote Address," Xinhua, July 7, 2017.
13. "Xi Proposes to Establish New Model of Party-to-Party Relations," *China Daily*, December 1, 2017.
14. "Department Profile."
15. "Department Profile."
16. Hackenesch and Bader, "The Struggle for Minds and Influence."
17. "Department Profile"; Luan Jianzhang, "Closer to China Special Series: Understanding the CPC" by Robert Lawrence Kuhn, CGTN, February 28, 2019.
18. State Council Information Office of the People's Republic of China, "White Paper: China and Africa in the New Era: A Partnership of Equals," Xinhua, November 26, 2021.
19. "Department Profile."
20. "Symmetry and Asymmetry in Negotiation," in *Power and Negotiation*, ed. William Zartman and Jeffrey Z. Rubin (Ann Arbor: University of Michigan Press, 2002), 271–93.
21. ID-CPC officials, personal communications with the authors, 2017; Ling Shengli, "主场外交、战略能力与全球治理" [Home diplomacy, strategic capability and global governance], *Foreign Affairs Review*, no. 4 (2019).
22. Chen Dongxiao, "China's 'Host Diplomacy': Opportunities, Challenges and Undertakings," *China International Studies* 5 (September/October 2014): 12–31.
23. ID-CPC officials, personal communication with the authors, 2017.
24. ID-CPC officials, personal communication with the authors, 2017.
25. "酒店介绍" [Hotel introduction], Wanshou Hotel.
26. Africans in the Wanshou Hotel, personal communication with the authors, 2014, 2015, 2016, 2017.
27. Personal communications with the authors by African guests in the Wanshou Hotel, 2016, 2017, and African former participants, 2018.
28. Wang Heming, "Closer to China Special Series: Understanding the CPC" by Robert Lawrence Kuhn, CGTN, 2019.
29. Wang Heming; Hackenesch and Bader, "The Struggle for Minds and Influence," 723; Lina Benabdallah, "Power or Influence? Making Sense of China's Evolving Party-to-Party Diplomacy in Africa," *Africa Studies Quarterly* 19, no. 3–4 (2020): 99.
30. James C. Scott, *Seeing Like a State: How Certain Schemes to Improve the Human Condition Have Failed* (New Haven, Conn.: Yale University Press, 1998), 183.

4. PARTY-TO-PARTY RELATIONS

31. Luan Jianzhang, "Closer to China Special Series."
32. Shinn and Eisenman, *China and Africa*, 66–68; David Shinn and Joshua Eisenman, "Evolving Principles and Guiding Concepts: How China Gains African Support for Its Core National Interests," *Orbis* 64, no. 2 (2020): 271–88.
33. "Department Profile."
34. Zhong Weiyun, "Inter-party Relations Promote Sino-African Strategic Partnership," *China.org.cn*, August 28, 2012.
35. ID-CPC officials, personal communication with the authors, 2017.
36. Xi Jinping, "Xi Jinping: Securing a Decisive Victory."
37. "China's Party System Is Great Contribution to Political Civilization: Xi," *China Daily*, March 3, 2018b.
38. Song Tao, "Africa: China Keen on Building a Moderately Prosperous Society," *Capital FM*, 2020.
39. Justin Yifu Lin, "中国改革开放给非洲带来三大机遇" [China's reform and opening-up bring three major opportunities to Africa], *People's Daily*, August 31, 2018.
40. Benabdallah, "Power or Influence?" 102.
41. Yun Sun, "Political Party Training: China's Ideological Push in Africa?" Brookings Institution Africa in Focus, 2016.
42. Yun Sun, "Implications of China's Presence and Investment in Africa, Statement Before the Subcommittee on Emerging Threats and Capabilities of the Committee on Armed Services United States Senate," 105th Cong. 9 (2018). Yun Sun is codirector, East Asia Program, and director of the China Program, Stimson Center.
43. Hackenesch and Bader, "The Struggle for Minds and Influence," 727.
44. Shinn and Eisenman, *China and Africa*, 71–75; Joshua Eisenman, "Comrades-in-Arms: The Chinese Communist Party's Relations with African Political Organizations in the Mao Era, 1949–76," *Cold War History* 18, no. 4 (2018): 429–45.
45. Cao Zhigang, comments at 8th U.S.-China Peace Forum, Washington, D.C., July 16–17, 2018; ID-CPC officials, personal communications with the authors, 2017, 2018.
46. ID-CPC official, personal communication with the authors, 2017.
47. Wang Juan, "非洲国家政党青年领导人研修班在我校开班" [Seminar for young leaders of political parties in African countries begins in our school], Central Communist Youth League of China, March 12, 2019; International Center for Cooperation and Exchange, "非洲政党党校建设专题研修班来我校交流学习" [Special seminar on Africa political party school construction arrived at our school for study and exchange], April 1, 2014.
48. Ouyang Cheng Yi, "非洲英语国家政党青年领导人研修班来我院研修" [Seminar for young African political leaders from English-speaking countries arrived at our school for study and exchange], Shanghai Municipal Committee Party School of the Communist Party of China, 2017.
49. Benabdallah, "Power or Influence?" 98.
50. "Tuju Admits Jubilee Party Has Its Challenges," *Nation*, June 7, 2020.
51. For examples of this rhetoric, see Xinhua, "CPPCC Chairman Meets Ugandan Guests," July 25, 2003; China Ministry of Foreign Affairs, "Africa Says 'NO' to 'China

4. PARTY-TO-PARTY RELATIONS

Threat'— Interview with Vice Chairman Msekwa of the Revolutionary Party of Tanzania," December 28, 2009; "Political Parties in Africa, China Convene Seminar to Share Development Experience," *Global Times*, February 4, 2015; Lily Kuo, "Beijing Is Cultivating the Next Generation of African Elites by Training Them in China," *Quartz Africa*, December 14, 2017; Xinhua, "China Donates Computers to South Sudan's Ruling SPLM Party," April 5, 2018; "China-Africa Ties Continue Growing at Different Circumstances: AU Commission Deputy Chairperson," *China.org.cn*, May 27, 2020; Okot Emmanuel, "Like Chinese Ruling Party, Kiir Claims SPLM Will Alleviate Poverty," *Eye Radio*, July 7, 2021.

52. African official, personal email communications, July 2021.
53. Chen Dongxiao, "China's 'Host Diplomacy,'" 12–31.
54. Wang Heming, "Closer to China."
55. Irving L. Janis, *Groupthink: Psychological Studies of Policy Decisions and Fiascoes* (Boston: Houghton Mifflin, 1982).
56. ID-CPC, "徐绿平出席第三届中非政党理论研讨会闭幕式" [Xu Luping attends closing ceremony of the Third China-Africa Political Party Theory Seminar], October 12, 2017.
57. Kunshan Municipal Committee Party School of the Communist Party of China, "非洲法语国家政党领导人研修班来昆山考察" [Seminar for young African political leaders from French-speaking countries visits Kunshan], November 25, 2019.
58. "中非青年领导人论坛召开，中共推出三年千人计划1000名非洲青年政治家将获邀赴华" [China holds the China-Africa Youth Leadership Forum and launches a three-year plan for inviting one thousand young African politicians to visit China], 南方都市报 [Southern metropolis daily]; Lily Kuo, "Beijing Is Cultivating the Next Generation of African Elites by Training Them in China," *Quartz Africa*, December 14, 2017.
59. Zhong Fei, "非洲国家政党青年领导人研修班来重庆市委党校学习交流" [Young African political leaders arrive at Chongqing Municipal Party School for study and exchange], Party School of the Central Committee CPC, 2019.
60. "Magufuli Launches Sh100bn Leadership School Project in Kibaha," *Citizen*, July 17, 2018; Xinhua, "尼雷尔领导力学院在坦桑尼亚奠基" [Nyerere Leadership Academy lays a foundation in Tanzania], July 17, 2018.
61. "Magufuli Launches."
62. International Center for Cooperation and Exchange, "非洲政党党校建设专题研修班来我校交流学习" [Special seminar on Africa Political Party School construction arrived at our school for study and exchange], 2014.
63. International Department Central Committee of CPC, "宋涛同非洲六党总书记举行会谈" [Song Tao holds talks with the general secretaries of six African political parties], October 13, 2016.
64. Xinhua, "中国共产党与世界政党高层对话会非洲专题会在坦桑尼亚开幕 宋涛出席并讲话" [Song Tao attends and speaks at the opening of the Africa special session of the CPC in Dialogue with World Political Parties high-level meeting in Tanzania], August 18, 2018; "Magufuli Launches."

4. PARTY-TO-PARTY RELATIONS

65. "Xi congratulates groundbreaking ceremony of Julius Nyerere Leadership School," *China Daily*, July 16, 2018.
66. International Department Central Committee of the CPC, "尼雷尔领导力学院竣工启用仪式举行" [Inauguration ceremony of Mwalimu Julius Nyerere Leadership School held], 2022.
67. Jevans Nyabiage, "China's Political Party School in Africa Takes First Students from Six Countries," *South China Morning Post*, June 21, 2022.
68. "China Sponsors Zanu PF," *Newsday*, May 24, 2022.
69. "Zanu PF Delegation in Tanzania," *Herald*, May 24, 2022.
70. Justina Crabtree, "Migration and Cheap Chinese Goods Worry South Africa's Largest Trade Union Group Over Pan-African Free Trade," *CNBC*, March 29, 2018; "A Chance to 'Reimagine South Africa,'" *Mail & Guardian*, April 21, 2020; Nkosikhona Duma, "COVID-19 Is an Opportunity for Govt to Revive Manufacturing Sector—COSATU," *Eyewitness News*, May 7, 2020.
71. Shinn/Eisenman interview with SACP, Johannesburg, June 6, 2018.
72. Interview with SACP party leaders, Johannesburg, June 6, 2018.
73. Email correspondence with SACP official, September 2021.
74. Shinn/Eisenman interview with SACP, Johannesburg, June 6, 2018.
75. Shinn and Eisenman, *China and Africa*, 345.
76. Mbeki served in the SACP Central Committee for decades and in 1989 chaired the SACP Seventh Congress held in Havana, Cuba. Email correspondence with SACP official, June 2020.
77. Email correspondence with SACP official, June 2020.
78. Email correspondence with SACP official, June 2020.
79. Shinn and Eisenman, *China and Africa*, 345–46.
80. Garth Shelton, "China, Africa and Asia Advancing South-South Co-operation," in *Politics and Social Movements in a Hegemonic World: Lessons from Africa, Asia and Latin America*, ed. Atilio A. Boron and Gladys Lechini (Buenos Aires: CLACSO, 2005), 184–203.
81. For work on CPC relations with other South African parties, see Shinn and Eisenman, *China and Africa*, 343–52.
82. Shinn and Eisenman, 82, 347, 351.
83. Jacob Zuma, "ANC: Zuma: Speech to the China Executive Leadership Academy (13/06/2008)," *Polity.org.za*, June 13, 2008.
84. Consulate General of the People's Republic of China in Cape Town, "习近平会见南非非国大全国执委研修班一行" [Xi Jinping meets with members of the Workshop of the ANC National Executive Committee of South Africa], October 10, 2011; Zhong Weiyun, "中非政党关系助力中非战略伙伴关系" [China-Africa political party relations boost Sino-African strategic partnership], *China News*, October 11, 2012; Martin Plaut, "Why Is the ANC Following the Example of the Chinese Communist Party?" *New Statesman*, January 6, 2015.
85. African National Congress, "60 Years of the Chinese Revolution, Lessons to Be Learnt"; ID-CPC, "Wang Jiarui Meets South African Guest," November 23, 2009.

4. PARTY-TO-PARTY RELATIONS

86. "African National Congress NGC 2015: Discussion Document," *Umrabulo*, 2015; Alex Newman, "South African Regime Embraces Chinese Communism, New World Order," *New American*, August 27, 2015.
87. Sam Ratner, "Illiberalism Isn't Just Rising—It's Spreading (Part II)," *World*, July 14, 2020; Hackenesch and Bader, "The Struggle for Minds and Influence," 731.
88. Thami Ka Plaatjie, "Lessons to Learn from Chinese Experience," *Sunday Independent*, August 2, 2015; Pan Junyu and Zhang Wei, "南非非洲人国民大会高级干部研修班一行访韶学习交流基层党组织建设的等先进经验" [Senior officials from South Africa's African National Congress visited Shaoguan to learn and exchange advanced experience in building grassroots party organizations], *Shaoguan Daily*, December 9, 2015; ID-CPC, "南非非国大高级干部研修感将访韶" [South Africa's ANC senior officials will visit China for a seminar], November 27, 2015.
89. Huaxia, ed., "Chinese Embassy in S. Africa Donate Food to Underprivileged Community," Xinhua, June 30, 2020.
90. Xinhua, "国家副主席李源潮10日在北京会见南非共总书记" [Vice President Li Yuanchao met with general secretary of South Africa's Communist Party in Beijing on September 10], September 10, 2013; ID-CPC, "南非共产党干部考察团将访华" [Official delegation from South Africa's Communist Party will visit China], June 8, 2016.
91. "Behalf of SACP Delegation," SACP China trip report, February 2019. This report was obtained directly from the SACP leadership in April 2020.
92. ID-CPC, "Li Mingxiang Attends Opening Ceremony of Online Training Workshop for SACP Senior Cadres," April 23, 2020.
93. Li Xiaoyu, "CPC and SACP Set to Enhance Their Cooperation and Exchanges on Occasion of Their Centennial Celebrations," *China Africa*, March 17, 2021.
94. ID-CPC, "Li Mingxiang Attends the 15th National Conference of the South African Communist Party," July 18, 2022.
95. Shinn/Eisenman interview with SACP, Johannesburg, June 2018.
96. Plaut, "Why Is the ANC Following the Example?"
97. Dan Mokonyane, *The Big Sellout: By the Communist Party of South Africa and the African National Congress* (Estate of Dan Mokonyane, 2011), 78.
98. Lizeka Tandala, "RET Is a Splinter Party Established in Magashule's Office, Says ANC EC Secretary," *Mail & Guardian*, March 23, 2021.
99. One noteworthy difference is that the TPLF (unlike the SACP) was the leading faction within the EPRDF and a regional and an ethnic party associated with the people of Tigray, the northernmost of Ethiopia's nine regions, who make up only about 6 percent of Ethiopia's population.
100. Interview in Addis Ababa, June 12, 2018.
101. Ai Ping, "Ethiopia in the New Century: A Chinese Perspective," in *China Comes to Africa: The Political Economy and Diplomatic History of China's Relations with Africa*, ed. Kinfe Abraham (Addis Ababa: Ethiopian International Institute for Peace and Development [EIIPD] and Horn of Africa Democracy and Development [HADAD], 2005), 237.

4. PARTY-TO-PARTY RELATIONS

102. "China Desires to Consolidate Bilateral Ties with Ethiopia," *Ethiopian Herald*, November 4, 2004.
103. Helen Tadesse, "Prosperity Party, Chinese Communist Party Agree to Boost Strategic Partnership," *Walta*, June 28, 2022.
104. Seifudein Adem, "The Logic of China's Diplomacy in Ethiopia," in *China's Diplomacy in Eastern and Southern Africa*, ed. Seifudein Adem (Burlington, Vt.: Ashgate, 2013), 152–53.
105. Aleksandra Gadzala,"Ethiopia: Toward a Foreign-Funded 'Revolutionary Democracy,'" in *Africa and China: How Africans and Their Governments Are Shaping Relations with China*, ed. Aleksandra Gadzala (Lanham, Md.: Rowman & Littlefield, 2015), 102.
106. Tang Xiaoyang, "埃塞俄比亚：复制中国模式?" [Ethiopia: Copying China's model?], *Modern Weekly*, August 29, 2014; Cai Linzhe, "埃塞俄比亚学习'中国模式'" [Ethiopia learns from "China's model"], *Phoenix Weekly*, May 15, 2013.
107. "中联部局长艾平谈于非洲政党的交往" [Director of ID-CPC talks about relations with African political parties], *Guangming Daily*, October 11, 2007.
108. Shinn and Eisenman, *China and Africa*, 274.
109. Yun Sun, "Political Party Training."
110. Bai Debin, "吴德刚会见埃塞俄比亚高级干部研修班一行" [Wu Degang met with Ethiopian senior Officials on a seminar], *Gansu Daily*, August 26, 2013; Research and Training Institute of NRTA, "埃塞俄比亚人民革命民主阵线党政干部考察团在京开班" [Ethiopian People's Revolutionary Democratic Front Party held study groups in Beijing], October 9, 2015; Jiang Xuelin, "埃塞俄比亚人民革命民主阵线干部考察团访问广西" [Official delegation from Ethiopian People's Revolutionary Democratic Front visited Guangxi Province], *China News*, February 29, 2016.
111. Arkebe Oqubay Metiku, "China-Africa Economic Ties: A New Dynamics of Development," keynote speech, 2017 Shanghai Forum, May 29, 2017.
112. Xiang Bo, "China's Top Legislator Visits Ethiopia to Boost Bilateral Ties," Xinhua, May 12, 2018; Shinn/Eisenman interview, Addis Ababa, June 13, 2018.
113. Liang Yu, "Xi Meets Ethiopian Prime Minister," Xinhua, September 2, 2018.
114. Xinhua, "中共代表郭业洲出席埃革阵十一大" [Chinese Communist Party representative Guo Yezhou attends Eleventh National Congress of EPRDF], October 5, 2018.
115. ID-CPC, "Song Tao Meets with EPRDF Cadre Study Group," December 14, 2018; April 23, 2019.
116. Shinn email correspondence with EPRDF cadre, August 18, 2020.
117. ID-CPC, "Li Mingxiang Attends Opening Ceremony of Online Training Workshop of Ethiopia's Prosperity Party," May 6, 2020.
118. Tadesse, "Prosperity Party."
119. David Shambaugh, "China's 'Quiet Diplomacy': The International Department of the Chinese Communist Party," *China: An International Journal* 5, no. 1 (2007): 32; Hackenesch and Bader, "The Struggle for Minds and Influence," 726.
120. Zhong Lianyan, ed., *International Relations of the Communist Party of China* (Beijing: China Intercontinental Press, 2007).
121. Shinn/Eisenman interview with NDC officials, Accra, June 21, 2018.

5. AFRICA-FOCUSED PROPAGANDA

122. Shinn/Eisenman interview with NDC officials, Accra, June 21, 2018.
123. The NDC is not unique in receiving material support from the CPC. For information on CPC material support to political parties in Zambia and Zimbabwe, see Shinn and Eisenman, *China and Africa*, 71–75.
124. "Statement: AFAG Questions $20-million NDC HQ Project," *Ghana Web*, December 6, 2011. For pictures of the headquarters, see "Why NDC Constructed Ultra-Modern Headquarters (Photos)," *Peace FM*, November 18, 2014.
125. "NDC Moves Into $20m Office," *Ghana Web*, October 14, 2014.
126. "Statement: AFAG Questions $20-Million NDC HQ Project," *Peace FM Online*; "NDC Moves."
127. Shinn/Eisenman interview with NDC officials, Accra, June 21, 2018.
128. Shinn/Eisenman interview with NDC officials, Accra, June 21, 2018.
129. Xinhua, "Ghana's Quartey Elected Vice Chair of AU Commission," January 31, 2017.
130. Xinhua, "China-Africa Ties Continue Growing at Different Circumstances: AU Commission Deputy Chairperson," June 8, 2020.
131. "NDC to Set Up 'Party School,'" *Citi FM Online*, May 11, 2014. Similarly, in Namibia, the ID-CPC provided SWAPO with computers and manuals and sent scholars from the ID-CPC and the Central Party School to Windhoek to help SWAPO create its own party school. Brigitte Weidlich, "SWAPO to Be Schooled Communist Party Way," *Namibian*, August 8, 2006.
132. "NDC to Set Up Party School: Asiedu Nketia Hints," *My Joy Online*, May 12, 2014.
133. Shinn/Eisenman interview with NDC officials, Accra, June 21, 2018.
134. Shinn/Eisenman interview with NPP official, Accra, June 18, 2018.
135. Nyawira Mwangi, "China Helps Ghana's Ruling Party to Fight COVID-19 with Medical Supplies," CGTN Africa, July 28, 2020. The ID-CPC also donated thirty thousand surgical face masks to Zambia's ruling Patriotic Front Party, whose leader called the donation "a practical demonstration of the goodwill that exists between the two parties." Huaxia, ed., "CPC Donates COVID-19 Medical Materials to Zambia's Ruling Party," Xinhua, June 20, 2020.
136. Shinn/Eisenman interview with NPP official, Accra, June 18, 2018.
137. Shinn/Eisenman interview with NPP official, Accra, June 18, 2018.
138. Shinn/Eisenman interviews, Addis Ababa, June 12, 2018.

5. AFRICA-FOCUSED PROPAGANDA

1. Chen Dongxiao, "China's 'Host Diplomacy': Opportunities, Challenges and Undertakings," *China Institute of International Studies* 48 (September/October 2014): 12–31.
2. "Forecast of the Total Population of Africa from 2020 to 2050," *Statista*, July 15, 2022; "How Will a Population Boom Change Africa?" *BBC*, September 11, 2015.
3. Mohamed Yahya, "Africa's Defining Challenge," United Nations Development Programme, August 7, 2017; United Nations Department of Economic and Social Affairs,

5. AFRICA-FOCUSED PROPAGANDA

Population Division, "Youth Population Trends and Sustainable Development," no. 2015/1, May 2015.

4. Liu Guangyuan, "Deepen China-Africa Media Cooperation and Enrich the China-Africa Community of Shared Destinies," November 18, 2013, China-Africa Media Cooperation Seminar, transcript, Chinese Embassy in Kenya.

5. Cited in Simon Allison, "Fixing China's Image in Africa, One Student at a Time," *The Guardian*, July 5, 2013.

6. "习近平:共同为改革想招 一起为改革发力" [Xi Jinping: Recruit together to make a powerful force for reform], Xinhua, August 18, 2014.

7. See Central Propaganda Department Cadre Bureau Writing Group, "新时期宣传思想工作" [Propaganda and ideological work in the new era], 2001, 188–89; David Shambaugh, "China's Propaganda System: Institutions, Processes and Efficacy," *China Journal*, no. 57 (2007): 49.

8. Dauti Kahura, "Enter the Dragon: China's Media War in Africa," *Elephant*, May 2, 2019.

9. Song Tao, "Africa: China Keen on Building a Moderately Prosperous Society—Minister," *Capitol FM (Nairobi)*, December 1, 2020; Anne-Marie Brady, "China's Foreign Propaganda Machine," in *Authoritarianism Goes Global: The Challenge to Democracy*, ed. Larry Diamond, Marc F. Plattner, and Christopher Walker (Baltimore: Johns Hopkins University Press), 189.

10. This objective was best summarized by Xi himself in his speech at the CPC's Nineteenth Congress in October 2017, when he claimed that China's system offers "a new option for other countries and nations who want to speed up their development while preserving their independence." Simon Denyer, "Move Over, America. China Now Presents Itself as the Model 'Blazing a New Trail' for the World," *Washington Post*, October 19, 2017.

11. Shambaugh, "China's Propaganda Systems," 29.

12. Chen Dongxiao, "China's 'Host Diplomacy.'" Also see "《习近平总书记系列重要讲话读本》之建立新型国际关系" [Readings from General Secretary Xi Jinping's series of important speeches on building a new type of international relations], *People's Daily*, 2014; Yu Yuanquan, "中国文化软实力建设任重道远" [Shouldering the heavy responsibility of building China's soft power], *International Communications*, no. 1 (2007): 44–46; Chen Xinguang, "美国软实力衰退与中国软实力提升" [U.S. soft power weakening, Chinese soft power rising], *China Daily*, June 23, 2015.

13. Raymond Zhong et al., "No 'Negative' News: How China Censored the Coronavirus," *New York Times*, January 13, 2021; Gary King, Jennifer Pan, and Margaret E. Roberts, "How the Chinese Government Fabricates Social Media Posts for Strategic Distraction, Not Engaged Argument," *American Political Science Review* 111, no. 3 (2017): 484–501.

14. China State Council, "习近平:讲好中国故事,传播好中国声音" [Xi Jinping: Tell China's stories well and spread China's voice well], September 4, 2013.

15. Wang Gengnian, "建设国际一流媒体积极争取国际话语权" [Build a world-class media and actively strive for the right to speak internationally], China State Council, January 5, 2010.

5. AFRICA-FOCUSED PROPAGANDA

16. Wang Gengnian, "中国国际传播的现状和发展趋势" [Current situation and development trend of international communication in China], *People's Daily*, September 12, 2013.
17. Shambaugh, "China's Propaganda Systems," 27.
18. Zhuang Pinghui, "China's Confucius Institutes Rebrand After Overseas Propaganda Rows," *South China Morning Post*, July 4, 2020.
19. Brady, "China's Foreign Propaganda Machine," 187–88.
20. 中国共产党建设大字典 *1921–1991* [An encyclopedia on the building of the CCP] (Chengdu: Sichuan Renmin Chubanshe, 1992), 676, cited in Shambaugh, "China's Propaganda Systems," 28.
21. In our previous volume we dedicated a chapter to these three topics. See David H. Shinn and Joshua Eisenman, *China and Africa: A Century of Engagement* (Philadelphia: University of Pennsylvania Press, 2012), 194–227. For Europe-focused propaganda work, see Vladimir Shopov, "Beijing's Megaphone: The Return of Party Propaganda in South-Eastern Europe," European Council on Foreign Relations, January 8, 2021. For China's Arab-focused propaganda, see Roie Yellinek, Yossi Mann, and Udi Lebel, "Chinese Soft-Power in the Arab world—China's Confucius Institutes as a Central Tool of Influence," *Comparative Strategy* 39, no. 6 (2020): 517–34.
22. Iginio Gagliardone, *China, Africa, and the Future of the Internet* (London: ZED Books, 2019).
23. Dani Madrid-Morales, "Sino-African Media Cooperation: An Overview of a Longstanding Asymmetric Relationship," in *It Is About Their Story: How China, Turkey and Russia Influence the Media in Africa* (Johannesburg: Konrad-Adenauer-Stiftung Regional Media Programme Sub-Saharan Africa, 2021), 20.
24. Celine Sui, "China Wants State Media to Peddle Its 'Soft Power' in Africa, but Tech Platforms Are a Better Bet," *Quartz*, October 29, 2019; Global System for Mobile Communications Association, "Mobile Internet Connectivity 2020: Sub-Saharan Africa Factsheet," September 2020.
25. Sui, "China Wants State Media to Peddle Its 'Soft Power.'"
26. Sarah Cook, "Beijing's Global Megaphone: The Expansion of Chinese Communist Party Media Influence Since 2017," *Freedom House Perspectives*, January 2020.
27. "China Is Spending Billions to Make the World Love It," *Economist*, March 23, 2017.
28. Cook, "Beijing's Global Megaphone."
29. Sarah Cook et al., "Beijing's Global Media Influence 2022: Authoritarian Expansion and the Power of Democratic Resilience," Freedom House, September 2022.
30. Shinn/Eisenman Beijing interviews, June 2017; Kenneth King, *China's Aid and Soft Power in Africa: The Case of Education and Training* (Oxford: James Currey/Boydell and Brewer, 2013), 74–75.
31. "Key Chinese University to Add Language Majors Amid Boosting Ties," *China Daily*, March 29, 2017.
32. Brady, "China's Foreign Propaganda Machine," 191.

5. AFRICA-FOCUSED PROPAGANDA

33. Sergio Grassi, "Changing the Narrative: China's Media Offensive in Africa," Friedrich Ebert Stiftung, April 2014, 3; Xinhua, "派驻国 (境) 外分支机构" [Branches outside the country of assignment], n.d.
34. Sui, "China Wants State Media to Peddle Its 'Soft Power'"; John Nduire, "Xinhua's Nairobi Office Tower Set for Completion in February," *Construction Kenya*, March 12, 2018.
35. "China Radio International Global Shortwave Schedule," *CRI*, October 29, 2017; Catie Snow Bailard, "China in Africa: An Analysis of the Effect of Chinese Media Expansion on African Public Opinion," *International Journal of Press/Politics* 21, no. 4 (2016): 446–71.
36. Xinhua, "组建中央广播电视总台，撤销央视、央广等建制" [The Central Radio and Television Station was established, and the establishment of CCTV and CCTV was abolished], March 21, 2018; Steven Jiang, "Beijing Has a New Propaganda Weapon: Voice of China," *CNN Business*, March 21, 2018.
37. Liu Guangyuan, "Opening Ceremony of CCTV Africa News Production Centre," January 11, 2012, Crowne Plaza Hotel, Nairobi, transcript, Chinese Embassy in Kenya.
38. Iginio Gagliardone, "China as a Persuader: CCTV Africa's First Steps in the African Media Sphere," *Ecquid Novi: African Journalism Studies* 34, no. 3 (2013): 29–30.
39. Jonathan Kaiman, "'China Has Conquered Kenya': Inside Beijing's New Strategy to Win African Hearts and Minds," *Los Angeles Times*, August 7, 2017; Eric Olander, "China's StarTimes Is Now One of Africa's Most Important Media Companies," *Medium* (blog), August 26, 2017.
40. "Ten Years of Contribution to Africa's Development from StarTimes," *New Times*, July 23, 2018.
41. Xinhua, "China's StarTimes Launches New TV Program in Kenya to Help Fight COVID-19 Pandemic," March 25, 2020; Javira Ssebwami, "Look Into the East: New StarTimes Programme Highlights Africa-China Connection," *PML Daily*, January 29, 2021.
42. Sui, "China Wants State Media to Peddle Its 'Soft Power.'"
43. Opera, "News App from Zero to More than 20 Million African Users," State of the Mobile Web 2019, 2019; Daniel Adeyemi, "Opera News Is Growing Fast in Africa but Has a Quality Problem," *Techcabal*, January 21, 2021.
44. "Video Social and Sharing App, Vskit Hits a Milestone of 10 Million Users in Africa," *Techpoint.africa*, January 17, 2019; Yu Jing and Bi Ran, "Chinese Video Apps Making Inroads Into Global Markets," CGTN, November 9, 2019; Emma Okonji, "Vskit Hits 51m Users in Three Years, Unveils New Plans," *This Day*, November 22, 2021; "Video Social and Sharing App, Vskit Hits a Milestone of 10 Million Users in Africa," *Techpoint Africa*, January 17, 2019.
45. Reuters, "Vodacom Partners with China's Alipay to Create 'Super App,' in South Africa," July 20, 2020.
46. Xinhua, "China to Promote Cultural Soft Power," January 1, 2014.
47. Permanent Mission of the People's Republic of China to the UN, "The China-Africa Institute Established in Beijing Yang Jiechi Reads the Congratulatory Message from President Xi Jinping and Delivers a Speech," April 9, 2019.

5. AFRICA-FOCUSED PROPAGANDA

48. Chinese Embassy in Republic of Kenya, "Deepen China-Africa Media Cooperation and Enrich the China-Africa Community of Shared Destinies," November 19, 2013.
49. Wang Gengnian, "建设国际一流媒体积极争取国际话语权" [Build a world-class media and actively strive for the right to speak internationally], State Council Information Office of the People's Republic of China, January 5, 2010. For Xinhua chief Li Congjun expressing a similar view, see Li Congjun, "牢牢掌握舆论工作主动权" [Firmly grasp the initiative of public opinion work], *People's Daily*, September 4, 2013.
50. For discussion of Xinhua's editorial policy prior to 2012, see Shinn and Eisenman, *China and Africa*, 199–201.
51. Emeka Umejei, *Chinese Media in Africa: Perception, Performance, and Paradox* (Lanham, Md.: Rowman and Littlefield, 2020), 76–77.
52. Shinn and Eisenman, *China and Africa*, 199–201.
53. Umejei, *Chinese Media in Africa*, 77.
54. Umejei, 69–70, 72–73.
55. Cited in Emeka Umejei, "Newspaper Coverage of China's Engagement with Nigeria: Protector or Predator?" in *China-Africa Relations: Building Images Through Cultural Cooperation, Media Representation and Communication*, ed. Kathryn Batchelor and Xiaoling Zhang (London: Routledge, 2017), 177.
56. "Tedros' Remarks on China's Zero-COVID 'Irresponsible,'" *Global Times*, May 11, 2022.
57. Sean Mantesso and Christina Zhou, "China's Multibillion-Dollar Media Campaign 'a Major Threat for Democracies' Around the World," *ABC News* (Australia), February 7, 2019.
58. Hao Yalin, "Chinese Official Stresses Role of 'Propaganda' During Beijing Olympics," Xinhua, January 31, 2008.
59. Brady, "China's Foreign Propaganda Machine," 190; "党的宣传工作文件选编 1988–1992" [Selection of the party's propaganda working documents: 1988–1992] (Beijing: CPC Central Party School Press, 1994).
60. Brady, "China's Foreign Propaganda Machine," 192; Cook, "Beijing's Global Megaphone."
61. Liu Qibao, "大力推动中华文化走向世界" [Vigorously promote Chinese culture to the world], *Guangming Daily*, May 22, 2014.
62. Brady, "China's Foreign Propaganda Machine," 192; Cook, "Beijing's Global Megaphone."
63. Shinn and Eisenman, *China and Africa*, 201–3; Gagliardone, "China as a Persuader," 25.
64. Xinhua, "Xinhua President Meets Heads of Four African News Agencies," June 13, 2007.
65. Ikenna Emewu, "Africa-China, Xinhua Sign Content Partnership," *Africa China Economy*, September 27, 2019; "Daily News Egypt Signs Content, Images Sharing Agreement with Xinhua," *Daily News Egypt*, October 19, 2019; Grassi, "Changing the Narrative," 3; Cook, "Beijing's Global Megaphone."
66. Herman Wasserman and Dani Madrid-Morales, "How Influential Are Chinese Media in Africa? An Audience Analysis in Kenya and South Africa," *International Journal of Communication* 12 (2018): 2212–31; Dani Madrid-Morales, "African News with Chinese

5. AFRICA-FOCUSED PROPAGANDA

Characteristics: A Case Study of CGTN Africa" (PhD diss., City University of Hong Kong, 2018).
67. Brady, "Authoritarianism Goes Global," 57.
68. Ikenna Emewu, "Exclusive: Covid-19 May Not Have Originated in China, Oxford University Expert Posits," *Africa China Economy*, July 5, 2020; He Wenping, "Demand Compensation from China, Devil in Hearts," *Daily News Egypt*, May 21, 2020.
69. Khaosod English, "Khaosod Signs Partnership with China's Xinhua," *Khaosod English*, July 25, 2019; "Xinhua, Lao News Agency Sign New Agreement for Enhanced Cooperation," *Xinhua Silk Road*, China Economic Information Service, October 25, 2018; Xinhua Servicios, "Xinhua," *La Estrella De Panamá*, October 18, 2021; Agencia Xinhua, "Xinhua," *El Comercio Perú*, December 15, 2021.
70. Breslin, "China's Global Cultural Interactions," 144.
71. Wu Yu-Shan, "The Rise of China's State-Led Media Dynasty in Africa," South African Institute of International Affairs, Occasional Paper no. 117, June 2012. Andy Sennitt, "Ni Hao! Togo, China Sign Broadcast Agreement," *Republic of Togo*, July 18, 2010.
72. Selma Mihoubi, "La Stratégie d'Implantation de Radio Chine Internationale (RCI) en Afrique Sahélienne," *Norois*, no. 252 (2019): 89–102.
73. Samuel Dweh, "Liberia: China Rejuvenates 'Old School' State-Owned Media," *FPA*, January 21, 2019; "Chinese Embassy Offers Technical Assistance to GNA," *Graphic Online*, October 6, 2021; Eric Olander, "China to Upgrade Equipment at Somalia's Government-Run Media Outlets," *China Africa Project*, November 8, 2021.
74. Cook, "Beijing's Global Megaphone."
75. Tai Nichols, "StarTimes to Expand TV Reach in Africa with SES 5," *Satellite Today*, September 23, 2013.
76. Sébastien Le Belzic, "The Chinese Will to Censor Critical Opinions in Africa Is Worrying," *Modern Ghana*, November 3, 2013.
77. Craig McKune, "Chinese Companies Scoop Shares in Independent News," *Mail and Guardian*, August 15, 2013; Geoffrey York, "Why China Is Making a Big Play to Control Africa's Media," *Globe and Mail*, September 11, 2013.
78. Interview with Eric Olander via Twitter direct message, December 8, 2020.
79. Reporters Without Borders, "China's Pursuit of a New World Media Order," October 2019, 38.
80. China Ministry of Foreign Affairs, "Forum on China-Africa Cooperation Dakar Action Plan (2022–2024)," November 30, 2021.
81. Bob Wekesa, "Chinese Media and Diplomacy in Africa," in Batchelor and Zhang, *China-Africa Relations*, 160.
82. Fang Aiqing, "Media Cooperation with Africa Growing," *China Daily*, June 27, 2018.
83. China Ministry of Foreign Affairs, "The 3rd Workshop for African Journalists Held in Beijing," March 14, 2006.
84. For a list and detailed description of each of the eight journalist-training workshops held between 2004 and 2011, see Shinn and Eisenman, *China and Africa*, 203–7.
85. Shinn and Eisenman, 205.

5. AFRICA-FOCUSED PROPAGANDA

86. Li Yan, ed., "The 2nd Forum on China-Africa Media Cooperation," *Global Times*, June 16, 2014.
87. "3rd China-Africa Media Cooperation Forum opens in Beijing," *CCTV.com*, June 22, 2016.
88. African Union, "3rd Forum on China-Africa Media Issues Joint Statement to Strengthen Cooperation Ties," June 27, 2016.
89. Fang Aiqing, "Media Cooperation with Africa Growing."
90. "中非媒体合作论坛在内罗毕举行 中非媒体人聚焦数字时代" [Forum on China-Africa Media Cooperation is Held in Nairobi, Chinese and African media people focus on the digital age], *China Radio International*, November 11, 2020.
91. Xinhua, "China, African Countries to Strengthen Media Cooperation," August 25, 2022.
92. All-China Journalists Association, "非洲记联主席欧杜拉·奥都西勒致辞" [Speech by Abdulwaheed Odusile, president of the African Journalism Federation], Xinhua, February 2, 2019.
93. All-China Journalists Association, "2018 Belt and Road Journalist Forum Held in Beijing," Xinhua, June 21, 2018.
94. Adagbo Onoja, "How China Lost Nigeria," *The Diplomat*, August 25, 2020; *Ethiopian News Agency*; *Thisday Newspaper* (Nigeria); *Independent Media* (South Africa); *Alintibaha Daily Newspaper* (Sudan); *Guardian Limited* (Tanzania); *Zambia Daily Mail*; BRNN Secretariat, "Belt and Road News Network," n.d.
95. Jordache Diala, "Coopération Chine—Afrique francophone/ 65 Journalistes Africains Participent à une Formation sur la Gestion de Média Cinématographique et Télévisuel," *La Prospérité*, July 14, 2021.
96. Shinn and Eisenman, *China and Africa*, 211–19.
97. Kenneth Leiberthal, *Governing China: From Resolution Through Reform* (New York: Norton, 2003), 8.
98. This reverence for teachers can be traced back to Confucius. For work on Chinese students' deference to Western teachers, see Leng Hui, "Chinese Cultural Schema of Education: Implications for Communication Between Chinese Students and Australian Educators," *Issues in Educational Research* 15, no. 1 (2005): 17–36.
99. James L. Hevia, *Cherishing Men from Afar: Qing Guest Ritual and the Macartney Embassy of 1793* (Durham, N.C.: Duke University Press, 1995), 20.
100. In the United States, for instance, the number of university students from China rose from less than 1,000 in 1979 to over 370,000 in 2019. Dan Kopf, "Data Show Chinese Students Are Steering Clear of the US," *Quartz*, October 28, 2020.
101. See China State Council Information Office, "新时代的中国国际发展合作" [China's international development cooperation in the new era], January 2021.
102. Zhao Suisheng, "Rethinking the Chinese World Order: The Imperial Cycle and the Rise of China," *Journal of Contemporary China* 24, no. 96 (2015): 982.
103. Forum on China-Africa Cooperation, "FOCAC Johannesburg Action Plan (2016–2018)," December 25, 2015.

5. AFRICA-FOCUSED PROPAGANDA

104. Forum on China-Africa Cooperation, "FOCAC Beijing Action Plan (2019–2021)," September 12, 2018.
105. "Forum on China-Africa Cooperation Dakar Action Plan (2022–2024)."
106. Statement of Yun Sun, *Implications of China's Presence and Investment in Africa*, before the Subcommittee on Emerging Threats and Capabilities of the Committee on Armed Services United States Senate, 105th Cong. 9 (2018).
107. Cited in Lina Benabdallah, *Shaping the Future: Knowledge Production and Network-Building in China-Africa Relations* (Ann Arbor: University of Michigan Press, 2020), 40.
108. Benabdallah, 11, 33, 39, 5.
109. Breslin, "China's Global Cultural Interactions," 149; Center for Strategic and International Studies, China Power Project, "Is China Both a Source and Hub for International Students?"
110. "Why African Students Are Choosing China Over the West," *Asia by Africa*, October 15, 2018.
111. China Foreign Ministry, "中华人民共和国外交部、国家移民管理局关于暂时停止持有效中国签证、居留许可的外国人入境的公告" [Announcement of the MFA of the PRC and the National Immigration Administration on temporary suspension of entry of foreigners holding valid Chinese visas and residence permits], March 27, 2020.
112. Lo Kinling, "Coronavirus Visa Uncertainty Turns Foreign Students Against China," *South China Morning Post*, December 26, 2020.
113. Lily Kuo, "Beijing Is Cultivating the Next Generation of African Elites by Training Them in China," *Quartz*, December 14, 2017.
114. Allison, "Fixing China's Image in Africa."
115. Xu Bu, "President's Message," China Institute of International Studies, November 27, 2020.
116. Peng Yuan, "China's International Strategic Thought and Layout for a New Era," *Contemporary International Relations* 28, no. 1 (2018): 28.
117. For work on China's conception of think tanks, see Nadège Rolland, "Commanding Ideas: Think-Tanks as Platforms for Authoritarian Influence," National Endowment for Democracy, December 2020.
118. Wang Lili, "加强'智库公共外交'提升国家话语权" [Strengthening 'think-tank public diplomacy' to enhance China's discourse power], *Guangming Network Theory Channel*, December 26, 201–9. Professor Wang is affiliated with the National Development and Strategy Research Institute at the Renmin University.
119. Breslin, "China's Global Cultural Interactions," 144.
120. Patrick C. P. Ho, "Some Thoughts About the Think-Tank Alliance," Silk Road Forum 2015; "The 3rd Forum on China-Africa Media Cooperation, Beijing, People's Republic of China," African Union, June 21, 2016.
121. Chen Dongxiao, "China's 'Host Diplomacy.'"
122. Ho, "Some Thoughts About the Think-Tank Alliance."

5. AFRICA-FOCUSED PROPAGANDA

123. "Objectives," Silk Road Forum 2015; "1st BRICS Think-Tank Forum on Pragmatic Cooperation," *Frontiere Rivista Di Geocultura*, May 22, 2017.
124. "FOCAC Johannesburg Action Plan (2016–2018)"; "FOCAC Beijing Action Plan (2019–2021)."
125. "Forum on China-Africa Cooperation Dakar Action Plan (2022–2024)."
126. Yun Sun, "China-Africa Think-Tanks Forum: China Broadens Soft Power Campaigns in Africa," Brookings, October 1, 2015.
127. "China-Africa Think-Tanks: The Way Ahead," *Africa*, December 9, 2011.
128. Xia Yuanyuan, "China-Africa Think-Tank Forum Held in Beijing," *ChinAfrica*, July 4, 2018.
129. Shen Shiwei, "China-Africa Think-Tanks Forum in Beijing to Boost Development," CGTN, August 26, 2019.
130. For a discussion of Confucius Institutes in Africa between 2004 and 2011, see Shinn and Eisenman, *China and Africa*, 214–17.
131. Zhuang, "China's Confucius Institutes Rebrand."
132. Sankulleh Gibril Janko, "UTG Signs MOU with Guizhou University of China," *The Point*, May 30, 2018,
133. Breslin, "China's Global Cultural Interactions," 150.
134. Confucius Institute, "Hanban"; Yun Sun, "China-Africa Think-Tanks."
135. Abhishek G. Bhaya, "Confucius Institutes a Bedrock of China's Growing Cultural Ties with Africa," *CGTN*, August 22, 2018; Hua Xia, "Confucius Institute for Chinese Medicine Launched in South Africa," *Xinhua*, September 13, 2019.
136. "The Minister of Education of Kenya stated that Confucius Institutes Promote Mutual Understanding and Kenya Will Continue to Support Chinese Education," *YQQLM*, December 20, 2020.
137. Lai Hongyi, "China's Cultural Diplomacy: Going for Soft Power," Singapore National University, East Asian Institute (EAI) Background Brief no. 308, 2006.
138. Xinhua, "Chinese Language Gains Appeal in Africa as Benefits Grow," October 27, 2019.
139. Xinhua, "Chinese Language Gains."
140. Paul Adude, "Chinese Language Teachers to Be Put on Govt Payroll—NCDC," *Daily Monitor*, April 7, 2022.
141. Xinhua, "Chinese Language Gains."
142. Degreume, "Professional Development of Local Chinese Teachers in Cameroon: Problems and Measures," *International Journal of Scientific and Research Publications* 11, no. 1 (January 2021): 146.
143. Lynsey Chutel, "Mandarin Is Putting in Extra Work to Catch Up with European Languages in South African Classrooms," *Quartz*, February 6, 2019; Xinhua, "Chinese Language Gains."
144. Xinhua, "Chinese Language Gains."
145. Liu Haifeng, "China-Africa Relations Through the Prism of Culture—the Dynamics of China's Cultural Diplomacy with Africa," *Journal of Current Chinese Affairs* 3, (2008): 15, 20.

5. AFRICA-FOCUSED PROPAGANDA

146. Liu Hai-feng, "China-Africa Relations," 13; Mao Zedong, *Selected Readings of Mao Zedong's Works*, vol. 2 (Beijing: People's Press, 1964), 726; King C. Chen, ed., *China and the Three Worlds: A Foreign Policy Reader* (London: Macmillan, 1979), 361.
147. Liu Haifeng, "China-Africa Relations," 14; Wu Di, "毛泽东和新中国对外文化交流" [Mao Zedong and China's external cultural exchanges], 中外文化交流中心 [China and world cultural exchange] 6 (1993): 4–6.
148. Liu Haifeng, "China-Africa Relations," 12; Mao Zedong, *Selected Readings*, 726.
149. Song Enfan et al., eds., 中华人民共和国外交大事记第一卷 [Memorabilia of diplomacy of People's Republic of China], vol. 1 (Beijing: World Affairs Publishing House, 1997), 341; Fan Zhonghui, "新中国对外文化交流50年（上）" [50 years of foreign cultural exchanges in the new China], 新文化史料 [Historical materials on new culture] 5 (1999): 16–18.
150. Miu Kaijin, "中国文化外交研究" [A study of China's cultural diplomacy] (PhD diss., Party School of the CPC Central Committee, 2006), 23.
151. Liu Haifeng, "China-Africa Relations," 14; Mao Zedong, *Selected Readings*. In 1962, Herbert Passin published his illuminating book *China's Cultural Diplomacy* (New York: Praeger, 1962).
152. Lin Songtian, "Remarks by Our President," Chinese People's Association for Friendship with Foreign Countries.
153. Milton C. Cummings, "Cultural Diplomacy and the United States Government: A Survey, Americans for the Arts," June 26, 2009. Cummings's approach stands in contrast to that of Liu Haifeng, who conflates the Western notion of "cultural diplomacy" with "foreign-focused propaganda work" in ways that gloss over important differences. Liu Haifeng, "China-Africa Relations," 12.
154. Jiang Zemin, "在全国对外出版工作会议上的讲话" [Speech on National Conference of External Publicity Works], *People's Daily*, 1997.
155. "The Tenth Conference for All Chinese Diplomats Held in Beijing," *People's Daily*, August 30, 2004.
156. Liu Haifeng, "China-Africa Relations," 18.
157. 中共中央文献研究室 [Party Literature Research Centre of the CPC Central Committee], ed., "中国共产党15大以来重要文献选编" [Selective compilation of important documents since Fifteenth CPCC] 15 (2003): 37.
158. David Shambaugh, "China's Soft-Power Push: The Search for Respect," *Foreign Affairs*, July–August 2015, 99.
159. "Cultural Centers: Bringing Real China to Global Audience," *China Daily*, September 14, 2017.
160. Feng Wenyan, ed., "习近平谈国家文化软实力: 增强做中国人的骨气和底气" [Xi Jinping discusses national cultural soft power: Strengthening Chinese character and integrity], Xinhua, June 25, 2015.
161. Xiang Bo, ed., "Xi Calls for Better Fulfilling Missions of Publicity Work," Xinhua, August 22, 2018.
162. Antony Funnell, "China Pushes to Expand Its Soft Power Through Cultural Exports," *ABC News (Australia)*, May 6, 2015.

5. AFRICA-FOCUSED PROPAGANDA

163. Coco Feng, "China in 'Culture Export' Push as It Seeks to Expand Soft Power Overseas with Global Media Platforms," *South China Morning Post*, October 29, 2021.
164. Examples of such websites can be found at http://www.acpfa.org/; http://www.focac.org/eng/; http://en.cadfund.com/; http://en.cabc.org.cn/; https://www.facebook.com/Director-General-Department-of-African-Affairs-MFA-China-108995937632751/; https://www.facebook.com/CIDCAofficial/.
165. Jorge Marinho, "China in Africa (2019): Facebook & Twitter as Part of Public Diplomacy," *Center on Public Diplomacy* (blog), August 14, 2020.
166. "Cultural Centers."
167. "Cultural Centers."
168. Edith Mutethya, "Spring Festival Celebrations Gain Popularity on Africa," *China Daily*, January 30, 2020.
169. "Forum on China-Africa Cooperation Addis Ababa Action Plan, 2004–2006," Xinhua, October 19, 2006. Also see FOCAC, "China-Africa Youth Festival Opens in Beijing," August 23, 2004.
170. Guo Yan, "China Launches Asian-African Youth Festival to Promote Bandung Spirit," *CRI English*, July 29, 2016.
171. China Soong Ching Ling Foundation, "China-Africa Youth Festival Opens," August 30, 2019.
172. FOCAC, "China-Africa Youth Festival Opens in Beijing for FOCAC Anniversary," October 28, 2020.
173. "Students from 44 African Nations Join Festival in Beijing," CGTN, October 20, 2021.
174. Steve Hess and Richard Aidoo, *Charting the Roots of Anti-Chinese Populism in Africa* (Cham, Switz.: Springer, 2015), 54.
175. Interview with African graduate students at Fudan University, 2017. Also see Benabdallah, *Shaping the Future*.
176. Eisenman interviews with African students in Harbin, Beijing, Nanjing, Wuhan, and Shanghai, 2000–2019.
177. Wasserman and Madrid-Morales, "How Influential Are Chinese Media." Also see Lauren Gorfinkel et al., "CCTV's Global Outreach: Examining the Audiences of China's 'New Voice' on Africa," *Media International Australia* 151, no. 1 (May 2014): 81–88; Abdirizak Garo Guyo and Hong Yu, "How Is the Performance of Chinese News Media in Kenya? An Analysis of Perceived Audience Reception and Motivation," *New Media and Mass Communication* 79 (2019): 54–67; Yu Xiang, "China in Africa: Refiguring Centre-Periphery Media Dynamics," in *China's Media Go Global*, ed. Daya Kishan Thussu, Hugo de Burgh, and Anbin Shi (Abingdon, UK: Routledge, 2018).
178. Dani Madrid-Morales and Herman Wasserman, "How Effective Are Chinese Media in Shaping Audiences' Attitudes Towards China? A Survey Analysis in Kenya, Nigeria, and South Africa," *Online Media and Global Communication* (2022).
179. Pew Research Center, "America's Global Image Remains More Positive than China's: But Many See China Becoming World's Leading Power," July 18, 2013, 24–33; Laura

5. AFRICA-FOCUSED PROPAGANDA

Silver et al., "China's Economic Growth Mostly Welcomed in Emerging Markets, but Neighbors Wary of Its Influence," Pew Research Center, December 5, 2019, 27–40.

180. Josephine Sanny and Edem Selormey, "AD489: Africans Welcome China's Influence but Maintain Democratic Aspirations," *Afrobarometer*, November 15, 2021.
181. Richard Turcsanyi et al., "US-China Rivalry in the Global South? Insights from a Public Opinion Survey," Central European Institute of Asian Studies, October 17, 2022.
182. Dani Madrid-Morales, "Who Set the Narrative? Assessing the Influence of Chinese Global Media on News Coverage of COVID-19 in 30 African Countries," *Global Media and China* 6, no. 2 (2021): 132.
183. Madrid-Morales, 138, 146.
184. Allison, "Fixing China's Image in Africa."
185. Chinese Embassy in Ghana, "Chinese Ambassador to Ghana H.E. Ms. Sun Baohong attended the Welcoming Reception Hosted by Ghana-China Friendship Association," December 24, 2014.
186. Chinese Embassy in Ghana.
187. "Ghana and China Celebrate Treaty of Friendship," *Ghana Business News*, September 3, 2018.
188. Xinhua, "China, Africa Working Together to Defeat COVID-19 in Africa," August, 19, 2020.
189. Benabdallah, *Shaping the Future*, 12.
190. African Union, "The 3rd Forum on China-Africa."
191. Kuo, "Beijing Is Cultivating the Next Generation."
192. Allison, "Fixing China's Image in Africa."
193. Kuo, "Beijing Is Cultivating the Next Generation."
194. Shinn/Eisenman interviews with African graduate students at Fudan University, Shanghai, July 2017.
195. Teng Fei, "美国德克萨斯大学马佳士教授访问北师大并发表围绕"一带一路"框架下的中美关系主旨演讲" [Professor Joshua Eisenman from the University of Texas visited Beijing Normal University and delivered a keynote speech on Sino-US relations under the framework of the "Belt and Road Initiative"], *BNU News*, May 24, 2019.
196. Shinn/Eisenman interviews, Shanghai, July 2017; Eisenman interviews with African students in Beijing, Nanjing, Wuhan, and Zhengzhou, 2012–2020.
197. Eric Olander and Cobus Van Staden, "2020 in Review: The Impact of the Guangzhou Incidents," *The China in Africa Podcast*, 01:12:19; Peter Jegwa, "Chinese Man Held Over Racist Videos," BBC, June 20, 2022.
198. Lo Kinling, "Coronavirus Visa Uncertainty."
199. Echo Huang and Lily Kuo, "A Museum in China Put on an Exhibit Called 'This Is Africa' That Compares Africans to Animals," *Quartz*, October 13, 2017.
200. Jane Perlez, "With Blackface and Monkey Suit, Chinese Gala on Africa Causes Uproar," *New York Times*, February 16, 2018; Wode Maya, "African React to Blackface on CCTV Chinese New Year Gala," YouTube video, February 17, 2018.

6. SECURITY STRATEGY AND INTERESTS

201. Peter Jegwa, "BBC Africa Eye Exposé: Chinese Man Extradited to Malawi Over Racist Videos," BBC, July 17, 2022.
202. Jean Comaroff, *Body of Power, Spirit of Resistance* (Chicago: University of Chicago Press, 1985), 127.

6. SECURITY STRATEGY AND INTERESTS

1. "National Security Law of the People's Republic of China," China Ministry of National Defense, July 1, 2015.
2. Liu Xuanzun, "China Amends National Defense Law, Shows Country's Sense of Global Justice," *Global Times*, December 27, 2020.
3. S. D. Pradhan, "Amendment of the Chinese National Defence Law: Xi Arrogates All Powers to Mobilise Military and Civil Resources," *Times of India*, January 6, 2021.
4. Shinn/Eisenman interview, Shanghai, June 30, 2017.
5. Nadège Rolland, *A New Great Game? Situating Africa in China's Strategic Thinking*, National Bureau of Asian Research Special Report no. 91, June 2021, 2.
6. China State Council Information Office, *China's Policies on Asia-Pacific Security Cooperation*, January 2017.
7. Xi Jinping, "New Asian Security Concept for New Progress in Security Cooperation (remarks at Shanghai Expo Center on May 21, 2014)," China Ministry of Foreign Affairs.
8. Austin Ramzy and Chris Buckley, "The Xinjiang Papers: 'Absolutely No Mercy': Leaked Files Expose How China Organized Mass Detentions of Muslims," *New York Times*, November 16, 2019.
9. China State Council Information Office, *China's Military Strategy*, May 26, 2015. See also Tiffany Ma, "The PLA at an Inflection Point," in *Securing the China Dream*, ed. Roy Kamphausen, David Lai, and Tiffany Ma (Seattle: National Bureau of Asian Research, 2020), 1–3.
10. For an elaboration of the "peaceful development" strategy, see Hend Elmahly and Degang Sun, "China's Military Diplomacy Towards Arab Countries in Africa's Peace and Security: The Case of Djibouti," *Contemporary Arab Affairs* 11, no. 4 (2018): 113–14, 125–26.
11. Andrea Ghiselli, *Protecting China's Interests Overseas: Securitization and Foreign Policy* (Oxford: Oxford University Press, 2021), 37–38.
12. Xinhua, "Full Text of Chinese President Xi Jinping's Speech at Opening Ceremony of 2018 FOCAC Beijing Summit," September 3, 2018.
13. China Ministry of Foreign Affairs, "Beijing Declaration—Toward an Even Stronger China-Africa Community with a Shared Future," September 5, 2018.
14. China State Council Information Office, *China's National Defense in the New Era*, July 2019.
15. Paul Nantulya, "Strategic Application of the Tao of Soft Power: The Key to Understanding China's Expanding Influence in Africa," *African Review* 47, no. 2 (2020): 19.

16. "China Attempts to Extend Its Global Security Reach, *ANI*, May 16, 2022. For a good explanation of this vague initiative, see Chris Cash, "What Is China's Global Security Initiative?" Council on Geostrategy, September 2022.
17. "Chinese FM Elaborates on China-Proposed Global Security Initiative, Stresses Nation Will Always Be the Backbone of Guarding World Peace," *Global Times*, April 24, 2022; Zhou Pingjian, "Global Security Initiative Path to Peace and Tranquility," *Sunday Nation*, May 22, 2022.
18. Pawlos Belete, "China's Global Security Initiative," *Walta*, May 6, 2022.
19. China Ministry of Foreign Affairs, "Joint Statement of the Coordinators' Meeting on the Implementation of the Follow-up Actions of the Eighth Ministerial Conference of the Forum on China-Africa Cooperation," August 22, 2022; Paul Nantulya, "China's Deepening Ties to Africa in Xi Jinping's Third Term," Africa Center for Strategic Studies, November 29, 2022.
20. Wang Xuejun, "Developmental Peace: Understanding China's Africa Policy in Peace and Security," in *China and Africa: Building Peace and Security Cooperation on the Continent*, ed. Chris Alden, Abiodun Alao, Zhang Chun, and Laura Barber (Cham, Switz.: Palgrave Macmillan, 2018), 68, 71–79.
21. U.S. Office of the Secretary of Defense, *Annual Report to Congress: Military and Security Developments Involving the People's Republic of China 2019* (Washington, D.C., May 2, 2019), 1–3.
22. Jenny Bavisotto, "China's Military-Civil Fusion Strategy Poses a Risk to National Security," U.S. State Department Bureau of International Security and Nonproliferation, January 30, 2020.
23. Daniel R. Russel and Blake H. Berger, "Weaponizing the Belt and Road Initiative," Asia Society Policy Institute, September 2020. For example, the PLA works with China's transportation and logistics firms. See China National People's Congress, "中华人民共和国国防交通法" [National Defense Traffic Law of the People's Republic of China], September 3, 2016.
24. U.S. Defense Intelligence Agency, *China Military Power: Modernizing a Force to Fight and Win* (Washington, D.C., 2019), 19, 33–78, 107.
25. Gordon Barrass and Nigel Inkster, "Xi Jinping: The Strategist Behind the Dream," *Survival* 60, no. 1 (February/March 2018): 61.
26. Kristen Gunness and Oriana Skylar Mastro, "A Global People's Liberation Army: Possibilities, Challenges, and Opportunities," *Asia Policy*, no. 22 (July 2016): 136–39; Anna Moller-Loswick, Thomas Wheeler, Richard Smith, and Showers Mawowa, "Promoting Peace Through Sustainable Development Goals: What Role for FOCAC?" *China Quarterly of International Strategic Studies* 1, no. 3 (2015): 413.
27. Nadège Rolland, "Securing the Belt and Road: Prospects for Chinese Military Engagement Along the Silk Road," in *Securing the Belt and Road Initiative: China's Evolving Military Engagement Along the Silk Roads*, ed. Nadège Rolland, National Bureau of Asian Research, Special Report no. 80, September 2019, 3.

6. SECURITY STRATEGY AND INTERESTS

28. Mathieu Duchâtel, "Overseas Military Operations in Belt and Road Countries: The Normative Constraints and Legal Framework," in Rolland, *Securing the Belt and Road Initiative*, 11.
29. Oriana Skylar Mastro, "The Stealth Superpower: How China Hid Its Global Ambitions," *Foreign Affairs* 98, no. 1 (January/February 2019): 31–33; Jonah Victor, "China's Security Assistance in Global Competition: The Case of Africa," in *The PLA Beyond Borders*, ed. Joel Wuthnow et al. (Washington, D.C.: National Defense University, 2021), 280. See also Elmahly and Sun, "China's Military Diplomacy," 119–20.
30. Timothy R. Heath, *China's Pursuit of Overseas Security* (Santa Monica, Calif.: RAND Corporation, 2018), 4.
31. Heath, 39–40; David Brewster, "The Red Flag Follows Trade: China's Future as an Indian Ocean Power," in *China's Expanding Strategic Ambitions*, ed. Ashley J. Tellis, Alison Szalwinski, and Michael Wills (Seattle: National Bureau of Asian Research, 2019), 201; Joel Wuthnow, Phillip C. Saunders, and Ian Burns McCaslin, "PLA Overseas Operations in 2035: Inching Toward a Global Combat Capability," Strategic Forum, May 2021, 4–6.
32. Obert Hodzi, "Delegitimization and 'Re-socialization': China and the Diffusion of Alternative Norms in Africa," *International Studies* 55, no. 4 (2018): 309.
33. Graham Allison, "China vs. America: Managing the Next Clash of Civilizations," *Foreign Affairs* 96, no. 5 (September/October 2017): 88; David Lai, *Learning from the Stones: A Go Approach to Mastering China's Strategic Concept, Shi* (Strategic Studies Institute, U.S. Army War College, May 2004); Gordon Barrass and Nigel Inkster make essentially the same point in "Xi Jinping: The Strategist Behind the Dream," 56.
34. Ronak Gopaldas, "China's Salami Slicing Takes Root in Africa," Institute for Security Studies, October 3, 2018.
35. Albert Rugaba, "A Rare Insider's View of the China-Africa Minerals Trade," interview by Eric Olander, China in Africa Project, March 22, 2019.
36. J. Alexander Nuetah and Xian Xin, "Has China's Investment Pattern in Sub-Saharan Africa Been Driven by Natural Resource Quest?" *Global Journal of Emerging Market Economies* 11, no. 3 (2019): 222–23. The authors actually conclude that China's investment is *not* driven by a natural resource quest because they also look at China's financing (loans) of infrastructure projects, which far exceeds FDI in value, and find that only about 6 percent of the financing goes to mineral-related activity. They include these loans as "investments." This argument is seriously flawed, however, in that these are commercial deals whereby African governments repay China's loans, much of which goes to a Chinese company that builds the infrastructure project.
37. China State Council, "China's Policy on Minerals," December 23, 2003.
38. See, for example, Mahamat K. Dodo, "The Securitization of China's Engagement with Africa: EU Energy Security Strategy," *Journal of Alternative Perspectives in the Social Sciences* 5, no. 4 (2014): 745; Linda Peasah Owusu and Thomas Prehi Botchway," *Asian Research Journal of Arts & Social Sciences* 7, no. 1 (2018): 1–16; Antonio Andreoni,

6. SECURITY STRATEGY AND INTERESTS

"Geopolitics of Critical Minerals in Renewable Energy Supply Chains," The African Climate Foundation, September 23, 2022.

39. Abdou Rahim Lema, "China in Africa's Peace and Security Landscape," *Diplomat*, December 12, 2019.
40. Jing Gu, "Is China's Role in African Fragile States Exploitative or Developmental?" Institute of Development Studies Policy Brief, no. 91 (March 2015).
41. Shinn/Eisenman interview, Addis Ababa, June 11, 2018.
42. Meeting in Washington, D.C., February 7, 2019, attended by Shinn.
43. U.S. Office of the Secretary of Defense, *Annual Report to Congress*, 12.
44. Reuters, "China's U.S. Crude Buying Binge to Set Off Global Sweet Oil Shake-up," January 16, 2020. The value in percentage terms of China's crude imports from its six leading African suppliers in 2007—Angola, Republic of Congo, Sudan, South Africa, Equatorial Guinea, and Libya—all fell by 2016. See Cyril Obi, "The Changing Dynamics of Chinese Oil and Gas Engagements in Africa," in *China-Africa and an Economic Transformation*, ed. Arkebe Oqubay and Justin Yifu Lin (Oxford: Oxford University Press, 2019), 174.
45. Daniel Workman, "Top 15 Crude Oil Suppliers to China," World's Top Exports, March 31, 2020.
46. "China's Strategy in Africa," *Enerdata*, January 21, 2020.
47. Comments by representatives of Libyan National Army on May 24, 2019, in Washington, D.C., at meeting attended by Shinn.
48. Philippe Copinschi et al., "La Belt and Road Initiative et la Stratégie de Sécurisation des Approvisionnements Énergétiques Chinois en Afrique," *Observatoire de la Sécurité des Flux et des Matières Énergétiques*, October 2019, 34; China Ministry of Foreign Affairs, "Policy Brief: Tanzania and China—New Pragmatic Dynamic Borne of Historical Links," September 18, 2017.
49. Guy C. K. Leung, Raymond Li, and Melissa Low, "Transitions in China's Oil Economy, 1990–2010," *Eurasian Geography and Economics* 52, no. 4 (2011): 483.
50. Copinschi et al., "La Belt and Road Initiative," 38–40. For a more detailed account of China's oil interests in Sudan and South Sudan, see Luke Patey, "Learning in Africa: China's Overseas Oil Investments in Sudan and South Sudan," *Journal of Contemporary China* 26, no. 107 (2017): 756–68. See also Moawia Ali Musa Ali, "China and the Conflict in South Sudan: Security and Engagement," *Journal of Economic, Administrative and Legal Sciences* 2, no. 2 (February 2018): 111–28. For a more detailed account of China's oil interests in Niger, see Jean-Pierre Cabestan, "Beijing's 'Going Out' Strategy and Belt and Road Initiative in the Sahel: The Case of China's Growing Presence in Niger," *Journal of Contemporary China* 28, no. 118 (2019): 597–601.
51. Copinschi et al., "La Belt and Road Initiative," 40–41.
52. Copinschi et al., 41; "Ethiopia and Djibouti Sign Deal to Build Gas Pipeline," Reuters, February 17, 2019.
53. Reuben Gregg Brewer, "8 Countries with the Largest Uranium Reserves," *Motley Fool*, October 18, 2017.

6. SECURITY STRATEGY AND INTERESTS

54. World Nuclear Association, "China's Nuclear Fuel Cycle," October 2019.
55. Peter Volberding and Jason Warner, "China and Uranium: Comparative Possibilities for Agency in Statecraft in Niger and Namibia," China Africa Research Initiative, working paper no. 11, March 2011, 10–11; Cabestan, "Beijing's 'Going Out,'" 595–96.
56. Volberding and Warner, "China and Uranium," 14–15; Meredith J. Deboom, "Nuclear (Geo) Political Ecologies: A Hybrid Geography of Chinese Investment in Namibia's Uranium Sector," *Journal of Current Chinese Affairs* 46, no. 3 (2017): 53–83.
57. "Rio Tinto Officially Hands Over Namibia's Rössing Uranium to Chinese Firm," Xinhua, July 26, 2019.
58. China State Council, "China's Policy on Minerals," December 23, 2003.
59. Copinschi et al., "La Belt and Road Initiative," 42–45.
60. M. Garside, "Tantalum Mine Production Worldwide in 2019, by country," *Statista*, February 18, 2020; Tiffany Ma, "China and Congo's Coltan Connection," Project 2049 Institute, June 22, 2009; Raimund Bleischwitz, Monika Dittrich, and Chiara Pierdicca, "Coltan from Central Africa, International Trade and Implications for Any Certification," Bruges European Economic Policy Briefings, no. 23 (2012), 24; Louis Putzel et al., "中国贸易和投资与刚果盆地的森林: 喀麦隆、刚果民主共和国和加蓬三国初步调究综合报告" [Chinese trade and investment with Congo basin forests: Preliminary synthesis reports for Cameroon, the Democratic Republic of the Congo, and Gabon], Center for International Forestry Research, Indonesia, working paper no. 135, 2014, 20–22.
61. "Global Cobalt Production Hits Record High in 2021, Boosted by EV Demand," *Mining*, February 7, 2022.
62. Melissa Pistilli, "Top Cobalt Production by Country," *Investing News*, June 21, 2021; "Global and China Cobalt Industry Report 2019–2023," *Research and Markets*, June 5, 2019; Stanis Bujakera, "Congo Launches Chinese-Owned Deziwa Copper and Cobalt Mine," *Investing News*, January 15, 2020; Reuters, "China Moly Buys 95% of DRC Copper-Cobalt Mine from Freeport for $550 Million," December 13, 2020; Dionne Searcey, Michael Forsythe, and Eric Lipton, "A Power Struggle Over Cobalt Rattles the Clean Energy Revolution," *New York Times*, November 20, 2021; Christian-Géraud Neema Byamungu, "Blue Metal Blues: Cobalt, the Democratic Republic of Congo, and China," South African Institute of International Affairs, May 2022, 1–14; Shinn/Eisenman interview with financial manager for several Chinese mining firms in the DRC, Shanghai, June 27, 2017.
63. "Research Report on Metal Mineral Import in China, 2019–2023," *Research and Markets*, December 2018; Georgia Williams, "10 Top Manganese-Producing Countries," *Investing News*, August 19, 2019; Liao Shumin, "China's Yahua to Pay Up to USD145 Million for Control of Four Namibian Lithium Mines," *Yicai*, November 25, 2022.
64. "Research Report on Metal Mineral Import in China, 2019–2023"; "Steel Industry Directory," *steelonthenet.com*; David Whitehouse, "Zimbabwe Well-Placed to Benefit from China's Thirst for Chromium," *Africa Report*, July 8, 2019.
65. "Mining the Future: How China Is Set to Dominate the Next Industrial Revolution," *Foreign Policy*, May 2019, 4–5; Daniel Workman, "Platinum Exports by Country,"

6. SECURITY STRATEGY AND INTERESTS

campaigns.sgs.com, March 7, 2020; "Profiling the Top Five Platinum Producing Countries in the World," *NS Energy*, October 4, 2019.

66. Debanjali Sengupta, "China's Bauxite Imports for the First Time Crossed 100 Million Tonnes in 2019," *Al Circle*, February 25, 2020; "Research Report on Metal Mineral Import in China, 2019–2023."
67. David Whitehouse, "China Closer to Control of Guinea's Simandou North," *Africa Report*, October 18, 2019.
68. "A Rocha Ghana, 20 CSOs Sue Ghana Gov't over Atewa Bauxite Mining," *Ghana Web*, January 15, 2020; "China's Voracious Bauxite Appetite Exposing Ghana's Environmental Fragility," *Stabroek News*, May 13, 2022.
69. "Research Report on Metal Mineral Import in China, 2019–2023"; Olivia Da Silva, "Top Copper Production by Country," *Investing News*, May 28, 2019; Patrick Smith, "China-Africa Copperbelt Key to the Race for the 21st Century," *Africa Report*, September 16, 2019; Andoni Maiza-Larrarte and Gloria Claudio-Quiroga, "The Impact of Sicomines on Development in the Democratic Republic of Congo," *International Affairs* 95, no. 2 (March 2019): 429–30.
70. Reuters, "China Leads the Race to Exploit Deep Sea Minerals: U.N. Body," October 23, 2019; Tang Damin, "Is China Ready to Mine the Deep Sea?" *China Dialogue Ocean*, March 25, 2019; Joycelyn Trainer, "The Geopolitics of Deep-Sea Mining and Green Technologies," US Institute of Peace, November 3, 2022.
71. International Seabed Authority, https://isa.org.jm.
72. David Shinn, "The Indian Ocean and Deep Seabed Mining," *Young Diplomats*, February 3, 2017; International Seabed Authority, "Deep Seabed Minerals Contractors."
73. Chelsea Zhaoxi Chen, "China's Domestic Law on the Exploration and Development of Resources in Deep Seabed Areas," in *Law of the Seabed: Access, Uses and Protection of Seabed Resources*, ed. Catherine Banet (Leiden: Brill Nijhoff, 2020), 335–70; Tang Damin, "Is China Ready to Mine the Deep Sea?"
74. Peng Yining, "China Seeks Cooperation with India for Sea Mining," *China Daily*, May 7, 2015; Deep Sea Mining Watch, interactive website, http://deepseaminingwatch.msi.ucsb.edu.
75. Xinhua, "China's New Manned Submersible Completes Expedition Mission," March 10, 2019.
76. James E. Fanell, "Asia Rising: China's Global Naval Strategy and Expanding Force Structure," *Naval War College Review* 72, no. 1 (Winter 2019): 29; Ryan D. Martinson and Peter A. Dutton, "China's Distant-Ocean Survey Activities: Implications for U.S. National Security," *China Maritime Report*, no. 3 (November 2018), 8–10.
77. Hobart M. King, "REE—Rare Earth Elements and Their Uses," *geology.com*; Gustavo Ferreira and Jamie Critelli, "China's Global Monopoly on Rare-Earth Elements," *Parameters* 52, no. 1 (Spring 2022): 67.
78. King, "REE"; Paul Haenle and Scott Kennedy, "What Exactly Is the Story with China's Rare Earths?" *China File*, May 31, 2019; John Xie, "California Mine Becomes Key Part of Push to Revive US Rare Earths Processing," *Voice of America*, December 31, 2020;

6. SECURITY STRATEGY AND INTERESTS

Jamil Hijazi and James Kennedy, "Caught Between Rare Earths and Chinese Dominance," *Mining*, 4 parts, April 22–23, 2021; Felix K. Chang, "China's Rare Earth Metals Consolidation and Market Power," Foreign Policy Research Institute, March 2, 2022; Larry M. Wortzel and Kate Selley, "Breaking China's Stranglehold on the U.S. Rare Earth Elements Supply Chain," American Foreign Policy Council, April 16, 2021; Gustavo Ferreira, "China's Global Monopoly on Rare-Earth Elements," *US Army War College Quarterly: Parameters* 52, no. 1 (2022): 67.

79. Gustavo Ferreira, Jamie Critelli, and Wayne Johnson, "The Future of Rare Earth Elements in Africa in the Midst of a Debt Crisis," Civil Affairs Association, August 15, 2020.
80. King, "REE."
81. Tasneem Bulbulia, "Pensana, Chinese Company to Cooperate at Angola Project," *Mining Weekly*, July 20, 2020.
82. Kristin Vekasi, "China's Control of Rare Earth Metals," National Bureau of Asian Research, August 13, 2019. For the official policy, see China State Council Information Office, 中国的稀土状况与政策 [China's rare earth status and policy], June 20, 2016.
83. Reuters, "Pentagon Eyes Rare Earth Supplies in Africa in Push Away from China," June 6, 2019.
84. China State Council, "Food Security in China," October 15, 2019; Zongyuan Zoe Liu, "China's Farmland is in Serious Trouble," Council on Foreign Relations, February 27, 2023.
85. Xiuli Xu et al., "Science Technology, and the Politics of Knowledge: The Case of China's Agricultural Technology Demonstration Centers in Africa," *World Development* 81 (2016): 83–84; David Shinn and Joshua Eisenman, *China and Africa: A Century of Engagement* (Philadelphia: University of Pennsylvania Press, 2012), 151–52.
86. China State Council, "Food Security in China."
87. China Ministry of Foreign Affairs, "The Forum on China-Africa Cooperation Johannesburg Action Plan (2016–2018), December 10, 2015.
88. Michael Bristow, "Chinese Migrants Are Following in the Footsteps of European Settlers, by Seeking Their Fortunes in Africa," *BBC*, November 29, 2007.
89. Shinn and Eisenman, *China and Africa*, 138–39.
90. Deborah Brautigam, *Will Africa Feed China?* (Oxford: Oxford University Press, 2015), 9, 73–74, 153–59; for a list of reported land leases in Africa and their status, see appendix 1, 165–68.
91. Development Reimagined, "China's Agricultural Technology Demonstration Centers: Do They Help Africa's Food Security Needs?" May 8, 2020.
92. Brautigam, *Will Africa Feed China?* 173–74; Xiuli Xu et al., "Science, Technology," 82–89.
93. Lauren Baker, "Bridging Perceptions: China in Mozambique," MacroPolo, August 27, 2019.
94. Manitra A. Rakotoarisoa, Massimo Lafrate, and Marianna Paschali, *Why Has Africa Become a Net Food Importer?* (Rome: FAO, 2011), 1–2.
95. Duncan Miriri and Joe Bavier, "Africa's Dream of Feeding China Hits Hard Reality," Reuters, June 28, 2022.
96. Julian May, "Strengthening African Food Systems: What Role Can China Play?" Italian Institute for International Political Studies, July 29, 2021.

6. SECURITY STRATEGY AND INTERESTS

97. Huang Ji-kun, Wei Wei, Cui Qi, and Xie Wei, "The Prospects for China's Food Security and Imports: Will China Starve the World Via Imports?" *Journal of Integrative Agriculture* 16, no. 12 (2017): 2933–34.
98. "Chinese Farming Is Changing Profoundly, but Gradually," *Economist*, January 13, 2018, 39.
99. Anna Woods, "China's Strategies in Pursuing Global Food Security," *SAIS China Studies Review*, October 29, 2019.
100. "China's Road Map to Food Security," *Gro Intelligence*, November 15, 2018; Hongzhou Zhang and Mingjiang Li, "Hunting for Food: A New Driving Force in Chinese Foreign Policy," *Harvard Asia Quarterly* 16, no. 1 (Spring 2014): 49.
101. Hongzhou Zhang, *Securing the "Rice Bowl": China and Global Food Security* (Singapore: Palgrave Macmillan, 2019), 46–48.
102. Peter Ford, "Big Promises, Few Results: Chinese Farms Falter in Uganda," *Christian Science Monitor*, September 10, 2019.
103. "World Integrated Trade Solution," *WITS Worldbank*; Wandile Sihlobo, "Should South Africa Boost Its Agricultural Exports to China?" *Agricultural Trade*, January 16, 2020.
104. Zhangi and Li, "Hunting for Food," 55–56; Zhang, *Securing the "Rice Bowl*," 53.
105. Mark Godfrey, "China to Revise Key Law on Distant-Water Fishing," *Seafood Source*, July 2, 2019.
106. Hongzhou Zhang, "China's Fishing Industry: Current Status, Government Policies, and Future Prospects," in *Becoming a Great 'Maritime Power': A Chinese Dream*, ed. Michael McDevitt (Washington, D.C.: CNA, June 2016): 100–116; Miren Gutiérrez et al., "China's Distant-Water Fishing Fleet: Scale, Impact and Governance," Overseas Development Institute, June 2020, 8, 21.
107. Stimson Center, "Shining a Light: The Need for Transparency Across Distant Water Fishing," November 1, 2019, 23.
108. Stimson Center, "Shining a Light," 15; comment by Sally Yozell, director of the Environmental Security Program at the Stimson Center in Washington, during a briefing on November 7, 2019, attended by Shinn.
109. Baker, "Bridging Perceptions."
110. Stop Illegal Fishing, "Madagascar Agrees to a 10 Year Fisheries Agreement with Chinese Consortium," September 22, 2018.
111. "Chinese Trawlers Bust in SA Waters Allowed to Depart," *Mail and Guardian*, April 29, 2020.
112. Reuters, "From Africa to South America, China's Fishing Fleet Outstrips the Competition," February 23, 2018.
113. Environmental Justice Foundation, "Fear, Hunger and Violence: Human Rights in Ghana's Industrial Trawl Fleet," 2020; Environmental Justice Foundation, "At What Cost? How Ghana Is Losing Out in Fishing Arrangements with China's Distant Water Fleet," March 23, 2021.
114. Mona Samari, "How Ghana's Weak Penalties Are Letting Trawlers Off the Hook," *China Dialogue Ocean*, October 3, 2019; Environmental Justice Foundation and Hen

7. PROTECTING INTERESTS AND MANAGING CONFLICT

Mpoano, "Stolen at Sea: How Illegal 'Saiko' Fishing Is Fueling the Collapse of Ghana's Fisheries," 2019; Gutiérrez, *China's Distant-Water Fishing Fleet*, 29.
115. Environmental Justice Foundation, "New Trawlers Arrive from China as Ghana's Fisheries Teeter on Brink of Collapse," May 27, 2020.
116. Eric Olander, "China's Distant Fishing Fleet Is Decimating What's Left of Ghana's Fish Stocks," China Global South Project podcast with Kofi Agbogah, July 24, 2019.
117. "Illegal Chinese Fishing Vessel Fined Over $1m," *Citi Newsroom*, October 10, 2019.
118. "Our Commitment to Ending Saiko is Very Strong—Akufo-Addo," *Modern Ghana*, August 21, 2020.
119. Environmental Justice Foundation, "Liberian Fishing Communities Threatened by Chinese Supertrawlers," July 14, 2020.
120. Chris Chase, "Liberia Refuses Licenses for Chinese-flagged Trawlers," *Seafood Source*, October 13, 2020.
121. Sherpa, "Mauritania-China Fisheries Agreement: Civil Society Appeals to EU and Mauritanian Government," April 17, 2014.
122. Mark Godfrey, "China's Contrasting Polices on Yangtze, Mauritania Reveal Its Global Fisheries Agenda," *Seafood Source*, September 24, 2020.
123. "China Loans Mauritania $87m for Port Construction," *North Africa Post*, January 8, 2020.
124. Louise Hunt, "Fishmeal Factories Threaten Food Security in The Gambia," *China Dialogue Ocean*, November 28, 2019; Louise Hunt, "Sea Shepherd Helps The Gambia Tackle Illegal Fishing," *Maritime Executive*, July 14, 2020. For China's account, see Chinese Embassy in The Gambia, Economic and Commerce Office, "鱼粉厂有关问题在冈比亚及次区域持续发酵" [Problems related to fishmeal factories continue to simmer in The Gambia and the subregion], October 25, 2019.
125. Mark Godfrey, "China's Distant-Water Fishing Sector Lobbies Government for Support for Fishing Bases," *Seafood Source*, May 29, 2020.
126. Woods, "China's Strategies in Pursuing Global Food Security."
127. Brautigam, *Will Africa Feed China?* 153–54, 156–58.

7. PROTECTING INTERESTS AND MANAGING CONFLICT

1. Rogier Creemers, "National Security Law of the People's Republic of China," *China Copyright and Media* (blog), July 2, 2015. Available in English and Chinese at https://chinacopyrightandmedia.wordpress.com.
2. Kristen Gunness and Oriana Skylar Mastro, "A Global People's Liberation Army: Possibilities, Challenges, and Opportunities," *Asia Policy*, no. 22 (July 2016): 137–38.
3. Wang Hongyi, "New Security Challenges in Africa: Implications for China-Africa Cooperation," *China International Studies*, no. 72 (September/October 2018): 82; Luke Patey, "Learning in Africa: China's Overseas Oil Investments in Sudan and South Sudan," *Journal of Contemporary China* 26, no. 107 (2017): 762–64.

7. PROTECTING INTERESTS AND MANAGING CONFLICT

4. Wang Duanyong and Zhao Pei, "Security Risks Facing Chinese Actors in Sub-Saharan Africa: The Case of the Democratic Republic of Congo," in *China and Africa: Building Peace and Security Cooperation on the Continent*, ed. Chris Alden, Abiodun Alao, Zhang Chun, and Laura Barber (Cham, Switz.: Palgrave Macmillan, 2018), 263.
5. Standard Bank, "FOCAC: 'Forum for China-Africa Cooperation': Africa Still Solidly in the Crosshairs of China Growth," August 23, 2018.
6. Hannah Postel, "We May Have Been Massively Overestimating the Number of Chinese Migrants in Africa," *African Arguments*, December 19, 2016.
7. China Africa Research Initiative, "Data: Chinese Workers in Africa," http://www.sais-cari.org/.
8. Wang Duanyong, "The Safety of Chinese Citizens Abroad: A Quantitative Interpretation of the 'Special Notices for Chinese Citizens Abroad' (2008–2010)," *Journal of Current Chinese Affairs* 42, no. 1 (2013): 170, 175, 180.
9. David Shinn and Joshua Eisenman, *China and Africa: A Century of Engagement* (Philadelphia: University of Pennsylvania Press), 179–81; Patey, "Learning in Africa," 765; Ulf Laessing and Sui-Lee Wee, "Kidnapped Chinese Workers Freed in Sudan Oil State," Reuters, February 7, 2012.
10. Shinn and Eisenman, *China and Africa*, 181–82; Reuters, "Two Killed as Chinese Workers Riot in Eq. Guinea," March 31, 2008; Lina Benabdallah, "China's Peace and Security Strategies in Africa: Building Capacity Is Building Peace?" *African Studies Quarterly* 16, no. 3–4 (December 2016): 27; BBC, "Angola Deports China 'Gangsters,'" August 25, 2012; Cheryl Mei-ting Schmitz, "Significant Others: Security and Suspicion in Chinese-Angolan Encounters," *Journal of Current Chinese Affairs* 43, no. 1 (2014): 41–69.
11. David Lumu, "Uganda Security Arrests 4 Chinese Gangsters," *New Vision*, January 8, 2022.
12. Richard Asante, "China's Security and Economic Engagement in West Africa: Constructive or Destructive?" *China Quarterly of International Strategic Studies* 3, no. 4 (2017): 589; Emmanuel Akyeampong, "China in West Africa's Regional Development and Security Plans," *Africa Development* 40, no. 4 (2015): 16.
13. Xu Weizhong, Yu Wensheng, and Wang Lei, "An Analysis of the Security Situation in Africa," in *International Strategic Relations and China's National Security*, ed. Institute for Strategic Studies National Defense University of the PLA, 2015, 283–84; "埃博拉阴影下中国在非投资现状如何？" [What is the status of China's investment in Africa under the shadow of Ebola?], *China Daily*, August 21, 2014.
14. Hannah Beech, "As More Chinese Fall Victim to Terrorism, Beijing Fumbles for a Response," *Time*, November 26, 2015; Xinhua, "习近平就3中国公民在马里人质劫持事件中遇害作出重要批示" [Xi Jinping makes important comments on the murder of three Chinese citizens in the hostage-taking incident in Mali], November 21, 2015.
15. "Chinese National Confirmed Dead in Somali Hotel Blast," *China Daily*, July 27, 2015.
16. Matthew T. Page, "The Intersection of China's Commercial Interests and Nigeria's Conflict Landscape," United States Institute of Peace, Special Report (September 2018): 7;

7. PROTECTING INTERESTS AND MANAGING CONFLICT

Chinedu Asadu, "Three Chinese Nationals Abducted in Nigeria, Police Say," Associated Press, January 6, 2022.
17. "Nigeria's Balanced and Diverse Relationship with China Is Key to Sustainability," *Belt and Road Advisory*, February 10, 2019.
18. "Consulate in Nigeria Urges Local Police to Rescue Kidnapped Chinese Workers: FM Spokesperson," *Global Times*, April 7, 2021; Shannon Tiezzi, "Kidnappings Plague Chinese Worksites in Nigeria," *Diplomat*, April 9, 2021.
19. "3 Chinese Nationals Killed in CAR Attack," *VOA*, October 5, 2018.
20. "China's MFA Speaks Out on Zambian-Chinese Tensions," *Africa Times*, November 23, 2018.
21. Reuters, "Congo Mine Attack Kills Three Chinese Nationals: Xinhua," April 6, 2020.
22. Associated Press, "China Says 5 Citizens Kidnapped from Congo Mining Operation," November 21, 2021.
23. John Wanjohi, "Al-Shabaab Militants Attack Chinese Construction Company in Lamu, Blow Up Construction Equipment," *Mwakilishi*, February 9, 2020; "Gunmen Burn Eight Lapsset Road Construction Vehicles in Lamu," *Horseed Media*, January 23, 2022; Agence France Presse, "Five Killed in Attack Near Kenya's Border with Somalia," March 12, 2022. For a study of attacks by Maasai workers on Chinese construction workers building Kenya's Standard Gauge Railway, see Weidi Zheng, "The Silent China: Toward an Anti-Essentialism Approach for South-South Encounters," *International Journal of Communication* 16 (2022): 1898–1917.
24. Siyanne Mekonnen, "News Analysis: Amhara State Deploys Its Forces to Neighboring Benishangul Gumuz State; Move Follows Recent Killings of Security Forces by Armed Rebels," *Addis Standard*, September 13, 2021.
25. Chinese Embassy in South Africa "Statement on the Recent Murder of Chinese Citizens in South Africa," August 24, 2020; Anna Cox, "We're Being Slaughtered by Criminals, Says Chinese Community in SA After Brutal Killing of Couple," *Star*, August 19, 2020.
26. Shinn/Eisenman interview with prominent member of Chinese community, Johannesburg, June 6, 2018; Shinn/Eisenman interview with Eric Wang, China-Africa Business Council, Beijing, June 22, 2017; Xu, Yu, and Wang, "Analysis of the Security Situation," 284; Wang Duanyong and Zhao Pei, "Security Risks," 260; "Liberia: Robberies Reports Scare Chinese Railway Investors," *Front Page Africa Online*, February 28, 2019.
27. Shinn/Eisenman interview with professor at Fudan University, Shanghai, June 28, 2017.
28. China House (Hongxiang Huang and Yanran Lyu) selected and monitored the students, who resided in China and countries around the world where they were studying. David Shinn designed the questions and provided guidance to each student group by Skype. In eleven of the countries the students completed 503 interviews using social media such as WeChat, QQ, Zhihu, Facebook, and email. In Kenya the students conducted mostly face-to-face interviews with 291 respondents. The response rate was 41 percent in Zimbabwe but averaged about 20 percent in the other ten countries where social media was the method for contact. Different teams of students, usually four, contacted the Chinese

7. PROTECTING INTERESTS AND MANAGING CONFLICT

communities in each country. There were nine students on the Kenya team. Many of the Chinese refused to respond because they did not fully understand how the information would be used or simply did not want to devote time to an interview. A few requested reimbursements for their time (not a chance). Several of the questions had to be modified as the survey progressed because it became clear they were too personal or were not capturing essential information. The different teams did not compile all the results in a manner that permitted precise comparisons. Consequently, even though the total number of responses was significant, we judge the results to be more anecdotal than scientific.

29. Shinn/Eisenman interview with Major General Zhu Chenghu, National Defense University, Beijing, June 21, 2017; Mathieu Duchâtel, Oliver Bräuner, and Zhou Hang, "Protecting China's Overseas Interests: The Slow Shift Away from Non-interference," SIPRI Policy Paper, no. 41 (June 2014): 53; Jonas Parello-Plesner and Mathieu Duchâtel, *China's Strong Arm: Protecting Citizens and Assets Abroad* (London: International Institute for Strategic Studies, 2015), 115.
30. Patey, "Learning in Africa," 764.
31. Obert Hodzi, *The End of China's Non-Intervention Policy in Africa* (Cham, Switz.: Palgrave Macmillan, 2019), 229–30.
32. Gunness and Mastro, "Global People's Liberation Army," 141–43; Xu, Yu, and Wang, "Analysis of the Security Situation," 284–85; Parello-Plesner and Duchâtel, *China's Strong Arm*, 134.
33. Shinn/Eisenman interview with He Wenping, Chinese Academy of Social Sciences, Beijing, June 20, 2017; Mathieu Duchâtel, Richard Gowan, and Manuel Lafont Rapnouil, "Into Africa: China's Global Security Shift," European Council on Foreign Relations Policy Brief, June 2016, 11.
34. James M. Dorsey, "Chinese Investments in the Arab Maelstrom," in *Securing the Belt and Road Initiative: Risk Assessment, Private Security and Special Insurances Along the New Wave of Chinese Outbound Investments*, ed. Alessandro Arduino and Xue Gong (Singapore: Palgrave Macmillan, 2018), 241.
35. Andrea Ghiselli, "Market Opportunities and Political Responsibilities: The Difficult Development of Chinese Private Security Companies Abroad," *Armed Forces and Society* 46, no. 1 (January 2020): 31.
36. Shinn/Eisenman interview with Africa specialists at the China Institute of International Studies, Beijing, June 23, 2017.
37. Evan Osnos, "Making China Great Again," *New Yorker*, January 8, 2018; Chris Alden and Lu Jiang, "Brave New World: Debt, Industrialization and Security in China-Africa Relations," *International Affairs* 95, no. 3 (2019): 652–53; Yu Xiang and Jinpu Wang, "Wolf Warrior II: What the Blockbuster Movie Tells Us About China's Views on Africa, *Conversation*, September 1, 2022.
38. Weidong Liu, *The Belt and Road Initiative: A Pathway Towards Inclusive Globalization* (London: Routledge, 2019), 83–84.
39. Patey, "Learning in Africa," 763–64.

7. PROTECTING INTERESTS AND MANAGING CONFLICT

40. Gunness and Mastro, "Global People's Liberation Army," 143–44; Parello-Plesner and Duchâtel, *China's Strong Arm*, 39–40.
41. Patey, "Learning in Africa," 765–66.
42. Duchâtel, Bräuner, and Zhou, "Into Africa," 59; Shinn/Eisenman interview with Africa specialists at the China Institute of International Studies, Beijing, June 23, 2017.
43. Shen Zhixiong, "On China's Military Diplomacy in Africa," in Alden et al., *China and Africa*, 108; Andrea Ghiselli, "Continuity and Change in China's Strategy to Protect Overseas Interests," *War on the Rocks*, August 4, 2021.
44. Ghiselli, "Market Opportunities," 32.
45. Ghiselli, 31.
46. UN Security Council, "Adopting Resolution 2155 (2014), Extends Mandate of Mission in South Sudan, Bolstering Its Strength to Quell Surging Violence," May 27, 2014, section 4(a)ii; Parello-Plesner and Duchâtel, *China's Strong Arm*, 138.
47. Shinn/Eisenman meeting with a dozen experts at Shanghai Academy of Social Sciences, Shanghai, June 30, 2017; Parello-Plesner and Duchâtel, *China's Strong Arm*, 50–53.
48. Jin Zheng and Christine Lagat, "Kenya's Railway Police Officers Look Forward to Training Stint in China," Xinhua, May 26, 2018.
49. Kristin Huang, "China Offers to Send Security Team to Nigeria," *South China Morning Post*, December 18, 2021.
50. Patey, "Learning in Africa," 767.
51. Shinn/Eisenman interview with the president of a Chinese company in Africa, Shanghai, June 29, 2017.
52. Shinn/Eisenman interview with Michael Sun, member of the Mayoral Committee for Public Safety, Johannesburg, June 6, 2018; Zhao Yanrong, "Center Brings Security to Chinese in Johannesburg," *China Daily*, March 25, 2013; Abdur Rahman Alfa Shaban, "South Africa Gets 13th Chinese Police Co-op Unit, Language Center," *Africa News*, November 2, 2018; Alden and Lu, "Brave New World," 655; Riaan Grobler, "Fake News: Reports About Chinese Police Stations Opening in SA Are Bogus, and 2 Years Old," *News 24*, May 13, 2020.
53. China House survey in South Africa, February–March 2019.
54. China House survey in Angola, February–March 2019.
55. BBC, "Uganda Orders Military to Protect Chinese Businesses," November 15, 2018; Baker Batte, "Army Gives LDUs Shoot-to-kill Orders," *Observer*, January 1, 2020; Chinese Embassy in Uganda, "乌干达总统穆塞韦尼指示安全部门全力保护在乌中国投资者" [Ugandan president Museveni instructs Security Department to fully protect Chinese investors in Uganda], November 14, 2018.
56. Shinn/Eisenman interview, Shanghai, June 29, 2017.
57. Changhong Pei and Wen Zheng, *China's Outbound Foreign Direct Investment Promotion System* (Heidelberg, Ger.: Springer, 2015), 162; remarks at press conference on December 2, 2015, by Qian Keming, vice minister of commerce, http://english.mofcom.gov.cn/.
58. Parello-Plesner and Duchâtel, *China's Strong Arm*, 41–50; for examples of embassy warnings to Chinese nationals, see CGTN News, "Zimbabwe Turmoil: Chinese Embassy in

7. PROTECTING INTERESTS AND MANAGING CONFLICT

Harare Warns Citizens to Stay Vigilant and Take Precautions," November 18, 2017; "On Reminding Chinese Citizens in Mozambique to Strengthen Safety Precautions," Chinese Embassy announcement, March 28, 2021; Yin Yeping and Tao Mingyang, "Chinese Projects in Sudan Face Uncertainty Due to Local Tensions," *Global Times*, October 26, 2021.

59. Lulu Chen and Chloe Whiteaker, "Where Hong Kong and Mainland China Have Extradition Pacts," *Bloomberg*, June 11, 2019; "Hide and Seek: China's Extradition Problem," Safeguard Defenders, February 2022, 8.
60. Abdi Guled, "Somali Pirates Say $4 Million Ransom Paid for Coal Ship," Reuters, December 27, 2009.
61. Parello-Plesner and Duchâtel, *China's Strong Arm*, 43, 133–34.
62. China House survey in Kenya, July 2019.
63. China House survey in Angola, February–March 2019.
64. China House survey in Ethiopia, August–September 2019.
65. China House survey in Nigeria, May–June 2019.
66. China House survey in Sudan, August–September 2019.
67. China House survey in all twelve countries, 2019.
68. Ghiselli, "Market Opportunities," 34–38; Alessandro Arduino, "Growing Demand in Africa for China's Private Security Contractors," interview by Eric Orlander, *The China in Africa Project*, December 3, 2019; Helena Legarda and Meia Nouwens, "Guardians of the Belt and Road: The Internationalization of China's Private Security Companies," Mercator Institute for China Studies, August 16, 2018, 4–5; Alessandro Arduino, "China's Private Army: Protecting the New Silk Road," *Diplomat*, March 20, 2018; Shinn/Eisenman interview with Michael Sun, Johannesburg, June 6, 2018; Christopher Spearin, "China's Private Military and Security Companies: 'Chinese Muscle' and the Reasons for U.S. Engagement," *Prism* 8, no. 4 (June 2020): 44; Paul Nantulya, "Chinese Security Contractors in Africa," Carnegie-Tsinghua Center for Global Policy, October 8, 2020.
69. Alessandro Arduino, "Chinese Private Security Firms Are Growing Their Presence in Africa: Why It Matters," *Conversation*, August 8, 2022.
70. Nantulya, "Chinese Security Contractors in Africa."
71. The PAP is a branch of the PLA that operates under the Ministry of Public Security but reports directly to the CPC's Central Military Commission.
72. Xie Wenting, "Chinese Security Companies in Great Demand as Overseas Investment Surges," *Global Times*, June 23, 2016; Legarda and Nouwens, "Guardians of the Belt and Road," 4–5, 14; Alessandro Arduino, "China's Private Security Companies: The Evolution of a New Security Actor," in Arduino and Xue Gong, *Securing the Belt and Road Initiative*, 95–98; M. B. van Meel, "Chinese Private Military Security Companies in Contemporary Africa" (M.A. thesis, Leiden University, 2019) 32–39; Paul Nantulya, "Chinese Security Firms Spread along the African Belt and Road," Africa Center for Strategic Studies, June 15, 2021. For a good overview of Chinese PSCs, see Sergey

7. PROTECTING INTERESTS AND MANAGING CONFLICT

Sukhankin, "Chinese Private Security Contractors: New Trends and Future Prospects," *China Brief* 20, no. 9 (May 15, 2020): 18–24.
73. Charles Clover, "Chinese Private Security Companies Go Global," *Financial Times*, February 26, 2017; Legarda and Nouwens, "Guardians of the Belt and Road," 13; Minnie Chan and Wendy Wu, "Why a Private US Military Firm Is of Value to China's Belt and Road Mission," *South China Morning Post*, July 15, 2018; Yunnan Chen, "China's Role in Nigerian Railway Development and Implications for Security and Development," United States Institute of Peace, Special Report no. 423 (April 2018): 6; van Meel, "Chinese Private Military," 27; Nantulya, "Chinese Security Contractors in Africa"; Shuwen Zheng and Ying Xia, "Private Security Companies in Kenya and the Impact of Chinese Actors," presentation at virtual conference hosted by the China Africa Research Initiative, Washington, D.C., October 1, 2020.
74. Frontier Services Group, http://fsgroup.com; Blake Schmidt, "Blackwater Mercenary Prince Has a New $1 Trillion Chinese Boss," *Bloomberg*, February 9, 2019; Anthony Loewenstein, "From Blackwater to Batteries," *Foreign Policy*, January 25, 2019; Alessandro Arduino, *China's Private Army: Protecting the New Silk Road* (Singapore: Palgrave Macmillan, 2018), 156–57; Alessandro Arduino, "China's Belt and Road Security: The Increasing Role of Insurance and Private Security Companies," in Arduino and Xue Gong, *Securing the Belt and Road Initiative*, 49.
75. China Overseas Security Group, http://www.cosg-ss.com/.
76. Legarda and Nouwens, "Guardians of the Belt and Road," 13; Xie Wenting, "Chinese Security Companies."
77. Liu Xin, "Private Security Companies Struggle to Go Abroad Due to Legal Restrictions," *Global Times*, December 23, 2015.
78. China Security Technology Group, http://cstghk.com.
79. Bose Simeon, "Nigerian Security Firm Signs Security Service Agreement with Chinese Company," *Nigeria Maritime 360*, February 21, 2019.
80. China House survey in Nigeria, May–June 2019.
81. Alessandro Arduino, "The Footprint of Chinese Security Companies in Africa," China Africa Research Initiative working paper no. 35, March 2020, 16; Hua Xin Zhong An, https://www.hkcorporationsearch.com/companies/1721225/; Nantulya, "Chinese Security Contractors in Africa."
82. Hanwei International Security Services Co., http.//hanweiss.com; Nantulya, "Chinese Security Contractors in Africa."
83. "Armed Escorts at the Maritime Level," Baidu Encyclopedia.
84. Veerle Nouwens, "Who Guards the 'Maritime Silk Road?'" *War on the Rocks*, June 24, 2020; Overseas Security Guardians (HK) Co., http://www.osgjh.com/en/; Zhongjun Hong Security Group, https://zjjhgroup.com.
85. China Overseas Security Services, http://www.cosg-ss.com/.
86. Lu Anqi, "For Safety's Sake," ChinAfrica Project, February 2015.
87. Cabestan, "China's Involvement," 601.

7. PROTECTING INTERESTS AND MANAGING CONFLICT

88. "Zambia's New Chinese Police Officers Removed After Outcry," *Tuesday's World Events*, January 9, 2018; Xinhua, "八名赞比亚华人入编赞预备役警察" [Eight Zambian Chinese join the Zambian reserve police], December 19, 2017.
89. Farayi Machamire, "Two Chinese Men Shoots ZANU PF MP's Son in Harare Over $8500," *Zimbabwe News*, February 21, 2018.
90. Shinn/Eisenman interview with researchers at China Institute of International Studies, Beijing, June 23, 2017.
91. Peter Connolly, "Chinese Evacuation Operations. Part I: A New Consideration for the Pacific," Australian National University, 2018.
92. Adam B. Siegel, *Eastern Exit: The Noncombatant Evacuation Operation (NEO) from Mogadishu Somalia, in January 1991* (Alexandria, Va.: Center for Naval Analyses, October 1991), 9; Christopher D. Yung and Ross Rostici, *China's Out of Area Naval Operations: Case Studies, Trajectories, Obstacles, and Potential Solutions* (Washington, D.C.: National Defense University Press, December 2010), 14.
93. Cindy Hurst, "Compelling Reasons for the Expansion of Chinese Military Forces," *Military Review* 97, no. 6 (November–December 2017): 30.
94. Xinhua, "Chinese Nationals Evacuated from Chad," February 2, 2008; "Fighting Intensifies in Chad; Chinese Moved to Safety," *China Daily*, February 4, 2008.
95. Xinhua, "Backgrounder: China's Major Overseas Evacuations in Recent Years," March 30, 2015; Duchâtel, Bräuner, and Zhou, "Into Africa," 51.
96. Shaio H. Zerba, "China's Libya Evacuation Operation: A New Diplomatic Imperative—Overseas Citizen Protection," *Journal of Contemporary China* 23, no. 90 (2014): 1093–94, 1100–1101; Peter Connolly, "Protecting Citizens Overseas: The Policy, the Power, and Now the Movie," in *China Story Yearbook 2018: Power*, ed. Jane Golley et al. (Canberra: ANU Press, 2019), 320; Parello-Plesner and Duchâtel, *China's Strong Arm*, 107–14; Ghiselli, *Protecting China's Interests Overseas*, 1, 33, 149.
97. Xinhua, "Chinese Nationals to Evacuate from Warring Libya," July 31, 2014; Xinhua, "134 Chinese Fly Home After Being Evacuated from Libya," August 3, 2014; Hurst, "Compelling Reasons," 33.
98. China Ministry of Foreign Affairs, "Foreign Ministry Spokesperson Hua Chunying's Regular Press Conference on December 31, 2012," January 1, 2013.
99. Xinhua, "Central African Republic: Murderers of 3 Chinese Nationals Not to 'Go Unpunished'—Central African President," October 23, 2018.
100. Yuwen Wu, "China's Oil Fears Over South Sudan Fighting," BBC, January 8, 2014.
101. "China Evacuates Oil Workers from South Sudan Oilfields Over Fighting: Report," *Sudan Tribune*, May 22, 2015.
102. Laura Zhou, "Chinese Firms Evacuate 330 Staff in South Sudan as Deadly Fighting Escalates," *South China Morning Post*, July 14, 2016.
103. "China Evacuates Embassy Staff and Medics from Juba," *South China Morning Post*, July 17, 2016; Xinhua, "49名我在南苏丹公民顺利撤离至乌干达" [49 of my citizens in South Sudan successfully evacuated to Uganda], July 17, 2016.

7. PROTECTING INTERESTS AND MANAGING CONFLICT

104. Reuters, "China's CNPC Says Evacuates Most of Its Staff from South Sudan," July 19, 2016.
105. Xu, Yu, and Wang, "Analysis of the Security Situation," 283–84.
106. Ian Taylor, "China's Response to the Ebola Virus Disease in West Africa," *Round Table* 104, no. 1 (2015): 49.
107. China State Council, *China's National Defense in the New Era*, July 2019; Ghiselli, *Protecting China's Interests Overseas*, 150–51.
108. Nathan Beauchamp-Mustafaga, "PLA Navy Used for First Time in Naval Evacuation from Yemen Conflict," *China Brief* 15, no. 7 (April 3, 2015): 1–3; Jane Perlez and Yufan Huang, "Yemen Evacuation Shows Chinese Navy's Growing Role," *New York Times*, March 31, 2015.
109. Connolly, "Protecting Citizens Overseas," 323–25; Robert Farley, "Operation Red Sea: The Chinese Public's Introduction to Beijing's New Navy," *Diplomat*, November 28, 2018.
110. Andrew Scobell and Nathan Beauchamp-Mustafaga, "The Flag Lags but Follows: The PLA and China's Great Leap Outward," in *Chairman Xi Remakes the PLA: Assessing Chinese Military Reforms*, ed. Phillip C. Saunders et al. (Washington, D.C.: National Defense University Press, 2019), 189–90.
111. Austin Bodetti, "What Ethiopia's Ethnic Unrest Means for China," *The Diplomat*, December 10, 2020.
112. Duchâtel, Bräuner, and Zhou, "Into Africa," 49–51; page 50 contains a list of all the Chinese institutions involved in the Libyan evacuation operation.
113. Marc Lanteigne, "Fire Over Water: China's Strategic Engagement of Somalia and the Gulf of Aden Crisis," *Pacific Review* 26, no. 3 (2013): 301; Zerba, "China's Libya Evacuation," 1103–4, 1107–12; David Brewster, "The Red Flag Follows Trade: China's Future as an Indian Ocean Power," in *Strategic Asia 2019: China's Expanding Strategic Ambitions*, ed. Ashley J. Tellis et al. (Seattle: National Bureau of Asian Research, 2019), 189.
114. Mathieu Duchâtel, "Overseas Military Operations in Belt and Road Countries," National Bureau of Asian Research special report no. 89 (September 2019): 16; for an assessment of China's planning for future evacuations, see Michael S. Chase, "The PLA and Far Seas Contingencies: Chinese Capabilities for Noncombatant Evacuation Operations," in *The People's Liberation Army and Contingency Planning in China*, ed. Andrew Scobell et al. (Washington, D.C.: National Defense University Press, 2015), 307–13.
115. Wang Xuejun, "Developmental Peace: Understanding China's Africa Policy in Peace and Security," in Alden et al., *China and Africa*, 76–78.
116. Comments by Dai Weilai, Anhui University, at conference in Washington, D.C., July 17, 2018.
117. Li Xinfeng, Zhang Chunyu, and Zhang Mengying, "China's Role in Peace and Security Cooperation in the Gulf of Guinea Region," *China International Studies* 66 (September/October 2017): 55.
118. "Mediation System," ChinaLawInfo Database, May 31, 2010.
119. United States Department of Justice, "Mediation," https://justice.gov.

7. PROTECTING INTERESTS AND MANAGING CONFLICT

120. Mordechai Chaziza, "China's Mediation Efforts in the Middle East and North Africa: Constructive Conflict Management," *Strategic Analysis* 42, no. 1 (2018): 30–31.
121. Xiaohui Wu and Cheng Qian, "Culture of China's Mediation in Regional and International Affairs," Belfer Center, January 2010, 5–8; Wang Xiaohong and Wang Qingxiao, "现代化前夕的中国调解" [Chinese mediation on the eve of modernization], *China Law Network*; Hong Liu, "试论调解在解决中非民商事争议中的地位" [On the status of mediation in resolving China-Africa civil and commercial disputes], *West Africa and Asia*, no. 2 (2020): 137–60.
122. David Shinn, "China and the Conflict in Darfur," *Brown Journal of World Affairs* 16, no. 1 (Fall/Winter 2009): 91–93.
123. Degang Sun and Yahia Zoubir, "China's Participation in Conflict Resolution in the Middle East and North Africa: A Case of Quasi-Mediation Diplomacy?" *Journal of Contemporary China* 27, no. 110 (2018): 231–32; Dan Large, "China's Role in the Mediation and Resolution of Conflict in Africa," Oslo Forum 2008, 39; Jian Junbo, "China in International Conflict Management: Darfur Issue as a Case," in Alden et al., *China and Africa*, 155–59; Xiaohui and Cheng, "Culture of China's Mediation."
124. Patey, "Learning in Africa," 763.
125. Comment made at meeting in Washington, D.C., January 11, 2019, attended by Shinn.
126. Comment made during an April 15, 2020, teleconference in Washington, D.C. See also Laura Barber, "China's Response to Sudan's Political Transition," United States Institute of Peace, special report no. 466, May 2020, 5.
127. Barber, "China's Response," 8–10.
128. Obert Hodzi, *The End of China's Non-Intervention Policy in Africa* (Cham, Switz.: Palgrave Macmillan, 2019), 187.
129. Yuwen Wu, "China's Oil Fears Over South Sudan Fighting," *BBC*, January 8, 2014; "王毅会见南苏丹冲突双方谈判代表" [Wang Yi meets with negotiators from both sides of the conflict in South Sudan], China Ministry of Foreign Affairs, January 7, 2014.
130. Xu, Yu, and Wang, "Analysis of the Security Situation," 280; Zhang Ying, "China's Diplomacy in Africa: Ideas and Practices,' *China International Studies* 69 (March/April 2018): 37–38.
131. Theo Neethling, "China's Evolving Role and Approach to International Peacekeeping: The Cases of Mali and South Sudan," *Australasian Review of African Studies* 38, no. 2 (2017): 24.
132. Daniel Wagner and Giorgio Cafiero, "In South Sudan, China Peacemaker Role Marks a First in Its Diplomacy," *South China Morning Post*, September 11, 2014.
133. Liesl Louw-Vaudran, "China's Role in South Sudan a Learning Curve," Institute for Security Studies, December 14, 2015; China Ministry of Foreign Affairs, "王毅：中国是南苏丹和平的积极促进者、坚定维护者和真心参与者" [Wang Yi: China is an active promoter, firm defender, and sincere participant of peace in South Sudan], January 13, 2015.
134. Comment made at meeting in Washington, D.C., October 24, 2017, attended by Shinn.
135. Comment made at meeting in Washington, D.C., November 7, 2018, attended by Shinn.

7. PROTECTING INTERESTS AND MANAGING CONFLICT

136. Xinhua, "Chinese Envoy Calls for Efforts to Advance Political Process in South Sudan," March 3, 2021.
137. "China's Participation in the Conflict Resolution in Sudan and South Sudan: A Case of 'Creative Mediation,'" *BRIQ* 1, no. 2 (Spring 2020): 20–21.
138. International Crisis Group, "China's Growing Role in UN Peacekeeping," *Asia Report*, no. 166, April 17, 2009, 16; Catherine Gegout, *Why Europe Intervenes in Africa: Security, Prestige and the Legacy of Colonialism* (New York: Oxford University Press, 2017), 106.
139. Saferworld, *China's Growing Role in African Peace and Security*, January 2011, 33–34; Sun and Zoubir, "China's Participation," 236.
140. Sun and Zoubir, "China's Participation," 239.
141. Samuel Ramani, "Where Does China Stand on the Libya Conflict?" *Diplomat*, June 18, 2019; China Ministry of Foreign Affairs, "外交部就利比亚首都爆发武装冲突等答问" [The Ministry of Foreign Affairs answers questions on the outbreak of armed conflict in the capital of Libya], September 3, 2018.
142. Hodzi, *The End of China's Non-Intervention Policy*, 155.
143. Sun and Zoubir, "China's Participation," 233.
144. Liu Zhen, "China Offers to Mediate Djibouti-Eritrea Border Row as It Expands Military Presence in Africa," *South China Morning Post*, July 25, 2017.
145. Shinn/Eisenman interview with a Chinese diplomat, Addis Ababa, June 13, 2018.
146. Shinn/Eisenman interview, Addis Ababa, June 11, 2018.
147. Joseph Sany and Thomas P. Sheehy, "Despite High Stakes in Ethiopia, China Sits on the Sidelines of Peace Efforts," U.S. Institute of Peace, January 19, 2022.
148. Ovigwe Eguegu, "What Does China's Horn of Africa Envoy Mean for Its Non-Intervention Principle?" *Diplomat*, February 17, 2022.
149. Agence France Presse, "China Wants Bigger Role in Horn of Africa Security—Envoy," June 22, 2022.
150. Conversation with Shinn in Washington, D.C., July 29, 2022. See also Paul Nantulya, "China's Diplomacy in the Horn—Conflict Mediation as Power Politics," Africa Center for Strategic Studies, October 12, 2022.
151. Ilaria Carrozza, "China's African Union Diplomacy: Challenges and Prospects for the Future," LSE Policy Brief No. 2/2018; Paul Nantulya, "Chinese Hard Power Supports Its Growing Strategic Interests in Africa," Africa Center for Strategic Studies, January 17, 2019.
152. Large, "China's Role," 37.
153. Comment by Princeton Lyman, former U.S. special envoy to Sudan and South Sudan, on November 7, 2017, in Washington, D.C., during briefing attended by Shinn.
154. He Yin, "China Rising and Its Changing Policy on UN Peacekeeping," in *United Nations Peace Operations in a Changing Global Order*, ed. Cedric de Coning and Mateja Peter (Cham, Switz.: Palgrave Macmillan, 2019), 255, 271–72; Marissa Gibson, "The Charm Offensive: Peacekeeping and Policy in China," *Canadian Military Journal* 19, no. 1 (Winter 2018): 7–9; Lei Yu, "China's Expanding Security Involvement in Africa: A Pillar for

'China-Africa Community of Common Destiny,'" *Global Policy* 9, no. 4 (November 2018): 494.

155. Bates Gill and Chin-Hao Huang, "China's Expanding Peacekeeping Role: Its Significance and the Policy Implications," SIPRI Policy Brief, February 2009, 2; Kossi Ayenagbo et al., "China's Peacekeeping Operations in Africa: From Unwilling Participation to Responsible Contribution," *African Journal of Political Science and International Relations* 6, no. 2 (February 2012): 25.

156. For China's official account of its contributions to UN peacekeeping operations, see China State Council, "China's Armed Forces: 30 Years of UN Peacekeeping Operations," September 2020.

157. "United Nations, African Union Reiterate Commitment to Sudan, as Joint Mission Ends Operations," *UN News*, December 31, 2020.

158. See United Nations Peacekeeping, https://peacekeeping.un.org. For a discussion of China's participation in UNMIL, see Guillaume Moumouni, "China and Liberia: Engagement in a Post-Conflict Country (2003–2013)," in Alden et al., *China and Africa*, 228–32. For a useful comparison of Chinese and Indian approaches to peacekeeping, see Garima Mohan and Olivia Gippner, "Chinese and Indian Approaches to United Nations Peacekeeping: A Theoretical Appraisal of Contribution Patterns and Decision-Making Structures," *Contemporary Readings in Law and Social Justice* 7, no. 1 (2015): 47–77.

159. Daniel M. Hartnett, "China's First Deployment of Combat Forces to a UN Peacekeeping Mission—South Sudan," U.S.-China Economic and Security Review Commission, March 13, 2012, 3; Sun Degang, "China's Soft Military Presence in the Middle East," *Dirasat*, January 2018, 13.

160. Jean-Pierre Cabestan, "China's Involvement in Africa's Security: The Case of China's Participation in the UN Mission to Stabilize Mali," *China Quarterly*, 235 (September 2018): 724.

161. Parello-Plesner and Duchâtel, *China's Strong Arm*, 138; Steven C. Y. Kuo, *Chinese Peace in Africa: From Peacekeeper to Peacemaker* (London: Routledge, 2020), 109; Songying Fang, Xiaojun Xi, and Fanglu Sun, "China's Evolving Motivations and Goals in UN Peacekeeping Participation," *International Journal* 73, no. 3 (2018): 470; Ghiselli, *Protecting China's Interests Overseas*, 218–20.

162. "China Sends Its First Helicopter Unit to UN Peacekeeping Missions," *CRI Online*, August 19, 2017.

163. Cabestan, "China's Involvement," 720–29; Neethling, "China's Evolving Role," 19–22; Niall Duggan, "The People's Republic of China and European Union Security Cooperation in Africa: Sino-EU Security Cooperation in Mali and the Gulf of Aden," *International Journal of China Studies* 8, no. 1 (April 2017): 12–14; Frans Paul van der Putten, "China's Evolving Role in Peacekeeping and African Security: The Deployment of Chinese Troops for UN Force Protection in Mali," *Clingendael Report*, September 2015, 9–24; Niall Duggan, "China's New Intervention Policy: China's Peacekeeping Mission to Mali," in Alden et al., *China and Africa*, 218–21; Lina Benabdallah and Daniel Large, "Development,

7. PROTECTING INTERESTS AND MANAGING CONFLICT

Security, and China's Evolving Role in Mali," China Africa Research Initiative, working paper no. 40, August 2020.
164. Jung Jae Kwon, "Red Under Blue: Chinese Humanitarian Action in UN Peacekeeping Missions," *International Peacekeeping* 27, no. 3 (2020): 430–32; Neethling, "China's Evolving Role," 22–27; van der Putten, "China's Evolving Role in Peacekeeping," 22.
165. Xinhua, "Chinese President Pledges Support for UN Peacekeeping," September 29, 2015; Shinn/Eisenman interview with Major General Zhu Chenghu, National Defense University, Beijing, June 21, 2017.
166. Ni Dandan, "The Art of Peace: A Young Chinese Woman's Unlikely Career Choice," *Sixth Tone*, March 26, 2018.
167. Sarah Zheng, "China Completes Registration of 8,000-strong UN Peacekeeping Force, Defence Ministry Says," *South China Morning Post*, September 29, 2017.
168. Associated Press, "China Says 8,000-Strong UN Peacekeeping Standby Force Ready," November 29, 2018.
169. Hong Xiao, "China Boosts Its Peacekeeping Role," *China Daily*, May 8, 2019.
170. Yin He, "China Rising," 257–58.
171. Jianwei Wang and Jing Zou, "China Goes to Africa: A Strategic Move?" *Journal of Contemporary China* 23, no. 90 (2014): 1120.
172. Paul D. Williams, "The Security Council's Peacekeeping Trilemma," *International Affairs* 96, no. 2 (2020): 483; Yin He, "China Rising," 262.
173. Lei Yu, "China's Expanding," 494–96.
174. Fang, Li, and Sun, "China's Evolving Motivations," 467–68.
175. Lei Yu, "China's Expanding," 493.
176. Philippe D. Rogers, "China and United Nations Peacekeeping Operations in Africa," *Naval War College Review* 60, no. 2 (Spring 2007): 16–17; Meicen Sun, "A Bigger Bang for a Bigger Buck: What China's Changing Attitude Toward UN Peacekeeping Says About Its Evolving Approach to International Institutions," *Foreign Policy Analysis* 13, no. 2 (April 2017): 345–46; Sunghee Cho, "China's Participation in UN Peacekeeping Operations Since the 2000s," *Journal of Contemporary China* 28, no. 117 (2019): 487; Joel Wuthnow, comments at a virtual conference at National Defense University, Washington, D.C., September 30, 2020.
177. Meicen Sun, "A Bigger Bang," 349; Songying Fang, Xiaojun Li, and Fanglu Sun, "China's Evolving Motivations," 469; Sunghee Cho, "China's Participation," 486; Lei Yu, "China's Expanding," 496; Marc Lanteigne, "The Role of UN Peacekeeping in China's Expanding Strategic Interests," United States Institute of Peace, special report no. 430 (September 2018): 3; Earl Conteh-Morgan and Patti Weeks, "Is China Playing a Contradictory Role in Africa? Security Implications of Its Arms Sales and Peacekeeping," *Global Security and Intelligence Studies* 2, no. 1 (Fall 2016): 95; Shen Zhixiong, "On China's Military Diplomacy in Africa," in Alden et al., *China and Africa*, 108–9.
178. Songying Fang and Fanglu Sun, "Gauging Chinese Public Support for China's Role in Peacekeeping," *Chinese Journal of International Politics* 12, no. 2 (2019): 200.

8. SECURITY DIPLOMACY

1. China State Council Information Office, *China's National Defense in the New Era*, July 2019; Yoro Diallo, "Le Forum Sino-Africain sur la Défense et la Sécurité, Instrument Inédit," *Chine Magazine*, December 12, 2018.
2. Argaw Ashine, "West Jittery as China Hosts Africa Military Chiefs," *East African*, July 4, 2018.
3. Nyshka Chandran, "China Says It Will Increase Its Military Presence in Africa," *CNBC Asia-Pacific*, June 27, 2018.
4. Joseph S. Margai, "China-Africa Defense and Security Forum," *Concord Times*, June 27, 2018; Jon Grevatt, "China Deepens Defence Engagement in Africa," *Jane's Defence Weekly*, July 3, 2018.
5. Richard D. Fisher, "China Militarizes Its Influence in Africa," *National Interest*, November 25, 2018; Xinhua, "中国人民解放军驻吉布提保障基地成立暨部队出征仪式在湛江举行" [Founding ceremony of the Chinese People's Liberation Army support base in Djibouti has been held in Zhanjiang], July 11, 2017.
6. Lina Benabdallah, "China-Africa Military Ties Have Deepened. Here are 4 Things to Know," *Washington Post* Monkey Cage Analysis, July 6, 2018.
7. Salem Solomon, "Deepening Military Ties Solidify China's Ambitions in Africa," *VOA*, July 15, 2018.
8. Xinhua, "1st China-Africa Peace, Security Forum Open in Beijing," July 15, 2019; Chen Liye et al., "Overview of 1st China-Africa Peace and Security Forum," *China Military Online*, July 17, 2019.
9. Xinhua, "State Councilor Meets Representatives from China-Africa Peace, Security Forum," July 18, 2019.
10. Chen Liye et al., "Overview of 1st China-Africa Peace and Security Forum," *China Military Online*.
11. Smail Chergui, "On Security Threats and Challenges Faced by Africa," African Union, July 14, 2019.
12. Ovigwe Eguegu, "China-Africa Peace and Security Forum: A New Partnership for Old Problems," *Ventures Africa*, July 22, 2019.
13. Jevans Nyabiage, "Global Security Initiative Helps Gain Military Standing in African Nations," *South China Morning Post*, August 1, 2022; Wang Xueyang and Zhang Dan, "Military Medicine Conference of Second China-Africa Peace and Security Forum Held in Beijing," *China Military Online*, November 15, 2022.
14. China Ministry of Foreign Affairs, "Forum on China-Africa Cooperation Dakar Action Plan (2022–2024)," November 30, 2021.
15. Tyler Jost and Austin Strange, "Delegated Diplomacy: Why China Uses the Military for Face-to-Face Exchanges," working paper, Harvard University, Cambridge, April 28, 2018; Dean Wingrin, "China Looks to Increase Defence Ties with South Africa," *Defence Web*, October 10, 2019.
16. Beatrice Marshall, "China, Africa Deepen Military Ties," CGTN, April 29, 2019.

8. SECURITY DIPLOMACY

17. Xu Yi, "Heads of Chinese and Foreign Ground Force Academies Exchange on Military Education," *China Military Online*, June 14, 2019.
18. "China's National Defense University Builds Ties with Military Academies in Above [*sic*] 100 Countries," *China Military Online*, August 2, 2018.
19. Jost and Strange, "Delegated Diplomacy"; Kenneth Allen, Phillip C. Saunders, and John Chen, *Chinese Military Diplomacy, 2003–2016: Trends and Implications* (Washington, D.C.: National Defense University, July 2017), 46–50, 62–66; David Shinn and Joshua Eisenman, *China and Africa: A Century of Engagement* (Philadelphia: University of Pennsylvania Press, 2012), 170; Shen Zhixiong, "On China's Military Diplomacy in Africa," in *China and Africa: Building Peace and Security Cooperation on the Continent*, ed. Chris Alden, Abiodun Alao, Zhang Chun, and Laura Barber (Cham, Switz.: Palgrave Macmillan, 2018), 106.
20. Shinn/Eisenman interview with Western defense attaché, Accra, June 19, 2018.
21. Donovan C. Chau, "Ally in the East: 21st Century Sino-Tanzanian Strategic Relations and Its Implications for U.S. Africa Policy," *Special Warfare* 26, no. 1 (January–March 2013): 49; "China, Tanzania Vow to Strengthen Cooperation," *Global Times*, June 1, 2010; "Fan Changlong Meets with Tanzanian Guests," *China Military Online*, April 18, 2013; China Ministry of Foreign Affairs, "China and Tanzania,"; "Tanzanian President Meets with Chang Wanquan," *China Military Online*, July 7, 2014; Zhang Zhihao, "China's Fan Changlong Promotes Military Ties with Tanzania," *China Daily*, November 22, 2016; China Ministry of National Defense, "Chinese Air Force Chief Meets with Tanzanian Counterpart," April 25, 2017; "China, Tanzania Pledge to Enhance Military Cooperation," *China Military Online*, May 24, 2018; "Chinese Defense Minister Holds Video Call with Tanzanian Counterpart," *China Military Online*, June 1, 2022.
22. Phillip C. Saunders and Jiunwei Shyy, "China's Military Diplomacy," in *China's Global Influence: Perspectives and Recommendations*, ed. Scott D. McDonald and Michael C. Burgoyne (Honolulu: Asia-Pacific Center for Security Studies, 2019), 213–14.
23. Judd Devermont, Marielle Harris, and Alison Albelda, "Personal Ties: Measuring Chinese and U.S. Engagement with African Security Chiefs," Center for Strategic and International Studies, August 2021, 3.
24. Jordan Link, "The Expanding International Reach of China's Police," Center for American Progress, October 2022, 4, 12.
25. Matsuda Yasuhiro, "An Essay on China's Military Diplomacy: Examination of Intentions in Foreign Strategy," *NIDS Security Reports*, no. 7 (December 2006): 7.
26. U.S. Office of the Secretary of Defense, *Annual Report to Congress: Military and Security Developments Involving the People's Republic of China 2019*, May 2, 2019, 26; U.S. Defense Intelligence Agency, *China Military Power: Modernizing a Force to Fight and Win* (Washington, D.C.: United States Defense Intelligence Agency, 2019), 19.
27. Heidi Holz and Kenneth Allen, "Military Exchanges with Chinese Characteristics: The People's Liberation Army Experience with Military Relations," in *The PLA at Home and Abroad: Assessing the Operational Capabilities of China's Military*, ed. Roy Kamphausen,

8. SECURITY DIPLOMACY

David Lai, and Andrew Scobell (Carlisle, Penn.: Strategic Studies Institute, June 2010), 436.
28. Susan Puska, "Resources, Security and Influence: The Role of the Military in China's Africa Strategy," *China Brief* 7, no. 11 (May 30, 2007): 2; Shinn and Eisenman, *China and Africa*, 169.
29. Based on survey of Chinese embassy websites and press accounts.
30. Shinn and Eisenman, *China and Africa*, 169.
31. List provided by Western military attaché in Beijing on April 4, 2018. The African attaché corps in Beijing once had a website with this information; it seems to have disappeared.
32. Paul Holtom and Irene Pavesi, "Trade Update 2018: Sub-Saharan Africa in Focus," Small Arms Survey, December 2018.
33. Michael J. Mazarr et al., *Security Cooperation in a Strategic Competition* (Santa Monica, Calif.: RAND Corporation, 2022), 104.
34. Ilaria Carrozza and Nicholas J. Marsh, "Great Power Competition and China's Security Assistance to Africa: Arms, Training, and Influence," *Journal of Global Security Studies* 7, no. 4 (2022): 9–10.
35. Link, "The Expanding International Reach of China's Police," 18–19.
36. Tom Bayes, *China's Growing Security Role in Africa: Views from West Africa, Implications for Europe* (Mercator Institute for China Studies, 2020), 36–37.
37. Mark Bromley, Mathieu Duchâtel, and Paul Holtom, "China's Exports of Small Arms and Light Weapons," SIPRI Policy Paper 38, October 2013, 2.
38. Paul Holtom, Mark Bromley, and Verena Simmel, "Measuring International Arms Transfers," SIPRI Fact Sheet, December 2012, 2.
39. Nan Tian and Fei Su, "Estimating the Arms Sales of Chinese Companies," SIPRI Insights on Peace and Security, no. 2, January 2020, 2–4; International Peace Information Service and Omega Research Foundation, "China North Industries Corporation," working paper no. 2, 2016 (paper includes list of exports to African countries).
40. Aude Fleurant et al., "Trends in International Arms Transfers, 2016," SIPRI Fact Sheet, February 2017.
41. Pieter D. Wezeman et al., "Trends in International Arms Transfers, 2021," SIPRI Fact Sheet, March 2022.
42. SIPRI Arms Transfers Database, generated June 12, 2022.
43. Andrew Hull and David Markov, "Chinese Arms Sales to Africa," Institute for Defense Analyses, 2012; Liu Xuanzun, "Chinese Weapons Appeal to Africa," *Global Times*, September 20, 2018.
44. Lukas Jeuck, "Arms Transfers to Zimbabwe: Implications for an Arms Trade Treaty," SIPRI Background Paper, March 2011, 2.
45. "China Sells CH-5 UAVs Armed with ATGM and Guided Bombs to Algeria, *bulgarianmilitary.com*, January 27, 2022.
46. Yahia H. Zoubir, "Algeria and China: Shifts in Political and Military Relations," *Global Policy*, July 27, 2022.

8. SECURITY DIPLOMACY

47. SIPRI Arms Transfers Database, generated June 4, 2020; Zhao Lei, "China Delivers Warship to Algeria," *China Daily*, July 20, 2016; "Algeria Displays New Chinese Artillery," *Defence Web*, May 29, 2017; Zhao Lei, "Nation's Drones Are in Demand," *China Daily*, April 21, 2016; "China Delivered PHL-03, or AR2, Multiple Rocket Launchers MLRS to Morocco," *defence.az*, March 10, 2020; Joe Saballa, "Morocco Buys Chinese Military Drones," *Defense Post*, October 4, 2022.
48. Lee Jeong-ho, "Chinese-Made Missiles and Drones Used in Libya Conflict, UN Experts Find," *South China Morning Post*, May 7, 2019.
49. Ryan Oliver, "The Strategic Implications of Chinese UAVs: Insights from the Libyan Conflict," *China Brief* 20, no. 15 (August 31, 2020): 26–28.
50. "Libya Commemorates Victims of Deadly UAE Drone Strike on Tripoli Military Academy," *Daily Sabah*, January 4, 2021.
51. "Mauritania Commissions New Chinese Offshore Patrol Boats," *Defence Web*, June 1, 2016; "毛里塔尼亚耗资4200万美元购买中国巡逻艇" [Mauritania spent $42 million to buy Chinese patrol boats], *Global Times*, May 27, 2016.
52. "China Begins Construction of Mauritanian Landing Ship," *Defence Web*, November 17, 2017.
53. SIPRI Arms Transfers Database, generated June 4, 2020.
54. SIPRI Arms Transfers Database, generated June 4, 2020.
55. Chau, "Ally in the East," 50; Alan Warnes, "The Rise and Rise of Tanzania's Air Force," *African Aerospace*, May 14, 2018.
56. SIPRI Arms Transfers Database, generated June 13, 2022.
57. Agence France Presse, "Ethiopia Shows Off Combat Drones at Military Ceremony," June 27, 2022.
58. Eric Biegon, "China Donates Military Equipment, Vehicles to Kenya," Kenya Broadcasting Corporation, April 4, 2022.
59. Patrick Kenyette, "China Donates Military Vehicles and Equipment to Somalia," *Military Africa*, March 21, 2022.
60. Dan Large, "Arms, Oil and Darfur: The Evolution of Relations Between China and Sudan," Small Arms Survey, HSBA Issue Brief no. 7, July 2007, 5–6.
61. SIPRI Arms Transfers Database generated June 4, 2020.
62. "First Sudanese FTC-2000 Unveiled," *Defence Web*, June 6, 2017; Sebastien Roblin, "You Might Soon See This Chinese Fighter All Over Africa and Latin America," *National Interest*, August 12, 2018.
63. "Sudan Discussing Acquisition of China's J-10C Fighters: New Squadron Could Be Africa's Finest," *Military Watch Magazine*, August 6, 2022.
64. SIPRI Arms Transfers Database, generated June 13, 2022.
65. "Nigerian Air Force Continues to Refurbish Its Fleet," *Defence Web*, November 9, 2020.
66. "Insurgency: Army Takes Delivery of Armoured Tanks, Artillery Trucks," *This Day*, April 8, 2020; "Buhari Administration's Fifth Anniversary Fact Sheet," *Premium Times*, June 7, 2020.

8. SECURITY DIPLOMACY

67. Dylan Malyasov, "Nigerian Anti-terrorism Operation Marks Combat Debut of Chinese VT4 Tank," *Defence Blog*, January 12, 2021.
68. Andrew McGregor, "Conflict at a Crossroads: Can Nigeria Sustain Its Military Campaign Against Boko Haram?" *Terrorism Monitor* 13, no. 13 (June 26, 2015): 9.
69. Liu Xuanzun, "Nigeria Receives China-made Armed Reconnaissance Drones: Reports," *Global Times*, November 11, 2020.
70. Richard Asante, "China's Security and Economic Engagement in West Africa: Constructive or Destructive?" *China Quarterly of International Strategic Studies* 3, no. 4 (2017): 580–82.
71. SIPRI Arms Transfers Database, generated June 4, 2020.
72. SIPRI Arms Transfers Database, generated June 4, 2020.
73. "China, Cameroon Sign Military Assistance Agreement," *Defence Web*, July 19, 2018.
74. SIPRI Arms Transfers Database, generated June 4, 2020.
75. Jyhjong Hwang, "Logics of Arms Deals: Multilevel Evidence from China-Zambia Relations," China Africa Research Initiative, working paper no. 37 (May 2020); Zhang Tao, "Zambia Air Force Commander Hopes to Buy More Chinese Aircraft," *China Military*, November 4, 2016.
76. SIPRI Arms Transfers Database, generated June 4, 2020; Shinn/Eisenman interview with Chinese embassy officer, Windhoek, June 7, 2018.
77. Huang Panyue, "Namibian President Commissions Chinese-Built Naval Vessels," *China Military*, October 30, 2017.
78. Shinovene Immanuel, "Nam's Chinese Arms Deal Blocked," *Namibian*, April 20, 2017.
79. SIPRI Arms Transfers Database, generated June 13, 2022.
80. "Angola Receives Final K-8W Jets from China," *Defence Web*, February 5, 2021.
81. Bayes, *China's Growing*, 34.
82. Paul Holtom and Irene Pavesi, "Trade Update 2018: Sub-Saharan Africa in Focus," Small Arms Survey, December 2018, 65.
83. Holtom and Pavesi, 11.
84. Bromley, Duchâtel, and Holtom, *China's Exports*, 36; United Nations, *The Global Reported Arms Trade*, Disarmament Study Series, no. 36 (2017): 19.
85. Bromley, Duchâtel, and Holtom, *China's Exports*, 6–8.
86. Bernardo Mariani and Elizabeth Kirkham, "China, Africa and the Arms Trade Treaty," in Alden et al., *China and Africa*, 344–46; UN Office for Disarmament Affairs, https://www.un.org/disarmament/.
87. Bromley, Duchâtel, and Holtom, *China's Exports*, 19–28.
88. Bromley, Duchâtel, and Holtom, 51.
89. Barney Walsh, "China's Pervasive yet Forgotten Regional Security Role in Africa," *Journal of Contemporary China* 28, no. 120 (2019): 978.
90. Xinhua, "Political Settlement Key to Control of Small Arms, Light Weapons: Chinese Envoy," February 5, 2020.
91. Holtom and Pavesi, "Trade Update 2018," 69.
92. "China Supplying Small Arms to Zimbabwe," *Defence Web*, November 14, 2011.
93. "Namibia Operating FN-6 Missiles," *Defence Web*, August 30, 2018.

8. SECURITY DIPLOMACY

94. Shinn/Eisenman interview with GAF officer, Accra, June 18, 2018.
95. "L'Algérie Opte pour le HJ-12, le Javelin Chinois," *Mena Defense*, July 20, 2020; "又一批红箭12导弹到货，北非一国交付前线陆军，准备对垒坦克" [Another batch of HJ-12 missiles arrives, delivered to North African country frontlines, prepared to fight against tanks], *Sina News*, August 5, 2020.
96. Earl Conteh-Morgan, "China's Arms Sales in Africa," *Sustainable Security*, April 19, 2017; Shinn and Eisenman, *China and Africa*, 175–79; Eric Olander, "Chinese Weapons and Military Equipment are Showing Up on the Battlefields of the Eastern DR Congo," China Global South Project, July 12, 2022.
97. Bromley, Duchâtel, and Holtom, *China's Exports*, 38.
98. Jonah Leff and Emile LeBrun, *Following the Thread: Arms and Ammunition Tracing in Sudan and South Sudan* (Geneva: Small Arms Survey, May 2014), 40–57, 71–73, 89–90, 101.
99. Leff and LeBrun, *Following the Thread*, 40–57.
100. Holtom and Pavesi, "Trade Update 2018," 69; Amnesty International, "South Sudan Arms Embargo Crucial After Massive Chinese Weapons Transfer," July 17, 2014; Shannon Tiezzi, "UN Report: China Sold $20 Million in Arms and Ammunition to South Sudan," *Diplomat*, August 27, 2015.
101. Shinn interview, Beijing, March 10, 2017; Shinn and Eisenman, *China and Africa*, 174–75.
102. Conflict Armament Research, *Weapon Supplies Into South Sudan's Civil War* (London: CAR, November 2018), 17.
103. Shinn/Eisenman interview with Western defense attaché, Accra, June 19, 2018.
104. Jordan Link, "Chinese Lending to Africa for Military and Domestic Security Purposes," *China in Africa: The Real Story*, April 9, 2019.
105. United States Defense Intelligence Agency, *China Military*, 2019, 107; U.S. Office of the Secretary of Defense, *Annual Report to Congress: Military and Security Developments Involving the People's Republic of China 2019*, 28; Jeremy Binnie, "US General Dismisses Chinese Kit in Africa," *Jane's Defence Weekly*, April 10, 2019, 16; Paul Nantulya, "China's Strategic Aims in Africa," testimony before U.S.-China Economic and Security Review Commission, May 20, 2020; Elijah N. Munyi, "Challenging Pax Americana: The Commercial Imperative in Chinese Arms Exports to Africa—A Case Study of Uganda and Kenya," China Africa Research Initiative, working paper no. 41 (September 2020): 20.
106. Shinn and Eisenman, *China and Africa*, 168–69.
107. Shinn/Eisenman interview, Accra, June 18, 2018.
108. Bayes, *China's Growing*, 38.
109. Shinn/Eisenman interview with U.S. ambassador, Accra, June 19, 2018.
110. Jonah Victor, "China's Security Assistance in Global Competition: The Case of Africa," in *The PLA Beyond Borders*, ed. Joel Wuthnow et al. (Washington, D.C.: National Defense University, 2021), 263.
111. Shen Zhixiong, "On China's," 111; Bayes, *China's Growing*, 41–42.
112. Earl Conteh-Morgan and Patti Weeks, "Is China Playing a Contradictory Role in Africa? Security Implications of Its Arms Sales and Peacekeeping," *Global Security and Intelligence Studies* 2, no. 1 (Fall 2016): 91.

8. SECURITY DIPLOMACY

113. Hu Yuwei, "Decades of Training Foreign Officers Boost China's Military Diplomacy," *Global Times*, October 14, 2019; for a listing of African military trainees in China from 1955 to 1978, see Ismail Debeche, "The Role of China in International Relations: The Impact of Ideology on Foreign Policy with Special Reference to Sino-African Relations (1949–1986)" (PhD diss., University of York, 1987), 1080.
114. Comment by Zhou Bo, director of the Center for Security Cooperation in the Ministry of National Defense, at a conference attended by Shinn in Beijing on March 8, 2017.
115. Paul Nantulya, "China Promotes Its Party-Army Model in Africa," Africa Center for Strategic Studies, July 28, 2020.
116. Nantulya, "China Promotes Its Party-Army Model in Africa," 3; Paul Nantulya, "China's Military Power Projection and U.S National Interests," testimony before U.S.-China Economic and Security Review Commission, February 20, 2020; Nantulya, "China's Strategic Aims in Africa."
117. Nantulya, "China's Military Power Projection."
118. John S. Van Oudenaren and Benjamin E. Fisher, "Foreign Military Education as PLA Soft Power," *Parameters* 46, no. 4 (Winter 2016–17): 111–14.
119. Guo Yuandan, "China Hosts Cadets from Military Academies Around the World, Boosting Ties and Mutual Understanding," *Global Times*, November 28, 2018.
120. "China and Russia Seek Bigger Security Role in Post-coup Burkina Faso," *South China Morning Post*, February 3, 2022.
121. Hu Yuwei, "PLA Trains Military Officers from Around the World, Boosting Ties and Understanding," *Global Times*, January 16, 2019.
122. China State Council, "China's National Defense in 2010," Xinhua, March 31, 2011.
123. Omatseye O'Weyinmi Nesiama, "China-Nigeria Security Cooperation Policies: Challenges and Prospects," International College of Defense Studies, 2013, 79–81.
124. China State Council Information Office, *China's National Defense in the New Era*, July 24, 2019.
125. Xinhua, "China Trains UN Peacekeeping Officers," June 6, 2016.
126. Shinn/Eisenman interview, Addis Ababa, June 12, 2018; Aaron Tesfaye, "China-Ethiopia Relations and the Horn of Africa," *ISPI Online*, September 20, 2019.
127. Shinn/Eisenman interview with senior Djiboutian Army officer, Djibouti, June 14, 2018.
128. Martin Bailey, "Tanzania and China," *African Affairs* 74, no. 294 (January 1975): 44.
129. "Tanzania-China Relations," *Global Security*, February 14, 2018.
130. "China, Tanzania Conclude 'Sincere Partners 2019' Joint Military Training," *China Military Online*, January 21, 2020.
131. Bayes, *China's Growing*, 40–41.
132. "The Confucius Institute at the University of Khartoum Offers a Chinese Training Course for the Sudanese Armed Forces," Confucius Institute, https://mp.weixin.qq.com/s/bKu5mMcjAD3ClQecToP_og, April 18, 2022; "Congo (Kinshasa) Confucius Institute Cooperates with the Military Language Institute to Build a Chinese Teaching Site," Confucius Institute, https://mp.weixin.qq.com/s/El97GxaCOCGY9nG6IoQkHQ, April 19, 2022.

8. SECURITY DIPLOMACY

133. Shinn/Eisenman interview with Western military attaché, Pretoria, June 5, 2018.
134. Nantulya, "China's Strategic Aims in Africa."
135. Shinn and Eisenman, *China and Africa*, 353; Shinn/Eisenman interview with senior police officer, Windhoek, June 7, 2018.
136. "Sudan vs S. Sudan, a Civil War Between Two Graduates of Chinese Military Academies?" *Defence Forum India*, April 17, 2012.
137. Sarah Zheng, "Rwandan Troops Trained by Chinese Military Mark 25th Anniversary of Liberation," *South China Morning Post*, July 7, 2019.
138. Shannon van Sant, "Why Is China Investing in the Comoros?" *CBS News*, November 12, 2014.
139. Nantulya, "China's Strategic Aims in Africa."
140. Large, "Arms, Oil and Darfur," 4–5.
141. Hilary Andersson, "China 'Is Fueling War in Darfur,'" *BBC*, July 13, 2008.
142. Adam Hartman, "President Commissions Submarines," *Namibian*, October 30, 2017.
143. Oscar Nkala, "Chinese Company Builds Growing African Presence," *Defense News*, October 10, 2015; Xinhua, "美媒：非洲空军教练机80%中国造 K8出口超30架" [U.S. media: 80% of African air force trainers are Chinese-made and over 30 K-8 aircraft exported], October 12, 2015.
144. Hull and Markov, "Chinese Arms Sales," 29–30.
145. Bayes, *China's Growing*, 40.
146. Chiemelie Ezeobi and Chinecherem Ojiako, "Insurgency: Army Takes Delivery of Armoured Tanks, Artillery Trucks," *This Day*, April 8, 2020.
147. Jeremy Binnie, "Nigeria to Get More Armed UAVs from China," *Janes*, October 14, 2020.
148. Comment by Chen Xiangyuan, Chinese People's Association for Peace and Development, at 8th U.S.-China Peace Forum in Washington, D.C., July 17, 2018, attended by Shinn.
149. Xinhua, "Langfang Home to Asia's Largest UN Police Training Center," August 19, 2002.
150. Zhang Yi, "Training Begins in Beijing for UN Police Missions," *China Daily*, August 9, 2016.
151. Tao Xu and Haiyan Fu, "Police Education and Training in China—The Case of Zhejiang Police College," *European Police Science and Research Bulletin* (2017): 101–3; "African Military Officials Visit China's Special Police College," *China Military*, July 17, 2019; Deng Xiaoci and Zhang Dan, "Beijing Police Working with Foreign Counterparts and Interpol to Hunt Down Fugitives," *Global Times*, April 28, 2019.
152. "Rwanda Sends Delegation to China for Law Enforcement Training," *Taarifa*, November 28, 2019.
153. Link, "The Expanding International Reach of China's Police," 15–17.
154. Zhang Jiexian, "Police Train to Fight Crime with King-fu," *Business Day*, December 17, 2015; Paul Nantulya, "China's Growing Police and Law Enforcement Cooperation in Africa," in *Political Front Lines: China's Pursuit of Influence in Africa*, ed. Nadège Rolland (Seattle: National Bureau of Asian Research, June 2022), 46–48.

8. SECURITY DIPLOMACY

155. "China Pledges More Support to Liberian Police Capacity Building," *Front Page Africa*, December 1, 2017.
156. "China to Train Uganda Police in Probing Crime," *APA News*, December 21, 2017; Nantulya, "China's Growing Peace and Law Enforcement," 53–54.
157. Edith Mutethya, "Kenya Railway Police to Train in Beijing," *China Daily*, May 23, 2018.
158. Shinn/Eisenman interview with senior police officer, Windhoek, June 7, 2018.
159. Saunders and Shyy, "China's Military Diplomacy," 214–16.
160. Omatseye O'Weyinmi Nesiama, "China-Nigeria Security Cooperation Policies," 81.
161. Kenneth Allen, Phillip C. Saunders, and John Chen, *Chinese Military Diplomacy, 2003–2016: Trends and Implications* (Washington, D.C.: National Defense University, July 2017), 34.
162. China Foreign Ministry, "Chinese-Built Military Training Centre Opens in Tanzania," *Defence Web*, February 14, 2018; "'东非解放军'迎来中国训练中心将诞生最强部队" ["East African Liberation Army" ushered in Chinese Training Center, the strongest force will be born], February 27, 2018.
163. "Chinese, Egyptian Navies Conduct Joint Maritime Drill in Mediterranean," *China Military Online*, September 9, 2015.
164. Allen, Saunders, and Chen, *Chinese Military Diplomacy*, 62–66.
165. Paul Nantulya, "Chinese Hard Power Supports Its Growing Strategic Interests in Africa," Africa Center for Strategic Studies, January 17, 2019.
166. Victor, "China's Security Assistance in Global Competition," 281.
167. Bayes, *China's Growing*, 44.
168. Link, "Chinese Lending to Africa."
169. Asante, "China's Security," 580–81. Shinn/Eisenman interview with senior military officer, Accra, June 18, 2018.
170. Daniel Nonor, "$100m Housing Project for Military Takes Off," *Finder*, July 5, 2019.
171. Musa C. Kaseke, "Namibia's President Geingob Opens Chinese-Funded Military College," Xinhua, October 18, 2019.
172. Shinn/Eisenman interview with former head of SWAPO Youth League, Windhoek, June 9, 2018; "Military Spending Despite Economic Crisis," *Namibian Sun*, September 30, 2019.
173. Joshua Meservey, "Government Buildings in Africa Are a Likely Vector for Chinese Spying," Heritage Foundation, *Backgrounder*, no. 3476 (May 20, 2020): 17.
174. Bailey, "Tanzania and China," 44.
175. Warnes, "The Rise and Rise of Tanzania's Air Force."
176. "Chinese-Built Military Training Centre Opens in Tanzania," *Defence Web*, February 14, 2018.
177. Nantulya, "China's Military Power Projection."
178. Meservey, "Government Buildings," 18.
179. Mary Wambui, "Uhuru Kenyatta Launches New Hospital for the Armed Forces," *Nation*, September 1, 2021.

8. SECURITY DIPLOMACY

180. Meservey, "Government Buildings," 18–19; Link, "Chinese Lending to Africa"; "China Supplying Small Arms to Zimbabwe," *Defence Web*, November 14, 2011; Arve Ofstad and Elling Tjønneland, "Zambia's Looming Debt Crisis—Is China to Blame?" *CMI Insight*, June 2019, 7.
181. Meservey, "Government Buildings," 13–18; Helen Tadesse, "Defense Ministry, China Sign Agreement to Build Modern Medical Laboratory," *Walta*, March 30, 2022.
182. Meservey, "Government Buildings," 1–2.
183. "National Intelligence Law of the People's Republic," Chinese National People's Congress Network, June 27, 2017.
184. China State Council, "China's Military Strategy," Xinhua, May 27, 2015.
185. Matthew Southerland, "The Chinese Military's Role in Overseas Humanitarian Assistance and Disaster Relief: Contributions and Concerns," U.S.-China Economic and Security Review Commission, July 11, 2019.
186. Tania M. Chacho, *Lending a Helping Hand: The People's Liberation Army and Humanitarian Assistance/Disaster Relief*, U.S. Air Force Institute for National Security Studies, 2009, 5–9.
187. Xiao-Bing Fu, "Military Medicine in China: Old Topic, New Concept," *Military Medical Research* 1, no. 2 (2014); "Background: Chinese Int'l Rescue Team," Xinhua, October 9, 2009; Liu Xin, "China Search and Rescue Team Completes First Overseas Mission," CGTN, April 17, 2019.
188. "Zambia Honors Chinese Military Medical Aid Team," *China Military Online*, January 15, 2019.
189. China State Council Information Office, "China's National Defense in the New Era," July 2019, 47.
190. Ying Li et al., "Chinese People's Liberation Army on Action of Fighting Against Ebola in Africa: Implications and Challenges," *Chinese Medical Journal* 128, no. 10 (May 20, 2015): 1420; Jean-Pierre Cabestan, "China's Response to the 2014–2016 Ebola Crisis: Enhancing Africa's Soft Security Under Sino-US Competition," *China Information* 35, no. 1 (March 2020): 7–11.
191. Yinying Lu et al., "Chinese Military Medical Teams in the Ebola Outbreak of Sierra Leone," *Journal of the Royal Army Medical Corps* 162, no. 3 (2016): 198.
192. Yanzhong Huang, "China's Response to the 2014 Ebola Outbreak in West Africa," *Global Challenges* 1, no. 2 (2017): 5.
193. Cabestan, "China's Response," 5; Jean-Pierre Cabestan remarks on September 30, 2020, at the China Africa Research Initiative conference in Washington, D.C., on "Strategic Interests, Security Implications: China, Africa, and the Rest."
194. Ian Taylor, "China's Response to the Ebola Virus Disease in West Africa," *Round Table* 104, no. 1 (2015): 41–54; Yinying Lu et al., "Chinese Military Medical," 201; Ying Li et al., "Chinese People's Liberation Army," 1420.
195. China State Council, "The Diversified Employment of China's Armed Forces," Xinhua, April 16, 2013.

8. SECURITY DIPLOMACY

196. "PLA's Logistical Base in Djibouti Donates Medical Materials to Djibouti Military Police," *China Military Online*, September 11, 2017.
197. Moritz Rudolf, "China's Health Diplomacy During Covid-19," German Institute for International and Security Affairs, *SWP Comment*, no. 9 (January 2021): 1–8.
198. "Chinese Armed Forces Donate COVID-19 Protective Gear to SANDF," *South African*, March 26, 2020; Xinhua, "Chinese Military Medical Experts Share Experience of Combating COVID-19 with S. African Counterparts," May 9, 2020; Tebogo Tshwane, "Beijing's Soft Power: China Offers 300,000 Vaccine Jabs to SANDF Soldiers," *amaBhungane*, December 14, 2021.
199. "China Donates More Medical Equipment to the SANDF," *Defence Web*, December 2, 2020; Chinese Embassy in South Africa, "中国企业助力南非国防军抗疫行动" [Chinese companies assist the South African National Defense Force in anti-epidemic operations], March 27, 2020.
200. Tonderayi Mukeredzi, "Zimbabwe Hails Medical Donation by Chinese Army," *China Daily*, June 8, 2020.
201. "Chinese Military Donates Anti-Pandemic Medical Supplies to Republic of Congo," *China Military Online*, June 8, 2020; Tabaro J. Croix, "Chinese Military Donates Medical Kits to Support RDF in Fight Against COVID-19," *KT Press*, June 3, 2020.
202. China Ministry of National Defense, "Chinese Military Provides COVID-19 Vaccines to Guinean Military," May 31, 2021; CGTN, "PLA Provides COVID-19 Vaccines to Armies of 3 African Countries," March 25, 2021.
203. Xu Wei, "Military Doctors Gain from Sudan Experience," *China Daily*, December 12, 2011.
204. Jung Jae Kwon, "Red Under Blue: Chinese Humanitarian Action in UN Peacekeeping Missions," *International Peacekeeping* 27, no. 3 (2020): 420–22.
205. Chacho, *Lending a Helping Hand*, 5.
206. Jung Jae Kwon, "Red Under Blue," 423–32; Xinhua, "Chinese Soldiers Implement UN Peacekeeping Missions Worldwide," July 30, 2012.
207. China's Permanent Mission in Geneva, "China's Experience in Mine Clearance," April 16, 2004.
208. China State Council Information Office, "The Diversified Employment of China's Armed Forces," April 2013.
209. Shen Zhixiong, "On China's," 111; "China: Practice Relating to Rule 83. Removal or Neutralization of Landmines," *IHL Database*; "China: Support for Mine Action," *Landmine & Cluster Munitions Monitor*, June 19, 2010; Xinhua, "China Donates Mine-sweepers to Eritrea," November 16, 2001; David Shinn, "Military and Security Relations: China, Africa, and the Rest of the World," in *China Into Africa: Trade, Aid, and Influence*, ed. Robert I. Rotberg (Washington, D.C.: Brookings Institution Press, 2008), 178.
210. Comment by Zhou Bo, director of the Center for Security Cooperation in the Ministry of National Defense, at a conference attended by Shinn in Beijing on March 8, 2017.
211. Vikash Chandra, "Rising Powers and International Organisations: The Case of China's Counter-terrorism Strategy at the United Nations," *China Report* 55, no. 2 (2019): 131–38;

8. SECURITY DIPLOMACY

Abdelhak Bassou, "China Faced with the Proliferation of the Terrorist Phenomenon in Africa," OCP Policy Center, March 16, 2016; Jacob Zenn, "China's Counter-Terrorism Calculus," *China Brief* 16, no. 2 (January 26, 2016): 10.

212. China Law Translate, "Unofficial Translation of the Counter-Terrorism Law of the People's Republic of China," December 27, 2015.
213. Joel Wuthrow, *China's Other Army: The People's Armed Police in an Era of Reform* (Washington, D.C.: National Defense University, April 2019), 3; Timothy R. Heath, *China's Pursuit of Overseas Security* (Santa Monica, Calif.: RAND Corporation, 2018), 36–37.
214. Murray Scot Tanner, "China's Response to Terrorism," Center for Naval Analyses, June 2016, 82–96.
215. Shinn/Eisenman interview with experts at Institute of West Asian and African Studies, Chinese Academy of Social Sciences, Beijing, June 20, 2017.
216. China Ministry of Foreign Affairs, "Forum on China-Africa Cooperation Dakar Action Plan (2022–2024)," November 30, 2021.
217. China Ministry of Foreign Affairs, "China's Arab Policy Paper," January 13, 2016.
218. Shinn and Eisenman, *China and Africa*, 234–35; "Al-Qaeda Targets China," *Maclean's*, July 14, 2009.
219. Comment by Yahia Zoubir, Brookings Doha Center, during webcast hosted by Hollings Center, June 24, 2020.
220. Xinhua, "China, Algeria Vow to Boost Counter-terrorism Cooperation," July 12, 2016.
221. China Foreign Ministry, "Assistant Foreign Minister Li Huilai Visits Algeria to Hold the First China-Algeria Counter-terrorism and Security Consultation," December 1, 2016.
222. Xinhua, "China, Egypt Oppose Linking Terrorism with Specific Nations, Religions," January 22, 2016.
223. China State Council Information Office, "China's National Defense in the New Era," 44.
224. China Foreign Ministry, "China, Egypt to Advance Comprehensive Strategic Partnership," September 1, 2018.
225. China Foreign Ministry, "China Contributes to Global Anti-terror Cause with Deradicalization Efforts in Xinjiang: FM," January 9, 2020.
226. Mohamed Mostafa and Mohamed Nagi, "'They Are Not Welcome . . .' Report on the Uyghur Crisis in Egypt," Association for Freedom Thought and Expression, October 1, 2017; Nour Youssef, "Egyptian Police Detain Uighurs and Deport Them to China," *New York Times*, July 6, 2017.
227. China Foreign Ministry, "Wang Yi: To Carry Out Strategic Friendship in All Aspects of China-Morocco Cooperation," June 4, 2014.
228. "Uyghur Exile Safely Returns to Turkey After Facing Deportation to China from Moroccan Authorities," *Radio Free Asia*, September 25, 2019.
229. Ehsan Azigh, "Moroccan Court Rules in China's Favor to Extradite Uyghur Accused of 'Terrorism,'" *Radio Free Asia*, December 16, 2021.

8. SECURITY DIPLOMACY

230. Benjamin David Baker, "After Deadly Attack in Mali, How Will China Protect Its Citizens Abroad?" *Diplomat*, November 29, 2015; Andrea Ghiselli, "Growing Overlap Between Counter-Terrorism and Overseas Interest Protection Acts as New Driver of Chinese Strategy," *China Brief* 16, no. 9 (June 2, 2016): 16.
231. "UN Peacekeeper Killed in Shelling by Al Qaeda Affiliate," *Global Times*, June 2, 2016.
232. China Foreign Ministry, "Foreign Ministry Spokesperson Hua Chunying's Regular Press Conference on June 3, 2016," June 4, 2016.
233. Response to question by Shinn during meeting in Washington, D.C., March 5, 2018.
234. Olawale Adeniyi, "Nigeria, China Sign Agreement on Counter-Terrorism," *Naija News*, December 2, 2020.
235. Xinhua, "China, Kenya Pledge to Boost Comprehensive Cooperative Partnership," May 11, 2014.
236. Hou Liqiang, "Somalia Offers Apology, Seeks China's Help," *China Daily*, July 30, 2015.
237. Abdullahi Abdille Shahow, "Al-Shabaab's Territory in Somalia Is a COVID-19 Powder Keg," *World Politics Review*, May 1, 2020.
238. Victor, "China's Security Assistance in Global Competition," 285–86. For an explanation of Chinese intelligence services, see United States Defense Intelligence Agency, *China Military Power*, 99–100.
239. Chergui, "On Security Threats," 6.
240. Xinhua, "China Stands Firm with Africa in Combating Terrorism," May 18, 2014.
241. Xu Weizhong, Yu Wensheng, and Wang Lei, "An Analysis of the Security Situation in Africa," in *International Strategic Relations and China's National Security*, ed. Institute for Strategic Studies National Defense University of the PLA, 2015, 282. For an historical account of China's efforts to collect intelligence in Africa, see Gérald Arboit, "The Chinese Intelligence Services in Africa," *Handbook on China and Globalization*, ed. Huiyao Wang and Lu Miao (Cheltenham, UK: Edward Elgar, 2019), 305–21.

9. MARITIME SECURITY

1. Teng Jianqun, "Understanding China's Maritime Policy—21st Century Maritime Silk Road," in *Indo-Pacific Security: Challenges and Cooperation*, ed. David Brewster (Canberra: Australian National University, July 2016), 51–54.
2. David Brewster, "An Indian Ocean Dilemma: Sino-Indian Rivalry and China's Strategic Vulnerability in the Indian Ocean," *Journal of the Indian Ocean Region* III, no. 1 (2015): 55.
3. "Mr. Biden's Multilateral Strategy: In Efforts to Counter China, the 'Quad' Is No Substitute for U.S. Strength," *Washington Post*, March 18, 2021.
4. Joel Wuthnow, "Just Another Paper Tiger? Chinese Perspectives on the U.S. Indo-Pacific Strategy," *Strategic Forum*, no. 305 (June 2020): 7.
5. Neil Melvin, "The Foreign Military Presence in the Horn of Africa Region," SIPRI Background Paper, April 2019, 20–24.

9. MARITIME SECURITY

6. Michael McDevitt, "Diego Garcia: An American Perspective," Lowy Institute, May 19, 2020.
7. Smruti S. Pattanaik, "Indian Ocean in the Emerging Geo-strategic Context: Examining India's Relations with Its Maritime South Asian Neighbors," *Journal of the Indian Ocean Region* 12, no. 2 (2016): 126; Richard Ghiasy, Fei Su, and Lora Saalman, "The 21st Century Maritime Silk Road: Security Implications and Ways Forward for the European Union," SIPRI, September 2018, 27.
8. Gaurav Sharma, "India—the Indian Ocean Region and Engagement with Four Littoral States: Sri Lanka, Maldives, Seychelles and Mauritius," German Institute for International and Security Affairs, October 2016, 2.
9. Saji Abraham, *China's Role in Indian Ocean—Its Implications on India's National Security* (New Delhi: Vij Books India, 2015), 120–23; Lindsay Hughes, "India's Naval Strategy," Future Directions International, October 4, 2016; Gulshan Rafique, "Countering India's Geopolitical Ambitions," *Pakistan Observer*, April 7, 2015; Zhu Li, "The Maritime Silk Road and India: The Challenge of Overcoming Cognitive Divergence," *Asia Policy*, no. 22 (July 2016): 23.
10. Saji Abraham, *China's Role*, 93.
11. Gerry Shih, "Facing Insecurity at Home, China's Xi Takes on the World," *Washington Post*, August 9, 2020.
12. Ijaz Khalid, Shaukat, and Azka Gul, "Indian Response to Chinese String of Pearls Doctrine," *Global Political Review* 2, no. 1 (2017): 28; Robert D. Kaplan, *Monsoon: The Indian Ocean and the Future of American Power* (New York: Random House, 2010), 10, 127.
13. Neil Melvin, "The New External Security Politics of the Horn of Africa Region," *SIPRI Insights on Peace and Security*, no. 2, April 2019, 23.
14. Zhou Bo, "The String of Pearls and the Maritime Silk Road," *China-US Focus*, February 11, 2014; Ma Jiali, "中国海军没有'珍珠链战略'" [The Chinese Navy does not have a "string of pearls" strategy], Xinhua, December 28, 2013.
15. Pankaj Jha, "Countering Chinese String of Pearls, India's 'Double Fish Hook' Strategy," *Modern Diplomacy*, August 8, 2020.
16. India Ministry of Defense, *Indian Maritime Doctrine*, 2015, 77.
17. H. I. Sutton, "Submarines May Sink Indian Navy's Plans for Future Aircraft Carrier," *Forbes*, February 23, 2020.
18. Roger Cliff, "A New U.S. Strategy for the Indo-Pacific," National Bureau of Asian Research, Special Report no. 86, June 2020, 45.
19. Satoru Nagao, "The Growing Militarization of the Indian Ocean Power Game and Its Significance for Japan," Sasakawa Peace Foundation, July 10, 2018. For a detailed account of Indian military cooperation with Mauritius and the Seychelles, see Gaurav Sharma, "India—the Indian Ocean Region," 13–17.
20. Vinitha Revi, "Seychelles and Assumption Island Project: Another Test for India," Observer Research Foundation, May 23, 2020; Aakriti Sharma, "India Looking to Setup a Military Base in Seychelles' Assumption Island to Counter China in the Indian Ocean?" *Eurasian Times*, December 12, 2020; Jean-Pierre Cabestan, "Seychelles: How a

9. MARITIME SECURITY

Small Island State Is Navigating Through the Emerging Competition Between India and China," *Seychelles Research Journal* 3, no. 1 (February 2021): 62.

21. Pramit Pal Chaudhuri, "India's 21st Century African Partner: Mozambique Was Modi's First Stop," *Hindustan Times*, July 7, 2016.
22. Shishir Upadhyaya, "Expansion of Chinese Maritime Power in the Indian Ocean: Implications for India," *Defence Studies* 17, no. 1 (2017): 73–76; Derek McDougall and Pradeep Taneja, "Sino-Indian Competition in the Indian Ocean Island Countries: The Scope for Small State Agency," *Journal of the Indian Ocean Region* 16, no. 2 (2020): 134.
23. Aman Thakker and Arun Sahgal, "U.S.-India Maritime Security Cooperation," Center for Strategic and International Studies, October 2019; Antara Ghosal Singh, "India, China and the US: Strategic Convergence in the Indo-Pacific," *Journal of the Indian Ocean Region* 12, no. 2 (2016): 170–71; Pramit Pal Chaudhuri, "New Delhi at Sea: The China Factor in the Indian Ocean Policy of the Modi and Singh Governments," *Asia Policy*, no. 22 (July 2016): 32.
24. Keitaro Ushirogata, "Japan's Commitment to Indian Ocean Security: A Vitally Important Highway, but Risks of Strategic Overextension?" in Brewster, *Indo-Pacific Maritime Security*, 65.
25. Luis Simón and Tomohiko Satake, "Rules-Based Connectivity, Maritime Security and EU-Japan Cooperation in the Indian Ocean," Elcano Royal Institute, May 14, 2020.
26. Ghiasy, Fei, and Saalman, "The 21st Century," 29.
27. Ushirogata, "Japan's Commitment," 63.
28. Yoichiro Sato, "Japan's Indo-Pacific Strategy: The Old Geography and the New Strategic Reality," *Air Force Journal of Indo-Pacific Affairs* 2, no. 3 (Winter 2019): 109; Christopher Len, "China's Maritime Silk Road and Energy Geopolitics in the Indian Ocean: Motivations and Implications for the Region," National Bureau of Asian Research, Special Report no. 68, November 2017, 51.
29. Cliff, "A New U.S. Strategy," 54.
30. Manu Pubby, "India, Japan Make Progress on Sharing Military Logistics," *Economic Times*, September 4, 2019; Don McLain Gill, "India Must Secure the Indian Ocean to Deter China's Assertion along the Border," RUSI, July 9, 2020.
31. Melvin, "The New External Security Politics," 26.
32. Melvin, "The Foreign Military Presence," 6–7.
33. Yves-Heng Lim, "China's Rising Naval Ambitions in the Indian Ocean: Aligning Ends, Ways and Means," *Asian Security* 16, no. 3 (2020): 397.
34. Jérôme Henry, "China's Military Deployments in the Gulf of Aden: Anti-Piracy and Beyond," *Notes de l'Ifri* 89 (November 2016): 12; Xu Qiyu, "National Security Interests and India Ocean: China's Perspective," University of Adelaide, RUMLAE Research Paper no. 16-11, January 12, 2016, 3; Brewster, "An Indian Ocean Dilemma," 49.
35. Comment by senior executive of international shipping company at conference attended by Shinn in Arlington, Virginia, March 7, 2019.
36. Liza Tobin, "Underway—Beijing's Strategy to Build China Into a Maritime Great Power," *Naval War College Review* 71, no. 2 (Spring 2018): 29; Ghiasy, Fei, and Saalman, "The 21st Century," 24–25.

9. MARITIME SECURITY

37. Jayanna Krupakar, "China's Naval Base(s) in the Indian Ocean—Signs of a Maritime Grand Strategy," *Strategic Analysis* 41, no. 3 (2017): 209–10.
38. U.S. Defense Intelligence Agency, *China Military Power: Modernizing a Force to Fight and Win* (Washington, D.C.: Defense Intelligence Agency, 2019), 66.
39. Li Jiacheng, "Developing China's Indian Ocean Strategy: Rationale and Prospects," *China Quarterly of International Strategic Studies* 3, no. 4 (2017): 489.
40. China State Council, *China's Military Strategy*, May 26, 2015.
41. You Ji, "China's Emerging Indo-Pacific Naval Strategy," *Asia Policy*, no. 22 (July 2016): 13.
42. Zhengyu Wu, "Towards Naval Normalcy: 'Open Seas Protection' and Sino-US Maritime Relations," *Pacific Review* 32, no. 4 (2019): 676–80; Lei Yu, "China's Expanding Security Involvement in Africa: A Pillar for 'China-Africa Community of Common Destiny,'" *Global Policy* 9, no. 4 (November 2018): 492.
43. Devin Thorne and Ben Spevack, "Harbored Ambitions: How China's Port Investments Are Strategically Reshaping the Indo-Pacific," C4ADS, 2017, 17.
44. Thorne and Spevack, 20.
45. Paraphrased in Xiaoyu Pu and Chengli Wang, "Rethinking China's Rise: Chinese Scholars Debate Strategic Overstretch," *International Affairs* 94, no. 5 (2018): 1030.
46. China State Council, "Full Text of the Vision for Maritime Cooperation Under the Belt and Road Initiative," Xinhua, June 20, 2017.
47. Jan Hornat, "The Power Triangle in the Indian Ocean: China, India and the United States," *Cambridge Review of International Affairs* 29, no. 2 (2016): 430–31; D. S. Rajan, "China in the Indian Ocean," South Asia Analysis Group, April 20, 2016. The latter study sheds light on China's strategy by quoting the views of officials and Chinese scholars from 2012 to 2016.
48. Ryan Martinson and Katsuya Yamamoto, "How China's Navy Is Preparing to Fight in the 'Far Seas,'" *National Interest*, July 18, 2017.
49. Mike Chia-Yu Huang, "A New Game Started? China's 'Overseas Strategic Pivots' in the Indian Ocean Region," *China Report* 54, no. 3 (2018): 271–73.
50. Lyle J. Goldstein, "Beijing at Sea: Is China Crafting an Atlantic Maritime Strategy?" *National Interest*, February 28, 2017.
51. Ryan D. Martinson, "China as an Atlantic Naval Power," *RUSI Journal* 164, no. 7 (September 2019): 18–19, 30–31.
52. Alice Ekman, "China in the Mediterranean: An Emerging Presence," *Notes de l'Ifri* (February 2018): 7–10.
53. Gurpreet S. Khurana, "China as an Indian Ocean Power: Trends and Implications," *Maritime Affairs: Journal of the National Maritime Foundation* 12, no. 1 (Summer 2016): 20.
54. Michael McDevitt, *Becoming a Great "Maritime Power": A Chinese Dream*, (Washington, D.C.: CNA, June 2016): 22–32, 118; Alan Burns, "The Role of the PLA Navy in China's Goal of Becoming a Maritime Power," in McDevitt, *Becoming a Great "Maritime Power,"* 28–30.
55. David Brewster, "The Red Flag Follows Trade: China's Future as an Indian Ocean Power," in *China's Expanding Strategic Ambitions*, ed. Ashley J. Tellis, Alison Szalwinski, and Michael Wills (Seattle: National Bureau of Asian Research, 2019), 198–201, 206;

9. MARITIME SECURITY

David Brewster, "Silk Roads and Strings of Pearls: The Strategic Geography of China's New Pathways in the Indian Ocean," *Geopolitics* 22, no. 2 (2017): 280.

56. Erickson, "Power vs Distance," 253.
57. Erickson, 258; Chad Peltier, "China's Logistics Capabilities for Expeditionary Operations," *Janes*, April 15, 2020, 36–37; Lucie Béraud-Sudreau et al., *Enabling a More Externally Focused and Operational PLA—2020 PLA Conference Papers*, (Carlisle Barracks, Penn: U.S. Army War College Press, 2022), 82–84.
58. For an analysis of China's plans to become a maritime power, see Ian Burns McCaslin and Andrew S. Erickson, "The Impact of Xi-Era Reforms on the Chinese Navy," in *Chairman Xi Remakes the PLA: Assessing Chinese Military Reforms*, ed. Phillip C. Saunders et al. (Washington, D.C.: National Defense University, 2019), 125–70; Lim, "China's Rising Naval Ambitions," 367–94.
59. Ronald O'Rourke, "China Naval Modernization: Implications for U.S. Navy Capabilities—Background and Issues for Congress," Congressional Research Service, May 21, 2020, 2, 25.
60. O'Rourke, 25; Lily Kuo and Cate Cadell, "China Unveils Cutting-edge Aircraft Carrier, First to Be Locally Designed," *Washington Post*, June 17, 2022. For a comparison of naval ship commissions by China and the United States since 1985, see Jerry Hendrix, "Sea Power Makes Great Powers," *Foreign Policy*, October 10, 2021, 38–39.
61. *China Military Power*, 64, 69–76; Bruce Vaughn, "China-India Great Power Competition in the Indian Ocean Region: Issues for Congress," Congressional Research Service, April 20, 2018, 28; "PLA Navy New Aircraft Carrier in Sea Trials as Scheduled," *China Military Online*, May 29, 2020; Zhou Bo, "Subdue the Enemy Without Using Force," *China-US Focus Digest* 14 (June 2017): 52–55.
62. McDevitt, *Becoming a Great "Maritime Power,"* 42–43; Erickson, "Power vs Distance," 261.
63. Peltier, "China's Logistics," 51.
64. O'Rourke, "China Naval Modernization," 4.
65. Shaurya Karanbir Gurung, "14 Chinese Navy Ships Spotted in Indian Ocean, Indian Navy Monitoring Locations," *Economic Times*, July 12, 2018; "中国潜艇被指平均每艘3年多轮到一次远洋巡逻" [Chinese submarines are said to average more than one oceangoing patrol every three years], *Sina Military*, April 9, 2013.
66. Xinhua, "Chinese Naval Fleet Stages Live-fire Drill in Indian Ocean," August 25, 2017.
67. Teddy Ng and Shi Jiangtao, "Chinese Navy's Live-fire Drill May Be Warning Shot to India Amid Ongoing Doklam Stand-off," *South China Morning Post*, August 26, 2017.
68. "China's Marines, and How They Compare with Those in the West," *Forces.net*, December 21, 2021.
69. U.S. Department of Defense, *Annual Report to Congress: Military and Security Developments Involving the People's Republic of China 2019*, May 2, 2019, 35; Jeffrey Becker et al., *China's Presence in the Middle East and Western Indian Ocean: Beyond Belt and Road* (Arlington, Va.: CNA, February 2019), 73; Dennis Blasko and Roderick Lee, "The Chinese Navy's Marine Corps, Part 1: Expansion and Reorganization," *China Brief* 19, no. 3 (February 1, 2019): 11.

9. MARITIME SECURITY

70. David Lague, "China Expands Its Amphibious Forces in Challenge to U.S. Supremacy Beyond Asia," *Reuters Special Report*, July 2, 2020.
71. Melvin, "The New External Security Politics," 20.
72. David Shinn and Joshua Eisenman, *China and Africa: A Century of Engagement* (Philadelphia: University of Pennsylvania Press, 2012), 181.
73. Marc Lanteigne, "Fire Over Water: China's Strategic Engagement of Somalia and the Gulf of Aden Crisis," *Pacific Review* 26, no. 3 (2013): 296–97.
74. Lanteigne, 298, 300–302; Cindy Cheng, "China and U.S. Anti-piracy Engagement in the Gulf of Aden and Western Indian Ocean Region," Carter Center, 2019, 5; Zhang Junshe, "Chinese/U.S. Naval Cooperation on Counterpiracy and Escort Missions," in *Beyond the Wall: Chinese Far Seas Operations*, ed. Peter A. Dutton and Ryan D. Martinson (Newport, R.I.: U.S. Naval War College, May 2015), 43; Niall Duggan, "The People's Republic of China and European Union Security Cooperation in Africa: Sino-EU Security Cooperation in Mali and the Gulf of Aden," *International Journal of China Studies* 8, no. 1 (April 2017): 10–11.
75. Terry McKnight, "End Piracy in the Gulf of Aden," *Proceedings of the US Naval Institute* 143, no. 6 (June 2017).
76. China Ministry of Foreign Affairs, "China's Arab Policy Paper," China Ministry of Foreign Affairs, January 2016; "Forum on China-Africa Cooperation Beijing Action Plan (2019–2021)," September 5, 2018.
77. Henry, "China's Military Deployments," 17–19; Zhang Junshe, "Chinese/U.S. Naval Cooperation," 43; Timothy R. Heath, *China's Pursuit of Overseas Security* (Santa Monica, Calif.: RAND Corporation, 2018): 29.
78. J. E. Dyer, "China Deploys Submarines to Gulf of Aden," *Liberty Unyielding*, October 5, 2014; Lawrence Chung, "China's Nuclear Sub Mission in Gulf of Aden 'Could Cause Unease Among Neighbours,'" *South China Morning Post*, April 27, 2015; Dinakar Peri, "U.S. Admiral Questions Logic of Chinese Submarines on Anti-piracy Missions," *Hindu*, January 9, 2016.
79. Lin Zihan and Zhao Huaning, "Making Contributions to Peace and Security in Africa," *China Military*, August 8, 2022.
80. Henry, "China's Military Deployments," 24–29; Gisela Grieger, "China's Growing Role as a Security Actor in Africa," European Parliamentary Research Service, October 2019, 11.
81. Matthew G. Minot-Scheuermann, "Chinese Anti-Piracy and the Global Maritime Commons," *Diplomat*, February 25, 2016.
82. Zhang Junshe, "Chinese/U.S. Naval Cooperation," 44.
83. Grieger, "China's Growing Role," 11; Cheng, "China and U.S.," 6; Lanteigne, "Fire Over Water," 301.
84. Cheng, "Cheng and U.S.," 8–9; Nana Raymond Lawrence Ofosu-Boateng, "Piracy Challenges in the Gulf of Guinea Along the Coast of Ghana, Togo, Benin and Nigeria in the Midst of Its Oil Find—A Case Study of Ghana," *Open Journal of Social Sciences* 6, no. 7 (July 2018): 191; Li Xinfeng, Zhang Chunyu, and Zhang Mengying, "China's Role

9. MARITIME SECURITY

in Peace and Security Cooperation in the Gulf of Guinea Region," *China International Studies* 66 (September/October 2017): 47; "Gulf of Guinea Kidnappings Makes 95% of 2020 Global Piracy Attacks," *Marine Insight*, January 20, 2021.

85. Agence France Presse, "Four Chinese Sailors Kidnapped in Gabon Are Free," January 14, 2020.
86. "Ocean Marine: We Rescued Chinese Vessel from Pirate Attack on Nigerian Waters," *Cable*, March 9, 2020.
87. Ian M. Ralby, "Nigerian Navy Thwarts Hijacking of Chinese Fishing Vessel," *Maritime Executive*, May 19, 2020.
88. "China Says Five Sailors Kidnapped off Nigeria from Singapore-flagged Ship Kota Budi," *Straits Times*, July 6, 2020; "5名中国籍船员在尼日利亚海域遭劫持！生命威胁有多大？海盗目的为何？" [Five Chinese crew members hijacked in Nigerian waters! How big is the threat? What is the purpose of piracy?], *China News Service*, July 8, 2020.
89. "Pirates Abduct 14 Seafarers from Heavy Lift Ship in Gulf of Guinea," *Maritime Executive*, November 17, 2020.
90. "Crew of Chinese Boat Freed after Ransom Payment: Nigeria Army," *Aljazeera*, March 7, 2021.
91. Grieger, "China's Growing Role," 11.
92. Richard Asante, "China's Security and Economic Engagement in West Africa," *China Quarterly of International Strategic Studies* 3, no. 4 (2017): 581.
93. China Ministry of Foreign Affairs, "Forum on China-Africa Cooperation Beijing Action Plan (2019–2021)," September 5, 2018.
94. Xinhua, "Navies of China, Gulf of Guinea Countries Discuss Maritime Security," May 26, 2022.
95. David Scott, "Chinese Maritime Strategy for the Indian Ocean," Center for International Maritime Security, November 28, 2017; U.S. Defense Intelligence Agency, *China Military Power*, 103–4; "Pakistan Gives China a 40-Year Lease for Gwadar Port," *Maritime Executive*, April 27, 2017; Thorne and Spevack, *Harbored Ambitions*, 39–53; Heath, *China's Pursuit of Overseas Security*, 24–25; Frédéric Grare, "Along the Road: Gwadar and China's Power Projection," EU Institute for Security Studies, July 2018.
96. Martin Humphreys et al., *Port Development and Competition in East and Southern Africa: Prospects and Challenges* (Washington, D.C.: World Bank, 2019), 47; McDevitt, *Becoming a Great "Maritime Power,"* 42.
97. John Lee, "China's Trojan Ports," *American Interest*, November 29, 2018.
98. China State Council, "Vision and Actions on Jointly Building Silk Road Economic Belt and 21st Century Maritime Silk Road," March 28, 2015.
99. Daniel J. Kostecka, "Places and Bases: The Chinese Navy's Emerging Support Network in the Indian Ocean," *Naval War College Review* 64, no. 1 (Winter 2011): 59–78; *China–South Asia Relations, Hearing Before the U.S.-China Economic and Security Review Commission*, 114 Cong. 38 (2016) (statement of David Brewster): 4.
100. Peltier, "China's Logistics," 24.

9. MARITIME SECURITY

101. Guifang Xue, "The Potential Dual Use of Support Facilities in the Belt and Road Initiative," *Securing the Belt and Road Initiative*, ed. Nadège Rolland (Seattle: National Bureau of Asian Research), 53–54.
102. Li Jiacheng, "Developing China's Indian Ocean Strategy," 495.
103. Thorne and Spevack, *Harbored Ambitions*, 21. Some Chinese analysts emphasize the economic benefits to the "investing parties" and the contribution they make "to a more effective and efficient African port industry." See Zhongzhen Yang, Yunzhu He, Hao Zhu, and Theo Notteboom, "China's Investment in African Ports: Spatial Distribution, Entry Modes and Investor Profile," *Research in Transportation Business & Management* 37 (December 2020): 1–24.
104. Daniel R. Russel and Blake H. Berger, *Weaponizing the Belt and Road Initiative* (New York: Asia Society Policy Institute, September 2020), 23.
105. *Hearing on China's Military Power Projection and U.S. National Interests Before the U.S.-China Economic and Security Review Commission*, 116 Cong. 1–2 (2020), statement of Isaac B. Kardon; Isaac B. Kardon, "China's Ports in Africa," in *(In)Roads and Outposts: Critical Infrastructure in China's Africa Strategy*, ed. Nadège Rolland (Seattle: National Bureau of Asian Research, May 2022), 12, 25–27.
106. Huang, "A New Game Started," 274–75.
107. Zhou Bo, "The String of Pearls and the Maritime Silk Road," *China-US Focus*, February 11, 2014.
108. "COSCO: China's Shipping Giant Expands Its Global Influence," *Hellenic Shipping News*, May 16, 2022.
109. Xinhua, "Chinese Naval Fleet Arrives in Greece for Friendly Visit," July 23, 2017.
110. Abdi Latif Dahir, "A Legal Tussle Over a Strategic African Port Sets Up a Challenge for China's Belt and Road Plan," *Quartz Africa*, February 28, 2019; "Djibouti Rejects Awarding Port Operations to Dubai Firm," *East African*, January 19, 2020.
111. Costas Paris, "China Tightens Grip on East African Port," *Wall Street Journal*, February 21, 2019.
112. Jevans Nyabiage, "China Merchants Signs US$350 Million Deal for Shekou-Style Revamp of Djibouti Port," *South China Morning Post*, January 5, 2021.
113. Judd Devermont, Amelia Cheatham, and Catherine Chiang, "Assessing the Risks of Chinese Investments in Sub-Saharan African Ports," Center for Strategic and International Studies, June 2019.
114. John Hursh, "Tanzania Pushes Back on Chinese Port Project," *Maritime Executive*, December 2, 2019; Michael Marray, "Tanzania Pushes Back Against Terms of Bagamoyo Port Concession," *Asset*, July 3, 2019; China Ministry of Commerce, "坦桑尼亚政府承认巴加莫约港项目没有进展" [The Tanzanian government admits that the Bagamoyo port project has not made progress], April 22, 2019.
115. "China Pushes for Implementation of Tanzania's Bagamoyo Port," *Maritime Executive*, April 29, 2022.
116. Xinhua, "Chinese Firm's Upgrade of Tanzania's Largest Port Set to Bolster Handling Capacity," July 13, 2020; Veda Vaidyanathan and Jumanne Gomera, "Building and

9. MARITIME SECURITY

Developing Port Infrastructure—Case Studies of Dar es Salaam and Bagamoyo Ports," in *China's Infrastructure Development in Africa: An Examination of Projects in Tanzania and Kenya,* ed. Veda Vaidyanathan (Delhi: Institute of Chinese Studies, November 2019), 71–73.
117. Humphreys et al., *Port Development*, 23–25.
118. Rodgers Luhwago, "Projects Linked to Mtwara Port Due for Kick Off March," *Daily News*, November 3, 2019.
119. Allan Mungai, "Uhuru and Abiy to Inspect Lamu Port," *Standard*, December 9, 2020; "Lamu Port Construction Project Updates, Kenya," *Construction Review Online*, May 29, 2022.
120. Charles Mghenyi, "The Sh40 Billion Kipevu Oil Terminal Now 84% Complete—KPA," *Star*, April 6, 2021.
121. Xinhua, "Chinese-Built Walvis Bay Container Terminal in Namibia Inaugurated," August 3, 2019.
122. Adam Hartman, "Chinese Naval Base for Walvis Bay," *Namibian*, November 19, 2014; "外媒称中国将在纳米比亚建基地该国军方称正商讨" [Foreign media says China will build a base in Namibia, the country's military says it is discussing], *Global Times*, November 24, 2014.
123. Shinn/Eisenman interview with Ambassador Zhang Yiming, Windhoek, June 7, 2018.
124. Shinn/Eisenman interview with senior Namibian police official, Windhoek, June 7, 2018.
125. Sakeus Likela, "Defense Mum on Chinese Troops in Namibia," *Namibian*, September 11, 2020; Sakeus Likela, "Defence Minister Claims LPM Reports to Foreign Countries," *Namibian*, September 16, 2020.
126. "New Beginnings for Angolan Port Projects," *Macauhub*, January 25, 2019; "Caio Deep Water Port Works Set to Resume This Month," *ANGOP*, January 26, 2020; "Minister Says New Port Key to Developing Angolan Province," Macao Forum, June 24, 2020; André dos Anjos, "Lobito Port Open to Private Capital," *Journal de Angola*, March 25, 2022.
127. Turloch Mooney, "Central Africa's Only Deep-Sea Port Takes Shape at Kribi," *JOC.com*, March 18, 2016; Information from the files of Isaac B. Kardon, Naval War College, and Wendy Leutert, Indiana University.
128. Thierry Pairault, "The China Merchants in Djibouti: From the Maritime to the Digital Silk Roads," *Africa News*, December 3, 2019.
129. "Lekki Port Project Receives First Installment of $630m Chinese Loan," *Global Construction Review*, May 5, 2021.
130. UNCTAD, "Investment Trends Monitor," no. 36, October 2020, 5.
131. "Deep Sea Port in Akwa Ibom, Nigeria," *Bolloré Ports*, November 30, 2018.
132. "China Merchant Group Will Invest in Industrial Sector, in Addition to Its Operations at Lomé Port," *Togo First*, September 6, 2018; Pairault, "The China Merchant's in Djibouti"; Loucoumane Coulibaly, "Ivory Coast Completes Second Shipping Container Terminal," Reuters, November 26, 2022.
133. SMB-Winning Consortium, http://smb-guinee.com/en/consortium-smb-winning/.
134. "Guinea Kimbo & Co. Port Construction Complete," *Asian Metal News*, July 26, 2019.

9. MARITIME SECURITY

135. "Mauritania to Get First Deepwater Port," *Global Construction Review*, April 10, 2018.
136. Stéphanie Pézard and Anne-Kathrin Glatz, "Arms in and Around Mauritania: National and Regional Security Implications," *Small Arms Survey*, June 2010, 11.
137. "Construction of the Port of N'Diago in Mauritania Nears Completion," *Sigma Plantfinder*, April 29, 2020.
138. "Mauritania Seeks Sorcerer to Make a $352 Million Port Project Profitable," *Archyde*, July 25, 2020.
139. "China Loans Mauritania $87m for Port Construction," *North Africa Post*, January 8, 2020.
140. Joanna Kakissis, "Chinese Firms Now Hold Stakes in Over a Dozen European Ports," *NPR*, October 9, 2018.
141. "Algeria to Build New Deepwater Port," *Maritime Executive*, February 10, 2017.
142. Algerie Presse Service, "Algeria Seeks to Engage in New Mode of Governance Based on Transparency, Efficiency," April 21, 2020.
143. Chris Devonshire-Ellis, "Algeria to Coordinate National Development Plans with China's Belt and Road Initiative," *Silk Road Briefing*, July 27, 2021.
144. Information from the files of Isaac Kardon and Wendy Leutert, as updated by authors from shipping company and press accounts.
145. Emma Scott, "China's Silk Road Strategy: A Foothold in the Suez, but Looking to Israel," *China Brief* 14, no. 9 (October 10, 2014): 1–14; "HPH Raises Its Stakes in Alexandria Complex," *World Cargo News*, March 16, 2016.
146. Xinhua, "Egypt Inks Deal with China's Port Giant to Build Container Terminal in Abu Qir Port," August 7, 2019; Haisam Hassanein, "Egypt Takes Another Step Toward China," Washington Institute for Near East Policy, August 19, 2019; "Hutchison Ports Partners with Egyptian Navy on Mega-ship Container Terminal in Abu Qir," *Safety4Sea*, August 31, 2020.
147. Xinhua, "China Now Biggest Investor in Suez," March 23, 2017; Xinhua, "China, Egypt Dream Big as Desert Is Converted Into Cooperation Zone," January 20, 2019.
148. Xinhua, "China's COSCO Shipping to Build Logistics Park in Egypt," November 8. 2017.
149. Kakissis, "Chinese Firms"; Charlotte So, "China Shipping Group Invests in Egyptian Port," *South China Morning Post*, November 28, 2007.
150. "China Invited to Set Up Anti-piracy Base in Seychelles." *Defence Web*, December 6, 2011.
151. "China Denies Seychelles Base," *News China Magazine*, February 2012; Cabestan, "Seychelles," 66; For an analysis of China-India competition in the Seychelles, see McDougall and Taneja, "Sino-Indian Competition," 136–39.
152. Seychelles Ministry of Foreign Affairs, "Seychelles to Boost Military Cooperation with China," November 23, 2016.
153. Kardon, *Hearing on China's Military Power*, 3.
154. Peltier, "China's Logistics," 22.
155. Xinhua, "South African Warship Ends China Visit," October 20, 2008.
156. Shinn and Eisenman, *China and Africa*, 189–90.
157. Kenneth Allen, Phillip C. Saunders, and John Chen, *Chinese Military Diplomacy, 2003-2016: Trends and Implications* (Washington, D.C.: National Defense University, July 2017),

62–66; Austin M. Strange, "China's Blue Soft Power," *Naval War College Review* 68, no. 1 (Winter 2015): 11–12; Martinson, "China as an Atlantic Naval Power," 22. Graham Benedict, George Washington University, updated the port visits drawing on press accounts. For a list of PLAN port calls at Djibouti until January 2020, see Peter A. Dutton, Isaac B. Kardon, and Conor M. Kennedy, "China Maritime Report No. 6: Djibouti: China's First Overseas Strategic Strongpoint," *CMSI China Maritime Reports* 6 (2020): 41–44.

158. Phillip C. Saunders and Jiunwei Shyy, "China's Military Diplomacy," in *China's Global Influence: Perspectives and Recommendations*, ed. Scott D. McDonald and Michael C. Burgoyne (Honolulu: Asia-Pacific Center for Security Studies, 2019), 216–17; Strange, "China's Blue Soft Power," 9–13.

159. SWAPO, "Chinese Navy Docks at Port"; Xinhua, "中国海军第十六批护航编队访问纳米比亚" [The 16th Chinese Navy Escort Fleet visits Namibia], June 12, 2014.

160. "Chinese and Nigerian Navies Conduct First Anti-piracy Joint Drill," *China Military Online*, May 29, 2014.

161. Zhu Linlin, "28th Chinese Naval Escort Taskforce Visits Cameroon," *China Military Online*, June 12, 2018; Zhu Linlin and Guo Bing, "Gabonese President Visits Chinese Frigate Yancheng in Libreville," *China Military Online*, June 20, 2018.

162. Philip Nwosu, "Nigeria, China, France, Portugal Navies Combat Piracy in Gulf of Guinea," *Sun*, June 3, 2018.

163. Lin Jian and Li Hao, "Chinese, Egyptian Navies Conduct Joint Maritime Exercise," *China Military Online*, August 21, 2019.

164. Andrew Scobell et al., *At the Dawn of Belt and Road: China in the Developing World* (Santa Monica, Calif.: RAND Corporation, 2018), 203; "China, Tanzania Carrying Out Month Long Joint Naval Drills," *Defence Web*, October 24, 2014.

165. Dean Wingrin, "Foreign Warships Arrive in Cape Town for Inaugural Naval Exercise," *Defence Web*, November 25, 2019; Peter Fabricius, "South Africa's Military Drills with Russia and China Raise Eyebrows," Institute for Security Studies, November 29, 2019; Hans Uwe Mergener, "'MOSI II' Naval Exercise Concluded, But Ramifications Continue," European Security and Defense, March 3, 2023.

166. Xu Yi, "Peace Ark Carries Cargo of Goodwill," *China Military*, December 13, 2019.

167. Claude Zanardi, "China's Soft Power with Chinese Characteristics: The Cases of Confucius Institutes and Chinese Naval Diplomacy," *Journal of Political Power* 9, no. 3 (2016): 438.

168. Xinhua, "It's a Pleasure to Exchange Medical Experiences with Chinese Navy Doctors," October 21, 2010.

169. Atmakuri Lakshmi Archana and Mingjiang Li, "Geopolitical Objectives Fuel China's Peace Ark," *East Asia Forum*, October 13, 2018.

170. "PLA Navy, on Humanitarian Mission, Visits Sierra Leone," *China Daily*, September 23, 2017.

171. "Chinese Naval Hospital Ship Wraps Up Visit to Republic of Congo," *China Military Online*, October 18, 2017; "Peace Ark Tightens the China-Africa Bond with Humanitarian

9. MARITIME SECURITY

Assistance," *People's Daily*, September 14, 2018; "Chinese Naval Hospital Ship Peace Ark Leaves Djibouti for Spain," *China Military Online*, September 1, 2017.
172. Thorne and Spevack, *Harbored Ambitions*, 23.
173. Kardon, *Hearing on China's Military Power*, 7.
174. "COSCO: China's Shipping Giant Expands Its Global Influence."
175. Nitin Agarwala and Rana Divyank Chaudhary, *Growth of Shipbuilding in China: The Science, Technology, and Innovation Route*, ICS Occasional Paper no. 31, Institute of Chinese Studies, Delhi, May 2019.
176. McDevitt, *Becoming a Great "Maritime Power,"* 84–88; Mathieu Duchâtel and Alexandre Sheldon Duplaix, *Blue China: Navigating the Maritime Silk Road to Europe*, European Council on Foreign Relations, April 2018, 21.
177. McDevitt, *Becoming a Great "Maritime Power,"* 89; Center for Strategic and International Studies, "How Is China Modernizing Its Navy?" January 9, 2019.
178. Agarwala and Chaudhary, "Growth of Shipbuilding."
179. Dennis J. Blasko, "China's Merchant Marine," in McDevitt, *Becoming a Great "Maritime Power,"* 92–95; James Kynge et al., "How China Rules the Waves," *Financial Times*, January 12, 2017; Virginia Marantidou, "Shipping Finance: China's New Tool in Becoming a Global Maritime Power," *China Brief* 18, no. 2 (February 13, 2018): 7.
180. Blasko, "China's Merchant Marine," 96–97; James E. Fanell, "Asia Rising: China's Global Naval Strategy and Expanding Force Structure," *Naval War College Review* 72, no. 1 (Winter 2019): 30.
181. Brewster, "The Red Flag Follows Trade," 201.
182. "China Has No Plan for Indian Ocean Military Bases," *Hindu*, September 4, 2012.
183. Shinn interview with representative of Shanghai Institutes for International Studies, Shanghai, May 6, 2016.
184. Shinn interview, Shanghai, May 11, 2016.
185. Huang, "A New Game Started," 273; Kristen Gunness and Oriana Skylar Mastro, "A Global People's Liberation Army: Possibilities, Challenges, and Opportunities," *Asia Policy*, no. 22 (July 2016): 145; Andrew Scobell and Nathan Beauchamp-Mustafaga, "The Flag Lags but Follows: The PLA and China's Great Leap Outward," in Saunders et al., *Chairman Xi Remakes the PLA*, 178.
186. Gunness and Mastro, "Global People's Liberation Army," 143.
187. Shen Dingli, "Don't Shun the Idea of Setting Up Overseas Military Bases," china.org.cn, January 28, 2010.
188. Conor Kennedy, "Strategic Strong Points and Chinese Naval Strategy," *China Brief* 19, no. 6 (March 22, 2019): 21.
189. "PLA's First Overseas Base in Djibouti," *China Military Online*, April 12, 2016.
190. Erica Downs, Jeffrey Becker, and Patrick deGategno, *China's Military Support Facility in Djibouti: The Economic and Security Dimensions of China's First Overseas Base*, Center for Naval Analyses, July 2017, 23.
191. Zach Vertin, *Great Power Rivalry in the Red Sea: China's Experiment in Djibouti and Implications for the United States*, Global China, Brookings Doha Center, June 2020, 6–7;

9. MARITIME SECURITY

François Soudan, "Ismaïl Omar Guelleh: 'Djibouti n'est Pas à Vendre,'" *Jeune Afrique*, April 25, 2018.

192. Scobell and Beauchamp-Mustafaga, "Flag Lags," 188.
193. Vertin, *Great Power Rivalry*, 6; H. I. Sutton, "Satellite Images Show That Chinese Navy Is Expanding Overseas Base," *Forbes*, May 10, 2020; Shinn/Eisenman interview with Western defense attaché, Djibouti, June 15, 2018.
194. Joel Wuthnow, "The PLA Beyond Asia: China's Growing Military Presence in the Red Sea Region," *Strategic Forum*, no. 303 (January 2020): 4; U.S. Department of Defense, *Annual Report to Congress 2019*, 61.
195. Zhao Lei and Zhou Jin, "Live-Fire Exercises Conducted by PLA Base in Djibouti," *China Daily*, November 25, 2017; Minnie Chan, "Live-Fire Show of Force by Troops from China's First Overseas Military Base," *South China Morning Post*, September 25, 2017.
196. "PLA Base in Djibouti Conducts Anti-terrorism Exercise," *People's Daily Online*, May 15, 2018.
197. James E. Fanell, "Asia Rising: China's Global Naval Strategy and Expanding Force Structure," *Naval War College Review* 72, no. 1 (Winter 2019): 27.
198. Hend Elmahly and Degang Sun, "China's Military Diplomacy Towards Arab Countries in Africa's Peace and Security," *Contemporary Arab Affairs* 11, no. 4 (2018): 129–32; Vertin, *Great Power Rivalry*, 10–11.
199. Downs, Becker, and deGategno, *China's Military Support*, 7–16.
200. Chris Alden and Zheng Yixiao, "China's Changing Role in Peace and Security in Africa," in *China and Africa: Building Peace and Security Cooperation on the Continent*, ed. Chris Alden et al. (Cham, Switz.: Palgrave Macmillan, 2018), 54.
201. Mathieu Duchâtel, "Overseas Military Operations in Belt and Road Countries: The Normative Constraints and Legal Framework," in *Securing the Belt and Road Initiative*, ed. Nadège Rolland, National Bureau of Asian Research, Special Report no. 80, September 2019, 12; David Styan, "China's Maritime Silk Road and Small States: Lessons from the Case of Djibouti," *Journal of Contemporary China* 29, no. 122 (2020): 199.
202. Xinhua, "Commentary: China's Djibouti Base Not for Military Expansion," July 13, 2017.
203. Downs, Becker, and deGategno, *China's Military Support*, 30–31; Krupakar, "China's Naval Base(s)," 209–10.
204. Vertin, *Great Power Rivalry*, 5; U.S. Department of Defense, *Annual Report to Congress 2019*, 16.
205. U.S. Defense Intelligence Agency, *China Military Power*, 29; Peter A. Dutton, Isaac B. Kardon, and Conor M. Kennedy, "China Maritime Report No. 6," 38–39.
206. Nathan Beauchamp-Mustafaga, "Where to Next? Considerations for Overseas Base Site Selection," *China Brief* 20, no. 18 (October 19, 2020): 28–29.
207. Conor M. Kennedy, "China Maritime Report No. 4: Civil Transport in PLA Power Projection," *CMSI China Maritime Reports* 4 (2019): 3.
208. "PLA's First Overseas Base in Djibouti."
209. Downs, Becker, and deGategno, *China's Military Support*, 40.

10. TECHNOLOGY AND INFORMATION SECURITY

210. Shinn/Eisenman interview, Shanghai, June 30, 2017.
211. CGTN America, "Victor Gao Discusses China-Africa Ties Amid Defense and Security Forum in Beijing," July 3, 2018, YouTube video.
212. Lee Jeong-ho, "How the Tiny African Nation of Djibouti Became the Linchpin in China's Belt and Road Plan," *South China Morning Post*, April 28, 2019.
213. China State Council Information Office, *China's National Defense in the New Era*, July 2019, 15.
214. House Committee on Armed Services, *National Security Challenges and U.S. Activities in Africa, 2018*: 3–42, 49–73.
215. U.S. Department of Defense, *Annual Report to Congress 2019*, 16.
216. Lolita C. Baldor, "General: China's Africa Outreach Poses Threat from Atlantic," Associated Press, May 6, 2021.
217. Michael M. Phillips, "U.S. Says China Eyes First Atlantic Navy Base—Alarmed by Findings, Biden Officials Urge Equatorial Guinea to Rebuff Beijing Overture," *Wall Street Journal*, December 6, 2021; Bonny Lin et al., "Is China Building a New String of Pearls in the Atlantic Ocean?" Center for Strategic and International Studies, December 20, 2021.
218. Eric A. Miller, "More Chinese Military Bases in Africa: A Question of When, Not If," *Foreign Policy*, August 16, 2022.
219. Thorne and Spevack, *Harbored Ambitions*, 24; Downs, Becker, and deGategno, *China's Military Support*, 40.
220. Lim, "China's Rising Naval Ambitions," 405–6.
221. Bharat Shakti, "Will Comoros Be China's Next 'Djibouti' in Indian Ocean Region?" *Dryad Global*, June 10, 2022; Peter Layton, "Indian Ocean Rivalries: China and India in the Indian Ocean," *Maritime Defence Monitor*, June 2022; Dipanjan Roy Chaudhury, "China Eyes Military Base in Indian Ocean Region in Madagascar," *Economic Times*, July 20, 2022.
222. Peltier, "China's Logistics," 25–83.
223. U.S. Office of the Secretary of Department of Defense, *Military and Security Developments Involving the People's Republic of China 2022: Annual Report to Congress*, 145. See also Paul Nantulya, "Considerations for a Prospective New Chinese Naval Base in Africa," Africa Center for Strategic Studies, May 12, 2022.
224. Cristina L. Garafola, Stephen Watts, and Kristin J. Leuschner, "China's Global Basing Ambitions: Defense Implications for the United States," Rand Corporation, 2022, 12.

10. TECHNOLOGY AND INFORMATION SECURITY

1. National People's Congress, "National Intelligence Law of the People's Republic of China," June 27, 2017.
2. Gu Bin, "Western Fears of Party Influence on Chinese Companies Are Overblown," *Financial Times*, February 18, 2019.

10. TECHNOLOGY AND INFORMATION SECURITY

3. Bonnie Girard, "The Real Danger of China's National Intelligence Law," *Diplomat*, February 23, 2019.
4. Bulelani Jili, "China's Surveillance Ecosystem and the Global Spread of Its Tools," Atlantic Council, October 2022, 6.
5. Rachel Schaer, an intern at the American Foreign Policy Council in 2019, helped with the research for this section.
6. "Nuclear: China as a Major Actor in Africa," *CAC International*; Chiponda Chimbelu, "African Countries Mull Nuclear Energy as Russia Extends Offers," *Deutsche Welle*, October 22, 2019.
7. China Ministry of Foreign Affairs, "China's Arab Policy Paper," January 2016.
8. Yuan Shenggao, "CZEC Powers African Cooperation," *China Daily*, September 4, 2018.
9. China Ministry of Foreign Affairs, "Forum on China-Africa Cooperation Dakar Action Plan (2022–2024)," November 30, 2021.
10. Abigail Sah et al., "Atoms for Africa: Is There a Future for Civil Nuclear Energy in Sub-Saharan Africa?" Center for Global Development, CDG Policy Paper, April 2018, 9.
11. World Nuclear Association, "Nuclear Power in South Africa," May 2020.
12. World Nuclear Association, "Nuclear Power in Egypt," June 2020.
13. Samuel Hickey, "China's Nuclear Diplomacy in the Middle East," *Diplomat*, October 9, 2018.
14. World Nuclear Association, "Emerging Nuclear Energy Countries," July 2020.
15. "Tunisia-China Cooperation in Nuclear Energy," *Tunisian Monitor Online News*, August 8, 2019.
16. Yuan Shenggao, "CZEC Powers African Cooperation."
17. Heba Taha, "Nuclear Revival in North Africa? Developments in Algeria, Libya, and Egypt," South African Institute of International Affairs, Occasional Paper no. 322, May 2021, 9.
18. World Nuclear Association, "Emerging Nuclear Energy Countries"; Hickey, "China's Nuclear Diplomacy."
19. Arnaud Lefevre, "The Chinese Investment in Sudan Nuclear Project," *NBN*, November 13, 2018.
20. "Emerging Nuclear Energy Countries."
21. "Sudan to Cooperate with China in Uranium Projects," *Anadolu Agency*, February 14, 2019.
22. "Emerging Nuclear Energy Countries."
23. "Emerging Nuclear Energy Countries"; Nobert Atukunda and Frederic Musisi, "Russia Beats China to Uganda's Nuclear Deal," *Monitor*, September 19, 2019.
24. Petr Chakrov and Thomas Hanlon, "Nigeria Converts Its Research from HEU to LEU Fuel," International Atomic Energy Agency, December 20, 2018; Andrea Rezzonico and Christine Parthemore, "Converging Risks in Nigeria: Nuclear Energy Plans, Climate Fragility, and Security Trends," Council on Strategic Risks, Briefer no. 3, August 28, 2019.
25. Nigeria Atomic Energy Commission, "Nigeria China Memorandum of Understanding."

10. TECHNOLOGY AND INFORMATION SECURITY

26. Chinese Embassy in Ghana, "Made-in-China Helps Ghana's Nuclear Energy Development," August 7, 2019; Richard Stone, "U.S.-China Mission Rushes Bomb-Grade Nuclear Fuel Out of Africa," *sciencemag.org*, August 31, 2017; Ghana Ministry of Foreign Affairs, "Ghana and China Sign Eight Cooperation Agreements, Memoranda of Understanding," September 5, 2018.
27. "Emerging Nuclear Energy Countries."
28. Agence de Presse Africaine, "Chinese Firm to Build a Nuclear Plant in Namibia," April 3, 2017.
29. China State Council, "Vision and Actions on Jointly Building Silk Road Economic Belt and 21st Century Maritime Silk Road," March 28, 2015.
30. "Forum on China-Africa Cooperation Dakar Action Plan (2022–2024)."
31. Bonnie S. Glaser and Namrata Goswami, "China's Outer Space Ambitions with Dr. Namrata Goswami," July 14, 2021, in *China Global*, podcast produced by the German Marshal Fund, 29:30.
32. Jevans Nyabiage, "China Aims to Lift Africa's Space Ambitions in Drive to Beat US Domination," *South China Morning Post*, September 8, 2022.
33. China State Council Information Office, "China's Space Program: A 2021 Perspective," January 2022.
34. "China and Africa Are Collaborating on Youth Space Education Programme," *Space in Africa*, January 7, 2022.
35. Kate Bartlett, "Why China, African Nations Are Cooperating in Space," *VOA*, September 13, 2022.
36. Michael S. Chase, "The Space and Cyberspace Components of the Belt and Road Initiative," in *Securing the Belt and Road Initiative: China's Evolving Military Engagement Along the Silk Road*, ed. Nadège Rolland (Seattle: National Bureau of Asian Research, September 2019), 21–22.
37. Julie Michelle Klinger, "China, Africa, and the Rest: Recent Trends in Space Science, Technology, and Satellite Development" China Africa Research Initiative, Working Paper no. 38, May 2020, 5.
38. Comment by Julie Klinger on September 25, 2020, at China Africa Research Initiative virtual conference in Washington, D.C.
39. Klinger, "China, Africa and the Rest," 15–19.
40. Daniel R. Russel and Blake H. Berger, *Weaponizing the Belt and Road Initiative* (New York: Asia Society Policy Institute, September 2020), 21–22. For an analysis of BeiDou as a competitor to GPS, see David R. Millner et al., "BeiDou: China's GPS Challenger Takes Its Place on the World Stage," *Joint Force Quarterly* 105, 2nd Quarter (2022): 23–31.
41. Zhao Lei, "China and Africa Will Strengthen Cooperation on Beidou Satellite System," *China Daily*, November 6, 2021.
42. China Ministry of Foreign Affairs, "China's Arab Policy Paper"; Deng Xiaoci, "China, Arab States Ink New Action Plan over BDS Cooperation," *Global Times*, December 9, 2021.

10. TECHNOLOGY AND INFORMATION SECURITY

43. CGTN, "China, Arab States to Deepen Cooperation on Satellite Navigation," April 3, 2019.
44. Joseph Ibeh, "China Plans to Double Down on Capital Investments in Egypt," *Africa News*, September 30, 2019.
45. "EgyptSat-2 Reaches New Milestone as China Strengthens Space Relationship with Egypt," *Africa News*, July 11, 2020; Mohammad Hanafi, "Egypt Plans to Launch First Satellite to Monitor Climate Changes in Africa," *Al-Monitor*, October 30, 2022.
46. China State Council Information Office, "China's Space Activities in 2016," December 27, 2016.
47. Julie Michelle Klinger, "China, Africa and the Rest," 14–15; Zhao Lei, "China Helps Algeria Put First Satellite in Orbit," *China Daily*, April 9, 2018.
48. Tabisa Raziya, "SA Joins BRICS Space Programme," African News Agency, July 4, 2017.
49. Joshua Faleti, "SANSA Signs MoU with China Satellite Network Office," *Space in Africa*, December 1, 2021.
50. "China's Space Program: A 2021 Perspective."
51. Klinger, "China, Africa and the Rest," 13–14; Iginio Gagliardone, *China, Africa, and the Future of the Internet* (London: Zed, 2019), 26–27.
52. Reuters, "Nigeria Agrees $550 Million Satellite Deal with China," January 3, 2018.
53. "Sudan's First Satellite SRSS-1 Launched by China," *Spacewatch Africa*, November 3, 2019.
54. Shen Shiwei, "China Boosts Ethiopia's Space Program," *Global Times*, December 22, 2019; Ogechi Onuoha, "ETRSS-1 Captures First Test Images," *Space in Africa*, January 6, 2020; Zhao Lei, "Ethiopia Takes Over Operation of Chinese-built Satellite," *China Daily*, December 14, 2020.
55. Andrew Jones, "China Launches First Long March 8 from Wenchang Spaceport," *Space News*, December 22, 2020; Tesfa-Alem Tekle, "Ethiopia Readies to Launch Second Satellite, Plans for 10 More by 2035," *East African*, September 30, 2020.
56. Klinger, "China, Africa and the Rest," 12.
57. "China-Namibia Relationship on Space Is One of the Best in Africa—Chinese Ambassador to Namibia," *Space in Africa*, September 3, 2019.
58. "Namibia-China Relations Undergo Major Surgery," *New Era*, April 6, 2018.
59. Sophie Tendane, "China Strengthens Space Cooperation with Nam," *Namibian*, September 7, 2022.
60. "Missile-Tracking Chinese Ship Makes Rare Visit," *Mercury*, March 25, 2020.
61. Luciano Anselmo, "Orbital Analysis of the Shenzhou-6 Manned Mission in Support of the Malindi Tracking Station" Istituto di Scienza e Technologie dell'Informazione, Space Flight Dynamics Laboratory, Technical Report, January 27, 2006.
62. Gitonga Njeru, "Prepare for Lift Off," *ChinAfrica*, April 10, 2018.
63. Xinhua, "Kenya Seeks to Cooperate with China on Satellite Technology," July 5, 2019.
64. Brian Ngugi, "Kenya, Chinese Space Station Deal Alarms US," *Business Daily*, September 25, 2020; Ben Payton, "Chinese and American Interests Vie for Kenyan Spaceport,"

10. TECHNOLOGY AND INFORMATION SECURITY

African Business, August 16, 2022; Marco Battaglia and Emanuele Rossi, "Watch Out for China in Kenyan Satellite Base, Warns COPASIR," *Decode 39*, July 12, 2022.
65. Council on Foreign Relations, "Assessing China's Digital Silk Road Initiative."
66. Joe McReynolds, "China's Evolving Perspectives on Network Warfare: Lessons from the *Science of Military Strategy*," *China Brief* 15, no. 8 (April 17, 2015): 3–6.
67. David Ignatius, "Russia and China's Hypocritical Attempt to Control Cyberspace," *Washington Post*, July 20, 2021; Daria Impiombato, "Chinese Telecommunications Giants and Africa's Emerging Digital Infrastructure," in *(In)Roads and Outposts: Critical Infrastructure in China's Africa Strategy*, ed. Nadège Rolland (Seattle: National Bureau of Asian Research, May 2022): 45–58.
68. Kenton Thibaut, "Chinese Discourse Power: Aspirations, Reality, and Ambitions in the Digital Domain," Atlantic Council, August 2022.
69. Alina Polyakova and Chris Meserole, "Exporting Digital Authoritarianism," Brookings Institution, August 2019, 6.
70. *Countering China: Ensuring America Remains the World Leader in Advanced Technologies and Innovation, Before the Subcommittee on Information Technology Committee on Oversight and Government Reform House of Representatives*, 105th Cong. 20 (2018) (statement of Sarah Cook).
71. Sam Olsen, "China Is Wining the War for Global Tech Dominance," *Hill*, October 4, 2020.
72. Niels Nagelhus Schia, "The Chinese Cyber Sovereignty Concept," *Asia Dialogue*, September 7, 2018.
73. Adam Segal, "China's Vision for Cyber Sovereignty and the Global Governance of Cyberspace," in *An Emerging China-Centric Order*, ed. Nadège Rolland (Seattle: National Bureau of Asian Research, August 2020), 88.
74. China State Council, "Vision and Actions."
75. Wu Peng, "Focus Both Immediate and Long-Term," *China Daily*, August 21, 2020.
76. China Ministry of Foreign Affairs, "International Strategy of Cooperation on Cyberspace," March 1, 2017; "China Proposes China-Africa Partnership Plan on Digital Innovation," *GhanaWeb*, August 30, 2021.
77. Elsa B. Kania, "Technology and Innovation in China's Strategy and Global Influence," in *China's Global Influence: Perspectives and Recommendations*, ed. Scott D. McDonald and Michael C. Burgoyne (Honolulu: Asia-Pacific Center for Security Studies, 2019), 232, 242–43.
78. Alexander Chipman Koty, "What Is the China Standards 2035 Plan and How Will It Impact Emerging Industries?" *China Briefing*, July 2, 2020; Naomi Wilson, "China Standards 2035 and the Plan for World Domination—Don't Believe China's Hype," Council on Foreign Relations, June 3, 2020.
79. Bevin Fletcher, "Huawei Still Dominates Telecom Equipment Market," *Fierce Wireless*, December 16, 2021.
80. Will Reno and Jesse Humpal, "As the US Slumps Away, China Subsumes African Security Arrangements," *Defense One*, October 21, 2020.

10. TECHNOLOGY AND INFORMATION SECURITY

81. Polyakova and Meserole, "Exporting Digital Authoritarianism," 2.
82. Democratic Staff, "The New Big Brother: China and Digital Authoritarianism" U.S. Senate Committee on Foreign Relations, July 21, 2020, 6, 30.
83. Thomas Blaubach, "Chinese Technology in the Middle East: A Threat to Sovereignty or an Economic Opportunity?" Middle East Institute, March 2021, 6.
84. Cave et al., "Mapping China's Technology Giants," 8.
85. Elsa Kania, Samm Sacks, Paul Triolo, and Graham Webster, "China's Strategic Thinking on Building Power in Cyberspace: A Top Party Journal's Timely Explanation Translated," *New America* (blog), September 25, 2017.
86. Cave et al., "Mapping China's Technology Giants," 9; James Griffiths, "Democratic Republic of Congo Internet Shutdowns Shows How Chinese Censorship Tactics Are Spreading," *CNN*, January 2, 2019; Matthew J. Slaughter and David H. McCormick, "Data Is Power," *Foreign Affairs* 100, no. 3 (May/June 2021): 59–60.
87. Catalin Cimpanu, "China's Great Firewall Is Blocking Around 311k Domains, 41k by Accident," *The Record*, July 11, 2021.
88. "Targeted, Cut Off, and Left in the Dark: The #KeepItOn Report on Internet Shutdowns in 2019," *Access Now*, 3, 6.
89. Nick Bailey, "East African States Adopt China's Playbook on Internet Censorship," Freedom House Perspectives, October 24, 2017; Abdi Latif Dahir, "China Is Exporting Its Digital Surveillance Methods to African Governments," *Quartz Africa*, November 1, 2018.
90. Huawei, https://www.huawei.com/us/media-center.
91. Benjamin Tsui, "Do Huawei's Training Programs and Centers Transfer Skills to Africa?" China Africa Research Initiative, Policy Brief no. 14, July 2016.
92. Melanie Hart and Jordan Link, "There Is a Solution to the Huawei Challenge," Center for American Progress, October 14, 2020.
93. Segal et al., "Is an Iron Curtain"; Cave et al., "Mapping China's Technology Giants," 6; Chiponda Chimbelu, "Investing in Africa's Tech Infrastructure. Has China Won Already?" *Deutsche Welle*, May 3, 2019.
94. Paul Adepoju, "China's Suspicious Interest in Africa's Internet Networks," *Guardian*, September 17, 2018; Andrea Marshall, "China's Mighty Telecom Footprint in Africa," *New Security Learning*, February 14, 2011.
95. Leonard Sengere, "Half of All Smartphones Sold in Africa Are Transsion Brands. How Did Itel, Tecno and Infinix's Parent Get So Dominant?" *Techzim*, March 9, 2022.
96. Comments by Connor Fairman, Council on Foreign Relations, on September 25, 2020, at virtual China Africa Research Initiative conference, Washington, D.C.; Sengere, "Half of All Smartphones."
97. Rong Wang, François Bar, and Yu Hong, "ICT Aid Flows from China to African Countries: A Communication Network Perspective," *International Journal of Communication* 14 (2020): 1–25. Chinese lending for technology projects in Africa was greater before the launch of the DSR than after. See Henry Tugendhat and Julia Voo, "China's Digital Silk Road in Africa and the Future of Internet Governance," China Africa Research Initiative, Working Paper no. 50, August 2021.

10. TECHNOLOGY AND INFORMATION SECURITY

98. "Huawei Marine Networks Co., Ltd.: Marine Successfully Delivers Hannibal Submarine Cable System for Tunisie Telecom," *M2 Presswire*, December 10, 2009.
99. "LITC and Huawei Marine Launch Silphium Submarine Cable Between Libya and Greece," *offshore-energy.biz*, January 7, 2013.
100. Jack Hasler, "Huawei Is Better Positioned to Spy on Us than We Think," *Washington Post*, March 13, 2019.
101. Mifrah Haq, "China Builds Digital Silk Road in Pakistan to Africa and Europe," *Nikkei Asia*, January 29, 2021; Thomas Blaubach, "Connecting Beijing's Global Infrastructure: The Peace Cable in the Middle East and North Africa," Middle East Institute, March 2022.
102. "Huawei to Sell 51pc Stake in Undersea Cable Business after US Trade Blacklist," *Bloomberg*, June 3, 2019; David Herbling, "Huawei-Backed Cable Linking China, Europe, Africa Lands in Kenya," *Bloomberg*, March 29, 2022; Dale Aluf, "China's Tech Outreach in the Middle East and North Africa," *Diplomat*, November 17, 2022.
103. Edith Mutethya, "China Mobile Teams Up to Build Subsea Cable for Africa, Middle East," *China Daily*, May 15, 2020.
104. Iginio Gagliardone and Frederick Golooba-Mutebi, "The Evolution of the Internet in Ethiopia and Rwanda: Towards a 'Developmental' Model?" *Stability: International Journal of Security & Development* 5, no. 1 (2016): 14–15; Iginio Gagliardone, "China and the Shaping of African Information Societies," in *Africa and China*, ed. Aleksandra W. Gadzala (Lanham, Md.: Rowman & Littlefield, 2015), 48–52; Gagliardone, *China, Africa, and the Future of the Internet*, 73, 78–79.
105. Fentaw Abitew, "The Case for Partial Privatization of Ethio Telecom," *Ethiopia Insight*, August 31, 2020; Emmanuel Abara Benson, "Ethio Telecom Launches Ethiopia's 5G Network, One of Few in Africa," *Business Insider Africa*, May 11, 2022.
106. Sanne van der Lugt, "Exploring the Political, Economic, and Social Implications of the Digital Silk Road Into East Africa: The Case of Ethiopia," in *Global Perspectives on China's Belt and Road Initiative*, ed. Florian Schneider (Amsterdam: Amsterdam University Press, 2021), 334, 337.
107. Iginio Gagliardone, "China and the Africa Internet: Perspectives from Kenya and Ethiopia," *Index Communicación* 3, no. 2 (2013): 78–79; Gagliardone, *China, Africa, and the Future of the Internet*, 68–70.
108. Xinhua, "Kenya Partners with Huawei to Train Public Servants to Enhance Technology Knowledge," October 30, 2020.
109. Xinhua, "Huawei to Support Kenya's Bid to Expand Digital Infrastructure," April 16, 2022.
110. "Kenya Signs 5G Deal with Huawei," *newsbeezer.com*, June 27, 2022.
111. Gagliardone, *China, Africa, and the Future of the Internet*, 68–70.
112. Abu Bakarr Jalloh, "A New Government Data Center Has Been Built in Senegal with the Aim of 'Guaranteeing Senegalese Digital Sovereignty,'" *African Dream*, June 23, 2021.
113. Dan Swinhoe, "Malawi Launches National Data Center," *Data Center Dynamics*, July 28, 2022.

10. TECHNOLOGY AND INFORMATION SECURITY

114. Ma Si, "China Unicom Enters S African Market," *China Daily*, July 19, 2018.
115. "China Mobile International Limited Establishes South Africa Office," *Bloomberg*, September 11, 2018.
116. Catherine Sheglia, "South Africa Is Still Several Years Away from Mass 5G Adoption," *RCR Wireless*, January 27, 2020; Reuters, "South Africa's Telkom Launches 5G Network with Huawei," October 27, 2022.
117. Momoko Kidera, "Huawei's Deep Roots Put Africa Beyond Reach of US Crackdown," *Nikkei Asian Review*, August 15, 2020.
118. Wandiri Gitogo, "Vodacom and Alipay Partner to Bring Super App in South Africa," *Kenyan Wall Street*, July 21, 2020.
119. Bradley Prior, "Huawei 5G Equipment Not under Threat in South Africa," *My Broadband*, August 18, 2020.
120. Jerry Omondi, "South African President Rallies Behind Huawei, Says U.S. is 'Jealous,'" CGTN, July 6, 2019.
121. Sheridan Prasso et al., "The Digital Iron Curtain," *Bloomberg Businessweek*, January 14, 2019.
122. "Huawei Faces Outcry Over Telecom Towers in Zambia," *PCWorld News*, February 13, 2015.
123. Alan Burkitt-Gray, "MTN Zambia to Create Global Hub in Lusaka Via Fibre to Namibia," *Capacity Media*, October 5, 2020.
124. Rong Wang, François Bar, and Yu Hong, "ICT Aid Flows," 19; Tawanda Karombo, "Zimbabwe Launches First Computer Plant," *Web Africa*, January 20, 2020.
125. "Zim, China Sign ICT Pact," *Herald*, September 11, 2019.
126. Bryce F. Neary, "China's Digital Silk Road in Morocco: The Implications of Digital Sector Dominance," Moroccan Institute for Policy Analysis, May 23, 2022.
127. Thomas Blaubach, "Chinese Technology in the Middle East: A Threat to Sovereignty or an Economic Opportunity?" Middle East Institute, March 2021, 6, 9.
128. "Artificial Intelligence (AI)," *IBM Cloud Education*, June 3, 2020.
129. Pei Wang, "On Defining Artificial Intelligence," *Journal of Artificial General Intelligence* 10, no. 2 (2019): 1, 28.
130. "Huawei, Africa and the Global Reach of Surveillance Technology," *Deutsche Welle*, September 12, 2019.
131. Email from Richard M. Harrison, American Foreign Policy Council, September 16, 2022.
132. Bulelani Jili, "The Spread of Surveillance Technology in Africa Stirs Security Concerns," Africa Center for Strategic Studies, December 11, 2020.
133. Steven Feldstein, "The Global Expansion of AI Surveillance," Carnegie Endowment for International Peace, September 2019, 3, 14.
134. Katherine Atha et al., "China's Smart Cities Development," SOS International LLC, January 2020, 60–61.
135. Scott N. Romaniuk and Tobias Burgers, "How China's AI Technology Exports Are Seeding Surveillance Societies Globally," *Diplomat*, October 18, 2018; Crystal Tse, Lulu Yilun Chen, and Vinicy Chan, "World's Largest AI Startup Said to Ready $2bn

10. TECHNOLOGY AND INFORMATION SECURITY

Fundraising," *Bloomberg*, January 10, 2019; "Chinese AI Unicorn CloudWalk Raises $253M, Accelerates IPO Schedule," *China Money AI*, May 14, 2020; Amanda Lentino, "This Chinese Facial Recognition Start-up Can Identify a Person in Seconds," *CNBC*, May 16, 2019.

136. Email from Richard M. Harrison, September 16, 2022.
137. Lydia Khalil, "Digital Authoritarianism, China and COVID," Lowy Institute, November 2020, 8.
138. China State Council, "New Generation of Artificial Intelligence Development Plan," trans. Flora Sapio, Weiming Chen, and Adrian Lo, Foundation for Law and International Affairs, July 8, 2017.
139. Gregory C. Allen, "Understanding China's AI Strategy: Clues to Chinese Strategic Thinking on Artificial Intelligence and National Security," Center for a New American Security, February 2019, 3; Gloria Shkurti Özdemir, "Artificial Intelligence Application in the Military: The Case of United States and China," SETA Foundation for Political, Economic, and Social Research, 2019, 18–19.
140. Alexander Chipman Koty, "What Is the China Standards?"; Brigitte Dekker, Maaike Okano-Heijmans, and Eric Siyi Zhang, "Unpacking China's Digital Silk Road," Clingendael Institute, July 2020, 17.
141. Kania, "Technology and Innovation," 245.
142. Khalil, "Digital Authoritarianism," 26; Arthur Gwagwa, "How AI Is Impacting National Governance Structures and Foreign Policy Decisions with a Focus on China," Geopolitics of Artificial Intelligence Symposium, March 12, 2019.
143. China Ministry of Foreign Affairs, "FOCAC Beijing Action Plan (2019–2021)," September 5, 2018.
144. Jonah Victor, "China's Security Assistance in Global Competition: The Case of Africa," in *The PLA Beyond Borders*, ed. Joel Wuthnow et al. (Washington, D.C.: National Defense University, 2021), 287.
145. Freedom House, "The Rise of Digital Authoritarianism: Freedom on the Net 2018," October 2018, 9.
146. Jonathan E. Hillman and Maesea McCalpin, "Watching Huawei's 'Safe Cities,'" Center for Strategic and International Studies, November 2019. The countries are Ghana, South Africa, Mauritius, Botswana, Nigeria, Uganda, Cote d'Ivoire, Madagascar, Kenya, Ethiopia, Cameroon, Angola, Tunisia, Morocco, Algeria, and Egypt.
147. Sheena Chestnut Greitens, "Dealing with Demand for China's Global Surveillance Exports," *Global China*, April 2020, 6.
148. Arthur Gwagwa, "Exporting Repression? China's Artificial Intelligence Push Into Africa," Council on Foreign Relations, December 17, 2018.
149. Cave et al., "Mapping China's Technology Giants," 9.
150. Itai Mushekwe, "China, Russia and Iran Helping Zimbabwe to Set-up Own NSA," *Bulawayo 24 News*, March 23, 2018.
151. Problem Masau, "Zimbabwe: Chinese Tech Revolution Comes to Zimbabwe," *Herald*, October 9, 2019.

10. TECHNOLOGY AND INFORMATION SECURITY

152. Gwagwa, "Exporting Repression?"; Democratic Staff, "The New Big Brother," 35.
153. Amy Hawkins, "Beijing's Big Brother Tech Needs African Faces," *Foreign Policy*, July 24, 2018; Kudzai Chimhangwa, "How Zimbabwe's Biometric ID Scheme (and China's AI Aspirations) Threw a Wrench into the 2018 Election," *Global Voices*, January 30, 2020.
154. Cave et al., "Mapping China's Technology Giants," 12.
155. David Gilbert, "Zimbabwe Is Trying to Build a China Style Surveillance State," *VICE News*, December 1, 2019.
156. Sheridan Prasso, "China's Digital Silk Road Is Looking More like an Iron Curtain," *Bloomberg Businessweek*, January 10, 2019.
157. "Huawei Offers Free AI Training to South African Students," *Gadget*, August 25, 2020.
158. Ray Mwareya, "Is Namibia Walking a Fine Line Between Chinese and European Spy Technology?" *Global Voices Advocacy*, July 20, 2020.
159. "China-Designed Big Data System Aids Angola's Intelligent Governance," *People's Daily*, August 24, 2018.
160. "First Integrated Public Security Center in the Country Opened on Monday," *Ver Angola*, January 6, 2020.
161. Scott N. Romaniuk and Tobias Burgers, "How China's AI Technology Exports Are Seeding Surveillance Societies Globally," *Diplomat*, October 18, 2018; Human Rights Watch, "Ethiopia: Telecom Surveillance Chills Rights," March 25, 2014; Bulelani Jili, "The Spread of Chinese Surveillance Tools in Africa: A Focus on Ethiopia and Kenya," in *Africa-Europe Cooperation and Digital Transformation*, ed. Chux Daniels, Benedikt Erforth, and Chloe Teevan (London: Routledge, 2022), 38–41.
162. Bulelani Jili, "Chinese Surveillance Tools in Africa," Research Brief no. 8/2019, China, Law and Development Project, June 30, 2020.
163. Elias Biryabarema, "Uganda's Cash-Strapped Cops Spend $126 Million on CCTV from Huawei," Reuters, August 15, 2019; Tom Wilson and Madhumita Murgia, "Uganda Confirms Use of Huawei Facial Recognition Cameras," *Bloomberg*, August 20, 2019.
164. James Griffiths, *The Great Firewall of China* (London: Zed, 2019), 303.
165. Atha et al., "China's Smart Cities Development," 61, 67–71.
166. Bulelani Jili, "Chinese ICT and Smart City Initiatives in Kenya," *Asia Policy* 17, no. 1 (2022): 41.
167. Hawkins, ""Beijing's Big Brother Tech."
168. "Reps Say Chinese Contractor Scammed Nigeria in $470 Million CCTV Project," *Pulse*, January 26, 2016; David Z. Morris, "China's ZTE Under Investigation in Nigerian Security Network Failure," *Fortune*, February 16, 2016.
169. "FG Engages Huawei for Electronic Surveillance of Land Borders," *News Direct*, October 10, 2022.
170. "China Exim Bank Lends $56 Mln to Cote d'Ivoire for Video Surveillance System in Abidjan," *Ecofin Agency*, September 2, 2016.
171. "National Security Installs 7000 CCTV Cameras to Check Crimes," *Daily Guide Network*, July 7, 2020.

10. TECHNOLOGY AND INFORMATION SECURITY

172. Muriel Edjo, "Burkinabe Govt to Build 800km of Optical Fiber and Install 900 Surveillance Cameras," *Ecofin Agency*, July 13, 2021.
173. Allison McManus, "Egypt and China's Telecoms: A Concerning Courtship," *Power 3.0*, February 20, 2020.
174. Prasso, "China's Digital Silk Road."
175. "Chinese Cooperation Strengthens Security in Angola and Cabo Verde," *Macauhub*, January 6, 2020.
176. "Forum on China-Africa Cooperation Dakar Action Plan (2022–2024)."
177. Brigitte Dekker, Maaike Okano-Heijmans, and Eric Siyi Zhang, "Unpacking China's Digital Silk Road," 12; Nigel Inkster, "The Huawei Affair and China's Technology Ambitions," *Survival* 61, no. 1 (February–March 2019): 109.
178. Tom Cotton and John Cornyn, "Keep the Chinese Government Away from 5G Technology," *Washington Post*, April 1, 2019.
179. Lucy Fisher and Michael Evans, "CIA Warning Over Huawei," *Times* (London), April 20, 2019.
180. Bill Gertz, *Deceiving the Sky: Inside Communist China's Drive for Global Supremacy* (New York: Encounter Books, 2019), 162.
181. Richard M. Harrison, "The Promise and Peril of 5G," *National Interest*, May 21, 2019.
182. David E. Sanger, Julian E. Barnes, Raymond Zhong, and Marc Santora, "America Pushes Allies to Fight Huawei in New Arms Race with China," *New York Times*, January 26, 2019.
183. Charlie Campbell, "The Battle for 5G," *Time*, June 3–10, 2019, 47.
184. Heidi Swart, "Visual Surveillance and Weak Cyber Security, Part One: When Cameras Get Dangerous," *Daily Maverick*, June 13, 2019.
185. Kai von Carnap, "Worried About Huawei? Then Worry About Chinese Blockchains, Too," Mercator Institute for China Studies, March 26, 2019.
186. Heidi Swart, "Part One: Are South Africans Safe with Huawei? It's All About the Risk," *Daily Maverick*, March 5, 2020.
187. "Communication Breakdown: How a Giant Chinese Telecoms Firm Became Mired in Political Controversy," *Economist*, April 27, 2019, 17.
188. "Communication Breakdown," 17.
189. Joan Tilouine and Ghalia Kadiri, "A Addis-Abeba, le Siège de l'Union Africaine Espionné par Pékin," *Le Monde Afrique*, January 27, 2018.
190. Associated Press, "China, African Union Deny Report Bloc's Building Was Bugged," February 8, 2018.
191. Aaron Maasho, "China Denies Report It Hacked African Union Headquarters," Reuters, January 29, 2018.
192. Tilouine and Kadiri, "A Addis-Abeba."
193. Xinhua, "China's Huawei, AU Sign MoU to Strengthen Technical Partnership on ICT," June 1, 2019.
194. Meeting with Shinn in Addis Ababa, June 20, 2019; "Across East Africa, Big Brother Is Watching Your Every Move," *East African*, December 3, 2022.

10. TECHNOLOGY AND INFORMATION SECURITY

195. Joe Parkinson, Nicholas Bariyo, and Josh Chin, "Huawei Technicians Helped African Governments Spy—Chinese Giant's Staff Aided Cybersecurity Forces' Snooping on Opposition," *Wall Street Journal*, August 15, 2019.
196. "Bronze President," Threat Profiles, https://www.secureworks.com/research/threat-profiles/bronze-president.
197. Raphael Satter, "Exclusive—Suspected Chinese Hackers Stole Camera Footage from African Union-Memo," Reuters, December 16, 2020.
198. Satter, "Exclusive."
199. Shinn/Eisenman meeting at the Ministry of Foreign Affairs, Accra, June 22, 2018.
200. "Kenya Dismisses US in Chinese 5G Spy Claims," *Business Daily*, March 29, 2021.
201. Shinn/Eisenman meeting at the Armed Forces Command and Staff College, Accra, June 18, 2018.
202. David Ehi, "Africa Embraces Huawei Technology Despite Security Concerns," *Deutsche Welle*, February 8, 2022.
203. Cobus van Staden, "Africa Could Be the Winner as the US Attempts to Stifle Huawei," *Daily Maverick*, February 24, 2020.
204. Mathieu Olivier, "Entre Surveillance des Opposants et des Terroristes, Le Juteux Marché de l'Espionnage en Afrique," *Jeune Afrique*, January 29, 2020.
205. Nir Kshetri, "Cybercrime and Cybersecurity in Africa," *Journal of Global Information Technology Management* 22, no. 2 (2019): 78.
206. Tomslin Samme-Nlar, "Cyberspace Security in Africa—Where Do We Stand?" *Circle ID* (blog), February 9, 2020.
207. Simnikiwe Mzekandaba, "Huawei's African Operations Weather US Pushback," *IT Web*, April 6, 2020.

11. PROJECTING TRENDS IN CHINA-AFRICA STRATEGIC RELATIONS

1. Xinhua, "China, African Countries to Strengthen Media Cooperation," August 25, 2022.
2. He Yafei, "China's Major-Country Diplomacy Progresses on All Fronts," *China.org.cn*, March 6, 2016.
3. Jevans Nyabiage, "Chinese Foreign Minister Wang Yi Looks to Boost Ties with Africa on Five-Nation New Year Tour," *South China Morning Post*, January 4, 2020.
4. "China Slams UN Report Alleging Litany of Rights Abuses in Xinjiang," *ChannelNewsAsia*, September 1, 2022.
5. Joshua Eisenman and Eric Heginbotham, "Building a More 'Democratic' and 'Multipolar' World: China's Strategic Engagement with Developing Countries," *China Review* 19, no. 4 (November 2019): 55–83.
6. Curtis Stone, "Deal or No Deal, the Brexit Mess Shows How Western-Style Democracy Can Fail," *People's Daily*, April 11, 2019.

7. Xi Jinping, "Working Together to Build a Better World: Keynote Speech at the CPC in Dialogue with World Political Parties High-Level Meeting," China Ministry of Foreign Affairs, December 1, 2017.
8. Liu Yuejin, "论总体国家安全观的五个'总体'" [On the five components of the "overall national security concept"], 人民论坛·学术前沿 [Frontiers], no. 11 (2014): 14–20; Liu Yuejin, "非传统的总体国家安全观" [Nontraditional concept of overall national security], *Journal of International Security Studies*, no. 6 (2014): 3–25.
9. Xinhua, "Full Text of Chinese President Xi Jinping's Speech at Opening Ceremony of 2018 FOCAC Beijing Summit," September 3, 2018.
10. Shu Zhan, "The '3c' Principle of Sustainable Security in Africa: For a Common, Comprehensive, Cooperative and Sustainable Security," Forum on China Africa Cooperation, March 14, 2016.
11. "China Told Sudan to Adopt UN's Darfur Plan—Envoy," *Bloomberg*, February 6, 2007.
12. MacDonald Dzirutwe, Joe Brock, and Ed Cropley, "Special Report: 'Treacherous Shenanigans'—The Inside Story of Mugabe's Downfall," Reuters, November 26, 2017.
13. Richard Wike, "5 Charts on America's (Very Positive) Image in Africa," Pew Research Center, July 23, 2015.
14. Laura Silver, Kat Devlin, and Christine Huang, "China's Economic Growth Mostly Welcomed in Emerging Markets, but Neighbors Wary of Its Influence," Pew Research Center, December 5, 2019, 27–40.
15. Pew Research Center, "America's Global Image Remains More Positive than China's, but Many See China Becoming World's Leading Power," July 18, 2013, 24–33; Silver, Devlin, and Huang, "China's Economic Growth."
16. Silver, Devlin, and Huang, "China's Economic Growth."
17. Reuters, "China's Xi Strikes Conciliatory Note, Broadens Diplomatic Focus," November 30, 2014.

INDEX

Page numbers in *italics* refer to figures and tables.

Abiy Ahmed, 25, 29, 60, 111, 112
Abraham, Colonel Saji, 258
African Centres for Disease Control and Prevention, 66
African Parliamentary Union, 54
African Political Party School Construction Special Training Course, 101
AFRICOM (United States Africa Command), 242, 291
Agbogah, Kofi, 176
agriculture, 18, 172–74, 178
Ahidjo, Ahmadou, 23
AI (artificial intelligence), 19, 296, 315–20, 341
Aidoo, Richard, 148
Ai Ping, 109
Akufo-Addo, Nana, 176
Algeria, 9, 29, 56, 187, 203; in AMU, 77; arms transfers from China, 223–24, 225, 232; BRI (Belt and Road Initiative) and, 61; Chinese-built military facilities in, 244;

Chinese communities in, 17; Chinese IT companies in, 309, 314; Chinese military attachés in, 220; "comprehensive strategic relationship" with, 25; diplomatic relations established with PRC, 345; extradition treaty with China, 188; infrastructure projects in, 210; Internet shutdowns in, 308; military attachés in China, 221; military-to-military relations and, 218; nuclear cooperation with China, 298; in OIC, 78; oil fields in, 165; PLAN port calls in, *282*; PLA's HADR intervention in, 245; political commissar system in military, 236; protection of Chinese nationals and interests in, 192; satellites launched by China for, 301, *302*; space cooperation with China, 303; threats to Chinese nationals in, 182, 184, 185; Western Sahara conflict and, 226; Xinjiang issue and, 250

INDEX

Alibaba Group Holding Limited (Alibaba), 246, 308, 309, 313
All-China Youth Federation, 147
Allison, Graham, 162
Allison, Simon, 152
Amoo-Gottfried, Kojo, 151
AMU (Arab Maghreb Union), 51, 64, 77–78
ANC [African National Congress] (South Africa), 86–87, 101, 103–8, 332; CPC relationship with, 239, 330; number of exchanges with ID-CPC, *105*; One China Policy, 104
Angola, 9, 36, 47; arms transfers from China, 225–26; BRI (Belt and Road Initiative) and, 60; Chinese communities in, 17; Chinese military attachés in, 221; diplomatic relations established with PRC, 348; in ECCAS, 76; extradition treaty with China, 188; in Forum Macao, 62; ID-CPC and, 86; military attachés in China, 221; military-to-military relations and, 218; oil exports to China, 164, 400n44; party-to-party relations and, 101; *Peace Ark* hospital ship in, 284; perceptions of China and United States in, 149; PLAN port calls in, *282*; police officers trained in China, 241; political commissar system in military, 236; port development in, 276; prospective Chinese military bases in, 292; protection of Chinese nationals and interests in, 188, 192; in SADC, 69; "strategic partnership" with, 25; surveillance technology provided by China, 318; threats to Chinese nationals in, 184
AQIM (al-Qaeda in the Islamic Maghreb), 182, 250, 251
Arab countries, 51, 53, 57; BRI (Belt and Road Initiative) and, 60; nuclear cooperation with China, 297
Arab Satellite Communication Organization, 301

"Arab Spring," 56, 77, 195
Argentina, 5
Arkebe Oqubay, 111
arms transfers. *See* military assistance
ASEAN+1 framework, 10
Asiedu-Nketia, Johnson, 115
ATDCs (Agricultural Technology Demonstration Centers), 173
Atlantic Ocean, 264
Attor, Kofi, 113
AU (African Union), 11, 22, 25, 44, 83; Addis Ababa headquarters, 27, 84, 109, 311, 323; China's security strategy and, 158, 159; on Chinese versus U.S. diplomacy, 29; COMESA and, 73; conflict mediation and, 201, 203; Convention on Cybersecurity and Personal Data Protection, 317; countries recognized by, 64–65; cybersecurity breaches against, 323–25, 341; FOCAC and, 54; importance to China's Africa policy, 63, 64; intelligence cooperation with China endorsed by, 252; Peace and Security Architecture, 66, 67, 70; peacekeeping operations, 67, 207, 338; as replacement for OAU, 64; security forums and, 214, 215, 216; space/satellite cooperation and, 301; subregional communities of, 51; Task Force on Africa's Strategic Partnership with Emerging Powers, 65
Australia, 167, 257
AVIC (Aviation Industry Corporation of China), 223, 229, 240
Awolu Abdi, 112

Baguma, Grace, 142
Baidu company, 309
Bandung Conference [Asia-Africa Conference] (1955), 80–81, 144, 147
Bangladesh, UN peacekeeping in Africa and, 205
Bao Yuping, Major General, 284

INDEX

Barrass, Gordon, 160
al-Bashir, Omar, 10, 200, 338
bauxite, 168
BDS (BeiDou Global Satellite Navigation System), 301–2
Benabdallah, Lina, 8, 13, 14, 93; on African perceptions of training programs, 151; on training workshops hosted in Beijing, 135
Benin, 47, 70; China Cultural Center in, 146; Chinese state media and, 129; diplomatic relations established with PRC, 347; Internet shutdowns in, 308; military attachés in China, 221; in OIC, 78
Berger, Blake, 273
biaotai (affirmations), 97
Biden, Joe, 31
Big Sell Out, The (Mokonyane), 108
bilateral relationships, 1, 9, 17, 22, 63, 83, 329, 344; COMESA and, 73; Confucius Institutes (CIs) and, 139; "core interests" of China and, 42; diplomatic recognition and, 23; EAC and, 75–76; ID-CPC and, 86, 104–5, 110; in interlocking relations, 9; power asymmetry in favor of China, 52
Blackwater security firm, 191, 192
Blay, Frederick Armah, 115, 116
Blue Book (*Annual Report on the Development of the Indian Ocean Region*, 2013), 263
Blue Book of Non-Traditional Security (2014–2015), 59
Bo'ao Forum (2013), 6
Bodomo, Adams, 152
Boko Haram (Nigeria, Cameroon), 182, 183, 228
Botswana, 37, 45, 147, 184, 329; diplomatic relations established with PRC, 348; high-level diplomatic visits to, 28; military attachés in China, 221; party-to-party relations and, 100; in SADC, 69
Brady, Anne-Marie, 129
Brautigam, Deborah, 177
Brazil, 5, 62, 167, 311

Breslin, Shaun, 13, 139
Brewster, David, 265
BRI (Belt and Road Initiative), 57, 69, 80, 123; AI (artificial intelligence) and, 316; BRI Forum for International Cooperation, 25, 44, 51, 53, 58–62, 83; Forum Macao and, 63; IORA and, 78, 82; IT (information technology) and, 306; maritime security and, 255, 256, 261, 262, 263, 264; OIC and, 79; security strategy and, 156, 159, 161, 178, 292; Sino-African media collaboration and, 132; space technology and, 300, 301, 302
BRICS (Brazil, Russia, India, China, and South Africa), 52, 78, 82–83, 259; New Development Bank, 83; space technology and, 301; Think-Tank Forum (2017), 138
"Bronze President" group, cyberattack by, 324
"Building a Community of Shared Future for China and Africa" (ID-CPC seminar, 2017), 98
Burkina Faso: defense of China's Xinjiang policies, 39; in OIC, 78; switch of diplomatic recognition from Taiwan to China, 24, 34, 237; Taiwan recognition by, 30
Burundi, 26, 29, 36, 67, 76, 329; COMESA and, 72; diplomatic relations established with PRC, 346; in EAC, 75; in ECCAS, 76; high-level diplomatic visits to, 28; Hong Kong issue and, 42; military attachés in China, 221; rare earth elements in, 171, 172; UN peacekeeping operation in, 206; UN resolutions and, 30

cadre training workshops, 85, 87, 93, 97, 100–102, 116; for Ethiopian political party members, 111; for Ghanian political party members, 114–15; for South African political party members, 103, 106–7

459

INDEX

Cai Fuchao, 132

Cameroon, 31–32, 36, 67, 311; arms transfers from China, 229; Chinese communities in, 17; Chinese-language instruction in, 142–43; Chinese military attachés in, 221; Chinese-sponsored training session for journalists from, 133; diplomatic relations established with PRC, 347; military attachés in China, 221; naval exercises with PLAN, 242, 283; in OIC, 78; PLAN port calls in, *282*; port development in, *280*, 340; protection of Chinese nationals and interests in, 191; threats to Chinese nationals in, 182, 184

Canada, 40, 75

Cao Zhigang, 96

Cape Verde, 24, 61, 320; diplomatic relations established with PRC, 348; in ECOWAS, 70; in Forum Macao, 62; political commissar system in military, 236

Carnap, Kai von, 322

Carrozza, Ilaria, 13

CASC (China Aerospace Science and Technology Corporation), 223

CASCF (China-Arab States Cooperation Forum), 10, 40, 51, 53; Arab League and, 68–69; composition of, 56; energy security and, 56–57; maritime security and, 264; overlapped membership with AMU, 78; political issues and, 57–58

CATTF (China-Africa Think-Tank Forum), 138–39

CCCC (China Communications Construction Company), 275–76

CCM [Chama Cha Mapinduzi] (Tanzania), 101

CCTV (closed circuit television cameras), 318–20

CEIAS (Central European Institute of Asian Studies), 149, 150

CEN-SAD (Community of Sahel-Saharan States), 51, 64, 76–77

censorship, 121, 124, 307, 308

center–periphery relations, 12

Central African Republic, 76, 77, 183, 196; diplomatic relations established with PRC, 346; evacuation of Chinese nationals from, 337; military attachés in China, 221; UN peacekeeping operation in, *206*

Central Asia, 4, 5, 10, 164, 249

CGC Overseas Construction Group, 71, 195

CGN (China General Nuclear Power Corporation), 297, 299

CGTN (China Global Television Network), 120, 343; Africans employed by, 128–29; foreign-language broadcasting, 123–24; propaganda editorial line and, 127, 128

Chad, 24, 28; BRI (Belt and Road Initiative) and, 61; conflict mediation by China and, 202; defense of Xinjiang policies, 39; diplomatic relations established with PRC, 347; in ECCAS, 76; evacuation of Chinese nationals from, 195, 337; insurgents with Chinese weapons, 232; military attachés in China, 221; in OIC, 78; oil fields in, 165; protection of Chinese nationals and interests in, 191

Chang Wanquan, 338

Chang Zhenming, 192

Chase, Michael, 301

CHEC (China Harbor Engineering Company), 275, 276, 277, 278, *280*

Chen Dongxiao, 13, 27–28, 90, 98

Chen Shui-bian, 23

Chen Xiaodong, *141*

Cheng Qian, 199

Chergui, Smail, 216

China, "core interests" of, 2–3, 22, 32–34, 87, 273, 309; Hong Kong, 32, 41–43, 49; human rights, 32, 35–36, 49; South China Sea, 32, 40–41, 49; Taiwan issue, 32, 34–35, 49; Tibet, 32, 36–37, 49; treatment of Muslim minorities, 32, 36, 37–40, 49

INDEX

China-Africa Community of Shared Future, 2, 8–14, 9, 21
China-Africa Defense and Security Forum, 213, 214–15
China-Africa Development Fund, 130, 280
China-Africa Institute, 126, *141*
China-Africa Peace and Security Forum, 11, 213, 214, 215–17
China-Africa Research Institute (Peking University), *141*
China-Africa Summit on Solidarity Against COVID-19, 42
China-Africa Youth Festival, 147–48
China and Africa: A Century of Engagement (Shinn and Eisenman, 2012), 15, 133
China-Arab Civilization Dialogue, 56
China-Brazil Earth Resource Satellite for Africa Program, 301
China–Caribbean Economic and Trade Cooperation Forum, 10
China Center for Contemporary World Studies, 137
China Central Television, 123, 124, 125. *See also* CGTN (China Global Television Network)
China Daily (newspaper), 123, 128, 147, 343
China Daily Africa, 124
China Electronics Technology Group, 309
China Energy Group, 197
China Export Import Bank, 45
ChinAfrica (magazine), 124
China Great Wall Industry Corporation, 303
China Harbor Engineering Company, 197
China Hongqiao Group Limited, 277, *280*
China House (Nairobi-based NGO), 17, 184, 187, 188–89
China Institute of International Studies, *141*
China International Television Corporation, 130
China Jiangxi International, 243
China Mobile company, 309, 311, 321
China Molybedenum company, 167

China National Space Administration, 301
China Road and Bridge Corporation, 191, 276
China Standards 2035 Plan, 307
China State Construction Engineering Company, 114, 274, 278
China Telecom company, 309, 321
China Unicom company, 309, 321
Chinese-African People's Friendship Association, 146
"Chinese Dream," 6, 21, 134, 160, 237; maritime power and, 265; space exploration and, 300
Chinese People's Association for Cultural Relations with Foreign Countries, 144
Chinese People's Political Consultative Conference, 54
Chissano, Joaquim, 235
Chiwenga, Constantino, 338
CICIR (China Institutes of Contemporary International Relations), 137
CISAR (China International Search and Rescue) team, 245
CITIC (China International Trust and Investment Corporation), 191–92
civil society organizations, 17, 31, 137, 159; criticism of China by, 33, 48, 153; environmental damage from mining and, 168
climate change, 54, 173, 177, 327
CloudWalk Technology (AI company), 315, 317
CMPorts (China Merchants Port Holdings), 274, 275, 277, 278, 280, 285
CNNC (China National Nuclear Corporation), 166, 297, 298–300
CNOOC (China National Offshore Oil Corporation), 164, 165
CNPC (China National Petroleum Corporation), 164, 165, 181, 186, 187, 191; conflict mediation by China and, 202; evacuation of Chinese nationals and,

CNPC (China National Petroleum Corporation) (*continued*) 196–97; PSCs (private security companies) and, 194
cobalt, 18, 47, 163, 166, 167, 178, 335
Cold War, 3, 230
colonialism, European, 235, 336
COMESA (Common Market for Eastern and Southern Africa), 51, 64, 72–74, 330
Community of Shared Future for Mankind, 2, 57, 80; desire to reshape international relations and, 6–8; IORA and, 82; security forums and, 215, 216
Comoros (Comoro Islands), 28, 31, 56, 256, 291, 329; COMESA and, 72; diplomatic relations established with PRC, 348; in IORA, 81; military personnel trained in China, 239; in OIC, 78; in SADC, 69
Confucianism, 12
Confucius Institutes (CIs), 46, 139, 142–43, 239
Congo (Brazzaville), Republic of, 29, 39; BRI (Belt and Road Initiative) and, 61; Chinese military attachés in, 221; COVID-19 vaccine delivered by PLA, 247; diplomatic relations established with PRC, 346; in ECCAS, 76; high-level diplomatic visits to, 28; military-to-military relations and, 218; oil exports to China, 164, 165, 400n44; *Peace Ark* hospital ship in, 284; PLAN port calls in, *282*; votes in UN, 31
Connolly, Peter, 194–95
Contemporary World (CPC journal), 262
Cook, Sarah, 124, 129
copper mines, 168–69
Cornyn, John, 321
Correia e Silva, José Ulisses da, 24
corruption, 46, 47, 184
COSATU (Congress of South African Trade Unions), 103
COSCO Shipping Corporation, 190, 274, 279, *280*; merchant shipping and, 286; ship building and, 285

COSG (China Overseas Security Group), 192
COSS (China Overseas Security Services), 193
Côte d'Ivoire, 70, 71, 277, 320; Chinese-controlled fishing vessels in, 175; diplomatic relations established with PRC, 348; military attachés in China, 221; in OIC, 78; pirates operating in waters off, 271; PLAN port calls in, *282*; port development in, *280*; UN peacekeeping operation in, 206
Cotton, Tom, 321
counterterrorism, 24, 38, 39, 55, 57, 253; arms transfers from China and, 228; CEN-SAD and, 77; China's security concept and, 156, 158; COMESA and, 73; counterterrorism diplomacy and intelligence sharing, 248–53; ECCAS and, 76; IORA and, 81; military-to-military relations and, 220; as OIC priority issue, 78; PLA Special Forces and, 161; security forums and, 214; threat to Chinese nationals and companies, 181, 183, 184, 249–50; UN peacekeeping operations and, 208
COVID-19 pandemic, 1, 2, 16, 19, 133, 146, 339–40, 342; African agency and, 48; African critics of China and, 48, 252; BRI (Belt and Road Initiative) and, 61; China's "zero-COVID" strategy, 128, 132, 139; Chinese nationals and companies in Africa and, 180; coverage in Chinese media, 150; educational programs curtailed by, 135, 136, 143; face masks delivered by China, 115–16, 344; health diplomacy and, 55; high-level diplomatic visits curtailed by, 28; lockdowns of Chinese cities, 328; military cooperation affected by, 235; naval port calls interrupted by, 283, 339; negative views of China in Africa

INDEX

during, 152–53, 342; number of multilateral exchanges before and after, 99–100, *100*; organization meetings shifted online during, 53, 63, 86, 96, 99, 107, 344; party-to-party relations temporarily halted by, 85, 94, 96, 112, 117; PLA's HADR activities and, 246–47; security diplomacy and, 213; security forums and, 216–17; setbacks to cultural propaganda programs from, 149; travel restrictions and, 90, 219, 333; uncertainty of future prediction and, 327
CPC (Communist Party of China), 32, 79, 90, 137, 272; African critics of, 97–98; Central Committee, 105, 121, 122, 126; Central Party School, 105, 111, 114, 240, 334; CMC (Central Military Commission), 215, 216, 218, 219, 240–41, 249; Communist Youth League of China, 147; constitution of, 58; controls on information flows and messaging, 343; foreigners' public displays of admiration for, 97; intelligence gathering and, 244, 295; International Department, 262; international public opinion as concern of, 153; IT companies and, 307–8, 322; legitimacy of, 179; military controlled by, 157, 236; Party and the World Dialogue, 91, 101; Politburo, 198, 218; as "political mentor" for African parties, 109; primary objectives of, 58–59; propaganda apparatus of, 121–23; Propaganda Department, 125, 129, 131, 132, 145; relations with African and Arab organizations, 85; relations with African political parties, 17–18, 87; United Front groups, 146. *See also* ID-CPC; National Congresses, of CPC
CRI (China Radio International), 121, 123, 125, 130, 149, 343
crime, transnational, 72, 81, 220
CSCLF (China Soong Ching Ling Foundation), 147, 148

CSGC (China South Industries Group Corporation), 223
CSIC (China Shipbuilding Industry Corporation), 223, 285
CSSC (China State Shipbuilding Corporation), 223, 285
CSTG (China Security Technology Group), 193
Cuba, 39, 42
cultural programs, 1, 18; Chinese New Year events, 146–47, 153; culture as politics, 143–48; propaganda and, 120, 122, 125
Cummings, Milton, Jr., 144, 394n153
cybersecurity, 19, 55, 158, 295, 321–26, 341; IORA and, 81; police training and, 241; state-centric view of, 306
CZEC (Zhongyuan Engineering Corporation), 298

Dahua Technology, 315, 319
Dai Bing, *140*
Dai Bingguo, 195
Dalai Lama i, 37
debt relief, 48, 54, 171
Déby, Idriss, 202
Declaration on the Conduct of Parties in the South China Sea, 41
decolonization, 64
Defense White Paper (China, 2019), 4, 5, 7
de Klerk, F. W., 37
democracy, 4, 18, 73, 74, 150, 151, 331; China's conception of, 332; democracy protestors in Hong Kong, 108; impact of free elections on party-to-party relations, 92; IORA and, 81; multiparty democracies, 113, 116; pejorative meaning of propaganda and, 121; PRC autocracy's assertion of superiority over, 120, 154, 331–32; as threat to Chinese model of governance, 97–98; U.S.-style liberal democracy, 92, 93
Deng Li, *141*, 148

463

INDEX

Deng Xiaoping, 5, 133–34
desalination, 296, 298
developing countries, 4, 135; China as alternative model of political governance for, 331; China's political system "offered" to, 92–93; China's self-description as developing country, 52, 81; "newly emerging powers," 5; political parties of, 92; scholarship on China's relations with, 15, 16; Sinocentric diplomacy and, 12; think tanks and, 138
DeWe Security Services, 191
"Digital Silk Road," 305, 306, 314
Ding Tai An Yuan Security Technology Research Institute, 192
Diong, Ibrahim, 45
Diop, Abdoulaye, *141*
diplomacy, 4, 5, 15, 17, 327; "host diplomacy," 13–14, 90, 94, 138; language skills of Chinese diplomats, 24; *Peace Ark* (hospital ship) and, 281, 284; recognition of PRC over Taiwan, 22–25, 104, 346–49; Sinocentric, 98; "UN-centered," 10. *See also* security diplomacy
disaster relief. *See* HADR
Djibouti, 9, 17, 32, 273, 311, 329; agency vis-à-vis China, 46–47, 48; arms transfers from China, 288; border dispute with Eritrea, 203; BRI (Belt and Road Initiative) and, 59, 60; CASCF and, 56; China's first overseas military base in, 19, 43–44, 160, 162, 258, 267, 286–91, 337–38, 344; Chinese military attachés in, 221; COMESA and, 72; defense of Xinjiang policies, 39; diplomatic relations established with PRC, 348; Doraleh Multipurpose Port, 288, 289; French military base in, 260, 288; high-level diplomatic visits to, 28; ID-CPC and, 86; in IGAD, 74; indebtedness to China, 43; medical supplies donated by PLA, 246; military-to-military relations and,

218; as Muslim-majority country, 38; in OIC, 78; *Peace Ark* hospital ship in, 284; PLAN port calls in, 281, 282, *282*; police officers trained in China, 241; protection of Chinese nationals and interests in, 191; "strategic partnership" with, 25; U.S. military base in, 257; votes in UN, 31
Doha Declaration (2016), 40–41, 57
DRC (Democratic Republic of the Congo), 29, 47, 48, 188, 329; Chinese communities in, 17; Chinese IT companies in, 309; Chinese military attachés in, 220; Chinese-sponsored training session for journalists from, 133; COMESA and, 72; conflict mediation by China and, 202; Confucius Institutes (CIs) in, 239; diplomatic relations established with PRC, 346; in EAC, 75; in ECCAS, 76; high-level diplomatic visits to, 28; PLA's HADR intervention in, 248; protection of Chinese nationals and interests in, 191; in SADC, 69; strategic minerals in, 163, 167, 168–69, 336; "strategic partnership" with, 25; threats to Chinese nationals in, 180, 182, 184; UN peacekeeping operation in, 205, *206*, *207*, 209, 247
drug smuggling, 81
Dube, Alfred, 45
Duval, Xavier-Luc, 320

EAC (East African Community), 11, 51, 64, 75–76
East Turkestan Islamic Movement, 251
Ebola outbreak (2014), 182, 197, 245–46
ECCAS (Economic Community of Central African States), 51, 76
ECOWAS (Economic Community of West African States), 11, 51, 64, 83, 330; Abuja (Nigeria) headquarters, 27, 71, 84; membership and structure of, 70–71; peacekeeping and security activities, 71–72

464

INDEX

educational programs, 1, 18, 54, 85, 116, 133; building of relationships and, 133–34; growth in number of African students in China, 136–37, *136*; Mandarin language courses, 139, 142–43, 187, 239; propaganda and, 120, 122; reverence for teachers in Chinese tradition, 133, 391n98; scholarships to study in China, 104, 109, 134; training and higher education, 134–37

Eguegu, Ovigwe, 216

Egypt, 5, 9, 17, 28, 33, 311, 329; agency vis-à-vis China, 47, 48; BRI (Belt and Road Initiative) and, 61; BRI News Network and, 132; CASCF and, 56; CEN-SAD and, 77; China Cultural Center in, 146; Chinese communities in, 17; Chinese IT companies in, 309, 314–15; Chinese media platforms in, 126; Chinese military attachés in, 220; Chinese state media and, 129; COMESA and, 72; "comprehensive strategic relationship" with, 25; diplomatic relations established with PRC, 345; evacuation of Chinese nationals from, 195; high-level diplomatic visits to, 28; Hong Kong issue and, 42; ID-CPC and, 86; military personnel trained in China, 237; military-to-military relations and, 217, 218; as Muslim-majority country, 38; natural gas reserves, 164; nuclear cooperation with Russia, 297–98; in OIC, 78; party-to-party relations and, 96, *96*; perceptions of China and United States in, 149; PLAN port calls in, 281, 282, *282*; port development in, 278, *280*, 340; satellites launched by China for, 302–3, *302*; threats to Chinese nationals in, 184; U.S. arms transfers to, 223; Xinjiang issue and, 250–51

elites, African, 1, 17, 327, 331–32; "cadre training" workshops for, 85; China's Africa-focused propaganda and, 120; CPC cultural programs and, 154; educational programs in China and, 137

energy security, 56–57, 335

Eperjesi, John, 12

EPRDF (Ethiopian People's Revolutionary Democratic Front), 87, 108–12, 329, 383n99; disintegration of, 111–12, 332; number of exchanges with ID-CPC, *110*

Equatorial Guinea, 27, 36; BRI (Belt and Road Initiative) and, 61; COVID-19 vaccine delivered by PLA, 247; diplomatic relations established with PRC, 347; in ECCAS, 76; military attachés in China, 221; oil exports to China, 400n44; prospective Chinese military bases in, 291, 292

Erickson, Andrew S., 266

Eritrea, 29, 36, 195, 203, 282, 329; COMESA and, 72; diplomatic relations established with PRC, 349; high-level diplomatic visits to, 28; in IGAD, 74; political commissar system in military, 236; UN peacekeeping operation in, *206*

Essa, Azad, 130

Eswatini (formerly Swaziland): ID-CPC and, 86, 94; as only African country with no diplomatic ties to Beijing, 349; in SADC, 69; Taiwan recognition by, 22, 34, 40, 53, 65, 349

Ethiopia, 5, 9, 17, 24–25, 329; agency vis-à-vis China, 46, 47; arms transfers from China, 225–26, 227; border dispute with Eritrea, 338; BRI (Belt and Road Initiative) and, 59, 60; BRI News Network and, 132; Chinese communities in, 17; Chinese IT companies in, 309, 310, 311–12; Chinese military attachés in, 220; COMESA and, 72; "comprehensive strategic relationship" with, 25;

465

INDEX

Ethiopia (*continued*)
 diplomatic relations established with PRC, 347; evacuation of Chinese nationals from, 198, 337; extradition treaty with China, 188; FOCAC and, 55; high-level diplomatic visits to, 28–29; Hong Kong issue and, 42; ID-CPC and, 86; in IGAD, 74, 75; Internet shutdowns in, 308; military personnel trained in China, 239; military attachés in China, 221; military exercises with PLA, 242; military-to-military relations and, 218; ONLF insurgency in, 181; party-to-party relations and, 18, 86, 96, 96, 102, 108–12, *110*, 117; political commissar system in military, 236; Prosperity Party, 87, 112; protection of Chinese nationals and interests in, 192; satellites launched by China for, 301, *302*; South China Sea issue and, 41; surveillance technology provided by China, 318–19; threats to Chinese nationals in, 181, 183, 184, 188; UN peacekeeping operation in, 206. *See also* EPRDF; TPLF
European Union (EU), 4, 68, 74, 75, 270
Export-Import Bank (China), 45, 167, 289; African fisheries and, 176; Chinese farmers in Africa and, 172; IT (information technology) projects and, 309, 312, 313; military procurement and, 229; port development in Africa and, 276, 277–78; space technology and, *302*, 303, 304; surveillance technology and, 320

Facebook, 123
facial recognition technology, 315–17, 326
Fara, Adam, 112
Faure, Danny, 279
Feng Chuanlu, 262
Feng Zhongping, 4
fishing, illegal, 81, 82, 174–76

FOCAC (Forum on China-Africa Cooperation), 8, 10–11, 13, 17, 29, 44, 45, 63; AI technology and, 316; antipiracy operations and, 272; Beijing Action Plan, 135; as Chinese-inspired organization, 53–55; conflict mediation by China and, 204; counterterrorism cooperation and, 249; creation of, 51, 53, 104, 367n5; Dakar Action Plan, 130–31, 135; Forum on China-Africa Media Cooperation, 131, 132; intelligence cooperation and, 252; Johannesburg Action Plan, 65, 67, 134; maritime security and, 264; as most important regional organization, 330; nuclear power cooperation and, 297; political cooperation, 54; security policy and, 54–55, 157–59; think tanks and, 138, *141*
food security, 54, 78, 172–77, 335
food-sharing, diplomacy and, 14
"Former Liberation Movements of Southern Africa Leading Cadres Workshop," 102
Forum Macao, 51, 53, 62–63
Forum on China-Africa Media Cooperation, 328
Fourie, Reneva, 107
"Four Principles and Five Propositions," 308
"461 Framework," 252
France, 30, 40, 47, 169, 225, 283, 311; arms transfers to Africa, 230; Djibouti military base, 260, 288; military interventions in Africa, 72; Sagem (IT company), 312; satellites launched for African countries, 301
FRELIMO (Mozambique Liberation Front Party), 101
"friends of China," 129, 154
FSG (Frontier Services Group), 191–92
Fu Quanyou, 218
Fu Ying, 7

INDEX

Gabon, 28, 165, 292; Chinese military attachés in, 221; Chinese-sponsored training session for journalists from, 133; diplomatic relations established with PRC, 348; in ECCAS, 76; military attachés in China, 221; military exercises with PLA, 242; naval exercises with PLAN, 283; in OIC, 78; *Peace Ark* hospital ship in, 284; pirates operating in waters off, 271; PLAN port calls in, *282*; protection of Chinese nationals and interests in, 191; rare earth elements in, 171; strategic minerals in, 167; "strategic partnership" with, 25

Gambia, 34, 41, 72; BRI (Belt and Road Initiative) and, 60, 61; Chinese-built police facilities in, 244; Chinese-controlled fishing vessels in, 177; Confucius Institutes (CIs) and, 139; diplomatic relations established with PRC, 348; in ECOWAS, 70; in OIC, 78; security forums and, 215

Gao, Victor Zhikai, 290

Geingob, Hage, 229, 243

geostrategy, of China: Africa's ascendant position in, 2; BRI (Belt and Road Initiative) and, 59, 62; China-Africa relations in context of, 15, 16; educational programs and, 134; "going out" strategy, 3, 334; naval security deployments and, 19; naval strategy, 157; rivalry with India, 47; soft and hard balancing against United States, 5, 352n18

Germany, 4, 39, 169

Ge Yezhou, 111

G5 Sahel Joint Force, 24

Ghana, 9, 17, 29, 44–45; antipiracy operations and, 271; arms transfers from China, 228–29, 232, 234–35; AU (African Union) and, 372n72; Bui Dam project, 46; Chinese-built military facilities in, 243, 334; Chinese-controlled fishing vessels in, 175, 176; Chinese cultural propaganda activities in, 148; Chinese IT companies in, 312; Chinese state media and, 129, 150; cybersecurity and, 325; debt relief talks with China, 48; diplomatic relations established with PRC, 345; FOCAC and, 55; Hong Kong issue and, 42; ID-CPC and, 86; military attachés in China, 221; military exercises with PLAN, 242; military-to-military relations and, 218; multiparty democracy in, 329; naval exercises with PLAN, 283; nuclear cooperation with China, 300; party-to-party relations and, 18, 86, 96, 102, 113–16, *114*, 117, 329–30; perceptions of China and United States in, 149; PLAN port calls in, *282*; strategic minerals in, 167, 168. *See also* NDC; NPP

Ghana–China Friendship Association, 151

Gheit, Ahmed Aboul, 69

Ghiselli, Andrea, 10, 157

Gizenga, Antoine, 346

Global Counterterrorism Forum, 249

Global Development Initiative, 61, 82, 178

Global Military journal, 273

global relationships, 1, 9, 17, 329, 344

Global Security Initiative, 178, 217, 255

Global South, 1, 2, 5, 15, 328, 344; Beijing's claims to leadership of, 150, 151; party-to-party relations in, 85; propaganda laundering in, 130; regional-level interaction with, 10; South–South solidarity, 13, 79–80, 330–31; think-tank forums and, 138

"going out" strategy, 3

Gopaldas, Ronak, 162

Gordon, Sue, 322

Governance of China (Xi Jinping), 115

government buildings diplomacy, 25–26

government-to-government diplomacy, 17, 21

Great Wall Counter-Terrorism International Forum, 250

INDEX

G-77 (Group of 77), 52, 78, 79–80
guanxi connections, 8
Gu Bin, 295
Guelleh, Ismaïl Omar, 24
guerrilla warfare, 23
Guinea, 28, 60, 175, 192, 282; COVID-19 vaccine delivered by PLA, 247; Ebola outbreak (2014), 182, 245; in ECOWAS, 70; evacuation of Chinese nationals from, 197, 337; military attachés in China, 221; in OIC, 78; port development in, 277, 280; strategic minerals in, 168; "strategic partnership" with, 25; votes in UN, 31
Guinea-Bissau, 26, 71, 176; diplomatic relations established with PRC, 347; Ebola outbreak (2014), 245; in ECOWAS, 70; in Forum Macao, 62; in OIC, 78; political commissar system in military, 236
Guizhou Aircraft Industries Corporation, 228
Gulf of Aden, 19, 55, 59, 193, 196, 255; antipiracy operations in, 256, 264, 268, 274, 286, 292, 337; China's naval strategy in, 256; India's maritime security and, 257–58; SLOCs (sea lines of communication) in, 289
Gulf of Guinea, 19, 55, 72, 242, 271, 272
Gulf States, 74
Gu, Jing, 163
Guo Chu, 7
Guo Yezhou, 107
Gwadar port (Pakistan), 258, 272, 274
Gwagwa, Arthur, 325

HADR (humanitarian assistance and disaster relief), 19, 74, 158, 213, 245–48, 253, 266; China as minor player in, 19, 213; Djibouti military base and, 289; IORA and, 81
Haftar, Khalifa, 164

Hanwei International Security Services Co., 193
"harmonious world" slogan, 6, 199, 284
Harrison, James P., 11
Hawkins, Amy, 319
Heath, Timothy, 161
Hess, Steve, 148
Hevia, James, 133
He Yafei, 4, 8, 269
He Yin, 205
high-level visits, 17, 22, 27–29, 54
Hikvision company, 309, 315, 317, 319, 322
Ho, Patrick, 138
Hodzi, Obert, 161, 162
holistic security, 3, 18, 121, 157
Hong Kong, 22, 286; China's territorial claims over, 120; as "core interest" of China, 32, 41–43, 49; democracy protestors in, 108; "one country, two systems" principle, 41
host diplomacy, 13–14, 90, 94, 138
Hsiung, James C., 12, 13
Huang Jing, 4
Huang Ju, 218
Huang, Mike Chia-Yu, 263, 274
Huawei company, 19, 123, 195, 296, 310, 341; AI (artificial intelligence) and, 318; China Standards 2035 Plan and, 307; CPC connections of, 308, 322; cybersecurity and, 323–24, 325; Huawei Marine Networks, 310–11; IT projects in African countries, 309, 311–14; surveillance technology and, 315, 317, 320
Hua Xin Zhong An (maritime security firm), 193
Hua-Yanan (Beijing) Security Services Co., 193
Hu Changming, 215
Hu Jintao, 3, 56, 69, 81, 200, 331; on cultural diplomacy as priority, 144–45; educational programs and, 133; "Harmonious World" concept, 6, 199,

284; Indian Ocean strategy and, 263–64; party-to-party relations and, 94, 99, *100*; on protection of Chinese nationals and interests, 185; on role of Ethiopia in China's Africa strategy, 109; on strategic periphery, 4; Sudan visit (2007), 338
humanitarian assistance. *See* HADR
human rights, 4, 22, 31, 74, 103, 308; in African countries, 33; arms transfers and, 231; China's concept of, 332; as "core interest" of China, 32, 35–36, 49; as OIC priority issue, 78; weak record of CPC, 116; Western concept of, 35–36; in Xinjiang, 38–40
Hutchison [CK] Port Holdings, 275, 278, 280
HW Raid Security, 194
Hyperspace Opportunity for Pioneering Education program, 301

ID-CPC (International Department of the Central Committee of CPC), 17, 94, 333–34, 385n135; African political parties and, 18, 85–87; bilateral exchanges and, 93–94, *95*, 96–98, *96*, 116–17; Ethiopia as case study of party-to-party relations, 102, 108–12, *110*; expanding role in China's foreign policy, 88–93; Ghana as case study of party-to-party relations, 102, 113–16, *114*; "group-think" effect created by, 98; "host diplomacy" of, 90; legibility of, 91–92; multilateral exchanges and, 98–102, *99*, *100*, 117; number of political parties engaged with, 89, 96; South Africa as case study of party-to-party relations, 102, 103–8, *105*; think tanks associated with, 137. *See also* party-to-party relations
IGAD (Intergovernmental Authority on Development), 51, 74–75, 76
IMF (International Monetary Fund), 332
imperialism, U.S. and Western, 108, 112, 134

India, 5, 169, 279; in BRICS, 82, 83; China's geostrategic rivalry with, 19, 47; IORA and, 81; maritime security and, 257–60; "Quad" partnership and, 257; UN peacekeeping in Africa and, 205
Indian Ocean, 19, 47, 81, 280; BRI (Belt and Road Initiative) and, 62; China's maritime interests in, 260–68; China's maritime strategy in, 286–87; competing security interests in, 256–60; deep seabed mining in, 18, 156, 169–70, 178, 336; fishing in, 175; maritime security in, 255; security in, 193
Indonesia, 5
Industrial and Commercial Bank of China, 297
industrialization, 47, 54
Infinity Security (Nigeria), 193
information security, 3, 295–96; AI (artificial intelligence) and surveillance technology, 315–20; IT (information technology) networks, 19, 296, 305–15; space and satellite technology, 300–305. *See also* cybersecurity
infrastructure, 29, 175, 293; BRI (Belt and Road Initiative) and, 58, 62; CASCF and, 56; civilian government, 243; COMESA and, 73; dependence on China for, 40; EAC and, 76; ECOWAS and, 71; financed by Chinese loans, 399n36; FOCAC and, 54; food production and, 174; Forum Macao and, 63; infrastructure-for-oil deals, 47; investment and loans for, 25; military and police facilities, 243–44; for oil export, 200
Inkster, Nigel, 160
Instagram, 123
internal affairs, noninterference in, 21, 33, 57, 162; China's role in conflict mediation, 180, 198–204, 338–39; as evolving principle, 336–39

INDEX

International Criminal Court, 10
Internet governance, 306–8
Internet of Things, 307, 312, 318, 323
IORA (Indian Ocean Rim Association), 52, 78, 81–82
Iran, 5, 230, 317
ISA (International Seabed Authority), 169
Isaias Afwerki, 235
Islamic Association of China, 79
IT (information technology), 19, 296, 305–15, 341; 5G Internet, 309, 312–13, 318, 321–22, 323; Great Firewall of China and, 308. *See also* cyber security

Jack Ma Foundation, 246
Japan, 4, 15, 38, 75, 169; Djibouti military base, 287; maritime security and, 259–60; "Quad" partnership and, 257
JEM [Justice and Equality Movement] (Sudan), 181
Jiang Zemin, 10, 69, 104, 110, 144
Jibril, Mahmoud, 202
Jili, Bulelani, 319
Jubilee Party (Kenya), 97, 143
Julius Nyerere Leadership School (Tanzania), 86, 100–102, 117
Jung Kae Kwon, 247

Kabila, Joseph, 48, 235
Kabila, Laurent, 202
Kabila, Laurent-Désiré, 235
Kagame, Paul, 323
Kardon, Isaac, 273
Kavalski, Emilian, 14
Kazakhstan, 5
Kenya, 9, 27, 32, 41, 45, 329; arms transfers from China, 227; BRI (Belt and Road Initiative) and, 59, 60; Chinese-built military facilities in, 244; Chinese communities in, 17; Chinese IT companies in, 309, 312; Chinese-language instruction in, 143; Chinese military attachés in, 221; Chinese state media and, 125, 126, 129, 150; COMESA and, 72; "comprehensive strategic relationship" with, 25; Confucius Institutes (CIs) in, 139, 142, 147; counterterrorism in, 252; cybersecurity and, 325; diplomatic relations established with PRC, 346; in EAC, 75; high-level diplomatic visits to, 28; Hong Kong issue and, 42; ID-CPC and, 86; in IGAD, 74; India's defense cooperation with, 259; in IORA, 81; military attachés in China, 221; military-to-military relations and, 218; nuclear cooperation with China, 299; party-to-party relations and, 97; perceptions of China and United States in, 149, 342; PLAN port calls in, 282; police officers trained in China, 241–42; port development in, 275–76; prospective Chinese military bases in, 292; protection of Chinese nationals and interests in, 192; rare earth elements in, 171; space cooperation with China, 305; surveillance technology provided by China, 317, 319; threats to Chinese nationals in, 183, 184
Kenyatta, Uhuru, 60
Khama, Ian, 37
Khurana, Gurpreet S., 265
Korea, North, 230
Korea, South, 169
Koussa, Moussa, 23
Krebs, Christopher, 321

Lai, David, 162
Lala, Ratsirahonana Norbert, 99
Latin America, 5
League of Arab States (Arab League), 56, 64, 68–69, 297, 338
Lei Yu, 6
Lema, Rahim, 163
Lesotho, 41, 70, 188, 239, 349, 364n102

INDEX

Liang Guanglie, 33, 279
Liang Liming, *140*
Liberia, 40, 42, 176, 282; arms transfers from China, 232; BRI (Belt and Road Initiative) and, 61; Chinese-built military facilities in, 244; Chinese military attachés in, 220; Chinese nationals evacuated from, 197; CRI broadcasts on Liberian radio, 130; diplomatic relations established with PRC, 348; Ebola outbreak (2014), 182, 245–46; in ECOWAS, 70; PLA's HADR intervention in, 247, 248; police officers trained in China, 241; UN peacekeeping operation in, 205, *206*, 207, 209–10, 247
Libya, 23, 56, 220, 221, 282; in AMU, 77; arms transfers from China, 226–27; CEN-SAD and, 76–77; COMESA and, 72; diplomatic relations established with PRC, 348; evacuation of Chinese nationals from, 185, 195–96, 198, 270, 286, 337; LNA (Libyan National Army), 226; military attachés in China, 221; NTC (National Transitional Council), 202; in OIC, 78; oil exports to China, 164, 400n44; PLA's HADR intervention in, 246; protection of Chinese nationals and interests in, 193; regime change crisis (2011), 338; threats to Chinese nationals in, 188; UN resolutions and, 30
Li Changchun, 125
Li Chunpang, 290
Lieberthal, Kenneth, 133
Li Jiacheng, 261
Li Jie, 197
Li Keqiang, 252–53
Li Mingxiang, 107, 112
Li Qiangmin, 131
Li Ruogu, 172
Li Yuanchao, 29
Li Zhanshu, 29, 111
Lin Songtian, *140*, 144

lithium, 166, 167, 178, 335
Liu Guangyuan, 125, 127
Liu Guijin, 200, 202
Liu Haifeng, 144, 394n153
Liu Jianchao, 109, 112
Liu Jiasheng, 290
Liu Qibao, 129
Liu Yunshan, 129
LNG (liquefied natural gas), 164, 165, 191, 335
Lopes, Carlos, 45
Lu Ke, 153
Luan Jianzhang, 89, 91–92
Luo Ning, 192

Macao, 62–63, 195
Machel, Samora, 235
Madagascar, 39, 168, 169, 175, 256, 291; Chinese military attachés in, 221; COMESA and, 72; diplomatic relations established with PRC, 347; in IORA, 81; maritime security and, 259; PLAN port calls in, *282*; rare earth elements in, 171; in SADC, 69
Madrid-Morales, Dani, 150
Magafuli, John, 244, 275
Mahachi, Ammanuel, 102
Mahama, John, 115
Mahamat, Moussa Faki, 66, *140*, 323
Malawi, 70, 150, 153; Chinese IT companies in, 313; COMESA and, 72; diplomatic relations established with PRC, 349; military attachés in China, 221; rare earth elements in, 171, 172
Mali, 24, 70–72, 202–3; Chinese military attachés in, 221; counterterrorism in, 251–52; diplomatic relations established with PRC, 346; military attachés in China, 221; in OIC, 78; threats to Chinese nationals in, 182, 192, 250; UN peacekeeping operation in, 186–87, 205, 207, 208, 209–10, 247, 251–52; UN resolutions and, 30; votes in UN, 31

INDEX

Mandela, Nelson, 104
manganese, 18, 167–68, 178, 335
Mao Zedong, 15, 144
Mapaila, Solly, 107
Mara, Moussa, *141*
maritime security, 255–56; African port development and, 272–81, *280*; China's interests and naval strategy in African waters, 260–68; competing security interests in Indian Ocean, 256–60; counterpiracy operations, 268–72; "Mediterranean strategy" and, 264; merchant fleet of China and, 286; port calls and naval exercises, 281–84, *282*, 292, 328; ship building and, 284–86; SLOCs (sea lines of communication), 256–60, 261, 262, 265, 266, 268, 289
Maritime Silk Road, 58, 59, 256, 262, 264, 273
Martinson, Ryan, 264
Marxism, 23, 103, 107, 108
Mauritania, 24, 56, 130, 176, 282, 291; in AMU, 77; arms transfers from China, 226–27; Chinese-controlled fishing vessels in, 175; COMESA and, 72; defense of Xinjiang policies, 39; diplomatic relations established with PRC, 347; natural gas reserves, 164; in OIC, 78; political commissar system in military, 236; port development in, 277–78, 340; votes in UN, 31
Mauritius, 70, 147, 169, 256; BRI (Belt and Road Initiative) and, 60; China Cultural Center in, 146; diplomatic relations established with PRC, 347; high-level diplomatic visits to, 28; India's defense cooperation with, 259; in IORA, 81; maritime security and, 259; PLAN port calls in, *282*; surveillance technology provided by China, 320
Mayotte, 260
Mbayu, Felix, *141*
Mbeki, Thabo, 104, 382n76

McDevitt, Michael, 265
Megvii Technology (AI company), 315, 316
Melese Alemu Hirboro, 111
Meles Zenawi, 110, 111
MEND [Movement for the Emancipation of the Niger Delta] (Nigeria), 181
Meserole, Chris, 306
Meservey, Joshua, 244
MFA [Ministry of Foreign Affairs] (China), 42, 56, 90; Africa-focused propaganda and, 131–32, 137; China-Africa Youth Festival and, 147–48; military attachés and, 220; state-to-state diplomacy and, 88; think-tank forums and, *140*; threats to Chinese nationals and, 181, 188, 195, 197
MIC [Military Industrial Corporation] (Sudan), 233
Michel, James, 279
Middle East, 5, 58
military assistance, 55, 72, 222–23, *224*; (dis)advantages of Chinese weapons, 234–35; African Standby Force, 55, 67; construction of military and police facilities, 243–44; conventional weapons, 223–26, *225*; decline in Chinese arms transfers to Africa, 340; to East Africa, 227–28; military exercises, 242; military training, 235–40; to North Africa and the Sahel, 226–27; SALW (small arms and light weapons), 222–23, 226, 230–34, 240, 253; to Southern Africa, 229–30; to West and Central Africa, 228–29
military-to-military relations, 9, 88, 119, 213, 334; military attachés, 220–22; military exchange visits, 19, 217–20
minerals, strategic, 18, 47, 163, 178, 335–36; deep seabed mining, 18, 156, 169–70, 178, 336; mineral security, 166–69. *See also specific minerals*
Ministry of Culture (China), 122, 146
Ministry of National Defense (China), 214, 215, 216, 220

INDEX

Ministry of State Security (China), 90, 137
Mnangagwa, Emmerson, 338
Moghalu, Kingsley, 48
Mokonyane, Dan, 108
Morocco, 17, 22, 39, 205, 251; in AMU, 77; arms transfers from China, 225; BRI (Belt and Road Initiative) and, 61; CASCF and, 56; Chinese-controlled fishing vessels in, 175; Chinese IT companies in, 309; Chinese military attachés in, 220; diplomatic relations established with PRC, 345; extradition treaty with China, 188; ID-CPC and, 86; military attachés in China, 221; military-to-military relations and, 218; in OIC, 78; party-to-party relations and, 96, 96; PLAN port calls in, 282; port development in, 278, 280, 340; prospective Chinese military bases in, 292; strategic minerals in, 167; "strategic partnership" with, 25; U.S. arms transfers to, 223; votes in UN, 31; Western Sahara conflict and, 77, 203, 226
Motshekga, Angie, 143
Moumié, Félix, 23
Moungui, Medi, 31–32
MOUs (memoranda of understanding), 61, 69, 71, 74, 113; Confucius Institutes (CIs) and, 139; on counterterrorism, 252; IT (information technology) and, 313, 314; on nuclear energy cooperation, 299; surveillance technology and, 317
Moussa, Amr Mahmoud, 69
Mozambique, 26, 45–46, 175, 176; ATDC in, 173; BRI (Belt and Road Initiative) and, 60, 61; Chinese-built military facilities in, 244; Chinese military attachés in, 220; "comprehensive strategic relationship" with, 25; diplomatic relations established with PRC, 348; in Forum Macao, 62; India's defense cooperation with, 259; in IORA, 81; military attachés in China, 221; military-to-military relations and, 218; natural gas reserves, 164; in OIC, 78; party-to-party relations and, 101; *Peace Ark* hospital ship in, 284; PLAN port calls in, 282; PLA's HADR intervention in, 245; political commissar system in military, 236; protection of Chinese nationals and interests in, 192; rare earth elements in, 171; in SADC, 69; UN peacekeeping operation in, 205, 206
MPLA (People's Movement for the Liberation of Angola), 101
Mugabe, Robert, 10, 235, 338
multilateral exchanges: ID-CPC and, 86; international forums, 4; number and location of, 99–100, 99, 100
multipolar world order, 6
Museveni, Yoweri, 43, 188
Muslim minorities in China, mistreatment of, 22, 37–40, 157; CASCF and, 57–58; as "core interest" of China, 32, 36, 49; OIC and, 79; threats against Chinese nationals in Africa and, 182, 250; Xinjiang seen as hotbed of terrorism, 248–49. *See also* Uighurs; Xinjiang
Mutambara, Arthur G. O., 64
Mwencha, Erastus, 151
Myanmar, 38, 291

NAM (Non-Aligned Movement), 52, 78, 80–81
Namibia, 9, 17, 36; agency vis-à-vis China, 46; AI technology provided by China in, 318; arms transfers from China, 229–30, 232; BRI (Belt and Road Initiative) and, 60; Chinese-built military facilities in, 243, 334; Chinese military attachés in, 220; "comprehensive strategic relationship" with, 25; diplomatic relations established with PRC, 349; extradition treaty with China, 188;

473

INDEX

Namibia (*continued*)
  high-level diplomatic visits to, 28; Hong Kong issue and, 41; ID-CPC and, 86; military attachés in China, 221; military personnel trained in China, 239; military-to-military relations and, 218; naval exercises with PLAN, 283; party-to-party relations and, 96, *96*, 101; PLAN port calls in, *282*; police officers trained in China, 241; port development in, 276, 340; prospective Chinese military bases in, 292; rare earth elements in, 171; in SADC, 70; space cooperation with China, 304–5, 325; strategic minerals in, 167; UN peacekeeping operation in, *206*; uranium reserves in, 165, 166, 300; votes in UN, 31
Nantulya, Paul, 58–59
National Congresses, of CPC: Fifteenth (1997), 10; Sixteenth (2002), 145; Eighteenth (2012), 145, 185, 262, 316; Nineteenth (2017), 6, 58, 66, 92, 262, 386n10
National Defense Law (China, 1997), 155
National Development and Reform Commission (China), 61
National Intelligence Law (China), 244, 321
national reunification, as "core interest" of China, 3
national security, as "core interest" of China, 3
National Security Law (China, 2015), 155, 179
NATO (North Atlantic Treaty Organization), 30
Naval Affairs (PLAN journal), 263
Ndayishimiye, Evariste, 42
NDC [National Democratic Congress] (Ghana), 87, 113–16, *114*
NECSA [Nuclear Energy Corporation SOC Limited] (South Africa), 297
NEPAD (New Partnership for Africa's Development), 67–68
Ngwenya, Sindiso, 73

Nie Chenxi, 131
Niger, 24, 46, 130; BRI (Belt and Road Initiative) and, 60, 61; defense of Xinjiang policies, 39; diplomatic relations established with PRC, 348; in ECOWAS, 70; in OIC, 78; party-to-party relations and, 96; protection of Chinese nationals and interests in, 194; threats to Chinese nationals in, 181–82; Tuareg rebels in, 181–82; uranium reserves in, 165, 166; votes in UN, 31
Nigeria, 5, 329; agency vis-à-vis China, 47; arms transfers from China, 225, 234; BRI (Belt and Road Initiative) and, 60; BRI News Network and, 132; China Cultural Center in, 146; Chinese communities in, 17; Chinese IT companies in, 309; Chinese media platforms in, 126; Chinese military attachés in, 220; Chinese state media and, 129; counterterrorism and, 252; defense of Xinjiang policies, 39; diplomatic relations established with PRC, 347; in ECOWAS, 70; high-level diplomatic visits to, 28; Hong Kong issue and, 42; MEND insurgency in, 181; military attachés in China, 221; military exercises with PLAN, 242; military personnel trained in China, 240; military-to-military relations and, 217; naval exercises with PLAN, 283; nuclear cooperation with China, 299–300; in OIC, 78; perceptions of China and United States in, 149, 342; PLAN port calls in, *282*; port development in, *280*, 340; protection of Chinese nationals and interests in, 189–90, 191, 192, 193; satellites launched by China for, 301, *302*; space cooperation with China, 303–4; "strategic partnership" with, 25; surveillance technology provided by China, 320; Taiwan's relations with,

INDEX

34–35; threats to Chinese nationals in, 180, 183, 184; votes in UN, 31
Nkrumah, Kwame, 23, 345
Nkunda, Laurent, 202
NORINCO (China North Industries Group Corporation), 223, 228, 232, 233–34
North Africa, 9, 222, 250
NPP [New Patriotic Party] (Ghana), 87, 113, *114*, 115–16
nuclear power, 3, 19, 164, 296–300, 325, 341
Nujoma, Sam, 235
Nzimande, Blade, 104
Nzo, Alfred, 104

OAU (Organization of African Unity), 64, 67, 367n5
Odusile, Abdulwaheed, 132
Office for International Military Cooperation, of the CMC, 215, 216
OIC (Organization of Islamic Cooperation), 38, 52, 78–79
One China Principle, 23, 35, 54, 57
Oniosun, Temidayo, 301
ONLF [Ogaden National Liberation Front] (Ethiopia), 181
Opera app, 126
Operation Red Sea (film, 2018), 197

Pakistan, 5, 258, 270, 272, 291, 311
pan-Africanism, 109
Pan-African Parliament, 54
Pang, Victor, 322
PAP (People's Armed Police), 190, 193, 207, 209, 410n71; counterterrorism missions of, 249, 289; police training for Africans, 235, 240–42; UN peacekeeping operations and, 240
party-to-party relations, 1, 9, 18, 21, 85–87, 119, 329–30; bilateral, 93–94, *95*, 96–98, *96*; electoral democracies and, 113; ideological differences and, 92, 108, 333;

multilateral, 98–102, *99*, *100*; national diplomatic relations and, 91; Xi Jinping's vision for, 88–89. *See also* ID-CPC
Patriotic Front Party (Zambia), 385n135
Paul, Antonio, 101
Peace Ark (hospital ship), 281, 284
Peace Cable International Network, 311
"peaceful rise" slogan, 6
Pensana Rare Earths company, 171
People's Daily (CPC newspaper), 132
people-to-people relations, 9, 21, 143–48
Perceival Security (Nigeria), 193
Percent Corporation, 318
Persian Gulf, 164, 256, 257
PetroChina company, 192, 195
Philippines, 40
Ping, Jean, 66
piracy, 55, 69, 81, 82, 184, 197, 256, 268–72; PLA Navy deployed against, 196, 255, 261, 264, 265, 266–67, 281, 286, 337; private security companies used against, 190, 193; security forums and, 214; U.S. navy as deterrence to, 257
PLA (People's Liberation Army), 3, 18, 88, 155; Academy of Military Science, 246; arms transfers to Africa and, 229, 231; Army Engineering University, 237; CDS (College of Defense Studies), 237; *China Military Science* journal, 61; counterterrorism missions of, 249, 289; defense of China's overseas interests and, 179; evacuation of Chinese nationals and, 211; HADR (humanitarian assistance and disaster relief), 19, 213, 245–48; International College of Defense Studies, 214, 236; IT (information technology) and, 305–6; military exchange visits and, 217–19; military training provided to Africans, 235–40; National Defense University, 287; National University of Defense Science and Technology, 217, 236; NDU

INDEX

PLA (People's Liberation Army) (*continued*) (National Defense University), 216, 217, 235, 236; officers as military attachés, 220; "other than war" missions of, 161, 242; political schools of, 236, 239, 240; security strategy and, 159, 160–61; space technology and, 301; in UN peacekeeping operations, 207–8, 210; veterans in private security, 190, 191, 193

PLA Air Force, 161, 195, 196, 266

PLAN (People's Liberation Army Navy), 1, 19, 47, 219, 255, 305; antipiracy operations, 196, 255, 261, 264, 265, 266–67, 270–71; BRI (Belt and Road Initiative) and, 62; China's naval strategy and, 263–68; Dalian Naval Academy, 290; Djibouti base and, 289; evacuation of Chinese nationals and, 195, 196, 197, 198; growth of naval power projection around Africa, 339–40; inventory and capabilities of, 266; Marine Corps (PLANMC), 267, 269, 270, 288; maritime security and, 261; military attachés and, 221; military exercises with African navies, 242; naval exercises with African navies, 283–84; plans for future operations in the Atlantic, 264; port calls in Africa, 281–84, *282*, *293*; port development and, 273–76, 279; quest for military bases, 291; security strategy and, 161; submarine force, 170

platinum, 18, 166, 168, 178, 335

POLISARIO Front, 205

Polyakova, Alina, 306

POLY-GCL Petroleum, 165, 191

Poly Technologies, 277

Portugal, 62, 264, 283

Pradhan, S. D., 155

Prince, Eric, 191, 192

propaganda, Africa-focused, 18, 119–20, 153–54, 327; China's propaganda apparatus, 121–23; Confucius Institutes (CIs) and, 139, 142–43; content localization, 128–30; cultural, 122, 123, 125, 143–48, 394n153; educational, 122, 123; evaluation of, 148–53; future increased investment in, 342–43; hosting and training of African media, 130–33; journalists and the editorial line, 126–27; media, 122; media outlets, 123–26; public content versus "internal reference" reports, 127; think tanks and, 137–39, *140–41*. See also educational programs

Prosperity Party (Ethiopia), 87, 112

PSCs (private security companies), 190–94, 211

P3 (permanent member-states of UN Security Council), 30, 31

PTI (Poly Technologies Incorporated), 228–29, 230

Pye, Lucian, 12

al-Qadhafi, Mu'ammar, 23, 202, 338

al-Qaeda, 182, 252

Qian Qichen, 69, 104

Qin Taqing, 11

Qiushi (CPC journal), 306

Quadrilateral Security Dialogue ("Quad"), 257

Quartey, Kwesi, 115

Qu Dongyu, 31

racism, 152, 153

Raid Private Security (South Africa), 194

Ramaphosa, Cyril, 105–6, 313

rare earth elements, 163, 164, 170–72

Red Sea, 256, 259, 261, 268, 280

regional relationships, 1, 9, 17, 329, 344

Réunion, 260

Rolland, Nadège, 58, 137, 156

Russel, Daniel, 273

Russia, 4, 15, 82, 164, 169, 325; arms transfers to Africa, 222, 223, 224, 230, 234, 340; Internet governance structure and, 306; nuclear cooperation with African countries, 296, 297–98, 299; satellites launched for African countries, 301; surveillance technology of, 317; Wagner Group mercenaries, 191

Rwanda, 47, 67, 125; COMESA and, 72; conflict mediation by China and, 202; diplomatic relations established with PRC, 347; in EAC, 75; high-level diplomatic visits to, 28; military personnel trained by PLA, 239, 240; political commissar system in military, 236; strategic minerals in, 163, 167; surveillance technology provided by China, 317

SACP (South African Communist Party), 87, 103–8, 330, 383n99; Central Committee, 382n76; number of exchanges with ID-CPC, *105*; scholarships for cadres to study in China, 104

SADC (Southern African Development Community), 51, 64, 69–70, 330

Sangay, Lobsang, 37

SANSA (South African National Space Agency), 303

São Tomé and Principe, 34, 271; diplomatic relations established with PRC, 348; in ECCAS, 76; in Forum Macao, 62, 63

Saudi Arabia, 5, 203

Science of Military Strategy, The (PLA publication, 2013), 266, 287, 290, 306–7

Scott, James C., 91

security diplomacy, 213–14; construction of military and police facilities, 243–44; counterterrorism cooperation and intelligence sharing, 248–53; forums on security, 214–17; HADR (humanitarian assistance and disaster relief), 245–48; military and police training, 235–42; military attachés, 220–22; military exchange visits, 19, 217–20. *See also* diplomacy; military assistance

security relations, 3, 15, 16, 21, 155–56, 177–78; access to energy and minerals, 162–64, 178; deep seabed mining and, 169–70; energy security, 164–66; food security, 172–77; Global Security Initiative, 158, 159; military exchange visits, 19; mineral security, 166–69, 178; new security challenges, 18; police training, 240–42; rare earth elements and, 170–72; security strategy of China, 156–62

security threats: attacks against Chinese nationals and interests, 179, 180–85, 336–37, 339; conflict prevention and management, 198–204; emergency evacuation of Chinese nationals, 194–98; protection of Chinese nationals and interests, 185–94, 337

Segal, Adam, 306

Seifudein Adem, 109

Senegal, 9, 130; Chinese-controlled fishing vessels in, 175; Chinese IT companies in, 312–13; Chinese-sponsored training session for journalists from, 133; Chinese state media and, 129; diplomatic relations established with PRC, 347; in ECOWAS, 70; high-level diplomatic visits to, 28; military attachés in China, 221; natural gas reserves, 164; in OIC, 78; PLAN port calls in, *282*; "strategic partnership" with, 25

SenseTime (AI company), 315–16

Seychelles, 28, 47, 48, 70, 256, 311, 329; COMESA and, 72; diplomatic relations established with PRC, 348; India's defense cooperation with, 259, 279; in IORA, 81; PLAN port calls in, 281, 282, *282*; port development in, 279; prospective Chinese military bases in, 291, 292

al-Shabaab (Somalia, Kenya), 157, 182–83, 252

Shambaugh, David, 113, 121, 124

Shandong Huawei Security Group, 194

INDEX

Shanghai Construction Company, 26–27, 244
Shanghai Cooperation Organization, 10, 259
Shanghai Institutes for International Studies, 138, 156
Shen Dingli, 287
Shen Xiaolei, 367n5
Shenzhen Aerospace Oriental Red Sea Satellite Co., 304
Shikwati, James, 45
Sierra Leone, 27, 28, 168, 175–76, 215; arms transfers from China, 232; Chinese-built military facilities in, 244; "comprehensive strategic relationship" with, 25; defense of China's Xinjiang policies, 39; diplomatic relations established with PRC, 347; Ebola outbreak (2014), 182, 245; in ECOWAS, 70; evacuation of Chinese nationals from, 197, 337; military attachés in China, 221; military exercises with PLA, 242; military personnel trained by PLA, 240; in OIC, 78; *Peace Ark* hospital ship in, 284; PLAN port calls in, *282*; UN peacekeeping operation in, 205, *206*
Silk Road Think-Tanks Network, 138
Singapore, 5
Sino-African strategic relations, 2–6; academic literature on, 15–16, 357n78; multitier and interlocking, 2, 8–11, *9*; Sinocentric, 2
Sino-Africa Young Political Leaders Forum, 100
Sinocentrism, 2, 11–14, 98, 117, 154; in Chinese relations with foreigners, 133; off-putting effect on some African elites, 154
Sinopec (Chinese oil company), 164, 165, 181, 188
al-Sisi, Abdel-Fattah, 60, 250
16+1 Cooperation, 10
SNPTC [State Nuclear Power Technology Corporation] (China), 297

socialism, 103, 107; "modernized" view of, 108; "socialism with Chinese characteristics," 92, 106
social media, 123, 185, 319, 324, 342
soft power, *140*, 284; China's security strategy and, 158; port calls and, 283; propaganda and, 145, 342–43
Somalia, 24, 31, 56, 257, 282, 311; arms transfers from China, 227; COMESA and, 72; diplomatic relations established with PRC, 346; evacuation of Chinese nationals from, 337; in IGAD, 74; in IORA, 81; in OIC, 78; pirates operating from, 190, 193, 268, 337; al-Shabaab insurgency in, 157, 182–83; Somaliland secession from, 35; threats to Chinese nationals in, 180, 182–83; U.S.-led operation in (1992–1993), 64; votes in UN, 31
Song Tao, 88, 93, 101, 102, 109, 111
South Africa, 5, 9, 17, 30, 82; Africa Aerospace and Defence Trade Show, 215, 224; agency vis-à-vis China, 47; in BRICS, 82–83; BRI News Network and, 132; Chinese communities in, 17; Chinese IT companies in, 309, 313; Chinese-language instruction in, 143; Chinese media platforms in, 126; Chinese military attachés in, 221; "comprehensive strategic relationship" with, 25; Confucius Institutes (CIs) in, 139; cultural propaganda activities in, 147; Dalai Lama in, 36–37; diplomatic relations established with PRC, 349; end of apartheid regime, 103; exiled Tibetan president's visit to, 33; extradition treaty with China, 188; FOCAC and, 104; food exports to China, 174; high-level diplomatic visits to, 28; Hong Kong issue and, 42; ID-CPC and, 86; India's defense cooperation with, 259; in IORA, 81; military personnel trained in China,

478

INDEX

237, 239; military-to-military relations and, 217, 218; naval exercises with PLAN, 284; nuclear cooperation with China, 297; oil exports to China, 400n44; party-to-party relations and, 18, 86, 96, *96*, 102–8, *105*, 117; perceptions of China and United States in, 342; PLAN port calls in, 281, 282, *282*; protection of Chinese nationals and interests in, 192; rare earth elements in, 171; in SADC, 70; SANDF (South African National Defense Force), 246–47; South China Sea issue and, 41; strategic minerals in, 167, 168; Taiwan's relations with, 35; textile industry, 46; threats to Chinese nationals in, 183–84, 187, 188; uranium reserves in, 165. *See also* ANC; SACP

South Asia, 4, 5, 249

South China Sea, 22, 57; China's incremental strategy in, 162; as "core interest" of China, 32, 40–41, 49; UN ruling against China's territorial claims, 330

Southeast Asia, 4, 5, 249

South Sudan, 30, 31, 36, 64, 80; arms transfers from China, 233; Chinese military attachés in, 221; civil war in, 157; conflict mediation by China in, 201–2, 204; diplomatic relations established with PRC, 349; in EAC, 75; evacuation of Chinese nationals from, 196–97, 337; IGAD and, 74, 75; military attachés in China, 221; military personnel trained in China, 239; oil fields in, 165, 208, 337; PLA's HADR intervention in, 248; political commissar system in military, 236; protection of Chinese nationals and interests in, 191; threats to Chinese nationals in, 180, 181; UN peacekeeping operation in, 206, 207, 209, 247

Southwest Indian Ridge, in Indian Ocean, 169, 170

Soviet Union, 15, 230

space and satellite cooperation, 19, 296, 300–305, *302*, 325, 341

SPLA (Sudan People's Liberation Army), 233

Sri Lanka, 291

SSI (Sonangol Sinopec International), 165

StarTimes (TV company), 125, 130, 313, 341

State Administration for Science, Technology and Industry for National Defense (China), 231

state sovereignty, as "core interest" of China, 3, 21, 32, 33; AU (African Union) and, 66; limitation on Western influence in Africa and, 162; UN peacekeeping operations and, 210

state-to-state relations, 9, 88, 112, 113

Strait of Malacca, 258, 259, 261, 263, 274

subregional relationships, 1, 9, 17, 63–64, 329, 344

Sudan, 10, 26, 56; Abyei border conflict, 205, 206; arms transfers from China, 225, 228, 232–33; BRI (Belt and Road Initiative) and, 61; BRI News Network and, 132; Chinese communities in, 17; Chinese military attachés in, 220; COMESA and, 72; conflict mediation by China in, 199–202, 204, 338; Confucius Institutes (CIs) in, 239; Darfur conflict, 157, 181, 199–200, 204, *206*, 207, 232, 338; diplomatic relations established with PRC, 345; ID-CPC and, 86; in IGAD, 74, 75; Internet shutdowns in, 308; military exercises with PLA, 242; military-to-military relations and, 218; nuclear cooperation with China, 298–99; in OIC, 78; oil exports to China, 400n44; oil fields in, 165; party-to-party relations and, 96, *96*; PLAN port calls in, *282*; protection of Chinese nationals and interests in, 191; satellites launched by China for, 301, *302*, 304; "strategic

479

Sudan (*continued*)
    partnership" with, 25; threats to Chinese nationals in, 180, 184; UN peacekeeping operation in, 206, 209; UN resolution criticizing Darfur actions, 30; votes in UN, 31
Suez Canal, 59, 60, 256, 268, 278–79, 281, 320
Sultan, Hend Elmahly Mahhoud, 202
Sun Degang, 202
Sun, Yun, 14, 93–94, 135, 139, 380n42
Sun Jianguo, Admiral, 290
supply chains, global, 18, 170, 171
surveillance technology, 19, 296, 307, 315–20, 341
SWAPO [South-West Africa People's Organization] (Namibia), 101
Syria, 230, 303

Taiwan (Republic of China), 22, 103, 172; China's territorial claims over, 120; China's UN seat and, 29, 34; as "core interest" of China, 32, 34–35, 49; diplomatic recognition of, 21, 22, 53, 63, 346–49
Tang Xiaoyang, 110
tantalum, 18, 163, 166–67, 178, 335
Tanzania, 8, 9, 29, 67, 147, 329; air force pilots trained in China, 239; arms transfers from China, 225, 227; BRI News Network and, 132; China Cultural Center in, 146; China's interest in resources of, 164; Chinese-built military facilities in, 243–44, 334; Chinese communities in, 17; Chinese-language instruction in, 143; Chinese military attachés in, 221; "comprehensive strategic relationship" with, 25; "core interests" of China and, 33; diplomatic relations established with PRC, 346; in EAC, 75, 76; high-level diplomatic visits to, 28; Hong Kong issue and, 41; in IORA, 81; military-to-military relations and, 218–19; natural gas reserves, 164; naval exercises with PLAN, 283–84; party-to-party relations and, 86, 96, *96*, 100–101, 116; *Peace Ark* hospital ship in, 284; PLAN port calls in, 281, 282, *282*; police officers trained in China, 241; political commissar system in military, 236; port development in, 275, *280*, 340; prospective Chinese military bases in, 291, *292*; rare earth elements in, 171; in SADC, 70; surveillance technology provided by China, 319; threats to Chinese nationals in, 184; TPDF (Tanzanian People's Defense Force), 218, 219, 227, 239, 244; votes in UN, 31
TEDA (Tianjin Economic-Technological Development Area), 278–79
Tedros Adhanom Ghebreyesus, 128
television, as propaganda conduit, 125
Tencent company, 308
territorial integrity, as "core interest" of China, 3, 32, 33, 61; African affirmations of, 97, 117; AU (African Union) and, 66; CPC propaganda and, 120; Hong Kong, 41; party-to-party relations and, 85
terrorism, efforts to combat. *See* counterterrorism
Thailand, 5
Third World, 15
"This Is Africa" exhibit (Hubei Provincial Museum, 2017), 153
tianxia ("all-under-heaven") system, 12
Tibet, 22, 36–37, 49, 120
Timor-Leste, 62
Togo, 26, 28, 33; BRI (Belt and Road Initiative) and, 60; Chinese state media and, 129; CRI broadcasts on Togolese radio, 130; diplomatic relations established with PRC, 347; in ECOWAS, 70; military-to-military relations and, 218; naval exercises with

INDEX

PLAN, 283; in OIC, 78; port development in, *280*
TopStar Communications Company, 130, 313
Townsend, General Stephen, 291
TPLF [Tigray People's Liberation Front] (Ethiopia), 87, 108–12, *110*, 383n99
trade deficits, 22, 43, 44, 49
trade unions, African, 46, 47
Transsion Holdings company, 310
Transsnet company, 126
tributary system, of imperial China, 13
Tuju, Raphael, 97, 143
Tunisia, 56, 302; in AMU, 77; Chinese IT companies in, 309, 314; Chinese military attachés in, 220; COMESA and, 72; COVID-19 vaccine delivered by PLA, 247; diplomatic relations established with PRC, 346; extradition treaty with China, 188; military attachés in China, 221; military-to-military relations and, 218; nuclear cooperation with China, 298; in OIC, 78; perceptions of China and United States in, 149–50, 342; PLAN port calls in, *282*; PLA's HADR intervention in, 246
Turkey, 38, 251
Tutu, Archbishop Desmond, 37
20+20 Cooperation Plan for Chinese and African Institutions of Higher Learning, 135
Twitter, 123

Uganda, 26, 43; BRI (Belt and Road Initiative) and, 61; Chinese-built military facilities in, 244, 334; COMESA and, 72; Confucius Institutes (CIs) in, 142; diplomatic relations established with PRC, 346; in EAC, 75; Hong Kong issue and, 41; in IGAD, 74, 75; military attachés in China, 221; military-to-military relations and, 218; nuclear cooperation with China, 299; in OIC, 78; oil fields in, 165; police officers trained in China, 241; protection of Chinese nationals and interests in, 188; surveillance technology provided by China, 319; UPDF (Uganda People's Defense Forces), 244; votes in UN, 31
Uighurs, 37–38, 39, 83, 250, 251, 252, 320. *See also* Muslim minorities in China, mistreatment of; Xinjiang
Umejei, Emeka, 127
UN (United Nations), 17, 21, 67, 222; ATT (Arms Trade Treaty), 231; Charter, 10, 158, 330; China-Africa collaboration at, 22, 29–32, 49, 361n46; China's seat in, 27, 29; conflict prevention and, 199; Convention on the Law of the Sea, 40; Economic Commission for Africa, 45; General Assembly, 30–31, 32, 34, 40; G-77 (Group of 77), 52, 78, 79–80; Human Rights Council, 29–30, 31, 36, 38, 39–40, 42, 330, 361n46; Libya crisis (2011) and, 338; official languages of, 123; POA (Program of Action), 231; ROCA (Register of Conventional Arms), 231; Security Council, 29, 30, 32, 36, 67, 269, 330, 338; specialized agencies of, 31–32; UN-centered diplomacy, 10. *See also* UN peacekeeping operations
UNCLOS (UN Convention on the Law of the Sea), 169–70
United Arab Emirates, 203, 225, 226
United Kingdom [UK] (Britain), 4, 30, 42, 169, 256; military presence in Indian Ocean region, 260; think tanks in, 137
United States, 4, 18, 47, 169; Africans' positive perceptions of, 149–50, 154; African students in, 136; arms transfers to Africa, 222, 223, 230; AU (African Union) and, 68; China's geostrategic rivalry with, 19; China's promotion of anti-U.S. sentiment, 116, 117, 119, 150, 237;

481

INDEX

United States (*continued*)
contentious relationship with China, 5, 331; criticized for racial discrimination, 36; Defense Department, 159; deterioration in China's relations with, 16; DIA (Defense Intelligence Agency), 160; diplomatic ties with African countries, 22–23; GPS (Global Positioning System) of, 301; "hegemony" of, 2, 87, 154, 331; ideological struggle for influence and, 15; "imperialism" of, 108, 112; as IT (information technology) leader, 305; maritime power of, 256–57; military bases in Indian Ocean and Persian Gulf, 257, 259; "Quad" partnership and, 257; rare earth elements and, 171–72; satellites launched for African countries, 301; security relations with African countries, 24; State Department, 31; think tanks in, 137; on threat of Chinese IT companies, 322, 325, 341; Trump administration, 29; UN Security Council and, 30; viewed as a power in decline, 120

UN peacekeeping operations, 10, 18, 54, 58, 63, 155, 180; China's participation in, 186–87, 204–5, 206, 207–11, 221, 266, 289; in Darfur region of Sudan, 186, 200, 206; in Mali, 72, 186; mandate to protect foreigners, 337; military and police training for, 237, 238, 240–41; security strategy of China and, 158, 160–62; in South Sudan, 187, 337

UPC (Union des Populations du Cameroon), 23

uranium, 46, 165–66, 297, 300

Veterans Security Services Security Group, 192
Victor, Jonah, 316
Voice of China, 125
Vskit, 126

Waitara, General George, 218
Waldhauser, General Thomas, 291
Wang, Philippe, 323
Wang Dongming, 105
Wang Gengnian, 121–22, 127
Wang Guanzhong, General, 279
Wang Heming, 91, 98
Wang Jiarui, 88, 147, 148
Wang Lili, 137
Wang Xuejun, 159
Wang Yi, 28, 32, 66, 69; AU cyberbreach allegations and, 323; conflict mediation and, 201; OIC and, 79; think-tank forums and, *140*; visits to African countries, 329; on Xinjiang issue, 250–51
Wanshou Hotel (Beijing), African party delegates in, 90–91
Wei Fenghe, 216, 217
Wekesa, Bob, 131
Wen Jiabao, 79, 185
West African Cable System, 311
Western countries (the West), 15, 274, 296; AI technology and, 315, 316; Bandung Conference and solidarity against, 144; China's promotion of postcolonial grievance against, 237; China's strategic vision in competition with, 7, 98, 177–78, 325; developing countries and, 8; human rights concept of, 35; IT (information technology) and, 305; liberal democracy and, 120; oil companies, 165; Western values of the United States, 117
Western Sahara, 22, 77, 203; China's neutrality in conflict, 226; Sahrawi Arab Democratic Republic, 64; UN peacekeeping operation in, 205, 206, 207, 221
Westphalian system, 11
Woods, Anna, 177
World Bank, 45, 332
World Health Organization, 128
World Trade Organization, 330

INDEX

Wu Xiaohui, 199
Wuchang Shipbuilding Industry Group, 227
Wu Haitao, 231–32
Wu Zhengyu, 62, 262

Xiao Qiang, 121
Xi Jinping, 1, 4, 21, 34, 42, 343, 386n10; African leaders received in Beijing by, 111; AI technology and, 316; Arab League and, 69; AU (African Union) and, 66; BRI (Belt and Road Initiative) and, 58, 60, 61, 255, 256, 264; CASCF and, 56–57; China's increased interaction with Africa and, 51; on China's participation in UN peacekeeping operations, 209; Community of Shared Future for Mankind concept, 2, 6, 7, 215, 216; "comprehensive strategy" concept and, 335; on cooperative security, 81, 156–57; on cultural "soft power," 145; desire to elevate China to great-power status, 160; on development as basis of security, 157; on "Digital Silk Road," 305; on "five major pillars" of China-Africa relationship, 88; FOCAC and, 11; "Four Principles and Five Propositions," 308; as general secretary of CPC, 85; Global Security Initiative and, 217, 255; *Governance of China*, 115; on "holistic security," 3, 157–58; maritime power as ambition of, 263, 265, 268; NAM (Non-Aligned Movement) and, 80–81; OIC and, 79; overseas military bases and, 290; party-to-party relations and, 86, 88–89, 94, 101–2, 333; on promotion of China's political system, 92–93; on propaganda strategy, 120, 121, 126, 342; protection of China's overseas interests and, 179; security laws and, 155–56; on training of foreign peacekeepers, 240–41; vision for China-Africa Community, 8; visits to African countries, 28, 250

Xinhua news agency, 59, 68, 123, 124, 142, 150, 289; African states' agreements with, 129; "big four" propaganda outlets and, 343; public content in daily reports of, 127
Xinjiang, 69, 79, 83, 157, 250–51; forced labor in, 10, 39–40, 330; PSCs (private security companies) in, 192; "re-education centers" in, 37–38; seen as hotbed of domestic terrorism, 248–49. *See also* Muslim minorities in China, mistreatment of; Uighurs
Xiong Guangkai, 3
Xue Bing, 203
Xue Guifang, 273
Xu Hui, 216
Xu Jinghu, 53–54
Xu Luping, 101

Yang Jiechi, 126, *140*
Yantai Port Group Company, 277, *280*
Yan Xuetong, 5
Yemen, Chinese nationals evacuated from, 197, 270
Yitu Technology (AI company), 315, 316
You Ji, 262
Young African Leaders Training Course (2019), 100
YouTube, 123
Yuan Peng, 137

Zambia, 48, 153; arms transfers from China, 229; BRI News Network and, 132; Chinese-built military facilities in, 244, 334; Chinese IT companies in, 313–14; Chinese military attachés in, 220; Chinese military doctors in, 245; Chinese state media and, 129; COMESA and, 72; defense of Xinjiang policies, 39; diplomatic relations established with PRC, 346; high-level diplomatic visits to, 28; Hong Kong issue and, 42; military exercises with PLA,

483

Zambia (*continued*)
242; military-to-military relations and, 218; party-to-party relations and, 385n135; police officers trained in China, 241; protection of Chinese nationals and interests in, 194; rare earth elements in, 171; in SADC, 70; strategic minerals in, 168–69; students sent to China, 136; surveillance technology provided by China, 317, 318; threats to Chinese nationals in, 183

ZANU-PF (Zimbabwe African National Union–Patriotic Front), 101, 102

Zhai Jun, 139, *140*

Zhang Dejiang, 196

Zhang Jun, 201

Zhang Yanqiu, 150–51

Zhao Jingman, 205

Zhao Qi, *141*

Zhao Suisheng, 11–13, 134

Zhao Tingyang, 12

Zhao Xiyuan, 142

Zhejiang Huayou Cobalt company, 167

Zheng Jiwei, *140*

Zhong Jianhua, 201

Zhongjie Security Group Co., 192

Zhongjun Hong Security Group, 193

Zhong Weiyun, 92, 113

Zhou Bo, 274

Zhou Enlai, 27, 78, 80, 144

Zhou Pingjian, 27

Zhu Congjiu, *141*

Zhu Jing, 115–16

Zhu Kezhen (oceanographic research ship), 281

Zhu Rongji, 69

Zimbabwe, 9, 10, 26, 329; arms transfers from China, 226, 232, 234; AU (African Union) and, 65; Chinese communities in, 17; Chinese IT companies in, 310, 314; Chinese military attachés in, 220; Chinese state media and, 129; COMESA and, 72; "comprehensive strategic relationship" with, 25; diplomatic relations established with PRC, 348; high-level diplomatic visits to, 28; party-to-party relations and, 96, *96*, 101, 102; police officers trained in China, 241; political commissar system in military, 236; protection of Chinese nationals and interests in, 194; in SADC, 70; strategic minerals in, 168; surveillance technology provided by China, 317–18; threats to Chinese nationals in, 184; UN sanctions and, 30; votes in UN, 31

ZNU (Zhejiang Normal University), Institute of African Studies at, 138, *140–41*

ZTE company, 19, 123, 195, 296, 310, 341; China Standards 2035 Plan and, 307; IT projects in African countries, 309, 311–14; surveillance technology and, 315

Zuma, Jacob, 105

GPSR Authorized Representative: Easy Access System Europe, Mustamäe tee 50, 10621 Tallinn, Estonia, gpsr.requests@easproject.com

www.ingramcontent.com/pod-product-compliance
Lightning Source LLC
Chambersburg PA
CBHW031227290426
44109CB00012B/189